The WHEELOCK'S LATIN Series

WHEELOCK'S LATIN
Frederic M. Wheelock, revised by Richard A. LaFleur

WORKBOOK FOR WHEELOCK'S LATIN
Paul Comeau, revised by Richard A. LaFleur

WHEELOCK'S LATIN READER:
SELECTIONS FROM LATIN LITERATURE
Frederic M. Wheelock, revised by Richard A. LaFleur

WHEELOCK'S LATIN READER

Selections from Latin Literature

WHEELOCK'S LATIN READER

Selections from Latin Literature

Frederic M. Wheelock

Revised by

Richard A. LaFleur

2nd Edition

HarperResource
An Imprint of HarperCollins *Publishers*

ACKNOWLEDGMENTS

Maps

pp. xxiii–xxv, 7, 257: All maps copyright by Richard A. LaFleur, Tom Elliott, Nicole Feldl, Alexandra Retzleff, and Joyce Uy. Copyright 2001, Ancient World Mapping Center (http://www.unc.edu/depts/awmc)

Photographs

cover and pp. 2, 15, 23, 27, 45, 53, 57, 63, 79, 81, 96, 109, 115, 117, 141, 161, 165, 171, 175, 177, 181, 198, 203, 223, 233, 237, 247, 248, 253, 255, 259, 285, 290, 292, 293, 316, 318, 322, 326: Scala/Art Resource, NY; pp. 4, 47, 59, 139, 157, 191, 196, 281: Alinari/Art Resource, NY; pp. 11, 13, 19, 20, 25, 29, 61, 65, 67, 83, 100, 107, 135, 145, 147, 173, 207, 221, 225, 229, 314, 324, 327: Erich Lessing/Art Resource, NY; pp. 17, 42, 169: James C. Anderson, jr.; pp. 35, 277: Robert I. Curtis; pp. 49, 111, 137, 163, 235, 275, 283: Réunion des Musées Nationaux/Art Resource, NY; p. 69: SEF/Art Resource, NY; pp. 76, 149, 153, 193, 205, 217, 219, 239, 261, 308, 320: Giraudon/Art Resource, NY; pp. 123, 227, 286: Tate Gallery, London/Art Resource, NY; p. 162: Kimbell Art Museum/CORBIS; p.167: Clore Collection, Tate Gallery, London/Art Resource, NY; p. 209: Whitford & Hughes, London, UK/ Bridgeman Art Library; p. 211: Gianni Dagli Orti/CORBIS; pp. 213, 215: Arte & Immagini srl/CORBIS; p. 231: Art Resource, NY; p. 241: Bettmann/CORBIS; p. 243: The Pierpont Morgan Library/Art Resource, NY; p. 263: Werner Forman/ Art Resource, NY; p. 266: Sarah Spence; p. 302: Image Select/Art Resource, NY; p. 310: Alinari/Regione Umbria/Art Resource, NY

DOROTHEAE CONIVGI
MARTHAE DEBORAEQUE FILIABVS
CARISSIMIS PATERFAMILIAS
FREDERICVS
D.D.

CONTENTS

PREFACE

The genesis of this book derives from the demand for an intermediate Latin reader that could be readily employed as a sequel to *Wheelock's Latin* and other beginning texts. The volume's purpose is to provide, not a survey of all Latin literature, but an interesting and stimulating selection from a variety of important authors, together with notes that assume and enlarge upon the student's knowledge of basic Latin grammar. Students who complete the readings in this text, or a generous sampling of them, will be well prepared to move on to more advanced work in Latin prose and verse; at the same time, those who do not continue with the language can with this book enjoy the rewards of reading selections from some of the most interesting and influential works of Latin literature, ranging from the late republic and the empire to the late Middle Ages, and including Cicero, Livy, Ovid, Pliny the Younger, St. Jerome's translation of the Latin Bible (the so-called Vulgate edition), and a variety of medieval writers.

In deciding upon the passages for this volume, preference was given to including longer selections from fewer authors rather than brief snippets from a wider array of works (the only exception being the sampling from medieval texts presented at the end of the book). Whenever a student comes to a new Latin author, some time is required to become familiar and comfortable with the characteristics of that author's style, and it is easy to imagine the compounding of those challenges in a text that ranges through numerous authors, works, and subjects in a multitude of short passages. Moreover, a very positive advantage in an anthology of longer readings is that each excerpt can provide a better sense of the character of the work as a whole.

All the readings included in this volume, unlike those in some intermediate textbooks, are authentic, unadapted Latin. The only liberty taken with the original texts is the use of classical spelling in the medieval Latin selections and the occasional omission of passages that are either too difficult or digressive or of too little interest. The majority of the passages, including most of Cicero's and Pliny's letters and the selections from Ovid's *Metamorphoses,* and the several medieval texts, are in fact unexcerpted, and those that have been excerpted are identified as such and provided with references to the full original text.

In the notes, outright translations are given as seldom as possible.

Instead, words that are likely to be unfamiliar are glossed, and comments on grammar and context are provided to help students comprehend the Latin and arrive at an accurate understanding of the text through their own abilities.

Finally, the end vocabulary includes English meanings for all Latin words appearing in the text, the sole exception being certain personal names and other proper nouns that are adequately defined in the notes. Macrons, though not appearing in the text (since the Romans themselves did not ordinarily employ them and they are not used in advanced Latin textbooks), are provided in the vocabulary.

To Professor Edwin S. Ramage of Indiana University I am very grateful for his most conscientious and critical survey of the manuscript of the passages and notes; many of his suggestions have led to improvements. Likewise I am grateful to Professors Joseph J. Prentiss of West Virginia University and W. M. Read of the University of Washington for submitting lists of corrigenda for the book's second printing. To the keen observation, good judgment, and acute queries of Dr. Gladys Walterhouse of Barnes and Noble I am also deeply indebted. Finally, my heartfelt and abiding thanks to my very patient and very devoted wife, Dorothy, who typed the manuscript so accurately and so understandingly, and to my daughter Deborah for her very faithful and accurate assistance in proofreading the galleys.

FREDERIC M. WHEELOCK
Amherst, New Hampshire
Summer, 1969

The Revised Edition

In many respects *Wheelock's Latin Reader* (originally titled *Latin Literature: A Book of Readings*) is one of the very best intermediate Latin texts published in the last generation. When the book first appeared in 1967, reviewers extolled the accessibility and comprehensiveness of its readings from Cicero, Livy, Ovid, and Pliny, praised its incorporation of selections from medieval Latin and the Vulgate as "a particularly happy innovation," and hailed the volume as "a solid companion" to *Wheelock's Latin,* the author's best-selling beginning Latin textbook.

The book's primary virtues were, and remain, these two: the wide range of selections from both classical and medieval Latin—about 3,400 lines altogether—and Professor Wheelock's judicious annotations. From

Cicero are included a rich and diverse sampling of his widely varied works, constituting nearly half the volume's readings: the extensive excerpts from Cicero's orations against Verres, the corrupt governor of Sicily whom he courageously prosecuted in 70 B.C., provide valuable insights into the political and judicial proceedings of the late republic and a marvelous specimen of Ciceronian rhetoric; the selections from two of his philosophical treatises, the *De Officiis* and the *De Amicitia,* probingly examine ethical and moral issues that continue to be of great concern to us today; and the several letters (most of them included in their entirety), addressed to family, friends, and associates, give us some remarkably candid glimpses into the personal and political life of that most famous orator and statesman.

The selections from Livy's *Ab Urbe Condita,* which include the story of Romulus and Remus and other legends of early Rome, as well as an account of Hannibal's assault on Italy during the Second Punic War, are at once invaluable historical documents and lively, captivating narratives. The four transformation tales from Ovid's *Metamorphoses*—the tragic love stories of Pyramus and Thisbe, and of Orpheus and Eurydice, the myths of Daedalus and Icarus and of Midas' golden touch—make for delightful reading and provide an ideal introduction to classical Latin poetry. The selections from Pliny's literary epistles present an interesting contrast with Cicero's more spontaneous letters and contain important and interesting information on social and political institutions of the early empire, as well as detailed evidence for both the catastrophic eruption of Mt. Vesuvius in A.D. 79 and the Roman government's policies regarding practices of the early Christian church during the reign of the emperor Trajan.

The passages from St. Jerome's Vulgate edition of the Bible, including the Ten Commandments, the Sermon on the Mount, the Prodigal Son, and others, are an excellent introduction to that profoundly influential document and to the vulgar Latin (the Latin of the *vulgus,* the common people) of the early fifth century. And finally, the several selections drawn from Latin literature of the Middle Ages demonstrate the evolution of the language from the eighth to the fourteenth centuries as well as the remarkable diversity of matter and manner seen in such disparate works as Bede's *Historia Ecclesiastica Gentis Anglorum,* the allegorizing tales of the *Gesta Romanorum,* the sometimes reverent, sometimes raucous *Carmina Burana,* and the hypnotic power of that most powerful of medieval hymns, the *Dies Irae.*

It would be difficult to improve upon so rich a selection from Latin literature, ranging as it does over the prose and verse of some 1,400 years and including ample material from which to pick and choose for a semester's course in college or, if read straight through, for up to two college semesters or a year's work in high school. Thus I have made few changes to the content of the reading passages. Here and there I have restored some of the Latin that Professor Wheelock omitted, but only when the level of interest was high and the difficulty low, and often in order to reconstitute a continuous, unexcerpted passage (as, for example, in some of the letters, the Ovid selections, and all the readings from the Vulgate). In a very few instances I have deleted passages that seemed to me inordinately difficult for students at the intermediate level (including the notoriously abstruse preface to Livy's history). Perhaps most obviously, the layout of the Latin text has been entirely redesigned and set in a more legible 12-point font.

The layout of the notes has likewise been redesigned, removing them from the back of the book and setting them in a larger font on pages facing the text. I have made considerable changes to the content of the notes as well, deleting some that seemed to provide unnecessary information, adding others where intermediate students might need more help. The glossing of vocabulary has been systematized; within each unit definitions are provided for words that students are not likely to have encountered in their previous study (including words not found in the Latin-English end vocabulary to *Wheelock's Latin*) and whose meanings cannot be easily deduced based on English derivatives; several definitions are usually given in each gloss, so the student must select the one that best suits the context; vocabulary glosses, usually including the nominative singular for a noun and the second principal part for a verb, are provided at a word's first occurrence within a unit and are repeated at the first occurrence in subsequent units, since some teachers and students may not read all the selections in the text or may not read them in the order in which they appear. In any case, as noted earlier in Professor Wheelock's preface, nearly every word in the text is defined in the extensive end vocabulary, which has been expanded in this edition and indicates those words that occur five or more times in the text and which therefore should be memorized.

Difficult or unusual grammatical constructions, figures of speech, and poetic and rhetorical devices that merit comment are printed in SMALL CAPITAL LETTERS LIKE THESE to focus the student's attention; in some instances, explanations or definitions are provided, but in most the teacher is expected to elaborate.

Each unit has been provided with a short introduction, drawn in part from comments previously included in Professor Wheelock's endnotes; and the brief bibliography, listing works useful for background and supplemental information, has been completely updated. Also new to this edition are several maps listing nearly every placename mentioned in the Latin text and many of those in the notes, as well as dozens of photographs which are intended to enrich the reader's understanding and appreciation of the text.

Once again it has been a pleasure and a privilege to have the opportunity of revising one of Frederic Wheelock's books, thus completing the "Wheelock's Latin Series" and rendering the three volumes (*Wheelock's Latin,* Paul Comeau's *Workbook for Wheelock's Latin,* and this *Wheelock's Latin Reader*) more serviceable, it may be hoped, for a new generation of Latin students. I am particularly grateful to Professor Wheelock's daughters, Martha Wheelock and Deborah Wheelock Taylor, my "sisters-in-Latin," for extending me this opportunity, and to my editor at Harper-Collins, Greg Chaput, for supporting my work on all the Wheelock projects every step of the way.

Thanks are due to many others as well: to my stalwart graduate assistants Brandon Wester and Jim Yavenditti for their service in a wide range of research and proofreading tasks; to Tom Elliott, Nicole Feldl, Alexandra Retzleff, and Joyce Uy of the Ancient World Mapping Center at the University of North Carolina, for their expert assistance in producing the maps newly included in this edition; to Tim McCarthy of Art Resource for his generous help in researching literally hundreds of photo options for the book; to my friend and Senior Associate Editor on the staff of *The Classical Outlook,* Mary Ricks, for reading and commenting ever so helpfully on numerous drafts of the typescript; to my colleagues Jim Anderson, Bob Curtis, Timothy Gantz, Bob Harris, Sallie Spence, Fran Teague, Erika Thorgerson, and Ann Williams, for their assistance in providing illustrations and information on topics beyond my very limited areas of competence; and finally, most emphatically and most affectionately, to my dear wife Laura, for her constant love and her unceasingly cheerful tolerance of all my little undertakings.

RICHARD A. LaFLEUR
Athens, Georgia
Spring, 2001

BIBLIOGRAPHY

The following brief bibliography contains works consulted for this new edition and recommended to students and instructors for background and other supplemental information.

Ackroyd, P.R., and C.F. Evans, eds. *The Cambridge History of the Bible.* 3 vols. Cambridge ENG: Cambridge Univ. Press, 1963–70.

Anderson, William S., ed. *Ovid's Metamorphoses: Books 1–5.* Norman OK: Univ. of Oklahoma Press, 1997.

———. *Ovid's Metamorphoses: Books 6–10.* Norman OK: Univ. of Oklahoma Press, 1972.

Barsby, John. *Ovid.* New Surveys in the Classics, 12. Oxford ENG: Clarendon Press, 1978.

Dickison, Sheila, ed. *Cicero's Verrine Oration II.4.* Detroit MI: Wayne State Univ. Press, 1992.

Dorey, T.A., ed. *Cicero.* Studies in Latin Literature and Its Influence. New York NY: Basic Books, 1965.

Dyck, Andrew R. *A Commentary on Cicero, De Officiis.* Ann Arbor MI: Univ. of Michigan Press, 1996.

Fisher, M.B., and M.R. Griffin. *Selections from Pliny's Letters: Handbook.* Cambridge ENG: Cambridge Univ. Press, 1977.

Gould, H.E., and J.L. Whiteley, eds. *Cicero: De Amicitia.* 1941. Reprint. Wauconda IL: Bolchazy-Carducci, 1999.

———. *Titus Livius: Book One.* Blasingstoke ENG: Macmillan, 1952.

Harrington, K.P., ed. *Medieval Latin.* 2nd ed. Rev. Joseph Pucci. Chicago IL: Univ. of Chicago Press, 1997.

Herman, József. *Vulgar Latin.* Rev. ed. Trans. Roger White. Univ. Park, PA: Pennsylvania State Univ., 2000.

Hill, D.E., ed. and trans. *Ovid: Metamorphoses IX-XII.* Warminster ENG: Aris and Phillips, 1999.

Hornblower, Simon, and Antony Spawforth, eds. *Oxford Classical Dictionary.* 3rd ed. Oxford ENG: Oxford Univ. Press, 1996.

How, W.W., and A.C. Clark, eds. *Cicero: Select Letters.* London ENG: Oxford Univ. Press, 1962.

Kelly, J.N.D. *Jerome: His Life, Writings, and Controversies.* New York NY: Harper and Row, 1975.

Kenney, E.J., and W.V. Clausen, eds. *The Cambridge History of Classical Literature.* Vol. 2. *Latin Literature.* Cambridge ENG: Cambridge Univ. Press, 1982.

Luce, T.J. *Livy: The Composition of His History.* Princeton NJ: Princeton Univ. Press, 1977.

Mack, Sara. *Ovid.* New Haven CT: Yale Univ. Press, 1988.

Mantello, F.A.C., and A.G. Rigg, eds. *Medieval Latin: An Introduction and Bibliographical Guide.* Washington DC: Catholic Univ. of America Press, 1996.

Ogilvie, R.M. *A Commentary on Livy Books 1–5.* Oxford ENG: Clarendon Press, 1965.

Powell, J.G.F., ed. and trans. *Cicero: Laelius, On Friendship.* Warminster ENG: Aris and Phillips, 1990.

Raby, F.J.E. *A History of Christian Latin Poetry from the Beginnings to the Close of the Middle Ages.* 2nd ed. London ENG: Oxford Univ. Press, 1953.

Shackleton Bailey, D.R., ed. and trans. *Cicero's Letters.* Vols. 1–10. Cambridge ENG: Cambridge Univ. Press, 1965–81.

Sherwin-White, A.N. *The Letters of Pliny: A Historical and Social Commentary.* London ENG: Oxford Univ. Press, 1966.

Stockton, David, ed. *Thirty-five Letters of Cicero.* London ENG: Oxford Univ. Press, 1969.

Thompson, John, and F.S. Plaistowe, eds. *Livy: Book XXII.* Bristol ENG: Bristol Classical Press, 1988.

Walsh, P.G. *Livy: His Historical Aims and Methods.* Cambridge ENG: Cambridge Univ. Press, 1961.

———, ed. *Livy: Book XXI.* Bristol, ENG: Bristol Classical Press, 1985.

Westcott, J.H., ed. *Selected Letters of Pliny.* Norman OK: Univ. of Oklahoma Press, 1965.

ABBREVIATIONS

The following abbreviations are employed in the notes and vocabulary:

abl.	ablative case	indecl.	indeclinable
abs.	absolute	indef.	indefinite
acc.	accusative case	indic.	indicative mood
act.	active voice	inf(s).	infinitive(s)
A.D.	after Christ (Lat. *anno Domini,* lit., *in the year of the Lord*)	interj(s).	interjection(s)
		interrog.	interrogative
		Lat.	Latin
adj(s).	adjective(s), adjectival	lit.	literally
adv(s).	adverb(s), adverbial	loc.	locative case
appos.	appositive, apposition, appositional	m.	masculine gender
		n.	neuter gender
B.C.	before Christ	nom.	nominative case
ca.	about (Lat. *circa*)	obj(s).	object(s), objective
cent.	century	partic(s).	participle(s)
cl(s).	clause(s)	pass.	passive voice
class.	classical	perf.	perfect (present perfect) tense
compl.	complement, complementary		
		pers.	person, personal
conj(s).	conjunction(s)	pl.	plural
cp.	compare (Lat. *compara*)	plpf.	pluperfect tense
dat.	dative case	pred.	predicate
decl.	declension	prep(s).	preposition(s), prepositional
dir.	direct		
eccl.	ecclesiastical	pres.	present tense
e.g.	for example (Lat. *exempli gratia*)	pron(s).	pronoun(s)
		ref.	reference
Eng.	Engli	rel.	relative
etc.	and others (Lat. *et cetera*)	sc.	supply, namely (Lat. *scilicet*)
f.	feminine gender	sent(s).	sentence(s)
fut.	future tense	sg.	singular
gen.	genitive case	subj(s).	subject(s)
hist.	historical	subjunct.	subjunctive mood
i.e.	that is (Lat. *id est*)	vb(s).	verb(s)
imper.	imperative	voc.	vocative case
impers.	impersonal	vs.	as opposed to, in comparison with (Lat. *versus*)
impf.	imperfect tense		
ind. quest(s).	indirect question(s)		
ind. state(s).	indirect statement(s)		

MAPS

ANCIENT ITALY

Map by Richard A. LaFleur, Tom Elliott, Nicole Feldl, Alexandra Retzleff, and Joyce Uy.
Copyright 2001, Ancient World Mapping Center (http://www.unc.edu/depts/awmc)

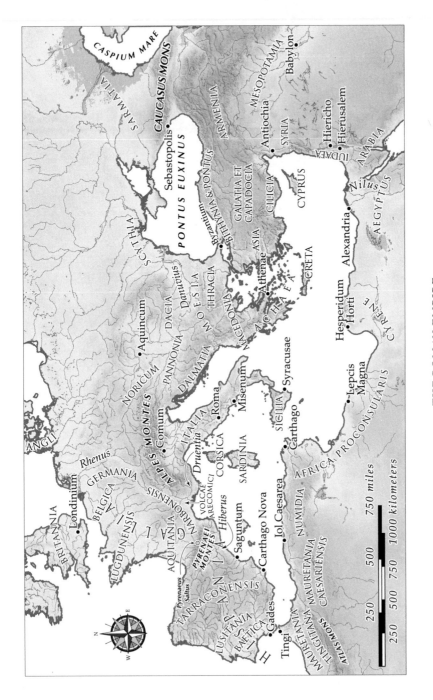

THE ROMAN EMPIRE

Map by Richard A. LaFleur, Tom Elliott, Nicole Feldl, Alexandra Retzleff, and Joyce Uy. Copyright 2001, Ancient World Mapping Center (http://www.unc.edu/depts/awmc)

ANCIENT GREECE AND THE AEGEAN

Map by Richard A. LaFleur, Tom Elliott, Nicole Feldl, Alexandra Retzleff, and Joyce Uy. Copyright 2001, Ancient World Mapping Center (http://www.unc.edu/depts/awmc)

WHEELOCK'S LATIN READER
Selections from Latin Literature

Cicero's Orations against Verres

Marcus Tullius Cicero was ancient Rome's most famous orator, an eminent statesman, and one of the best known, most prolific, and most admired of all classical Latin authors. Born in Arpinum in central Italy on January 3, 106 B.C., Cicero's family was wealthy and well-connected. His father saw to it that the young man received an excellent education, and after a brief stint in the army when he was only 17 years old, Cicero turned to the study of law, serving an apprenticeship with some of the leading jurists of the day. He argued his first case in 81 B.C., and in the following year his successful defense of Sextus Roscius in his trial for murder—a case in which he risked incurring the enmity of the dictator Sulla—earned him a reputation as a bold and highly competent lawyer. In 79 his wife Terentia gave birth to their daughter Tullia.

During the early 70's Cicero continued his study of philosophy and rhetoric in Greece and returned to Rome to commence a political career, which began with his election to the quaestorship in 75 B.C., to the praetorship in 66, and, despite his status as a *novus homo* (a candidate whose family had no tradition of office-holding), to the consulship in 63. Cicero's year as consul was notable for his suppression of the conspiracy of Lucius Sergius Catilina, an episode of Roman history richly docu-

"Cicero Denouncing Catiline in the Roman Senate"
Cesare Maccari, 19th century, Palazzo Madama, Rome, Italy

mented in a monograph written by the contemporary historian Sallust and especially in Cicero's four highly celebrated Catilinarian orations.

Cicero's speeches were so persuasive, and the evidence so compelling, that Catiline fled Rome immediately and joined his rebel troops. Soon he and his army were outlawed, five conspirators who had remained in Rome were arrested and executed, and in early 62 Catiline and nearly all his forces fell in battle at Pistoria, in northern Etruria, in a bloody confrontation with the Roman legions sent in their pursuit. Thanks to Cicero's personal courage, his political adroitness, and his oratorical skills (well evidenced in the excerpts you are about to read from his earlier Verrine orations), he managed to suppress a rebellion that could have had far more sweeping, and violent, consequences.

In executing several of the Catilinarian conspirators, Cicero had acted under the authority of an emergency decree of the senate; nevertheless, the legality of the action was open to question and Cicero's political adversaries ultimately engineered his banishment from Rome in 58 B.C. With the support of Pompey the Great, Cicero was recalled the next year; but under the shadow of Pompey's alliance with Gaius Julius Caesar and Marcus Licinius Crassus (the so-called "first triumvirate"), he played a less active role in politics during the mid-50's, devoting his time instead to the courts and to writing a number of oratorical and political treatises, including the *De Oratore,* the *De Republica,* and the *De Legibus.*

In 52 B.C. he was elected to the augurate, a prestigious state priesthood, and then in 51–50 he was dispatched to serve as proconsular governor of Cilicia, taking with him his young son Marcus (born in 65). When he returned to Rome this time, Cicero found the state embroiled in civil war after the split between Caesar and Pompey. Pompey was soon defeated, and, to Cicero's great dismay, Caesar was elected to a series of consulships and ultimately appointed dictator for life. During this same period Cicero divorced Terentia for suspected financial improprieties, and, plunged into despair over their daughter's death in 45, he withdrew entirely from public life and turned to philosophy, authoring several important works on ethics and religion (discussed below in the introduction to "Cicero's *Philosophica*").

After Caesar's assassination in 44, Cicero returned briefly but with a passion to the political scene, vehemently attacking Caesar's former lieutenant and would-be successor, Mark Antony, in a series of speeches known as the "Philippics." When Antony joined ranks in the "second triumvirate" with Marcus Aemilius Lepidus and Octavian (Caesar's adoptive son and the future emperor Augustus), Cicero's fate was sealed; at Antony's insistence, his name was included among those proscribed on the triumvirs' enemies list and he was hunted down and beheaded on the 7th of December, 43 B.C.—a grim and unmerited conclusion to a brilliant life and career.

One of the many bright moments in that career was in 75 B.C., when at the age of 31 Cicero took his first step on the traditional course of political offices known as the *cursus honorum* and was elected to the financial post of quaestor. Cicero served his quaestorship in the province of Sicily, and he administered the office with such integrity that he won the enduring esteem and affection of the provincials. In 70 B.C., after the notoriously corrupt and rapacious Gaius Verres had governed the island for three years (73–71), the Sicilians called upon Cicero to represent them in prosecuting their former governor in the extortion courts for his crimes against the province and its people. Verres enjoyed the support of not a few prominent men in Rome and had every expectation of escaping justice through his influence, bribery, and the postponement of his trial to the following year, when the composition of the court would be more favorable to his defense. Cicero, however, by his rapid amassing of evi-

Cicero, 1st century B.C.
Museo Capitolino, Rome, Italy

dence and the immediate presentation of witnesses during the trial's opening phase, the so-called *Actio Prima,* provided such damning testimony that Verres' lawyer, Quintus Hortensius Hortalus, withdrew from the case and Verres fled into voluntary exile in Massilia (modern Marseilles).

This stunning victory made unnecessary the more formal presentation of the case which Cicero had prepared for the second phase of the trial, the *Actio Secunda,* but he nevertheless polished and published in five volumes the text of his planned speeches, rightly considering them good publicity for a political aspirant and a rising orator. Hortensius' reputation as the leading lawyer of the day was soon eclipsed by Cicero's; and Verres himself died in exile, proscribed by Mark Antony, ironically, for his art collection, much of which had been stolen from the Sicilians.

The passages from the Verrines excerpted in this book include some of the most interesting sections of both the *Actio Prima* and the *Actio Secunda.* Focusing on the enormity of Verres' crimes, in particular his plundering of Syracuse, capital of the province, and his torture and crucifixion of Publius Gavius, a Roman citizen who had dared to speak out against Verres, the selections provide valuable insights into provincial administration and the juridical process in the first century B.C. as well as a generous sampling of Cicero's spectacular rhetorical powers.

1. **quod:** the antecedent is **id** (3).
    unum: *alone* or *especially.*
2. **vestri ordinis:** OBJ. GEN.; i.e., the senatorial class (vs. the equestrians, or busi-
    nessmen, and the urban plebs, or common people). Senatorial juries,
    commonly biased in favor of any fellow senator who was tried before
    them on the charge of extortion, had a bad reputation, hence **invidiam**
    and **infamiam.** In this case, however, Cicero felt that he had managed to
    secure a reliable jury and wanted to indict Verres as quickly as possible,
    since both he and Verres had reason to believe that the senatorial court
    of the following year would be more easily swayed by Verres and acquit
    him.
    vestri . . . vobis (4): some manuscripts have **nostri . . . nobis,** which could be
    the correct reading, since Cicero, as a former quaestor, was himself a
    member of the senate.
    iudiciorum: iudicium can mean not only a *judgment* or *trial* but also a *court*
    or *jury* (i.e., those who gave the judgment).
    sedandam: sedare, *to settle, check, stop, mitigate.*
3. **prope:** adv., *nearly, almost.*
    divinitus: adv., *divinely, providentially.*
4. **summo:** here, *most critical.*
5. **inveteravit: inveterascere,** *to grow old, become established;* note the emphasis
    achieved both by placing the main verb at the beginning of the sentence
    and by employing CHIASMUS (the ABBA order in the phrase **perniciosa
    rei publicae vobisque periculosa**).
7. **exteras nationes:** i.e., the provinces.
    sermone: not *sermon,* but *conversation, talk;* the IND. STATE. **pecuniosum . . .
    posse** (8–9) depends on this speech word.
    percrebruit: percrebrescere, *to spread abroad.*
8. **pecuniosum:** i.e., as long as he is wealthy.
    neminem: emphatic for **nullum.**
9. **discrimine: discrimen,** *turning point, crisis, critical moment;* a bill had been
    proposed (and was subsequently passed) limiting the authority of the
    senate over the courts.
10. **qui . . . conentur (11):** REL. CL. OF PURPOSE, *(when men are ready) to attempt.*
    contionibus: contio, *meeting, assembly, speech.*
11. **reus:** *defendant.*
12. **vita atque factis:** ABL. OF CAUSE.
    omnium: depends on **opinione.**
13. **pecuniae . . . absolutus (14):** sc. **sed;** both the omission of the conj. (ASYNDE-
    TON) and the parallelism of the two cls. emphasize the contrast between
    damnatus and **absolutus.**
    praedicatione: praedicatio, *proclamation, declaration;* with **spe,** *according to
    his own hopeful assertion,* an example of HENDIADYS (use of two nouns
    connected by a conj., instead of one modified noun, to convey vividly a
    single complex idea).
14. **absolutus: absolvere,** *to absolve, acquit.*

IN C. VERREM: ACTIO PRIMA

Confidence in the incorruptibilty of the senatorial jury, which now has the opportunity to redeem Rome's honor in the eyes of the world.

Quod erat optandum maxime, iudices, et quod unum ad invidiam vestri ordinis infamiamque iudiciorum sedandam maxime pertinebat, id non humano consilio sed prope divinitus datum atque oblatum vobis summo rei publicae tempore videtur.
5 Inveteravit enim iam opinio perniciosa rei publicae vobisque periculosa, quae non modo apud populum Romanum sed etiam exteras nationes omnium sermone percrebruit: his iudiciis, quae nunc sunt, pecuniosum hominem, quamvis sit nocens, neminem posse damnari. Nunc in ipso discrimine ordinis iudiciorumque
10 vestrorum, cum sint parati qui contionibus et legibus hanc invidiam senatus inflammare conentur, reus in iudicium adductus est C. Verres, homo vita atque factis omnium iam opinione damnatus, pecuniae magnitudine sua spe ac praedicatione absolutus.

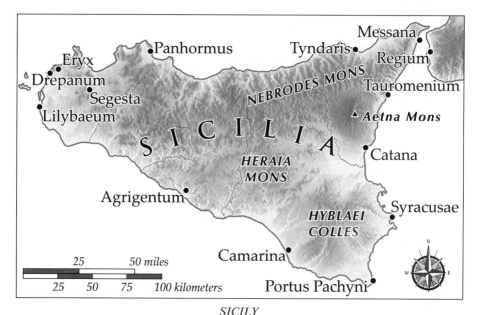

SICILY
Map by R. A. LaFleur, Tom Elliott, Nicole Feldl, Alexandra Retzleff,
and Joyce Uy. Copyright 2001, Ancient World Mapping Center
(http://www.unc.edu/depts/awmc)

16. **actor:** here, not *actor,* but *prosecutor, attorney.*
     augerem: augere, *to increase, enlarge.*
17. **communi:** i.e., which both the senate and Cicero himself shared.
18. **reconciliare:** here, not *reconcile,* but *win back.*
     existimationem: existimatio, *judgment, good name, reputation.*
20. **depeculatorem: depeculator,** *plunderer, embezzler.*
     aerari: aerarium, *treasury.*
     Asiae atque Pamphyliae (21): the Roman province of Asia and Pamphylia, during Cicero's day part of the province of Cilicia (of which Cicero himself became proconsular governor in 51–50 B.C.), were both in Asia Minor, where Verres had served the corrupt governor Dolabella.
21. **praedonem: praedo,** *robber;* the allusion is to Verres' term as praetor urbanus in 74 B.C.
     labem atque perniciem (22): from **labes** and **pernicies,** *ruin and destruction.*
22. **religiose:** adv., *conscientiously.*
23. **haerebit: haerere,** *to cling, stick, persist.*
24. **quam ob rem (25):** here = **cur.**
25. **proficere:** *to gain, accomplish.*
26. **intellegere non possum:** because the current praetor (Manius Acilius Glabrio) and panel **(consilium)** are reliable.
27. **reiectione: reiectio,** *challenging, rejection;* during the selection of a panel, prospective jurors could be challenged and rejected.
27. **ea spe . . . ut (28):** lit., *with such hope . . . that;* the cl. is in appos. with **unum illud.**
28. **praeditum:** *endowed (with)* + abl.; freely, *his hopes were such that.*
     constitueret: constituere, *to place, establish, determine, decide.*
29. **sibi . . . adiumento: adiumentum,** *help, assistance;* DAT. OF REF. + DAT. OF PURPOSE (together sometimes called the DOUBLE DAT.).
     fore: a common alternate form for **futurum esse.**
32. **quae . . . possit (34):** REL. CL. OF RESULT.
34. **aliqua ex parte:** *in any way, even partially.*
36. **indicia:** *proofs, evidence.*
39. **aliquando:** adv., *at some time, at any time, ever, at last.*
40. **hoc praetore:** ABL. ABS.; the governor of Sicily was a propraetor (i.e., a former praetor).
41. **communia:** *common to all men, universal.*
43. **imprudentiam:** lit., *lack of foresight.*
     superfuit: superesse, *to be more than enough (for).*
44. **nutum:** *nod (of approval), command.*
     pecuniae: *sums of money.*
45. **aratorum: arator,** *plowman, farmer, tenant;* in Sicily much of the land was regarded as owned by the state and was rented out to the **aratores** for a tithe of their crops.
     bonis: *goods.*
     instituto: institutum, practice, custom.
     coactae: sc. **sunt;** Cicero and other writers frequently omitted forms of **sum** in the perf. pass. system, employing only the perf. pass. partic. (so **existimati, cruciati,** etc., later in this sent.).

15   Huic ego causae, iudices, cum summa voluntate et exspectatione populi Romani, actor accessi, non ut augerem invidiam ordinis sed ut infamiae communi succurrerem. Adduxi enim hominem in quo reconciliare existimationem iudiciorum amissam, redire in gratiam cum populo Romano, satisfacere exteris
20   nationibus possetis—depeculatorem aerari, vexatorem Asiae atque Pamphyliae, praedonem iuris urbani, labem atque perniciem provinciae Siciliae. De quo si vos vere ac religiose iudicaveritis, auctoritas ea, quae in vobis remanere debet, haerebit. Quid iste speret et quo animum intendat facile perspicio. Quam
25   ob rem vero se confidat aliquid proficere posse, hoc praetore et hoc consilio, intellegere non possum. Unum illud intellego (quod populus Romanus in reiectione iudicum iudicavit) ea spe istum fuisse praeditum ut omnem rationem salutis in pecunia constitueret, hoc erepto praesidio ut nullam sibi rem adiumento fore
30   arbitraretur. (I.1–10, excerpts)

A summary of Verres' crimes, especially in Sicily.

     Etenim quod est ingenium tantum, quae tanta facultas dicendi aut copia, quae istius vitam, tot vitiis flagitiisque convictam, iam pridem omnium voluntate iudicioque damnatam, aliqua ex parte possit defendere?
35   Iam vero omnium vitiorum suorum plurima et maxima constituit monumenta et indicia in provincia Sicilia, quam iste per triennium ita vexavit ac perdidit ut ea restitui in antiquum statum nullo modo possit, vix autem per multos annos innocentisque praetores aliqua ex parte recreari aliquando posse videatur. Hoc praetore, Siculi neque suas leges neque nostra senatus
40   consulta neque communia iura tenuerunt. Tantum quisque habet in Sicilia quantum hominis avarissimi et libidinosissimi aut imprudentiam subterfugit aut satietati superfuit. Nulla res per triennium nisi ad nutum istius iudicata est. Innumerabiles pecuniae ex aratorum bonis novo nefarioque instituto coactae;
45

46. **socii:** not allies in the international sense, but non-Roman members of communities within the Roman state which had special rights such as local independence.

  existimati: existimare, *to estimate, think, consider.*

47. **cruciati: cruciare,** *to crucify, torture;* it was illegal to inflict serious physical punishment on a Roman citizen except as a result of a trial by peers at Rome.

48. **integerrimi: integer,** *untouched, blameless, honest.*

49. **indicta:** lit., *not spoken = untried, unheard;* with **causa** (49), ABL. ABS.

  eiecti: i.e., into exile.

  portus: *ports, harbors.*

52. **fame: fames,** *hunger, starvation.*

  classes: classis, *fleet;* maintained by the Sicilians as a defense against pirates.

  opportunissimae: here, *most serviceable.*

54. **partim:** adv., *partly.*

55. **locupletissimorum: locuples,** *rich, wealthy.*

  illi: the antecedent is **regum;** e.g., Hiero II, king of Syracuse ca. 270–216 B.C.

  ornamento urbibus: DOUBLE DAT.

56. **imperatorum:** e.g., Marcus Claudius Marcellus, who recaptured Syracuse from the Carthaginians in 212 B.C. and spared its public monuments, and Scipio Aemilianus, who after his victory in the Third Punic War restored to the Sicilians a number of statues that had been removed to Carthage.

57. **spoliavit: spoliare,** *to rob, plunder.*

59. **delubra: delubrum,** *shrine, temple.*

60. **in:** *in the case of, in respect to.*

  stupris: stuprum, *debauchery.*

  flagitiis: flagitium, *shameful act, disgrace.*

63. **consili:** PARTITIVE GEN.

  profecto: adv., *surely, actually, really.*

  taciti: agrees with the subj. of **dabitis.**

  egomet: **-met** is a suffix appended to prons. for emphasis.

64. **necessario:** adv.

65. **legitimo:** i.e., the time allotted by law for Cicero's prosecution of the case.

66. **ut ... videatur (68):** NOUN CL. OF RESULT, common after **perficere, efficere, accidere,** etc.

  post: our idiom says *within.*

67. **compositior: compositus,** *put together, arranged, prepared, calm.*

68. **reus ne elabatur (69): elabi,** *to slip away, escape;* FEAR CL., dependent on **periculum est.**

70. **absconditum:** *concealed, hidden.*

71. **perpetua:** *uninterrupted, complete.*

72. **hominem:** here, contemptuous compared with **virum.**

  tabulis: tabula, *board, writing tablet, document, record.*

  testibus: testis, *witness.*

socii fidelissimi in hostium numero existimati; cives Romani servilem in modum cruciati et necati; homines nocentissimi propter pecunias iudicio liberati; honestissimi atque integerrimi, absentes rei facti, indicta causa, damnati et eiecti; por-
50   tus munitissimi, maximae tutissimaeque urbes piratis praedonibusque patefactae; nautae militesque Siculorum, socii nostri atque amici, fame necati; classes optimae atque opportunissimae, cum magna ignominia populi Romani, amissae et perditae. Idem iste praetor monumenta antiquissima, partim regum
55   locupletissimorum, quae illi ornamento urbibus esse voluerunt, partim etiam nostrorum imperatorum, quae victores civitatibus Siculis aut dederunt aut reddiderunt, spoliavit nudavitque omnia. Neque hoc solum in statuis ornamentisque publicis fecit, sed etiam delubra omnia sanctissimis religionibus consecrata
60   depeculatus est. In stupris vero et flagitiis, nefarias eius libidines commemorare pudore deterreor. (I.10–14, excerpts)

Cicero's strategy: immediate presentation of evidence and witnesses without formal development of the case.

Nunc ego, iudices, iam vos consulo quid mihi faciendum putetis. Id enim consili mihi profecto taciti dabitis quod egomet mihi necessario capiendum intellego. Si utar ad dicendum meo
65   legitimo tempore, mei laboris, industriae, diligentiaeque capiam fructum, et ex accusatione perficiam ut nemo umquam post hominum memoriam paratior, vigilantior, compositior ad iudicium venisse videatur. Sed in hac laude industriae meae, reus ne elabatur summum periculum est. Quid est igitur quod fieri possit? Non obscurum, opinor, neque absconditum. Fructum istum laudis, qui ex perpetua oratione percipi potuit, in alia tempora reservemus; nunc hominem tabulis, testibus, privatis publicisque litteris auctoritatibusque accusemus.

Doric temple, 5th century B.C.
Segesta, Sicily, Italy

74.   **mihi certum est:** *I am determined.*
    committere: here, *permit* + **ut** cl.
    praetor: Glabrio, the incumbent praetor, was unbiased, but the praetor-elect, under whom the case of Verres would be tried if delayed to the next year, was prejudiced in Verres' favor.
    nobis: DAT. OF REF., implying disadvantage.
75.   **mutetur:** sg. because the compound subj. is viewed as a single entity.
76.   **homines:** here, simply *human beings.*
77.   **supplices: supplex,** *suppliant.*
    omnis: = **omnes;** this alternate acc. pl. form for **i**-stems is common in Cicero and other class. authors.
78.   **verum:** conj., *but.*
    deplorandi: deplorare, *to weep, lament the loss of, complain of.*
80.   **ut . . . statim:** noun cl. in appos. with **hoc non novum.**
81.   **testis:** acc. pl. (cp. **omnis** in 77).
    quod . . . explicem (82): in appos. to **illud . . . novum;** instead of delivering the usual opening argument, providing an overview of the case, Cicero will introduce witnesses to support each charge as he enumerates them, a clever ploy allowing him to produce evidence before the defense attorney (Quintus Hortensius Hortalus) has an opportunity to counter with his own opening remarks.
    constituam: here, *arrange, deploy.*
82.   **crimen:** *charge, accusation.*
83.   **altera actione:** excerpts from this *second action,* i.e., the second part of the trial, are included below.
87.   **quadringentiens sestertium:** = **quadringentiens (centena milia) sestertium,** *400 x 100,000 sesterces = 40,000,000 sesterces;* a **sestertius** was a *sesterce,* and **sestertium,** *1,000 sesterces,* when used with a numeral adv., stood for 100,000 sesterces.
89.   **statuatis: statuere,** *to set up, decide, determine.*
    spatium: *space, time, opportunity.*
90.   **nostro commodo: commodum,** *convenience, advantage;* ABL. OF ACCORDANCE, *according to our convenience.*
91.   **oratione:** ABL. OF MEANS with the idiom **opus est,** *there is need of* (lit., *there is work to be done by . . .*).
    nihil: emphatic for **non.**
    dixi: indicating the end of his opening remarks; depositions and the testimony of witnesses followed.
93.   **Syracusarum: Syracusae,** pl. in form but sg. in meaning; Syracuse was capital of the province of Sicily.
    direptionem: direptio, *plundering.*

Mihi certum est non committere ut in hac causa praetor no-
75 bis consiliumque mutetur. Non patiar rem in id tempus adduci
ut homines miseri, antea socii atque amici populi Romani, nunc
servi ac supplices, non modo ius suum fortunasque omnis amit-
tant, verum etiam deplorandi iuris sui potestatem non habeant.

Faciam hoc non novum, sed ab eis qui nunc principes nos-
80 trae civitatis sunt ante factum, ut testibus utar statim; illud a
me novum, iudices, cognoscetis quod ita testis constituam ut
crimen totum explicem. Si quis erit qui perpetuam orationem
accusationemque desideret, altera actione audiet.

Haec primae actionis erit accusatio: dicimus C. Verrem, cum
85 multa libidinose, multa crudeliter in civis Romanos atque in
socios, multa in deos hominesque nefarie fecerit, tum praeterea
quadringentiens sestertium ex Sicilia contra leges abstulisse.
Hoc testibus, hoc tabulis privatis publicisque auctoritatibus ita
vobis planum faciemus ut hoc statuatis, etiam si spatium ad di-
90 cendum nostro commodo vacuosque dies habuissemus, tamen
oratione longa nihil opus fuisse. Dixi. (I.32–33, 53–56, excerpts)

IN C. VERREM: ACTIO SECUNDA

Verres' Plundering of Syracuse

Contrast the treatment of Syracuse by Marcellus in war and by Verres in peace.

Unius etiam urbis omnium pulcherrimae atque ornatissi-
mae, Syracusarum, direptionem commemorabo. Nemo fere

Temple G, 6th century B.C.
Selinunte, Sicily, Italy

94. **vestrum:** PARTITIVE GEN.

quin: when used to introduce a REL. CL. OF CHARACTERISTIC after a generalizing negative word (here **nemo**) has the force of **qui non.**

M. Marcello: Hiero II, the Syracusan king, had been friendly to the Romans in the Second Punic War, but on his death in 216 B.C. the city went over to the Carthaginians; Marcus Claudius Marcellus, a former consul and commander of Rome's legions in Sicily, then besieged Syracuse and finally won it back for Rome in 212 B.C.

95. **audierit:** = **audiverit,** perf. subjunct., one of the common short forms of perf. system tenses which drop the **v** (and sometimes an accompanying vowel as well, e.g., **amasset** for **amavisset**).

annalibus: annales, *annals* = *history;* Roman historical writings were frequently annalistic.

96. **conferte:** the contrast between Marcellus and Verres was not quite so sharp as Cicero suggests, for Marcellus, as a victorious general, did permit considerable plundering, and he sent many art treasures to Rome; however, the acts of Marcellus in war were hardly so heinous as those of Verres in peace.

97. **cohortem:** commonly a military term but here = *band, retinue.*

99. **conditas . . . captas:** sc. **esse.**

constitutas: here, *well established.*

101. **omitto:** a good example of the common rhetorical device known as PRAETERITIO ("passing over"), where a speaker says that he will not talk about something and then proceeds to do so.

102. **introitu:** introitus, *entrance.*

103. **purum:** PRED. ADJ. after **servatum esset.**

servatum esset: subjunct. in a SUBORDINATE CL. IN IND. STATE.

id: refers back to **forum** as subj. of the IND. STATE.

104. **redundasse:** = **redundavisse;** from **redundare,** *to overflow.*

portum . . . patuisse (106): note the close structural similarity of this and the preceding cl. (**forum . . . redundasse**); this sort of parallelism is a recurring feature of Cicero's style.

105. **classibus:** dat.; Marcellus had not been able to enter the harbor during his siege of Syracuse.

Carthaginiensium: possessive gen. with **classibus,** balancing **nostris.**

106. **eum:** refers to **portum** and picks up the idea after the interruption caused by the rel. cl., just as **id** looked back to **forum** in the preceding cl.

isto praetore: ABL. ABS.; **iste** often, as here, has a contemptuous force.

Cilicum: Cilices, *Cilicians,* the people of Cilicia in southern Asia Minor. At this time pirates **(praedones)** were sailing at will all over the Mediterranean; in 67 B.C. Pompey was commissioned to wipe out this menace and did so in the amazingly brief space of three months.

mitto: = **omitto;** Latin authors often employed the simple form of a vb. in place of the expected compound form.

adhibitam: adhibere, *to hold to, apply, employ (against).*

95 vestrum est quin quem ad modum captae sint a M. Marcello Syracusae saepe audierit, non numquam etiam in annalibus legerit. Conferte hanc pacem cum illo bello, huius praetoris adventum cum illius imperatoris victoria, huius cohortem impuram cum illius exercitu invicto, huius libidines cum illius continentia: ab illo qui cepit, conditas, ab hoc qui constitutas accepit,
100 captas dicetis Syracusas.

Ac iam illa omitto quae disperse a me multis in locis dicentur et dicta sunt: forum Syracusanorum, quod introitu Marcelli purum a caede servatum esset, id adventu Verris Siculorum innocentium sanguine redundasse; portum Syracusanorum, qui
105 tum et nostris classibus et Carthaginiensium clausus fuisset, eum isto praetore Cilicum praedonibus patuisse. Mitto adhibi-

Relief of warship, temple of Fortuna Primigenia, 1st century A.D.
Praeneste, Italy
Museo Pio Clementino, Vatican Museums, Vatican State

107. **ingenuis:** *native, freeborn.*
    familias: an archaic form of the gen. **familiae** which survived in the phrases **pater familias,** *the head of a household,* and **mater familias,** *matron.*
    quae: n. pl. referring to the crimes described in the preceding cl.
108. **neque . . . neque (109):** the repeated conjs. (POLYSYNDETON) are emphatic and do not negate but intensify the preceding **non.**
111. **illis rebus:** Verres' thefts of works of art in other parts of Sicily were detailed earlier in the speech.
112. **Graecarum . . . omnium (113):** sc. **urbium.**
113. **audistis:** = **audivistis;** see above on **audierit (96).**
115. **Insula:** Ortygia (here called simply *the Island*), site of the original city and connected to the mainland by a bridge over a narrow channel.
116. **aedes:** *sanctuaries, temples.*
    complures: *several.*
117. **antecellant:** **antecellere,** *to surpass.*
    Dianae: gen., *(one) Diana's.*
118. **extrema:** not *the farthest* but *the farthest part of;* some adjs. which indicate a sequence can be used to indicate a part of an object (e.g., **medius,** *middle, middle of*), the so-called partitive use of an adj.
119. **fons:** *spring, source, fountain.*
    dulcis: i.e., *fresh.*
    cui: DAT. OF POSSESSION.
    Arethusa: associated with the river nymph Arethusa, whose waters were said to flow beneath the earth from Elis in Greece to Syracuse.
120. **urbs:** here, *district.*
    Syracusis: loc.
122. **porticus:** one of the few f. nouns of the fourth decl.; in Greek cities porticoes were commonly employed for shelter, the conduct of business and academic lectures, etc.
    prytaneum: *town hall.*
123. **egregium:** *uncommon, extraordinary.*
    ceterae: i.e., in contrast to the public center.
124. **lata:** *broad, wide.*
    transversis: sc. **viis.**
125. **continentur:** *are occupied, filled.*
126. **fanum:** *temple, shrine.*
    Tycha: *Tyche* is Greek for **Fortuna,** the goddess of fate or luck.
128. **Neapolis:** Greek for *New-city;* cp. Naples in Italy.
129. **quam ad summam:** = **et ad summam eam,** *and at the highest point of it;* for the partitive sense of **summam,** see above on **extrema (118).**
    theatrum: sc. **est** (forms of **esse** are often omitted in Lat. and their equivalents must be supplied in translation); the theatre Cicero mentions survives to this day.

tam vim ingenuis, matres familias violatas, quae tum in urbe
capta commissa non sunt neque odio hostili neque licentia militari neque more belli neque iure victoriae; mitto, inquam, haec
110 omnia, quae ab isto per triennium perfecta sunt. Ea, quae coniuncta cum illis rebus sunt de quibus antea dixi, cognoscite.
(IV.115–16, excerpts)

Description of Syracuse.

Urbem Syracusas maximam esse Graecarum, pulcherrimam
omnium saepe audistis. Est, iudices, ita ut dicitur. Ea tanta est
urbs ut ex quattuor urbibus maximis constare dicatur, quarum
115 una est Insula, in qua domus est quae Hieronis regis fuit, qua
praetores uti solent. In ea sunt aedes sacrae complures, sed duae
quae longe ceteris antecellant: Dianae et altera, quae fuit ante
istius adventum ornatissima, Minervae. In hac insula extrema
est fons aquae dulcis, cui nomen Arethusa est, incredibili mag-
120 nitudine, plenissimus piscium. Altera autem est urbs Syracusis,
cui nomen Achradina est, in qua forum maximum, pulcherrimae porticus, ornatissimum prytaneum, amplissima est curia
templumque egregium Iovis Olympii; ceteraeque urbis partes,
quae, una via lata perpetua multisque transversis divisae, priva-
125 tis aedificiis continentur. Tertia est urbs quae, quod in ea parte
Fortunae fanum antiquum fuit, Tycha nominata est, in qua
gymnasium amplissimum est et complures aedes sacrae. Quarta
autem est quae, quia postrema coaedificata est, Neapolis nomi-
natur; quam ad summam theatrum maximum. Praeterea duo

Roman theater, replacing a Greek original, with Mt. Aetna in background
1st century A.D.*, Taormina, Sicily, Italy*

130. **Cereris:** gen. of **Ceres;** Ceres was the Roman goddess of grain, equivalent to the Greek Demeter, and thus an important deity on Sicily, where grain was a major agricultural product.

   Liberae: *Libera,* another Italian agricultural deity, was associated with Proserpina (Persephone), daughter of the grain goddess.

   signum: here, *statue.*

131. **Apollinis:** gen. of **Apollo,** god of the sun, who at Syracuse had the epithet "Temenites."

132. **portare:** *to carry;* the cult statues in ancient temples were typically huge.

134. **qui:** *for he;* the so-called "conjunctive" use of the rel. pron. at the beginning of a sentence, often to be translated *and he (qui = et is),* is very common in Cicero.

   vi copiisque (135): *by force and troops = by force of troops = by military force;* HENDIADYS.

135. **hoc:** explained by the appos. inf. phrase **hanc . . . exstinguere.**

136. **praesertim:** adv., *especially.*

   ex qua . . . ostenderetur (137): a REL. CAUSAL CL., *since from it. . . .*

138. **publicis privatis, sacris profanis:** a highly effective ASYNDETON, imparting a terse, staccato effect.

139. **in:** *in the matter of, in respect to.*

140. **habuit . . . habuit:** ANAPHORA (word repetition, especially at the beginning of successive phrases) and ASYNDETON emphasize the reasonableness and decency of Marcellus.

   victoriae rationem: OBJ. GEN., *consideration (regard) for his victory.*

   humanitatis: also with **rationem,** and positioned at the end of the sentence for emphasis; not always an easy word to translate, it seems here to connote *kindness, courtesy, decency.*

   victoriae . . . esse (141): PRED. GEN. OF POSSESSION, lit., *that it was of victory;* freely, with **deportare,** *that it was appropriate to his victory to carry off.*

142. **humanitatis:** construed, like **victoriae** in the preceding cl., with **putabat esse** and the inf. **exspoliare.**

143. **quam . . . voluisset:** another rel. cl. with causal force (see on **ex qua . . . ostenderetur,** 136–37).

   ornatus: OBJ. GEN.

145. **quae:** sc. **ea** as antecedent and dir. obj. of **videmus.**

   aedem Honoris et Virtutis (146): this temple was just south of Rome on the Via Appia.

146. **item:** adv., *also, likewise.*

   nihil . . . nihil . . . nihil (147): again ANAPHORA combined with ASYNDETON for emphasis—a favorite Ciceronian device.

   aedibus: aedes in pl. often = *house.*

147. **suburbano:** sc. **praedio,** *estate, villa.*

   urbis ornamenta domum suam . . . domum suam ornamento urbi (149): CHIASMUS underscores the contrasting idea.

149. **permulta:** per- as a prefix often has an intensive force such as *very.*

130   templa sunt egregia, Cereris unum, alterum Liberae, signumque
Apollinis, qui Temenites vocatur, pulcherrimum et maximum,
quod iste si portare potuisset, non dubitasset auferre. (IV.117–
19, excerpts)

Marcellus spared Syracuse when he captured the city in 212 B.C.

    Nunc ad Marcellum revertar, ne haec a me sine causa com-
memorata esse videantur. Qui, cum tam praeclaram urbem vi
135   copiisque cepisset, non putavit ad laudem populi Romani hoc
pertinere, hanc pulchritudinem, ex qua praesertim periculi nihil
ostenderetur, delere et exstinguere. Itaque aedificiis omnibus,
publicis privatis, sacris profanis, sic pepercit quasi ad ea defen-
denda cum exercitu, non oppugnanda venisset. In ornatu urbis
140   habuit victoriae rationem, habuit humanitatis. Victoriae putabat esse multa Romam deportare quae ornamento urbi esse
possent; humanitatis non plane exspoliare urbem, praesertim
quam conservare voluisset. In hac partitione ornatus non plus
victoria Marcelli populo Romano appetivit quam humanitas
145   Syracusanis reservavit. Romam quae apportata sunt, ad aedem
Honoris et Virtutis itemque aliis in locis videmus. Nihil in aedibus, nihil in hortis posuit, nihil in suburbano: putavit, si urbis
ornamenta domum suam non contulisset, domum suam ornamento urbi futuram. Syracusis autem permulta atque egregia

"Ruins of the Theater at Taormina"
Achille-Etna Michallon, 1821
Louvre, Paris, France

151. **qua:** f. nom. sg. of indef. adj. modifying **iniuria.**
153. **adventum et comitatum:** *a governor's arrival and his retinue.*
156. **attigit: attingere,** *to touch.*
158. **consuetudinis: consuetudo,** *custom.*
160. **Agathoclis:** gen. of **Agathocles,** tyrant and later king of Syracuse 317–289 B.C.
161. **nobilius:** here, *more famous, celebrated.*
162. **visendum: visere,** *to go to see, visit.*
163. **profana:** *secular, not sacred,* because when a city was conquered, its gods were thought to have abandoned it; OBJ. COMPL. with **omnia.**
164. **diuturnam:** *longlasting.*
165. **sacra religiosaque:** again OBJ. COMPL.; with the passing of time, the paintings were again deemed sacred.
167. **saecula: saeculum,** *century, generation.*
169. **is:** repeats the subj. **Marcellus** and parallels the use of **Verres/is** in the next, very similarly structured cl. (and see the note on **eum,** 105).
       aedificaturus: aedificare, *to build.*
170. **qui . . . deberet (171):** REL. CL. OF CHARACTERISTIC, *the sort of person who . . ..*
171. **quem ad modum ille:** we would say *in the way that he (Marcellus) had.*
       vota: votum, *prayer.*
173. **meretriciam:** *of a prostitute, meretricious;* Verres allegedly kept a mistress in his home.
178. **cognitione formarum:** lit., *by recognition of their forms* = *by familarizing people with their personal appearance.*
       quanto: ABL. OF DEGREE OF DIFFERENCE.
       taetrior: taeter, *offensive, hateful.*
179. **superiorum:** here, *predecessors.*
       tamen: i.e., although they were tyrants.
180. **ornarint:** = **ornaverint,** perf. subjunct., like **sustulerit,** in the CUM CAUSAL CL.
       hic: ASYNDETON emphasizes the contrast between **illi** and **hic.**

Temple to Castor and Pollux, 5th century B.C.
Agrigentum, Sicily, Italy

150   reliquit; deum vero nullum violavit, nullum attigit. Conferte
Verrem, non ut hominem cum homine comparetis, ne qua tali
viro mortuo fiat iniuria, sed ut pacem cum bello, leges cum vi,
forum et iurisdictionem cum ferro et armis, adventum et comitatum cum exercitu et victoria conferatis. (IV.120–21)

Verres plundered the temple of Minerva, including the paintings.

155   Aedis Minervae est in Insula, de qua ante dixi: quam Marcellus non attigit, quam plenam atque ornatam reliquit, quae ab
isto sic spoliata atque direpta est, non ut ab hoste aliquo, qui
tamen in bello religionem et consuetudinis iura retineret, sed ut
a barbaris praedonibus vexata esse videatur. Pugna erat eques-
160   tris Agathoclis regis in tabulis picta; his autem tabulis interiores
templi parietes vestiebantur. Nihil erat ea pictura nobilius, nihil
Syracusis quod magis visendum putaretur. Has tabulas M. Marcellus, cum omnia victoria illa sua profana fecisset, tamen religione impeditus non attigit. Iste, cum illa propter diuturnam
165   pacem fidelitatemque populi Syracusani sacra religiosaque accepisset, omnes eas tabulas abstulit; parietes, quorum ornatus
tot saecula manserant, tot bella effugerant, nudos ac deformatos
reliquit. Et Marcellus qui, si Syracusas cepisset, duo templa se
Romae dedicaturum voverat, is id quod erat aedificaturus eis
170   rebus ornare quas ceperat noluit; Verres qui non Honori neque
Virtuti, quem ad modum ille, sed Veneri et Cupidini vota deberet, is Minervae templum spoliare conatus est. Ille deos deorum
spoliis ornari noluit, hic ornamenta Minervae virginis in meretriciam domum transtulit. Viginti et septem praeterea tabulas
175   pulcherrime pictas ex eadem aede sustulit in quibus erant ima-
gines Siciliae regum ac tyrannorum, quae non solum pictorum
artificio delectabant, sed etiam commemoratione hominum et
cognitione formarum. Ac videte quanto taetrior hic tyrannus
Syracusanis fuerit quam quisquam superiorum: cum illi tamen
180   ornarint templa deorum immortalium, hic etiam illorum monumenta atque ornamenta sustulerit. (IV.122–23)

182. **valvis: valvae,** *doors.*
      commemorem: DELIBERATIVE SUBJUNCT., used in questions implying doubt or, as here, indignation.
183. **augere:** here, *exaggerate.*
184. **liquido:** adv., *with certainty.*
185. **ebore: ebur,** *ivory.*
      perfectiores: lit., *more thoroughly made, more carefully wrought.*
186. **incredibile dictu: dictu** is a supine used as an ABL. OF SPECIFICATION, *incredible to say.*
187. **scriptum:** *writing, account, record;* Cicero's point is that the Greeks were extremely fond of the arts and hence suffered deeply from Verres' wholesale looting.
188. **mirentur atque efferant:** POTENTIAL SUBJUNCT. with **forsitan,** *they may perhaps. . . .*
      esto: fut. imper. of **esse,** *let it be = granted.*
189. **honestius est:** *it is more honorable* (not *more honest*) *for* + the inf. phrase **imperatorem . . . reliquisse.**
      ea: obj. of **reliquisse** and **abstulisse.**
192. **argumenta:** *subjects, scenes,* carved in relief on panels attached to the doors.
      curavit: *he took care (that), saw to it (that).*
193. **Gorgonis:** gen. of **Gorgo,** *Gorgon.* The three Gorgons (Medusa the best known of them) were female monsters with snakes for hair who turned anyone who gazed upon them into stone; images of their faces were often attached to temples as apotropaic devices.
      cinctum: perf. partic. of **cingere,** *to surround, bind.*
      anguibus: anguis, *snake.*
      revellit: revellere, *to tear away, pull off.*
195. **quaestu: quaestus,** *gain, profit.*
      bullas: ornamental *bosses* or *bolt heads.*
197. **pondere: pondus,** *weight.*
200. **Sappho:** i.e., a statue of Sappho, the celebrated Greek lyric poet of the seventh century B.C.
      tibi iustam excusationem (201): Cicero addresses Verres directly in a highly sarcastic tone.
201. **concedendum . . . videatur:** an impers. pass. construction; lit., *it seems to have to be permitted and even pardoned = it seems we should permit and even pardon (you).*
202. **Silanionis:** *Silanion,* a famous Athenian sculptor of the fourth century B.C.
203. **quisquam . . . haberet (204):** POTENTIAL SUBJUNCT., *who should have had.*
205. **nimirum:** adv., *doubtless, of course, surely.*
206. **delicati:** *fastidious;* more sarcasm.

He stole the ornaments from the temple doors.

Iam vero quid ego de valvis illius templi commemorem? Vereor ne haec qui non viderunt, omnia me nimis augere atque ornare arbitrentur. Confirmare hoc liquido, iudices, possum valvas
185　magnificentiores, ex auro atque ebore perfectiores, nullas umquam ullo in templo fuisse. Incredibile dictu est quam multi Graeci de harum valvarum pulchritudine scriptum reliquerint. Nimium forsitan haec illi mirentur atque efferant. Esto; verum tamen honestius est rei publicae nostrae, iudices, ea quae illis
190　pulchra esse videantur imperatorem nostrum in bello reliquisse, quam praetorem in pace abstulisse. Ex ebore diligentissime perfecta argumenta erant in valvis: ea detrahenda curavit omnia. Gorgonis os pulcherrimum, cinctum anguibus, revellit atque abstulit; et tamen indicavit se non solum artificio sed etiam pretio
195　quaestuque duci. Nam bullas aureas omnes ex eis valvis, quae erant multae et graves, non dubitavit auferre, quarum iste non opere delectabatur, sed pondere. Itaque eius modi valvas reliquit ut quae olim ad ornandum templum erant maxime, nunc tantum ad claudendum factae esse videantur. (IV.124, excerpts)

The statue of Sappho was stolen from the city hall.

200　Sappho quae sublata de prytaneo est dat tibi iustam excusationem, prope ut concedendum atque ignoscendum esse videatur. Silanionis opus tam perfectum, tam elegans, tam elaboratum quisquam non modo privatus sed etiam populus potius haberet quam homo elegantissimus atque eruditissimus, Verres?
205　Nimirum contra dici nihil potest. Nostrum enim unus quisque—qui tam beati quam iste est non sumus, tam delicati esse non possumus—si quando aliquid istius modi videre volet, eat ad

Gorgon, 6th century B.C.
Museo Archeologico, Syracuse, Sicily, Italy

208. **aedem Felicitatis:** *the temple of Fortune,* built ca. 150 B.C. and filled with art objects taken from the conquered city of Corinth.

    monumentum Catuli: a portico constructed by Quintus Lutatius Catulus with the spoils from his successful campaign against the Cimbri in 101 B.C.

    porticum Metelli: ca. 146 B.C. Quintus Caecilius Metellus Macedonicus enclosed with a portico two temples (to Juno and Jupiter Stator) in the Campus Martius; the buildings served much as art museums.

209. **det operam:** a common idiom, *let him take care (to), make an effort (to)* + JUSSIVE NOUN CL.

    istorum: i.e., Verres and his friends.

    Tusculanum: sc. **praedium,** *Tusculan villa, estate;* Tusculum, a beautiful spot about 15 miles southeast of Rome, where many wealthy Romans had estates, among whom later was Cicero.

210. **suorum:** i.e., statues and other works of art; PARTITIVE GEN. with **quid.**

    aedilibus: the *aediles* were in charge of state entertainments and might borrow art objects from wealthy associates for public display.

    commodarit: = **commodaverit,** fut. perf. indic. of **commodare,** *to loan;* FUT. MORE VIVID CONDITION, with an imper. in the apodosis, paralleling **si . . . volet, eat** in 207.

211. **habeat . . . habeat (212):** JUSSIVE SUBJUNCTS., paralleling **det** and **spectet;** Verres should have his own private art collection, Cicero sarcastically asserts, so that he need not stoop to visit the public galleries and so that he can accommodate the aediles when they require assistance.

    ornamentis: ABL. OF MEANS with **plenam** and **refertas** *(crammed full, packed).*

    oppidorum: **oppidum,** *town.*

212. **plenam domum, villas refertas:** CHIASMUS and ASYNDETON underscore Cicero's indignation.

    etiam: here, *still, even now.*

213. **operari:** **operarius,** *day-laborer.*

    delicias: *delights, pleasures.*

214. **animo et corpore:** ABL. OF SPECIFICATION.

    appositior: **appositus,** *suitable, suited.*

215. **ferenda . . . auferenda:** i.e., to carry them on his back as a day laborer rather than to carry them off as a connoisseur, a delightful play on the two forms of **fero.**

    haec . . . reliquerit (216): the IND. QUEST. is dependent on **dici vix potest,** *it can hardly be said how great.*

216. **desiderium sui:** lit., *desire of itself* = *loss.*

217. **cum . . . tum:** *not only . . . but also.*

    epigramma: *inscription.*

218. **basi:** abl. sg. of **basis,** *pedestal, base.*

    quod: conjunctive rel. = **et hoc epigramma,** obj., along with **unam litteram,** of **scisset,** i.e., *and if he had understood this epigram, had understood even a single letter of Greek, he would not have . . ..*

    Graeculus: *little Greek, Greekling;* the diminutive has contemptuous force.

220. **sustulisset:** sc. **statuam.**

221. **fuerit:** sc. **ibi.**

aedem Felicitatis, ad monumentum Catuli, in porticum Metelli; det operam ut admittatur in alicuius istorum Tusculanum; spec-
210 tet forum ornatum, si quid iste suorum aedilibus commodarit; Verres haec habeat domi, Verres ornamentis fanorum atque oppidorum habeat plenam domum, villas refertas. Etiamne huius operari studia ac delicias, iudices, perferetis?—qui ita natus, ita educatus est, ita factus et animo et corpore ut multo appositior
215 ad ferenda quam ad auferenda signa esse videatur. Atque haec Sappho sublata quantum desiderium sui reliquerit dici vix potest. Nam cum ipsa fuit egregie facta, tum epigramma Graecum pernobile incisum est in basi; quod iste eruditus homo et Graeculus, qui haec subtiliter iudicat, qui solus intellegit, si unam litteram Graecam scisset, certe non sustulisset. Nunc enim quod
220 scriptum est inani in basi, declarat quid fuerit, et id ablatum indicat. (IV.126–27)

"Sappho Playing the Lyre"
Leopold Burthe, 1848
Musée des Beaux-Arts
Carcassone, France

223. **quid:** *what about this?*
     Paeanis: *Paean* was an epithet of Apollo the healer, father of Aesculapius, god of medicine.
224. **non:** = **nonne,** as also in line 225.
226. **Liberi:** *Liber* was the Roman equivalent of Bacchus.
     Aristaei: *Aristaeus,* a son of Apollo and protector of flocks, bees, the grapevine, and olives.
229. **simul:** adv., *at the same time, along with.*
230. **olei:** oleum, *(olive) oil.*
     una: adv., *together, along (with).*
232. **quanto honore:** ABL. OF DESCRIPTION, used here in the pred.; lit., *of what great esteem* = *how greatly esteemed.*
233. **recordari:** deponent, *to recall, remember.*
234. **specie:** species, *appearance;* **eadem specie ac forma** = ABL. OF DESCRIPTION with **signum.**
235. **Capitolio:** the *Capitolium* was the magnificent temple of Jupiter Capitolinus on the Capitoline Hill.
     Flamininus: the consul *Titus Quinctius Flamininus* defeated Philip V of Macedon in 197 B.C. and proclaimed the liberty of Greece the following year.
236. **ferebantur: ferre** often, as here, means *to report, say.*
     uno in genere (237): *of one type, of the same type.*
238. **vidimus:** past tense, as the statue and the temple that housed it were both destroyed by fire in 83 B.C.
     in Ponti ore et angustiis: *at the mouth and narrows of the Black Sea,* i.e., where the Black Sea and the Bosporus meet.
240. **ita:** *so, as (he did);* **ut . . . poneret (239–40)** is a PURPOSE CL., not result.
     sua: refers, not to the subj. (Flamininus), as might be expected, but rather to **illud (signum),** which has been placed at the beginning of the sentence as the focus of Cicero's point.
     hoc est: parenthetical, like **id est,** *that is.*
     terrestri domicilio: the Romans regarded their capital city, the seat of the Roman empire, as the proper *earthly home* of Jupiter.
241. **introitum:** introitus, *entrance.*
242. **emerserint:** emergere, *to come forth, emerge.*
     porro: adv., *straight on, forward,* or, here, *in turn.*
243. **invecta sint:** invehere, *to carry into, bring in.*
     hanc diem: dies is treated variously as m. or f., the latter especially when referring to a specific day or to time in general.
244. **quod . . . Syracusis, quod . . . viderat, quod . . . concesserat, quod . . . solebant (247):** a good example of TRICOLON CRESCENS, a common rhetorical device consisting of three (or more) consecutive cls., each longer and more complex than the one preceding and building to a climax.
246. **incolae:** incola, m., *inhabitant, resident.*
     advenae: advena, m., *stranger, foreigner.*
247. **id:** repeats **hoc tertium** in 243, following the elaborate tricolon.

Verres stole other statues as well, including a famous one of Jupiter.

Quid? signum Paeanis ex aede Aesculapi praeclare factum, sacrum ac religiosum, non sustulisti?—quod omnes propter pul-
225 chritudinem visere, propter religionem colere solebant. Quid? ex aede Liberi simulacrum Aristaei non tuo imperio palam ab-latum est? Quid? ex aede Iovis religiosissimum simulacrum Iovis Imperatoris, pulcherrime factum, nonne abstulisti? Atque ille Paean sacrificiis anniversariis simul cum Aesculapio apud
230 illos colebatur; Aristaeus, qui inventor olei esse dicitur, una cum Libero patre apud illos eodem erat in templo consecratus.

Iovem autem Imperatorem quanto honore in suo templo fu-isse arbitramini? Conicere potestis, si recordari volueritis quanta religione fuerit eadem specie ac forma signum illud quod ex
235 Macedonia captum in Capitolio posuerat T. Flamininus. Etenim tria ferebantur in orbe terrarum signa Iovis Imperatoris uno in genere pulcherrime facta: unum illud Macedonicum quod in Capitolio vidimus; alterum in Ponti ore et angustiis; tertium, quod Syracusis ante Verrem praetorem fuit. Illud Flamininus
240 ita ex aede sua sustulit ut in Capitolio, hoc est, in terrestri domi-cilio Iovis, poneret. Quod autem est ad introitum Ponti, id, cum tam multa ex illo mari bella emerserint, tam multa porro in Pontum invecta sint, usque ad hanc diem integrum inviola-tumque servatum est. Hoc tertium, quod erat Syracusis, quod
245 M. Marcellus armatus et victor viderat, quod religioni conces-serat, quod cives atque incolae Syracusani colere, advenae non solum visere verum etiam venerari solebant, id Verres ex templo Iovis sustulit.

Colossal head of Zeus
Otricoli, Italy
Museo Pio Clementino
Vatican Museums
Vatican State

249. **saepius:** lit., *rather often = once again.*
   habetote: 2nd pers. pl. of fut. imper., *think, consider.*
250. **esse . . . desideratos (251):** *have been missed = have been lost.*
   istius adventu . . . victoria Marcelli (251): CHIASMUS underscores the contrast; **adventu** and **victoria** are ABL. OF CAUSE.
251. **ille:** Marcellus.
   requisisse: = **requisivisse;** Marcellus hoped to save him at the capture of Syracuse.
252. **Archimedem illum:** when **ille** follows the noun it modifies, it generally means *that famous;* Archimedes, the renowned Greek mathematician and inventor, was born at Syracuse in 287 B.C. and was carelessly slain by some Roman soldiers during Marcellus' sack of the city in 212.
253. **quem:** = **et eum;** conjunctive use of the rel.
   permoleste: adv., *with much annoyance, with great distress.*
   tulisse: with **dicitur (251).**
254. **asportaret: asportare,** *to carry off.*
256. **eos:** the Syracusans.
261. **nimio opere:** *excessively* or perhaps, in a more positive sense, *exceedingly* (cp. **magnopere**); although Cicero here speaks somewhat patronizingly of the Greeks' devotion to art, Greek artworks were actually very popular among the Romans, as is shown by the fact that so many ancient Greek works are known to us through Roman copies.
   querimoniis: querimonia, *lament, complaint.*
264. **hosce:** emphatic for **hos,** *these (recent).*
   exterae nationes: see on line 7.
266. **huiusce modi:** GEN. OF DESCRIPTION with **spoliationes** = **tales spoliationes.**
268. **licet . . . dicat:** often construed with acc. + inf., **licet** can also take a subjunct. cl., as here; *it is permitted that he say = although he may say.*
   emisse: i.e., the various art objects he had stolen.
   sicuti: = **sicut.**
   credite hoc mihi (269): this cl. combines the two case constructions which may follow **credo,** (a) **credite hoc,** *believe this* (acc. of thing), (b) **credite mihi,** *believe me* (dat. of person), where Eng. might instead have, "believe me when I say this . . . ."
269. **tota Asia et Graecia:** sc. **in;** the prep. is often omitted in place constructions, especially where the placename is modified by **totus, medius,** or a similar adj.
   signum . . . urbis (270): this TRICOLON CRESCENS along with the ANAPHORA and the accumulation of indef. adv./adj./pron. **(umquam/ullum/ullum/ullum/cuiquam)** all intensify Cicero's point.
271. **scitote:** for the form, see on **habetote** in 248.
272. **emptionem: emptio,** *purchase.*
   qui: the indef. adj. is often used for the indef. pron. **quis.**

Ut saepius ad Marcellum revertar, iudices, sic habetote:
250 plures esse a Syracusanis istius adventu deos quam victoria
Marcelli homines desideratos. Etenim ille requisisse etiam dicitur Archimedem illum, summo ingenio hominem ac disci-
plina, quem cum audisset interfectum, permoleste tulisse; iste
omnia quae requisivit, non ut conservaret verum ut asportaret,
255 requisivit. (IV.127–31, excerpts).

The resentment of the Syracusans.

Quid tum? Mediocrine tandem dolore eos adfectos esse arbitramini? Non ita est, iudices: primum, quod omnes religione
moventur et deos patrios quos a maioribus acceperunt colendos
sibi diligenter et retinendos esse arbitrantur; deinde hic ornatus,
260 haec opera atque artificia, signa, tabulae pictae, Graecos homines nimio opere delectant. Itaque ex illorum querimoniis intellegere possumus haec illis acerbissima videri quae forsitan nobis
levia et contemnenda esse videantur. Mihi credite, iudices, cum
multas acceperint per hosce annos socii atque exterae nationes
265 calamitates et iniurias, nullas Graeci homines gravius ferunt ac
tulerunt quam huiusce modi spoliationes fanorum atque oppidorum.
Licet iste dicat emisse se, sicuti solet dicere, credite hoc
mihi, iudices: nulla umquam civitas tota Asia et Graecia signum
270 ullum, ullam tabulam pictam, ullum denique ornamentum urbis
sua voluntate cuiquam vendidit; acerbiorem etiam scitote esse
civitatibus falsam istam et simulatam emptionem quam si qui

Death of Archimedes, 18th century copy of 2nd century mosaic
Liebieghaus, Frankfurt am Main, Germany

273. **clam:** adv., *secretly, privately;* the contrast with **palam** is emphasized through CHIASMUS and the use of two compound vbs. of different meaning from the same root **(surripiant/eripiat).**
    surripiat: surripere, *to snatch (stealthily), steal.*
    turpitudinem . . . arbitrantur (274): with the inf. phrase **referri in tabulas publicas,** which in turn governs the IND. STATE. **pretio . . . abalienasse,** *for it to be entered into the public records that a state . . . .*
276. **abalienasse:** = **abalienavisse,** from **abalienare,** *to transfer (ownership of).*
    mirandum in modum (277): adv. phrase, *in a wonderful way.*
278. **esse apud illos:** *to remain in their possession.*
279. **imperio nostro:** i.e., as proud states within the Roman empire.
280. **florentissimique: florens,** *flowering, flourishing.*
    vectigalis: *subject to taxation.*
    stipendiarios: *required to pay tribute,* imposed on subject states originally to defray the costs of an occupying army.
281. **fecerant . . . relinquebant:** sc. as subj. **maiores nostri.**
282. **oblectamenta: oblectamentum,** *delight, pleasure.*
284. **quae apud quosque:** *what (works of art) among the several peoples;* in an omitted passage Cicero names more than a dozen works in different parts of the Greek world, each priceless to the Greeks and a number of them known to us today, including a statue of Venus from the island of Cnidus.
285. **mirum . . . auferantur (286):** this entire IND. STATE. is in appos. with **hoc.**
287. **Consano:** *of Consa,* possibly to be identified with Compsa, a city of the Hirpini in south central Italy.
    municipe: municeps, *a municipal, citizen of a free town* (a **municipium**); in Cicero's day the citizens of Italy's self-governing **municipia** enjoyed extensive rights.
290. **tametsi:** conj., *although.*
292. **negotiantur: negotiari,** *to be in business, trade.*
293. **Valentinorum:** *the people of Valentia* (also known as Vibo), in Bruttium, the toe of Italy.
294. **Reginorum:** *the people of Regium (Rhegium),* a Greek city on the very tip of the Italian toe, opposite Sicily.
295. **Messanae:** *Messana* (or *Zancle*) was on the extreme northeast tip of Sicily opposite Regium.
    dedi: here, *I produced.*
    priore actione: i.e., in the first phase of the trial, where numerous witnesses were called and extensive evidence presented.
    testium: testis, *witness;* PARTITIVE GEN. with **tantum,** lit., *so much of witnesses* = *so many witnesses.*
297. **iam . . . dicam (298):** the common idiomatic use of pres. tense with words indicating duration of time, = *I have already spoken.*
    genere: here, *topic.*
300. **quem ad modum:** *in what manner, how.*
301. **in medio:** i.e., *before you.*

clam surripiat aut eripiat palam atque auferat. Nam turpitudinem summam esse arbitrantur referri in tabulas publicas, pretio
275   adductam civitatem (et pretio parvo) ea quae accepisset a maioribus vendidisse atque abalienasse. Etenim mirandum in modum Graeci rebus istis, quas nos contemnimus, delectantur.
Itaque maiores nostri facile patiebantur haec esse apud illos
quam plurima: apud socios, ut imperio nostro quam ornatissimi
280   florentissimique essent; apud eos autem quos vectigalis aut sti-
pendiarios fecerant, tamen haec relinquebant ut illi quibus haec
iucunda sunt (quae nobis levia videntur) haberent haec oblectamenta et solacia servitutis. Longum est et non necessarium
commemorare quae apud quosque visenda sunt tota Asia et
285   Graecia; verum existimare vos hoc volo—mirum quendam dolorem accipere eos ex quorum urbibus haec auferantur. (IV.132–
35, excerpts)

The Crucifixion of Publius Gavius

The case of Gavius is almost unbelievable.

Quid ego de P. Gavio, Consano municipe, dicam, iudices?
aut qua vi vocis, qua gravitate verborum, quo dolore animi dicam? Crimen eius modi est ut, cum primum ad me delatum est,
290   usurum me illo non putarem; tametsi enim verissimum esse in-
tellegebam, tamen credibile fore non arbitrabar. Coactus lacrimis omnium civium Romanorum qui in Sicilia negotiantur,
adductus Valentinorum, hominum honestissimorum, omnium-
que Reginorum testimoniis multorumque equitum Romanorum
295   qui casu tum Messanae fuerunt, dedi tantum priore actione tes-
tium, res ut nemini dubia esse posset.
Quid nunc agam? Cum iam tot horas de uno genere ac de
istius nefaria crudelitate dicam, cum prope omnem vim verborum eius modi, quae scelere istius digna sint, aliis in rebus con-
300   sumpserim, quem ad modum de tanta re dicam? Opinor, unus
modus atque una ratio est: rem in medio ponam, quae tantum

302. **gravitatis:** with **tantum.**
     mea: with **eloquentia.**
304. **in illo numero:** earlier in the speech Cicero told how Verres had brutally
     incarcerated in the quarries at Syracuse fugitives from the army of
     Quintus Sertorius, a revolutionary who had been defeated by Pompey
     (Gnaeus Pompeius Magnus) a few years earlier.
305. **nescio qua:** **nescio qui/quae/quod** taken together form a frequently used indef.
     adj., *some* (lit., *I do not know what*).
306. **lautumiis:** **lautumiae,** *stone-quarry;* presumably the same quarries in which
     the remnant of the Athenian force to Sicily came to an ignominious end
     during the Peloponnesian War and which can still be seen today.
307. **Reginorum:** Regium was only four miles across the strait from Messana.
308. **tenebris:** **tenebrae,** *shadows, darkness, gloom.*
311. **sibi:** DAT. OF POSSESSION, with **iter esse Romam,** lit., *that he had a journey to
     Rome = that he was going to Rome.*
     recta: sc. **via,** i.e., *directly.*
     praesto: adv., *on hand, ready, waiting for.*
     advenienti: *for him arriving = on his arrival,* i.e., ready to prosecute him on
     his return, a threat that clearly cost Gavius his life.
312. **interesse:** the basic vb. means *to be between, in the midst of,* but the frequently
     used impers. sense employed here = *to be important, of interest, of con-
     cern, make a difference;* with **nihil** here, *it made no difference.*
313. **praetorio:** **praetorium,** *general's tent, governor's residence.*
314. **iste:** Cicero repeatedly uses this word, with its contemptuous force, of Verres.
     delegerat: **deligere,** *to pick out, choose, select.*
     quam haberet: REL. CL. OF PURPOSE, *to have it (as).*
     adiutricem . . . consciam (315): TRICOLON CRESCENS.
315. **furtorum:** **furtum,** *theft, stolen property.*
     consciam: here, *accomplice.*
316. **Mamertinum:** a name applied to the residents of Messana, the Mamertini
     were originally Campanian mercenaries who served Agathocles, tyrant
     of Messana, and after his death seized the town for themselves (289
     B.C.).
318. **esse civem:** IND. STATE. suggested by **res defertur,** *that there was . . ..*
319. **quem:** conjunctive rel. = **et eum.**
320. **minitantem:** **minitari** + dat., *to threaten.*
321. **in eum . . . quod videretur:** i.e., *what seemed best to do with him.*
324. **eminebat:** **eminere,** *to project, stand out, be conspicuous.*
325. **quo tandem:** *just how far.*
     quidnam: **quisnam,** an emphatic form of the interrog. pron., *who/what in the
     world.*
327. **deligari:** **deligare,** *to bind.*
     virgas: **virga,** *stick, rod.*
     expediri: **expedire,** *to let loose, prepare, procure.*
     clamabat: the impf. suggests that Gavius cried out repeatedly.
328. **meruisse:** sc. **se** as subj.; from **merere,** *to earn (one's pay), serve as a soldier.*

habet ipsa gravitatis ut neque mea (quae nulla est) neque cuius-
quam ad inflammandos vestros animos eloquentia requiratur.
(V.158–59, excerpts)

Gavius voiced complaints which were reported to Verres.

Gavius hic, quem dico, Consanus, cum in illo numero civi-
305 um Romanorum ab isto in vincula coniectus esset et nescio qua
ratione clam e lautumiis profugisset Messanamque venisset—
qui tam prope iam Italiam et moenia Reginorum, civium Romanorum, videret et ex illo metu mortis ac tenebris, quasi luce
libertatis et odore aliquo legum recreatus, revixisset—loqui Mes-
310 sanae et queri coepit se, civem Romanum, in vincula coniectum,
sibi recta iter esse Romam, Verri se praesto advenienti futurum.
Non intellegebat miser nihil interesse utrum haec Messanae an
apud istum in praetorio loqueretur. Nam (ut antea vos docui)
hanc sibi iste urbem delegerat quam haberet adiutricem sce-
315 lerum, furtorum receptricem, flagitiorum omnium consciam.
Itaque ad magistratum Mamertinum statim deducitur Gavius:
eoque ipso die casu Messanam Verres venit. Res ad eum defertur: esse civem Romanum qui se Syracusis in lautumiis fuisse
quereretur; quem, iam ingredientem in navem et Verri nimis
320 atrociter minitantem, ab se retractum esse et adservatum, ut
ipse in eum statueret quod videretur. (V.160)

Though Gavius protested that he was a Roman citizen, Verres had him
beaten and prepared a cross for his crucifixion.

Agit hominibus gratias et eorum benivolentiam erga se dili-
gentiamque collaudat. Ipse, inflammatus scelere et furore, in forum venit. Ardebant oculi; toto ex ore crudelitas eminebat. Ex-
325 spectabant omnes quo tandem progressurus aut quidnam
acturus esset; cum repente hominem proripi atque in foro medio
nudari ac deligari et virgas expediri iubet. Clamabat ille miser
se civem esse Romanum, municipem Consanum; meruisse cum

329. **equite:** here, *knight, equestrian,* i.e., a member of the equestrian class, wealthy Roman businessmen.

Panhormi: loc. of **Panhormus,** an important town in northwest Sicily, modern Palermo.

330. **iste:** sc. **dixit.**

comperisse: comperire, *to find out, learn, discover.*

331. **speculandi: speculari,** *to spy.*

a ducibus fugitivorum: the gladiator Spartacus and his fellow **fugitivi** *(runaway slaves)* held out against the Roman armies and ravaged Italy until finally defeated by Marcus Licinius Crassus in 71 B.C.

332. **cuius rei . . . esset (333):** REL. CL. OF CHARACTERISTIC, not part of what Verres claimed to have found out, but rather **res,** the incorporated antecedent of the cl., refers to Verres' charge, *a circumstance of which there was . . ..*

index: *witness, informer.*

vestigium: *track, trace, evidence.*

334. **verberari: verberare,** *to beat.*

caedebatur: caedere, *to cut, beat, slay;* the imperf. tense, with its idea of continuous action, adds vividness and pathos.

335. **gemitus:** *groan.*

336. **crepitum: crepitus,** *rattling, rustling, noise.*

plagarum: plaga, *blow, wound.*

337. **commemoratione: commemoratio,** *mention, remembrance.*

338. **cruciatum: cruciatus,** *torture, torment.*

340. **ut . . . deprecaretur: deprecari,** *to avert, ward off (by entreaty);* NOUN CL. OF RESULT, in appos. with **hoc.**

341. **usurparet: usurpare,** *to claim, employ, repeatedly mention.*

crux: *cross.*

342. **aerumnoso:** *distressed, troubled.*

345. **lex Porcia:** passed ca. 198 B.C., this law forbade the infliction of capital or corporal punishment by a magistrate without the right of appeal and a trial before the assembly.

leges . . . Semproniae: these laws, passed by Gaius Sempronius Gracchus in 123 B.C., granted a citizen the right of appeal even against an official to whom dictatorial power had been given.

346. **tribunicia potestas:** the tribunes were essentially the protectors and leaders of Rome's lower classes. By ca. 80 B.C. Sulla's reformed, pro-senatorial constitution had limited their powers considerably (hence, **graviter desiderata**); but in 70 B.C., just before Cicero's prosecution of Verres, the consuls Pompey and Crassus restored the tribunes' authority, including the right to try criminal cases before the assembly.

hucine: interrog. form of **huc,** *to this (place, point).*

347. **reciderunt: recidere,** *to fall back, return, be reduced.*

ut . . . caederetur (349): RESULT CL.

348. **foederatorum:** *allies* (allied with Rome by a treaty, **foedus**).

beneficio: i.e., by his election to the office of praetor.

349. **fascis et securis:** acc. pl., *rods and axes,* the familiar symbol of Roman officials, including praetors and consuls, who held the imperium.

L. Raecio, splendidissimo equite Romano, qui Panhormi nego-
330　tiaretur, ex quo haec Verres scire posset. Tum iste, se comperisse
eum speculandi causa in Siciliam a ducibus fugitivorum esse
missum—cuius rei neque index neque vestigium aliquod neque
suspicio cuiquam esset ulla. Deinde iubet undique hominem ve-
hementissime verberari. Caedebatur virgis in medio foro Mes-
335　sanae civis Romanus, iudices, cum interea nullus gemitus, nulla
vox alia illius miseri inter dolorem crepitumque plagarum audiebatur, nisi haec, "Civis Romanus sum." Hac se commemoratione civitatis omnia verbera depulsurum, cruciatumque a corpore deiecturum, arbitrabatur. Is non modo hoc non perfecit,
340　ut virgarum vim deprecaretur, sed, cum imploraret saepius
usurparetque nomen civitatis, crux—crux, inquam—infelici et
aerumnoso, qui numquam istam pestem viderat, comparaba-
tur. (V.161–62)

*Gavius' crucifixion was a brutal violation of the dignity and rights of
Roman citizenship.*

　　　O nomen dulce libertatis! O ius eximium nostrae civitatis! O
345　lex Porcia legesque Semproniae! O graviter desiderata, et aliquando reddita plebi Romanae, tribunicia potestas! Hucine
tandem omnia reciderunt, ut civis Romanus in provincia populi
Romani, in oppido foederatorum, ab eo qui beneficio populi
Romani fascis et securis haberet deligatus in foro virgis caedere-

Theater, 3rd century B.C.
Syracuse, Sicily, Italy

350.   **ardentes: ardere,** *to be on fire, blaze, burn.*
    laminae: lamina, *thin plate, layer;* here, *iron plates* (heated for torture).
    ceteri . . . cruciatus: *other forms of torture.*

353.   **fletu: fletus,** *weeping, lamentation.*
    commovebare: -re is a common alternate pass. ending for **-ris.**
    in crucem . . . agere: *to crucify.*

354.   **quemquam: quisquam** is regularly used after a negative or an implied nega-
    tive; here the incredulity implicit in the question provides the negative
    connotation.

355.   **exploratum est: explorare,** *to search out, ascertain.*
    loco: locus, because of its very meaning, is often used without a prep. in a
    place construction; here the meaning is figurative, *plight, condition.*

356.   **quid . . . sit:** i.e., what is going to happen to you; the fut. act. periphrastic
    often serves, as here, to indicate future action in a subjunct. cl.
    agam: here, *I shall deal.*

357.   **repentinum:** *unexpected, all of a sudden,* i.e., contrary to the original charge
    that he was a fugitive from Sertorius' army.
    in lautumias: a convicted spy would have received more severe treatment.

358.   **abs:** a common alternate form of **a/ab.**
    litteris: here, *records.*

359.   **aliquis . . . Gavius (360):** *someone with the name Gavius;* the name was com-
    mon, and so Verres might try to prove that the Gavius Cicero says had
    been compelled to labor in the quarries was in fact a different man than
    the one he had himself punished for spying.

360.   **fingere:** *to imagine, pretend, invent.*

361.   **ad arbitrium:** *at your bidding,* implying *to your heart's content.*

362.   **dicant:** REL. CL. OF PURPOSE; similarly **doceant** (362).

363.   **necessarios:** lit., *a necessary person = an intimate friend, a relative.*

364.   **sero:** adv., *too late;* ANAPHORA and asyndeton give the parallel phrases **te nunc
    sero . . . iudices non sero** an epigrammatic quality.

367.   **patronis:** the general meaning is *protector;* the specific meaning here is *ad-
    vocate.*

368.   **istuc:** adv., *to where you are, to what you mention;* here essentially = **istud.**
    tenebo: here, *I will grab hold of, seize upon.*

370.   **impetu: impetus,** *violent movement, violence, attack.*
    exsiluisti: exsilire, *to leap forth, start up.*

371.   **illum . . . clamitasse . . . sed . . . fuisse (373):** IND. STATE. depending on **elocu-
    tus es.**

372.   **ideo:** adv., *therefore.*
    clamitasse: = **clamitavisse,** from **clamitare,** frequentative form of **clamare,** *to
    shout, cry out (repeatedly).*

373.   **veri sunt:** i.e., they are telling the truth.

374.   **C. Numitorius:** *Gaius Numitorius* and all the other witnesses named here
    testified that they had heard Gavius crying out that he was a Roman
    citizen.

350 tur? Quid? cum ignes ardentesque laminae ceterique cruciatus admovebantur, si te illius acerba imploratio et vox miserabilis non inhibebat, ne civium quidem Romanorum qui tum aderant fletu et gemitu maximo commovebare? In crucem tu agere ausus es quemquam qui se civem Romanum esse diceret? (V.163)

It can be proven that Gavius was not a spy.

355 Nunc, quoniam exploratum est omnibus quo loco causa tua sit et quid de te futurum sit, sic tecum agam: Gavium istum, quem repentinum speculatorem fuisse dicis, ostendam in lautumias Syracusis abs te esse coniectum neque id solum ex litteris ostendam Syracusanorum, ne possis dicere me, quia sit aliquis
360 in litteris Gavius, hoc fingere et eligere nomen ut hunc illum esse possim dicere; sed ad arbitrium tuum testis dabo qui istum ipsum Syracusis abs te in lautumias coniectum esse dicant. Producam etiam Consanos, municipes illius ac necessarios, qui te nunc sero doceant, iudices non sero, illum P. Gavium, quem tu
365 in crucem egisti, civem Romanum et municipem Consanum, non speculatorem fugitivorum fuisse. (V.164)

Gavius' claim to Roman citizenship should have been investigated.

Cum haec omnia, quae polliceor, cumulate tuis patronis plana fecero, tum istuc ipsum tenebo, quod abs te mihi datur; eo contentum me esse dicam. Quid enim nuper tu ipse, cum
370 populi Romani clamore atque impetu perturbatus exsiluisti, quid, inquam, elocutus es? Illum, quod moram supplicio quaereret, ideo clamitasse se esse civem Romanum, sed speculatorem fuisse. Iam mei testes veri sunt. Quid enim dicit aliud C. Numitorius? quid M. et P. Cottii, nobilissimi homines, ex

375. **agro Tauromenitano:** *the district of Tauromenium,* a town in eastern Sicily (modern Taormina).

     argentariam: *silver business = banking business.*

376. **ceteri:** *all the others,* a strong, all-inclusive word (**alii** would have meant simply *others*).

377. **se vidisse:** therefore supremely important as eyewitnesses.

379. **illum clamitasse . . . nomen . . . valuisse (381):** the two inf. phrases are in appos. with **hoc.**

380. **se . . . Romanum:** this obviously and intentionally has become a refrain throughout this passage.

     apud te: *with you, in your estimation.*

381. **ut . . . ut . . . moram (382):** ANAPHORA, ASYNDETON, and the CHIASMUS **dubitationem . . . crucis . . . supplici . . . moram** all lend emphasis to Cicero's point.

     dubitationem . . . crucis: *some hesitancy to inflict crucifixion.*

382. **saltem:** adv., *at least.*

384. **hic haereo:** lit., *here I cling = I cling to this point.*

385. **induatur ac iuguletur:** from **induere,** *to clothe, wrap, entangle,* and **iugulare,** *to cut the throat, slay;* here, with **necesse est,** the passives can be translated reflexively, *he must inevitably entangle and destroy himself* (lit., *cut his own throat*).

386. **necesse est:** impers., *it is necessary (that);* the construction ordinarily takes **ut** + subjunct., but **ut** is often omitted.

     qui: *what kind of person* (Gavius was), i.e., a citizen or not.

     qui esset . . . dicebat (388): note how Cicero adapts his style to the excitement and tension of the passage with the stiletto thrusts of the short cls., the juxtaposition of **tua te,** the interlocked word-order of **tua te accuso oratione,** and the culminating refrain **civem . . . dicebat.**

     esse: sc. **eum (Gavium)** as subj.; such prons. are often omitted in Lat. when easily understood from the context.

388. **si . . . ducerere (389):** the pres. (vs. past) contrary to fact condition makes Cicero's point more vivid.

     Persas: *the Persians.*

     extrema: the partitive use of the adj.

389. **deprensus: deprehendere,** *to seize, arrest.*

390. **si . . . profuisset . . . potuit (396):** MIXED CONDITION.

     ignoto: *unknown, strange (a stranger);* dat. with **profuisset,** from **prosum, prodesse,** *to be useful, benefit, profit.*

     apud . . . positos (392): TRICOLON CRESCENS.

396. **adsequi:** *to overtake, reach, attain, gain.*

397. **tenues:** lit., *thin, slender;* here, *poor.*

     obscuro loco: i.e., of humble origin.

398. **quo:** adv. with **eis** as antecedent = **ad quos.**

399. **cognitoribus: cognitor,** *attorney, witness to one's identity.*

400. **fiducia:** *confidence, reliance, trust.*

401. **existimationis: existimatio,** *public opinion.*

     neque . . . solum (402): = **et non solum.**

375   agro Tauromenitano? quid Q. Lucceius, qui argentariam Regii
      maximam fecit? quid ceteri? Adhuc enim testes ex eo genere a
      me sunt dati, non qui novisse Gavium, sed se vidisse dicerent,
      cum is, qui se civem Romanum esse clamaret, in crucem agere-
      tur. Hoc tu, Verres, idem dicis; hoc tu confiteris, illum clami-
380   tasse se civem esse Romanum, apud te nomen civitatis ne tantum
      quidem valuisse ut dubitationem aliquam crucis, ut crudelissimi
      taeterrimique supplici aliquam parvam moram saltem posset
      adferre. (V.165)

Roman citizenship provides protection throughout the world.

      Hoc teneo, hic haereo, iudices. Hoc sum contentus uno;
385   omitto ac neglego cetera; sua confessione induatur ac iuguletur
      necesse est. Qui esset ignorabas; speculatorem esse suspicabare.
      Non quaero qua suspicione: tua te accuso oratione. Civem Ro-
      manum se esse dicebat. Si tu, apud Persas aut in extrema India
      deprensus, Verres, ad supplicium ducerere, quid aliud clami-
390   tares, nisi te civem esse Romanum? et si tibi ignoto apud ig-
      notos, apud barbaros, apud homines in extremis atque ultimis
      gentibus positos, nobile et illustre apud omnis nomen civitatis
      tuae profuisset—ille, quisquis erat, quem tu in crucem rapiebas,
      qui tibi esset ignotus, cum civem se Romanum esse diceret, apud
395   te praetorem, si non effugium, ne moram quidem mortis, menti-
      one atque usurpatione civitatis, adsequi potuit? (V.166)

The value of Roman citizenship is threatened by Verres' action.

      Homines tenues, obscuro loco nati, navigant; adeunt ad ea
      loca quae numquam antea viderunt, ubi neque noti esse eis quo
      venerunt, neque semper cum cognitoribus esse possunt. Hac
400   una tamen fiducia civitatis, non modo apud nostros magistra-
      tus, qui et legum et existimationis periculo continentur, neque
      apud civis solum Romanos, qui et sermonis et iuris et multarum

403. **quocumque:** adv., *to whatever place, wherever.*
404. **rem:** i.e., their Roman citizenship.
405. **tolle . . . praecluseris (412):** this highly climactic sent., characterized by exten-
     sive use of ANAPHORA, ASYNDETON, and TRICOLON CRESCENS, has the
     force of a FUT. MORE VIVID CONDITION, with a series of imper. vbs. di-
     rected at Catiline in the protasis **(tolle . . . tolle . . . constitue)** and the
     fut. perf. **praecluseris** (from **praecludere**) in the apodosis, *(if you) take
     away . . . you will soon have closed.*
     constitue: the imper. *(decide, determine)* governs the parallel IND. STATES.,
     nihil esse and **posse . . . praetorem aut alium quemlibet.**
406. **opis:** with **nihil,** *no force.*
407. **quemlibet:** quilibet, *any (you please).*
408. **constituere:** COMPL. INF. with **posse.**
409. **quis:** = **aliquis.**
413. **plura:** sc. **dicam.**
     quasi tu . . . fueris: Cicero continues to address Verres. The vb. is perf. sub-
     junct. in a CL. OF IMAGINED COMPARISON; related to conditions, these cls.
     are introduced by **quasi** or **velut si** and generally take vbs. in the pres. or
     pres. perf. tense, where Eng. would more often employ the plpf., *as if
     you had been.*
414. **infestus:** *dangerous, hostile (to).*
     generi: *class, society;* i.e., Verres has become the public enemy **(hostis)** of all
     Roman citizens, not merely the personal enemy of Gavius alone.
416. **quid . . . attinuit:** attinere, *to pertain to;* with the inf. cls. **(te iubere . . . et . . .
     addere),** lit., *what did it pertain to that you ordered . . . and that you
     added = what was the point of your ordering . . . and adding.*
     more atque instituto: HENDIADYS, *in accordance with their established practice*
     (ABL. OF ACCORDANCE).
417. **fixissent:** figere, *to attach, fasten, fix, set up.*
418. **fretum:** *strait, channel.*
     hoc: obj. of **addere** and in appos. with the IND. STATE. **te . . . deligere.**
420. **idcirco:** adv., *on that account, therefore;* the word often serves, as here, as
     antecedent to a purpose cl., *for this reason . . . that . . . .* This accusation
     amplifies Cicero's characterization of Verres' cruelty.
422. **post conditam Messanam (423):** lit., *after Messana having been founded =
     (for the first time) since the founding of Messana.*
425. **divisa:** sc. **esse.**
     servitutis: crucifixion was the form of execution for slaves.
428. **facinus . . . tollere (429):** note the climactic progression of both nouns and
     verbs, **facinus** *(bad deed),* **scelus** *(crime),* **parricidium** *(murder of a rela-
     tive),* and **vincire** *(to bind),* **verberare** *(to beat),* **necare** *(to murder),* and
     finally **(civem) in crucem tollere,** a violation so heinous, Cicero suggests,
     that it is beyond his power to describe **(quid dicam).**
430. **digno:** here, *fitting, appropriate.*
433. **unum hominem nescio quem:** *just some single human being.*

rerum societate iuncti sunt, fore se tutos arbitrantur; sed, quocumque venerint, hanc sibi rem praesidio sperant futuram.
405 Tolle hanc spem, tolle hoc praesidium civibus Romanis, constitue nihil esse opis in hac voce, "Civis Romanus sum," posse impune praetorem aut alium quemlibet supplicium quod velit in eum constituere qui se civem Romanum esse dicat, quod eum quis ignoret: iam omnis provincias, iam omnia regna, iam omnis
410 liberas civitates, iam omnem orbem terrarum, qui semper nostris hominibus maxime patuit, civibus Romanis ista defensione praecluseris. (V.167–68)

Verres is a menace to all Roman citizens.

Sed quid ego plura de Gavio? quasi tu Gavio tum fueris infestus, ac non nomini, generi, iuri civium hostis. Non illi,
415 inquam, homini sed causae communi libertatis inimicus fuisti. Quid enim attinuit, cum Mamertini more atque instituto suo crucem fixissent post urbem, in via Pompeia, te iubere in ea parte figere quae ad fretum spectaret et hoc addere—quod negare nullo modo potes, quod omnibus audientibus dixisti pa-
420 lam—te idcirco illum locum deligere, ut ille, quoniam se civem Romanum esse diceret, ex cruce Italiam cernere ac domum suam prospicere posset? Itaque illa crux sola, iudices, post conditam Messanam, illo in loco fixa est. Italiae conspectus ad eam rem ab isto delectus est ut ille, in dolore cruciatuque moriens,
425 perangusto fretu divisa servitutis ac libertatis iura cognosceret, Italia autem alumnum suum servitutis extremo summoque supplicio adfixum videret. (V.169)

The audacity of the crime.

Facinus est vincire civem Romanum, scelus verberare, prope parricidium necare: quid dicam in crucem tollere? Verbo satis
430 digno tam nefaria res appellari nullo modo potest. Non fuit his omnibus iste contentus; "Spectet," inquit, "patriam; in conspectu legum libertatisque moriatur." Non tu hoc loco Gavium, non unum hominem nescio quem, sed communem libertatis et civitatis causam in illum cruciatum et crucem egisti. Iam vero

435.   **nonne . . . defigere (437):** Cicero suggests that Verres aspires to be dictator, with the power to crucify citizens in the very strongholds of Rome *(the forum . . . the assembly place . . . the rostra);* hence he is a menace not only to someone like Gavius but to the state itself and all its citizens.

436.   **non . . . non (437):** ANAPHORA and ASYNDETON.

437.   **Quod . . . elegit (438):** = **elegit (id) quod . . . (esse) potuit,** *he chose that (place) which could be.*

   his locis: i.e., **foro . . . rostris;** dat. with **simillimum** and **proximum.**

438.   **celebritate:** *in its populousness.*

   regione: *location.*

440.   **praetervectione: praetervectio,** *passing place.*

441.   **ultro citroque:** adv., *up and down, back and forth.*

442.   **ad cives . . . ad scopulos (446):** another highly effective use of climax.

446.   **scopulos: scopulus,** *crag, cliff;* with **saxa,** used for any wild and desolate region.

   conqueri et deplorare: note the intensive force of the prefixes, *to complain loudly and lament bitterly,* and cp. **commoverentur** (447).

450.   **non . . . dignus:** sc. **iudicetur** from the next cl.; *that one citizen* (i.e., Verres) *may not be judged deserving.*

451.   **paulo:** adv., *a little, somewhat.*

452.   **nauarchorum: nauarchus,** *captain of a ship;* in an earlier passage Cicero told how pirates had destroyed the Syracusan fleet and killed the captains in the forum, and he implied that this had been done through Verres' connivance.

456.   **postulat: postulare,** *to demand.*

457.   **ubicumque:** adv., *wherever, anywhere, everywhere.*

459.   **commoda:** here, *interests.*

461.   **versari:** *to be turned, be busy, engaged, involved (in), depend (on).*

Limestone quarries
Syracuse, Sicily, Italy

435 videte hominis audaciam. Nonne eum graviter tulisse arbitramini, quod illam civibus Romanis crucem non posset in foro, non
in comitio, non in rostris defigere? Quod enim his locis in provincia sua celebritate simillimum, regione proximum potuit, elegit. Monumentum sceleris audaciaeque suae voluit esse in con-
440 spectu Italiae, vestibulo Siciliae, praetervectione omnium qui
ultro citroque navigarent. (V.170)

Cicero's confidence in a just decision.

Si haec non ad cives Romanos, non ad aliquos amicos nostrae civitatis, non ad eos qui populi Romani nomen audissent,
denique si non ad homines verum ad bestias, aut etiam (ut lon-
445 gius progrediar) si in aliqua desertissima solitudine ad saxa et
ad scopulos haec conqueri et deplorare vellem, tamen omnia
muta atque inanima tanta et tam indigna rerum acerbitate commoverentur. Nunc vero cum loquar apud senatores populi Romani, legum et iudiciorum et iuris auctores, timere non debeo
450 ne non unus iste civis Romanus illa cruce dignus, ceteri omnes
simili periculo indignissimi iudicentur. Paulo ante, iudices, lacrimas in morte misera atque indignissima nauarchorum non
tenebamus; et recte ac merito sociorum innocentium miseria
commovebamur; quid nunc in nostro sanguine tandem facere
455 debemus? Nam civium Romanorum sanguis coniunctus exis-
timandus est, quoniam id et salutis omnium ratio et veritas postulat. Omnes hoc loco cives Romani, et qui adsunt et qui ubicumque sunt, vestram severitatem desiderant, vestram fidem
implorant, vestrum auxilium requirunt; omnia sua iura, com-
460 moda, auxilia, totam denique libertatem in vestris sententiis
versari arbitrantur. (V.171–72)

CICERO'S LETTERS

The nearly 800 letters of Marcus Tullius Cicero which have come down to us cover the quarter century from 68 B.C. to 43 B.C. and provide us with unrivaled source material for the political and social life of that period—one of the most important in Roman history—as well as an intimate acquaintance with Cicero's thought and personality. A wide range of topics, both serious and light-hearted, are found here, from politics and literature to travel and the affairs of family and friends. Preserved in the collection are epistles to his wife Terentia and their children Tullia and Marcus, his younger brother Quintus Tullius Cicero, his life-long friend Titus Pomponius Atticus (there are altogether 16 books of *Epistulae ad Atticum*), his beloved freedman and personal secretary Marcus Tullius Tiro, and numerous other associates and politicians; in addition, there are, within the 16 volumes of the *Epistulae ad Familiares,* over 100 letters written to him by such public figures as Julius Caesar and Pompey the Great.

The letters survive thanks to Tiro, who collected and published the *Ad Familiares* after Cicero's death, as well as to Atticus, who likely published those in his possession, and to other ancient scholars who understood the inestimable value of the correspondence. Cicero himself did not consider his *Epistulae* formal literary productions, as Pliny the Younger clearly did, and appears to have had little idea of ever publishing more than an abbreviated selection. Hence his style, while occasionally formal and close to that of his speeches, is more often that of an educated man's *sermo cotidianus,* simple, colloquial, and free of the self-consciousness that often characterizes the letters of Pliny (as seen from the selections included later in this volume). These are the work not so much of Cicero the rhetorician and orator as of Cicero the man, revealing without inhibition his human feelings.

The selections chosen for this volume, nearly all of them complete and unexcerpted, include letters: to Atticus on a variety of topics, including the deteriorating relations between Pompey and Caesar; to his brother Quintus on the First Triumvirate and Clodius Pulcher's threats to prosecute him for executing the Catilinarians; to his wife and children, lamenting his exile in Greece in 58; to his friend Marcus Marius on the vulgarity of Pompey's public entertainments, an epistolary essay of sorts, like many of Pliny's more formal letters; to Tiro on the freedman's ill health and the volatile political situation in Rome following

Caesar's crossing of the Rubicon River in early 49; to Sulpicius Rufus, a friend who had written Cicero a *consolatio* on the death of his daughter Tullia in 45; to Basilus, one of the conspirators who assassinated Caesar on the Ides of March, 44; and finally, in the autumn of 44, to Cassius, in whom (together with his fellow assassin Brutus) Cicero placed all hope of ridding Rome of Caesar's successor, the "crazed gladiator" Mark Antony, and restoring the republic to senatorial control—a hope, of course, that was never to be realized.

A note on epistolary usages: Roman letters were typically written down, by the author or a secretary, using a reed pen on papyrus or, in the case of short notes, a stilus on a wax-covered folding tablet, then tied with a string, sealed with wax marked with a sealstone, and given to a slave or other courier for delivery. The salutation usually consists of the writer's name in the nominative case, the addressee's name in the dative, and some expression of greeting, generally abbreviated, such as *S.* or *Sal. (salutem,* sc. *dicit)* or *S.P.D. (salutem plurimam dicit).* The complimentary close, when there was one, was usually a simple *vale* or *cura ut valeas,* sometimes followed by the date (using abbreviations explained below in the notes). Often the past tenses are used to apply to the moment when the recipient reads a letter, not to the time it was written. In translating these so-called "epistolary tenses," one should employ standard English idiom; hence, *hanc epistulam Romae scribebam* is equivalent to "I am writing this letter at Rome," and *scripseram* to "I wrote."

Paquius Proculus (?) and wife
Fresco from Pompeii, house at region VII.ii.6, 1st century A.D.
Museo Archeologico Nazionale, Naples, Italy

1. **Cicero Attico Sal.:** i.e., **salutem dicit,** a standard epistolary salutation; lit., *Cicero says good health to Atticus,* = "Dear Atticus." Titus Pomponius Atticus, dedicatee of the *De Amicitia,* was Cicero's closest friend.
2. **ames:** *admire, approve;* **volo** takes a JUSSIVE NOUN CL. with or without **ut.**
    constantiam: *firmness, strength of character;* perhaps said somewhat tongue in cheek, as **non placet** can mean both *it does not seem advisable* (i.e., since in 59 B.C. the First Triumvirate were in control of Rome) and *it is not pleasing* (i.e., since Cicero does not enjoy the games anyway).
    Anti: loc. of **Antium,** *Antium* (modern Anzio), a town on the coast about 30 miles south of Rome and 12 miles west of the Appian Way.
3. *hyposoloicon:* Greek, *somewhat awkward;* Cicero, like most educated Romans of the period, spoke Greek as well as Latin and occasionally employed Greek words just as we might use a French or German or even a Latin word or phrase in a letter to a friend.
    vitare . . . suspicionem (4): perhaps because of the political tension revealed in the next letter.
    deliciarum: deliciae, *luxurious pleasures;* so **delicate** below, *luxuriously.*
4. *anaphainesthai:* Greek = **videri,** *to be seen.*
5. **inepte:** adv., *foolishly.*
    peregrinantem: peregrinari, *to travel abroad* or *about.*
    Nonas Maias: *the Nones of May;* the Nones = the 5th day of most months, the 7th in March, May, July, and October.
6. **Formiano:** sc. **praedio,** *my estate at Formiae,* on the coast of Latium considerably south of Antium.
    fac ut: a common idiom, **facere ut** = *to make sure that, see to it that.*
    visuri simus: FUT. ACT. PERIPHRASTIC in an IND. QUEST.
7. **ab Appi Foro:** sc. **hanc epistulum dabam,** *I am mailing this letter.* The *Forum of Appius* and *Three Taverns* **(Tres Tabernae)** were villages on the Appian Way east of Antium; Cicero stayed on the Appian Way and by-passed Antium completely.
    hora quarta: roughly 10:00 a.m., calculated from sunrise.
    dederam aliam: sc. **epistulam.** Letter-writers often used the impf. instead of the pres. and the plupf. instead of the perf., the so-called EPISTOLARY TENSES, depicting actions as they will appear to the recipient of the letter; in Eng. these are generally better translated as pres. and perf., respectively.
9. **Marcus Quinto Fratri:** sc. **salutem dicit** (the salutation was frequently omitted); note the familiar use of the sender's and recipient's **praenomina.** Plebeian aedile in 65 B.C. and praetor in 62, Quintus was governor of Asia 61–58, when Marcus sent him two long letters that have survived, including the one from which this selection has been excerpted.
10. **rem publicam:** three men, Gaius Julius Caesar, Gnaeus Pompeius Magnus (Pompey), and Marcus Licinius Crassus, were in effect ruling by their arbitrary power what had been a constitutional republic.
11. **funditus:** adv., *utterly, completely.*
    Cato: *Gaius Porcius Cato* (not the famous Marcus Cato, a kinsman), an opponent of Pompey's in the early 50's, when this letter was written, tribune in 57–56 and probably praetor in 55.

AD ATTICUM 2.10

On a trip to his villa at Formiae (on the coast of Latium, south of Rome), Cicero writes Atticus to tell him he has decided not to stop over for the games at Antium. April, 59 B.C.

Cicero Attico Sal.

Volo ames meam constantiam: ludos Anti spectare non placet; est enim *hyposoloicon,* cum velim vitare omnium deliciarum suspicionem, repente *anaphainesthai* non solum delicate sed
5   etiam inepte peregrinantem. Quare usque ad Nonas Maias te in Formiano exspectabo. Nunc fac ut sciam quo die te visuri simus. Ab Appi Foro, hora quarta; dederam aliam paulo ante a Tribus Tabernis. Vale.

AD QUINTUM FRATREM 1.2.15–16

Excerpt from a lengthy letter to his younger brother Quintus, then governor of Asia. The First Triumvirate dominates the state, quelling opposition by force, and Clodius threatens to prosecute Cicero. November (?), 59 B.C.

Marcus Quinto Fratri

10   Nunc ea cognosce quae maxime exoptas. Rem publicam funditus amisimus, adeo ut Cato, adulescens nullius consili sed

Portrait of a young woman with stilus and tabella, fresco from Pompeii
Museo Archeologico Nazionale, Naples, Italy

12.   **Cato:** *a Cato (nonetheless),* i.e., despite his lack of judgment.

13.   **Gabinium:** *Aulus Gabinius,* a politician working with the Triumvirate (not the
      Catilinarian conspirator), was consul-elect (along with Caesar's father-
      in-law) for 58.
      ambitu: ambitus, *bribery, electoral corruption.*
      postulare: *to demand, request, prosecute.*
      diebus aliquot (14): *for several days;* the ABL. OF DURATION OF TIME was some-
      times used instead of the acc. Cato had to make arrangements with the
      praetores (*praetors,* the leading judicial officers), before the trial, and
      they in the interests of the triumvirate refused to see him.

14.   **contionem: contio,** *meeting, assembly.*
      escendit: escendere, *to go, arise;* since Cato held no public office at this time,
      some magistrate must have invited him to speak.
      privatum: i.e., *self-appointed,* one not elected by due constitutional process.

15.   **propius . . . quam:** lit., *nothing was more nearly done than (that);* i.e., he was
      very nearly killed.
      ut occideretur (16): NOUN CL. OF RESULT.
      qui: interrog. adj. agreeing with **status.**

18.   **nostrae . . . causae:** = **meae causae** (Cicero typically employs first pers. pl. for
      sg., cp. **nos** below). Cicero's political enemies, especially Publius Clodius
      Pulcher (brother of the notorious Clodia/Lesbia of Catullus' poems),
      were attempting to prosecute him on the grounds that he had executed
      Roman citizens without right of appeal—as indeed he had done in the
      case of the Catilinarian conspirators in 63 B.C. Despite his confidence
      here, his adversaries did finally secure his banishment in 58 B.C.
      defuturi: deesse, + dat., *to be wanting, fail;* here, *likely to fail.*
      mirandum in modum (19): *in a way to be marveled at, in a marvelous fashion.*
      profitentur: profiteri, *to speak out openly.*
      offerunt se: i.e., in his support.
      pollicentur: polliceri, *to promise, make promises.*

20.   **spe . . . maxima . . . maiore . . . animo:** CHIASMUS; the ABL. OF DESCRIPTION,
      regularly with an adj. as here, is continued in the following cls. (**spe . . .
      animo**) without one.
      animo: here, *courage, confidence.*
      superiores: i.e., victorious in the political struggle; PRED. ADJ. with **fore** (=
      futuros esse) **nos,** IND. STATE. depending on **spe** (*of the hope that . . .*).

21.   **ut . . . pertimescam (22):** RESULT CL. with **animo** (sc. **tanto**).

22.   **se . . . habet:** an idiom common in Cicero; lit., *the situation thus has itself* =
      the situation is this.
      diem . . . dixerit: *appoints a day, fixes a date* (for trial); sc. **Clodius.**

23.   **concurret:** i.e., to support Cicero and oppose Clodius.
      discedamus: from court, i.e., escape the charges.
      sin: conj., *but if.*

tamen civis Romanus et Cato, vix vivus effugerit, quod, cum
Gabinium de ambitu vellet postulare neque praetores diebus
aliquot adiri possent, in contionem escendit et Pompeium "pri-
15   vatum dictatorem" appellavit. Propius nihil est factum quam ut
occideretur. Ex hoc qui sit status totius rei publicae videre
potes.

    Nostrae tamen causae non videntur homines defuturi; mi-
randum in modum profitentur, offerunt se, pollicentur. Equidem
20   cum spe sum maxima, tum maiore etiam animo: spe, superiores
fore nos; animo, ut in hac re publica ne casum quidem ullum
pertimescam. Sed tamen se res sic habet: si diem nobis dixerit,
tota Italia concurret, ut multiplicata gloria discedamus; sin

Pompey
1st century B.C.
Louvre
Paris, France

24.   **vi agere:** the possibility of violence on the part of Clodius and his followers
          is in ugly contrast to the legal procedure suggested at the beginning of
          the sent.; the resort to force was all too common in the 1st century B.C.
       spero fore ... ut ... resistamus (25): fore (= futurum esse) + a subjunct.
          RESULT CL. was a common circumlocution for the fut. inf.
       studiis: pl. because **amicorum** and **alienorum** are pl.

25.   **alienorum:** i.e., those who were not of Cicero's immediate political party.
       vi: ABL. OF MEANS or possibly (though the form is rare) dat. with **resistamus.**

26.   **clientis:** acc. pl. of **cliens,** *dependent, client, follower;* wealthy Roman patrons
          (patroni) typically had dozens or even hundreds of dependents, to whom
          they provided financial and other assistance in return for political
          support.
       libertos: libertus, *freedman, former slave.*

27.   **antiqua:** Cicero likely has in mind those who had supported him against
          Catiline in 63 B.C.
       bonorum: an epithet frequently applied by Cicero to members of his political
          faction, the Optimates.
       nostri: again = **mei;** OBJ. GEN.

28.   **qui:** interrog. pron., indef. after **si.**

29.   **horum regum:** the word **rex,** boldly applied here to the triumvirs, was de-
          spised in Roman politics.

31.   **comparatione: comparatio,** *preparation.*
       tribuni ... designati: *tribunes-elect;* we know half a dozen of the 10 plebeian
          tribunes for 58 B.C., some of them, including Clodius himself, hostile to
          Cicero, and others sympathetic.

32.   **consules:** if Cicero means the consuls-elect, as seems to be the case, then his
          comment here is wishful thinking, or rather encouragement for his
          brother, since one of the two was Aulus Gabinius and the other Caesar's
          father-in-law Calpurnius Piso (see note on 13 above).
       praetores: the four men named were praetors-elect for 58.

34.   **alios:** i.e., some of the other four praetors.
       fac: idiom, sc. **ut,** *see to it that.*

36.   **faciam te ... certiorem:** idiom, *I shall keep you informed.*
       crebro: adv., *frequently.*

39.   **distinear: distinere,** *to distract.*

41.   **voculae: vocula,** diminutive of **vox;** here = *my weak voice,* probably strained
          from speaking.
       dictavi: a slave would take down Cicero's dictation, typically his much ad-
          mired **scriba,** Tiro (see *Ad Familiares* 16.11 below).
       ambulans: walking was considered good for the voice.

43.   **illud:** *the following,* obj. of **scire** and explained by the following infs. in IND.
          STATE.
       Sampsiceramum: obj. of **paenitere** and subj. of **cupere.** *Sampsiceramus* was a
          petty Syrian monarch whom Pompey had defeated; here and elsewhere
          Cicero applied this and similar oriental names to Pompey in ridiculing
          his growing arrogance and eastern mannerisms.

autem vi agere conabitur, spero fore studiis non solum amico-
25   rum sed etiam alienorum ut vi resistamus. Omnes et se et suos
amicos, clientis, libertos, servos, pecunias denique suas pollicentur. Nostra antiqua manus bonorum ardet studio nostri
atque amore. Si qui antea aut alieniores fuerant aut languidi-
ores, nunc horum regum odio se cum bonis coniungunt. Pom-
30   peius omnia pollicetur et Caesar; quibus ego ita credo ut nihil
de mea comparatione deminuam. Tribuni plebis designati sunt
nobis amici; consules se optime ostendunt; praetores habemus
amicissimos et acerrimos civis, Domitium, Nigidium, Mem-
mium, Lentulum; bonos etiam alios. Quare magnum fac ani-
35   mum habeas et spem bonam. De singulis tamen rebus quae cotidie gerantur faciam te crebro certiorem.

AD ATTICUM 2.23

*News of Pompey's political problems and of Clodius' vicious campaign for the tribune-
ship. August or September, 59* B.C.

Cicero Attico Sal.

Numquam ante arbitror te epistulam meam legisse nisi mea
manu scriptam. Ex eo colligere poteris quanta occupatione dis-
40   tinear. Nam cum vacui temporis nihil haberem et cum recrean-
dae voculae causa necesse esset mihi ambulare, haec dictavi am-
bulans.
Primum igitur illud te scire volo: Sampsiceramum, nostrum

44.　**sui status paenitere:** the impers. vb. **paenitet** takes an acc. of the repentant person + a gen. of the thing which causes the regret or displeasure; lit., with **Sampsiceramum,** *it repents Sampsiceramus of his status* = *Sampsiceramus is sorry about his status.* Pompey's position in 59 B.C. was that of neither general nor politician; he was simply a member of the unofficial triumvirate formed in 60 B.C. with Caesar and Crassus.

　　locum: i.e., as a general with extensive powers such as he had been in 67–61 B.C.

45.　**impertire:** *to impart to, share with.*

46.　**medicinam ... quaerere:** a common metaphor, applied here to Pompey's quest for a solution to his political ills.

　　aperte: adv., *openly.*

47.　**nullam:** to be translated as an emphatic adv., *not at all, in no way,* though it is an adj. with **quam.**

　　omnes ... fuisse (49): both IND. STATES. dependent on **te scire volo.**

　　partis: here, *(political) party.*

48.　**nullo adversario:** ABL. ABS., *though there is no opponent, no opposition.*

　　consenescere: *to grow very old* (figuratively) = *to lose power;* though the word is not etymologically connected with **consensionem,** Cicero juxtaposes the two terms and omits the conjunction in order to accentuate their AS-SONANCE.

　　universorum: = **omnium.**

　　nec voluntatis nec sermonis (49): i.e., men were never in greater agreement in what they wanted and what they said in their conversations.

50.　**nos ... intersumus (51):** *I am in the midst of* = *I take part in.*

51.　**totos:** Eng. would employ an adv., *entirely.*

　　forensem operam laboremque (52): i.e., *legal business* in the courts, as opposed to politics.

52.　**contulimus:** here, *applied, devoted.*

　　ex quo: = **et ex hoc,** *and as a result of this (situation);* conjunctive use of the rel. pron.

53.　**earum rerum:** depends on both **commemoratione** and **desiderio** *(longing);* Cicero had a weakness for dwelling on his own accomplishments, particularly his role in suppressing the Catilinarian conspiracy of 63 B.C.

　　versamur: versari, *to be busy, engaged (in), concerned (with).*

54.　*Boopidos:* Greek for *Ox-eyed (= big-eyed) girl,* an allusion to the notorious Clodia (the "Lesbia" of Catullus' poems), sister of Cicero's nemesis Clodius Pulcher (see note on line 18 above). Homer applies the term to the goddess Juno, and Cicero's use of the word, though intended disparagingly, shows that Clodia was famous for her large, lustrous eyes.

　　consanguineus: *of the same blood, related;* here, *brother.*

　　terrores: *terroristic threats.* Cicero had exposed Clodius, who was now running a ruthless campaign for election to the tribuneship in order to introduce, among other things, legislation which would lead to Cicero's banishment; through terrorist tactics he succeeded in both objectives.

55.　**denuntiat: denuntiare,** *to announce, declare, threaten* (not *denounce*).

　　negat ... fert ... ostentat (56): sc. **terrores** with each vb.

amicum, vehementer sui status paenitere, restituique in eum lo-
45　cum cupere ex quo decidit, doloremque suum impertire nobis
et medicinam interdum aperte quaerere, quam ego possum in-
venire nullam; deinde omnes illius partis auctores ac socios,
nullo adversario, consenescere, consensionem universorum nec
voluntatis nec sermonis maiorem umquam fuisse.
50　　　Nos autem (nam id te scire cupere certo scio) publicis consiliis nullis intersumus totosque nos ad forensem operam laboremque contulimus. Ex quo, quod facile intellegi possit, in multa
commemoratione earum rerum quas gessimus desiderioque versamur. Sed *Boopidos* nostrae consanguineus non mediocres ter-
55　rores iacit atque denuntiat, et Sampsiceramo negat, ceteris prae

"The Head of Pompey Presented to Caesar"
Bonifazio de' Pitati, 16th century
Coll. Berenson, Florence, Italy

56.   **quamobrem:** adv., *wherefore, therefore.*
      profecto: adv., *really, surely, actually, undoubtedly.*
57.   **expergiscere: expergisci,** *to wake up.*
      ingredere: ingredi, *to walk.*
58.   **advola:** *fly to (me).*
      quantum: obj. of **ponam,** *rely (on).*
59.   **quodque maximum est:** *and what is most important,* emphasizes the following
      quantum cl.; **(id) quod** is often used to refer to an entire phrase or cl.
62.   **permagni nostra interest:** idiom, with abl. sg. of possessive + inf. phrase as
      subj. (here, **te . . . esse**), *it is of very great importance to us (that).*
      comitiis: comitia, n. pl., *election;* sc. **in,** *at the election.* The elections for this
      year, in an act of political disruption typical of the period, had been
      delayed from July to October 18.
      potueris: sc. **esse.**
63.   **declarato: declarare,** *to make clear, declare, declare as elected to office.*
      cura ut valeas: a conventional closing remark; cp. Eng. "take care of your-
      self." No correspondence between Atticus and Cicero exists for the next
      four months, probably an indication that Atticus in fact complied with
      his request and returned to Rome, as Cicero requested in this letter.
64.   **Terentiae:** *Terentia,* Cicero's first wife and mother of his two children; she
      encouraged his activities against Catiline and later Clodius, and exerted
      herself on his behalf during his exile. The two were later divorced, in 48,
      due to Cicero's suspicions that she was mishandling their finances.
      Tulliolae: *little Tullia,* a diminutive form of the name of Cicero's daughter,
      used as a term of endearment. Born ca. 79 B.C., Tullia was 21 years old
      at this time and married to Gaius Calpurnius Piso Frugi, a quaestor
      who lobbied for Cicero's recall.
65.   **Ciceroni:** Cicero's son, named *Marcus Tullius Cicero* for his father; born in
      65, he was just seven years old at the time of his father's banishment.
66.   **perfertur: fero** and a number of its compounds are often used with the sense
      of *bringing news, reporting.*
67.   **incredibilem:** PRED. ADJ., placed at the beginning of its cl. for emphasis.
      tuam . . . te: Terentia; Cicero refers to each of the three family members,
      following the order in the salutation.
68.   **me miserum:** ACC. OF EXCLAMATION.
      te . . . incidisse (70): the inf. used independently (i.e., without an introductory
      main vb.) to express an exclamation, *(to think) that you have . . ..*
      ista virtute (69): ABL. OF DESCRIPTION, = *a person of such excellence.*
69.   **humanitate:** here, *human kindness.*
      aerumnas: aerumna, *hardship.*
70.   **patre:** logically with **ex eo** as antecedent of **quo,** the word is attracted into
      the rel. cl., common when the rel. cl. precedes its antecedent.
71.   **luctus:** *grief, sorrow, distress;* here, acc. pl.
72.   **sapere:** *to have understanding.*
73.   **quae:** = **et haec,** n. pl., referring to **dolores miseriasque.**
      facta: sc. **esse.**
74.   **paulo:** adv., *a little.*

se fert et ostentat. Quamobrem, si me amas quantum profecto amas, si dormis, expergiscere; si stas, ingredere; si vero ingredieris, curre; si curris, advola. Credibile non est quantum ego in consiliis et prudentia tua, quodque maximum est, quantum
60   in amore et fide ponam. Magnitudo rei longam orationem fortasse desiderat; coniunctio vero nostrorum animorum brevitate contenta est. Permagni nostra interest te, si comitiis non potueris, at declarato illo esse Romae. Cura ut valeas.

AD FAMILIARES 14.1

Clodius was elected tribune for 58 and authored a bill banishing Cicero for his role in the execution of the Catilinarians; from exile in Greece, Cicero writes to his wife Terentia and their daughter Tullia and son Marcus on a wide range of topics. Most of the letter was written in Thessalonica, with a postscript added in Dyrrhachium. November 25, 58 B.C.

Tullius Terentiae Suae, Tulliolae Suae,
65   Ciceroni Suo Salutem Dicit

Et litteris multorum et sermone omnium perfertur ad me incredibilem tuam virtutem et fortitudinem esse teque nec animi neque corporis laboribus defatigari. Me miserum!—te ista virtute, fide, probitate, humanitate in tantas aerumnas propter
70   me incidisse! Tulliolamque nostram, ex quo patre tantas voluptates capiebat, ex eo tantos percipere luctus! Nam quid ego de Cicerone dicam?—qui cum primum sapere coepit, acerbissimos dolores miseriasque percepit. Quae si, tu ut scribis, fato facta putarem, ferrem paulo facilius, sed omnia sunt mea culpa com-

75. **ab eis:** the senatorial party; from the beginning Cicero had to struggle against their grudging acceptance of him because he was a **novus homo,** and now, he felt, they were jealous **(invidebant)** of his accomplishments.

76. **qui petebant:** the triumvirs, Caesar in particular, who did invite Cicero to join them but whose political philosophy he could not accept.

77. **quod si:** *but if.*
     apud nos: *with me.*
     tantum: adv., *so much.*

78. **sermo:** here, *advice.*
     improborum: *wicked, dishonest, treacherous.*

80. **dabo operam: operam dare,** idiom, *to give attention, take care,* + **ut** cl.
     valetudo: in the next paragraph Cicero mentions a plague at Thessalonica, where he had been staying, possibly a source of Terentia's concern.

81. **quanto:** ABL. OF DEGREE OF DIFFERENCE.

82. **omnis . . . habemus:** i.e., with us, on our side.
     Lentulum: sc. **habemus;** *Publius Cornelius Lentulus Spinther* was consul-elect at this time, and then as consul in 57 B.C. he did much to secure Cicero's return from exile and to assist in the restoration of his property.

84. **est desperandum:** impers. pass.

85. **familia:** here, the household *slaves.*
     quo modo: *as (in what way);* what the friends had suggested is not clear, but Cicero himself had considered the possibility of freeing his slaves.
     de loco (86): *with regard to this place;* on fleeing into exile Cicero had gone to Gnaeus Plancius, quaestor of Macedonia, who provided him asylum at his residence in Thessalonica.

86. **quam diu:** *how long = as long as.*

87. **attigit: attingere,** *to touch, reach, affect.*

88. **Epiro:** *Epirus,* a remote section of northwest Greece.

89. **quo:** adv., *where.*
     Hispo: probably a pseudonym for Lucius Calpurnius Piso, Caesar's father-in-law and the incoming governor of Macedonia; as consul in 58 B.C. he had worked with Clodius to secure Cicero's banishment.

90. **decedat:** NOUN CL. OF RESULT; Plancius was about to retire from his post in Macedonia.

91. **complexum: complexus,** *embrace.*

92. **me ipsum:** i.e., his former position.
     recuperaro: = **recuperavero,** from **recuperare,** *to recover, regain.*

93. **pietatis:** *affection, loyalty* (not "piety" in our ordinary sense of the word).
     Pisonis: Tullia's husband (see note on line 64 above); Piso died in 57 B.C. just before Cicero's return, and Tullia remarried the following year.

94. **utinam:** adv., introducing wishes, *would that* + subjunct. (OPTATIVE SUBJUNCT.).

95. **ei voluptati:** the so-called DOUBLE DAT. = DAT. OF REF. + DAT. OF PURPOSE.

75 missa, qui ab eis me amari putabam, qui invidebant, eos non
sequebar, qui petebant.

Quod si nostris consiliis usi essemus neque apud nos tantum
valuisset sermo aut stultorum amicorum aut improborum, bea-
tissimi viveremus; nunc, quoniam sperare nos amici iubent,
80 dabo operam ne mea valetudo tuo labori desit. Res quanta sit,
intellego, quantoque fuerit facilius manere domi quam redire:
sed tamen, si omnis tribunos plebis habemus, si Lentulum tam
studiosum quam videtur, si vero etiam Pompeium et Caesarem,
non est desperandum.

85 De familia, quo modo placuisse scribis amicis, faciemus; de
loco, nunc quidem iam abiit pestilentia, sed quam diu fuit, me
non attigit. Plancius, homo officiosissimus, me cupit esse secum
et adhuc retinet. Ego volebam loco magis deserto esse in Epiro,
quo neque Hispo veniret nec milites, sed adhuc Plancius me re-
90 tinet; sperat posse fieri ut mecum in Italiam decedat—quem
ego diem si videro et si in vestrum complexum venero ac si et
vos et me ipsum recuperaro, satis magnum mihi fructum vide-
bor percepisse et vestrae pietatis et meae. Pisonis humanitas,
virtus, amor in omnis nos tantus est ut nihil supra possit. Uti-
95 nam ea res ei voluptati sit! Gloriae quidem video fore.

Julius Caesar
1st century B.C.
Museo Pio Clementino
Vatican Museums
Vatican State

96. **nihil:** = a strong **non.**

   te accusavi: Terentia and Quintus had had some disagreement, and Cicero, in attempting to mediate, apparently had given his wife the impression that he blamed her.

   vos: subj. of **esse;** also felt as subj. of **sitis.**

   praesertim: adv., *especially.*

98. **egi:** sc. **eis gratias,** with **eis** the antecedent of **quibus;** the antecedent of a rel. pron. was often omitted, especially when indef. or when, as here, the antecedent and rel. would be in the same case construction.

   certiorem factum esse: for the idiom, see note on line 36; in his letters to these men Cicero gave Terentia due credit for reporting to him their help.

99. **quod:** *as to the fact that.*

   vicum: vicus, *property, estate.*

100. **obsecro:** obsecrare, *to beg, beseech.*

101. **premet:** with **eadem** the sense is *will continue to oppress.*

   queo: = **possum.**

   reliqua: *the remaining (things), the other (things), the rest.*

103. **fletum:** fletus, *weeping, lamentation.*

   tantum: i.e., *only this much* (as follows).

   erunt in officio: *will do their duty.*

104. **deerit:** deesse, + dat., *to be lacking, wanting, fail.*

   efficere: here, *to manage.*

105. **per:** in oaths, *by.*

   vide ne puerum perditum perdamus: *see that we do not ruin* (i.e., financially, by your selling too much of your property) *the boy, who has (already) been ruined* (by the consequences of my exile).

106. **cui:** DAT. OF POSSESSION.

   mediocri virtute opus est: *there is need of (only) ordinary character* = *he will need only . . .;* i.e., if he can escape absolute poverty, he can manage well enough with just average character and a bit of luck.

107. **consequatur:** consequi, *to follow, follow up, gain.*

   fac valeas: cp. **cura ut valeas** at the end of the preceding letter.

108. **tabellarios:** tabellarius, *letter-carrier.*

109. **omnino:** adv., *wholly, completely, certainly, definitely.*

   exspectatio: *wait, waiting.*

110. **d. a. d. VI K. Decemb.:** = **(litterae) datae ante diem sextum Kalendas Decembres,** *given* (to the letter-carrier) *on the 6th day before the December Kalends* (= the first day of the month), i.e., Nov. 25. The first **d.** in such date formulations may also stand for **datum** or **dabam.** Many of Cicero's letters were dated in this way, using more or less standard abbreviations.

   Dyrrachi: loc.; *Dyrrachium* was on the west coast of the Balkan peninsula north of Epirus and approximately opposite the heel of Italy.

111. **Dyrrachium . . . scribam (113):** a postscript.

   libera civitas: technically not subject to Rome, and hence a place where Roman exiles could live unmolested.

De Quinto fratre nihil ego te accusavi, sed vos, cum praesertim tam pauci sitis, volui esse quam coniunctissimos. Quibus me voluisti agere gratias, egi, et me a te certiorem factum esse scripsi. Quod ad me, mea Terentia, scribis te vicum vendituram,

100 quid, obsecro te—me miserum!—quid futurum est? Et, si nos premet eadem fortuna, quid puero misero fiet? Non queo reliqua scribere—tanta vis lacrimarum est—neque te in eundem fletum adducam. Tantum scribo: si erunt in officio amici, pecunia non deerit; si non erunt, tu efficere tua pecunia non poteris.

105 Per fortunas miseras nostras, vide ne puerum perditum perdamus. Cui si aliquid erit ne egeat, mediocri virtute opus est et mediocri fortuna, ut cetera consequatur. Fac valeas et ad me tabellarios mittas ut sciam quid agatur et vos quid agatis. Mihi omnino iam brevis exspectatio est. Tulliolae et Ciceroni salutem

110 dic. Valete. D.a.d. VI K. Decemb. Dyrrachi.

Dyrrachium veni, quod et libera civitas est et in me officiosa

Cicero, 1st century B.C.
Vatican Museums, Vatican State

112. **celebritas:** *crowded condition,* because it was a major port for the traffic from Italy to Greece.

     alio: adv., *to another place, elsewhere.*

114. **S. D.: salutem dicit.**

     M. Mario: *Marcus Marius,* known only through a few of Cicero's letters as a person of taste and refinement who led a quiet lifestyle and suffered from ill health; possibly one of the Marii of Arpinum, Cicero's hometown, he had a villa at Stabiae near Cicero's.

115. **tenuit quominus . . . venires (116):** *kept you from coming;* vbs. of hindering and preventing are followed by **ne** or **quominus** + subjunct.

116. **ludos:** Pompey produced lavish games in August, 55 B.C., in connection with the dedication of his new theater, Rome's first permanent stone theater; the entertainments, which were so spectacular as to be mentioned a century later by Pliny the Elder, included plays, wild animal hunts, and athletic competitions.

     tribuo: tribuere, *to ascribe, attribute, give;* sc. **id.**

118. **posses:** sc. **venire.**

119. **utrumque:** *each of two, both.*

     laetor: laetari, *to be glad about, take delight in.*

     et . . . te fuisse et . . . valuisse: *both that you were . . . and that . . .;* both infs. are in appos. with **utrumque.**

121. **apparatissimi:** *most sumptuous;* sc. **erant.**

     stomachi: stomachus, *stomach, digestion, liking, taste.* We would say "to your taste"; and cp. the expression "I cannot stomach this."

122. **meo:** sc. **stomacho.**

     honoris causa . . . honoris causa (123): Cicero jokingly plays on two different meanings of **honor;** in the first instance he means *for the sake of the honor,* i.e., to honor Pompey on this occasion, and in the second, *for the sake of their own honor,* i.e., their (dwindling) reputation.

123. **scaenam: scaena,** *stage, theater.*

124. **deliciae:** lit., *delights;* but often, as here, the pl. is used in the sg. sense of *pet, favorite, darling.*

     noster Aesopus: *my friend Aesop;* in his younger days Clodius Aesopus was the most famous tragic actor at Rome and a friend of Cicero's.

125. **eius modi fuit:** *he was such;* he was so old and feeble that everyone was ready *for him to retire* (**ei desinere**).

     iurare: *to take an oath,* i.e., as a character in the play.

126. **sciens:** Eng. would use an adv., *knowingly.*

     fallo: fallere, *to deceive, cheat, disappoint, fail;* the joke is that, as Aesopus spoke the words from an oath, *if I . . . fail,* his voice in fact failed him.

127. **quid:** = **cur,** as often.

     narrem: DELIBERATIVE SUBJUNCT.

     nosti: = **novisti,** implying that Marius had already heard something of the games, not surprisingly, as they were a spectacular, if tasteless, event.

128. **leporis: lepos,** *charm, grace, wit;* PARTITIVE GEN. with **id.**

     mediocres: here, *ordinary.*

     apparatus . . . spectatio (129): *the spectacle (sight) of the elaborate display.*

·

et proxima Italiae; sed si offendet me loci celebritas, alio me conferam, ad te scribam.

AD FAMILIARES 7.1 (excerpts)

The public entertainments sponsored by Pompey at the dedication of his theater at Rome are vulgar displays which displeased Cicero and would have displeased his friend Marcus Marius as well; more formal than most of his correspondence, the letter is essentially an epistolary essay of the sort later written by Horace (in verse) and the younger Pliny. September or October, 55 B.C.

M. Cicero S. D. M. Mario

Marius' absence from the games.

115   Si te dolor aliqui corporis aut infirmitas valetudinis tuae tenuit quominus ad ludos venires, fortunae magis tribuo quam
sapientiae tuae; sin haec, quae ceteri mirantur, contemnenda
duxisti et, cum per valetudinem posses, venire tamen noluisti,
utrumque laetor, et sine dolore corporis te fuisse et animo valu-
120 isse, cum ea, quae sine causa mirantur alii, neglexeris.
    Omnino, si quaeris, ludi apparatissimi, sed non tui sto-
machi; coniecturam enim facio de meo: nam primum honoris
causa in scaenam redierant ei, quos ego honoris causa de
scaena decessisse arbitrabar; deliciae vero tuae, noster Aesopus,
125 eius modi fuit ut ei desinere per omnis homines liceret. Is iurare
cum coepisset, vox eum defecit in illo loco, "si sciens fallo."
Quid tibi ego alia narrem? Nosti enim reliquos ludos, qui ne id
quidem leporis habuerunt quod solent mediocres ludi; appara-

Gladiators fighting, terracotta relief
2nd century A.D.
Museo Nazionale Romano, Rome, Italy

129. **hilaritatem: hilaritas,** *enjoyment, amusement.*
130. **sescenti:** *600;* commonly used for an indefinite large number, here a hyperbole emphasizing the extravagance of the spectacle.

     muli: perhaps carrying Agamemnon's booty when he returned to Clytemnestra from Troy.

     Clytaemestra . . . Equo Troiano **(131):** *Clytemnestra* and *The Trojan Horse,* titles of two Roman tragedies presented during the **ludi;** they have not survived, but they clearly dealt with the Trojan cycle.
131. **creterrarum: creterra,** *mixing bowl,* for mixing water with wine as the ancients regularly did; here again possibly loot from the Trojan War.

     armatura: *armor, equipment.*

     peditatus et equitatus (132): both gen. sg., *of the infantry and cavalry.*
133. **attulissent:** sc. **si adfuisses.**
134. **Protogeni:** *Protogenes,* an educated Greek slave trained as a reader (in Greek, an ***anagnostes***); many cultivated Romans had such slaves.

     dummodo . . . legerit (135): this self-deprecating aside shows that Cicero did, after all, have a sense of humor and could even poke fun at himself.

     quidvis: quivis, *anyone, anything.*
135. **ne:** a Greek interjection, employed in Lat. only before prons., *surely, indeed.*

     haud paulo plus: i.e., *a great deal more;* LITOTES.
136. **nostrum:** gen. with **quisquam.**

     delectationis: depends on **plus.**
137. **venationes: venatio,** *animal-hunt;* wild beasts (lions, panthers, elephants, etc.) were turned loose in an arena to fight human beings and one another.

     binae: *two each (day).*
138. **polito:** *polished,* therefore *refined, cultivated.*
139. **imbecillus:** *weak, powerless,* by nature as compared with **bestiae,** and also because sometimes the gladiators were unarmed.

     laniatur: laniare, *to tear, mangle.*
140. **venabulo: venabulum,** *hunting spear.*

     transverberatur: transverberare, *to pierce through.*
142. **elephantorum . . . fuit:** we would say "was devoted to . . . ."
143. **admiratio:** not *admiration,* but *surprise, amazement.*

     vulgi atque turbae: *the vulgar throng;* HENDIADYS.

     exstitit: exsistere, *to stand out, show itself, appear.*
144. **quin:** here, *to the contrary.*

     misericordia: Pliny the Elder in his *Natural History* (8.21) reports that the terrified elephants seemed to plead with the spectators so pathetically that all the people arose with tears in their eyes and cursed Pompey.
145. **esse . . . societatem:** IND. STATE. depending on **opinio;** the symmetry of the phrase is appropriate to the bond that Cicero suggests was felt between man and beast.
147. **forte:** abl. of **fors** as adv., *by chance, perhaps.*
148. **dirupi: dirumpere,** *to burst, rupture.*

     paene: adv., *nearly, almost;* Eng. might say, "I practically killed myself."

130 tus enim spectatio tollebat omnem hilaritatem. Quid enim delectationis habent sescenti muli in *Clytaemestra*? aut in *Equo
Troiano* creterrarum tria milia? aut armatura varia peditatus et
equitatus in aliqua pugna? Quae popularem admirationem habuerunt; delectationem tibi nullam attulissent. Quod si tu per
eos dies operam dedisti Protogeni tuo (dummodo is tibi quidvis
135 potius quam orationes meas legerit), ne tu haud paulo plus
quam quisquam nostrum delectationis habuisti.

The wild animal hunts.

Reliquae sunt venationes binae per dies quinque, magnifi-
cae—nemo negat; sed quae potest homini esse polito delectatio,
cum aut homo imbecillus a valentissima bestia laniatur aut
140 praeclara bestia venabulo transverberatur? Quae tamen, si viden-
da sunt, saepe vidisti; neque nos, qui haec spectamus, quicquam novi vidimus. Extremus elephantorum dies fuit. In quo
admiratio magna vulgi atque turbae, delectatio nulla exstitit:
quin etiam misericordia quaedam consecuta est atque opinio
145 eius modi, esse quandam illi beluae cum genere humano societatem.

Cicero is extremely busy.

His ego tamen diebus (ludis scaenicis), ne forte videar tibi
non modo beatus sed liber omnino fuisse, dirupi me paene in

Gladiators, Roman mosaic, 3rd century A.D.
Galleria Borghese, Rome, Italy

149. **Galli Canini:** *Lucius Caninius Gallus* was a **tribunus plebis** in 56 B.C. and a supporter of Pompey, but we know nothing about this trial.

     familiaris: *friend, associate.*

     facilem populum: *an accommodating public;* another joke, since Aesopus' audience, as Cicero had noted earlier (124–25), were eager to be rid of him.

150. **mehercule:** interj., *by Hercules* = *good heavens!* or *so help me!*

     artem desinerem (151): i.e., to retire.

151. **nostri: similis** may be followed by either the dat. or the gen.

152. **non numquam:** common for *sometimes.*

153. **homines . . . meritos (152):** *men not deserving very much from me;* from **mereri,** *to earn, deserve, merit.*

155. **causas . . . vivendi:** *reasons for living.*

     aliquando: adv., *at some time, at last, finally.*

     arbitratu: arbitratus, *choice, pleasure;* ABL. OF ACCORDANCE.

156. **oti:** = **otii;** spelling with only one **-i** the gen. sg. of **-ius/-ium** nouns was common through the Ciceronian period.

157. **quodque:** *and as to the fact that;* the phrase introduced is in appos. with the following **hoc.**

     intervisis: intervisere, *to visit from time to time.*

158. **neque nos . . . neque te:** both are subjs. of **frui,** *for me to enjoy;* the entire cl. is highly elliptical, = **neque nos lepore tuo frui liceret neque te lepore meo (si qui est lepos in me) frui liceret.**

159. **qui:** indef. adj. after **si.**

160. **quibus:** = **et eis (occupationibus);** ABL. OF SEPARATION.

     relaxaro: = **relaxavero.**

161. **commentaris: commentari,** *to study, consider, practice;* with advs. such as **iam** and expressions of duration of time, such as **multos annos** here, Lat. uses the pres. where Eng. uses the perf., *have been studying.*

     humaniter: adv., *as a man* **(homo)** *should,* i.e., *in a refined manner.*

163. **sustenta: sustentare,** *to endure with courage.*

164. **tuere: tueri,** *to look at, guard, watch, protect.*

     lecticula: diminutive of **lectica,** *small litter.*

165. **concursare:** *to run about, travel about.*

166. **abundantia:** ABL. OF CAUSE.

167. **subinvitaras:** = **subinvitaveras,** from **subinvitare,** *to gently invite, suggest, hint.*

168. **quominus:** = **ne,** used to introduce a negative purpose cl.; lit., *by which . . . the less* = *so that . . . not.*

     paeniteret: for construction see note on line 44 above.

169. **quod:** = **et hoc.**

     minus: = **non,** as often.

170. **quod . . . vises:** cl. in appos. with **hoc.**

iudicio Galli Canini, familiaris tui. Quod si tam facilem popu-
150   lum haberem, quam Aesopus habuit, libenter mehercule artem
desinerem tecumque et cum similibus nostri viverem; neque
enim fructum ullum laboris exspecto, et cogor non numquam
homines non optime de me meritos rogatu eorum, qui bene
meriti sunt, defendere.
155   Itaque quaero causas omnis aliquando vivendi arbitratu
meo; teque et istam rationem oti tui et laudo vehementer et
probo; quodque nos minus intervisis, hoc fero animo aequiore,
quod, si Romae esses, tamen neque nos lepore tuo neque te—si
qui est in me—meo frui liceret propter molestissimas occupati-
160   ones meas; quibus si me relaxaro, te ipsum, qui multos annos
nihil aliud commentaris, docebo profecto quid sit humaniter
vivere.

A cordial conclusion.

     Tu modo istam imbecillitatem valetudinis tuae sustenta et
tuere, ut facis, ut nostras villas obire et mecum simul lecticula
165   concursare possis. Haec ad te pluribus verbis scripsi quam so-
leo, non oti abundantia sed amoris erga te, quod me quadam
epistula subinvitaras, si memoria tenes, ut ad te aliquid eius
modi scriberem, quominus te praetermisisse ludos paeniteret.
Quod si adsecutus sum, gaudeo; sin minus, hoc me tamen con-
170   solor, quod posthac ad ludos venies nosque vises.

Three comic actors
Fresco from Pompeii
1st century A.D.
Museo Archeologico Nazionale
Naples, Italy

172. **Q.Q.:** = **Quintus** (Cicero's brother) and **Quintus** (the son of Quintus); the fact that Cicero composed this letter in the names of all his family, as well as his use of **plurimam (salutem),** suggests the affection in which all held Tiro. Marcus Tullius Tiro, as he was called after being freed by Cicero, invented the first known system of shorthand (the so-called **Notae Tironianae**) for the purpose of taking down Cicero's speeches, and he was also important in the editing of Cicero's letters.
     dic.: dicit.
173. **opportunitatem:** here, *advantage.*
174. **te . . . valere:** IND. STATE. dependent on **doleo.**
175. **quartanam:** sc. **febrim** *(fever), quartan fever,* which recurred every fourth day and was taken to be a sign of convalescence from more serious illnesses.
176. **Curius:** a banker at Patrae in whose care Cicero had left Tiro.
177. **humanitatis tuae:** *characteristic of your human feeling* or *kindness;* PRED. GEN.
178. **quam commodissime:** here, *as expeditiously as possible.*
179. **ex desiderio labores:** *you suffer from being away.*
180. **nauseae molestiam:** *the annoyance of seasickness.*
     aeger: *sick, ill.*
181. **hieme: hiems,** *winter;* the ancients thought that winter was no time for navigation.
182. **ad:** = *to the vicinity of.* A general could not enter Rome without surrendering his **imperium,** unless the senate had granted him a triumph (**triumphum,** an honorary military parade through the city to the temple of Jupiter Capitolinus); Cicero was awaiting such a triumph for a victory in his province of Cilicia but it had not yet been decreed by the senate.
     pr. Non. Ian.: pridie Nonas Ianuarias, *the day before the Nones of January* = January 4 (49 B.C.).
     obviam: adv., *in the way, towards, to meet,* + dat.; with **mihi** and the impers. pass. **est proditum** (from **prodire**), lit., *it was come forth* (by the people) *to meet me* = *the people came out to meet me.*
183. **ornatius:** *more splendidly.*
     incidi: incidere, *to fall into, come upon.*
184. **cui:** = **et ei (bello).**
     mederi: *to heal, cure,* + dat.; actually there was practically no likelihood that Cicero's actions could have resolved the crisis, as Rome was clearly moving toward one-man rule of some sort.
186. **ex utraque parte:** *on both* (each of two) *sides,* i.e., the Caesarians and the senatorial aristocracy.
187. **omnino:** here, *the sum of the matter is this, in sum.*
     et . . . Caesar . . . et Curio (189): *both Caesar . . . and Curio;* Gaius Scribonius Curio, tribune in 50 B.C. and a Caesarian, read to the senate on January 1 the letter Cicero mentions here.
     amicus noster: ever the mediator, Cicero had attempted to maintain reasonably amicable relations with both Pompey and Caesar, so much so in fact that he was accused by some of fence-straddling.
     minacis: *threatening;* acc. pl.

AD FAMILIARES 16.11

When returning from his province of Cilicia in November, 50 B.C.*, Cicero had left behind in Patrae, Greece, his beloved freedman and secretary Tiro; in this letter to Tiro, Cicero expresses his concern both over his friend's health and over the dangers Rome faced on the very eve of civil war between Caesar and Pompey. January 12, 49* B.C.*, the day following Caesar's crossing of the Rubicon River.*

Tullius et Cicero, Terentia, Tullia,
Q. Q. Tironi Sal. Plurimam Dic.

Etsi opportunitatem operae tuae omnibus locis desidero, tamen non tam mea quam tua causa doleo te non valere; sed
175 quoniam in quartanam conversa vis est morbi—sic enim scribit Curius—spero te, diligentia adhibita, iam firmiorem fore. Modo fac (id quod est humanitatis tuae) ne quid aliud cures hoc tempore, nisi ut quam commodissime convalescas. Non ignoro quantum ex desiderio labores; sed erunt omnia facilia, si va-
180 lebis. Festinare te nolo, ne nauseae molestiam suscipias aeger et periculose hieme naviges.

Ego ad urbem accessi pr. Non. Ian. Obviam mihi sic est proditum ut nihil possit fieri ornatius; sed incidi in ipsam flammam civilis discordiae vel potius belli, cui cum cuperem mederi
185 et, ut arbitror, possem, cupiditates certorum hominum—nam ex utraque parte sunt qui pugnare cupiant—impedimento mihi fuerunt. Omnino et ipse Caesar, amicus noster, minacis ad sena-

Two ships with man overboard
Marble relief from a Roman sarcophagus, 2nd–3rd centuries A.D.
Ny Carlsberg Glyptotek, Copenhagen, Denmark

188. **qui . . . teneret (189):** REL. CL. OF RESULT with **erat adhuc impudens,** *he was still so shameless (defiant) that he . . . .* The senate had ordered Caesar to relinquish his extraordinary 10-year governorship of Gaul and return to Rome, where his enemies intended to prosecute him for illegal acts he had committed during his consulship in 59.

189. **provinciam:** Caesar had governed the triple province of Cisalpine Gaul, Transalpine (Narbonese) Gaul, and Illyricum.

190. **Antonius . . . et Q. Cassius:** partisans of Caesar and tribunes for 49 B.C. When the senate rejected the demands in Caesar's letter and decreed that he must disband his army or be regarded a public enemy, Antony and Cassius futilely interposed their veto against the senate's decree and were forced to flee; Caesar used their expulsion to justify his march on Rome.

191. **postea quam:** = **postquam.**

192. **nobis . . . pro consulibus (193):** Cicero (who had not yet entered the city and was thus still proconsul) and Pompey (who had been specially empowered by the senate); a proconsul was an ex-consul whose **imperium** had been extended by vote of the senate beyond his year of office, generally for service as a provincial governor.

193. **negotium:** *business, assignment.*

   ne . . . caperet (194): this was the wording of the **senatus consultum ultimum,** a decree of martial law issued by the senate and giving the magistrates extraordinary powers to deal with the crisis; a similar decree was passed during the Catilinarian conspiracy in 63 B.C.

194. **detrimenti: detrimentum,** *harm;* depends on **quid.**

196. **ex hac . . . parte:** *on our side.*

   comparatur: impers. pass.

197. **sero:** adv., *too late;* this adv. and the pres. tense of **comparatur** give evidence of Pompey's lack of preparation.

198. **frequens:** *crowded, full.*

   flagitavit: flagitare, *to demand.*

199. **Lentulus:** *Lucius Cornelius Lentulus Crus,* brother of Lentulus Spinther (line 82), he was elected consul for 49 as an anti-Caesarian.

   quo . . . faceret (200): i.e., to put Cicero more in his debt.

200. **simul atque:** *as soon as.*

201. **relaturum:** sc. **esse;** i.e., he would introduce a bill in the senate for a formal vote.

   discriptae sunt: discribere, lit., *to write separately* = *to distribute, assign.*

   quam . . . tueretur (202): an IND. QUEST., loosely appended in appos. to **regiones,** *(indicating) what part (the part which) each should defend.*

202. **Capuam:** *Capua,* one of the chief cities of Campania.

204. **etiam atque etiam:** repetition for emphasis = *again and again.*

205. **cui des:** sc. **aliquem** as antecedent; i.e., a letter-carrier.

206. **d. pr. Idus Ian.: datum** or **dabam** or **(litterae) datae pridie Idus Ianuarias,** *the day before the Ides of January* = January 12 (the Ides fell on the 13th of most months, the 15th in March, May, July, and October).

tum et acerbas litteras miserat, et erat adhuc impudens qui exercitum et provinciam invito senatu teneret, et Curio meus illum
190 incitabat. Antonius quidem noster et Q. Cassius, nulla vi ex-
pulsi, ad Caesarem cum Curione profecti erant postea quam
senatus consulibus, praetoribus, tribunis plebis, et nobis qui pro
consulibus sumus, negotium dederat ut curaremus ne quid res
publica detrimenti caperet. Numquam maiore in periculo civi-
195 tas fuit; numquam improbi cives habuerunt paratiorem ducem.
Omnino ex hac quoque parte diligentissime comparatur; id fit
auctoritate et studio Pompei nostri, qui Caesarem sero coepit
timere. Nobis inter has turbas senatus tamen frequens flagitavit
triumphum; sed Lentulus consul, quo maius suum beneficium
200 faceret, simul atque expedisset quae essent necessaria de re publica, dixit se relaturum. Italiae regiones discriptae sunt, quam
quisque partem tueretur: nos Capuam sumpsimus. Haec te
scire volui.

    Tu etiam atque etiam cura ut valeas litterasque ad me mit-
205 tas, quotienscumque habebis cui des. Etiam atque etiam vale.
D. pr. Idus Ian.

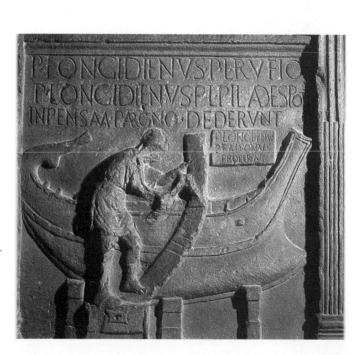

Funerary stele of
Publius Longidienus,
faber navalis
1st century B.C.
Museo Nazionale
Ravenna, Italy

208. **lippitudo: lippitudo,** *inflammation of the eyes;* Cicero frequently complained of problems with his eyes during this period.

     librari: librarius, *secretary.*

     manus: here, *handwriting;* Cicero often wrote out his own personal letters.

209. **scriberem . . . erat:** EPISTOLARY TENSES, to be translated as pres. (see note on line 7); similarly several of the vbs. following.

210. **omnis exspectatio nostra erat:** i.e., "we are eagerly awaiting."

     nuntiis Brundisinis: *the news from Brundisium;* after crossing the Rubicon in January, Caesar marched south and Pompey fled with his army to Brundisium, where he was preparing to cross over to Greece.

     nactus . . . esset (211): nancisci, *to find, get, obtain;* here = *if he has caught up with.*

211. **hic:** Caesar.

     Gnaeum: Pompey.

     dubia: here, not *dubious,* but *some, slight.*

     transmisisset: again epistolary, *has crossed* (to Greece).

212. **in quem hominem:** *to what kind of man* (i.e., Caesar); many had expected the worst of Caesar, but after his unexpected clemency in sparing the forces of Pompey who surrendered to him in a recent engagement at Corfinium, opinion throughout Italy began to turn in Caesar's favor.

214. **si . . . occiderit:** i.e., especially if there were to be no proscriptions (the public posting of names of political enemies to be liquidated), like those of Sulla.

     cuiquam: DAT. OF SEPARATION, common with vbs. that mean *to take away,* like **adimere** here; Cicero refers to the confiscations which regularly attended proscriptions.

216. **municipales homines:** *townspeople* (living in **municipia** outside of Rome).

     rusticani: *country people.*

217. **prorsus:** adv., *absolutely.*

     nisi . . . nummulos (218): ANAPHORA, ASYNDETON, TRICOLON CRESCENS, and the diminutives all serve to underscore Cicero's indignation over the people's apathy and fickleness.

218. **nummulos:** diminutive of **nummus,** *little sums of money.*

     illum: Pompey, who had posed as the champion of the senate and constitutionality.

219. **confidebant: confidere,** *to trust completely (in),* may take the dat. or, as here, the ABL. OF PLACE WHERE.

220. **nostris:** refers to the senatorial party.

221. **scripseram . . . exspectabam (222):** EPISTOLARY TENSES.

224. **valde:** adv., *greatly, very much.*

225. **quae apud Corfinium sunt gesta:** i.e., Caesar's clemency in releasing without injury Pompey's troops whom he had captured at Corfinium in central Italy.

226. **libentius:** with **hoc** (ABL. OF DEGREE OF DIFFERENCE), *the more gladly.*

     mea sponte: abl. used as adv., *voluntarily, of my own accord.*

     constitueram: constituere, *to place, determine, decide.*

227. **me praeberem:** here, *to show myself (to be).*

     Pompeium: with **reconciliarem** *(to regain, win back).*

AD ATTICUM 8.13

Whereas only recently Caesar had been feared and Pompey revered by many Romans, now, as Cicero complains to Atticus, in less than three months since the preceding letter and Caesar's crossing of the Rubicon, the public's attitude toward both men is changing. Written from his villa at Formiae, March 1, 49 B.C.

Cicero Attico Sal.

Lippitudinis meae signum tibi sit librari manus et eadem causa brevitatis, etsi nunc quidem quod scriberem nihil erat.
210 Omnis exspectatio nostra erat in nuntiis Brundisinis. Si nactus hic esset Gnaeum nostrum, spes dubia pacis; sin ille ante transmisisset, exitiosi belli metus. Sed videsne in quem hominem inciderit res publica, quam acutum, quam vigilantem, quam paratum? Si mehercule neminem occiderit nec cuiquam quidquam
215 ademerit, ab iis qui eum maxime timuerant maxime diligetur.
Multum mecum municipales homines loquuntur, multum rusticani; nihil prorsus aliud curant nisi agros, nisi villulas, nisi nummulos suos. Et vide quam conversa res sit; illum quo antea confidebant metuunt, hunc amant quem timebant. Id quantis
220 nostris peccatis vitiisque evenerit, non possum sine molestia cogitare. Quae autem impendere putarem, scripseram ad te et iam tuas litteras exspectabam.

AD ATTICUM 9.7c

Caesar wrote the following letter to Oppius and Cornelius, two of his agents in Rome, and a copy was sent to Cicero. He will not follow the extreme course of Sulla and others, but seeks reconciliation with Pompey and the senatorial party. March 5 (?), 49 B.C.

Caesar Oppio Cornelio Sal.

Gaudeo mehercule vos significare litteris quam valde probe-
225 tis ea quae apud Corfinium sunt gesta. Consilio vestro utar libenter et hoc libentius quod mea sponte facere constitueram ut quam lenissimum me praeberem et Pompeium darem ope-

228. **temptemus ... si possimus:** *let us try in case we should be able,* a FUT. LESS VIVID CONDITION equivalent to an IND. QUEST. = *let us try to see whether we can.*
229. **reliqui:** Cicero likely has in mind the massacres ordered by Gaius Marius and, certainly, the proscriptions of Lucius Cornelius Sulla, both in the civil wars of the 80's.
232. **liberalitate:** here, *generosity.*
236. **N. Magium:** *Numerius Magius,* one of Pompey's prefects of engineers, captured by Caesar after Corfinium and then dispatched by him to Pompey with a request that the two generals meet.
      scilicet: adv., *obviously, to be sure, of course.*
237. **instituto: institutum,** *custom, practice;* Caesar had demonstrated his **clementia** with other captured officers.
      missum feci: = *I dismissed, released.*
      duo praefecti: Magius was one, Vibullius Rufus the other.
238. **fabrum:** = **fabrorum,** from **faber,** *smith, engineer.*
240. **mihi ... iis:** both dat. with **amicus.**
241. **inimicissimi:** i.e., certain senators.
      artificiis: artificium, *scheme.*
244. **vellem:** *I could wish;* POTENTIAL SUBJUNCT.
      casu: here, *misfortune, distress.*
246. **ex eo ... quod:** *from the fact that.*
247. **aliquantum:** adv., *somewhat.*
      adquievi: adquiescere, *to become quiet, rest, calm down.*
249. **adhibuisti:** here, *you showed.*
      Servius ... tuus: i.e., Sulpicius' son.
250. **declaravit:** here, not *declared,* but *made clear, demonstrated.*
251. **faceret:** lit., *made of* = *esteemed.*
      animum: *attitude.*
253. **oratio tua:** i.e., his words.
254. **societas ... aegritudinis:** *partnership in my grief,* almost a translation of Greek *sympatheia,* which literally means *suffering with another,* as does also eccl. Lat. **compassio.**
      auctoritas: i.e., the influence of his advice.

ram ut reconciliarem. Temptemus hoc modo si possimus omnium voluntates reciperare et diuturna victoria uti, quoniam re-
230 liqui crudelitate odium effugere non potuerunt neque victoriam
diutius tenere praeter unum L. Sullam, quem imitaturus non
sum. Haec nova sit ratio vincendi ut misericordia et liberalitate
nos muniamus. Id quemadmodum fieri possit, nonnulla mihi in
mentem veniunt et multa reperiri possunt. De his rebus rogo
235 vos ut cogitationem suscipiatis.

   N. Magium, Pompei praefectum, deprehendi. Scilicet meo
instituto usus sum et eum statim missum feci. Iam duo praefecti
fabrum Pompei in meam potestatem venerunt et a me missi
sunt. Si volent grati esse, debebunt Pompeium hortari ut malit
240 mihi esse amicus quam iis qui et illi et mihi semper fuerunt inimicissimi, quorum artificiis effectum est ut res publica in hunc
statum perveniret.

AD FAMILIARES 4.6

*We have, preserved amid Cicero's correspondence (*Ad Familiares *4.5), a letter of
consolation on the death of his daughter Tullia written to him from Greece in April,
45* B.C., *by the noted jurist, orator, and politician Servius Sulpicius Rufus. In the following reply Cicero expresses gratitude for Servius' kindness but remarks that his
sorrow is still hard to bear, because he cannot in these times take an active role in the
political and forensic activities that might otherwise provide distraction from his grief.
Written from Atticus' villa at Ficulea, just to the east of Rome, April, 45* B.C.

M. Cicero S.D. Ser. Sulpicio

   Ego vero, Servi, vellem, ut scribis, in meo gravissimo casu
245 adfuisses; quantum enim praesens me adiuvare potueris et consolando et prope aeque dolendo, facile ex eo intellego quod,
litteris lectis, aliquantum adquievi. Nam et ea scripsisti quae
levare luctum possent, et in me consolando non mediocrem ipse
animi dolorem adhibuisti. Servius tamen tuus omnibus officiis,
250 quae illi tempori tribui potuerunt, declaravit et quanti ipse me
faceret et quam suum talem erga me animum tibi gratum pu-
taret fore; cuius officia iucundiora scilicet saepe mihi fuerunt,
numquam tamen gratiora. Me autem non oratio tua solum et
societas paene aegritudinis sed etiam auctoritas consolatur;

256. **praeditus:** *endowed.*
259. **Q. Maximus:** *Quintus Fabius Maximus,* dictator in 217 B.C. and hero in the
     war against Hannibal (see Livy's "Hannibal and the Second Punic War,"
     below); his son, consul in 213 (hence **consularem,** *ex-consul*), prede-
     ceased him.
     rebus gestis: *accomplishments.*
260. **L. Paullus:** *Lucius Aemilius Paullus,* victor over king Perseus at the battle of
     Pydna in 168 B.C. in the Third Macedonian War; his triumph was marred
     by the deaths of his two youngest sons in the same week.
     duo: sometimes, as here, used for **duos.**
261. **Gaius:** *Gaius Sulpicius Gallus,* called **vester** as a member of Servius Sulpicius'
     gens, served under Paullus at Pydna and also lost a son.
     M. Cato: *Marcus Porcius Cato,* the famous orator, politician, and censor of
     the early second century B.C.; four years before his own death, his son
     died after being elected praetor in 153.
262. **iis:** here, *such.*
     fuerunt: = **vixerunt.**
265. **ornamentis:** here, *distinctions, honors.*
266. **eram . . . adeptus: adipisci,** *to gain.*
     unum manebat illud solacium (267): under Caesar's rule, with his own politi-
     cal career eclipsed, Cicero's one comfort had been the love and under-
     standing of his daughter Tullia, who died in February, 45 B.C. (at the age
     of 33 or 34), two months before this letter was written.
268. **procuratione: procuratio,** *management, conduct.*
     impediebantur: here, *held in check.*
     cogitationes: i.e., his grief.
269. **in foro:** i.e., *in legal practice.*
     libebat: libere, libuit, impers., *it is pleasing.*
     curiam: *senate-house;* Caesar, now dictator, had greatly diminished the role
     of the senate.
270. **id quod erat: id** is in appos. with the whole cl. **existimabam . . . perdidisse,** *the*
     thing which was = as was the case.
272. **frangerem:** *I broke = I gained control over.*
273. **ferre:** sc. **me** as subj.
     quo: adv., lit., *whither = (a person) to whom;* with **confugerem,** REL. CL. OF
     PURPOSE.
     ubi: here, *with whom;* **quo, ubi,** and **cuius** refer to Tullia.
276. **consanuisse: consanescere,** *to become healthy, get well, heal.*
     recrudescunt: recrudescere, *to become raw again,* continuing the metaphor in
     vulnere.
     non: modifies **possum** (275).
277. **tum:** when Tullia was still alive.
     a re publica: i.e., *from the political world.*
     quae levaret: = **ut ea** (i.e., **domus**) **me levaret,** REL. CL. OF PURPOSE, and cp.
     the parallel **ut . . . adquiescam** below.
278. **maerens: maerere,** *to grieve, lament.*
279. **in eius bonis:** i.e., *in its good fortunes.*

255 turpe enim esse existimo me non ita ferre casum meum, ut tu
tali sapientia praeditus ferendum putas. Sed opprimor interdum
et vix resisto dolori, quod ea me solacia deficiunt, quae ceteris,
quorum mihi exempla propono, simili in fortuna non defuerunt.
Nam et Q. Maximus, qui filium consularem, clarum virum et
260 magnis rebus gestis, amisit, et L. Paullus, qui duo septem diebus, et vester Gaius, et M. Cato, qui summo ingenio, summa
virtute filium perdidit, iis temporibus fuerunt ut eorum luctum
ipsorum dignitas consolaretur ea quam ex re publica conseque-
bantur.

265   Mihi autem amissis ornamentis iis, quae ipse commemoras,
quaeque eram maximis laboribus adeptus, unum manebat illud
solacium, quod ereptum est. Non amicorum negotiis, non rei
publicae procuratione impediebantur cogitationes meae, nihil
in foro agere libebat; aspicere curiam non poteram; existim-
270 abam, id quod erat, omnes me et industriae meae fructus et fortunae perdidisse. Sed, cum cogitarem haec mihi tecum et cum
quibusdam esse communia, et cum frangerem iam ipse me co-
geremque illa ferre toleranter, habebam quo confugerem, ubi
conquiescerem, cuius in sermone et suavitate omnes curas dolo-
275 resque deponerem. Nunc autem hoc tam gravi vulnere etiam
illa, quae consanuisse videbantur, recrudescunt; non enim, ut
tum me a re publica maestum domus excipiebat, quae levaret,
sic nunc domo maerens ad rem publicam confugere possum, ut
in eius bonis adquiescam. Itaque et domo absum et foro, quod

281. **domesticum:** sc. **dolorem.**
282. **quo:** ABL. OF DEGREE OF DIFFERENCE, with **magis** = *all the more.*
283. **ratio nulla:** *no philosophical reasoning.*
284. **consuetudinis: consuetudo,** *custom, practice, close personal relationship;* with **coniunctio,** *the association of our daily lives.*

　　　quamquam: conj., *although,* or at the beginning of an independent cl., as here, *however, and yet.*

　　　sperabam . . . audiebam (285): EPISTOLARY TENSES.
286. **cum . . . tum:** = **non solum . . . sed etiam.**
287. **ante:** adv., *in advance,* i.e., before Caesar returns from Spain, where he had just defeated Pompey's sons at Munda.

　　　traducendum sit (288): traducere, *to pass, spend.*
288. **unius:** namely Caesar, modified by the four following adjs.; despite his aversion to dictatorship, Cicero can recognize good qualities in Caesar, as well as the necessity of political compromise.
290. **alieni:** here, *estranged.*

　　　amicissimi: Caesar had pardoned Sulpicius, a former supporter of Pompey, and appointed him governor of Achaia in 46 B.C.

　　　magnae . . . est deliberationis (291): *it is a matter for careful consideration.*
291. **ratio:** here, *plan*—and a plan not for action but for keeping quiet and out of Caesar's way.
292. **concessu et beneficio:** *with his permission and kindness;* probably a HENDIADYS, *by his kind permission.*
293. **Basilo:** *Lucius Minucius Basilus,* a former legate of Caesar's in Gaul who apparently served with him also in the civil war, joined the conspiracy after being denied a provincial governorship following his term as praetor in 45.
294. **gratulor: gratulari,** + dat., *to congratulate;* the brevity of this letter and its intense emotionality suggest to many historians that it was written within just hours after the assassination, to which Cicero may have been an eye-witness.
295. **quid agas:** *how you are;* a friend meeting another often commenced a conversation with **"Salve! Quid agis?"**

"Julius Caesar Proceeding
to the Senate on the
Ides of March"
Abel de Pujol
19th century
Musée des Beaux-Arts
Valenciennes, France

280   nec eum dolorem, quem de re publica capio, domus iam conso-
lari potest nec domesticum res publica.

Cicero longs to see Servius as soon as possible.

      Quo magis te exspecto teque videre quam primum cupio;
maius mihi solacium afferre ratio nulla potest quam coniunctio
consuetudinis sermonumque nostrorum; quamquam sperabam
285   tuum adventum (sic enim audiebam) appropinquare. Ego autem
cum multis de causis te exopto quam primum videre, tum etiam
ut ante commentemur inter nos qua ratione nobis traducendum
sit hoc tempus, quod est totum ad unius voluntatem accommo-
dandum et prudentis et liberalis et, ut perspexisse videor, nec a
290   me alieni et tibi amicissimi. Quod cum ita sit, magnae tamen
est deliberationis quae ratio sit ineunda nobis non agendi aliquid sed illius concessu et beneficio quiescendi. Vale.

AD FAMILIARES 6.15

*Cicero's apparent willingness to seek an accommodation with Caesar, as expressed in
the preceding letter, ultimately faded with the dictator's return to Rome in September of 45 and what seemed his ever-growing tyranny. In the following brief note,
almost certainly written on the Ides of March, Cicero congratulates one of Caesar's
assassins on the deed and, though not one of the conspirators himself nor even invited
to participate, he declares both his satisfaction and his support. Written in Rome,
March 15, 44 B.C.*

Cicero Basilo S.

      Tibi gratulor, mihi gaudeo; te amo, tua tueor; a te amari et,
295   quid agas quidque agatur, certior fieri volo.

296. **Cassio:** *Gaius Cassius Longinus,* a former Pompeian who had been pardoned
     and given a praetorship by Caesar, nonetheless joined with Marcus Jun-
     ius Brutus as one of the leaders in the assassination plot; he committed
     suicide in 42 B.C. after being defeated by Marc Antony's forces in the
     first battle at Philippi.

297. **laetor: laetari,** *to be glad.*
     tibi: DAT. OF REF.
     orationem meam (298): the so-called "First Philippic," delivered September
     2, 44 B.C., was the first of a series of vehement speeches delivered by
     Cicero against Antony that ultimately cost the orator his life; 14 of the
     speeches survive and at least three others have been lost.

298. **negoti:** PARTITIVE GEN. with **nihil,** = *it would not be difficult (to).*

299. **reciperare:** also spelled **recuperare,** *to regain.*
     homo amens: Marc Antony; Cicero used even harsher invective in his public
     denunciations of Antony, particularly in the acerbic Second Phillipic.

300. **nequior:** comparative of **nequam,** indecl. adj., *worthless, good for nothing,*
     wicked.
     ille: i.e., Caesar.
     nequissimum occisum esse (301): i.e., *was the wickedest man* (ever) *slain.*

301. **caedis: caedes,** *slaughter.*

302. **criminatur: criminari,** *to charge;* the charge was made by Antony following
     Cicero's First Philippic.
     nisi . . . incitentur (303): explains the **causam.**

303. **veterani:** Caesar's.

304. **modo:** here = **si modo,** *if only,* or **dummodo,** *provided that,* + subjunct.
     communicet: communicare, *to join.*

305. **Pisoni . . . mihi . . . Servilio (306):** each depends on **licet.** *L. Calpurnius Piso,*
     Caesar's father-in-law (see note on line 89 above), had been a political
     enemy of Cicero but, after Caesar's assassination, shared in his opposi-
     tion to Antony; *Publius Servilius Isauricus,* consul with Caesar in 48, also
     initially opposed Antony, though the two subsequently reconciled.
     invectus est: invehere, *to carry against;* pass., *to be carried against, inveigh*
     against.
     nullo adsentiente: i.e., without anyone else at that time supporting him in his
     opposition to Antony **(eum).**

306. **tricensimo: trice(n)simus,** *thirtieth;* Piso spoke against Antony in early Au-
     gust, and Cicero delivered his First Philippic on September 2.

307. **tuto:** adv., *safely.*
     gladiator: an insulting term for Antony.

308. **eius:** sc. **caedis.**
     a. d. XIII Kal. Octobr.: ante diem tertium decimum Kalendas Octobres, *the*
     13th day before the Kalends of October = September 19.
     a me: *from me* = *with me.*

AD FAMILIARES 12.2 (excerpts)

The assassination of Caesar has not restored the republic, Cicero laments, because Antony has taken over the state and is proving himself even worse than Caesar. Cicero has hope in the tyrannicides and professes in this letter his loyalty to Cassius, one of the leaders in the conspiracy against Caesar and the resistance to Antony and Octavian. September or October, 44 B.C.

Cicero Cassio S.

Vehementer laetor tibi probari sententiam et orationem meam; qua si saepius uti liceret, nihil esset negoti libertatem et rem publicam reciperare. Sed homo amens et perditus mul-
300 toque nequior quam ille ipse, quem tu nequissimum occisum esse dixisti, caedis initium quaerit nullamque aliam ob causam me auctorem fuisse Caesaris interficiendi criminatur, nisi ut in me veterani incitentur: quod ego periculum non extimesco, modo vestri facti gloriam cum mea laude communicet. Ita nec
305 Pisoni, qui in eum primus invectus est nullo adsentiente, nec mihi, qui idem tricensimo post die feci, nec P. Servilio, qui me est consecutus, tuto in senatum venire licet: caedem enim gladiator quaerit eiusque initium a. d. XIII Kal. Octobr. a me se fac-

"Death of Julius Caesar"
Vincenzo Camuccini, 19th century
Museo Nazionale di Capodimente, Naples, Italy

309.   **ad quem:** sc. **diem,** *on which day.*
      venerat: sc. **in senatum.**
      Metelli: *Quintus Caecilius Metellus Pius Scipio,* consul in 52 and a leading
          Pompeian; after the defeat of his army and his death at the Battle of
          Thapsus, his property, including a villa at Tibur, was confiscated.

310.   **complures:** *several;* in another of Cicero's letters (*Ad Atticum* 16.2) we are
          told that Antony practiced his speech against Cicero for 17 days.

311.   **lustris: lustrum,** *den, brothel, debauchery.*

312.   **vomere:** Cicero uses the same grotesque image in the Philippics.
      suo more (313): a slur on both his oratorical skills and his drinking habits.

313.   **quod scribis:** *as regards your writing (that).*

314.   **profici: proficere,** *to accomplish.*
      non nihil: = **aliquid;** common in Cicero, like **non numquam** for **interdum.**
      ut in tantis malis (315): lit., *as in such great evils* = *considering the grim situ-*
        ation.

316.   **consulares:** i.e., Cicero, Piso, Servilius as mentioned above.

317.   **locuti sint . . . possint:** subjunct. in SUBORDINATE CLS. IN IND. STATE.

318.   **vobis:** Cassius, Brutus, and their supporters.
      aliquid . . . gloria: i.e., action against Antony.
      velim: sc. **ut vos id faciatis.**

319.   **salvis nobis:** *while I am safe* (i.e., still alive). Cicero's wish, of course, was
          never realized, as he became a victim of the proscriptions, assassinated
          at Antony's order on December 7, 43 B.C., just over a year after the
          composition of this letter and several months before the defeat of Cas-
          sius and Brutus at Philippi.
      minus: = **non;** sc. **erit.** No matter what happens to Cicero, he is confident
          that the republic will soon be restored by Cassius and his followers.

320.   **tuis:** sc. **amicis.**

321.   **sive . . . sive:** conj., *whether . . . or.*
      ad me referent: *report (matters) to me* = *consult me.*

310 turum putavit, ad quem paratus venerat, cum in villa Metelli complures dies commentatus esset.

Quae autem in lustris et in vino commentatio potuit esse? Itaque omnibus est visus, ut ad te antea scripsi, vomere suo more, non dicere. Quare, quod scribis te confidere auctoritate et eloquentia nostra aliquid profici posse, non nihil, ut in tantis
315 malis, est profectum: intellegit enim populus Romanus tres esse consulares, qui, quia quae de re publica bene senserint libere locuti sint, tuto in senatum venire non possint. Quare spes est omnis in vobis; si aliquid dignum vestra gloria cogitatis, velim salvis nobis; sin id minus, res tamen publica per vos brevi tem-
320 pore ius suum reciperabit. Ego tuis neque desum neque deero: qui sive ad me referent sive non referent, mea tibi benevolentia fidesque praestabitur. Vale.

"Banquet of Anthony and Cleopatra"
Francesco Trevisani, 18th century
Galleria Spada, Rome, Italy

CICERO'S *PHILOSOPHICA:*
"ON MORAL RESPONSIBILITIES" AND "ON FRIENDSHIP"

Throughout his life Cicero was deeply interested in philosophy, and he studied in Rome and Greece, both as a young man in his 20's and later in life, with some of the leading Stoic, Epicurean, and Academic philosophers of his day. Partly as a consequence of this interest and partly due to his growing disenchantment with the political strife in Rome, Cicero ultimately turned to writing on a wide range of philosophical topics. Prior to his governorship in Cilicia he published, in 55 B.C., the *De Oratore,* one of several important works he authored on rhetoric, and, a few years later, the *De Republica* and the *De Legibus,* political treatises on the ideal state and laws, both much influenced by Stoicism.

Following his proconsulship in Cilicia, Cicero returned to a Rome on the brink of civil war. Soon, in despair over the demise of the Roman republic during the dictatorship of Julius Caesar, and grief-stricken over the death of his daughter Tullia in early 45, Cicero again turned to writing, rapidly producing between February 45 and November 44 a number of works on philosophy, ethics, and theology, with the purpose of translating and transforming much of Greek thought for a Roman audience. Dating to this period are: the *De Finibus Bonorum et Malorum,* a treatise on ethics and the various theories of the *summum bonum*—what man should regard as the highest good in life; the *Tusculanae Disputationes,* an exploration of death, fear, and the passions, and what can bring man happiness; and three religious tracts, the *De Natura Deorum, De Divinatione,* and *De Fato,* dealing with differing views of the gods, the validity of divination, and the divine role in human life.

The last of Cicero's *philosophica,* the *Cato Maior de Senectute,* a discussion and consolation on old age, *Laelius de Amicitia,* and the *De Officiis,* were among his most popular and influential works during the Middle Ages and remain favorites today. In addressing his prefatory remarks in the *De Amicitia* to his close friend Titus Pomponius Atticus, Cicero makes it clear that he wishes the whole essay to be a tribute to their life-long friendship. This purpose Cicero accomplishes by representing the intellectual Gaius Laelius engaged in a discourse on friendship soon after the death in 129 B.C. of Laelius' dearest friend, Scipio the Younger (Publius Cornelius Scipio Aemilianus). Laelius delivers the discourse in the framework of a conversation with his two sons-in-law, Gaius Fannius and Quintus Mucius Scaevola (the famous augur and jurist, whom Cicero had known when he was himself a very young man). The excerpts included in this volume explore, inter alia, the origin, nature, and benefits of friendship.

The *De Officiis* ("On Moral Responsibilities"), begun some months after Caesar's assassination on the Ides of March 44 B.C. and completed in November of that same year, was dedicated by Cicero to his son, Marcus, then a somewhat irresponsible 21-year-old studying philosophy in Athens. The treatise's three volumes were based closely upon a work by the second-century Greek philosopher, Panaetius of Rhodes, in which he discussed the nature of morally responsible action, an issue of interest to Cicero both intellectually and from the perspective of his ongoing political conflict with Mark Antony in the wake of Caesar's death. Despite evidence of haste, this practical moral work provides interesting, instructive reading and, like "On Friendship," has earned much praise. Among the selections included here are excerpts from Book One on the origin of morality and the cardinal virtues of wisdom, justice, courage, and moderation, and from Book Three on the conflict between moral right and expediency, a problem that still confronts us today.

A conversation among philosophers
Roman mosaic from Pompeii, 1st century A.D.
Museo Archeologico Nazionale, Naples, Italy

1. **quamquam:** conj., *although.*
   te ... abundare oportet (2): *you should be well equipped* (lit., *overflowing with*).
   annum: Cicero's son had gone to study in Athens in April or May of 45 B.C.
   audientem: *hearing the lectures of, studying under.*
   Cratippum: *Cratippus* was a well known Athenian philosopher of the day and a friend of Cicero's.
2. **idque:** *and that too.*
   institutis: institutum, *custom, institution, instruction, principle.*
3. **summam:** with **auctoritatem;** Cicero frequently separates adj. from noun, here for emphasis.
   urbis: Athens, though it had become politically insignificant, was still venerated as an intellectual capital.
4. **augere:** *increase, enlarge.*
5. **Latina:** n. acc. pl., *Latin matters, Latin studies.*
7. **censeo: censere,** *to estimate, think, advise.*
8. **orationis:** here = *speech, language;* all educated Romans of this period were bilingual.
   quam ob rem: lit., *on account of this fact;* common in Cicero for *wherefore, therefore.*
10. **illis:** i.e., Cicero's speeches; the philosophical works were almost as numerous.
    aequarunt: = **aequaverunt;** shortened forms of the perf. tense, dropping the **v** and often the following vowel, were common, especially with first conj. vbs.
11. **statuissem: statuere,** *to put, place, decide, determine.*
12. **ordiri:** *to begin, commence.*
    aetati: the younger Cicero was 21 at the time this treatise was written.
13. **sint:** with **disputata,** from **disputare,** *to discuss, examine;* perf. pass. vb. forms were frequently separated in this way.
15. **patere:** *lie open, extend,* and hence *apply.*
17. **forensibus: forensis,** *of the forum, public, forensic.*
18. **contrahas:** *negotiate with, deal with.*
19. **officio:** cp. the abl. with **careo.**
    et ... et (20): the conjs. imply fully coordinating phrases, i.e., **et in eo colendo omnis honestas sita est et in eo neglegendo omnis turpitudo sita est;** this sort of parallelism and ellipsis are quite common in Cicero.
    sita: *placed, situated.*
    honestas: *honor, virtue, worth;* not *honesty,* which is rather **probitas, fides.**
21. **nullis ... tradendis (22):** ABL. OF ATTENDANT CIRCUMSTANCE; *in giving no instructions* = *if he gives no instructions.*
22. **philosophum:** OBJ. COMPL.
23. **potissimum:** adv., *chiefly;* Cicero was himself an Academic and did not always subscribe to Stoic doctrine.
    Stoicos: many Romans found the Stoic emphasis on **virtus** and character very attractive.

DE OFFICIIS

The value of studying philosophy and learning both Greek and Latin.

Quamquam te, Marce fili, annum iam audientem Cratippum, idque Athenis, abundare oportet praeceptis institutisque
philosophiae propter summam et doctoris auctoritatem et urbis,
quorum alter te scientia augere potest, altera exemplis, tamen,
5   ut ipse ad meam utilitatem semper cum Graecis Latina con-
iunxi—neque id in philosophia solum sed etiam in dicendi exercitatione feci—idem tibi censeo faciendum ut par sis in utriusque orationis facultate. Quam ob rem magnopere te hortor,
mi Cicero, ut non solum orationes meas sed hos etiam de philo-
10   sophia libros, qui iam illis fere se aequarunt, studiose legas.
(I.1–3, excerpts)

The importance of moral duties is paramount, as the Stoics have shown.

Sed cum statuissem scribere ad te aliquid hoc tempore
(multa posthac), ab eo ordiri maxime volui quod et aetati tuae
esset aptissimum et auctoritati meae. Nam cum multa sint in
philosophia et gravia et utilia accurate copioseque a philosophis
15   disputata, latissime patere videntur ea quae de officiis tradita
ab illis et praecepta sunt. Nulla enim vitae pars—neque publicis
neque privatis neque forensibus neque domesticis in rebus, neque
si tecum agas quid neque si cum altero contrahas—vacare
officio potest; in eoque et colendo sita vitae est honestas omnis
20   et neglegendo turpitudo. Atque haec quidem quaestio communis est omnium philosophorum; quis est enim qui, nullis officii
praeceptis tradendis, philosophum se audeat dicere? Sequemur
hoc quidem tempore et hac in quaestione potissimum Stoicos.
(I.4–6, excerpts)

25. **Panaetio:** *Panaetius* of Rhodes was one of the foremost proponents of Stoicism in the second century B.C., and his works were an important source for the arguments Cicero employs in the *De Officiis*.

    praetermissum esse (26): praetermittere, *to pass over, omit, neglect.*

27. **institutio:** *education, instruction, teaching.*

29. **finem bonorum:** *the end, goal, summit of good things* = *the summum bonum.* This is the theory; the **alterum genus** provides the practical rules of conduct by which to implement the theory.

30. **in omnis partes:** *in all directions*

    usus: *practice, management, conduct.*

    conformari: conformare, *to shape, mold, fashion.*

32. **principio:** *in the first place* (i.e., at the beginning of our discussion).

    animantium: animans, *living being, creature, animal.*

33. **est . . . tributum: tribuere,** *to assign, ascribe, attribute, give.*

34. **tueatur: tueri,** *to look at, protect.*

    nocitura: the fut. act. partic. can have the meaning of *likely to . . ..*

35. **anquirat: anquirere,** *to seek, search after.*

    pastum: pastus, *food.*

36. **latibula: latibulum,** *hiding place, shelter.*

    commune: commune should agree with **appetitus,** but the n. ending makes the adj. essentially a pred. noun, *a common thing, characteristic.*

    item: adv., *also, likewise.*

39. **beluam: belua,** *beast.*

    hoc . . . interest, quod (40): *this makes a difference, (the fact) that . . ..*

40. **haec:** i.e., **belua.**

    tantum quantum: adv., *only to the extent that.*

41. **paulum admodum (42):** *very little.*

42. **praeteritum aut futurum:** an awareness of *past* and *future,* vs. only the present, was viewed as a major distinction between man and beast.

    quod . . . futuras (46): the thought is simply that, through his faculty of reason, man can understand the concatenation of cause and effect and can govern himself accordingly.

44. **praegressus: praegressus, -us,** *previous development, antecedent.*

    antecessiones: *antecedent (causes).*

45. **similitudines comparat:** i.e., *makes analogies.*

46. **adnectit: adnectere,** *to connect, associate.*

47. **degendam:** from **de+agere.**

49. **societatem:** here, *community, common bond.*

    in primis (50): = **imprimis,** adv., *particularly, especially.*

50. **praecipuum:** *especial, peculiar, distinguished.*

51. **impellitque ut . . . velit (52):** *drives (man) to want.*

    coetus et celebrationes: *meetings and assemblies;* subj. of both **esse** and **obiri.**

52. **obiri:** *to be visited, attended.*

    suppeditent ad (53): *are sufficient for.*

53. **cultum et . . . victum: cultus** refers to culture and refinement in living; **victus** refers to food and the other necessities of life.

    coniugi: coniunx, *wife.*

The need to define terms.

Placet igitur, quoniam omnis disputatio de officio futura est,
25   ante definire quid sit officium (quod a Panaetio praetermissum
esse miror). Omnis enim, quae ratione suscipitur de aliqua re,
institutio debet a definitione proficisci ut intellegatur quid sit id
de quo disputetur. Omnis de officio duplex est quaestio: unum
genus est quod pertinet ad finem bonorum; alterum, quod pos-
30   itum est in praeceptis quibus in omnis partes usus vitae con-
formari possit. (I.7)

Origin of the concepts of right, morality, and virtue.

(a) Self-preservation and procreation. Principio, generi animantium omni est a natura tributum ut se, vitam, corpusque
tueatur, declinet ea quae nocitura videantur, omniaque quae
35   sint ad vivendum necessaria anquirat et paret, ut pastum, ut
latibula, ut alia generis eiusdem. Commune item animantium
omnium est coniunctionis appetitus procreandi causa et cura
quaedam eorum quae procreata sint.
(b) Reason. Sed inter hominem et beluam hoc maxime in-
40   terest, quod haec, tantum quantum sensu movetur, ad id solum
quod adest quodque praesens est se accommodat, paulum admodum sentiens praeteritum aut futurum; homo autem—quod
rationis est particeps, per quam consequentia cernit, causas rerum videt earumque praegressus et quasi antecessiones non ig-
45   norat, similitudines comparat rebusque praesentibus adiungit
atque adnectit futuras—facile totius vitae cursum videt ad eamque degendam praeparat res necessarias.
(c) Society. Eademque natura vi rationis hominem conciliat
homini et ad orationis et ad vitae societatem, ingeneratque in
50   primis praecipuum quendam amorem in eos qui procreati sunt
impellitque ut hominum coetus et celebrationes et esse et a se
obiri velit ob easque causas studeat parare ea quae suppeditent
ad cultum et ad victum, nec sibi soli sed coniugi, liberis, cete-

54. **quae cura:** the antecedent of a rel. pron. is often attracted into the rel. cl., =
     and this concern (referring to the preceding cl.).
     exsuscitat: exsuscitare, *to arouse.*

55. **maiores:** sc. **eos** (i.e., **animos**); OBJ. COMPL.

56. **propria:** *appropriate (to), characteristic (of).*

58. **avemus: avere,** *to wish, be eager.*

59. **occultarum aut admirabilium:** i.e., the mysteries or miracles of science.

61. **sit:** subjunct. in a SUBORDINATE (REL.) CL. IN IND. STATE.

63. **principatus: principatus, -us,** *preeminence, rule, independence.*

64. **informatus:** for this metaphor of molding or shaping the intellect, cp. **con-
     formari** (31).
     praecipienti: practically synonymous with **docenti,** whereas **imperanti** is spe-
     cifically political.
     utilitatis . . . legitime (65): a ruler must keep in mind both what is useful and
     what is just and legal.

66. **humanarum . . . rerum:** the insignificant matters of life, as the Stoics saw it.

67. **nec . . . est:** i.e., **nec illa vis** (here, *manifestation*) **naturae rationisque est parva;**
     with the **quod** cl. in appos., *nor is that . . . a slight thing, the fact that.*

68. **quid sit quod deceat (69): decet,** impers., *is decorous, appropriate, decent;* i.e.,
     what (moral and aesthetic) propriety is.

69. **qui modus:** sc. **sit; modus** here = *moderation.*

71. **venustatem: venustas,** *charm, loveliness.*
     convenientiam: lit., *coming together,* here = *harmony.*
     quam similitudinem: *this resemblance,* i.e., the resemblance of the physical
     world to the spiritual world.

72. **natura ratioque:** the two are regarded as a single concept (= that which
     makes man distinctly different from other animals), and so they are
     modified by the sg. **transferens** and serve as the subj. of the sg. **putat,
     cavet,** etc.
     multo: ABL. OF DEGREE OF DIFFERENCE with **magis.**

73. **constantiam:** *consistency, constancy.*

74. **conservanda:** sc. **esse;** n. pl. to modify collectively the three subjs. of the
     IND. STATE.
     cavet: cavere, *to beware, be careful (to),* regularly takes a JUSSIVE NOUN CL.

75. **tum:** here, *and at the same time, and also.*

76. **libidinose:** adv., *impulsively, capriciously.*

78. **conflatur: conflare,** *to blow together, forge.*
     quaerimus: here, *investigate, inquire into.*
     honestum . . . honestum (79): we here have first **id honestum** (n. as a noun)
     meaning *virtue, moral excellence,* and then **honestum** (adj.), *honorable,
     proper;* cp. Cicero's comment in *De Finibus* II.45, **honestum igitur id intel-
     legimus quod tale est ut, detracta omni utilitate sine ullis praemiis fructi-
     busve per se ipsum possit iure laudari.**

79. **nobilitatum . . . sit: nobilitare,** *to make famous* (i.e., praised by the multitude);
     cp. **nobilis,** *well known.*

82. **ut ait Plato (83):** the Greek philosopher Plato makes a similar point in *Phae-
     drus* 250D.

risque quos caros habeat tuerique debeat; quae cura exsuscitat
55 etiam animos et maiores ad rem gerendam facit.

(d) Truth. In primisque hominis est propria veri inquisitio
atque investigatio. Itaque cum sumus necessariis negotiis cur-
isque vacui, tum avemus aliquid videre, audire, addiscere cog-
nitionemque rerum aut occultarum aut admirabilium ad beate
60 vivendum necessariam ducimus. Ex quo intellegitur quod verum,
simplex, sincerumque sit, id esse naturae hominis aptissimum.

(e) Independence. Huic veri videndi cupiditati adiuncta est
appetitio quaedam principatus, ut nemini parere animus bene
informatus a natura velit nisi praecipienti aut docenti aut uti-
65 litatis causa iuste et legitime imperanti; ex quo magnitudo animi
existit humanarumque rerum contemptio.

(f) Beauty and harmony. Nec vero illa parva vis naturae est
rationisque, quod unum hoc animal sentit quid sit ordo, quid sit
quod deceat, in factis dictisque qui modus. Itaque eorum ips-
70 orum quae aspectu sentiuntur, nullum aliud animal pulchritudinem, venustatem, convenientiam partium sentit. Quam similitudinem natura ratioque ab oculis ad animum transferens multo
etiam magis pulchritudinem, constantiam, ordinem in consiliis
factisque conservanda putat cavetque ne quid indecore effemi-
75 nateve faciat, tum in omnibus et opinionibus et factis ne quid
libidinose aut faciat aut cogitet.

(g) Hence the concept of moral excellence. Quibus ex rebus
conflatur et efficitur id, quod quaerimus, honestum, quod etiamsi nobilitatum non sit, tamen honestum sit, quodque vere
80 dicimus, etiamsi a nullo laudetur, natura esse laudabile. (I.11–14)

The four cardinal virtues: wisdom, justice, courage, temperance.

Formam quidem ipsam, Marce fili, et tamquam faciem honesti vides, "Quae si oculis cerneretur, mirabiles amores," ut ait
Plato, "excitaret sapientiae." Sed omne quod est honestum, id

84. **quattuor partium:** *of four sources;* in Greek thought there were four cardinal virtues, which Cicero translates as **sapientia (prudentia), iustitia, fortitudo,** and **temperantia,** and generally defines in the following list.
     perspicientia: *clear perception.*
85. **sollertia:** *skillful mastery, intellectual development.*
     versatur: *is engaged in, concerned with.*
86. **tribuendo . . . cuique:** i.e., in respecting the rights of others.
     fide: i.e., *the faithful observation (of).*
87. **excelsi:** *lofty, noble.*
     invicti: *unconquered,* and therefore *unconquerable.*
     robore: **robur,** *oak,* and therefore *strength.*
89. **modestia:** *moderation, restraint.*
90. **locis:** here, *topics, divisions.*
92. **attingit:** **attingere = ad + tangere.**
93. **pulchrum:** n. pred. adj. to agree with **excellere,** *we think it (is) admirable to excel;* the same construction is found in the next cl.
95. **genere:** *kind (of activity).*
97. **temere:** adv., *rashly, heedlessly.*
     quod vitium: see on **quae cura** (54).
98. **adhibebit:** **adhibere,** *to hold to, apply, devote.*
99. **quod:** *the fact that,* introducing a noun cl.; *the other fault is the fact that.*
104. **fonte: fons,** *fountain, spring, source;* this sent. effectively closes out the discussion of intellect.
106. **reliquis:** sc. *virtues, divisions.*
      latissime patet ea ratio: lit., *that principle extends most widely;* i.e., *the principle with the widest application is the one (by which).*
107. **continetur:** *is maintained.*
109. **beneficentia:** *beneficence, charity.*
110. **eandem: idem** can often be translated *likewise* or *also.*
      benignitatem: benignitas, *kindness.*
112. **munus:** essentially = **officium,** *duty, function.*
113. **communibus pro communibus (114):** i.e., the various resources that are free to the members of a community are to be used for the equal benefit of all.
114. **utatur:** the subj. is supplied from **quis** in the preceding cl.
      ut: *as,* balancing **pro** in the preceding phrase; the distinction is between public and private property.
      fundamentum: with **iustitiae.**
115. **dictorum: dictum,** n. of the perf. partic. used as a noun.
      conventorum: conventum, *agreement, pact.*

85 quattuor partium oritur ex aliqua: (1) aut enim in perspicientia
veri sollertiaque versatur, (2) aut in hominum societate tuenda
tribuendoque suum cuique et rerum contractarum fide, (3) aut
in animi excelsi atque invicti magnitudine ac robore, (4) aut in
omnium quae fiunt quaeque dicuntur ordine et modo, in quo
inest modestia et temperantia. (I.15)

Wisdom.

90 Ex quattuor autem locis in quos honesti naturam vimque
divisimus, primus ille, qui in veri cognitione consistit, maxime
naturam attingit humanam. Omnes enim trahimur et ducimur
ad cognitionis et scientiae cupiditatem, in qua excellere pulchrum putamus; labi autem, errare, nescire, decipi et malum et
95 turpe ducimus. In hoc genere et naturali et honesto duo vitia
vitanda sunt: unum, ne incognita pro cognitis habeamus hisque
temere assentiamur; quod vitium effugere qui volet (omnes
autem velle debent), adhibebit ad considerandas res et tempus et
diligentiam. Alterum est vitium quod quidam nimis magnum
100 studium multamque operam in res obscuras atque difficiles con-
ferunt easdemque non necessarias. Omnis autem cogitatio mo-
tusque animi aut in consiliis capiendis de rebus honestis et per-
tinentibus ad bene beateque vivendum aut in studiis scientiae
cognitionisque versabitur. Ac de primo quidem officii fonte dixi-
105 mus. (I.18–19, excerpts)

Justice.

De tribus autem reliquis latissime patet ea ratio qua societas
hominum inter ipsos et vitae quasi communitas continetur,
cuius partes duae sunt: iustitia, in qua virtutis splendor est maximus, ex qua viri boni nominantur, et huic coniuncta benefi-
110 centia, quam eandem vel benignitatem vel liberalitatem appellari licet.
(a) Justice proper. Sed iustitiae primum munus est ut ne cui
quis noceat nisi lacessitus iniuria, deinde ut communibus pro
communibus utatur, privatis ut suis. Fundamentum autem est
115 iustitiae fides, id est dictorum conventorumque constantia et
veritas.

117. **unum:** sc. **est.**
118. **inferunt:** sc. **iniuriam.**
     quibus: dat.
119. **propulsant: propulsare,** *to repel, ward off.*
     impetum: impetus, *attack.*
     quempiam: quispiam, *someone.*
121. **obsistit: obsistere** + dat., *to stand in the way, withstand, resist.*
122. **in vitio:** cp. Eng. "at fault."
123. **deserat: deserere,** *to desert, abandon.*
125. **de industria:** *on purpose, intentionally.*
127. **incommodo: incommodum,** *inconvenience, harm.*
     maximam . . . partem: *for the most part.*
128. **adipiscantur: adipisci,** *to obtain, acquire.*
129. **latissime patet:** cp. 106 above; here, *exercises the strongest influence.*
130. **interest:** the subj. of the impers. vb. is the double IND. QUEST. introduced by
     utrum . . . an.
131. **plerumque:** adv., *for the most part, generally.*
     consulto et cogitate: *intentionally and deliberately.*
132. **repentino:** *sudden.*
133. **accidunt: accidere,** *to happen.*
134. **vetant: vetare,** *to forbid, veto.*
     quicquam: quisquam, quidquam (=quicquam), *anyone, anything.*
     quod: introduces a REL. CL. OF CHARACTERISTIC **(dubites)** and at the same time
     provides the subj. for **sit** (IND. QUEST.); freely, *when you are uncertain
     whether it is right or wrong.*
135. **aequitas:** *fairness = justice.*
137. **incidunt: incidere,** *to happen, occur.*
140. **referri:** *to be carried back = to go back, return.*
142. **ne cui noceatur:** impers. pass., common with certain intransitive vbs. (cp.
     serviatur in the next cl.); lit., *that it not be harmed to anyone = that no
     one be harmed.*
143. **cum:** *when.*
146. **calumnia:** *deceit, chicanery.*
     malitiosa: *malicious.*
147. **summum . . . iniuria:** as A. Dyck explains, **ius** here refers to "rights over oth-
     ers (conferred by the law)," and so the proverb meant that one party's
     "right pushed to the maximum . . . is an **iniuria** for the other party."
     tritum: *well-worn, familiar, commonly used.*
148. **genere:** *sort (of injustice).*
     in re publica: i.e., at the national and international level and not just in pri-
     vate actions.
149. **ille qui:** the allusion is to the Spartan king Cleomenes III in the campaign
     against Argos.
150. **indutiae:** only in pl., *truce.*
     populabatur: populari, *to plunder, devastate.*

(b) Injustice. Iniustitiae genera duo sunt, unum eorum qui inferunt; alterum eorum qui ab iis quibus infertur, si possunt, non propulsant iniuriam. Nam qui iniuste impetum in quem-
120 piam facit aut ira aut aliqua perturbatione incitatus, is quasi manus afferre videtur socio; qui autem non defendit nec obsistit, si potest, iniuriae, tam est in vitio quam si parentes aut patriam deserat.

(c) Motives for injustice. Atque illae quidem iniuriae quae
125 nocendi causa de industria inferuntur, saepe a metu proficiscuntur, cum is qui nocere alteri cogitat timet ne, nisi id fecerit, ipse aliquo afficiatur incommodo. Maximam autem partem ad iniuriam faciendam aggrediuntur ut adipiscantur ea quae concupiverunt; in quo vitio latissime patet avaritia. Sed in omni
130 iniustitia permultum interest utrum perturbatione aliqua animi, quae plerumque brevis est et ad tempus, an consulto et cogitate fiat iniuria. Leviora enim sunt ea quae repentino aliquo motu accidunt quam ea quae meditata et praeparata inferuntur. Bene praecipiunt qui vetant quicquam agere quod dubites aequum sit
135 an iniquum. Aequitas lucet ipsa per se; dubitatio cogitationem significat iniuriae. (I.20–30, excerpts)

(d) Justice in special cases: (1) Promises. Sed incidunt saepe tempora cum ea quae maxime videntur digna esse iusto homine, eoque quem virum bonum dicimus, commutantur fiuntque con-
140 traria, ut reddere depositum, facere promissum. Referri enim decet ad ea quae posui principio fundamenta iustitiae—primum ut ne cui noceatur, deinde ut communi utilitati serviatur. Ea cum tempore commutantur, commutatur officium, et non semper est idem. Nec promissa igitur servanda sunt ea quae sint
145 iis, quibus promiseris, inutilia. Exsistunt etiam saepe iniuriae calumnia quadam et callida sed malitiosa iuris interpretatione. Ex quo illud "Summum ius summa iniuria" factum est iam tritum sermone proverbium. Quo in genere etiam in re publica multa peccantur, ut ille qui, cum triginta dierum essent cum
150 hoste indutiae factae, noctu populabatur agros, quod dierum

151. **essent pactae: paciscere,** *to arrange, negotiate, agree upon;* SUBJUNCT. OF QUOTED REASON.

noster: i.e., a fellow Roman, vs. the Greek Cleomenes.

152. **Q. Fabium Labeonem:** *Quintus Fabius Labeo,* consul in 183 B.C.; subj. of **locutum (esse)** in the IND. STATE. dependent on **verum est.**

seu: = **sive,** *or if, or.*

153. **auditum:** *hearsay.*

Nolanis . . . finibus (155): Labeo was appointed to arbitrate a border dispute between Nola and Naples.

154. **datum:** simply a partic. here, *appointed.*

155. **appetenter:** adv. from **ad**+**petens,** *greedily.*

156. **aliquantum:** *a good deal.*

159. **decipere:** used as a pred. noun, *this is deception (cheating).*

160. **quocirca:** adv., *therefore.*

sollertia: here, *trickery, chicanery.*

163. **haud scio an (164):** *I do not know whether* = *I am inclined to think.*

164. **eum . . . paenitere: paenitet,** impers., takes as dir. obj. the repentant person (**eum**) and a gen. of that of which he repents (**iniuriae**); thus, lit., *that it repent him of his injury* = *that he be repentant for his injury.*

lacessierit: = **lacessiverit;** intervocalic **v** was often dropped in such perf. system forms.

165. **ne quid tale:** sc. **faciat.**

166. **in re publica:** i.e., in international affairs (cp. 148 above).

168. **ut:** introduces **censuit (171).**

Regulus: *Marcus Atilius Regulus,* consul in 267 and 256 B.C. and a general in the First Punic War; the story briefly told here was a favorite example of Roman **fides.**

169. **Poenis: Poeni,** *Carthaginians.*

commutandis: commutare, *to exchange;* having been captured along with other Romans, Regulus was sent to Rome to see whether the Romans would ransom those held by the Carthaginians. In a meeting of the senate Regulus argued against the ransom of himself and his fellow captives, and then, loyal to his oath, returned voluntarily to Carthage and to certain death (see below, lines 448–69).

iurasset: = **iuravisset** (see on **aequarunt,** 10).

171. **propinquis: propinquus,** *kinsman, relative.*

173. **fallere:** *to deceive, be false to, violate.*

174. **meminerimus:** JUSSIVE SUBJUNCT. of the defective vb. **meminisse,** *let us remember.*

175. **infimos:** *the lowest, basest* (superlative of **inferus**).

176. **quibus:** = **et eis,** abl. with **uti.**

qui . . . mercennariis (177): = **qui iubent uti quibus** (= **servis**) **ita ut mercennariis** (*hired men, employees*).

177. **operam exigendam:** sc. **esse,** *(saying that) service ought to be . . ..*

iusta: *their just deserts,* e.g., food, clothing, shelter.

179. **elatio:** *exaltation.*

180. **iustitia:** ABL. OF SEPARATION with **vacat.**

essent pactae, non noctium indutiae. Ne noster quidem probandus, si verum est Q. Fabium Labeonem seu quem alium (nihil enim habeo praeter auditum) arbitrum Nolanis et Neapolitanis de finibus a senatu datum, cum ad locum venisset, cum utrisque
155 separatim locutum ne cupide quid agerent, ne appetenter, atque ut regredi quam progredi mallent. Id cum utrique fecissent, aliquantum agri in medio relictum est. Itaque illorum finis sic, ut ipsi dixerant, terminavit; in medio relictum quod erat, populo Romano adiudicavit. Decipere hoc quidem est, non iudicare.
160 Quocirca in omni est re fugienda talis sollertia.

(2) Duties in war and toward the enemy. Sunt autem quaedam officia etiam adversus eos servanda a quibus iniuriam acceperis. Est enim ulciscendi et puniendi modus; atque haud scio an satis sit eum qui lacessierit iniuriae suae paenitere, ut et ipse
165 ne quid tale posthac et ceteri sint ad iniuriam tardiores. Atque in re publica maxime conservanda sunt iura belli. Etiam si quid singuli, temporibus adducti, hosti promiserunt, est in eo ipso fides conservanda, ut primo Punico bello Regulus, captus a Poenis, cum de captivis commutandis Romam missus esset iu-
170 rassetque se rediturum, primum, ut venit, captivos reddendos in senatu non censuit, deinde, cum retineretur a propinquis et ab amicis, ad supplicium redire maluit quam fidem hosti datam fallere.

(3) Justice toward slaves. Meminerimus autem etiam adver-
175 sus infimos iustitiam esse servandam. Est autem infima condicio et fortuna servorum, quibus non male praecipiunt qui ita iubent uti ut mercennariis: operam exigendam, iusta praebenda. (I.31–41, excerpts)

Physical and moral courage.

(a) Courage must be based on justice. Ea animi elatio, quae
180 cernitur in periculis et laboribus, si iustitia vacat pugnatque non

181. **commodis: commodum,** *convenience, advantage.*
    in vitio: = **vitiosa.**
182. **consecutus est: consequi,** *to follow, pursue, gain.*
183. **adeptus: adipisci,** *to acquire, obtain.*
184. **illud:** *that (remark).*
185. **calliditas:** *cunning, cleverness.*
189. **concupieris:** = **concupiveris,** in the indef. 2nd pers. sg., *you* or *one.*
190. **quo . . . praeclarius (191):** *the more difficult (it is), the more admirable* (lit., *by what . . . by this);* ABL. OF DEGREE OF DIFFERENCE.
191. **tempus:** here, *occasion.*
195. **positum:** pred. adj. agreeing with **honestum illud.**
    principem: i.e., *foremost;* the truly magnanimous person prefers moral action to the mere appearance of morality.
198. **despicientia:** *contempt (of), indifference (to).*
199. **persuasum est:** impers. pass.; lit., *it has been persuaded* = *a person has been persuaded.*
    nihil . . . succumbere (202): the infs. are subjs. of the impers. vb. **oportere,** which in turn is subj. of **persuasum est,** i.e., **oportere** *(it is necessary)* **hominem admirari (optare, expetere) nihil nisi quod . . . sit** and **(oportere hominem) succumbere nulli homini neque perturbationi nec fortunae.**
204. **ut . . . geras:** RESULT CL., dependent on **altera est res,** *the other characteristic is such (that).*
    cum . . . animo: i.e., when one has true greatness of spirit.
206. **cum . . . tum:** *not only . . . but also.*
207. **ea . . . parva ducere (208):** *to regard those things . . . as trivial;* this inf. and **ea . . . contemnere** are the subjs. of **ducendum est,** *should be considered.*
    plerisque: plerique, pl., *the majority, most people.*
209. **fortis animi:** *(characteristic) of a brave mind,* PRED. GEN. OF POSSESSION; for the construction, cp. **robusti . . . constantiae** (207) and **angusti . . . parvi** (212).
210. **versantur:** lit., *are turned* = *are encountered.*
211. **nihil:** = a strong **non.**
213. **non est . . . consentaneum:** *it is not consistent (for)* + acc./inf.
214. **frangatur: frangere,** *to break, shatter, subdue.*
215. **a labore . . . a voluptate:** ABL. OF AGENT, with the abstract nouns personified.

Herm of Plato
Museo Pio Clementino
Vatican Museums
Vatican State

pro salute communi, sed pro suis commodis, in vitio est. Quocirca nemo qui fortitudinis gloriam consecutus est insidiis et
malitia laudem est adeptus; nihil enim honestum esse potest
quod iustitia vacat. Praeclarum igitur illud Platonis: "Non," in-
185 quit, "solum scientia quae est remota ab iustitia calliditas potius
quam sapientia est appellanda, verum etiam animus paratus ad
periculum, si sua cupiditate, non utilitate communi, impellitur,
audaciae potius nomen habeat quam fortitudinis." Difficile
autem est, cum praestare omnibus concupieris, servare aequita-
190 tem, quae est iustitiae maxime propria. Sed quo difficilius, hoc
praeclarius; nullum enim est tempus quod iustitia vacare debeat. Fortes igitur et magnanimi sunt habendi, non qui faciunt,
sed qui propulsant, iniuriam. Vera autem et sapiens animi magnitudo honestum illud, quod maxime natura sequitur, in factis
195 positum non in gloria iudicat, principemque se esse mavult
quam videri. (I.62–65, excerpts)

*(b) Two characteristics of courage: (1) Indifference to exter-
nal circumstance.* Omnino fortis animus et magnus duabus rebus
maxime cernitur, quarum una in rerum externarum despicientia
ponitur, cum persuasum est nihil hominem, nisi quod honestum
200 decorumque sit, aut admirari aut optare aut expetere oportere
nullique neque homini neque perturbationi animi nec fortunae
succumbere.

(2) Readiness to do the useful but dangerous. Altera est res
ut, cum ita sis affectus animo ut supra dixi, res geras magnas
205 illas quidem et maxime utiles sed vehementer arduas plenasque
laborum et periculorum cum vitae, tum multarum rerum quae ad
vitam pertinent. Nam et ea, quae eximia plerisque et praeclara
videntur, parva ducere eaque ratione stabili firmaque contemnere fortis animi magnique ducendum est, et ea quae videntur
210 acerba, quae multa et varia in hominum vita fortunaque versantur, ita ferre ut nihil a statu naturae discedas, nihil a dignitate sapientis, robusti animi est magnaeque constantiae.

(c) Courage to resist excessive desires. Non est autem consentaneum, qui metu non frangatur, eum frangi cupiditate nec,
215 qui invictum se a labore praestiterit, vinci a voluptate. Quam ob
rem et haec vitanda et pecuniae fugienda cupiditas; nihil enim
est tam angusti animi tamque parvi quam amare divitias, nihil

219. **conferre:** here, *to devote.*
221. **vacandum . . . est:** impers. pass., *one must be free from.*
222. **aegritudine: aegritudo,** *illness, sorrow, pain.*
227. **quaecumque: quicumque,** *whoever, whatever.*
     obliti: *heedless (of);* **oblivisci,** + gen., *to forget.*
230. **tutela:** *protection, guardianship.*
     procuratio: *administration.*
234. **populares:** the *populares,* or reform party, and the conservative "optimates"
     (**studiosi optimi cuiusque,** lit., *partisans of each best man*) were the two
     major political factions in Cicero's day.
235 **universorum:** *of all (the citizens) together.*
     hinc: i.e., from partisanship and the selfish use of power.
     apud Athenienses: the allusion is to the civil discord in Athens during the
     Peloponnesian War and afterward.
237. **bella civilia:** those of Marius and Sulla, Caesar and Pompey. In fact, the ugly
     situation continued after Cicero's death at the battles of Philippi and
     Actium, until Augustus finally established the Pax Romana. Vergil, Hor-
     ace, and many other Romans became heartily weary of civil war and
     were grateful to see Augustus embody many of the ideals expressed by
     Cicero here.
239. **consectabitur: consectari,** *to pursue, strive after.*
240. **criminibus: crimen,** *charge, accusation.*
242. **adhaerescet: adhaerescere,** *to stick to, cling to.*
243. **offendat: offendere,** *to suffer grief.*
     oppetat: oppetere, *to encounter.*
246. **ad:** *according to.*
     superbiam: superbia, *pride, insolence.*
247. **fastidium:** *haughtiness, disdain.*
248. **levitatis: levitas;** PRED. GEN., *(a sign) of weakness.*
     praeclara: though agreeing with **aequabilitas** *(equability, serenity),* this is
     pred. adj. with **vultus** and **frons** as well.
250. **Socrate . . . Laelio:** *Socrates* was known for his moderation and calm in the
     face of adversity, as was the Roman consul (in 140 B.C.) and intellectual
     Gaius Laelius; a member of the so-called "Scipionic Circle," Laelius was
     a friend of the Stoic philosopher Panaetius of Rhodes, whose treatise
     On Duty was a major influence on Cicero's *De Officiis.*
251. **sequitur ut:** + subjunct., a common idiom for *it remains that . . .* or *what
     comes next is that . . . .*
252. **verecundia:** *respect, reverence, modesty, propriety.*
     ornatus: *embellishment.*
     temperantia: *self-control, restraint, avoidance of excess, temperance.*

honestius magnificentiusque quam pecuniam contemnere, si non habeas, si habeas ad beneficentiam liberalitatemque conferre.
220 Cavenda etiam est gloriae cupiditas, ut supra dixi; eripit enim libertatem. Vacandum autem omni est animi perturbatione, cum cupiditate et metu, tum etiam aegritudine et voluptate nimia et iracundia ut tranquillitas animi et securitas adsit, quae affert cum constantiam, tum etiam dignitatem. (I.66–69, excerpts)

(d) Political leaders should serve the interests of state and not
225 *merely those of self or party.* Omnino qui rei publicae praefuturi sunt, duo Platonis praecepta teneant: unum, ut utilitatem civium sic tueantur ut, quaecumque agunt, ad eam referant, obliti commodorum suorum; alterum, ut totum corpus rei publicae curent, ne, dum partem aliquam tuentur, reliquas deserant. Ut
230 enim tutela, sic procuratio rei publicae ad eorum utilitatem qui commissi sunt, non ad eorum quibus commissa est, gerenda est. Qui autem parti civium consulunt, partem neglegunt, rem perniciosissimam in civitatem inducunt, seditionem atque discordiam; ex quo evenit ut alii populares, alii studiosi optimi cui-
235 usque videantur, pauci universorum. Hinc apud Athenienses magnae discordiae, in nostra re publica non solum seditiones, sed etiam pestifera bella civilia; quae gravis et fortis civis et in re publica dignus principatu fugiet atque oderit, tradetque se totum rei publicae, neque opes aut potentiam consectabitur, to-
240 tamque eam sic tuebitur ut omnibus consulat. Nec vero criminibus falsis in odium aut invidiam quemque vocabit, omninoque ita iustitiae honestatique adhaerescet ut, dum ea conservet, quamvis graviter offendat mortemque oppetat potius quam deserat illa quae dixi. (I.85–86)
245 *(e) Arrogance and flattery are to be avoided.* Atque etiam in rebus prosperis et ad voluntatem nostram fluentibus, superbiam magnopere, fastidium, arrogantiamque fugiamus. Nam ut adversas res, sic secundas immoderate ferre levitatis est, praeclaraque est aequabilitas in omni vita et idem semper vultus eademque
250 frons, ut de Socrate idemque de C. Laelio accepimus. (I.90)

Moderation and self-control.

Sequitur ut de una reliqua parte honestatis dicendum sit, in qua verecundia et, quasi quidam ornatus vitae, temperantia et

254.   **hoc loco:** *under this heading.*

decorum: *decorum, propriety, that which is fitting;* cp. **decet,** *it is fitting, proper, becoming, decent.*

255.   **vis:** *force, essence.*

ea: = **talis,** pred. adj.

queat: = **possit;** from **queo, quire,** defective vb. found chiefly in pres.

259.   **hac parte honestatis (260):** i.e., moderation.

260.   **disserendum est:** impers. pass. from **disserere,** *to discuss.*

tribus superioribus (261): wisdom, justice, courage, the other three cardinal virtues, each of which is briefly touched upon below in connection with this discussion of proper and decorous behavior.

261.   **uti:** this and the three infs. following are subjs. of **decet.**

264.   **mente esse captum:** lit., *to have been seized in (respect to) the mind* = *to be insane, mad.*

266.   **ratio fortitudinis:** i.e., *the reasoning in the case of courage.*

270.   **huc et illuc:** *here and there, in one direction and another.*

272.   **obtemperet: obtemperare,** *to obey, submit.*

274.   **agere:** dependent on **debet,** but supply **quisquam** *(anybody)* as subj.

probabilem: *commendable, acceptable.*

275.   **descriptio:** *definition.*

276.   **oboediant: oboedire,** *to listen to, obey.*

277.   **pigritiam: pigritia,** *laziness, indolence.*

ignaviam: ignavia, *listlessness.*

sintque: sc. **homines** as subj.

279.   **appetitus:** with **ii,** antecedent of **qui** but incorporated into the rel. cl., *those appetites which.*

evagantur: evagari, *to wander, spread.*

285.   **gestiunt: gestire,** *to exult, be excited.*

286.   **status:** *state (of mind), attitude.*

287.   **illud:** the following inf. phrases are in appos., *that is understood, the fact that all appetites . . . .*

formam: *outline, description.*

288.   **contrahendos: contrahere,** *to contract, control.*

Socrates
Copy of a 4th century
B.C. *original by Lysippus*
Louvre
Paris, France

modestia omnisque sedatio perturbationum animi et rerum modus cernitur. Hoc loco continetur id quod dici Latine decorum

255   potest. Huius vis ea est ut ab honesto non queat separari; nam
et quod decet honestum est, et quod honestum est decet. Qualis
autem differentia sit honesti et decori facilius intellegi quam ex-
planari potest. Quidquid est enim quod deceat, id tum apparet
cum antegressa est honestas. Itaque non solum in hac parte

260   honestatis de qua hoc loco disserendum est, sed etiam in tribus
superioribus quid deceat apparet. Nam et ratione uti atque oratione prudenter, et agere quod agas considerate, omnique in re
quid sit veri videre et tueri decet; contraque falli, errare, labi,
decipi tam dedecet quam delirare et mente esse captum; et iusta

265   omnia decora sunt, iniusta contra, ut turpia, sic indecora. Similis est ratio fortitudinis. Quod enim viriliter animoque magno
fit, id dignum viro et decorum videtur, quod contra, id ut turpe,
sic indecorum. (I.93–94, excerpts)

    *(a) The dual nature of the soul: (1) appetite; (2) reason, to
govern the appetites.* Duplex est enim vis animorum atque na-

270   tura: una pars in appetitu posita est, quae hominem huc et illuc
rapit; altera, in ratione, quae docet et explanat quid faciendum
fugiendumque sit. Ita fit ut ratio praesit, appetitus obtemperet.
Omnis autem actio vacare debet temeritate et neglegentia, nec
vero agere quidquam cuius non possit causam probabilem red-

275   dere; haec est enim fere descriptio officii. Efficiendum autem est
ut appetitus rationi oboediant eamque neque praecurrant nec
propter pigritiam aut ignaviam deserant, sintque tranquilli
atque omni animi perturbatione careant; ex quo elucebit omnis
constantia omnisque moderatio. Nam qui appetitus longius eva-

280   gantur et tamquam exultantes non satis a ratione retinentur, ii
sine dubio finem et modum transeunt; relinquunt enim et abici-
unt oboedientiam nec rationi parent, cui sunt subiecti lege naturae; a quibus non modo animi perturbantur sed etiam corpora.
Licet ora ipsa cernere iratorum aut eorum qui aut libidine ali-

285   qua aut metu commoti sunt aut voluptate nimia gestiunt; quorum omnium vultus, voces, motus, statusque mutantur. Ex
quibus illud intellegitur (ut ad officii formam revertamur) appetitus omnes contrahendos sedandosque esse excitandamque di-

293. **quo:** ABL. OF DEGREE OF DIFFERENCE.
294. **animadvertatur: animadvertere,** *to notice, consider;* here impers., *that it should be observed.*
296. **postulet: postulare,** *to demand, require, request.*
297. **liberalem:** *gentlemanly, befitting a free man.*
     speciem: species, *appearance*
298. **modus:** here, *rule, method* (for accomplishing all this).
     decus: a variant for **decorum.**
299. **praestantissimum: praestans,** *excellent, important.*
301. **species:** here, *specious form.*
     utilitatis: here, *advantage, expediency*
     commoveri: sc. **nos,** *for us to be greatly moved, affected.*
302. **attenderis:** sc. **ad eam,** *you give your attention to it.*
304. **intellegendum:** sc. **est;** impers. pass.
306. **celandi et occultandi:** from **celare** and **occultare;** both mean *to hide, conceal* (here, one's actions).
     opinio: here, *thought, expectation.*
307. **nobis . . . persuasum esse debet (308):** impers. pass.; lit., *it ought to have been persuaded to us = we should have been persuaded.*
     profecimus: proficere, *to gain, accomplish.*
308. **celare:** here, *to hide from, escape the attention of.*
     nihil . . . nihil (309): ANAPHORA (repetition) and ASYNDETON (omission of conjunctions) add emphasis to the point.
309. **incontinenter:** adv., *immoderately, intemperately.*
311. **hinc:** i.e., for purposes of illustrating this point.
312. **Gyges:** king of Lydia in the 7th cent. B.C.; antecedent of **qui.**
     a Platone: in Book II of the *Republic.*
     discessisset: *had gone apart = had opened up.*
313. **imbribus: imber,** *violent rain, storm;* ABL. OF CAUSE.
     hiatum: hiatus, *opening, gap.*
     aeneum: *bronze.*
314. **lateribus: latus,** *side.*
     fores: foris, *door,* usually pl. referring to *folding doors.*
316. **invisitata:** *not seen = unusual.*
     anulum: anulus, *ring.*
317. **induit: induere,** *to put on.*
     pastor: *shepherd.*
     se . . . recepit (318): *he took himself,* i.e., *he went.*
318. **palam: pala,** *bezel, mounted gem* (of a ring).
319. **rursus:** adv., *again.*
321. **stuprum:** *dishonor, (illicit) sexual intercourse;* with **intulit** (+ dat.) = *he seduced.*
     adiutrice: adiutrix, *assistant,* here, *accomplice;* ABL. ABS.
322. **interemit: interimere,** *to kill.*

290 ligentiam ut ne quid temere ac fortuito, inconsiderate neglegen-
terque agamus. (I.101–03, excerpts)

(b) In every action three tenets should be observed: (1) re-
straint of appetites, (2) proportion, (3) moderation. In omni
autem actione suscipienda tria sunt tenenda: primum ut appetitus rationi pareat, quo nihil est ad officia conservanda accom-
modatius; deinde ut animadvertatur quanta illa res sit quam
295 efficere velimus, ut neve maior neve minor cura et opera suscipi-
atur quam causa postulet; tertium est ut caveamus ut ea, quae
pertinent ad liberalem speciem et dignitatem, moderata sint.
Modus autem est optimus decus ipsum tenere, de quo ante dixi-
mus, nec progredi longius. Horum tamen trium praestantissi-
300 mum est appetitum obtemperare rationi. (I.141)

Expediency and moral right.

Cum igitur aliqua species utilitatis obiecta est, commoveri
necesse est; sed si, cum animum attenderis, turpitudinem videas
adiunctam ei rei quae speciem utilitatis attulerit, tum non utilitas relinquenda est, sed intellegendum, ubi turpitudo sit, ibi
305 utilitatem esse non posse. Atque etiam ex omni deliberatione
celandi et occultandi spes opinioque removenda est. Satis enim
nobis, si modo in philosophia aliquid profecimus, persuasum
esse debet, si omnes deos hominesque celare possimus, nihil tamen avare, nihil iniuste, nihil libidinose, nihil incontinenter
310 esse faciendum.

Illustrated by Plato's story about the ring of Gyges. Hinc ille
Gyges inducitur a Platone, qui, cum terra discessisset magnis
quibusdam imbribus, descendit in illum hiatum aeneumque
equum, ut ferunt fabulae, animadvertit, cuius in lateribus fores
315 essent. Quibus apertis, corpus hominis mortui vidit magnitudine invisitata anulumque aureum in digito; quem ut detraxit,
ipse induit (erat autem regius pastor), tum in concilium se pas-
torum recepit. Ibi cum palam eius anuli ad palmam converterat,
a nullo videbatur, ipse autem omnia videbat; idem rursus vide-
320 batur, cum in locum anulum inverterat. Itaque, hac opportuni-
tate anuli usus, reginae stuprum intulit; eaque adiutrice, regem
dominum interemit, sustulit quos obstare arbitrabatur, nec in

323. **facinoribus: facinus,** *deed, misdeed, crime.*
324. **exortus est: exoriri,** *to arise, rise (to become), emerge (as).*
327. **bonis viris:** DAT. OF REF., with somewhat more emotional force than the more factual ABL. OF AGENT, *in the case of good men.*
328. **hoc loco:** here, *on this point.*
     philosophi quidam: possibly an allusion to the Epicureans, who would assert that one should avoid immoral or criminal acts simply in order to avoid punishment or the other consequences of having one's misdeeds discovered.
329. **fictam: fingere,** *to mold, fashion, imagine.*
     commenticiam: *invented, fictitious.*
330. **quasi . . . defendat (331):** CL. OF IMAGINED COMPARISON.
335. **negant . . . posse:** i.e., that an immoral act can be concealed from both men and gods.
336. **quidnam: quisnam, quidnam,** interrog. pron., *who/what in the world.*
337. **tamquam . . . adhibemus (338):** *we are, so to speak, applying.*
338. **tormenta: tormentum,** *an instrument of torture.*
340. **omnia . . . concedant:** i.e., they would have to concede Cicero's (and the Stoics') point.
341. **incidunt: incidere,** *to happen, occur.*
     causae: here, *cases, situations.*
342. **hoc:** explained by the appos. cl. (an IND. QUEST.) **relinquendane . . . magnitudinem.**
344. **illud:** parallel to **hoc,** i.e., **cum illud deliberetur,** explained by the cl. **possitne . . . turpiter.**
346. **Collatino collegae:** DAT. OF SEPARATION; Lucius Tarquinius Collatinus was one of the Roman republic's first two consuls, along with his colleague, Lucius Junius Brutus, who led the uprising against the city's last king, Tarquinius Superbus.
     imperium abrogabat (347): *was taking away the imperium,* which was the supreme power of command possessed by the consuls.
349. **consilium hoc:** explained by the following appos. inf. phrase.
     cognationem: *family, kindred.*
351. **quod:** the antecedent is **id.**
354. **in:** *in the case of.*
356. **solum:** sc. **se,** subj. of **regnare.**
     fratrem: Remus; for the story, see Livy's account in "Legends of Early Rome," below.

his eum facinoribus quisquam potuit videre. Sic repente, anuli beneficio, rex exortus est Lydiae.

325 *The point of the story.* Hunc igitur ipsum anulum si habeat sapiens, nihilo plus sibi licere putet peccare, quam si non haberet; honesta enim bonis viris, non occulta quaeruntur. Atque hoc loco philosophi quidam, minime mali illi quidem, sed non satis acuti, fictam et commenticiam fabulam prolatam dicunt a

330 Platone—quasi vero ille aut factum id esse aut fieri potuisse defendat! Haec est vis huius anuli et huius exempli: si nemo sciturus, nemo ne suspicaturus quidem sit, cum aliquid divitiarum, potentiae, dominationis, libidinis causa feceris, si id dis hominibusque futurum sit semper ignotum, sisne facturus?

335 Negant id fieri posse. Sed quaero, quod negant posse, id si posset, quidnam facerent. Cum enim quaerimus si celare possint, quid facturi sint, non quaerimus possintne celare, sed tamquam tormenta quaedam adhibemus ut, si responderint se impunitate proposita facturos quod expediat, facinorosos se esse fateantur,

340 si negent, omnia turpia per se ipsa fugienda esse concedant. (III.35–39, excerpts)

Some examples of expediency vs. justice.

Incidunt multae saepe causae quae conturbent animos utilitatis specie, non, cum hoc deliberetur—relinquendane sit honestas propter utilitatis magnitudinem (nam id quidem improbum est)—sed illud—possitne id quod utile videatur fieri non

345 turpiter.

Brutus and Collatinus. Cum Collatino collegae Brutus imperium abrogabat, poterat videri facere id iniuste; fuerat enim in regibus expellendis socius Bruti consiliorum et adiutor. Cum autem consilium hoc principes cepissent—cognationem Su-

350 perbi nomenque Tarquiniorum et memoriam regni esse tollendam—quod erat utile, patriae consulere, id erat ita honestum ut etiam ipsi Collatino placere deberet. Itaque utilitas valuit propter honestatem, sine qua ne utilitas quidem esse potuisset.

Romulus. At in eo rege qui urbem condidit non item; species

355 enim utilitatis animum pepulit eius; cui cum visum esset utilius solum quam cum altero regnare, fratrem interemit. Omisit hic

357. **pietatem: pietas,** *loyalty, devotion* (to family and friends, to country, to the gods).

358. **muri causam:** *the excuse of the wall* (over which Remus is said to have leaped to show his scorn of Romulus' modest fortifications on the Palatine).

360. **pace ... Quirini:** lit., *with the peace of Quirinus* = *with all due respect to Quirinus* (the name given to Romulus after his death and deification).
      dixerim: POTENTIAL SUBJUNCT., *I would say.*

362. **suae cuique utilitati ... serviendum est (363):** lit., *it should be served by each person to his own advantage.*

363. **quod ... fiat:** REL. CL. OF CHARACTERISTIC, with the antecedent implied in the main cl., *whatever may be done, as far as one may do.*

364. **scite:** adv., *cleverly.*
      Chrysippus ut multa ... inquit: = **Chrysippus inquit ut multa dicit,** i.e., in his colorful, vivid language. Chrysippus (ca. 280–207 B.C.), head of the Stoic school after Zeno and Cleanthes, was famous for his systematization of Stoic doctrine.
      stadium: *a race in the stadium.*
      eniti: *to struggle.*

365. **supplantare:** *to trip up.*

366. **certet: certare,** *to struggle, contend, compete.*

369. **illa:** sc. **exempla sunt.**

371. **cum ... tum:** *not only ... but also;* Latin is fond of stating the general idea first and then following with a specific example.

372. **Cannensi: Cannensis,** *at Cannae,* a town in Apulia where, during the second Punic war in 216 B.C. the Romans suffered a calamitous loss at the hands of Hannibal; see Livy's account in "Hannibal and the Second Punic War," below.

376. **impetum:** the allusion is to the battle of Thermopylae in 480 B.C., which the Greeks lost to the invading Persians and their king Xerxes but which was made famous by the heroic stand and death of the Spartan king Leonidas and his men.

378. **Troezene:** loc.; *Troezen,* an old city across the Saronic Gulf southwest of Athens.
      conscenderent: conscendere, *to ascend, go on board.*

379. **classe: classis,** *fleet, navy;* the Greeks did in fact defeat the Persians at sea at the decisive battle of Salamis in 480 B.C. under the leadership of the Athenian commander Themistocles.
      Cyrsilum: *Cyrsilus,* an otherwise unknown Athenian.

381. **lapidibus: lapis,** *stone, rock.*
      videbatur: i.e., **sibi.**

384. **contione: contio,** *assembly* (convened especially to hear a speech by a magistrate).

385. **salutare: salutaris,** *healthful, advantageous.*
      sciri: i.e., publicly; inf. subj. of the impers. **opus esse,** *to be necessary.*

et pietatem et humanitatem ut id, quod utile videbatur neque erat, assequi posset; et tamen muri causam opposuit, speciem honestatis nec probabilem nec sane idoneam. Peccavit igitur—
360 pace vel Quirini vel Romuli, dixerim.

In the stadium. Nec tamen nostrae nobis utilitates omittendae sunt aliisque tradendae, cum iis ipsis egeamus, sed suae cuique utilitati, quod sine alterius iniuria fiat, serviendum est. Scite Chrysippus ut multa, "Qui stadium," inquit, "currit, eniti
365 et contendere debet quam maxime possit, ut vincat; supplantare eum quocum certet aut manu depellere nullo modo debet. Sic in vita sibi quemque petere quod pertineat ad usum non iniquum est, alteri deripere ius non est." (III.40–42)

In the Second Punic War. Illa praeclara in quibus publicae
370 utilitatis species prae honestate contemnitur. Plena exemplorum est nostra res publica cum saepe, tum maxime bello Punico secundo; quae, Cannensi calamitate accepta, maiores animos habuit quam umquam rebus secundis: nulla timoris significatio, nulla mentio pacis. Tanta vis est honesti ut speciem utilitatis ob-
375 scuret.

The Athenians in 480 B.C. Athenienses cum Persarum impetum nullo modo possent sustinere statuerentque ut urbe relicta, coniugibus et liberis Troezene depositis, naves conscenderent libertatemque Graeciae classe defenderent, Cyrsilum
380 quendam, suadentem ut in urbe manerent Xerxemque reciperent, lapidibus obruerunt. At ille utilitatem sequi videbatur; sed ea nulla erat, repugnante honestate.

Themistocles and Aristides. Themistocles, post victoriam eius belli quod cum Persis fuit, dixit in contione se habere consilium
385 rei publicae salutare, sed id sciri non opus esse; postulavit ut

Chrysippus
3rd century B.C.
Louvre
Paris, France

386. **quicum:** = **quocum.**

   Aristides: an Athenian statesman so famous for his incorruptibility that he was called "the Just."

387. **ille:** sc. **dixit.**

   Lacedaemoniorum: *Laecdaemonians, Spartans,* with whom the Athenians were in conflict.

   subducta esset . . . esset (389): SUBORDINATE CLS. IN IND. STATE.

388. **Gytheum:** *Gytheum,* a Spartan port.

   quo facto: ABL. ABS.

389. **necesse esset:** impers.; here, *it was inevitable.*

390. **exspectatione:** i.e., of all the people; ABL. OF ATTENDANT CIRCUMSTANCE.

   perutile: note the force of the prefix.

393. **auctore Aristide (394):** i.e., at his instigation.

395. **id:** i.e., the issue of the conflict between expediency and moral action.

   alias: adv., *at another time, other times.*

   Pyrrhi: *Pyrrhus,* king of the Greek state of Epirus, championed the Greek cities of southern Italy against Roman imperialism; after victories against Rome in 280 and 279 B.C., in which he won the battles but lost large numbers of his own soldiers (giving us the term "Pyrrhic victory"), he ultimately lost the war and withdrew from Italy.

396. **C. Fabricio:** *Gaius Fabricius Luscinus,* consul in 282 and 278 B.C. and censor in 275, became for the Romans an example of frugality and incorruptibility.

   iterum: i.e., *for the second time.*

   iudicatum est (397): *was decided.*

397. **ultro:** adv., *voluntarily, without provocation.*

398. **certamen:** *contest, struggle, fight.*

   generoso: *noble.*

399. **perfuga:** *deserter.*

   est pollicitus: **polliceri,** *to promise.*

400. **ut:** *just as;* with this meaning **ut** ordinarily takes the indic., but here the vb. is subjunct. in a SUBORDINATE CL. IN IND. STATE.

401. **rediturum et . . . necaturum:** sc. **esse.**

403. **si . . . quaerimus . . . sustulisset (405):** MIXED CONDITION, with a past contrary to fact apodosis following a simple pres. protasis.

406. **quicum:** the antecedent is **eum;** for the form, see above on line 386.

   eum . . . superatum (407): sc. **esse;** inf. phrase with **flagitium fuisset,** *it would have been a disgrace for him . . ..*

407. **utrum . . . utilius:** sc. **erat;** with **armis . . . certare an venenis** in 409–10, *which (of the two actions) was more expedient, to contend . . ..*

409. **seiunxit:** **seiungere,** *to separate.*

411. **sin:** conj., *but if.*

aliquem populus daret quicum communicaret. Datus est Aristides. Huic ille classem Lacedaemoniorum quae subducta esset ad Gytheum clam incendi posse, quo facto frangi Lacedaemoniorum opes necesse esset. Quod Aristides cum audisset, in con-
390 tionem magna exspectatione venit dixitque perutile esse consilium quod Themistocles adferret, sed minime honestum. Itaque Athenienses, quod honestum non esset, id ne utile quidem putaverunt totamque eam rem, quam ne audierant quidem, auctore Aristide repudiaverunt. (III.47–49)
395   *Fabricius and Pyrrhus.* Id quidem cum saepe alias, tum Pyrrhi bello a C. Fabricio consule iterum et a senatu nostro iudicatum est. Cum enim rex Pyrrhus populo Romano bellum ultro intulisset, cumque de imperio certamen esset cum rege generoso ac potenti, perfuga ab eo venit in castra Fabricii eique est polli-
400 citus, si praemium sibi proposuisset, se, ut clam venisset, sic clam in Pyrrhi castra rediturum et eum veneno necaturum. Hunc Fabricius reducendum curavit ad Pyrrhum idque eius factum laudatum a senatu est. Atqui, si speciem utilitatis opinionemque quaerimus, magnum illud bellum perfuga unus et gravem ad-
405 versarium imperii sustulisset, sed magnum dedecus et flagitium fuisset, quicum laudis certamen fuisset, eum non virtute sed scelere superatum. Utrum igitur utilius vel Fabricio, qui talis in hac urbe qualis Aristides Athenis fuit, vel senatui nostro, qui numquam utilitatem a dignitate seiunxit, armis cum hoste cer-
410 tare an venenis? Si gloriae causa imperium expetendum est, scelus absit, in quo non potest esse gloria; sin ipsae opes expetuntur quoquo modo, non poterunt utiles esse cum infamia.

Themistocles
Museo Archeologico Nazionale
Naples, Italy

413. **L. Philippi Q. f.:** = **Luci Philippi Quinti fili,** *of Lucius Philippus the son of Quintus.*

414. **sententia:** *opinion, proposal,* i.e., **ut . . . redderemus.**

    quas civitates: the antecedent is incorporated into its rel. cl. = **eae civitates quas.**

    L. Sulla: *Lucius Cornelius Sulla,* conservative military and political rival of Gaius Marius and finally, in 82–79 B.C., dictator.

    pecunia accepta: i.e., after a lump-sum payment to Rome's treasury.

    ex: *in accordance with.*

415. **vectigales: vectigalis,** *tributary, liable to taxes* (**vectigal**).

417. **est adsensus: adsentiri,** *to agree with, assent to.*

418. **at . . . igitur:** an imagined objection to Cicero's point.

    quousque: adv., *how far, how long.*

420. **fultum esse: fulcire,** *to prop up, support.*

421. **odium et infamia: potest** and **utile** agree with **odium,** the nearer of the two subjs.

424. **Sol:** i.e., *Apollo,* here in his role as god of the sun.

426. **currum: currus,** *chariot.*

    constitit: here, *stood firmly* (on the ground).

427. **ictu: ictus,** *blow, stroke.*

    fulminis: fulmen, *lightning, thunderbolt.*

    deflagravit: deflagrare, *to destroy by fire* or, here, *be destroyed by fire.*

    fuerat: for the more usual contrary to fact **fuisset,** *it would have been.*

    promissum . . . non esse servatum (428): *for the promise . . .,* subj. of **fuerat.**

429. **quid quod:** *what of the fact that.*

    Theseus: the legendary hero and king of early Athens. As a special favorite, Theseus had received from Neptune the promise to fulfill any three requests which Theseus might make of him; when Theseus wrongly suspected Hippolytus, his son, of having an affair with his wife Phaedra, he prayed for his son's death.

431. **interitum: interitus,** *destruction, ruin.*

    patri: DAT. OF AGENT.

432. **noverca:** *stepmother.*

    impetrato: impetrare, *to obtain, gain, accomplish, succeed in a request.*

    luctibus: luctus, *grief, sorrow.*

434. **Agamemnon:** the commander of the Greek forces in the Trojan war, Agamemnon sacrificed his daughter Iphigenia to Diana to atone for a crime and thus gain favorable winds for his expedition to Troy.

435. **devovisset: devovere,** *to vow, consecrate.*

    Dianae: *Diana* (the Greek Artemis), goddess of the hunt.

436. **immolavit: immolare,** *to sacrifice.*

    qua: ABL. OF COMPARISON.

438. **taetrum: taeter,** *hideous, offensive.*

Even Romans can err. Non igitur utilis illa L. Philippi Q. f. sententia, quas civitates L. Sulla pecunia accepta ex senatus
415 consulto liberavisset, ut eae rursus vectigales essent neque iis pecuniam, quam pro libertate dederant, redderemus. Ei senatus est adsensus. Turpe imperio! Piratarum enim melior fides quam senatus. "At aucta vectigalia, utile igitur." Quousque audebunt dicere quidquam utile quod non honestum? Potest autem ulli
420 imperio, quod gloria debet fultum esse et benevolentia sociorum, utile esse odium et infamia? (III.86–88)

Promises may be broken when inexpedient for those to whom they have been made.

Ac ne illa quidem promissa servanda sunt quae non sunt iis ipsis utilia quibus illa promiseris.
The case of Phaethon. Sol Phaethonti filio (ut redeamus ad
425 fabulas) facturum se esse dixit quidquid optasset; optavit ut in currum patris tolleretur; sublatus est. Atque is, antequam constitit, ictu fulminis deflagravit. Quanto melius fuerat in hoc promissum patris non esse servatum!
Theseus and Hippolytus. Quid quod Theseus exegit promissum a Neptuno? Cui cum tres optationes Neptunus dedisset,
430 optavit interitum Hippolyti filii, cum is patri suspectus esset de noverca. Quo optato impetrato, Theseus in maximis fuit luctibus.
Agamemnon and Iphigenia. Quid quod Agamemnon, cum
435 devovisset Dianae quod in suo regno pulcherrimum natum esset illo anno, immolavit Iphigeniam, qua nihil erat eo quidem anno natum pulchrius? Promissum potius non faciendum quam tam taetrum facinus admittendum fuit.

"Phaedra and Hippolytus"
Pierre N. Guerin, 1802
Louvre, Paris, France

439. **facienda:** sc. **est;** here, *should be kept.*
440. **non numquam:** *not never = sometimes.*
      deposita: depositum, *something deposited* or *entrusted.*
      si . . . reddere (441): deposuerit and **repetat** are the vbs. of the protasis of this
           fut. less vivid condition, and **sit,** to be taken with both **reddere** (as its
           subj.) **peccatum** (*a sin,* pred. nom.) and the parallel phrase **officium non
           reddere,** is the vb. of the apodosis. The structure is highly rhetorical,
           with both parts of the sent. characterized by ASYNDETON (**deposuerit/
           repetat** and **reddere peccatum/officium non reddere**) and CHIASMUS (ABBA
           word order: [A] **sana mente,** [B] **deposuerit,** [B] **repetat,** [A] **insaniens,** and
           [A] **reddere,** [B] **peccatum,** [B] **officium,** [A] **non reddere**).
444. **facias:** POTENTIAL SUBJUNCT., essentially the conclusion of an understood
           condition ("if you should return the deposit, then *you would . . .*").
446. **conventis: conventum,** *agreement.*
448. **Regulus:** after winning a number of victories in the First Punic War, Regulus
           was finally captured by the Carthaginians in 255 B.C. Although the exact
           circumstances of his death are somewhat disputed today, the story which
           Cicero here outlines (and see above, lines 168–73) became a paradigm
           for Roman courage and morality.
      consul: actually proconsul, having served his second consulship during the
           previous year.
449. **iuratus:** act. and governing the **ut** cl., *having sworn that.*
452. **quae:** the antecedent is **utilitatis speciem,** i.e., *the apparent advantage,* ex-
           plained by the three inf. phrases following.
453. **quam calamitatem:** the antecedent is attracted into the rel. cl., = **calamitatem**
           (obj. of **iudicantem**) **quam.**
454. **fortunae bellicae:** dat. with **(calamitatem) communem.**
      iudicantem: acc. to agree with the understood subj. of **tenere,** *(for him), judg-
           ing that . . ., to retain.*
455. **gradum: gradus,** *position, rank.*
457. **mandata: mandatum,** *orders* (which he had from the Carthaginians).
      recusavit: vbs. meaning *to refuse* and *to hinder* are often followed by **ne** +
           subjunct.; here, *he refused to state his opinion* (saying that . . .).
458. **esse se senatorem:** IND. STATE. depending on the reported speech implicit in
           recusavit.
459. **illud:** sc. **dixit** or **fecit.**
      dixerit quispiam: POTENTIAL SUBJUNCT., *someone may say.*
461. **confectum: conficere,** *to accomplish, finish, wear out, weaken.*
465. **exquisita:** *sought ought,* i.e., *carefully chosen.*
466. **vigilando:** *by staying awake,* i.e., *by being kept awake;* other sources in-
           clude starvation along with sleep deprivation as the cause of Regulus'
           death.
467. **causa:** here, *state* or *situation.*
      senex: here used as an adj. with **captivus,** *an aged (former) prisoner of war.*
      periurus: *perjured, lying.*
      consularis: here a noun, *ex-consul, a man of consular rank.*

A promise to return something. Ergo et promissa non faci-
440 enda non numquam; neque semper deposita reddenda. Si gladium quis apud te sana mente deposuerit, repetat insaniens, reddere peccatum sit, officium non reddere. Quid si is qui apud
te pecuniam deposuerit bellum inferat patriae, reddasne depositum? Non credo; facias enim contra rem publicam, quae
445 debet esse carissima. Sic multa, quae honesta natura videntur
esse, temporibus fiunt non honesta: facere promissa, stare conventis, reddere deposita, commutata utilitate, fiunt non honesta.
(III.94–95)

The famous example of Regulus in the First Punic War.

M. Atilius Regulus, cum consul iterum in Africa ex insidiis
captus esset, iuratus missus est ad senatum ut, nisi redditi essent
450 Poenis captivi nobiles quidam, rediret ipse Carthaginem. Is cum
Romam venisset, utilitatis speciem videbat sed eam, ut res declarat, falsam iudicavit; quae erat talis: manere in patria; esse
domui suae cum uxore, cum liberis; quam calamitatem accepisset in bello communem fortunae bellicae iudicantem, tenere
455 consularis dignitatis gradum. Quis haec negat esse utilia? Magnitudo animi et fortitudo negat. Itaque quid fecit? In senatum
venit; mandata exposuit; sententiam ne diceret recusavit: quam-
diu iure iurando hostium teneretur, non esse se senatorem.
Atque illud etiam ("O stultum hominem," dixerit quispiam, "et
460 repugnantem utilitati suae!"): reddi captivos negavit esse utile;
illos enim adulescentes esse et bonos duces, se iam confectum
senectute. Cuius cum valuisset auctoritas, captivi retenti sunt;
ipse Carthaginem rediit, neque eum caritas patriae retinuit nec
suorum. Neque vero tum ignorabat se ad crudelissimum hostem
465 et ad exquisita supplicia proficisci, sed ius iurandum conservan-
dum putabat. Itaque tum cum vigilando necabatur, erat in meli-
ore causa quam si domi senex captivus, periurus consularis re-
mansisset. Potest autem, quod inutile rei publicae sit, id cuiquam
civi utile esse? (III.99–101, excerpts)

470. **laudandus:** sc. **est.**

    iure: sc. **iurando.**

    decem illi (471): subj. of **redierunt** and **vituperandi (sunt)** in 473.

471. **Cannensem:** see Livy's account of Rome's defeat at the battle of Cannae in "Hannibal and the Second Punic War," below.

472. **se . . . redituros:** IND. STATE. depending on **iuratos.**

    quorum: **potiri,** *to gain possession of,* takes the gen. (sometimes the abl.); **castra . . . ea** is the antecedent.

473. **redimendis: redimere,** *to buy back, ransom.*

    redierunt: a simple fact condition, since there were varying accounts of the incident and whether the 10 men all returned or not.

    vituperandi: sc. **sunt;** from **vituperare,** *to blame, censure.*

474. **non omnes:** sc. **auctores,** i.e., historians.

    Polybius: a Greek historian of the 2nd century B.C. who lived at Rome as a political hostage 167–151 B.C.; he wrote in Greek a sober and reliable history of Rome's rise to imperial power during the period of the Punic wars.

477. **paulo:** ABL. OF DEGREE OF DIFFERENCE, with **post quam** as with comparatives, = *a little after.*

478. **reditu: reditus,** *return.*

479. **interpretabatur: interpretari,** *to explain, interpret.*

    fraus: *deceit, fraud.*

480. **adstringit: adstringere,** *to bind, tighten;* here, by contrast with **dissolvit** *(to loosen, absolve),* = *to aggravate, make worse.*

    calliditas: *skill, shrewdness, cunning.*

482. **veterator:** *experienced person, old hand* (often, as here, pejorative).

    vinctus: vincire, *to bind.*

483. **illud maximum:** sc. **est;** i.e., the most important part of the story.

485. **Paulo . . . Varrone:** Lucius Aemilius Paulus and Gaius Terentius Varro were the two consuls whose army was crushed by Hannibal at Cannae; see Livy's "Hannibal and the Second Punic War," below.

487. **insitum: inserere,** + dat., *to implant, instill.*

    emori: *to die.*

489. **idem:** *the same man,* i.e., Polybius.

    adflictis: adfligere, *to dash down, shatter.*

    excelso: *lofty, high;* the CHIASMUS in **rebus afflictis . . . excelso animo** emphasizes the intended contrast.

Two examples after the defeat of the Romans at Cannae in the Second Punic War.

470   Sed, ut laudandus Regulus in conservando iure, sic decem illi quos post Cannensem pugnam iuratos ad senatum misit Hannibal se in castra redituros ea, quorum erant potiti Poeni, nisi de redimendis captivis impetravissent, si non redierunt, vituperandi. De quibus non omnes uno modo: nam Polybius, bo-
475 nus auctor in primis, ex decem nobilissimis, qui tum erant missi, novem revertisse dicit, re a senatu non impetrata; unum ex decem, qui, paulo post quam erat egressus e castris, redisset quasi aliquid esset oblitus, Romae remansisse; reditu enim in castra liberatum se esse iure iurando interpretabatur—non recte, fraus
480 enim adstringit, non dissolvit periurium. Fuit igitur stulta calliditas, perverse imitata prudentiam. Itaque decrevit senatus ut ille veterator et callidus, vinctus, ad Hannibalem duceretur. Sed illud maximum: octo hominum milia tenebat Hannibal, non quos in acie cepisset aut qui periculo mortis diffugissent, sed
485 qui relicti in castris fuissent a Paulo et a Varrone consulibus. Eos senatus non censuit redimendos (cum id parva pecunia fieri posset) ut esset insitum militibus nostris aut vincere aut emori. Qua quidem re audita, fractum animum Hannibalis scribit idem quod senatus populusque Romanus rebus adflictis tam ex-
490 celso animo fuisset. Sic honestatis comparatione ea, quae videntur utilia, vincuntur. (III.113–14)

"The Oath of Hannibal"
Johann Heinrich Schoenfeld, 17th century
Germanisches Nationalmuseum, Nuremberg, Germany

1. **Scaevola:** *Quintus Mucius Scaevola* (ca. 170–87 B.C.) was consul in 117 B.C., an augur, and a famous Roman jurist, with whom Cicero studied for about two years (ca. 90–88 B.C.); a son-in-law of Gaius Laelius, after whom the *De Amicitia* was titled, both men are characters in the dialogue that follows. Scaevola is depicted as relating the conversation to Cicero in 88 B.C.

   Laeli: *Gaius Laelius* (born ca. 190 B.C.), consul in 140, a celebrated orator, and, as the closest friend of Publius Cornelius Scipio Aemilianus (victor over the Carthaginians in the Third Punic War), a member of the so-called "Scipionic Circle"; the principal figure in this dialogue, he also appeared in Cicero's *De Republica.*

2. **genero:** gener, *son-in-law.*

   C. Fannio: *Gaius Fannius,* consul in 122, a student of the philosopher Panaetius of Rhodes, son-in-law of Laelius, and the third character in the dialogue.

3. **diebus:** ABL. OF DEGREE OF DIFFERENCE.

   post mortem Africani: i.e., the younger Africanus, Scipio Aemilianus, who died in 129 B.C. (the dramatic date of the dialogue Scaevola reports). He earned the honorary title *Africanus* for his victory over Carthage in 146 B.C.; his illustrious adoptive grandfather, P. Cornelius Scipio Africanus Maior, had been given the same title because of his victory over Hannibal in 202 B.C.

   sententias: i.e., the ideas rather than the exact words.

4. **mandavi:** mandare, *to commit, entrust.*

5. **coram:** adv., *face to face, personally.*

6. **ageres:** here, *you were pleading;* the subj. is Titus Pomponius Atticus (born 110 B.C.), Cicero's dearest friend from their childhood days and the addressee of this work.

7. **cum . . . tum (8):** = **non solum . . . sed etiam.**

   cognitione: cognitio, *study, consideration.*

8. **familiaritate:** familiaritas, *close friendship.*

9. **prodessem:** prosum, *to be useful to, benefit.*

11. **persona:** originally *mask* (worn by an actor); hence *personality, character.*

    ea ipsa: not with **amicitia,** but n. pl. dir. obj.

12. **dissereret:** disserere, *to discuss, argue;* with **quae,** a REL. CL. OF RESULT.

    disputata: sc. **esse.**

14. **plus:** with **gravitatis.**

15. **amicissimus:** = *a completely devoted friend;* a fine tribute to Cicero's friendship with Atticus.

17. **socerum:** socer, *father-in-law.*

19. **te ipse cognosces:** Cicero complimented Atticus not only by dedicating the *De Amicitia* to him but by imagining their relationship as equal to the proverbially close friendship of Scipio and Laelius.

20. **quaerunt:** the subj. is general, *people ask.*

    quonam: from the interrog. adj. **quinam, quaenam, quodnam,** *who, which, what (in the world).*

    pacto: pactum, *pact, agreement, way.*

LAELIUS DE AMICITIA

Preface and dedication to Atticus.

Tum Scaevola exposuit nobis sermonem Laeli de amicitia habitum ab illo secum et cum altero genero C. Fannio paucis diebus post mortem Africani. Eius disputationis sententias memoriae mandavi, quas hoc libro exposui arbitratu meo; quasi
5 enim ipsos induxi loquentes ut tamquam a praesentibus coram haberi sermo videretur. Cum enim saepe mecum ageres ut de amicitia scriberem aliquid, digna mihi res cum omnium cognitione tum nostra familiaritate visa est. Itaque feci non invitus ut prodessem multis rogatu tuo. Cum accepissemus a patribus
10 maxime memorabilem C. Laeli et P. Scipionis familiaritatem fuisse, idonea mihi Laeli persona visa est quae de amicitia ea ipsa dissereret quae disputata ab eo meminisset Scaevola. Genus autem hoc sermonum, positum in hominum veterum auctoritate et eorum illustrium, plus videtur habere gravitatis. (Sed hoc
15 libro ad amicum amicissimus de amicitia scripsi.) Nunc Laelius, amicitiae gloria excellens, de amicitia loquitur. C. Fannius et Q. Mucius ad socerum veniunt post mortem Africani. Ab his sermo oritur, respondet Laelius, cuius tota disputatio est de amicitia, quam legens te ipse cognosces. (3–5, excerpts)

Introductory conversation: how Laelius bore the loss of Scipio.

20   FANNIUS. Itaque ex me quaerunt quonam pacto mortem Africani feras.
SCAEVOLA. Quaerunt quidem, C. Laeli, multi, ut est a

Scipio Africanus the Elder
Museo Archeologico Nazionale
Naples, Italy

23. **animum adverti:** taken as a unit, *I have noticed, perceived.*
25. **nec potuisse non:** a common formulation, *you were unable not (to), you could not have failed (to).*
27. **viderint:** a parenthetical POTENTIAL SUBJUNCT.; i.e., if Laelius should deny his grief (philosophers would understand and approve such denial), he would be concealing the truth.
28. **sapientes:** *philosophers,* particularly the Stoics, whose ideal of imperturbability would theoretically not permit them to be disturbed by any circumstance.
     mentiar: mentiri, *to lie.*
29. **orbatus: orbare,** + abl., *to deprive of.*
     recordatione: recordatio, *recollection.*
30. **fruor: frui,** + abl., *to enjoy.*
31. **ista:** with **sapientiae . . . fama,** *that reputation for wisdom.*
32. **quam . . . quam (33):** the first is a rel. pron. with **fama** as antecedent; the second a correlative conj. with **tam.**
     falsa: *(since it is) untrue.*
     praesertim: adv., *especially (since).*
33. **quod:** *the fact that,* introducing a noun cl. that, like **fama,** is a subj. of **delectat.**
     sempiternam: *enduring, eternal.*
34. **fore:** = **futuram esse.**
     eo: ABL. OF DEGREE OF DIFFERENCE with **magis,** *more by this much* = *this much more.*
     cordi: cor, *heart;* DAT. OF PURPOSE, lit., *(it is) for the heart* = *(it is) pleasing.*
35. **saeculis: saeculum,** *century, generation.*
     paria: n. of the adj. **par,** used as a noun, *pairs;* the pairs of friends most famous in legend were Theseus and Pirithous, Achilles and Patroclus, Orestes and Pylades, Damon and Pythias.
39. **pergratum:** note the force of the prefix **per-.**
     disputaris: = **disputaveris,** fut. perf. in a FUT. MORE VIVID CONDITION.
40. **qualem:** sc. **amicitiam esse;** i.e., what the nature of friendship is.
     existimes: existimare, *to estimate, reckon, think.*
42. **gravarer: gravare,** *to weigh down, burden,* pass., *to be reluctant.*
44. **magnum opus est:** i.e., a thorough philosophical discussion.
45. **exercitatione: exercitatio,** *exercise, training, practice.*
     quamobrem: = **quam ob rem,** *wherefore, therefore.*
     quae: sc. **ea** as antecedent of **quae** and obj. of **petatis.**
46. **eis . . . qui . . . profitentur: profiteri,** *to declare openly, profess;* i.e., professional philosophers or Sophists.
     censeo: censere, *to estimate, think, advise, recommend.*
     petatis: ut is often omitted in a JUSSIVE NOUN CL.
50. **bonis:** i.e., *good men.*
52. **rerum:** OBJ. GEN. with **consensio,** *an agreement on all matters.*
     qua: ABL. OF COMPARISON with **nihil melius.**
53. **haud scio an:** idiom introducing an IND. QUEST., *I do not know whether* = *I am inclined to think.*
     excepta sapientia: ABL. ABS. = *with the exception of . . . .*

Fannio dictum; sed id respondeo quod animum adverti: te dolorem quem acceperis cum summi viri tum amicissimi morte
25   ferre moderate, nec potuisse non commoveri.

     LAELIUS. Recte tu quidem, Scaevola, et vere. Ego si Sci-
pionis desiderio me moveri negem—quam id recte faciam viderint sapientes—sed certe mentiar. Moveor enim tali amico
orbatus qualis, ut arbitror, nemo umquam erit. Sed tamen re-
30   cordatione nostrae amicitiae sic fruor ut beate vixisse videar,
quia cum Scipione vixerim. Itaque non tam ista me sapientiae,
quam modo Fannius commemoravit, fama delectat (falsa praesertim) quam quod amicitiae nostrae memoriam spero sempi-
ternam fore. Idque mihi eo magis est cordi quod ex omnibus
35   saeculis vix tria aut quattuor nominantur paria amicorum, quo
in genere sperare videor Scipionis et Laeli amicitiam notam
posteritati fore.

     FANNIUS. Quoniam amicitiae mentionem fecisti et sumus
otiosi, pergratum mihi feceris si de amicitia disputaris quid sen-
40   tias, qualem existimes, quae praecepta des.

     SCAEVOLA. Mihi vero erit gratum. (7–16, excerpts)

Laelius' observations on the nature of friendship.

     LAELIUS. Ego vero non gravarer, si mihi ipse confiderem;
nam et praeclara res est, et sumus, ut dixit Fannius, otiosi. Sed
quis ego sum? Aut quae est in me facultas? Magnum opus est
45   egetque exercitatione non parva. Quamobrem quae disputari de
amicitia possunt, ab eis censeo petatis qui ista profitentur. Ego
vos hortari tantum possum ut amicitiam omnibus rebus humanis anteponatis; nihil est enim tam naturae aptum, tam con-
veniens ad res vel secundas vel adversas. Sed hoc primum sen-
50   tio: nisi in bonis amicitiam esse non posse.

     Est autem amicitia nihil aliud nisi omnium divinarum hu-
manarumque rerum cum benevolentia et caritate consensio, qua
quidem haud scio an, excepta sapientia, nihil melius homini sit

56. **beluarum: belua,** *animal, beast.*
    hoc extremum: *this end, objective;* i.e., the last mentioned, **voluptates.**
    superiora: i.e., *earlier ones* (**divitias, valetudinem,** etc.); sc. **sunt.**
    caduca: *falling, frail, perishable, transitory.*
58. **temeritate:** here, *impulse, accident.*
59. **illi:** sc. **agunt.**
    gignit: gignere, *to beget, bring forth.*
61. **talis:** = **tales,** i.e., **bonos.**
    opportunitates: here, *advantages.*
62. **queo:** = **possum.**
    qui: adv., *how.*
    vitalis: *worth living.*
63. **Ennius:** *Quintus Ennius* (239–169 B.C.), one of the earliest Roman poets and
    author of the epic poem, the *Annales,* was much admired and frequently
    quoted by Cicero.
64. **quid:** sc. **est.**
    quicum: sc. **aliquem,** *(someone) with whom; qui,* an old abl. form used with
    cum.
65. **qui:** adv., as in 62 above.
    haberes: sc. **aliquem.**
66. **aeque ac tu:** *as much as you; ac (atque)* means *as* after words of comparison
    and similarity.
67. **sine eo:** serves to introduce a conditional cl., = *if there were not a person
    (who).*
68. **singulae . . . singulis (69):** the repetition emphasizes the limited nature and
    service of aims other than friendship, = *individually for generally single
    (i.e.,* limited) *purposes.*
69. **utare:** = **utaris,** sc. **eis.**
71. **fungare: fungi,** + abl., *to perform, discharge, complete.*
72. **quoquo:** adv., indefinite of **quo,** *wherever.*
    praesto: adv., *at hand, ready.*
74. **locis:** ABL. OF PLACE WHERE without a prep. is common with **locus.**
75. **splendidiores:** OBJ. COMPL.
    adversas: obj. both of the partics. and of the understood **facit.**
    partiens: partire, *to divide, distribute.*
    communicans: communicare, *to share, take a share in.*
77. **cum . . . tum (78):** *since . . . also.*
78. **illa:** sc. **commoditate;** ABL. OF SPECIFICATION.
    nimirum: adv., *doubtless, of course, to be sure.*
    bonam spem praelucet in posterum (79): *it (friendship) shines (a ray of) good
    hope into the future.*
80. **intuetur: intueri,** *to look upon, behold.*
    exemplar: here, *likeness, image.*

a dis immortalibus datum. Divitias alii praeponunt, bonam alii
55 valetudinem, alii potentiam, alii honores, multi etiam voluptates. Beluarum hoc quidem extremum; illa autem superiora ca-
duca et incerta, posita non tam in consiliis nostris quam in fortunae temeritate. Qui autem in virtute summum bonum ponunt,
praeclare illi quidem; sed haec ipsa virtus amicitiam et gignit et
60 continet, nec sine virtute amicitia esse ullo pacto potest. (17–
20, excerpts)

The benefits of friendship.

Talis igitur inter viros amicitia tantas opportunitates habet
quantas vix queo dicere. Principio, qui potest esse vita vitalis,
ut ait Ennius, quae non in amici mutua benevolentia conquies-
cit? Quid dulcius quam habere quicum omnia audeas sic loqui
65 ut tecum? Qui esset tantus fructus in prosperis rebus, nisi haberes qui illis aeque ac tu ipse gauderet? Adversas vero ferre
difficile esset sine eo qui illas gravius etiam quam tu ferret. Denique ceterae res quae expetuntur opportunae sunt singulae rebus fere singulis: divitiae, ut utare; opes, ut colare; honores, ut
70 laudere; voluptates, ut gaudeas; valetudo, ut dolore careas et
muneribus fungare corporis; amicitia res plurimas continet.
Quoquo te verteris praesto est; nullo loco excluditur; numquam
intempestiva, numquam molesta est. Itaque non aqua, non igni,
ut aiunt, pluribus locis utimur quam amicitia. Nam et secundas
75 res splendidiores facit amicitia, et adversas partiens communi-
cansque leviores.

Cumque plurimas et maximas commoditates amicitia con-
tineat, tum illa nimirum praestat omnibus, quod bonam spem
praelucet in posterum nec debilitari animos aut cadere patitur.
80 Verum etiam amicum qui intuetur, tamquam exemplar aliquod

81. **quocirca:** adv., *therefore.*
    et . . . et (82): POLYSYNDETON emphasizes the point.
    et absentes: *(friends) even though absent.*
82. **imbecilli:** *weak.*
83. **desiderium:** *longing, grief.*
    amicorum: SUBJECTIVE GEN.
84. **illorum . . . horum:** i.e., the deceased and their surviving friends.
    beata . . . laudabilis: PRED. ADJS., contrasted through CHIASMUS.
    quod si (85): *but if.*
85. **exemeris:** eximere, *to take away.*
    coniunctionem: here, *bond.*
87. **id:** i.e., the assertion in the preceding sentence.
    minus: adv. = **non.**
    concordiae . . . discordiis (88): Cicero plays on the shared etymology of the
    two words, both of which are based on **cor, cordis,** *heart.*
89. **quae non . . . everti:** REL. CL. OF RESULT.
90. **discidiis:** discidium, *division, disagreement.*
    funditus: adv., *completely.*
91. **si quando:** *if ever.*
    officium: *dutiful action, service.*
92. **exstitit:** exsistere, *to stand forth, arise, appear.*
    adeundis: adire, here = *to incur.*
93. **efferat:** REL. CL. OF CHARACTERISTIC.
    clamores: sc. some appropriate vb. such as **facti (auditi, sublati) sunt.**
    tota cavea: *in the entire theater* (strictly the auditorium); the ABL. OF PLACE
    WHERE is regularly used without a prep. when the noun is modified by
    totus.
94. **M. Pacuvii:** *Marcus Pacuvius,* a tragic poet of the second cent. B.C. whose
    plays have not survived, despite his fame in antiquity; Laelius, as this
    passage indicates, was his patron.
    fabula: the regular word for *play* as well as *story.* This play was apparently
    based on Euripides' *Iphigenia among the Taurians,* in which the famous
    friends Orestes and Pylades are arrested by Thoas, king of the Taurians.
    Thoas has condemned Orestes to death but does not know which of the
    two strangers actually is Orestes, hence the setting for this display of
    loyalty between friends.
96. **ita ut erat:** i.e., *as was the case.*
97. **perseveraret:** perseverare, *to persevere, persist, insist.*
    stantes: i.e., the audience at the play.
    ficta: fingere, *to invent, imagine, make up.*
101. **hactenus:** adv., *thus far.*
102. **si quae . . . sunt:** *if there are any (other) things.*
    praeterea: adv., *beyond, besides.*
    eis: the professional philosophers alluded to in line 46.
    si videbitur (103): *if it seems best, if you please.*
103. **quaeritote:** fut. imper., a formal equivalent of **quaerite.**

intuetur sui. Quocirca et absentes adsunt et egentes abundant
et imbecilli valent et, quod difficilius dictu est, mortui vivunt;
tantus eos honos, memoria, desiderium prosequitur amicorum.
Ex quo illorum beata mors videtur, horum vita laudabilis. Quod
85 si exemeris ex rerum natura benevolentiae coniunctionem, nec
domus ulla nec urbs stare poterit; ne agri quidem cultus per-
manebit. Id si minus intellegitur, quanta vis amicitiae concordi-
aeque sit ex dissensionibus atque discordiis percipi potest. Quae
enim domus tam stabilis, quae tam firma civitas est quae non
90 odiis et discidiis funditus possit everti?—ex quo quantum boni
sit in amicitia iudicari potest. Itaque si quando aliquod officium
exstitit amici in periculis aut adeundis aut communicandis, quis
est qui id non maximis efferat laudibus? Qui clamores tota cavea
nuper in hospitis et amici mei M. Pacuvii nova fabula cum, ig-
95 norante rege uter esset Orestes, Pylades Orestem se esse diceret
ut pro illo necaretur; Orestes autem, ita ut erat, Orestem se esse
perseveraret. Stantes, plaudebant in re ficta: quid arbitramur in
vera facturos fuisse? Facile indicabat ipsa natura vim suam cum
homines, quod facere ipsi non possent, id recte fieri in altero
100 iudicarent. (22–24, excerpts)

Transition to a new topic.

Hactenus mihi videor de amicitia quid sentirem potuisse dicere. Si quae praeterea sunt (credo autem esse multa), ab eis, si
videbitur, qui ista disputant, quaeritote.

"Pylades and Orestes Brought as Victims before Iphigenia"
Benjamin West, 1766
Tate Gallery, London, Great Britain

104. **a te:** sc. **quaerimus.**

    quamquam: conj., *although* or, at the beginning of a sent. or a main cl., *and yet.*

105. **aliud quoddam (106):** lit., *a certain other thing* = *something quite different.*

106. **filum:** *thread,* hence metaphorically *style;* sc. **est.**

108. **illud:** subj. of **solet** and in appos. to the **utrum . . . an** cl., a double IND. QUEST.

    considerandum: PRED. ADJ., *deserving of consideration.*

109. **inopiam:** inopia, *need, want.*

110. **meritis:** meritum, *benefit, service.*

    quod . . . acciperet (111): = **(ut) quisque ab alio acciperet id quod ipse per se (accipere) minus posset.**

111. **vicissim:** adv., *in turn.*

    an: *or,* introducing the second part of the IND. QUEST., which itself has two parts, (1) **hoc esset proprium,** (2) **sed alia causa (esset) antiquior . . ..**

    hoc: i.e., the desire of mutual advantage just mentioned.

113. **profecta:** here, *derived.*

    alia causa: sc. **amicitiae esset.**

    amor . . . est (114): more etymologizing (see above on line 88).

114. **princeps est:** lit., *is foremost* = *is the chief principle.*

    coniungendam: coniungere, *to unite,* here *generate, show.*

115. **ab eis percipiuntur:** *are gained from those.*

116. **observantur:** here, *are honored.*

    temporis causa: *for the purposes of the moment.*

117. **quidquid est:** i.e., **in amicitia.**

118. **voluntarium:** *spontaneous.*

119. **orta:** sc. **esse.**

    applicatione: applicatio, *attachment, inclination.*

120. **cogitatione:** *from a consideration (of).*

    utilitatis: with **quantum.**

121. **quod:** = **et hoc** (i.e., this instinct which gives rise to friendship), conjunctive use of rel., subj. of the IND. QUEST.

122. **animadverti:** animadvertere, *to notice, observe.*

125. **caritate:** caritas, *affection, love.*

    dirimi: dirimere, *to sunder, break off, end.*

127. **nacti sumus:** nancisci, *to find.*

128. **congruamus:** congruere, *to come together, harmonize, agree.*

    lumen: *light.*

130. **adliciat:** adlicere, *to allure, attract.*

    quippe: adv. common in explanations, *indeed, certainly; quippe cum, inasmuch as.*

132. **C. Fabrici . . . M'. Curi:** *Gaius Fabricius Luscinus* and *Manius Curius Dentatus,* popular heroes in the war against Pyrrhus, were regarded as exemplars of honesty and virtuous living.

133. **usurpet:** usurpare, *to use, employ;* with **memoriam,** *cherish.*

134. **Tarquinium Superbum:** *Tarquinius Superbus,* Rome's last king, an Etruscan hated by the Romans and expelled in 510 B.C. (see Livy's "Legends of Early Rome" below).

FANNIUS. Nos autem a te potius: quamquam etiam ab
105 istis saepe quaesivi et audivi non invitus equidem, sed aliud
quoddam filum orationis tuae. (24–25)

The origin and basis of friendship is love, not practical advantage.

LAELIUS. Saepissime igitur mihi de amicitia cogitanti
maxime illud considerandum videri solet, utrum propter imbe-
cillitatem atque inopiam desiderata sit amicitia ut dandis reci-
110 piendisque meritis, quod quisque minus per se ipse posset, id
acciperet ab alio vicissimque redderet, an esset hoc quidem pro-
prium amicitiae, sed antiquior et pulchrior et magis a natura
ipsa profecta alia causa. Amor enim, ex quo amicitia nominata
est, princeps est ad benevolentiam coniungendam. Nam uti-
115 litates quidem etiam ab eis percipiuntur saepe qui simulatione
amicitiae coluntur et observantur temporis causa. In amicitia
autem nihil fictum est, nihil simulatum; et quidquid est, id est
verum et voluntarium. Quapropter a natura mihi videtur potius
quam indigentia orta amicitia, applicatione magis animi cum
120 quodam sensu amandi quam cogitatione quantum illa res utilitatis esset habitura. Quod quidem quale sit etiam in bestiis
quibusdam animadverti potest, quae ex se natos ita amant ad
quoddam tempus et ab eis ita amantur ut facile earum sensus
appareat. Quod in homine multo est evidentius—primum ex ea
125 caritate quae est inter natos et parentes, quae dirimi nisi de-
testabili scelere non potest; deinde, cum similis sensus exstitit
amoris, si aliquem nacti sumus cuius cum moribus et natura
congruamus, quod in eo quasi lumen aliquod probitatis et virtutis perspicere videamur. Nihil est enim virtute amabilius; nihil
130 quod magis adliciat ad diligendum, quippe cum propter virtutem et probitatem etiam eos quos numquam vidimus quodam
modo diligamus. Quis est qui C. Fabrici, M'. Curi non cum caritate aliqua et benevolentia memoriam usurpet, quos numquam
viderit? Quis autem est qui Tarquinium Superbum non oderit?

135.   **est decertatum:** impers. pass., *it was fought to the finish* = *we fought to the finish.*

  Pyrrho et Hannibale (136): *Pyrrhus,* king of the Greek state of Epirus, led the Greeks of south Italy in their resistance to Roman encroachment (280–275 B.C.); *Hannibal,* of course, was the Carthaginian leader in the Second Punic War (218–201 B.C.—see Livy's "Hannibal and the Second Punic War," below).

136.   **propter probitatem:** Pyrrhus was respected by the Romans, not least for an incident in which he returned to them a number of prisoners of war without ransom.

137.   **alienos:** here, *unfriendly.*

  crudelitatem: Roman views of Hannibal were especially hostile, as he had brought their empire to the brink of disaster.

142.   **usu:** *by experience,* i.e., by close social contact.

  perspicere: *to observe, note.*

144.   **studio:** here, *affection.*

145.   **consecutae sunt: consequi,** *to follow, result, follow up, pursue, gain.*

147.   **eius:** = **amicitiae.**

148.   **conglutinaret: conglutinare,** *to cement together.*

  dissolveret: sc. **amicitiam;** friendship would not be able to stand the test of adversity.

149.   **idcirco:** adv., *therefore, for that reason.*

150.   **ortum: ortus,** *rising, origin, source.*

151.   **perge: pergere,** *to continue.*

156.   **nam:** sc. **dicebat.**

  ut . . . ut (157): both **ut** cls. are subjs. of **incidere,** *to befall, happen* = *it often happened that.*

  non idem expediret: *the same thing was not expedient* or *useful* (to both the friends); i.e., their objectives and priorities had changed.

158.   **alias . . . alias:** adv., *at one time . . . at another.*

159.   **ingravescente: ingravescere,** *to grow heavy, become burdensome.*

  discidia: discidium, *separation, disagreement, alienation.*

  plerumque: adv., *generally.*

160.   **postularetur: postulare,** *to demand.*

161.   **adiutores: adiutor,** *helper, assistant.*

162.   **quatenus:** adv., *how far.*

163.   **Coriolanus:** *Coriolanus,* a patrician, was banished from Rome early in the 5th cent. B.C. for resisting the authority of the tribunes; subsequently he marched on Rome with a Volscian army but was dissuaded from his attack by his mother.

135   Cum duobus ducibus de imperio in Italia est decertatum, Pyrrho et Hannibale: ab altero propter probitatem eius non nimis alienos animos habemus; alterum propter crudelitatem semper haec civitas oderit.

    Quod si tanta vis probitatis est ut eam vel in eis quos num-
140 quam vidimus, vel—quod maius est—in hoste etiam diligamus, quid mirum est si animi hominum moveantur, cum eorum quibuscum usu coniuncti esse possunt virtutem et bonitatem perspicere videantur? Quamquam confirmatur amor et beneficio accepto et studio perspecto. Sed quamquam utilitates multae et
145 magnae consecutae sunt, non sunt tamen ab earum spe causae diligendi profectae. Sic amicitiam, non spe mercedis adducti, sed quod omnis eius fructus in ipso amore inest, expetendam putamus. Nam si utilitas conglutinaret, eadem commutata dissolveret. Sed quia natura mutari non potest, idcirco verae ami-
150 citiae sempiternae sunt. Ortum quidem amicitiae videtis.

    FANNIUS. Tu vero perge, Laeli.

    SCAEVOLA. Recte tu quidem. Quamobrem audiamus. (26–33, excerpts)

The difficulties of maintaining friendship throughout life.

    LAELIUS. Audite vero, optimi viri, ea quae saepissime inter me et Scipionem de amicitia disserebantur; quamquam ille
155 quidem nihil difficilius esse dicebat quam amicitiam usque ad extremam vitae diem permanere: nam vel ut non idem expediret incidere saepe, vel ut de re publica non idem sentiretur; mutari etiam mores hominum saepe dicebat, alias adversis rebus, alias aetate ingravescente; magna etiam discidia et plerumque iusta
160 nasci cum aliquid ab amicis quod rectum non esset postularetur, ut aut libidinis ministri aut adiutores essent ad iniuriam. (33–35, excerpts)

The proper use of friendship.

    Quamobrem id primum videamus, si placet, quatenus amor in amicitia progredi debeat. Numne, si Coriolanus habuit amicos, ferre contra patriam arma illi cum Coriolano debue-

166. **conciliatrix:** *uniter, promoter.*
    opinio: here, (a friend's) *belief (in).*
168. **sanciatur: sancire,** *to make sacred, ratify.*
170. **pro . . . fidem:** idiomatic in exclamations, *by the faith (of), in the name (of).*
    ut: in a limiting cl., as here, = *on the condition that, with the proviso that.*
171. **circumfluere:** *to overflow (with).*
172. **copiis:** i.e., *resources, wealth.*
177. **coluntur:** sc. **tyranni.**
    dumtaxat: adv., *at least, at any rate, only.*
179. **quod:** *and this,* obj. of **dixisse,** referring to the point made in the preceding
    sent. and in appos. with the IND. STATE. **se intellexisse.**
    Tarquinium: for *Tarquinius,* see note on line 134.
    exsulantem: exsulare, *to go into exile.*
182. **superbia:** *arrogance,* ABL. OF CAUSE.
    importunitate: importunitas, *insolence, inconsiderateness.*
186. **complexa est: complecti,** *to embrace.*
    efferuntur: *they are carried away,* i.e., with their arrogance and self-
    importance.
187. **fastidio: fastidium,** *scorn, disdain.*
    contumacia: *obstinacy, haughtiness.*
    insipiente: as **sapiens** is a *wise man,* **insipiens** is a fool.
188. **hoc:** obj. of **videre** and in appos. with the inf. phrases following, *you may
    observe this, that . . ..*
189. **commodis . . . moribus:** PRED. ABL. OF DESCRIPTION, *of agreeable character.*
190. **amicitias:** subj. of **sperni.**
    indulgeri: impers. pass. of an intransitive vb. + dat., *it is indulged in* = *they
    indulge in, enjoy.*
191. **cum plurimum . . . possint (192):** *when they are the most able* = *when they have
    the greatest influence.*
    facultatibus: facultas, *opportunity, means.*
193. **famulos: famulus,** *household slave.*
    vestem: vestis, *clothing.*
    egregiam: *extraordinary, splendid.*
    vasa pretiosa: we would say "fine china."
    amicos: sc. **sed.**
194. **ut ita dicam:** *so to speak,* used to qualify a somewhat extreme metaphor.
    supellectilem: supellex, *furniture, equipment.*

165 runt? Nulla est igitur excusatio peccati si amici causa peccaveris;
nam, cum conciliatrix amicitiae virtutis opinio fuerit, difficile
est amicitiam manere, si a virtute defeceris. Haec igitur lex in
amicitia sanciatur ut neque rogemus res turpis nec faciamus rogati. (36–40, excerpts)

The blessings of friendship cannot be bought.

170   Quis est—pro deorum fidem atque hominum!—qui velit, ut
neque diligat quemquam nec ipse ab ullo diligatur, circumfluere
omnibus copiis atque in omnium rerum abundantia vivere? Haec
enim est tyrannorum vita, nimirum in qua nulla fides, nulla caritas, nulla stabilis benevolentiae potest esse fiducia; omnia sem-
175 per suspecta atque sollicita, nullus locus amicitiae. Quis enim
aut eum diligat quem metuat, aut eum a quo se metui putet?
Coluntur tamen simulatione dumtaxat ad tempus. Quod si
forte, ut fit plerumque, ceciderint, tum intellegitur quam fuerint
inopes amicorum. Quod Tarquinium dixisse ferunt exsulantem:
180 tum se intellexisse quos fidos amicos habuisset, quos infidos,
cum iam neutris gratiam referre posset. Quamquam miror illa
superbia et importunitate si quemquam amicum habere potuit.
Atque ut huius, quem dixi, mores veros amicos parare non potuerunt, sic multorum opes praepotentium excludunt amicitias
185 fideles. Non enim solum ipsa fortuna caeca est, sed eos etiam
plerumque effecit caecos quos complexa est. Itaque efferuntur
fere fastidio et contumacia, nec quidquam insipiente fortunato
intolerabilius fieri potest. Atque hoc quidem videre licet—eos
qui antea commodis fuerunt moribus, imperio, potestate, pros-
190 peris rebus immutari, sperni ab eis veteres amicitias, indulgeri
novis. Quid autem stultius quam, cum plurimum copiis, facul-
tatibus, opibus possint, cetera parare quae parantur—pecunia,
equos, famulos, vestem egregiam, vasa pretiosa—amicos non
parare, optimam et pulcherrimam vitae, ut ita dicam, supellec-
195 tilem? (52–55)

197. **querebatur:** sc. **Scipio** as subj.
     omnibus in rebus: sc. **aliis;** i.e., besides friendship.

198. **capras . . . esse (200):** each of these two pairs of cls. is marked by parallelism,
     ASYNDETON, AND CHIASMUS **(dicere posse . . . non posse dicere** and **adhi-
     bere curam . . . neglegentis esse);** the devices are common in Cicero, who
     frequently uses CHIASMUS, as here, to underscore a contrast.
     capras: capra, *she-goat.*
     ovis: ovis, *sheep.*

199. **posse:** sc. **eos (homines)** here, and with the several infs. following, as subj. of
     the IND. STATE. depending on the speech implied in **querebatur.**

200. **deligendis: deligere,** *to choose, select.*
     neglegentis: acc., PRED. ADJ.

201. **notas: nota,** *mark.*

202. **sunt . . . eligendi (203):** sc. **homines (amici).**

203. **penuria:** *scarcity, lack.*
     iudicare . . . est (204): sc. **aliquem** as subj. of the inf.

204. **expertum:** agrees with the subj. of **iudicare;** with **nisi,** *unless having tested (a
     person)* = *unless he has tested (a person).*

205. **ita . . . potestatem (206):** i.e., in order to know the true worth of a friend, one
     must first make him a friend, so one cannot exercise perfect judgment
     in this matter without first taking a chance.

206. **prudentis:** PRED. GEN. OF POSSESSION, *it is the part of a prudent man.*
     sustinere: here, *to check, hold back.*
     ut cursum: *as (he would) a race;* as clarified by **equis temptatis** in the next
     line, the simile compares the rush to form a friendship with a chariot-
     race (a very popular form of entertainment among the Romans).

207. **quo:** = **ut,** introducing a PURPOSE CL.

208. **aliqua parte:** *in some degree, to some extent.*
     periclitatis: periclitari, *to test;* sometimes the perf. partic. of a deponent vb.
     has a pass. meaning, as here in this ABL. ABS.

209. **in parva pecunia:** i.e., in some transaction involving a small sum of money.
     leves: here, *unreliable.*

210. **parva . . . magna:** sc. **pecunia.**

211. **sin:** conj., *but if.*

212. **sordidum:** sc. **esse,** *that it is base.*

214. **ex altera parte:** Eng. would say *on one side* or *on the one hand.*
     ius: here, *bond;* the word refers to both the responsibilities and the privileges
     that friendship entails.

216. **obscuratum iri (217): obscurare,** *to hide, conceal, forget;* here, the relatively
     rare fut. pass. inf.

219. **versantur: versari,** *to be engaged in, take part in.*
     invenias: *would you find;* POTENTIAL SUBJUNCT.

220. **haec:** the considerations of wealth and power just discussed.

221. **plerisque:** *very many, most.*

Choosing friends.

Sed (saepe enim redeo ad Scipionem cuius omnis sermo erat de amicitia) querebatur quod omnibus in rebus homines diligentiores essent: capras et ovis quot quisque haberet dicere posse, amicos quot haberet non posse dicere; et in illis quidem
200 parandis adhibere curam, in amicis deligendis neglegentis esse nec habere quasi signa quaedam et notas, quibus eos qui ad amicitiam essent idonei iudicarent. Sunt igitur firmi et stabiles et constantes eligendi, cuius generis est magna penuria; et iudicare difficile est sane nisi expertum, experiendum autem est in
205 ipsa amicitia: ita praecurrit amicitia iudicium tollitque experiendi potestatem. Est igitur prudentis sustinere, ut cursum, sic impetum benevolentiae, quo utamur, quasi equis temptatis, sic amicitia, aliqua parte periclitatis moribus amicorum. Quidam saepe in parva pecunia perspiciuntur quam sint leves. Quidam
210 autem quos parva movere non potuit, cognoscuntur in magna. Sin vero erunt aliqui reperti qui pecuniam praeferre amicitiae sordidum existiment, ubi eos inveniemus qui honores, magistratus, imperia, potestates, opes amicitiae non anteponant, ut, cum ex altera parte proposita haec sint, ex altera ius amicitiae, non
215 multo illa malint? Imbecilla enim est natura ad contemnendam potentiam, quam etiam si neglecta amicitia consecuti sint, obscuratum iri arbitrantur, quia non sine magna causa sit neglecta amicitia. Itaque verae amicitiae difficillime reperiuntur in eis qui in honoribus reque publica versantur. Ubi enim istum invenias qui honorem amici anteponat suo? Quid?—haec ut omit-
220 venias qui honorem amici anteponat suo? Quid?—haec ut omittam, quam graves, quam difficiles plerisque videntur calamita-

222. **societates: societas,** *partnership, association, sharing.*
     ad quas: i.e., the depths of another's misfortunes.
     inventu qui: sc. **eos (homines)** as obj. of the supine and antecedent of the REL.
     CL. OF CHARACTERISTIC.
223. **Ennius:** see on line 63 above.
     amicus ... cernitur: the ALLITERATION and ASSONANCE are characteristic of
     Ennius' poetry; cp. our proverb, "A friend in need is a friend indeed."
224. **haec duo:** *these two points,* i.e., the two just discussed and summarized in **aut
     ... deserunt.**
     levitatis: *of fickleness;* GEN. OF THE CHARGE with **convincunt,** *convict.*
225. **bonis rebus:** i.e., their own good fortune.
     contemnunt: sc. **amicos.**
     malis: their friends' misfortune.
227. **hunc:** sc. **esse.**
230. **quamquam:** here, *to be sure, indeed.*
232. **tenuis:** *slender, modest, simple.*
     victus: *mode of living, food.*
     cultus: *lifestyle, refinement.*
     delectat: sg. because both subjs. constitute a single idea.
235. **cetera:** obj. of **putent.**
236. **nihilo:** **nihilum** is used as a collateral form of **nihil** when case distinction is
     necessary.
     ad unum: *to a man.*
237. **serpit: serpere,** *to creep, permeate.*
     nescio quo modo: a kind of parenthetical cl. equivalent to an adv., *I do not
     know how = somehow.*
238. **degendae: degere,** *to pass* (one's life), *live.*
     expertem: expers, + gen., *without a share in, free from, devoid of.*
240. **adminiculum:** *prop* (for vines), *support;* with **aliquod tamquam,** *some support,
     as it were.*
     adnititur: adniti, *to struggle toward, lean on.*
     in amicissimo quoque: *in the case of one's dearest friend as well.*
242. **illa prima:** i.e., to his first major points, that virtue is the source of friendship
     and that true friendship, therefore, can exist only among good men
     (above, lines 50–60).
     aliquando: adv., *at last.*
243. **conciliat: conciliare,** *to bring together, unite.*
244. **in ea ... in ea (245):** the ANAPHORA and ASYNDETON here are among several
     rhetorical devices that lend intensity to Laelius' closing remarks.
     convenientia: *harmony, agreement.*
247. **exardescit: exardescere,** *to become hot, glow, blaze forth;* the vb. continues the
     metaphor begun in **lumen.**
     sive ... sive (248): conj., *whether ... or.*
249. **amare:** the vb. has a more emotional and physical connotation than **diligere,**
     the sense of which is more rational and intellectual.
250. **efflorescit: efflorescere,** *to begin to flower, blossom;* another vivid metaphor.
251. **minus:** = **non.**

tum societates, ad quas non est facile inventu qui descendant. Quamquam Ennius recte: "Amicus certus in re incerta cernitur." Tamen haec duo levitatis et infirmitatis plerosque convincunt:
225 aut si in bonis rebus contemnunt aut in malis deserunt. Qui igitur utraque in re gravem, constantem, stabilem se in amicitia praestiterit, hunc ex maxime raro genere hominum iudicare debemus et paene divino. (62–64)

The universal appeal of friendship.

Una est enim amicitia in rebus humanis de cuius utilitate
230 omnes uno ore consentiunt; quamquam a multis virtus ipsa contemnitur et ostentatio esse dicitur. Multi divitias despiciunt, quos parvo contentos tenuis victus cultusque delectat. Honores vero, quorum cupiditate quidam inflammantur, quam multi ita contemnunt ut nihil inanius, nihil esse levius existiment; item-
235 que cetera, quae quibusdam admirabilia videntur, permulti sunt qui pro nihilo putent. De amicitia omnes ad unum idem sentiunt. Serpit enim nescio quo modo per omnium vitas amicitia, nec ullam aetatis degendae rationem patitur esse expertem sui. Sic natura solitarium nihil amat, semperque ad aliquod tam-
240 quam adminiculum adnititur quod in amicissimo quoque dulcissimum est. (86–88, excerpts)

Recapitulation and conclusion.

Ad illa prima redeamus eaque ipsa concludamus aliquando. Virtus, virtus inquam, C. Fanni et tu Q. Muci, et conciliat amicitias et conservat. In ea est enim convenientia rerum, in ea
245 stabilitas, in ea constantia; quae cum se extulit et ostendit suum lumen et idem aspexit agnovitque in alio, ad id se movet vicissimque accipit illud quod in altero est, ex quo exardescit sive amor sive amicitia. Utrumque enim dictum est ab amando; amare autem nihil est aliud nisi eum ipsum diligere quem ames,
250 nulla utilitate quaesita, quae tamen ipsa efflorescit ex amicitia, etiam si tu eam minus secutus sis. Sed quoniam res humanae

256. **vivit tamen semperque vivet:** CHIASMUS emphasizes Laelius' point.
259. **tribuit:** tribuere, *to grant, bestow.*
260. **quod . . . senserim (261):** idiom, *so far as I observed.*
261. **una . . . erat (262):** sc. **nobis,** = *we had . . ..*
262. **communis:** *shared.*
     militia: *military service.*
263. **peregrinationes:** peregrinatio, *foreign travel.*
     rusticationes: rusticatio, *visit to the country.*
     quid . . . dicam (264): *why should I speak;* the DELIBERATIVE SUBJUNCT. is often
        more rhetorical than real, as here, where the meaning in effect is *there is
        no need for me to speak.*
266. **contrivimus:** conterere, *to wear out, consume, spend.*
     una: adv., *along, together.*
268. **illa:** i.e., his experiences with Scipio.
269. **augentur:** augere, *to increase.*
270. **magnum . . . solacium:** the wide separation of adj. and noun is likely meant
        to emphasize the degree of solace Laelius felt.
     aetas: i.e., his own age. Laelius was about 60 at the time of the dialogue; the
        date of his death is unknown, though the remarks Cicero attributes to
        him here suggest that he may not have lived much later than 129 B.C.,
        the year that Scipio died and the dramatic date of this dialogue.
271. **in hoc desiderio:** *in this state of bereavement.*
273. **haec . . . dicerem:** a conventional formula for concluding a discussion, =
        these are the things I had to say.
     ut . . . locetis (274): *that you place* or *rank.*
275. **praestabilius:** *more excellent, better.*

fragiles caducaeque sunt, semper aliqui anquirendi sunt quos diligamus et a quibus diligamur; caritate enim benevolentiaque
255 sublata, omnis est e vita sublata iucunditas. Mihi quidem Scipio, quamquam est subito ereptus, vivit tamen semperque vivet; virtutem enim amavi illius viri quae exstincta non est.

Equidem ex omnibus rebus, quas mihi aut fortuna aut natura tribuit, nihil habeo quod cum amicitia Scipionis possim
260 comparare. Numquam illum ne minima quidem re offendi quod quidem senserim; nihil audivi ex eo ipse quod nollem. Una domus erat, idem victus isque communis; neque militia solum sed etiam peregrinationes rusticationesque communes. Nam quid ego de studiis dicam cognoscendi semper aliquid atque dis-
265 cendi, in quibus, remoti ab oculis populi, omne otiosum tempus contrivimus? Quarum rerum recordatio et memoria si una cum illo occidisset, desiderium coniunctissimi atque amantissimi viri ferre nullo modo possem. Sed nec illa exstincta sunt alunturque potius et augentur cogitatione et memoria mea; et si illis plane
270 orbatus essem, magnum tamen affert mihi aetas ipsa solacium, diutius enim iam in hoc desiderio esse non possum; omnia autem brevia tolerabilia esse debent etiam si magna sunt.

Haec habui quae de amicitia dicerem. Vos autem hortor ut ita virtutem locetis, sine qua amicitia esse non potest, ut, ea
275 excepta, nihil amicitia praestabilius putetis. (100–04, excerpts)

"School of Athens" (with Plato and Aristotle at center)
Raphael, 1508
Stanze di Raffaelo, Vatican Palace, Vatican State

LIVY'S HISTORY OF ROME: "LEGENDS OF EARLY ROME" AND "HANNIBAL AND THE 2ND PUNIC WAR"

Titus Livius, "Livy" as he is commonly known, is one of the most highly regarded of Rome's historians. Born in the prosperous north Italian town of Patavium (modern Padua), possibly in 59 B.C., he was likely educated there before moving to Rome. Concerning his life we have remarkably few details: he was married (perhaps to a Cassia Prima), had two sons and a daughter, and came to know well and in many respects admire the emperor Augustus. The region around Patavium was noted for its stern moral conservatism, which proved to be an important influence on Livy's works, a corpus that included some early philosophical dialogues (now lost) and his monumental 142-volume history of Rome, the *Ab Urbe Condita* ("From the Founding of the City").

Writing during the reign of Augustus, Livy shared the emperor's concern over the moral decline that plagued Roman society; "we can tolerate neither our vices nor their remedies" *(nec vitia nostra nec remedia pati possumus),* he wrote in the Preface to his history. Nevertheless, as he also makes clear in his Preface, he intended his work to be a kind of remedy, a moral remedy, and many of his narratives, especially those looking back to the early republic, were designed and choreographed to portray the glory days of a heroic past as an exemplum for present and future generations. Although Livy was obviously not, therefore, a strictly scientific historian in our sense of the word, he did employ a range of literary sources, often comparing different accounts, and his rich pages provide an accurate assessment of what his fellow Romans thought about the *mores* and *gravitas* and *fides* and *virtus* of their forebears.

Livy's ethical didacticism and the frequently epic qualities of his narrative have caused his work, and rightly so, to be regarded in certain respects as the prose counterpart to the *Aeneid,* the grand epic of his somewhat older contemporary Vergil. Not only does the *Ab Urbe Condita* begin with an account of Aeneas' wanderings, which Livy acknowledges is more akin to the tales poets tell than to genuine history, but the diction of his writing is very often, and deliberately, dramatic and rhetorical (with its many speeches in both direct and indirect discourse), and highly poetic. The first-century A.D. rhetorician and educator Quintilian referred to the "milky richness" *(lactea ubertas)* of his style, a quality that readers of the following selections will come to savor.

Of Livy's original 142 volumes, composed over a period of about 40 years (ca. 25 B.C.–A.D. 17, the year of his death) and ranging from Rome's founding down to 9 B.C., only Books 1–10 and 21–45 survive essentially intact; we have, in addition, some fragments and quotations from later authors, as well as brief summaries *(periochae),* composed in the fourth century, of nearly all the missing books. The passages excerpted for this volume include, from Books One and Two, some of the best known legends of early Rome (Romulus and Remus, the Horatii and the Curiatii, the expulsion of the Tarquins, Horatius at the bridge) and, from Books 21–22, Hannibal's invasion of Italy and his stunning victories over the Romans at Trasimene in 217 B.C. and the next year at Cannae, one of the most disastrous military defeats in European history. Readers will appreciate throughout these selections Livy's consummate narrative skill and his steadfastly patriotic aim of demonstrating the valor and high moral character of the Roman people and their heroes even in the face of catastrophic adversity.

Battle of Cannae
Illuminated manuscript
Inv. RF 5271
Louvre
Paris, France

1. **Proca:** Livy has just recounted the legend of Aeneas' founding of Lavinium, of his son Ascanius' transfer of the people to Alba Longa, and of the succession of Alban kings down to Proca, the father of Numitor and Amulius.

   regnat: Livy frequently employs the HIST. PRES. tense.

2. **stirpis: stirps,** *trunk, stock, family, lineage.*

   maximus: i.e., in years, *oldest.*

   Silviae gentis (3): so-called after Silvius, the son of Ascanius.

3. **legat: legare,** *to appoint, bequeath.*

4. **plus ... potuit:** i.e., *had greater power.*

   verecundia: *respect, reverence;* with **aetatis,** the respect due to Numitor's seniority.

6. **interemit: interimere,** *to take away, destroy, kill.*

   filiae Reae Silviae: in Eng. usually spelled *Rhea Silvia;* DAT. OF SEPARATION with **adimit.**

   speciem: species, *view, appearance, semblance.*

7. **Vestalem:** the Vestal Virgins in the service of the goddess of hearth fire took a vow of chastity; breaking this vow meant death.

8. **partus:** gen. of **partus,** *offspring, giving birth.*

   adimit: adimere, *to take away.*

9. **debebatur ... fatis:** a recurrent theme also in Vergil's *Aeneid;* the vb. is sg. as the subjs. **origo** and **principium** constitute a single idea.

10. **secundum:** prep. + acc., *following, after.*

11. **edidisset: edere,** *to give forth, give birth to.*

    seu ... seu: = **sive ... sive,** *whether ... or.*

    rata: reri, *to think, believe;* sc. **est.**

    deus auctor (12): i.e., *(having) a god as. . . .*

12. **honestior:** *more honorable,* pred. adj.

    Martem: *Mars,* the god of warriors and warfare, second only to Jupiter in his importance to the Romans.

13. **nuncupat: nuncupare,** *to name.*

    dii: = **dei; dii** and **di** are alternative nom. pl. forms.

14. **vincta: vincire,** *to bind.*

15. **iubet:** sc. **rex.**

16. **divinitus:** adv., *divinely, providentially.*

    ripas: ripa, *bank (of a river).*

    Tiberis: *Tiber River;* subj. of both **poterat** and **dabat.**

    effusus: effundere, *to pour out.*

17. **stagnis: stagnum,** *standing water, pool;* sc. **in.**

    iusti ... amnis: i.e., *of its regular stream.*

    posse ... infantes (18): IND. STATE., depending on **spem ... dabat; infantes** serves as both obj. of **ferentibus** and subj. of **posse mergi.**

18. **quamvis languida ... aqua:** *by the water however sluggish.*

19. **velut:** adv., *as, just as, as if.*

    defuncti: defungi, *to perform, discharge, complete* + abl.; the partic. here is nom., agreeing with the subj. of **exponunt.**

    adluvie: adluvies, *overflow, pool, floodwater.*

LEGENDS OF EARLY ROME

Romulus and Remus

The birth of Romulus and Remus and their abandonment on the banks of the Tiber River.

Proca deinde regnat. Is Numitorem atque Amulium procreat; Numitori, qui stirpis maximus erat, regnum vetustum Silviae gentis legat.

Plus tamen vis potuit quam voluntas patris aut verecundia
5 aetatis. Pulso fratre, Amulius regnat. Addit sceleri scelus: stirpem fratris virilem interemit, fratris filiae Reae Silviae per speciem honoris, cum Vestalem eam legisset, perpetua virginitate spem partus adimit.

Sed debebatur, ut opinor, fatis tantae origo urbis maximique
10 secundum deorum opes imperii principium. Vi compressa Vestalis cum geminum partum edidisset, seu ita rata seu quia deus auctor culpae honestior erat, Martem incertae stirpis patrem nuncupat. Sed nec dii nec homines aut ipsam aut stirpem a crudelitate regia vindicant: sacerdos vincta in custodiam datur;
15 pueros in profluentem aquam mitti iubet.

Forte quadam divinitus super ripas Tiberis effusus lenibus stagnis nec adiri usquam ad iusti cursum poterat amnis et posse quamvis languida mergi aqua infantes spem ferentibus dabat. Ita velut defuncti regis imperio in proxima adluvie, ubi nunc

She-wolf with Romulus and Remus
Etruscan bronze, ca. 500 B.C. (the infants a later addition)
Museo Capitolino, Rome, Italy

20.   **ficus Ruminalis:** *the fig-tree Ruminalis,* on the slope of the Palatine hill where there was a temple of Rumina, goddess of suckling infants.

Romularem: *of Romulus;* the Romans were fond of etymologizing and readily associated the name **Ruminalis** with their founding king Romulus.

vocatam: sc. **esse;** agreeing in gender with **ficus,** which, like most trees (and the word **arbor**), is f.

21.   **solitudines:** in contrast to the dense population in Livy's time.

22.   **tenet fama:** cp. our idiom "rumor has it"; the expression takes an IND. STATE. **(lupam . . . flexisse; eam . . . praebuisse).**

fluitantem: **fluitare,** *to flow, float.*

alveum: alveus, *trough, tub, basket.*

23.   **tenuis:** *slender, thin;* here, *shallow, receding.*

in sicco: siccus, *dry;* sc. **loco.** Livy often employs adjs. substantively.

24.   **vagitum: vagitus,** *crying.*

25.   **adeo:** adv., *to such a degree, so.*

mitem: with **eam,** *gently;* Lat. often uses an adj. in the pred. where Eng. would employ an adv.

26.   **lambentem: lambere,** *to lick.*

pecoris: pecus, *flock.*

Faustulo . . . nomen (27): i.e., **nomen fuisse (ei) Faustulo; Faustulo** is attracted into the case of the understood pron. **ei** (DAT. OF POSSESSION), *he had the name Faustulus.*

27.   **ferunt:** *they say;* the vb. is common in this sense (cp. **fertur** below, *is said*) and often, as here, takes an IND. STATE.

ad stabula: *at his hut;* from **stabulum,** *stable, lodging.*

28.   **datos:** sc. **esse** and **pueros** as subj., still dependent on **tenet fama.**

29.   **Albana re:** sc. **publica,** *the Alban state;* after Romulus and Remus had reached maturity, they discovered their true identities, murdered Amulius, and restored Numitor to the throne at Alba Longa.

30.   **urbis condendae (31):** depends on **cupido;** the phrase recalls the title of Livy's history, *Ab Urbe Condita.*

31.   **supererat: superesse,** *to be left over, survive,* here *to be excessive;* Alba Longa had become overpopulated.

32.   **ad id:** *to this* (number).

accesserant: adcedere, *to go to, approach, be added;* i.e., the population had also been increased by the shepherds (among whom Romulus and Remus had been reared).

qui . . . facerent: *who altogether could easily hope,* i.e., whose combined numbers were so great that they were encouraged in their plans; a REL. CL. OF RESULT.

33.   **parvam:** PRED. ADJ. with **Albam . . . fore.**

prae: prep. + abl.; here, *in comparison with.*

conderetur: SUBORDINATE CL. IN IND. STATE.

34.   **avitum:** *ancestral,* referring in particular to Amulius and Numitor.

35.   **foedum:** *foul, base, shameful.*

certamen: *contest, struggle, fight.*

coortum: sc. **est;** from **cooriri,** *to arise, break out.*

20   ficus Ruminalis est (Romularem vocatam ferunt), pueros expo-
nunt. Vastae tum in his locis solitudines erant.

The twins are suckled by a wolf and reared by Faustulus.

Tenet fama, cum fluitantem alveum, quo expositi erant
pueri, tenuis in sicco aqua destituisset, lupam sitientem ex montibus, qui circa sunt, ad puerilem vagitum cursum flexisse; eam
25   summissas infantibus adeo mitem praebuisse mammas ut lingua lambentem pueros magister regii pecoris invenerit—Faustulo fuisse nomen ferunt; ab eo ad stabula Laurentiae uxori
educandos datos.

Now grown, the twins wish to found a city on the Palatine and agree to
decide the leadership by augury.

Ita Numitori Albana re permissa, Romulum Remumque cu-
30   pido cepit in iis locis, ubi expositi ubique educati erant, urbis
condendae. Et supererat multitudo Albanorum Latinorumque;
ad id pastores quoque accesserant qui omnes facile spem facerent parvam Albam, parvum Lavinium prae ea urbe quae conderetur fore. Intervenit deinde his cogitationibus avitum ma-
35   lum, regni cupido, atque inde foedum certamen coortum a satis

"Romulus and Remus"
Peter Paul Rubens
17th century
Museo Capitolino
Rome, Italy

36.   **miti:** here, *innocent* or *uncontroversial.*
       essent: SUBJUNCT. OF QUOTED REASON.
37.   **ut . . . legerent (38):** dependent on the main vb. **capiunt.**
       quorum . . . essent: lit., *of whose protection these places were = under whose*
          protection the region was; the vb. is SUBJUNCT. BY ATTRACTION.
38.   **auguriis: augurium,** *augury, omen;* also known as "taking the auspices" (from
          avis, *bird*), this was the practice of determining the will of the gods by
          interpreting the flight of birds or similar omens.
       qui . . . daret, qui . . . regeret (39): REL. CL. OF PURPOSE, or, construing **qui** as
          interrogative (= **uter**), IND. QUEST.
39.   **Palatium Romulus, Remus Aventinum:** CHIASMUS; the Palatine and Aventine
          hills are adjacent.
       inaugurandum: inaugurare, *to take the auguries.*
40.   **templa:** *as sacred precincts,* in appos. with **Palatium** and **Aventinum;** originally
          templum indicated simply a sacred area marked out in the sky or on the
          ground as a place for taking omens or as a spot sacred to a divinity.
41.   **priori Remo:** *for Remus first (sooner),* DAT. OF REF.; the position of **priori** at
          the beginning of the sentence emphasizes Remus' advantage in time;
          Romulus' advantage was in quantity.
       sex vultures: in appos. with **augurium.**
43.   **multitudo:** i.e., of supporters.
       tempore . . . praecepto (44): lit., *the time (of the omen) having been taken as*
          foremost, i.e., on the grounds that they had received their omen sooner;
          CHIASMUS **(tempore illi . . . hi numero)** accentuates the conflicting claims.
44.   **trahebant:** *kept claiming.*
       cum altercatione: *in a dispute, in conflict of words.*
45.   **certamine:** ABL. OF CAUSE.
       irarum: the pl. emphasizes the *angry feelings* on both sides.
       caedem: caedes, *cutting, slaughter, murder.*
       ibi . . . cecidit (46): the very brevity of the sentence emphasizes the quickness
          with which the hotheaded brawl was over.
46.   **ictus: icere,** *to strike, hit.*
       vulgatior: not *more vulgar* but *more commonly known.*
       fama est: this construction typically governs an IND. STATE, here **Remum . . .**
          transiluisse . . . inde . . . interfectum (esse).
       ludibrio: ludibrium, *mockery, derision;* DAT. OF PURPOSE.
47.   **transiluisse: transilire,** *to leap over.*
       muros: murus, *wall.* According to this version, Romulus had apparently de-
          cided for himself that his omens were superior and had immediately
          begun constructing his walls, to a height of perhaps three or four feet,
          by the time Remus happened along; the walls followed the pomerium, a
          consecrated plowed boundary around the city, and so Remus' leap was
          actually an act of sacrilege.
       inde: adv., *thence, after that, thereupon.*
48.   **increpitans: increpitare,** *to call out to, reproach, rebuke.*
       sic: sc. **pereat.**
       quicumque: *whoever.*

miti principio. Quoniam gemini essent nec aetatis verecundia discrimen facere posset, ut dii, quorum tutelae ea loca essent, auguriis legerent qui nomen novae urbi daret, qui conditam imperio regeret, Palatium Romulus, Remus Aventinum ad inaugurandum templa capiunt.

40

Remus is killed in an ensuing quarrel, and Romulus gains sole power.

Priori Remo augurium venisse fertur, sex vultures; iamque nuntiato augurio cum duplex numerus Romulo sese ostendisset, utrumque regem sua multitudo consalutaverat. Tempore illi praecepto, at hi numero avium regnum trahebant. Inde cum altercatione congressi, certamine irarum ad caedem vertuntur. Ibi in turba ictus Remus cecidit. Vulgatior fama est ludibrio fratris Remum novos transiluisse muros, inde ab irato Romulo, cum verbis quoque increpitans adiecisset "Sic deinde quicumque

45

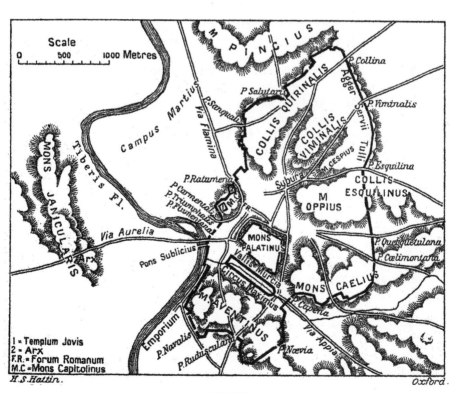

ROME

49. **potitus . . . appellata (50):** sc. **est** with each; like other Lat. writers, Livy often omits forms of **esse** when easily understood from the context.

51. **duobus . . . exercitus:** i.e., of Rome and Alba Longa. After Romulus had firmly established the Roman state and its constitution, and then mysteriously vanished in a storm and was transformed into the god Quirinus, the people elected as their king Numa, a man of peace and piety who was credited with having systematized Roman religious institutions. Rome's third king was the warlike Tullus Hostilius, among whose campaigns was one against Alba, the very city from which Romulus had come. To avoid great bloodshed in what amounted to a civil war, both sides agreed to the plan recounted in the following passage.

     trigemini: *triplet.*

52. **aetate . . . viribus:** ABL. OF SPECIFICATION with **dispares.**

53. **constat:** impers., *it is agreed.*

     nec ferme: *and scarcely, and hardly.*

     res: here, *story, tradition.*

     nobilior: *more renowned, well known.*

54. **error:** *confusion, uncertainty.*

     utrius populi: i.e., whether Roman or Alban.

55. **utroque:** adv., *in both directions;* i.e., Livy's sources were divided over the question.

     trahunt: sc. **nos.**

56. **qui . . . vocent:** REL. CL. OF CHARACTERISTIC.

     Horatios: OBJ. COMPLEM.

57. **agunt:** *negotiate, arrange.*

     dimicent: dimicare, *to fight, struggle;* **quisque** often takes a pl. vb., *they should each . . ..*

58. **fore:** depends on idea of speech implicit in the preceding cl.

59. **convenit: convenire,** *to come together, meet, be agreed upon;* often impers., *it is agreed* (so **convenerat,** 63). Here, where we would say *are agreed upon,* the compound subj. is thought of as a single idea, hence the sg. vb.

     dimicarent: the ANTICIPATORY SUBJUNCT. is used with **antequam** and **priusquam** to express anticipation or purpose, *before they should fight.*

     foedus: *treaty, pact.*

     ictum . . . est (60): the thought develops from striking a sacrificial victim by which a treaty is sanctified to simply ratifying or "striking" a treaty.

60. **his legibus:** *on these conditions* (lit., *in accordance with these laws*), which are explained by the appos. cl. **ut . . . imperitaret.**

     cuius populi: *whichever nation's.*

61. **vicissent:** SUBJUNCT. BY ATTRACTION within the JUSSIVE NOUN CL.

     is: sc. **populus** from the preceding **populi.**

     cum bona pace: i.e., *in peace and harmony.*

alius transiliet moenia mea!" interfectum. Ita solus potitus im-
50   perio Romulus; condita urbs conditoris nomine appellata.
(I.3.10–7.3, excerpts)

The Horatii and the Curiatii

*Arrangements for settling a war between Rome and Alba by a fight
between two sets of triplets, one from each city.*

    Forte in duobus tum exercitibus erant trigemini fratres nec
aetate nec viribus dispares. Horatios Curiatiosque fuisse satis
constat, nec ferme res antiqua alia est nobilior; tamen in re tam
clara nominum error manet, utrius populi Horatii, utrius Cu-
55   riatii fuerint. Auctores utroque trahunt; plures tamen invenio
qui Romanos Horatios vocent; hos ut sequar inclinat animus.
    Cum trigeminis agunt reges ut pro sua quisque patria dimi-
cent ferro: ibi imperium fore unde victoria fuerit. Nihil recusa-
tur, tempus et locus convenit. Priusquam dimicarent, foedus ic-
60   tum inter Romanos et Albanos est his legibus ut, cuius populi
cives eo certamine vicissent, is alteri populo cum bona pace imperitaret.

"The Oath of the Horatii"
Jacques Louis David, 18th century
Louvre, Paris, France

64.   **sui:** *their own (people),* i.e., the people of each side.

    utrosque: their own set of triplets.

    deos . . . intueri (66): the IND. STATE., with its several subjs. and two objs. **(arma . . . manus)** is dependent on the speech act implied in **adhortarentur,** *urged them on (saying that . . .).*

65.   **quidquid . . . quidquid . . . illorum . . . illorum (66):** note how Livy's use of short, rapid-fire phrases, together with ANAPHORA, ASYNDETON, and ALLITERATION **(patrios, patriam, parentes),** add intensity to the narrative.

    civium: PARTITIVE GEN. with the indef. **quidquid.**

66.   **et . . . et:** the regular order would be **et feroces . . . et pleni.**

    suopte: **-pte** is an indecl. suffix with intensive force, *very own.*

    pleni: the adj. can be used with either the gen. (as in the Eng. idiom) or the abl. (of means), as here.

69.   **expertes: expers,** adj. + gen., *having no part in, free from.*

    quippe: adv., *for, indeed.*

    agebatur: *was at stake.*

72.   **infestis:** *unsafe, dangerous, hostile.*

    terni: distributive numeral, *three each = the three young men on each side.*

74.   **increpuere:** = **increpuerunt;** from **increpare,** *to rattle, make a loud noise, reproach, rebuke.*

    arma: strictly the defensive arms, and here probably the shields.

    micantes: micare, *to shake, shine, flash, sparkle.*

75.   **spectantis:** = **spectantes.**

    perstringit: perstringere, *to affect deeply, strike, move.*

    neutro: adv., *to neither side.*

    torpebat . . . spiritusque (76): torpere, *to be stiff, sluggish, numb, stupefied;* i.e., they seemed unable to speak or even breathe.

    consertis . . . manibus: conserere, *to connect, join, engage (in battle);* i.e., in hand to hand fighting.

77.   **anceps:** here, *on both sides.*

    telorum: telum, *missile, javelin, spear, weapon.*

78.   **vulnera . . . et sanguis:** HENDIADYS = *bloody wounds.*

    spectaculo essent: *were for a sight* (DAT. OF PURPOSE) = *were to be seen.*

80.   **corruerunt: corruere,** *to fall together, fall to the ground.*

    quorum: = **eorum;** where Eng. would use a pers. pron., Livy, like other class. authors, often employed the rel. pron. at the beginning of a sentence, with its antecedent in the preceding sentence.

81.   **legiones: legio,** *legion* or, here, any *military force.*

82.   **deseruerat: deserere,** *to desert.*

    exanimes: *lifeless, breathless* (here, with horror).

    vice: vicis, *change, vicissitude, lot, plight, fate;* ABL. OF CAUSE.

83.   **ut . . . sic (84):** *as . . . so,* but here better rendered *although . . . nevertheless.*

    universis: *all together.*

    nequaquam: adv., *by no means.*

As the armies of both cities watch the contest, the tension mounts.

Foedere icto, trigemini sicut convenerat arma capiunt. Cum
sui utrosque adhortarentur, deos patrios, patriam ac parentes,
65   quidquid civium domi, quidquid in exercitu sit, illorum tunc
arma, illorum intueri manus, feroces et suopte ingenio et pleni
adhortantium vocibus, in medium inter duas acies procedunt.
Consederant utrimque pro castris duo exercitus, periculi magis
praesentis quam curae expertes; quippe imperium agebatur in
70   tam paucorum virtute atque fortuna positum. Itaque ergo erecti
suspensique in minime gratum spectaculum animos intendunt.

The battle begins, and one surviving Roman kills the three Albans.

Datur signum infestisque armis, velut acies, terni iuvenes
magnorum exercituum animos gerentes concurrunt. Ut primo
statim concursu increpuere arma micantesque fulsere gladii,
75   horror ingens spectantis perstringit; et neutro inclinata spe, tor-
pebat vox spiritusque. Consertis deinde manibus, cum iam non
motus tantum corporum agitatioque anceps telorum armorum-
que sed vulnera quoque et sanguis spectaculo essent, duo Romani super alium alius, vulneratis tribus Albanis, expirantes
80   corruerunt. Ad quorum casum cum conclamasset gaudio Albanus exercitus, Romanas legiones iam spes tota, nondum tamen
cura deseruerat, exanimes vice unius quem tres Curiatii circum-
steterant. Forte is integer fuit, ut universis solus nequaquam par,
sic adversus singulos ferox. Ergo ut segregaret pugnam eorum,

Battle scene between
Romans and barbarians
Relief on sarcophagus
Portonaccio, Italy
1st–3rd centuries A.D.
Museo Nazionale Romano
Rome, Italy

85.   **capessit:** from **capere** + the desiderative infix **-ess-**, which indicates eagerness.
  ita . . . ut: *in such a way as,* i.e., as quickly as; **ut** in this sense ordinarily takes
   an indic. but here introduces **sineret** (from **sinere,** *to allow*), subjunct. in
   a SUBORDINATE CL. WITHIN IND. STATE.
  ratus: reri, *to think, suppose.*
  secuturos: i.e., **eos secuturos esse.**
86.   **aliquantum spatii:** *some distance,* ACC. OF EXTENT OF SPACE + PARTITIVE GEN.
87.   **videt . . . sequentes (88):** sc. **eos.**
88.   **sequentes . . . abesse:** note the easy shift from partic. phrase to IND. STATE.
  procul: adv., *far off, at a distance.*
89.   **uti:** a common alternate form of **ut.**
90.   **caeso: caedere,** *to cut, beat, slay.*
91.   **qualis . . . solet (92):** i.e., **qualis clamor ex insperato faventium** (from **favere,**
   to support, favor) **esse solet,** freely, *such as is customary of supporters at*
   an unexpected turn of events.
  ex insperato: lit., *out of the unhoped for.*
93.   **prius . . . quam: priusquam** is often separated into its component elements,
   as here.
  alter . . . alterum (94): *the one* (the more distant of the two remaining Curiatii) . . . *the other* (the closer of the two).
94.   **et:** as often, = **etiam,** *also,* i.e., as well as the first brother.
  conficit: conficere, *to accomplish, finish, destroy, kill.*
  Marte: here, as often, *fight, contest.*
95.   **singuli:** *one on each side.*
  alterum: i.e., Horatius; the word must be obj. of **dabat,** since both in position
   and in usage it balances **alter** at the beginning of the next cl.
  intactum . . . corpus et geminata victoria (96): both are nom., subj. of **dabat.**
96.   **ferocem:** OBJ. COMPL. with **alterum,** the phrase neatly surrounding the compound subj.
97.   **fessum . . . fessum:** *weary, exhausted;* ANAPHORA and ASYNDETON effectively
   intensify the scene's pathos.
98.   **strage: strages,** *ruin, slaughter;* with **fratrum,** OBJ. GEN.
  obicitur: reflexive use of the pass. (sometimes called the MIDDLE VOICE), indicating the subj. acting upon himself; lit., *is cast before = casts himself*
   before, opposes.
  nec . . . fuit (99): i.e., the fight was so one-sided, it was not a real contest.
100. **manibus: manes,** *shades, ghosts;* the two slain Curiatii he regards as a kind of
   sacrifice to the dead, as in the case of Achilles' slaying of Hector.
  huiusce: the suffix **-ce** intensifies the demonstrative.

85   capessit fugam, ita ratus secuturos ut quemque vulnere adfectum corpus sineret. Iam aliquantum spatii ex eo loco ubi pugnatum est aufugerat, cum respiciens videt magnis intervallis sequentes, unum haud procul ab sese abesse. In eum magno impetu rediit, et dum Albanus exercitus inclamat Curiatiis uti
90   opem ferant fratri, iam Horatius, caeso hoste victor, secundam pugnam petebat. Tum clamore, qualis ex insperato faventium solet, Romani adiuvant militem suum et ille defungi proelio festinat. Prius itaque quam alter, qui nec procul aberat, consequi posset, et alterum Curiatium conficit. Iamque aequato Marte
95   singuli supererant, sed nec spe nec viribus pares. Alterum intactum ferro corpus et geminata victoria ferocem in certamen tertium dabat; alter, fessum vulnere, fessum cursu trahens corpus victusque fratrum ante se strage, victori obicitur hosti. Nec illud proelium fuit. Romanus exsultans "Duos," inquit, "fra-
100   trum manibus dedi; tertium causae belli huiusce, ut Romanus

"Battle of the Horatii and the Curiatii"
Cavaliere d'Arpino (Giuseppe Cesari), 17th century
Museo Capitolino, Rome, Italy

101. **male:** here, *scarcely, with difficulty;* the rapidity of this final sentence patheti-
      cally harmonizes with the words **nec illud proelium fuit.**

      sustinenti: sc. **ei,** DAT. OF REF.

      superne: adv., *from above.*

102. **iugulo: iugulum,** *throat;* sc. **in.** Like some other writers, especially the poets,
      Livy frequently omits a prep. where one would ordinarily be expected in
      class. Lat.

      defigit: defigere, *to fix, fasten, drive down.*

      spoliat: spoliare, *to strip, despoil, rob;* stripping the armor from a victim was
      common practice.

103. **ovantes: ovare,** *to rejoice, exult.*

      eo maiore . . . quo (104): *all the greater as.*

104. **res:** *the matter,* i.e., *the fight.*

      sepulturam: sepultura, *burial.*

106. **alteri . . . alteri:** *the one group . . . the other group.*

      aucti: augere, *to increase, enlarge,* or here *exalt.*

      dicionis alienae facti: *subjected to foreign control;* PRED. GEN. OF POSSESSION, a
      construction found often in Livy.

107. **quo . . . loco:** *where.*

108. **distantia locis:** *standing apart in their locations = separated.*

      ut et: *as also, just as.*

110. **addita:** sc. **est,** *was added,* i.e., to his other condemnatory remarks. Sextus
      Tarquinius (son of Lucius Tarquinius Superbus, the seventh king of
      Rome) had raped Lucretia, the wife of Tarquinius Collatinus, a trusting
      fellow army officer. Then, when she had called upon Collatinus, Lucius
      Junius Brutus, and others to swear vengeance against Sextus, Lucretia
      committed suicide and was buried at Collatia. Vowing the ouster of Su-
      perbus ("the Arrogant") and his family, Brutus hurried to Rome and
      delivered to an assembly in the Forum an intense oration, which Livy
      here recounts, about the fate of Lucretia and the crimes of Superbus.

112. **regi:** DAT. OF SEPARATION.

      abrogaret: abrogare, *to repeal, abrogate, take away.*

113. **coniuge: coniunx,** *wife.*

      ultro: adv., *to the farther side, beyond, voluntarily.*

114. **concitandum: concitare,** *to stir up, excite.*

115. **Ardeam:** *Ardea,* a town in Latium which Tarquinius Superbus was besieging
      at the time.

116. **Lucretio:** *Lucretius,* father of the dead Lucretia.

      praefecto: praefectus, *overseer, commander, prefect.*

117. **re nova:** a *new thing* politically is a *revolution.*

118. **pergeret: pergere,** *to go on, keep on, continue, proceed.*

119. **obvius fieret:** *become in the way = meet.*

121. **clausae . . . indictum:** sc. **sunt** and **est.**

122. **inde:** i.e., **ex castris.**

125. **regnatum:** sc. **est;** impers. pass., *it was ruled = kings ruled.*

      ad liberatam: sc. **urbem,** *to the liberation of . . ..*

Albano imperet, dabo." Male sustinenti arma gladium superne
iugulo defigit; iacentem spoliat.

The dead are buried and the Albans accept Roman rule.

Romani ovantes ac gratulantes Horatium accipiunt, eo maiore cum gaudio quo prope metum res fuerat. Ad sepulturam
105 inde suorum nequaquam paribus animis vertuntur, quippe imperio alteri aucti, alteri dicionis alienae facti. Sepulcra exstant
quo quisque loco cecidit, duo Romana uno loco propius Albam, tria Albana Romam versus, sed distantia locis, ut et pugnatum est. (I.24.1–25.14, excerpts)

The End of the Kingdom and the Beginning of the Republic

The last of the Etruscan Tarquins are expelled from Rome.

110 Addita superbia ipsius regis miseriaeque et labores plebis.
His atrocioribusque aliis memoratis, incensam multitudinem
perpulit ut imperium regi abrogaret exsulesque esse iuberet
L. Tarquinium cum coniuge ac liberis. Ipse, iunioribus qui ultro
nomina dabant lectis armatisque, ad concitandum inde adver-
115 sus regem exercitum Ardeam in castra est profectus. Imperium
in urbe Lucretio, praefecto urbis iam ante ab rege instituto, re-
linquit. Harum rerum nuntiis in castra perlatis, cum re nova
trepidus rex pergeret Romam ad comprimendos motus, flexit
viam Brutus (senserat enim adventum) ne obvius fieret; eodem-
120 que fere tempore diversis itineribus Brutus Ardeam, Tarquinius
Romam venerunt. Tarquinio clausae portae exsiliumque indictum; liberatorem urbis laeta castra accepere, exactique inde
liberi regis.

*In place of a king, two consuls are appointed, Lucius Junius Brutus and
Lucius Tarquinius Collatinus.*

L. Tarquinius Superbus regnavit annos quinque et viginti.
125 Regnatum Romae ab condita urbe ad liberatam annos ducentos

126. **consules:** an anachronism, as the two chief republican magistrates were originally called "praetors."

    comitiis centuriatis: the *comitia centuriata,* regularly pl. as here, was one of a number of Roman assemblies of the people.

127. **ex commentariis:** *according to the regulations;* according to tradition, Servius Tullius, the sixth Roman king, had created the centuriate assembly and a number of new political procedures.

129. **nescio an:** *I am unsure whether* (strictly speaking, **an** introduces the second part of a double question **utrum . . . an**).

    nimis: with **muniendo.**

    undique: adv., *from* or *on all sides, everywhere.*

    eam: sc. **libertatem,** i.e., the Romans' newly gained liberty.

    minimis . . . rebus: *in the most trivial details,* as indicated in the following episode.

130. **modum excesserint:** sc. **Romani;** Livy wonders whether the Romans may have gone too far in their efforts at protecting their freedom from tyranny.

    alterius: i.e., one of the two.

    nihil aliud offenderit (131): i.e., *he gave no other offense.*

    nomen: i.e., Tarquinius.

132. **adsuesse:** = **adsuevisse;** this and the following infs. are part of an understood IND. STATE. giving the people's reasons for **invisum,** i.e., *(people said that) the Tarquins had been too accustomed,* etc.

    penes: prep. + acc., *in the possession of.*

133. **Tarquinios:** subj. of **nescire,** *did not know how.*

    privatos: PRED. ADJ. after **vivere.**

135. **contionem: contio,** *assembly* (especially for a magistrate to address the people).

    populum Romanum: subj. of **credere** in an IND. STATE. depending on an understood speech verb ("Brutus argued that . . . ").

139. **absolve:** *free,* i.e., *complete.*

141. **auctore me:** freely, *at my request, under my authority.*

    deest: deesse, *to be lacking.*

    amicus: nom. not voc., *as a friend.*

142. **forsitan:** adv., *perhaps.*

143. **animis:** i.e., of the citizens; dat. with **persuasum est,** here an impers. pass., where Eng. would say, *the citizens' hearts have been persuaded.*

    regnum: here, *kingship, monarchy;* subj. of **abiturum (esse),** inf. in IND. STATE. after the impers. **persuasum est.**

144. **Lavinium:** a town in Latium said to have been founded by Aeneas; Collatinus would hardly dare to go to an Etruscan city because of his part in the expulsion of Tarquinius Superbus.

145. **tulit:** sc. **legem.**

147. **P. Valerium:** Brutus is generally regarded as an historical figure, but Collatinus and Valerius likely were not.

    quo adiutore: adiutor, *assistant;* ABL. ABS., freely, *with whose assistance.*

quadraginta quattuor. Duo consules inde comitiis centuriatis a praefecto urbis ex commentariis Servi Tulli creati sunt: L. Iunius Brutus et L. Tarquinius Collatinus. (I.59.9–60.4, excerpts)

Collatinus, though loyal, is asked to leave Rome because of his name.

  Ac nescio an, nimis undique eam minimisque rebus muni-
130 endo, modum excesserint. Consulis enim alterius, cum nihil aliud offenderit, nomen invisum civitati fuit: nimium Tarquinios regno adsuesse; pulso Superbo, penes Collatinum imperium esse; nescire Tarquinios privatos vivere; non placere nomen, periculosum libertati esse. Sollicitam suspicione plebem Brutus ad
135 contionem vocat: non credere populum Romanum solidam libertatem reciperatam esse; regium genus, regium nomen non solum in civitate sed etiam in imperio esse; id obstare libertati. "Hunc tu," inquit, "tua voluntate, L. Tarquini, remove metum. Meminimus, fatemur, eiecisti reges; absolve beneficium tuum,
140 aufer hinc regium nomen. Res tuas tibi non solum reddent cives tui, auctore me; sed, si quid deest, munifice augebunt. Amicus abi; exonera civitatem vano forsitan metu; ita persuasum est animis cum gente Tarquinia regnum hinc abiturum." Abdicavit se consulatu; rebusque suis omnibus Lavinium translatis, civi-
145 tate cessit. Brutus ex senatus consulto ad populum tulit ut omnes Tarquiniae gentis exsules essent. Collegam sibi comitiis centuriatis creavit P. Valerium, quo adiutore reges eiecerat.

"Tarquin and Lucretia"
Jan Sanders van Hemessen, 16th century
Musée des Beaux-Arts, Lille, France

148. **Lartem:** an Etruscan name or title.
    Clusinum: *of Clusium,* one of the most important Etruscan cities; many rich Etruscan tombs have been found in the vicinity.
149. **se:** here, as often, the reflex. pron. refers to the subj. of the vb. in the main clause (the Tarquins) rather than to the subject of its own clause (Porsenna).
150. **oriundos:** gerundive of **oriri,** *to rise, spring from;* here essentially = **ortos.**
152. **inultum:** *unavenged;* sc. **esse.**
    cum regem esse Romae tum (153): *not only for there to be a king at Rome but also;* the inf. phrase depends on **ratus.**
153. **amplum Tuscis ratus:** sc. **esse,** *thinking it was an important thing for the Etruscans.*
154. **alias:** adv., *at another time, elsewhere.*
155. **res:** sc. **publica.**
158. **saepiunt: saepire,** *to hedge in, enclose, protect.*
    alia . . . alia: *some things (= parts of the city) . . . others.*
    Tiberi obiecto (159): *with the Tiber situated in (= blocking) the way.*
159. **sublicius:** *built on piles,* in contrast to the regular use of arches; the old wooden bridge survived to the fifth century A.D.
160. **ni:** = **nisi.**
    Horatius Cocles: the cognomen means *one-eyed;* his story is one of the most famous and oldest Roman legends.
    id munimentum: i.e., Horatius.
162. **Ianiculum:** the *Janiculum,* a hill across the Tiber opposite the city of Rome.
164. **reprehensans:** frequentative intensive of **reprehendere,** *seizing and holding back.*
    obsistens: obsistere, *to stand in the way, withstand, resist.*
165. **obtestans: obtestari,** *to call to witness, implore, entreat.*
    deum: poetic form = **deorum.**
    testabatur: testari, *to bear witness to, declare, assert;* governing both **fugere** and **fore** in IND. STATE.
    nequiquam: adv., *in vain, to no purpose.*
166. **transitum pontem:** *the bridge, after they had crossed it* (lit., *the crossed bridge*).
    a tergo: we would say *at their rear* or *behind them.*
167. **Capitolio: Capitolium;** the *Capitoline hill* and the Palatine were situated in Rome across the Tiber from the Janiculum.
169. **monere, praedicere:** the HIST. INF. (with subj., if there is one, in the nom.) can be used as the main vb. in a passage of lively, rapid narration and is regularly translated as a past tense; here, *he warned, he instructed.* ASYN-DETON adds further speed and intensity to the narrative.
170. **interrumpant: interrumpere,** *to break down.*
    se . . . excepturum (171): sc. **esse** and some speech vb., e.g., *saying that.*
    quantum: adv. *in so far as.*
171. **posset obsisti:** impers. pass.
    vadit: vadere, *to go, rush.*
    aditum: aditus, *approach, entrance.*

Some Ordeals of the Early Republic

The Tarquins flee to Lars Porsenna of Clusium, who leads an army against Rome.

Iam Tarquinii ad Lartem Porsennam, Clusinum regem, per-
fugerant. Ibi miscendo consilium precesque nunc orabant ne se,
150 oriundos ex Etruscis, eiusdem sanguinis nominisque, egentes
exsulare pateretur; nunc monebant etiam ne orientem morem
pellendi reges inultum sineret. Porsenna, cum regem esse Romae tum Etruscae gentis regem amplum Tuscis ratus, Romam
infesto exercitu venit. Non umquam alias ante tantus terror se-
155 natum invasit: adeo valida res tum Clusina erat magnumque
Porsennae nomen. (II.2.2–9.5, excerpts)

Horatius Cocles is posted to defend the bridge at Rome.

Cum hostes adessent, pro se quisque in urbem ex agris de-
migrant, urbem ipsam saepiunt praesidiis. Alia muris, alia Ti-
beri obiecto videbantur tuta. Pons sublicius iter paene hostibus
160 dedit, ni unus vir fuisset, Horatius Cocles: id munimentum illo
die fortuna urbis Romanae habuit. Qui positus forte in statione
pontis, cum captum repentino impetu Ianiculum atque inde ci-
tatos decurrere hostes vidisset, trepidamque turbam suorum
arma ordinesque relinquere, reprehensans singulos, obsistens
165 obtestansque deum et hominum fidem, testabatur nequiquam
deserto praesidio eos fugere; si transitum pontem a tergo reli-
quissent, iam plus hostium in Palatio Capitolioque quam in Ianiculo fore.

Cocles orders the bridge to be destroyed behind him, while he holds the Etruscans at the entrance.

Itaque monere, praedicere ut pontem ferro, igni, quacumque
170 vi possint, interrumpant; se impetum hostium, quantum corpore
uno posset obsisti, excepturum. Vadit inde in primum aditum

172. **insignis . . . inter . . . terga:** lit., *conspicuous among the visible backs of those yielding to the fight* = *conspicuous among those who were clearly turning their backs to the fight.*

173. **comminus:** adv., *hand to hand, at close quarters.*

174. **obstupefecit:** obstupefacere, *to astonish, amaze.*

175. **Sp. Larcium ac T. Herminium:** *Spurius Larcius and Titus Herminius;* both family names are of Etruscan origin.
      ambos: *both.*

176. **procellam:** procella, *storm, onset.*
      tumultuosissimum: *the most turbulent part of.*

177. **parumper:** adv., *for a little while.*
      exigua: *scanty, small, little.*

178. **revocantibus:** sc. **eis** as antecedent of **qui;** those dismantling **(rescindere)** the bridge were calling out to Larcius and Herminius to retreat.

179. **circumferens . . . oculos:** Eng. would say *casting . . . glances.*
      truces: *savage, fierce.*
      minaciter: adv., *menacingly, threateningly.*

180. **proceres:** procer, *chief, noble.*
      provocare . . . increpare: both HIST. INFS.

181. **servitia:** = **servos.**
      immemores . . . venire (182): sc. **eos,** *(saying) that they, forgetful . . ., were coming.*

182. **alienam:** sc. **libertatem,** obj. of **oppugnatum.**
      oppugnatum: *to attack,* acc. of the supine.

183. **alius alium . . . circumspectant:** idiomatic, *one looked at one, one at another,* hence the pl. vb.

185. **quae cum . . . cuncta:** = **cum haec cuncta,** sc. **tela;** the INTERLOCKED WORD ORDER (ABAB: **quae . . . obiecto cuncta scuto**), common in poetry and in Livy's often poetic style, is perhaps meant to create a WORD PICTURE, with the word **cuncta** (= **omnia**) contained within the phrase **obiecto . . . scuto,** just as *all (the spears)* are themselves pictured as stuck within the circle of *the shield.*
      haesissent: haerere, *to cling, stick.*

186. **ingenti pontem . . . gradu:** another WORD PICTURE with Cocles' *huge stride* actually spanning *the bridge.*

187. **detrudere:** *to thrust down, dislodge.*
      simul fragor . . . simul clamor (188): ANAPHORA, ASYNDETON, and ASSONANCE all contribute to the poetic quality of the passage.
      fragor: *breaking, crash, noise.*

189. **pavore:** pavor, *trembling, terror.*

190. **Tiberine pater:** Cocles ritually prays to the god of the Tiber; river deities were regularly conceived of as male.
      precor: precari, *to pray, beseech, invoke.*

191. **accipias:** sc. **ut,** JUSSIVE NOUN CL. with **precor.**

193. **incolumis:** *uninjured, safe.*
      tranavit: tranare, *to swim across.*

pontis, insignisque inter conspecta cedentium pugnae terga, obversis comminus ad ineundum proelium armis, ipso miraculo audaciae obstupefecit hostes. Duos tamen cum eo pudor tenuit,
175 Sp. Larcium ac T. Herminium, ambos claros genere factisque. Cum his primam periculi procellam et quod tumultuosissimum pugnae erat parumper sustinuit; deinde eos quoque ipsos, exigua parte pontis relicta, revocantibus qui rescindebant, cedere in tutum coegit. Circumferens inde truces minaciter oculos ad
180 proceres Etruscorum, nunc singulos provocare, nunc increpare omnes, servitia regum superborum, suae libertatis immemores alienam oppugnatum venire. Cunctati aliquamdiu sunt, dum alius alium, ut proelium incipiant, circumspectant. Pudor deinde commovit aciem, et, clamore sublato, undique in unum hostem
185 tela coniciunt. Quae cum in obiecto cuncta scuto haesissent, neque ille minus obstinatus ingenti pontem obtineret gradu, iam impetu conabantur detrudere virum, cum simul fragor rupti pontis, simul clamor Romanorum alacritate perfecti operis sublatus, pavore subito impetum sustinuit.

Cocles leaps to safety in the Tiber and is honored by the Romans.

190 Tum Cocles "Tiberine pater," inquit, "te, sancte, precor, haec arma et hunc militem propitio flumine accipias!" Ita sic armatus in Tiberim desiluit, multisque superincidentibus telis, incolumis ad suos tranavit, rem ausus plus famae habituram ad posteros quam fidei. Grata erga tantam virtutem civitas fuit:

Lunette with Fortitude and Temperance above and Lucius Licinius, Leonidas,
Horatius Cocles, Scipio Africanus the Elder, Pericles, and Cincinnatus
Pietro Perugino, 15th century
Collegio del Cambio, Palazzo dei Priori (Comunale), Perugia, Italy

195. **statua:** Pliny the Elder reports that an ancient statue of Cocles was still to be seen in Rome in his own day (the first century A.D.).

agri: PARTITIVE GEN. with **quantum,** *as much land as.*

datum: i.e., **ei datum est.**

198. **obsidendam: obsidere,** *to besiege.*

199. **accitis: accire,** *to summon, send for.*

et ad . . . et ut (200): *both for . . . and so that.*

200. **frumenti: frumentum,** *grain.*

201. **praedatum:** supine of **praedari,** *to plunder.*

202. **brevi:** sc. **tempore.**

203. **cetera:** i.e., the rest of their belongings.

204. **propellere:** sc. **pecus.**

206. **obsidio erat: obsidio,** *siege;* i.e., *the siege continued.*

nihilo minus: i.e., despite a temporarily successful Roman action against some Etruscan foragers.

caritate: caritas, here, *high price.*

207. **inopia:** *want, lack, need.*

208. **cum:** *when,* should introduce **constituit,** but the cl. becomes so involved that after **fuderit** Livy starts all over with **itaque.**

C. Mucius: *Gaius Mucius Scaevola,* whose bold venture described here is another very old Roman legend.

indignum videbatur: *it seemed disgraceful that,* governing the IND. STATE. that follows.

209. **servientem, cum . . . esset:** lit., *being in slavery when under the kings* = *when enslaved under the kings.*

210. **liberum eundem populum (211):** sc. **sed.**

212. **fuderit:** sc. **populus Romanus;** strictly speaking, the hist. sequence of tenses requires **fudisset** in this SUBORDINATE CL. IN IND. STATE., but Livy often employs primary tenses in hist. sequence.

facinore: facinus, *deed, crime.*

213. **sponte:** a defective noun, used chiefly in the abl. = *of (one's) own accord, voluntarily, freely.*

214. **iniussu:** another specialized abl. used adverbially, *without the orders.*

216. **ut transfuga:** *as a deserter.*

fortuna . . . adfirmante: ABL. ABS. giving the circumstances which would justify the accusation that Mucius was a **transfuga.**

crimen: here, as often, *charge, accusation,* rather than *crime.*

218. **praedo:** *robber, pirate, plunderer.*

populationum: populatio, *plundering, devastation;* OBJ. GEN. with **ultor.**

in vicem (219): *in turn.*

219. **approbant:** Livy's narrative becomes suspenseful at this point, as the **patres** know the **facinus** and we as yet do not.

221. **abdito: abdere,** *to put away, hide.*

vestem: vestis, *clothing, garment.*

confertissima: confertus, *closely packed, dense, crowded.*

222. **prope:** prep. + acc., *near;* adv., *nearly, almost.*

195   statua in comitio posita; agri quantum uno die circumaravit datum. (II.10.1–12)

Porsenna now besieges Rome.

Porsenna primo conatu repulsus, consiliis ab oppugnanda
urbe ad obsidendam versis, praesidio in Ianiculo locato, ipse in
plano ripisque Tiberis castra posuit, navibus undique accitis, et
200   ad custodiam, ne quid Romam frumenti subvehi sineret, et ut
praedatum milites trans flumen per occasiones aliis atque aliis
locis traiceret; brevique adeo infestum omnem Romanum agrum
reddidit ut non cetera solum ex agris sed pecus quoque omne
in urbem compelleretur, neque quisquam extra portas propel-
205   lere auderet.

Gaius Mucius resolves to do something about the desperate situation.

Obsidio erat nihilo minus et frumenti cum summa caritate
inopia, sedendoque expugnaturum se urbem spem Porsenna habebat, cum C. Mucius, adulescens nobilis, cui indignum videbatur populum Romanum servientem, cum sub regibus esset,
210   nullo bello nec ab hostibus ullis obsessum esse, liberum eundem
populum ab isdem Etruscis obsideri quorum saepe exercitus
fuderit—itaque magno audacique aliquo facinore eam indigni-
tatem vindicandam ratus, primo sua sponte penetrare in hostium castra constituit. Dein metuens ne, si consulum iniussu et
215   ignaris omnibus iret, forte deprehensus a custodibus Romanis
retraheretur ut transfuga, fortuna tum urbis crimen adfirmante,
senatum adit. "Transire Tiberim," inquit, "patres, et intrare, si
possim, castra hostium volo, non praedo nec populationum in
vicem ultor: maius, si di iuvant, in animo est facinus." Appro-
220   bant patres.

Mucius enters the Etruscan camp and is arrested as he attempts to as-
sassinate Porsenna.

Abdito intra vestem ferro proficiscitur. Ubi eo venit, in confertissima turba prope regium tribunal constitit. Ibi cum sti-

223. **pari . . . ornatu (224):** ABL. OF DESCRIPTION with **scriba.**
224. **vulgo:** adv., here *openly.*
225. **sciscitari:** *to inquire, seek to know.*
      semet: **-met** is an intensive suffix occasionally added to pers. prons.
226. **aperiret: aperire,** *to open, reveal.*
      quo: adv., *whither, where* (motion to which—as opposed to **qua** in the next
          sent. = *where* in the sense of *at which place*); sc. something like *proceed-
          ing,* looking ahead to the next cl., i.e., *proceeding where.*
227. **obtruncat: obtruncare,** *to cut down, kill.*
      vadentem: sc. **Mucium,** in a general way parallel to **comprehensum** and obj.
          of **retraxissent;** in view of the complexity of the sent., this phrase is per-
          haps best translated as an independent cl. = *(He walked away) from
          there (the scene), proceeding where he had made . . ..*
228. **cruento:** *bloody.*
      mucrone: mucro, *sharp point (of a sword), sword.*
229. **satellites: satelles,** *attendant.*
230. **minas: mina,** *threat.*
232. **vocant:** sc. **me.**
233. **animi:** PARTITIVE GEN. with **minus;** we would say *nor am I less prepared.*
234. **Romanum:** PRED. ADJ. (cp. **errare humanum est**); a fine epigram by which to
          describe Roman character at its best.
235. **idem:** with **decus** *(honor),* i.e., **longus ordo (virorum) idem decus petentium.**
      proinde: adv., *therefore.*
      in hoc discrimen: *for this hazard, critical danger,* explained by the two cls. **ut
          dimices** and **(ut) habeas.**
236. **accingere:** reflexive pass. 2nd pers. sg. imper., *arm yourself (be armed).*
      in singulas horas: *from hour to hour.*
      capite: = **vita,** ABL. OF PRICE, a kind of instrumental abl. denoting the price
          or cost of the action; here, *for your life.*
      dimices: dimicare, *to fight, struggle.*
237. **regiae: regia,** *palace.*
      hoc . . . bellum (238): adj. and noun, often widely separated in Livy, here
          frame the entire sentence, adding emphasis to Mucius' bold declaration.
238. **nullam . . . timueris (239):** **ne** or a similar negative + the perf. subjunct. in
          2nd pers. = a negative command.
239. **uni . . . erit:** *the affair will be between you alone and (us) one by one.*
240. **infensus:** *hostile.*
      circumdari ignes (241): lit., *fires to be put around him* = *him to be burned.*
241. **minitabundus:** *threatening.*
      expromeret: expromere, *to disclose, tell.*
      propere: adv., *quickly.*
242. **quas insidiarum . . . minas:** = **quas minas insidiarum.**
      ambages: *ambiguous words, riddles.*
      en: interj., *behold, see.*
      tibi: *for yourself,* DAT. OF REF.
243. **vile:** *cheap, worthless.*

pendium militibus forte daretur, et scriba cum rege sedens pari
fere ornatu multa ageret, eumque milites vulgo adirent, timens
225   sciscitari uter Porsenna esset, ne ignorando regem semet ipse
aperiret quis esset, quo temere traxit fortuna facinus, scribam
pro rege obtruncat. Vadentem inde, qua per trepidam turbam
cruento mucrone sibi ipse fecerat viam, cum concursu ad clamorem facto comprehensum regii satellites retraxissent, ante
230   tribunal regis destitutus, tum quoque inter tantas fortunae minas metuendus magis quam metuens, "Romanus sum," inquit,
"civis; C. Mucium vocant. Hostis hostem occidere volui, nec ad
mortem minus animi est quam fuit ad caedem: et facere et pati
fortia Romanum est. Nec unus in te ego hos animos gessi; lon-
235   gus post me ordo est idem petentium decus. Proinde in hoc discrimen, si iuvat, accingere, ut in singulas horas capite dimices
tuo, ferrum hostemque in vestibulo habeas regiae. Hoc tibi iu-
ventus Romana indicimus bellum. Nullam aciem, nullum proelium timueris; uni tibi et cum singulis res erit."

*Boldly demonstrating his courage, Mucius wins Porsenna's admiration
and is released.*

240   Cum rex, simul ira infensus periculoque conterritus, cir-
cumdari ignes minitabundus iuberet, nisi expromeret propere
quas insidiarum sibi minas per ambages iaceret, "En tibi," inquit, "ut sentias quam vile corpus sit eis qui magnam gloriam

Roman soldier mosaic
Imperial palace, Istanbul, Turkey

244. **dextram:** sc. **manum.**
     foculo: foculus, *little fire, brazier.*
     quam cum (245): = **cum eam,** i.e., **dextram.**
245. **velut alienato . . . animo:** ABL. ABS.
     torreret: torrere, *to burn, roast.*
     attonitus: *thunderstruck, astonished.*
248. **macte:** in origin the voc. of **mactus,** *honored,* but treated as indecl.; the common idiomatic phrase **macte virtute,** which often = *well done, congratulations,* here with **iuberem esse** means something like *honored for your courage.*
251. **meritum:** *merit, service.*
     quando quidem: conj. (sometimes written as a single word), *since.*
253. **nequisti:** = **nequivisti,** from **nequire,** *to be unable;* the implied main cl. follows, "I will tell you what you want to know."
254. **hac via:** *in this way* or *manner.*
     grassaremur: grassari, *to proceed (against).*
255. **cuiusque . . . primi:** sc. **sors,** *the lot of each one first* = *of each in order.*
     quoad: conj., *how long, as long as, until.*
     opportunum: lit., *suitable;* here, *accessible (to us), vulnerable.*
257. **Scaevolae:** from **scaevus,** *left,* dat. by attraction to **cui;** we would say *to whom the cognomen Scaevola* (the "Left-handed") *was given.*
     clade: clades, *destruction, loss.*
     cognomen: the formal Roman name was composed of three elements, the **nomen** (indicating the **gens** or family), the **praenomen** (the given name, which stood before the **nomen**), and the **cognomen** (which stood after the **nomen** and in origin must have been rather like what we call a nickname, often based on some physical characteristic as here in the case of Gaius Mucius Scaevola).
258. **et . . . casus . . . et . . . dimicatio (260):** both subjs. of **moverat.**
259. **casus:** here, *experience.*
     texisset . . . superessent (260): the reasons for dispatching ambassadors expressed in these two cls. are those Livy attributes to Porsenna **(eum)** and not his own, hence the SUBJUNCT. OF QUOTED REASON.
260. **subeunda dimicatio:** freely, *having to undergo an assault.*

*"Mucius Scaevola
Confronting King Porsenna"
Bernardo Cavallino
1650
Kimbell Art Museum
Fort Worth, Texas*

vident," dextramque accenso ad sacrificium foculo inicit. Quam
245   cum velut alienato ab sensu torreret animo, prope attonitus miraculo rex, cum ab sede sua prosiluisset amoverique ab altaribus
iuvenem iussisset, "Tu vero abi," inquit, "in te magis quam in
me hostilia ausus. Iuberem macte virtute esse, si pro mea patria
ista virtus staret: nunc iure belli liberum te intactum invio-
250   latumque hinc dimitto."

The terrified Porsenna offers to make peace with Rome.

Tunc Mucius quasi remunerans meritum, "Quando quidem,"
inquit, "est apud te virtuti honos, ut beneficio tuleris a me quod
minis nequisti: trecenti coniuravimus principes iuventutis Romanae ut in te hac via grassaremur. Mea prima sors fuit; ceteri,
255   ut cuiusque ceciderit primi, quoad te opportunum fortuna dede-
rit, suo quisque tempore aderunt." Mucium dimissum, cui postea
Scaevolae a clade dextrae manus cognomen inditum, legati a
Porsenna Romam secuti sunt: adeo moverat eum et primi periculi casus, a quo nihil se praeter errorem insidiatoris texisset, et
260   subeunda dimicatio totiens quot coniurati superessent, ut pacis
condiciones ultro ferret Romanis. (II.11.1–13.2, excerpts)

"Romulus and Remus Given Shelter by Faustulus"
Pietro da Cortona, 17th century
Louvre, Paris, France

2. **in se convertit:** *attracted to him.*

Hamilcarem: *Hamilcar Barca,* father of Hannibal and a Carthaginian general in the First Punic War (264–241 B.C.).

3. **veteres milites:** veterans of the First Punic War, nom. subj. of the HISTORICAL INFS. **credere** and **intueri.**

vigorem in vultu vimque: ALLITERATION, just one of the many poetic features of Livy's style, adds emphasis; cp. the Eng. expression "vim and vigor."

4. **habitum oris:** *expression.*

lineamenta: lineamentum, *line,* (pl.) *(facial) features.*

intueri: here, *they beheld, saw.*

brevi: sc. **tempore.**

5. **pater in se:** *the father (Hamilcar) in him,* i.e., *his similarity to his father.*

momentum: here, *influence, importance;* PRED. NOUN.

6. **parendum . . . imperandum (7):** gerunds in appos. with **res.**

7. **habilius: habilis,** *handy, fit, skillful.*

discerneres: POTENTIAL SUBJUNCT. in the indef. 2nd pers. sg., *you could decide.*

8. **Hasdrubal:** son-in-law of Hamilcar, and the general currently in command of Spain; subj. of **malle.**

9. **praeficere:** *to put in command.*

quid: *anything.*

10. **agendum esset:** Livy uses the impf. and plpf. subjunct. to indicate repeated action; hence **ubi** = *whenever.*

alio duce: ABL. ABS.

11. **capessenda: capessere,** *to seize eagerly, enter upon.*

12. **erat:** sc. **ei;** i.e., *he had.*

13. **caloris: calor,** *heat.*

patientia par: sc. **erat;** forms of **esse** are omitted from several of the following cls., accelerating the narrative.

cibi potionisque (14): with **modus,** *measure* or, here, *consumption;* Livy has Stoic ideals in mind.

14. **vigiliarum somnique (15):** with **tempora;** the word order deliberately parallels that of **cibi . . . modus** above.

15. **discriminata:** *were separated/demarcated.*

id quod (16): i.e., **id tempus quod.**

16. **gerendis rebus:** dat. with the compound vb. **superesset;** lit., *that (time) which was more than enough for doing things* = *that (time) which was not required for things which had to be done.*

ea: i.e., **quies.**

17. **strato: stratum,** *bed, blanket.*

accersita: = **arcessita,** from **arcessere,** *to summon, obtain, induce.*

sagulo: sagulum, *military cloak.*

opertum: operire, *to cover.*

19. **vestitus:** *clothing.*

nihil: here = a strong **non.**

inter aequales: i.e., *in comparison to his fellow soldiers.*

excellens: *superior, extravagant.*

HANNIBAL AND THE SECOND PUNIC WAR

The nature and character of Hannibal.

Missus Hannibal in Hispaniam primo statim adventu omnem exercitum in se convertit: Hamilcarem iuvenem redditum
sibi veteres milites credere; eundem vigorem in vultu vimque in
oculis, habitum oris lineamentaque intueri. Dein brevi effecit ut
5   pater in se minimum momentum ad favorem conciliandum esset. Numquam ingenium idem ad res diversissimas, parendum
atque imperandum, habilius fuit. Itaque haud facile discerneres
utrum imperatori an exercitui carior esset; neque Hasdrubal
alium quemquam praeficere malle, ubi quid fortiter ac strenue
10   agendum esset, neque milites alio duce plus confidere aut au-
dere. Plurimum audaciae ad pericula capessenda, plurimum consilii inter ipsa pericula erat. Nullo labore aut corpus fatigari aut
animus vinci poterat. Caloris ac frigoris patientia par; cibi potionisque desiderio naturali, non voluptate, modus finitus; vi-
15   giliarum somnique nec die nec nocte discriminata tempora: id
quod gerendis rebus superesset quieti datum; ea neque molli
strato neque silentio accersita; multi saepe militari sagulo opertum humi iacentem inter custodias stationesque militum con-
spexerunt. Vestitus nihil inter aequales excellens; arma atque

"Hamilcar Asks Hannibal to Swear His Hatred of the Romans"
Giovanni Battista Pittoni, 18th century
Pinacoteca di Brera, Milan, Italy

20. **conspiciebantur:** *were conspicuous.*
     peditum: pedes, *foot-soldier;* pl., *infantry.*
21. **conserto: conserere,** *to connect, join, engage (in battle).*
23. **perfidia plus quam Punica:** since to the Romans **fides Punica** was proverbial
     for utter faithlessness and treachery, this characterization is the ulti-
     mate insult.
     deum: = **deorum.**
24. **nullum ius iurandum:** *no oath* = *no respect for oaths.* This entire characteriza-
     tion reflects the Romans' bitter hatred of Hannibal, who had nearly de-
     feated Rome and for over a decade had roamed the heartland of Italy at
     will; in fact, based on the account of the historian Polybius and even
     some other passages in Livy, it is generally agreed that descriptions like
     the one here exaggerated the enormity of Hannibal's sins.
     indole: indoles, *nature, disposition, talent;* here, *natural endowment.*
25. **triennio:** a not uncommon use of the ABL. OF TIME WITHIN WHICH where we
     might have expected the ACC. OF DURATION OF TIME.
     meruit: merere, *to earn (pay), serve as a soldier.*
26. **nulla re . . . praetermissa (27):** ABL. ABS.
28. **Druentia:** *the Durance,* a tributary of the Rhone in southeastern Gaul.
     campestri: lit., *like a field, level;* i.e., the march was largely through open
     country.
29. **cum bona pace:** i.e., *with the good will;* ABL. OF ATTENDANT CIRCUMSTANCE.
     incolentium: incolere, *to inhabit.*
30. **praecepta . . . erat:** *had been anticipated.*
     ex propinquo: Livy is fond of using a prep. and the n. of an adj. with adv. or
     adj. force: *from a near thing, close at hand, at close range.*
31. **nives: nix,** *snow.*
     caelo: dat. with **immixtae.**
     prope: prep. + acc., *near;* adv., *nearly, almost.*
     tecta: tectum, *roof, dwelling, house.*
32. **imposita:** we might say *perched on.*
     rupibus: rupes, *rock, cliff.*
     pecora: pecus, *cattle, herd.*
     iumenta: iumentum, *beast of burden, pack animal.*
     torpida: *stiff, numb.*
33. **intonsi et inculti:** *unshaven and unkempt.*
34. **gelu:** *frost, cold.*
     cetera . . . foediora: i.e., *more dreadful* than words can describe.
     erigentibus . . . agmen (35): *to those directing their line of march* = *to those
     marching.*
35. **clivos: clivus,** *slope, hill.*
     imminentes: modifies **tumulos,** here *hilltops,* obj. of **insidentes montani** *(moun-
     taineers).*
36. **consistere signa:** *to set up the standards,* i.e., to encamp.

20   equi conspiciebantur. Equitum peditumque idem longe primus
      erat: princeps in proelium ibat, ultimus conserto proelio excede-
      bat. Has tantas viri virtutes ingentia vitia aequabant: inhumana
      crudelitas, perfidia plus quam Punica, nihil sancti, nullus deum
      metus, nullum ius iurandum, nulla religio. Cum hac indole vir-
25   tutum atque vitiorum triennio sub Hasdrubale imperatore me-
      ruit nulla re, quae agenda videndaque magno futuro duci esset,
      praetermissa. (XXI.4.1–10)

*In crossing the Alps Hannibal's army suffers from both the cold and the
hostility of the natives.*

      Hannibal a Druentia campestri maxime itinere ad Alpes
      cum bona pace incolentium ea loca Gallorum pervenit. Tum,
30   quamquam fama prius praecepta res erat, tamen ex propinquo
      visa montium altitudo nivesque caelo prope immixtae, tecta in-
      formia imposita rupibus, pecora iumentaque torpida frigore,
      homines intonsi et inculti, animalia inanimaque omnia rigentia
      gelu, cetera visu quam dictu foediora, terrorem renovarunt. Eri-
35   gentibus in primos agmen clivos apparuerunt imminentes tu-
      mulos insidentes montani. Hannibal consistere signa iussit;

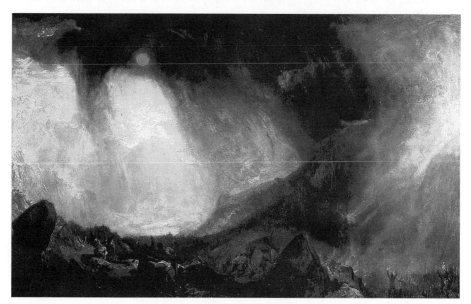

"Snow Storm: Hannibal and His Army Crossing the Alps"
Joseph Mallord William Turner, 1812
Tate Gallery, London, Great Britain

37. **quam . . . valle (38):** sc. **in;** Livy often omits the prep. in ABL. OF PLACE WHERE constructions, as again with **tumulis** below (39).
38. **die . . . consumpto (39):** ABL. ABS.
     aliud: Hannibal actually fortified his camp, but he pretended that he would try to lead his army through the pass at the foot of the heights held by the mountaineers. At the end of the day, however, when the natives finally realized that Hannibal was not going to carry out this apparent intention, they withdrew from their posts on the heights and returned home in the evening; Hannibal then built a large number of camp fires to make the enemy think that his army was spending the night in camp.
40. **expeditis:** sc. **militibus,** *his light-armed soldiers.*
     quoque: from **quisque.**
41. **raptim:** adv., *quickly, hurriedly.*
     angustias: angustiae, pl., *narrow pass, defile.*
     evadit: evadere, *to go forth, escape, travel over;* here, *marched up to* (i.e., out of the valley).
42. **prima . . . luce:** i.e., *at daybreak.*
     mota: sc. **sunt.**
43. **castellis:** castellum, *fort, fortified village.*
45. **alios . . . alios:** both with **hostes** (46).
     via: *by the (regular) road,* which ran along at the foot of the heights; ABL. OF ROUTE, a common construction related to the ABL. OF MEANS.
46. **iuxta:** *equally.*
     in . . . adsueti: *(the mountaineers) being accustomed to.*
47. **ab iniquitate:** the prep., not usual with an ABL. OF MEANS, is here employed to balance **ab hostibus.**
48. **plus:** with **certaminis** (PARTITIVE GEN.) **erat.**
     quoque: from **quisque.**
49. **ut . . . primus:** *he might be the first to.*
     certaminis: certamen, *contest, struggle, fight.*
50. **infestum:** *unsafe, hostile, dangerous;* OBJ. COMPL.
     qui . . . consternabantur (52): the basic structure of the rel. cl. is **qui et . . . territi trepidabant, et icti . . . consternabantur.**
51. **nemora:** nemus, *grove.*
     repercussae: *re-echoing.*
     augebant: augere, *to increase, amplify.*
52. **trepidabant:** trepidare, *to be agitated, alarmed, anxious.*
     icti: icere, *to strike, hit, stab.*
     adeo: adv., *to such a degree, so, even.*
53. **stragem:** strages, *ruin, slaughter.*
     sarcinarum: sarcina, *soldier's pack, baggage.*
54. **turba:** here, *crowding.*
     deruptae: *steep.*
55. **utrimque:** adv., *on both sides.*
     immensum altitudinis: a poetic circumlocution, using the n. adj. as a noun with a PARTITIVE GEN., lit., *an immensity of depth = an immense depth.*
56. **ruinae . . . modo:** *in the manner of a falling building.*

Gallisque ad visenda loca praemissis, castra quam extentissima
potest valle locat. Die deinde simulando aliud quam quod para-
tur consumpto, ubi primum digressos tumulis montanos laxa-
40 tasque sensit custodias, ipse cum expeditis, acerrimo quoque
viro, raptim angustias evadit iisque ipsis tumulis, quos hostes
tenuerant, consedit. Prima deinde luce castra mota, et agmen
reliquum incedere coepit. Iam montani, signo dato, ex castellis
ad stationem solitam conveniebant, cum repente conspiciunt
45 alios arce occupata sua supra caput imminentes, alios via transire hostes; diversis rupibus, iuxta in vias ac devia adsueti, decurrunt. Tum vero simul ab hostibus simul ab iniquitate locorum
Poeni oppugnabantur, plusque inter ipsos, sibi quoque tendente
ut periculo primus evaderet, quam cum hostibus certaminis
50 erat. Equi maxime infestum agmen faciebant, qui et clamoribus
dissonis, quos nemora etiam repercussaeque valles augebant,
territi trepidabant, et icti forte aut vulnerati adeo consternaban-
tur ut stragem ingentem simul hominum ac sarcinarum omnis
generis facerent; multosque turba, cum praecipites deruptaeque
55 utrimque angustiae essent, in immensum altitudinis deiecit,
quosdam et armatos; sed, ruinae maxime modo, iumenta cum

Mont Blanc, viewed from the southeast

57. **quae:** = **haec.**
58. **parumper:** adv., *for a little while.*
61. **inde:** adv., *then, after that, thereupon.*
    caput: i.e., *the principal town.*
    viculos: viculus, *hamlet.*
    capit et . . . aluit (62): sc. **Hannibal.**
62. **cibo: cibus,** *food.*
    triduum: *a period of three days.*
63. **nono die:** i.e., from the time when they began their ascent.
    iugum: *yoke, ridge.*
    perventum est: a common impers. vb., where Eng. would say *they arrived.*
    pleraque: *very many.*
64. **errores:** here, *circuitous routes, detours.*
    stativa habita: sc. **castra,** *a stationary camp was made.*
    fessis: *tired, exhausted;* with **militibus,** a favorite device of word order in Livy
        (and in Lat. verse), framing an entire cl. with adj. + modified noun.
67. **fessis:** sc. **eis,** dat. with **adiecit.**
    taedio: taedium, *weariness, disgust.*
    nivis: with **casus,** *snow-fall, snow-storm.*
68. **sidere Vergiliarum:** *the constellation of the Pleiades,* which set toward the end
        of October, signalling the onset of wintry weather.
69. **oppleta: opplere,** *to fill, cover.*
    segniter: adv., *sluggishly, slowly.*
70. **pigritia:** *sluggishness, disinclination (to act).*
    emineret: eminere, *to project, stand out, be conspicuous.*
71. **praegressus: praegredi,** + acc., *to precede, go in advance of;* Hannibal was
        likely proceeding on the basis of some special information.
72. **consistere iussis militibus . . . ostentat (73):** Eng. would use two vbs. rather
        than the partic., *he ordered them to stop and he showed them . . .;* **ostentat,**
        to eagerly point out, display, is frequentative or intensive of **ostendere,** an
        indication of Hannibal's mood.
73. **subiectos:** + dat., *lying at the foot of, adjacent to.*
    circumpadanos: *surrounding the Po;* from **Padus,** the Po River, the largest
        river in northern Italy.
    campos: campus, *field, plain.*
74. **eos . . . transcendere:** IND. STATE., like the following inf. phrases, with *he said
        that* or some such speech vb. understood.
75. **cetera:** i.e., *the rest (of their journey).*
    plana, proclivia: *level, downhill;* the ASYNDETON emphasizes the eagerness of
        Hannibal's assurances.
    fore: a common alternative form for **futurum esse,** fut. inf. of **sum.**
    summum: adv., *at most.*
76. **in manu ac potestate:** a quasi-legal expression indicating total control.

oneribus devolvebantur. Quae quamquam foeda visu erant, stetit parumper tamen Hannibal ac suos continuit ne tumultum ac trepidationem augeret. Sed is tumultus momento temporis,
60 postquam liberata itinera fuga montanorum erant, sedatur. Castellum inde, quod caput eius regionis erat, viculosque capit et captivo cibo ac pecoribus per triduum exercitum aluit. (XXI.32.6–33.11, excerpts)

Having passed the summit of the Alps, Hannibal shows his men the Po Valley spreading southward.

Nono die in iugum Alpium perventum est per invia pleraque et errores. Biduum in iugo stativa habita, fessisque labore
65 ac pugnando quies data militibus; iumentaque aliquot, quae prolapsa in rupibus erant, sequendo vestigia agminis in castra pervenere. Fessis taedio tot malorum nivis etiam casus, occidente iam sidere Vergiliarum, ingentem terrorem adiecit. Per omnia nive oppleta cum, signis prima luce motis, segniter agmen
70 incederet, pigritiaque et desperatio in omnium vultu emineret, praegressus signa, Hannibal in promuntorio quodam, unde longe ac late prospectus erat, consistere iussis militibus Italiam ostentat subiectosque Alpinis montibus circumpadanos campos, moeniaque eos tum transcendere non Italiae modo sed etiam
75 urbis Romanae: cetera plana, proclivia fore; uno aut summum altero proelio arcem et caput Italiae in manu ac potestate ha-

Sarcophagus with battle between Romans and Germans
Museo Nazionale Romano, Rome, Italy

77.   **nihil ne hostibus . . . temptantibus (78):** the double negative simply emphasizes the negative force, *with the enemy* (the mountaineers) *not even trying anything at all (against them).*

78.   **furta: furtum,** *theft;* pl. here, *raids.*
per occasionem: i.e., *as the opportunity arose.*
ceterum: adv., *but;* if the mountaineers were now no trouble, the steep southern slopes of the Alps proved more difficult than the western and northern ones had been.

80.   **ferme:** = **fere.**
praeceps: *steep.*

82.   **ventum:** sc. **est;** cf. **perventum est** (63).
rectis: here, *perpendicular, sheer;* ABL. OF DESCRIPTION with **rupem.**

83.   **expeditus:** *unimpeded, unencumbered, light-armed.*
temptabundus: *feeling his way.*

84.   **virgulta: virgultum,** *shrub, bush.*
stirpes: stirps, *trunk, root.*

85.   **velut:** conj., *as, just as, as if.*

87.   **nequiquam:** adv., *in vain, to no avail.*

89.   **id ipsum:** *this very purpose.*
fodiendum: fodere, *to dig up.*

90.   **ad rupem muniendam:** on the model of **viam munire,** *to build* (lit., *fortify*) *a
road* = *to build a road along the cliff.*
unam: = **solam.**

91.   **ducti:** actually a partic. agreeing with **milites,** subj. of **faciunt,** but translate
as if the reading were **milites ducti sunt et . . . struem faciunt.**
caedendum esset: caedere, *to cut, beat, slay.*

92.   **circa:** *in the vicinity.*
immanibus: *huge, immense.*
detruncatis: here, *stripped of their branches.*
struem: strues, *heap, pile.*

93.   **lignorum: lignum,** *wood, log.*
et: = **etiam.**

94.   **succendunt: succendere,** *to set on fire.*
ardentia: *hot, glowing.*
infuso aceto: *with vinegar (wine) poured onto them;* there is some additional
ancient evidence for this process of softening or breaking up rocks by
heating them and then pouring vinegar over them, but Livy's account
here is generally seen as exaggerated.
putrefaciunt: putrefacere, *to soften, make brittle.*

95.   **ferro:** i.e., with iron tools.
pandunt: pandere, *to extend, spread, lay open.*
molliunt: *make gentler.*

96.   **anfractibus: anfractus,** *turn, bend;* here, *zigzag paths.*
modicis: *moderate, easy, gentle.*
clivos: clivus, *slope, hill.*

bituros. Procedere inde agmen coepit, iam nihil ne hostibus quidem praeter parva furta per occasionem temptantibus. Ceterum iter multo, quam in ascensu fuerat, difficilius fuit. Omnis
80 enim ferme via praeceps, angusta, lubrica erat ut non sustinere se a lapsu possent. (XXI.35.4–12, excerpts)

Hannibal breaks up a gigantic boulder which blocks his way, and completes the descent into Italy.

Ventum deinde ad multo angustiorem rupem atque ita rectis saxis ut aegre expeditus miles, temptabundus manibusque retinens virgulta ac stirpes circa eminentes, demittere sese posset.
85 Ibi cum velut ad finem viae equites constitissent, miranti Hannibali quae res moraretur agmen nuntiatur rupem inviam esse. Digressus deinde ipse ad locum visendum. Tandem nequiquam iumentis atque hominibus fatigatis, castra in iugo posita, aegerrime ad id ipsum loco purgato—tantum nivis fodiendum atque
90 egerendum fuit. Inde ad rupem muniendam, per quam unam via esse poterat, milites ducti, cum caedendum esset saxum, arboribus circa immanibus deiectis detruncatisque struem ingentem lignorum faciunt eamque, cum et vis venti apta faciendo igni coorta esset, succendunt ardentiaque saxa infuso aceto pu-
95 trefaciunt. Ita torridam incendio rupem ferro pandunt molliuntque anfractibus modicis clivos ut non iumenta solum sed

Barbarian fighting a Roman legionary
Roman stone relief, 2nd century A.D.
Louvre, Paris, France

97. **elephanti:** *war-elephants* were first employed against the Romans (and with great success) by the Greek general Pyrrhus in 280–279 B.C. Although the Carthaginians' elephants helped to terrify the natives in Hannibal's march through the Alps, they were apparently otherwise little used during the Second Punic War.

98. **fame: fames,** *hunger, starvation.*
    cacumina: cacumen, *top, peak (of a mountain).*

99. **pabuli: pabulum,** *fodder, grass, pasture;* here, PARTITIVE GEN. with **si quid,** *whatever grass (there was).*
    inferiora: sc. **loca.**

100. **apricos:** *sunny, warm.*
     colles: collis, *hill.*
     rivos: rivus, *stream.*

101. **cultu: cultus,** *culture, life, occupation;* abl. with **dignus.**
     muniendo: ABL. OF CAUSE with **fessis;** refers to **ad rupem muniendam** (90).

103. **hoc maxime modo:** *in this way for the most part;* since Livy's dramatic narrative of Hannibal's crossing of the Alps is more rhetorical than geographically literal, much uncertainty exists about the exact route taken.
     quinto mense: the march is usually dated May–September, 218 B.C.

104. **Carthagine Nova:** *New Carthage* in southeastern Spain, the point of departure for Hannibal's march to Italy.
     quidam auctores: the Greek historian Polybius is one important source.

106. **nobilis:** *well-known.*
     Trasumennum: *Lake Trasimene,* in central Italy, west of Perugia; several months after crossing the Alps into Italy, on the 21st of July 217 B.C., Hannibal's army of some 60,000 men dealt the Romans a devastating blow at this site, slaughtering 15,000 of their 25,000 troops along with their commander, the consul Gaius Flaminius.
     inter paucas memorata (107): i.e., *memorable as only a few are;* three other losses at Hannibal's hands were at Ticinus, Trebia, and Cannae.

107. **clades:** *calamity, disaster, slaughter.*

109. **urbem:** Rome.
     petiere: = **petierunt;** -**ere** is a common alternate ending for the 3rd pers. perf. tense.

112. **frequentis contionis modo:** *in the manner of a crowded assembly.*

113. **versa:** middle or reflexive use of the pass., *having turned itself to* or *turning to.*
     comitium et curiam: the meeting places for the assemblies and the senate.

114. **pugna ... victi sumus (115):** laconic enough to suit even the Spartans, and undoubtedly intended to emphasize that **gravitas** *(seriousness, dignity, morale)* which was for so long one of the most noble and valuable characteristics of the Romans.

115. **quamquam:** conj., *although.*

116. **alius ab alio impleti rumoribus:** an example of the distributive sense of **alius,** meaning lit., *one person having been filled with rumors by one person and another by another,* or more smoothly, *filling one another with rumors.*

elephanti etiam deduci possent. Quadriduum circa rupem con-
sumptum, iumentis prope fame absumptis; nuda enim fere ca-
cumina sunt, et si quid est pabuli, obruunt nives. Inferiora valles
100 apricosque colles habent rivosque prope silvas et iam humano
cultu digniora loca. Ibi iumenta in pabulum missa, et quies mu-
niendo fessis hominibus data.

Hoc maxime modo in Italiam perventum est, quinto mense
a Carthagine Nova, ut quidam auctores sunt, quinto decimo die
105 Alpibus superatis. (XXI.36.1–38.1, excerpts)

Aftermath of the Romans' defeat at Lake Trasimene.

Haec est nobilis ad Trasumennum pugna atque inter paucas
memorata populi Romani clades. Quindecim milia Romanorum
in acie caesa; decem milia, sparsa fuga per omnem Etruriam,
diversis itineribus urbem petiere; duo milia quingenti hostium
110 in acie, multa postea ex vulneribus periere. Romae ad primum
nuntium cladis eius cum ingenti terrore ac tumultu concursus
in forum populi est factus. Et cum, frequentis contionis modo,
turba in comitium et curiam versa magistratus vocaret, tandem
haud multo ante solis occasum M. Pomponius praetor "Pugna,"
115 inquit, "magna victi sumus"; et quamquam nihil certius ex eo
auditum est, tamen alius ab alio impleti rumoribus domos re-

Allegory of Africa, Mosaic from Roman villa
Piazza Armerina, Sicily, Italy, 4th century A.D.

117. **caesum:** sc. **esse;** inf. in IND. STATE. after **referunt,** *they carry back to their homes the report that . . ..*
  superesse: from **supersum,** *to be left over, survive.*
119. **quot casus ... fuerant:** *however many had been the misfortunes,* i.e., loss of life, flight, or capture.
120. **propinqui:** *relatives.*
  C. Flaminio: *Gaius Flaminius,* consul for the second time in 217, was a major political figure and reformer; his defeat at Trasimene was blamed by some on his failure to take the auspices and observe other religious practices.
121. **ignorantium:** modifies **eorum.**
122. **satis certum habet:** *know with any degree of certainty.*
123. **praetores:** the *praetors* had judicial functions and presided over the senate in the absence of the consuls.
  aliquot: indecl. adj., *several, some.*
  ab orto: sc. **sole,** *from the risen sun* = *from sunrise.*
124. **quonam duce:** *by what leader, pray;* the intensive suffix **-nam** adds a sense of urgency and desperation to the question.
125. **resisti ... Poenis:** the impers. pass. inf. takes the same dat. noun it would have in the act. voice; idiomatic Eng., of course, would use an act. construction, *they might be able to resist the victorious Carthaginians.*
126. **adhibitum: adhibere,** *to hold to, apply, employ.*
127. **dictatorem dicendum:** in appos. with **remedium,** *a dictator to be appointed* = *the appointment of a dictator.* A sole dictator could be appointed to meet a specific emergency; his term was six months unless he completed his mission in less time, and his power was absolute.
128. **uno:** = **solo.**
  videbatur: sc. **dictator.**
130. **quod:** the **(id) quod** cl. looks forward to and is in appos. with the cl. **populus creavit.**
  eam diem (131): dies, usually m., was f. when referring to a specific day.
131. **Q. Fabium Maximum:** *Quintus Fabius Maximus* was a former consul and censor; his campaigns against Hannibal, including his famous delaying tactics, contributed much to the Romans' ultimate victory.
132. **magistrum equitum:** the *master of the horse,* usually appointed by the dictator himself, was his second in command.
  M. Minucium Rufum: *Marcus Minucius Rufus,* also a former consul, was subsequently elevated to the extraordinary position of joint dictator with Fabius; he died fighting in the battle of Cannae.
133. **muros: murus,** *wall.*
  turres: turris, *tower.*
134. **locis: locus** is often used without a prep. of place.
  videretur: *it seemed best;* SUBJUNCT. BY ATTRACTION.
  rescinderent: rescindere, *to tear away, tear down.*

ferunt consulem cum magna parte copiarum caesum, superesse
paucos aut fuga passim per Etruriam sparsos aut captos ab
hoste. Quot casus exercitus victi fuerant, tot in curas distracti
120   animi eorum erant, quorum propinqui sub C. Flaminio consule
meruerant, ignorantium quae cuiusque suorum fortuna esset;
nec quisquam satis certum habet quid aut speret aut timeat.
Senatum praetores per dies aliquot ab orto usque ad occiden-
tem solem in curia retinent, consultantes quonam duce aut
125   quibus copiis resisti victoribus Poenis posset. (XXII.7.1–14, excerpts)

Quintus Fabius Maximus appointed dictator.

Itaque ad remedium iam diu neque desideratum nec adhibitum, dictatorem dicendum, civitas confugit. Et quia et consul
aberat, a quo uno dici posse videbatur, nec per occupatam armis
Punicis Italiam facile erat aut nuntium aut litteras mitti, nec
130   dictatorem praetor creare poterat, quod numquam ante eam
diem factum erat, dictatorem populus creavit Q. Fabium Maximum et magistrum equitum M. Minucium Rufum; hisque negotium ab senatu datum ut muros turresque urbis firmarent et prae-
sidia disponerent quibus locis videretur, pontesque rescinderent

Battle scene, base of the column of Antoninus Pius
2nd century A.D.
Vatican Palace, Vatican State

135. **fluminum:** the Tiber and the Anio.

penatibus: penates, *penates,* the household gods; the people's efforts now were to be devoted to the defense of the city and their homes rather than to the rest of Italy.

dimicandum esse: dimicare, *to fight, struggle;* impers. pass. of the PASS. PERIPHRASTIC in an IND. STATE. governed by an understood speech vb.

136. **tueri:** *to protect, defend.*

nequissent: nequire, *to be unable.*

137. **viam Latinam:** the *Via Latina,* a major road leading south from Rome, somewhat parallel to the Appian Way, only more inland.

139. **ducit:** sc. **exercitum.**

nullo loco . . . commissurus (140): *intending to entrust himself to fortune in no place;* i.e., *determined not to entrust himself to (mere) luck in any place.* This policy of caution and watchful waiting earned Fabius the epithet **Cunctator** *(the Delayer)* and has given us the terms "Fabian tactics" and "Fabian socialism"; disregard of the policy in 216 B.C. led to the tremendous Roman defeat at Cannae.

nisi . . . cogeret: the vb. is subjunct. in a SUBORDINATE CL. IN IND. STATE., depending on Fabius' intention implied in **commissurus.**

141. **nulla mora facta quin:** sc. **est,** *no delay was made but that = without delay.*

Poenus: i.e., Hannibal.

educeret: sc. **milites.**

copiam . . . pugnandi faceret (142): idiomatic, *and prepared for battle.*

143. **increpans: increpare,** *to make a loud noise, shout angrily.*

144. **Martios:** *of Mars, martial, warlike.*

Romanis: DAT. OF REF.

145. **demum:** adv., *at length, at last, finally.*

146. **quaesissent:** SUBJUNCT. OF QUOTED REASON, indicating that the reason given for Hannibal's anxiety was his own, not Livy's.

147. **extemplo:** adv., *immediately.*

constantiam: i.e., Fabius'.

hauddum: = **nondum,** *not yet.*

148. **crebro:** adv., *frequently.*

populando: populari, *to devastate, plunder.*

151. **omitteret:** here, *lose contact with.*

152. **magistrum equitum:** Minucius, Fabius' second in command.

153. **ferox:** *impetuous.*

consiliis ac lingua: ABL. OF SPECIFICATION.

154. **pro . . . compellabat (155):** sc. as dir. obj. **eum** (Fabius), with **segnem** and **timidum** functioning as OBJ. COMPL., *he kept calling him sluggish instead of one who delays . . . ;* note the effect of the impf.

adfingens: adfingere, *to fashion, invent.*

156. **aquas Sinuessanas:** *the waters (= mineral springs) of Sinuessa,* a coastal town in Latium, near its border with Campania.

populatio: *devastation;* Hannibal's plundering of Rome's allies continues.

135 fluminum: pro urbe ac penatibus dimicandum esse, quando
Italiam tueri nequissent. (XXII.8.5–7)

*Fabius' tactics save the day but irritate some of his own people no less
than Hannibal.*

Dictator, exercitu consulis accepto, in viam Latinam est
egressus, unde itineribus summa cum cura exploratis ad hostem
ducit, nullo loco, nisi quantum necessitas cogeret, fortunae se
140 commissurus. Quo primum die in conspectu hostium posuit
castra, nulla mora facta quin Poenus educeret in aciem copi-
amque pugnandi faceret. Sed ubi quieta omnia apud hostes nec
castra ullo tumultu mota videt, increpans quidem victos tandem Martios animos Romanis, in castra rediit. Ceterum tacita
145 cura animum incessit, quod tum demum, edocti malis, Romani
parem Hannibali ducem quaesissent. Et prudentiam quidem
novi dictatoris extemplo timuit. Constantiam hauddum expertus, agitare ac temptare animum movendo crebro castra po-
pulandoque in oculis eius agros sociorum coepit. Fabius per
150 loca alta agmen ducebat modico ab hoste intervallo, ut neque
omitteret eum neque congrederetur. Sed non Hannibalem magis
infestum tam sanis consiliis habebat quam magistrum equitum.
Ferox rapidusque consiliis ac lingua immodicus—primo inter
paucos, dein propalam in vulgus—pro cunctatore segnem, pro
155 cauto timidum, adfingens vicina virtutibus vitia, compellabat.
Usque ad aquas Sinuessanas populatio pervenit. Ingentem

157. **tamen ... latius:** the actual destruction was enormous, but the area from which people fled was greater. Undoubtedly Hannibal was counting on this sort of thing coupled with spectacular victories to break the loyalty of the members of the Roman federation and cause wholesale desertions, thus bringing Rome to her knees and obviating the need for a siege. In this Hannibal made his greatest miscalculation.
     Numidae: *the Numidians,* i.e., the Carthaginians.
158. **flagrarent: flagrare,** *to blaze, be inflamed.*
159. **videlicet:** adv., *clearly, of course, to be sure.*
160. **abnuebant: abnuere,** *to deny, refuse.*
     quod: the antecedent is **melioribus parere.**
     melioribus: i.e., the Romans.
161. **Volturnum flumen:** *the Volturnus river,* in Campania.
     castra: sc. **Hannibalis.**
162. **exurebatur: exurere,** *to burn up.*
     amoenissimus: *the most lovely.*
     ager: here, *district, countryside.*
163. **Massici montis:** *Mount Massicus,* along the border of Latium and Campania, north of the Volturnus.
164. **de integro:** *anew.*
     accensa: accendere, *to kindle, set on fire, stir up, incite;* sc. **est.**
     in suos ... intentus (165): *alert to his own men.*
167. **infamem:** *unpopular.*
169. **actum est:** impers. pass.; **agere** here = *discuss.*
170. **enimvero:** adv., *indeed, certainly.*
171. **dictatorem:** subj. of the IND. STATE., which continues through the next several cls. to the end of the sent., following an understood speech vb.
     rei bene gerendae: freely, *the proper management of matters;* dat. with **obstitisse.**
172. **gestae:** sc. **rei bene,** paralleling **rei bene gerendae;** the ever-cautious Fabius had expressed reluctance to celebrate even a recent battle in which the Romans had enjoyed a minor victory.
     sedulo: adv., *deliberately.*
173. **quo:** *by which action,* but essentially = **ut; quo** was often used to introduce a PURPOSE CL. containing a comparative adj. or adv.
174. **promulgaturum:** sc. **se** as subj. of the IND. STATE.; with **rogationem,** *to introduce a bill.*
175. **de aequando ... iure:** the whole purpose of the dictatorship was to secure in an emergency greater efficiency by granting all the imperium to one man instead of two consuls; thus the measure here proposed was by no means **modicam,** as it nullified the original intent of the dictatorship. After being appointed co-dictator, Minucius and his army were trapped by Hannibal until they were rescued by Fabius; thereafter Minucius had the good sense to recognize Fabius as his superior until the end of Fabius' six-month term.

cladem, fugam tamen terroremque latius Numidae fecerunt;
nec tamen is terror, cum omnia bello flagrarent, fide socios di-
movit, videlicet quia iusto et moderato regebantur imperio, nec
160   abnuebant, quod unum vinculum fidei est, melioribus parere.
(XXII.12.1–13.11, excerpts)

Disagreement with Fabius increases both in the army and at Rome.

Ut vero, postquam ad Volturnum flumen castra sunt posita,
exurebatur amoenissimus Italiae ager villaeque passim incen-
diis fumabant, per iuga Massici montis Fabio ducente, tum
prope de integro seditio accensa. Fabius pariter in suos haud
165   minus quam in hostes intentus, prius ab illis invictum animum
praestat. Quamquam probe scit non in castris modo suis sed
iam etiam Romae infamem suam cunctationem esse, obstinatus
tamen tenore eodem consiliorum, aestatis reliquum extraxit. De
iis rebus persaepe et in senatu et in contione actum est. Tum
170   M. Metilius, tribunus plebis, id enimvero ferendum esse negat:
non praesentem solum dictatorem obstitisse rei bene gerendae,
sed absentem etiam gestae obstare, et in ducendo bello sedulo
tempus terere, quo diutius in magistratu sit solusque et Romae
et in exercitu imperium habeat; nunc modicam rogationem pro-
175   mulgaturum de aequando magistri equitum et dictatoris iure;

"The Banquet of Syphax"
(with Scipio Africanus)
Geraert van der Strecken
17th century
Palazzo Labia
Venice, Italy

176. **nec . . . ne ita quidem:** the double negatives do not cancel each other, *and not even so.*

prius . . . quam (177): *sooner . . . than, until.*

mittendum: sc. **esse,** still IND. STATE.

177. **Flamini:** who had died at Trasimene.

suffecisset: sufficere, *to suffice, supply, substitute, appoint* (in place of another).

178. **suasor:** *recommender, advocate.*

C. Terentius Varro: praetor in 218, *Gaius Terentius Varro* became consul in 216, when, along with Lucius Aemilius Paulus, he led the Roman army that Hannibal crushed at the battle of Cannae.

179. **loco . . . sordido:** ABL. OF ORIGIN, a common construction, usually, as here, without a prep.; his father was a butcher and he was himself a plebeian and, in Livy's somewhat biased account, a demagogue.

180. **cum:** conj.

orationibus: delivered by a tribune who had inveighed against the patricians.

181. **rogando collegae:** *for electing a colleague,* DAT. OF PURPOSE.

182. **experta: experiri;** lit., *having tried = realizing from experience.*

competitoribus: one of the two consuls had to be a plebeian and the other a patrician, but the patrician vote had been split among several candidates, so that none had received the required majority and only Varro had been initially elected; thus the patricians were especially eager to find a candidate who would be a strong match for his plebeian colleague.

183. **plebei:** an alternate fifth decl. form for **plebi;** Paulus had earlier been consul, in 219 B.C., and was involved in an indictment brought by the people against his colleague, hence his hostility.

recusantem: recusare, *to decline, refuse, protest.*

184. **ad petitionem:** *to the campaign for election, to run for election.*

185. **eum proficiscentem:** i.e., Paulus; Fabius, no longer dictator, addresses the consul as he leaves for the war.

186. **tui:** gen. of **ego,** *like you;* some adjs. like **similis** which usually take the dat. may be modified by a gen. as here.

187. **supervacanea:** *superfluous.*

189. **nescio an:** *I do not know whether = I am inclined to suppose.*

190. **adversarius:** *political opponent.*

maneat te: *may await you = may prove to be.*

191. **rem . . . hunc (192):** a highly effective ASYNDETON.

192. **nobilior:** here, *more notorious.*

193. **ita res se habet:** a common idiom, *= the situation (the fact of the matter) is this.*

194. **ratio:** here, *method, system.*

195. **stultorum:** it is the mark of a fool to learn simply by trial and error, simply by experience undirected by reason.

196. **ratio:** here, *reasoning, judgment.*

donec: conj., *as long as.*

197. **sede: sedes,** *seat, abode, home.*

solo: solum, *soil, earth.*

199. **commeatibus: commeatus,** *supplies, provisions.*

nec tamen ne ita quidem prius mittendum ad exercitum Q. Fabium quam consulem in locum C. Flamini suffecisset. Unus inventus est suasor legis, C. Terentius Varro, qui priore anno praetor fuerat, loco non humili solum sed etiam sordido ortus. (XXII.14.1–25.18, excerpts)

Gaius Terentius Varro, a plebeian, and Lucius Aemilius Paulus, a patrician, are elected consuls.

180 Cum his orationibus accensa plebs esset, C. Terentius consul unus creatur ut in manu eius essent comitia rogando collegae. Tum experta nobilitas parum fuisse virium in competitoribus, L. Aemilium Paulum infestum plebei, diu ac multum recusantem, ad petitionem compellit. (XXII.35.1–3, excerpts)

Fabius exhorts Paulus as the latter sets out with Varro against Hannibal.

185 Q. Fabius Maximus sic eum proficiscentem adlocutus fertur: "Si aut collegam, id quod mallem, tui similem, L. Aemili, haberes aut tu collegae tui esses similis, supervacanea esset oratio mea. Erras enim, L. Paule, si tibi minus certaminis cum C. Terentio quam cum Hannibale futurum censes: nescio an infestior
190 hic adversarius quam ille hostis maneat te. Atqui si hic, quod facturum se denuntiat, extemplo pugnaverit, aut ego rem militarem, belli hoc genus, hostem hunc ignoro, aut nobilior alius Trasumenno locus nostris cladibus erit. Ita res se habet: una ratio belli gerendi adversus Hannibalem est, qua ego gessi. Nec
195 eventus modo hoc docet—stultorum iste magister est—sed eadem ratio, quae fuit futuraque, donec res eaedem manebunt, immutabilis est. In Italia bellum gerimus, in sede ac solo nostro; omnia circa plena civium ac sociorum sunt; armis, viris, equis, commeatibus iuvant iuvabuntque—id iam fidei documentum in
200 adversis rebus nostris dederunt; meliores, prudentiores, con-

201. **tempus diesque:** = *each day that passes.*
203. **illi:** DAT. OF POSSESSION.
204. **usquam:** adv., *anywhere.*
      in diem rapto (205): *by what he has plundered for the day.*
205. **eius:** here a weak demonstrative with **exercitus,** delayed by attraction to the
      rel. cl., *of that army.*
      Hiberum: *the Ebro river,* in eastern Spain.
206. **fame quam ferro:** ALLITERATION emphasizes the contrast; the style throughout
      this speech is highly rhetorical.
207. **victus:** *food.*
      suppeditat: suppeditare, *to supply, furnish, suffice (for).*
208. **superaturi simus:** *we are going to overcome;* the ACT. PERIPHRASTIC, sometimes
      termed the "fut. subjunct.," formed with the fut. act. partic. + subjunct.
      of **sum,** here with a CL. OF IDEAL CERTAINTY after **dubitas quin,** *do you
      doubt that.*
210. **idem . . . idem (211):** i.e., an immediate battle.
      tui: nom. pl.; sc. **milites.**
212. **resistas oportet (213): oportet** may take a JUSSIVE SUBJUNCT. or an inf.
215. **falsa infamia:** i.e., the unfounded charges which his political enemies would
      make against him.
      nimis saepe: with **laborare.**
216. **aiunt:** often employed, as here, with a proverbial expression.
217. **sine . . . vocent (218): sine** from **sinere,** *let them call you;* **ut** is often omitted
      as the introductory word in a JUSSIVE NOUN CL.
218. **metuat: volo** and its compounds may take the subjunct. (with or without **ut/
      ne**) as well as the more common inf.
221. **tuae potestatis:** PRED. GEN. OF POSSESSION = *in your own control.*
223. **desis: deesse** + dat., *to be wanting, fail.*
224. **properanti: properare,** *to hasten, act in haste.*
226. **sane:** adv., *indeed, truly, certainly.*
      fatentis: agrees with **consulis** but explains **haud laeta,** *admitting that those
      things.*
227. **factu:** abl. of the supine with **facilia.**
      consuli: DAT. OF POSSESSION.
228. **virium atque auctoritatis:** PARTITIVE GEN. with **quid.**
229. **fore:** implied IND. STATE. (continued in the next sent.); although **quid** should
      technically introduce an IND. QUEST., the cl. has the force of an emphatic
      statement, and hence the inf. is used.
230. **telis: telum,** *missile, javelin, spear, weapon.*
231. **caput:** i.e., *his life.*

stantiores nos tempus diesque facit. Hannibal contra in aliena,
in hostili est terra, inter omnia inimica infestaque, procul ab
domo, ab patria; neque illi terra neque mari est pax; nullae eum
urbes accipiunt, nulla moenia; nihil usquam sui videt; in diem
205   rapto vivit; partem vix tertiam exercitus eius habet quem Hi-
berum amnem traiecit; plures fame quam ferro absumpti, nec
his paucis iam victus suppeditat. Dubitas ergo quin sedendo
superaturi simus eum?

    "Haec una salutis est via, L. Paule, quam difficilem in-
210   festamque cives tibi magis quam hostes facient. Idem enim tui
quod hostium milites volent; idem Varro consul Romanus quod
Hannibal Poenus imperator cupiet. Duobus ducibus unus resistas oportet. Resistes autem, si adversus famam rumoresque
hominum satis firmus steteris, si te neque collegae vana gloria
215   neque tua falsa infamia moverit. Veritatem laborare nimis saepe
aiunt, exstingui numquam: vanam gloriam qui spreverit, veram
habebit. Sine timidum pro cauto, tardum pro considerato, im-
bellem pro perito belli vocent. Malo te sapiens hostis metuat
quam stulti cives laudent. Omnia audentem contemnet Hanni-
220   bal, nihil temere agentem metuet. Nec ego, ut nihil agatur, moneo, sed ut agentem te ratio ducat, non fortuna; tuae potestatis
semper tu tuaque omnia sint; armatus intentusque sis; neque
occasioni tuae desis neque suam occasionem hosti des. Omnia
non properanti clara certaque erunt; festinatio improvida est et
225   caeca." (XXII.38.13–39.22, excerpts)

Paulus replies firmly but with apprehension.

    Adversus ea consulis oratio haud sane laeta fuit, magis fa-
tentis ea, quae diceret, vera quam facilia factu esse: quid consuli
adversus collegam seditiosum ac temerarium virium atque auctoritatis fore? Se optare ut omnia prospere evenirent; sed si quid
230   adversi caderet, hostium se telis potius quam suffragiis iratorum
civium caput obiecturum. (XXII.40.1–3, excerpts)

232. **satis exploratis:** this much, at least, the Romans had learned from Flaminius' fatal carelessness at Trasimene.

Poenum ... Poenum (233): the first **Poenum** may refer to Hannibal (cp. 141 above) but the second, a collective sg., clearly means *the Carthaginians.*

233. **Cannas:** *Cannae,* a town on the Aufidus River in Apulia in southeast Italy.

bina castra (234): *two camps,* one on either side of the river; with nouns like **castra** that were normally used only in the pl. the Romans regularly employed distributive numerals (**singuli, bini, terni,** etc.) instead of cardinals.

234. **nactus:** nancisci, *to find, obtain;* here = *entertaining* (the hope).

facturos: sc. **esse;** for the idiom **copiam pugnandi facere,** see 141–42 above.

235. **procursatione:** procursatio, *a charge, skirmish.*

236. **sollicitari:** HIST. INF.; the subj., **Romana castra,** is delayed.

seditione: *dissension, quarrel;* the soldiers were quarreling over the best tactics to employ, just as their consular generals were.

238. **speciosum:** *beautiful, splendid;* but, when sarcastic, as here, = *specious.*

240. **postero die:** Paulus had been in command on the day before and had restrained the Romans from attacking; only one consul at a time had command of the troops, on alternate days.

sors: *lot, fate;* with **imperii,** *responsibility for command.*

nihil: = **non,** *not at all.*

243. **cornua:** Eng. would say *the wings.*

tenuere: for the form, see on **petiere** (109).

244. **laevum:** *left, left-hand.*

Gemino Servilio: *Gnaeus Geminus Servilius,* consul in 217, here was given command of the center of the army.

245. **tuenda data:** *was given to be looked after, was given for command.*

246. **quosque:** i.e., *each of his units.*

247. **Hasdrubal ... Maharbal ... Magone (248):** respectively, one of Hannibal's unit commanders (not the Hasdrubal mentioned above in line 8), his chief cavalry officer, and his youngest brother, Mago.

248. **adversus:** here, an adj. agreeing with **ventus,** *against, adverse (to).*

249. **pulvere:** pulvis, *dust.*

250. **ademit:** adimere, *to take away.*

251. **parte altera:** Paulus had been in command of the right wing of the army, but when those troops had been routed he moved to the **altera pars,** i.e., the center.

252. **funda:** *sling-stone.*

et: = **etiam.**

253. **confertis:** *closely packed, dense, crowded;* here, sc. **equitibus,** *with his cavalrymen in close formation.*

254. **omissis ... equis:** *their horses having been let go* = *having dismounted.*

255. **pepulerunt:** sc. **hostes** as subj.

256. **superantes:** here, *surviving.*

dissipati sunt: dissipare, *to scatter.*

258. **praetervehens:** *riding by.*

259. **cruore:** cruor, *blood, gore.*

The battle of Cannae: the consuls Varro and Paulus find Hannibal ready to fight but are themselves disunited.

Consules satis exploratis itineribus sequentes Poenum, ut ventum ad Cannas est et in conspectu Poenum habebant, bina castra communiunt. Hannibal, spem nactus facturos copiam
235 pugnandi consules, dirigit aciem lacessitque Numidarum procursatione hostes. Inde rursus sollicitari seditione militari ac discordia consulum Romana castra, cum Paulus Flaminii temeritatem Varroni, Varro Paulo speciosum timidis ac segnibus ducibus exemplum Fabium obiceret. (XXII.44.1–5, excerpts)

The lines of battle are finally drawn up.

240 Postero die Varro, cui sors eius diei imperi erat, nihil consulto collega, signum proposuit instructasque copias flumen traduxit, sequente Paulo, quia magis non probare quam non adiuvare consilium poterat. Consules cornua tenuere, Terentius laevum, Aemilius dextrum; Gemino Servilio media pugna
245 tuenda data.
Hannibal prima luce quosque in acie locabat. Duces cornibus praeerant, sinistro Hasdrubal, dextro Maharbal; mediam aciem Hannibal ipse cum fratre Magone tenuit. Ventus adversus Romanis coortus, multo pulvere in ipsa ora volvendo, pros-
250 pectum ademit. (XXII.45.5–46.9, excerpts)

The bravery and death of Paulus, and the rout of the Romans.

Parte altera pugnae Paulus, quamquam primo statim proelio funda graviter ictus fuerat, tamen et occurrit saepe cum confertis Hannibali et aliquot locis proelium restituit, protegentibus eum equitibus Romanis, omissis postremo equis quia
255 consulem et ad regendum equum vires deficiebant. Pepulerunt tamen iam paucos superantes et labore ac vulneribus fessos; inde dissipati omnes sunt equosque ad fugam qui poterant repetebant. Cn. Lentulus, tribunus militum, cum praetervehens equo sedentem in saxo cruore oppletum consulem vidisset,
260 "L. Aemili," inquit, "quem unum insontem culpae cladis ho-

262. **comes:** *companion, comrade.*
263. **ne . . . feceris:** JUSSIVE SUBJUNCT., *do not make.*
    funestam: *disastrous,* i.e., more catastrophic than it already is.
264. **luctus:** *grief, sorrow;* gen.
265. **macte virtute esto:** idiomatic, *be honored for your courage, bravo.*
266. **cave:** (sometimes **cave ne**) + the JUSSIVE SUBJUNCT. **absumas,** a prohibition,
    lit., *beware of wasting* = *do not waste.*
    miserando: miserari, *to pity.*
    exiguum: *scanty, small, little.*
269. **Fabio:** sc. **nuntia;** the vb. takes a JUSSIVE SUBJUNCT. in the preceding cl., an
    IND. STATE. here.
270. **memet:** emphatic for **me.**
271. **patere:** imper. of **patior.**
    reus: *defendant;* Paulus had earlier been charged with misappropriation of
    booty (in 219 B.C.) but not convicted.
    e: *as a result of, after.*
272. **alieno crimine:** lit., *by a charge belonging to another,* i.e., *by incriminating an-
    other.*
274. **haec . . . agentes:** i.e., as Lentulus and Paulus were engaged in this ex-
    change.
276. **undique:** adv., *from all sides, on all sides.*
    effuse: adv., *far and wide.*
277. **consul alter:** Varro.
    insertus: inserere, *to introduce, join.*
278. **Venusiam:** *Venusia,* the modern Venosa, a town in Apulia about 30 miles
    southwest of Cannae.
281. **tantadem prope . . . pars (282):** *nearly the same proportion.*
282. **caesi:** sc. **esse.**
283. **haec est:** Eng. would say *such was.*
284. **ceteri:** i.e., in contrast to Maharbal.
    circumfusi: circumfundere, *to pour around;* pass., *to gather around.* Eng.
    would use a finite vb., not a partic., in parallel with **gratularentur** and
    suaderent, *when the others had gathered round and were . . . .*
285. **ut . . . et . . . sumeret et . . . daret (286):** JUSSIVE NOUN CL., depending on
    suaderent, *that he should both . . . and . . . .*
    perfunctus: perfungi + abl., *to perform, complete.*
    bello: these Carthaginians considered that the war, and not merely the battle,
    had been won.
    diei: PARTITIVE GEN. with **quod reliquum esset,** *what was left of the day.*
287. **cessandum:** sc. **esse,** impers. pass., *that there ought to be no delay at all.*
288. **immo:** adv., *on the contrary, indeed.*
289. **Capitolio: Capitolium** was used both of the temple and the hill, apparently
    regarded as the **caput** of Rome; here either *on the Capitoline* or *in the
    Capitol.*
    epulaberis: epulari, *to banquet, feast.*
    equite: here used as a collective noun.

diernae dei respicere debent, cape hunc equum, dum et tibi
virium aliquid superest et comes ego te tollere possum ac prote-
gere. Ne funestam hanc pugnam morte consulis feceris; etiam
sine hoc lacrimarum satis luctusque est."

265   Ad ea consul: "Tu quidem, Cn. Corneli, macte virtute esto;
sed cave, frustra miserando, exiguum tempus e manibus hostium evadendi absumas. Abi; nuntia publice patribus urbem
Romanam muniant ac, priusquam victor hostis advenit, praesidiis firment; privatim Q. Fabio Aemilium, praeceptorum eius
270 memorem, et vixisse adhuc et mori. Memet in hac strage militum meorum patere exspirare, ne aut reus iterum e consulatu
sim aut accusator collegae exsistam ut alieno crimine inno-
centiam meam protegam."

    Haec eos agentes prius turba fugientium civium, deinde
275 hostes oppressere; consulem ignorantes quis esset, obruere telis;
Lentulum inter tumultum abripuit equus. Tum undique effuse
fugiunt. Consul alter, seu forte seu consilio nulli fugientium in-
sertus agmini, cum quinquaginta fere equitibus Venusiam per-
fugit. (XXII.49.1–14, excerpts)

The Romans' catastrophic losses.

280   Quadraginta quinque milia quingenti pedites, duo milia
septingenti equites, et tantadem prope civium sociorumque
pars caesi dicuntur. Capta eo proelio tria milia peditum et
equites mille et quingenti dicuntur. Haec est pugna Cannensis.
(XXII.49.15–50.1, excerpts)

Hannibal fails to follow up his victory.

    Hannibali victori cum ceteri circumfusi gratularentur sua-
285 derentque ut, tanto perfunctus bello, diei quod reliquum esset
noctisque insequentis quietem et ipse sibi sumeret et fessis daret
militibus, Maharbal, praefectus equitum, minime cessandum
ratus, "Immo ut quid hac pugna sit actum scias, die quinto,"
inquit, "victor in Capitolio epulaberis. Sequere; cum equite, ut

290. **prius venisse quam venturum:** sc. **esse** with **venturum** and **te** as subj. of both infs.; cp. Eng., "you will be there before they know it."

291. **maiorque quam ut:** *and greater than (that) he could = too great for him to be able;* the **ut** clause is result.

293. **pensandum: pensare,** *to weigh carefully.*
    opus esse: *there is need, it is necessary;* in this common phrase, **opus** is indecl. and can be accompanied by various constructions including the abl. (very common), the gen. (less commonly), the inf.

294. **nimirum:** adv., *doubtless, of course, to be sure.*

295. **saluti . . . urbi atque imperio (296):** DAT. OF PURPOSE + DAT. OF REF., sometimes called the DOUBLE DAT., *for the salvation for (of) the city and the empire.*

297. **nulla . . . esset:** POTENTIAL SUBJUNCT. Throughout this entire passage we see Roman character at its best; surely one of the clearest reasons for Rome's greatness is this morale and pertinacity, this **gravitas** and **virtus,** which had an epic quality that both Vergil and Livy appreciated, admired, and recorded for the inspiration of their readers.
    profecto: adv., *surely, actually, really.*
    mole: moles, *mass, large structure;* with **cladis,** Eng. would use an adj., *so massive a calamity.*

298. **praetores:** again in the absence of the consuls.
    curiam Hostiliam (299): the *Curia Hostilia* was the regular meeting place of the senate down to the time of Caesar; located in the Roman Forum, it was said to have been built by Tullus Hostilius, Rome's third king.

301. **expeditos:** *light-armed* and therefore swift.

302. **Appia et Latina via:** the two major highways leading south from Rome.
    obvios: *those in the way opposite = those whom they met;* i.e., fugitives straggling back to Rome.
    percunctando: percunctari, *to question.*

303. **referant:** REL. CL. OF PURPOSE; note that, for a more vivid narrative, Livy uses primary sequence after a historical main vb.

304. **quid:** with **reliquum . . . fecerint;** freely, *have left any remnant.*
    nominis: here, *power.*

305. **quo:** adv., *where.*

306. **acturus . . . sit:** *what he is going to do;* ACT. PERIPHRASTIC, commonly employed to indicate fut. tense in an IND. QUEST.
    haec . . . esse (307): IND. STATE., in parallel with **equites . . . mittendos,** depending on **censuit** in the preceding sent.

307. **impigros:** *energetic*
    illud: *the following,* looking ahead to, and explained by, the lengthy series of appositional JUSSIVE NOUN CLS. that follow.
    patres: = **patres conscripti, senatores; per patres,** like **per impigros iuvenes,** in place of the DAT. OF AGENT.

308. **tollant: tollere** can mean either *to raise up* or *to suppress,* here the latter.
    publico: i.e., indoors and away from public places.

309. **arceant: arcere,** *to keep away, restrain, prevent.*
    comploratus: *loud wailing, lamentations,* acc. pl.

312. **nisi . . . salvis (313):** ABL. ABS. with conditional force.

290 prius venisse quam venturum sciant, praecedam." Hannibali
nimis laeta res est visa maiorque quam ut eam statim capere
animo posset. Itaque voluntatem se laudare Maharbalis ait, ad
consilium pensandum temporis opus esse. Tum Maharbal: "Non
omnia nimirum eidem di dedere: vincere scis, Hannibal; victo-
295 ria uti nescis." Mora eius diei satis creditur saluti fuisse urbi
atque imperio. (XXII.51.1–4)

Action at Rome as the news reaches the city.

Nulla profecto alia gens tanta mole cladis non obruta esset.
P. Furius Philus et M. Pomponius, praetores, senatum in curiam
Hostiliam vocaverunt ut de urbis custodia consulerent; neque
300 enim dubitabant, deletis exercitibus, hostem ad oppugnandam
Romam venturum. Tum Q. Fabius Maximus censuit equites expeditos et Appia et Latina via mittendos, qui obvios percunc-
tando referant quae fortuna consulum atque exercituum sit et,
si quid dii immortales reliquum Romani nominis fecerint, ubi
305 eae copiae sint; quo se Hannibal post proelium contulerit, quid
paret, quid agat acturusque sit. Haec exploranda noscendaque
per impigros iuvenes esse; illud per patres ipsos agendum ut
tumultum ac trepidationem in urbe tollant, matronas publico
arceant, comploratus familiarum coerceant, silentium per ur-
310 bem faciant, nuntios rerum omnium ad praetores deducendos
curent, custodesque praeterea ad portas ponant qui prohibeant
quemquam egredi urbe, cogantque homines nullam nisi urbe ac
moenibus salvis salutem sperare.

Tum demum litterae a C. Terentio consule adlatae sunt:

Via Appia, with ruins of tombs

315. **Canusii: Canusium,** modern Canosa, a town in Apulia.
316. **naufragio: naufragium,** *shipwreck.*
317. **vulgatae sunt (318): vulgare,** *to communicate, announce.*
318. **sacrum . . . Cereris (319):** the major ritual celebration of the grain-goddess, Ceres, was the Cerealia, held on April 19; as the battle of Cannae took place on August 2, Livy must have in mind some other festival.
321. **dilectu: dilectus,** *levy, draft.*
322. **praetextatos:** boys under 17; the **toga praetexta** with its crimson band around the edge was worn until a boy became of age at 17 or 18 and assumed the **toga virilis.**
     scribunt: *enroll.*
323. **Latinum . . . nomen:** *(those of) Latin status,* a class of allies who had special privileges; on the principle of **divide et impera,** Rome had a separate treaty with each of her allies.
     ad . . . accipiendos (324): *to enlist.*
     ex formula: *in accordance with their treaty.*
324. **arma, tela:** the former primarily defensive, the latter offensive.
325. **spolia . . . detrahunt:** to be used in case of need against the enemy.
326. **quanto:** ABL. OF DEGREE OF DIFFERENCE.
327. **vel:** here, adv., *even.*
     indicio: DAT. OF PURPOSE.
     quod: *the fact that,* introducing a noun cl. in appos. with **res.**
     eam diem: for the gender, see on 130–31 above.
328. **labare:** *to waver.*
     nulla . . . alia: with **de re.**
330. **moverunt:** sc. **animos.**
331. **consulis Romam adventum:** i.e., the return of Varro to Rome after his defeat at Cannae.
332. **quo in tempore ipso (333):** the prep. **in** was used in an ABL. OF TIME construction when a situation, rather than an exact time, was being described.
333. **magno animo:** ABL. OF DESCRIPTION.
     consuli . . . redeunti (334): dat. with the compound adv. **obviam,** *toward, to meet.*
334. **fuisset:** SUBJUNCT. BY ATTRACTION, within the RESULT CL.
     et . . . et (335): *both . . . and.*
     itum . . . ab omnibus ordinibus sit (335): impers. pass. with ABL. OF AGENT, *all classes went;* this must have included even senators, some of whom had favored another battle with Hannibal.
335. **frequenter:** adv., *in throngs.*
336. **desperasset:** the subjunct. shows that this is the people's reason, not Livy's; *because (as they said) he had not despaired.* When one considers what a scapegoat Varro might have been, Livy is showing us here Roman character at its best; this magnificent morale plus the fact that, for whatever reason, Hannibal did not march directly on Rome enabled the Romans to survive Cannae and to persevere until (as was the rule in Roman history) they won the final victory, at the battle of Zama in 202 B.C.

315 L. Aemilium consulem exercitumque caesum; sese Canusii esse, reliquias tantae cladis velut ex naufragio colligentem; Poenum sedere ad Cannas. Tum privatae quoque per domos clades vulgatae sunt, adeoque totam urbem opplevit luctus ut sacrum anniversarium Cereris intermissum sit. Inde dictator ex auctori-

320 tate patrum dictus M. Iunius et Ti. Sempronius magister equitum, dilectu edicto, iuniores ab annis septendecim et quosdam praetextatos scribunt. Quattuor ex his legiones et mille equites effecti. Item ad socios Latinumque nomen ad milites ex formula accipiendos mittunt. Arma, tela, alia parari iubent, et vetera

325 spolia hostium detrahunt templis porticibusque. (XXII.54.10–57.10, excerpts)

The remarkable morale of the Romans.

Quanto autem maior ea clades superioribus cladibus fuerit, vel ea res indicio est, quod fides sociorum, quae ad eam diem firma steterat, tum labare coepit, nulla profecto alia de re quam quod desperaverant de imperio. Nec tamen eae clades defecti-

330 onesque sociorum moverunt ut pacis usquam mentio apud Romanos fieret, neque ante consulis Romam adventum nec postquam is rediit renovavitque memoriam acceptae cladis; quo in tempore ipso adeo magno animo civitas fuit ut consuli ex tanta clade, cuius ipse causa maxima fuisset, redeunti et obviam itum

335 frequenter ab omnibus ordinibus sit et gratiae actae quod de re publica non desperasset. (XXII.61.10–14, excerpts)

"Battle of Zama" (Scipio's defeat of Hannibal, 202 B.C.)
Anonymous (circle of Giulio Romano), ca. 1521
Pushkin Museum of Fine Arts, Moscow, Russia

Ovid's *Metamorphoses*

Ovid (Publius Ovidius Naso) was born to a wealthy equestrian family on March 20, 43 B.C., the year of Cicero's death and the year after the assassination of Julius Caesar. His father sent him to study in Rome and Athens, hoping the young man would embark upon a career in law and politics. But Ovid was far more inclined to literature, and in his early 20's he published his first books of verse (begun when he was only a teenager), the *Amores,* sprightly elegiac poems written to and about his fictional mistress, Corinna. Though quite self-consciously following the tradition of Catullus, Tibullus, and Propertius (these last two friends of his), his elegies were at once more contrived and more playful, almost a parody of his predecessors' work.

"Whatever I tried to compose became verse" *(quod temptabam scribere versus erat),* Ovid later wrote (*Tristia* 4.10), reflecting back on his career. And indeed he was an enormously prolific poet, publishing one book after another over a period of more than 40 years; most of his early work was sportively erotic, in the manner of the *Amores,* including: the *Heroides,* verse epistles from famous mythological heroines to their absent husbands or paramours (e.g., Medea to Jason, Dido to Aeneas); the only partially extant *Medicamina Faciei Femineae,* a how-to manual on ladies' cosmetics; the *Ars Amatoria,* another tongue-in-cheek didactic poem on how to attract and seduce a lover, with two volumes of instructions (some rather naughtily detailed) for men and another for women; and then, aptly concluding the series, the *Remedia Amoris,* a handbook on extricating oneself from a love affair, once one has had enough.

If all of this sounds ahead of its time and rather lacking in Roman *gravitas,* so it was. By the time the "Art of Love" first appeared, ca. 1 B.C., Octavian had long since been proclaimed "Augustus," his monarchy was firmly established, and his program of moral reform was well underway. In this context, Ovid's poetry, which routinely trumpeted adultery, travestied the sanctity of marriage, and poked fun at authority, could be easily viewed as subversive. It is not surprising, therefore, that in A.D. 8 Ovid was banished by Augustus to Tomis on the Black Sea. Writing from exile, the poet insists that his relegation was the consequence, not of any crime, but of a *carmen* and an *error;* the exact nature of the "mistake" has never been ascertained, but the offending poetry certainly included the *Ars Amatoria,* and the combined offense was so considerable that neither Augustus himself nor his successor Tiberius gave in to the poet's unceasing pleas for a recall from Tomis, where he remained, embittered, until his death in A.D. 17 (the same year that Livy died) at the age of 60.

During the decade of his exile, Ovid continued work on two enormously important poetical works which he had begun earlier, the *Fasti* and the *Metamorphoses.* The former, a verse calendar describing the major historical events, legends, and festivals associated with each month of the Roman year, remains an invaluable source for these topics, though we have only the first six books (for January through June). The latter, a rich compendium of classical myths in 15 dactylic hexameter volumes, has remained over the centuries Ovid's most popular and influential work.

Set in a quasi-chronological framework and woven together with ingeniously crafted interconnections, the *Metamorphoses* recounts some 250 tales of transformation, from the creation of the world out of chaos to the deification of Julius Caesar. In this *carmen perpetuum,* as he called his greatest poem, Ovid presents us with dazzling narratives (in many cases the best known, or only, ancient source for a particular myth), which range in tone from the tragic to the comic, the heroic to the grotesque, the patriotic to the erotic, some of them charged with political (and occasionally anti-Augustan) undertones, and all of them providing astute insights into the human condition. A supreme manipulator of the language, Ovid has given us too a production that is remarkably "audiovisual," abounding in cinematographic effects and with a musicality perhaps unparalleled in classical Latin verse.

The four selections included in this book are among Ovid's best known. The story of the two star-crossed Babylonian lovers, Pyramus and Thisbe, may have originated in the near east, but Ovid is our earliest source; the two young people (teenagers most likely) were neighbors who, once acquainted, fell rapturously in love, only to have their parents forbid their relationship. At first communicating with each other through a crack in the wall connecting their homes, they soon conspire to slip away for a nocturnal, and ultimately fatal, rendezvous just outside the city. This story of young love and its tragic ending has charmed readers for centuries and was a major influence on Shakespeare's *Romeo and Juliet.* The similarly ill-fated love of Orpheus and Eurydice was well known to Ovid's readers from Vergil's longer and more dramatic narration in the *Georgics.* The lovely Eurydice dies of a snakebite on her wedding day, and her bridegroom boldly descends into the Underworld to bring her back from the kingdom of the dead; Ovid's perfunctory retelling, which focuses on Orpheus' almost legalistic pleading with Pluto and Persephone in Hades, is regarded by many readers as a parody of his Vergilian model.

Also familiar to modern readers is Ovid's story of Midas, the Phrygian king who, granted one wish by the wine-god Bacchus, wasted the opportunity by asking that all he touched be turned to gold. Ovid's narration is spectacularly visual, as he shows us the king moving from one object to another, gleefully transforming each into gold, until too late he realizes that even his food and drink and his own body are being similarly metamorphosed. In the tale of the Athenian inventor Daedalus and his young son Icarus, another error of judgment leads to unfortunate, and in this case fatal, consequences; imprisoned by Minos, king of Crete, Daedalus constructs miraculous wings for himself and his son to aid in their escape from the island, and Icarus, with the impetuosity of youth, disregards his father's warnings and flies too near the sun, thus melting the wax that held together his wings and plummeting to his death in the sea.

"Daedalus and Icarus"
Antonio Canova
1779
Museo Correr
Venice, Italy

Exhibiting a variety that is characteristic of the *Metamorphoses,* two of these stories, those of Pyramus and Thisbe and of Daedalus and Icarus, focus on more or less ordinary human beings, their passions and their frailties, while the other two involve the agency of the gods, Bacchus and the king and queen of the Underworld. All involve miracles or transformations. And all are told in Ovid's lively, fluid, highly visual, and musical style.

Some Aspects of Ovid's Style

Ovid is one of the easiest of Roman authors to read and enjoy, and students will quickly become accustomed to the peculiarities of his style, many of which are characteristic of Latin verse in general and most of which are commented upon in the notes accompanying the selections below. Following are a few important points to keep in mind, as you begin to read, especially if this is your first extensive introduction to Latin poetry.

Word order: Word order is much freer in poetry than it is in prose, and Ovid is no exception. Words that logically belong together, e.g., an adjective and its noun or a preposition and its object, are often separated for emphasis or some other poetic effect (and, of course, for metrical considerations). For instance, an adjective may appear as the first word in a line and its noun as the last (a device referred to as "framing"), or a noun-adjective pair may even be split between two lines; a prepositional phrase may occur between a noun and its adjective or may itself be broken up by other words, or a preposition may follow its object ("anastrophe"); a relative pronoun may precede its antecedent or be placed late in the clause which it is supposed to introduce, or the antecedent may be attracted into the relative clause. A key word or phrase may be delayed and carried over to the beginning of the next verse ("enjambement").

"Chiasmus" (ABBA order, e.g., object-verb-verb-object, *omnia possideat . . . possidet aera,* "Daedalus and Icarus," line 187), often used to emphasize some contrast, is a favorite device, as is "interlocked word order," especially of the ABAB variety (e.g., adjective[A]-adjective[B]-noun[A]-noun[B], *una duos . . . nox . . . amantes,* "Pyramus and Thisbe," 108); an elaboration of this interlocked order known as a "golden line" places the verb at the center of the line with two adjectives preceding and two nouns following, in an ABCAB arrangement (*scelerata fero consumite viscera morsu,* "Pyramus," 113). Sometimes interlocked order is meant to create a "word-picture," where the words are arranged in a way that suggests visually the image that is being described (*obscurum timido pede fugit in antrum,* "Pyramus," 100, where the fearful Thisbe is literally inside the "dark . . . cave").

Ellipsis is common in poetry as well (especially omission of forms of *sum* and the subject of an infinitive in indirect statement), and in Ovid one must frequently supply in one phrase a word from another adjacent phrase. The notes provided along with the text below will often call attention to such devices, but students, in reading and translating poetry, need to be aware of these and other variants of word order and thus be all the more attentive to the word endings that signal syntactical relationships.

Morphology and syntax: Latin poetry in general is characterized by a wider variety of forms and syntax than usual in prose; again, these are often commented upon in the notes, but students should be generally aware of these differences before beginning to read. The predicate geni-

Augustus of Prima Porta
1st century B.C.
Vatican Museums
Vatican State

tive (of description or possession) is commonly used in place of a predicate nominative; the dative is more freely used, often in place of the ablative, as in the dative of separation, the dative with verbs of mixing, and the dative of agent with passive forms other than the gerundive; the ablative instead of the accusative is employed for duration of time, the ablative of route is common, and the ablative of agent is used instead of the ablative of means, for purposes of personification. The so-called "poetic plural" is employed where prose would use the singular; and Greek forms appear frequently, especially with proper nouns.

Common too are: omission of prepositions where prose would require them, especially in place constructions; the use of simple verbs instead of their compounds; use of *-ere* for *-erunt* for the third person plural of the perfect indicative; use of the genitive plural *-um* in place of *-orum/-arum.*

Rhetorical and poetic devices and sound effects: Ovid employs a wide range of these devices, including anaphora, apostrophe, hendiadys, metonymy, personification, simile, synecdoche, and transferred epithet, many of which are identified in the notes. One of the most musical of Latin poets, Ovid also makes extensive use of alliteration, assonance, and onomatopoeia, as well as the various metrical effects discussed in the next section.

The Scansion and Reading of Ovid's Verse

In order to associate his poem with epic, Ovid deliberately composed the *Metamorphoses* in the metrical form known as dactylic hexameter, the same meter employed by Homer in his *Iliad* and *Odyssey* and by Vergil in the *Aeneid.* Like these authors, Ovid meant for his poetry to be read aloud, to be recited (from the Latin word *recitare,* which quite aptly means "to bring back to life"), hence the importance of such features as alliteration and assonance. But the most prominent sound effect in the poem is, of course, the meter itself; and in order to appreciate fully the work's musicality and indeed to experience it as the author intended, one must read aloud. The most important step in this regard is also the easiest, and that is, as the late Professor Gareth Morgan remarked, simply to read the words correctly and with attention to what they mean. The point is to read the poem as one would read a story in prose to a group of eager listeners, with proper pronunciation of course, but, in particular, expressively. Read the text aloud in just this way, each time you pick it up (and certainly before you commence the artificial exercise of translation into English), and you will find yourself well on your way to a proper appreciation of Ovid's poetry; beyond that, one needs to know just a bit about the technicalities of dactylic hexameter verse.

Meter: From the Latin *metrum* (Greek *metron,* "measure"), poetic meter is simply the measured arrangement of syllables in a regular rhythmical pattern. In English poetry, meter is based upon the patterned alternation of accented and unaccented syllables (Jáck and Jíll went úp the híll"); the system is called "qualitative," as it depends upon the quality (stressed/unstressed) of the syllables. Medieval Latin verse works the same way, as we shall see later on in this book. But in classical Latin poetry the meter was "quantitative" (a system borrowed, like much else in Roman verse, from the Greeks), based on the alternation of long and short syllables.

Syllable quantity and elision: The syllables of a word may be long or short, as you learned in your first Latin course in order to know which syllable of a word is accented. A long syllable (indicated here by underlining) is one that contains either a long vowel (e.g., *amō*—macrons indicating long vowels are provided in the Vocabulary at the end of this book), or a diphthong (*ae, oe, ei, ui, au, eu;* e.g., *saepe*), or a short vowel followed by two or more consonants or the double consonant **x** (e.g., *quantus*). Exceptions to this last rule are as follows: *h* does not count as a consonant; *ch, ph, th,* and *qu* count only as single consonants; and when a stop *(p, b, c, g, d, t)* is followed by a liquid *(1, r),* the syllable may be treated as either long or short according to the requirements of the meter (*patria* or *patria*). In poetry the two-consonant rule also holds when the final syllable of a word within (not at the end of) a verse ends with a consonant and the next word begins with a consonant (*enim* pater).

When a word ends with a vowel (or diphthong) or a vowel + *-m* and the following word begins with a vowel/diphthong or *h-* + a vowel/diphthong, the two syllables involved were generally "elided," i.e., reduced to a single syllable, usually with the vowel in the first syllable muted or dropped altogether and the quantity of the second syllable determining the quantity of the resultant single syllable. For example, *quantum erat* ("Pyramus," 74) was pronounced *quant'erat* and the resultant elided syllable *(t'e)* is short, whereas *foribusque excedere* ("Pyramus," 85) would be pronounced *foribusqu'excedere* and the elided syllable *(qu'ex)* is long.

In the context of this discussion, it should be recalled that initial *i*- followed by a vowel functions as a consonant with the sound of *y*, and thus prevents elision (*quoque iure*, "Pyramus," 60, is not elided) and can make a preceding syllable long (*et iacuit*, "Pyramus," 121). Likewise intervocalic -*i*- serves both as a vowel producing a diphthong with the preceding vowel, and as a consonant; e.g., *huius* is scanned as if spelled "hui-yus."

Dactylic hexameter: The dactylic hexameter line consists of six measures, or feet, with the basic pattern of the first five feet being a dactyl, i.e., a long syllable followed by two shorts ($-\,\smile\smile$). A spondee (two long syllables, $-\,-$) is often substituted for a dactyl in the first four feet of the line, rarely in the fifth (a line with a fifth-foot spondee is in fact called a "spondaic line"—see "Midas," line 93), and the sixth foot is always a spondee (or a trochee [$-\,\smile$], which here has the force of a spondee, due to the slight pause naturally occurring at the end of the verse). The pattern of dactyls and possible spondees may be thus schematized:

$$-\quad-\quad-\quad-\quad(-)$$
$$-\,\mathsf{u}\,\mathsf{u}\,/\,-\,\mathsf{u}\,\mathsf{u}\,/\,-\,\mathsf{u}\,\mathsf{u}\,/\,-\,\mathsf{u}\,\mathsf{u}\,/\,-\,\mathsf{u}\,\mathsf{u}\,/\,-\,-$$

An author may vary the balance of dactyls and spondees in a line to achieve some special effect, using more dactyls to describe rapid actions (e.g., "Pyramus," line 92, where the opening series of dactyls suggests the quick coming of nightfall) or more spondees to describe some slow, or deliberate, or solemn action (e.g., "Pyramus," 62, where the heavy spondees emphasize the unwavering intensity of the lovers' passion). Each foot in a dactylic hexameter line begins with a long syllable, and in reading aloud this syllable should be pronounced with a slight stress accent, known as an "ictus," which may or may not coincide with the normal word accent; poets sometimes manipulate the coincidence or "conflict" (non-coincidence) of ictus and accent for special effect, coincidence producing a smoother, more rapid flow, and conflict creating a harsher, staccato rhythm.

Each line generally contains a principal pause, sometimes two, generally coinciding with the end of some sense unit such as a phrase or a clause; if the principal pause occurs within a foot, it is called a "caesura," and if it occurs at the division between two feet (which is less common), it is called a "diaeresis." The commonest pattern in dactylic hexameter involves a major caesura in the third foot, though occasionally there are two equivalent caesurae in the second and fourth feet (marking off some phrase within the line), and there are other patterns as well, thus producing greater rhythmical variety.

Scansion: Scansion is the process of marking the long and short syllables in a line of verse and indicating the feet and the principal pause(s), while keeping in mind the several points made in the preceding discussion. Conventionally, long syllables are indicated with a line over the syllable (⁻), short syllables with a micron (ᵘ); the individual feet are marked off with a slash (/), and the principal pause(s) with a double slash (//). Elisions are marked with parentheses, and the mark indicating the long or short quantity of the resultant single syllable is placed above the space between the two elided syllables.

With practice, students can scan lines with ease, from beginning to end, as the procedure is quite straightforward. But beginners may wish at first to follow these steps: 1) mark all elisions; 2) mark the last two syllables long, as the sixth foot may always be treated as a spondee; 3) mark all syllables long that contain a diphthong or what you know to be a long vowel; then 4) mark all remaining syllables, keeping in mind that the first syllable of each foot must be long, that the fifth foot is nearly always a dactyl, and that, whenever you identify a short syllable in the first five feet, there must always be a second short syllable adjacent to it. Consider the following examples, all drawn from the story of "Pyramus and Thisbe":

55   Pyramus / et This/be, // iuve/num pul/cherrimu/s alter,

56   altera, // quas ori/ens habu/it, // prae/lata pu/ellis

74   Quan(tum e)ra/t ut sine/res // to/to nos / corpore / iungi

75   aut, hoc / si nimi/(um est) // vel a/d oscula / danda pa/teres?

Reading aloud: Scansion is merely a mechanical procedure designed to familiarize students with meter. Once you have had sufficient practice with scanning lines and then reading them aloud, you will find it a fairly easy matter to recite a text rhythmically without needing to scan the lines first. Let me repeat the cardinal rule stated earlier in this introduction: in order to properly recite a text, you need only read the words correctly and think about what they mean. The poet has done most of the work for you, after all, by arranging the words in each verse with the appropriate alternation of long and short syllables; if you simply pronounce each word according to the rules you learned in beginning Latin and have practiced ever since, you will hear and even feel the quantitative rhythms the author has built into the line. Remembering that in the ancient world poetry was performance, you should read aloud yourself as if you were reading a story to a receptive audience; read expressively, with attention to meaning, pausing just briefly at the appropriate points, usually at the end of a phrase or clause (without any exaggerated pause at the end of a line, especially where there is enjambement), and adding the slight verse accent, or ictus, to the first syllable in each foot.

Whenever you pick up a Latin text—whether prose or verse, in fact—read it aloud. Then, once you have read, and translated, and thought about, and discussed a passage in class, and before you pack up your books, read that passage aloud again; as a consequence you will come to appreciate more fully not only the matter of an author's text but also the manner, often sonorous and dramatic, in which he expected his audience to experience it.

"Ovid"
Luca Signorelli, 15th century
Duomo, Orvieto, Italy

55. **Pyramus et Thisbe:** there were rivers with these names in Cilicia, but the two characters are known from no source earlier than Ovid.

   iuvenum ... alter ... altera ... puellis (56): CHIASMUS; the device is very common in Ovid.

56. **quas:** antecedent is **puellis.**

   praelata: praeferre, *to prefer.*

57. **tenuere:** = **tenuerunt** (so also **vetuere, potuere,** etc., below).

   dicitur: the subj. is **Semiramis,** wife of the Assyrian king Ninus, reputed to have been the builder of Babylon.

   altam: with **urbem,** both positioned at line's end; adj.-noun pairs are often widely separated in Ovid, frequently for some special effect (as here, perhaps, to suggest the grandeur of the city).

58. **coctilibus:** lit., *cooked* or *baked,* hence *made of brick.*

   muris: murus, *wall.*

   cinxisse: cingere, *to surround.*

59. **notitiam: notitia,** *acquaintance.*

   gradus: acc. pl., *steps;* sc. **amoris,** or this may be, with **notitiam,** a HENDIADYS *(the first steps of their relationship).*

   vicinia: *proximity,* i.e., their being neighbors.

60. **taedae: taeda,** *torch, marriage torch* (carried in the wedding procession).

   iure: here, *(legal) bond.*

   coissent: coire, *to come together, be joined;* POTENTIAL SUBJUNCT.

61. **vetuere: vetare,** *to forbid, prevent.*

   quod: *what, that which;* the following cl. is antecedent.

62. **ex aequo:** idiom, *equally;* the line's symmetry and the spondaic rhythms help to emphasize the equality and intensity of the lovers' feelings.

   captis ... mentibus: sc. **amore.**

63. **conscius:** *witness.*

   abest: note the shift from the perf. tenses of the preceding sent. to the HIST. PRES. in this sent., lending further intensity and vividness to the narrative.

   nutu: nutus, *nod.*

64. **quoque:** = **et quo,** ABL. OF DEGREE OF DIFFERENCE; **quoque magis ... (eo) magis,** *and the more . . . the more.*

   magis tegitur, tectus magis: CHIASMUS.

   aestuat: aestuare, *to burn, blaze;* **ignis** is subj. of both this vb. and **tegitur.**

65. **fissus erat: findere,** *to split;* the subj. is **paries,** *wall* (of a house).

   tenui: *slender, thin.*

   rima: *crack.*

   duxerat: here, *had developed.*

66. **utrique:** *each.*

67. **vitium:** here, *flaw, defect.*

   nulli: dat. with **notatum,** *known (to).*

   saeculum: *age, generation.*

68. **primi:** as often, Lat. employs an adj. where Eng. would use an adv. (so also **tutae,** *safely,* in 69).

   amantes: the partic. functions as a noun, *lovers;* Ovid addresses the two in a dramatic APOSTROPHE.

PYRAMUS AND THISBE

Metamorphoses. **4.55–166**

Pyramus and Thisbe, two young lovers in Babylon, occupy adjoining houses, but their parents determine to keep them apart.

55   Pyramus et Thisbe, iuvenum pulcherrimus alter,
        altera, quas oriens habuit, praelata puellis,
        contiguas tenuere domos, ubi dicitur altam
        coctilibus muris cinxisse Semiramis urbem.
        Notitiam primosque gradus vicinia fecit;
60   tempore crevit amor; taedae quoque iure coissent,
        sed vetuere patres. Quod non potuere vetare,
        ex aequo captis ardebant mentibus ambo.
        Conscius omnis abest; nutu signisque loquuntur,
        quoque magis tegitur, tectus magis aestuat ignis.
65   Fissus erat tenui rima, quam duxerat olim,
        cum fieret, paries domui communis utrique.
        Id vitium nulli per saecula longa notatum
        (quid non sentit amor?) primi vidistis amantes,

"Semiramis Building Babylon"
Edgar Degas, 1860–62
Musée d'Orsay, Paris, France

69. **vocis . . . iter:** *a passage for your speech,* an image elaborated in the next cl.
     tutae . . . murmure blanditiae minimo (70): this sort of ABAB arrangement,
         known as INTERLOCKED WORD ORDER, is a favorite device of Ovid's.
70. **blanditiae: blanditia,** *blandishment, endearment.*
71. **constiterant: constare,** *to stand firm, take a position.*
     hinc . . . illinc: *on this side . . . on that side;* the CHIASMUS here neatly suits
         the image.
72. **in . . . vices:** idiom, *in turn.*
     fuerat captatus: = captatus erat, *had been seized at.*
     anhelitus: *gasping, panting, breathing;* the young lovers are pictured longingly
         gasping at one another's breath through the crack in the wall.
73. **invidus:** *envious, jealous;* the lovers imagine the wall as a living creature.
     quid: = cur.
74. **quantum erat:** more vivid than **esset,** *how great a matter was it (to).*
     sineres: sinere, *to allow, permit.*
     toto . . . iungi: the lovers' wishes here become explicit.
77. **quod:** *the fact that;* the entire cl. is obj. of **debere.**
     amicas: here, *loving, of a lover.*
78. **nequiquam:** adv., *in vain.*
79. **sub:** here, *at the approach of, just before.*
     parti . . . oscula . . . suae . . . pervenientia (80): INTERLOCKED WORD ORDER.
     dedere . . . quisque (80): the pron. often takes a pl. vb., *they each gave.*
80. **contra:** adv., *to the other side.*
81. **postera:** *following, next.*
     nocturnos . . . ignes: i.e., the stars.
     Aurora: goddess of the dawn.
82. **pruinosas:** *frost-covered.*
     radiis: radius, *rod, spoke, ray.*
     siccaverat: siccare, *to dry.*
     herbas: herba, *grass.*
83. **coiere: = coierunt,** from **coire,** *to come together.*
84. **statuunt: statuere,** *to decide, determine,* introducing here a series of subjunct.
         vbs. in JUSSIVE NOUN CLS.
85. **fallere:** *to deceive, elude, disappoint.*
     custodes: i.e., their parents.
     foribus: foris, *door.*
     temptent: temptare, *to try, attempt.*
86. **tecta: tectum,** *roof, building.*
87. **neve: = et ne,** *and so that . . . not,* here introducing **sit errandum,** a PASS.
         PERIPHRASTIC vb. in the negative PURPOSE CL.
     spatiantibus: spatiari, *to walk (about);* sc. **eis,** DAT. OF AGENT.
88. **busta: bustum,** often pl. for sg., *tomb.*
     Nini: Ninus, king of Assyria and husband of Semiramis.
     lateant: latere, *to lie hidden, hide.*

et vocis fecistis iter; tutaeque per illud
70   murmure blanditiae minimo transire solebant.
Saepe, ubi constiterant hinc Thisbe, Pyramus illinc,
inque vices fuerat captatus anhelitus oris,
"Invide," dicebant, "paries, quid amantibus obstas?
Quantum erat ut sineres toto nos corpore iungi
75   aut, hoc si nimium est, vel ad oscula danda pateres?
Nec sumus ingrati; tibi nos debere fatemur,
quod datus est verbis ad amicas transitus aures."

The lovers plan a rendezvous in the night.

Talia diversa nequiquam sede locuti,
sub noctem dixere, "Vale," partique dedere
80   oscula quisque suae non pervenientia contra.
Postera nocturnos Aurora removerat ignes,
Solque pruinosas radiis siccaverat herbas;
ad solitum coiere locum. Tum, murmure parvo
multa prius questi, statuunt ut nocte silenti
85   fallere custodes foribusque excedere temptent,
cumque domo exierint, urbis quoque tecta relinquant,
neve sit errandum lato spatiantibus arvo,
conveniant ad busta Nini lateantque sub umbra

Aurora, from the tomb of Lorenzo, duke of Urbino
Michelangelo, 1521–34
Medici Chapel, S. Lorenzo, Florence, Italy

89. **ibi:** syllables normally short were sometimes lengthened (DIASTOLE), when occurring, as here, under the ictus as the first syllable of a foot.

    niveis: the fruit of the mulberry tree **(morus)** is imagined here as white, before its metamorphosis later in the story.

    uberrima: *very rich.*

90. **ardua:** *tall, high;* the gender of Lat. words for trees is regularly f.

    gelido: *cool, cold.*

    contermina: *adjacent (to), near,* + dat.

    fonti: fons, *spring, fountain.*

91. **pacta: pactum,** *agreement;* poetry often uses pl. for sg.

    lux: *daylight;* the rest of the day seemed to drag because of the lovers' eagerness.

92. **praecipitatur aquis . . . aquis . . . exit:** sc. **in** with the first noun, **ex** with the second; Ovid aptly employs CHIASMUS to describe the opposing actions and dactyls to suggest the rapidity of the sun's setting.

93. **callida:** *skillful, clever;* here, perhaps, with adv. force.

    tenebras: tenebrae, *shadows, darkness, gloom;* the imagery of darkness permeates the rest of the tale.

    cardine: cardo, *door-hinge;* with **versato,** lit., *with the hinge turned = opening the door.*

94. **suos:** her parents; cp. **fallere custodes** in 85 above.

    adoperta . . . vultum: *having covered her face;* the pass. form **adoperta (adoperire)** is employed as a reflexive with a dir. obj. **vultum,** a common poetic usage (cp. **oblita rictus** in 97).

96. **audacem faciebat amor:** sc. **eam;** Ovid was a master of the short, epigrammatic statement, which he liked to alternate with longer, more complex sents.

    ecce: interj., *look, behold.*

97. **caede: caedes,** *cutting, slaughter, murder;* note the deliberately harsh ALLITERATION with **recenti caede.**

    leaena: *lioness.*

    boum: gen. pl. of **bos,** *bull, ox, cow.*

    spumantes: spumare, *to foam.*

    oblita: oblinere, *to smear;* for the construction with **rictus** *(open mouth, jaws),* see note on **adoperta . . . vultum** (94).

98. **depositura:** *intending to quench* (lit., *put aside*); the fut. partic. frequently expresses purpose.

    sitim: sitis, *thirst;* for this acc. sg. form, cp. **vim** from **vis.**

    unda: *wave, water.*

99. **quam:** = **leaenam.**

    procul: adv., *far off, at a distance.*

    ad: here, *by.*

arboris (arbor ibi niveis uberrima pomis,
90   ardua morus, erat gelido contermina fonti).
Pacta placent, et lux tarde discedere visa,
praecipitatur aquis, et aquis nox exit ab isdem.

Thisbe, fleeing from a lioness, loses her veil, which the lioness then finds
and tears to shreds with her bloody mouth.

Callida per tenebras, versato cardine, Thisbe
egreditur fallitque suos, adopertaque vultum
95   pervenit ad tumulum dictaque sub arbore sedit.
Audacem faciebat amor. Venit ecce recenti
caede leaena boum spumantes oblita rictus,
depositura sitim vicini fontis in unda;
quam procul ad lunae radios Babylonia Thisbe

"Thisbe"
J. W. Waterhouse, 1909
Private collection

100. **timido:** logically applying to Thisbe, a TRANSFERRED EPITHET, another common poetic device.

   fugit: perf. in this line, pres. in the next, as the meter indicates.

   antrum: *cave;* the adj.-noun pair, **obscurum** (*shadowy,* continuing the imagery of darkness) . . . **antrum,** surrounds the rest of the cl., creating a typically Ovidian WORD-PICTURE that helps depict the girl's enclosure within the cave.

101. **tergo:** tergum, *back;* sc. **de.** With **lapsa,** Eng. would use a cl. rather than a participial phrase, *which had slipped (from).*

   velamina: velamen, *veil;* poetic pl. for sg. (see note on **pacta** in 91).

102. **lea:** = **leaena.**

   saeva: *savage, fierce.*

   compescuit: compescere, *to check, restrain;* with **unda,** *to satisfy, quench.*

103. **inventos:** with **amictus,** *robe, veil,* poetic pl.; the two words frame the cl.

   forte: abl. of **fors** as adv., *by chance.*

   ipsa: i.e., Thisbe.

104. **cruentato:** *stained with blood.*

   laniavit: laniare, *to tear (to pieces).*

105. **serius:** compar. of **sero,** adv., *late.*

   vestigia: vestigium, *track, footprint.*

106. **pulvere:** pulvis, *dust.*

   ferae: *wild, savage;* sc. **bestiae.**

   expalluit: expallescere, *to turn very pale.*

107. **vestem:** vestis, *clothing, clothes, garment.*

   sanguine: sanguis, *blood.*

   tinctam: tingere, *to wet, dip, dye, stain.*

108. **una . . . amantes:** the INTERLOCKED WORD ORDER neatly juxtaposes the contrasting numerals **una duos.**

110. **nostra:** = **mea.**

   nocens: partic. of **nocere** employed as an adj., *harmful, guilty.*

111. **venires:** sc. **ut,** JUSSIVE NOUN CL. instead of the usual inf. with **iussi.**

112. **divellite:** divellere, *to tear apart.*

113. **scelerata . . . morsu:** a special sort of interlocking word order known as a GOLDEN LINE, with a vb. at the center, adjs. preceding, and nouns following in an ABCAB arrangement (adj.^A, adj.^B, vb.^C, noun^A, noun^B).

   viscera: n. pl., *vitals, entrails, flesh.*

   morsu: morsus, *biting, bite, teeth.*

114. **quicumque:** *whatever;* the suffix **-cumque** added to a rel. makes it indef.

   habitatis: habitare, *to live, dwell.*

   rupe: rupes, *rock, cliff.*

1T5. **timidi est:** *it is (the part) of a cowardly person;* PRED. GEN. OF POSSESSION.

   necem: nex, *murder, violent death.*

   Thisbes: Greek gen. sg.

116. **pactae:** *agreed upon,* modifies **arboris.**

   umbram: with **ad,** delayed to the end of the line for emphasis.

100 vidit et obscurum timido pede fugit in antrum,
dumque fugit, tergo velamina lapsa reliquit.
Ut lea saeva sitim multa compescuit unda,
dum redit in silvas, inventos forte sine ipsa
ore cruentato tenues laniavit amictus.

*When Pyramus finds the torn and bloody veil, he thinks Thisbe has
been slain, and commits suicide.*

105 Serius egressus vestigia vidit in alto
pulvere certa ferae totoque expalluit ore
Pyramus. Ut vero vestem quoque sanguine tinctam
repperit, "Una duos," inquit, "nox perdet amantes,
e quibus illa fuit longa dignissima vita;
110 nostra nocens anima est. Ego te, miseranda, peremi,
in loca plena metus qui iussi nocte venires,
nec prior huc veni. Nostrum divellite corpus,
et scelerata fero consumite viscera morsu,
o quicumque sub hac habitatis rupe leones.
115 Sed timidi est optare necem." Velamina Thisbes
tollit et ad pactae secum fert arboris umbram,

Mosaic with Pyramus and Thisbe
2nd–3rd century A.D.
House of Dionysus, Paphos, Cyprus

117. **notae:** *well-known, familiar;* with **vesti.** Ovid frequently splits a noun/adj. pair in this way between two closely connected cls., here joined by the pathetic ANAPHORA of **dedit . . . dedit.**

118. **haustus:** *drink, draft.*

119. **quoque:** = **et quo;** the antecedent is **ferrum.**
      erat accinctus: accingere, *to gird, arm.*
      ilia: n. pl., *groin, genitals, entrails.*

120. **nec mora:** idiom, sc. **erat** = **et sine mora.**
      ferventi: *bleeding* (lit., *boiling*).
      traxit: sc. **ferrum.**

121. **resupinus:** *on the back.*
      cruor: *blood.*
      emicat: emicare, *to dart forth, spurt out.*

122. **non . . . cum:** a conventional expression used to introduce a simile.
      vitiato: *faulty, defective.*
      fistula: *tube, pipe, water-pipe.*
      plumbo: plumbum, *lead.*

123. **scinditur: scindere,** *to cut, split.*
      stridente: stridere, *to hiss.*
      foramine: foramen, *hole, perforation.*

124. **eiaculatur: eiaculari,** *to shoot out, spurt forth.*
      aquas: i.e., *streams of water.*
      ictibus: ictus, *blow, stroke;* here, *pulsing.*
      aera: aer, *air.*
      rumpit: rumpere, *to burst (through), break open.*

125. **fetus:** lit., *offspring* = *fruit.*
      adspergine: adspergo, *spray, sprinkling.*

126. **faciem: facies,** *form, face, appearance.*
      madefacta: *drenched.*
      radix: *root.*

127. **purpureo:** *purple, dark red;* the adj.-noun pair **purpureo . . . colore** frames the line, a favorite device of Ovid's, which here creates a kind of WORD-PICTURE, with the berries literally surrounded by the *purple color.*
      pendentia: pendere, *to hang, be suspended.*
      mora: morum, *mulberry* (the fruit, vs. the tree, **morus**).

128. **posito:** = **deposito;** Ovid often uses a simple vb. in place of a compound.

130. **vitarit:** = **vitaverit.**
      gestit: gestire, *to desire eagerly, be eager.*

131. **utque . . . sic (132):** *and although . . . still.*
      visa . . . in arbore formam: lit., *the shape in the seen tree* = *the shape of the tree which she saw.*

132. **incertam:** OBJ. COMPL. agreeing with **eam** understood.
      pomi: pomum, *fruit.*
      haeret: haerere, *to stick, hesitate, be uncertain.*
      an: conj., *or, whether.*
      haec sit: sc. **arbor.**

utque dedit notae lacrimas, dedit oscula vesti,
"Accipe nunc," inquit, "nostri quoque sanguinis haustus."
Quoque erat accinctus, demisit in ilia ferrum;
120 nec mora, ferventi moriens e vulnere traxit
et iacuit resupinus humo. Cruor emicat alte,
non aliter quam cum vitiato fistula plumbo
scinditur, et tenui stridente foramine longas
eiaculatur aquas, atque ictibus aera rumpit.
125 Arborei fetus adspergine caedis in atram
vertuntur faciem, madefactaque sanguine radix
purpureo tingit pendentia mora colore.

Thisbe returns to the scene and, finding Pyramus dead, kills herself.

Ecce metu nondum posito, ne fallat amantem,
illa redit iuvenemque oculis animoque requirit,
130 quantaque vitarit narrare pericula gestit.
Utque locum et visa cognoscit in arbore formam,
sic facit incertam pomi color. Haeret an haec sit.

"Pyramus and Thisbe"
Jacopo Tintoretto (Jacopo Robusti)
1650–1660

133. **tremebunda ... membra (134):** *trembling limbs,* subj. of **pulsare.**
     cruentum ... solum (134): *bloody soil.*
134. **retro:** adv., *backward.*
134. **ora ... gerens (135):** instead of *bearing her features* we say *with features.*
     buxo: buxum, *box-tree, boxwood.*
135. **exhorruit: exhorrere,** *to shudder.*
     aequoris: aequor, *level surface, sea.*
     instar: indecl. n. noun, *image, likeness;* + gen., *like.*
136. **exigua:** *scanty, small, slight.*
     summum: *its surface.*
     stringitur: stringere, *to touch lightly, graze.*
     aura: *air, breeze, wind.*
137. **remorata: remorari,** *to linger.*
     amores: here, as often, *lover.*
138. **percutit: percutere,** *to strike.*
     claro: here, *loud.*
     plangore: plangor, *striking, blow, lamentation, wailing;* the repetition of the
        long **o** sound (ASSONANCE) is perhaps onomatopoetic.
     lacertos: lacertus, *upper arm.*
139. **laniata: laniare,** *to tear (at);* reflexive pass. with dir. obj.
     comas: coma, *hair* (of the head).
     amplexa: amplecti, *to embrace.*
140. **supplevit: supplere,** *to fill up.*
     fletum: fletus, *weeping.*
     cruori: misceo may be used with the dat. as here, or with **cum.**
141. **vultibus:** this word is often pl. for sg.
     figens: figere, *to fix, imprint.*
142. **clamavit: clamare,** *to cry, shout, call out.*
     quis ... casus: = **qui casus.**
     mihi: *from me;* DAT. OF SEPARATION.
     ademit: adimere, *to take away.*
144. **nominat: nominare,** *to call by name;* note the emphatic placement of the
        names in 142–43.
145. **a morte:** use of the prep. (ABL. OF AGENT instead of ABL. OF MEANS) has the
        effect of personifying death.
146. **recondidit: recondere,** *to conceal again* = *to close again.*
147. **quae:** conjunctive use of the rel.
     postquam ... suam cognovit: a deliberate echo of **postquam ... suos cognovit,**
        identically positioned in 137; like the repetition of **tua te** in 143 and 148,
        an example of the pervasive musicality of Ovid's verse.
     -que ... et: = **et ... et,** *both ... and.*
     ense: ensis, *sword;* ABL. OF SEPARATION with **vacuum,** *empty.*
148. **ebur:** *ivory;* here, by SYNECDOCHE, = *ivory scabbard.*

Dum dubitat, tremebunda videt pulsare cruentum
membra solum retroque pedem tulit, oraque buxo
135 pallidiora gerens exhorruit aequoris instar,
quod tremit exigua cum summum stringitur aura.
Sed postquam remorata suos cognovit amores,
percutit indignos claro plangore lacertos,
et laniata comas amplexaque corpus amatum
140 vulnera supplevit lacrimis fletumque cruori
miscuit, et gelidis in vultibus oscula figens,
"Pyrame," clamavit, "quis te mihi casus ademit?
Pyrame, responde! tua te carissima Thisbe
nominat. Exaudi vultusque attolle iacentes!"
145   Ad nomen Thisbes oculos a morte gravatos
Pyramus erexit visaque recondidit illa.
Quae postquam vestemque suam cognovit et ense
vidit ebur vacuum, "Tua te manus," inquit, "amorque

"Pyramus and Thisbe"
Gregorio Pagani
16th–early 17th century

149. **perdidit:** use of a sg. vb. with a compound subj. was not uncommon.

     et: = **etiam** both in this line and in the next.

     mihi: DAT. OF POSSESSION.

     in unum hoc (150): *for this one thing;* **in** is used similarly in the next line.

150. **hic:** sc. **amor; hic,** the pron., has a long **i** where the meter requires.

151. **exstinctum:** sc. **te.**

     leti: letum, *death;* with **tui,** framing the cl.

152. **comes:** *companion.*

     quique: = **et (tu) qui.**

     morte revelli ... poteras, poteris ... morte revelli (153): revellere, *to tear away;* an extraordinarily effective use of ANAPHORA, CHIASMUS, and end-line rhyme.

153. **sola:** with **morte,** not **me.**

     nec: here, *not even.*

154. **hoc ... estote rogati:** *you shall be asked for this;* **estote** is fut. imper. of **sum. Rogare** and similar vbs. of asking take two accs., one of the pers. asked, one of the thing; in the pass. the latter acc. is retained.

     amborum: *of both.*

155. **multum miseri meus:** ALLITERATION of **m** is often meant to add a somber tone.

     meus: sg. perhaps because she is thinking only of her father.

156. **ut ... non invideatis (157):** JUSSIVE NOUN CL. in appos. with **hoc,** *that you not be unwilling to allow* + the inf. phrase **(nos) componi eodem tumulo; ut ... non** is used instead of **ne** to give negative emphasis to **invideatis.**

     novissima: here, *last.*

158. **tu, quae ... arbor:** = **tu, arbor, quae.**

     ramis: ramus, *branch.*

159. **tegis ... es tectura:** sc. **et,** as both vbs. belong to the rel. cl.

     unius ... duorum: cp. **una duos ... nox perdet amantes** (108); Thisbe's response to Pyramus' suicide echoes his response to what he thought was her death.

     es tectura: sc. **corpora;** FUT. ACT. PERIPHRASTIC.

160. **pullos:** *dark.*

     luctibus: luctus, *grief, sorrow.*

162. **aptato: aptare,** *to place, adapt.*

     mucrone: mucro, *point of a sword.*

     sub imum: *at the lowest part of.*

163. **incubuit: incumbere,** *to lean on;* with **ferro,** *fall on.*

     adhuc: adv., *still.*

     tepebat: tepere, *be warm.*

164. **vota: votum,** *prayer;* ANAPHORA, ASYNDETON, and the resounding ALLITERATION make this line a very effective introduction to the story's two, highly dramatic closing verses.

perdidit infelix. Est et mihi fortis in unum
150   hoc manus, est et amor; dabit hic in vulnera vires.
Persequar exstinctum letique miserrima dicar
causa comesque tui; quique a me morte revelli
heu sola poteras, poteris nec morte revelli.
Hoc tamen amborum verbis estote rogati,
155   o multum miseri meus illiusque parentes,
ut quos certus amor, quos hora novissima iunxit,
componi tumulo non invideatis eodem.
At tu, quae ramis arbor miserabile corpus
nunc tegis unius, mox es tectura duorum,
160   signa tene caedis, pullosque et luctibus aptos
semper habe fetus, gemini monumenta cruoris."
Dixit et, aptato pectus mucrone sub imum,
incubuit ferro quod adhuc a caede tepebat.
Vota tamen tetigere deos, tetigere parentes;

"Pyramus and Thisbe"
Lucas Cranach the Elder, 1520–25
Neue Residenz, Bamberg, Germany

165. **nam . . . ater:** this verse, with the metamorphosis of the tree's berries from snowy-white (**niveis,** line 89) to black, reveals the gods' response (**tetigere deos**) to Thisbe's prayer in 158–61, while the following verse shows the parents' response (**tetigere parentes**) to the entreaty of 154–57.

166. **quod:** sc. **id** (i.e., their ashes) as antecedent of **quod** and subj. of **requiescit.**
   rogis: rogus, *funeral pyre;* sc. **ex.**
   superest: superesse, *to be left over, survive.*
   una . . . in urna: the ASSONANCE especially, and the ALLITERATION of **r,** add a charming sound effect to the tale's closing line.

183. **Daedalus:** a legendary Athenian inventor and craftsman (which is the meaning of his name, Greek *daidalos*), he was regarded as the earliest sculptor. Having murdered his nephew in a jealous rage over the young man's talents, he fled to the court of King Minos in Crete, where he constructed the fabulous labyrinth to contain the Minotaur. Later, when Minos imprisoned him and his son Icarus in the labyrinth, Daedalus contrived to fly away as we read in the following story.
   Creten: Greek acc. of **Creta.**
   perosus: *hating, loathing.*

185. **pelago: pelagus,** *sea.* Either Daedalus was shut in *by the sea* (which barred his escape) or he was shut off (excluded) *from the sea* (i.e., Minos denied him access to the sea); in view of **undas obstruat** in the next sent., the latter option may have more to recommend it.
   licet . . . obstruat (186): licet, here *although,* may be used with the inf. or with the subjunct., as here, *he* (i.e., Minos) *may block.*

186. **illac:** adv., *by that route.*

187. **omnia possideat . . . possidet aera:** CHIASMUS underscores the contrast.
   possideat: sc. **licet,** *although he may possess.*
   aera: Greek acc. of **aer,** *air.*

188. **ignotas:** *unknown, unfamiliar.*

189. **novat: novare,** *to make new, change, alter.*
   pennas: penna, *feather.*

190. **a minima coeptas:** sc. **penna;** we would say, *beginning with . . ..*
   longam breviore sequenti: i.e., **breviore penna sequenti longam pennam;** although the entire description is somewhat impressionistic, Ovid may mean that long feathers were alternated with shorter ones, giving the wing's edge a serrated effect.

191. **ut . . . putes:** RESULT CL., *(in such a way) that . . ..*
   clivo: clivus, *slope;* sc. **in.**
   rustica . . . fistula (192): *a rustic pipe* = a Pan's pipe, or primitive harmonica, made of several small pipes of graduated lengths, each producing a different note.
   quondam: i.e., *from ancient times.*

192. **disparibus:** *unequal, varying.*
   paulatim: adv., *gradually.*
   surgit: *rises* or, here, *tapers.*
   avenis: avena, *reed.*

165   nam color in pomo est, ubi permaturuit, ater,
      quodque rogis superest una requiescit in urna.

DAEDALUS AND ICARUS: THE FIRST FLIGHT

Metamorphoses **8.183–235**

Daedalus constructs wings for himself and his son Icarus.

      Daedalus interea Creten longumque perosus
      exsilium, tactusque loci natalis amore,
185   clausus erat pelago. "Terras licet," inquit, "et undas
      obstruat, et caelum certe patet; ibimus illac!
      Omnia possideat, non possidet aera Minos."
      Dixit et ignotas animum dimittit in artes,
      naturamque novat. Nam ponit in ordine pennas
190   a minima coeptas, longam breviore sequenti,
      ut clivo crevisse putes (sic rustica quondam
      fistula disparibus paulatim surgit avenis);

"Daedalus Attaching
Icarus' Wings"
Joseph Marie Vien
1754
École des Beaux-Arts
Paris, France

193. **lino: linum,** *linen, thread, cord.*
     medias et . . . imas atque . . . compositas (194): sc. **pennas.**
     ceris: cera, *wax.*
     alligat: alligare, *to tie, bind.*
     imas: *lowest, bottommost.*
194. **flectit: flectere,** *to bend.*
195. **aves: avis,** *bird.*
     una: adv., *together;* sc. **cum patre.**
196. **tractare:** *to handle.*
197. **renidenti: renidere,** *to shine, beam, smile.*
     modo . . . modo (198): both are advs.
     vaga: *wandering, shifting.*
198. **captabat: captare,** *to try to seize, catch, snatch at, pluck at.*
     plumas: = **pennas.**
     flavam: *yellow, golden.*
     pollice: pollex, *thumb.*
199. **mollibat:** = **molliebat.**
     lusu: lusus, *playing, sport.*
200. **manus ultima:** *the last hand = the finishing touch.*
     coepto: coeptum, *a thing begun = undertaking, project.*
201. **opifex:** *worker, artisan.*
     libravit: librare, *to balance, poise.*
     alas: ala, *wing.*
202. **mota:** i.e., by the movement of his wings.
203. **et:** = **etiam.**
     natum: natus, partic. of **nasci** used as a noun, = **filius.**
     limite: limes, *path, way;* ABL. OF ROUTE.
204. **demissior:** *too low.*
205. **celsior:** *too high.*
206. **utrumque:** *each, the two;* i.e., keep to the middle course.
     Booten aut Helicen (207): Greek acc., constellations of *the Plowman* and *the Great Bear;* Icarus should not try to set an independent course by the stars but should simply follow Daedalus.
207. **strictum: stringere,** with **ensis** *(sword),* = *to draw.* Orion is a constellation prominent to the south, the Plowman and the Great Bear to the north; so the order is a recapitulation of that in 206.
209. **umeris: umerus,** *shoulder, upper arm.*
     accommodat: accommodare, *to adapt, adjust, fit.*
210. **monitus:** acc. pl., *warnings.*
     genae: gena, *cheek.*
     maduere: madere, *to be wet;* sc. **lacrimis,** because of his anxiety for Icarus.
211. **patriae:** adj. with **manus.**
212. **repetenda:** *to be repeated* or *sought again.*
     levatus: levare, *to lighten, raise, lift up.*
213. **velut:** *just as.*
     ales: *bird.*
     ab alto: with **nido (nidus,** *nest),* producing an end-line rhyme.

tum lino medias et ceris alligat imas,
atque ita compositas parvo curvamine flectit,
195 ut veras imitetur aves. Puer Icarus una
stabat et, ignarus sua se tractare pericla,
ore renidenti modo, quas vaga moverat aura,
captabat plumas, flavam modo pollice ceram
mollibat, lusuque suo mirabile patris
200 impediebat opus. Postquam manus ultima coepto
imposita est, geminas opifex libravit in alas
ipse suum corpus motaque pependit in aura.

Daedalus instructs and warns Icarus.

Instruit et natum, "Medio"que "ut limite curras,
Icare," ait "moneo, ne, si demissior ibis,
205 unda gravet pennas, si celsior, ignis adurat:
inter utrumque vola. Nec te spectare Booten
aut Helicen iubeo strictumque Orionis ensem:
me duce, carpe viam!" Pariter praecepta volandi
tradit et ignotas umeris accommodat alas.
210 Inter opus monitusque genae maduere seniles,
et patriae tremuere manus; dedit oscula nato
non iterum repetenda suo, pennisque levatus
ante volat comitique timet, velut ales ab alto

"Daedalus and Icarus"
Charles Paul Landon
1799
Musée Municipal des Beaux-Arts
Alençon, France

214. **teneram:** *tender, delicate, young.*
     prolem: **proles,** *offspring.*
215. **sequi:** sc. **natum** as subj.
     damnosas: *destructive.*
     erudit: erudire, *to teach.*
216. **alas:** with both **movet** and **respicit;** see note on **notae** (117).
217. **hos:** obj. of **videt** and **obstipuit,** antecedent of **qui,** and subj. of **esse.**
     tremula: *shaking,* because there is a fish on the line, or *trembling,* because
          the fisherman is frightened at the sight of the two men flying.
     harundine: harundo, *rod.*
     pisces: piscis, *fish.*
218. **pastor . . . arator:** *a shepherd leaning on* **(inniti)** *his staff* **(baculus)** *or a plow-
          man (leaning on) the handle of his plow* **(stiva);** CHIASMUS.
219. **obstipuit: obstipescere,** *to be amazed, astounded.*
     aethera: Greek acc. of **aether,** *heaven, sky.*
     carpere: here, *to pass through.*
220. **laeva parte (221):** *on their left side.*
221. **Samos:** sc. **erat;** called **Iunonia** because it was *sacred to Juno.* Samos, Delos,
          Paros, Lebinthos, and Calymne are all Greek islands in the Aegean Sea.
222. **dextra:** nom., as the meter indicates, though it balances **laeva parte.** Having
          flown north from Crete and past Delos and Paros, the pair are now fly-
          ing east, with Samos to the north, Lebinthos and Calymne to the south,
          and approaching what was to be named, after Icarus' disaster, the Icar-
          ian Sea.
     fecunda: *fertile, rich.*
223. **audaci:** logically with **puer,** a TRANSFERRED EPITHET; and note the ASSONANCE
          with **gaudere.**
224. **deseruit: deserere,** *to desert, abandon.*
225. **rapidi:** here, *ravaging, fierce.*
226. **odoratas:** *fragrant.*
227. **tabuerant: tabescere,** *to waste away, melt;* the plpf. indicates sudden action.
     nudos: i.e., *stripped* (of their wings).
     quatit: quatere, *to shake.*
228. **remigio: remigium,** *oarage, set of oars;* Ovid's use of this term for Icarus'
          wings deliberately anticipates the boy's fall from the sky into the sea.
     percipit: percipere, *to receive, catch.*
229. **ora . . . aqua (230):** the complex interlocking order (ABCACB) suits Ovid's
          violent and pathetic image of the youth's drowning.
     caerulea: lit., *sky-blue,* mirroring the **caelum** (224) from which Icarus has
          fallen; similarly **excipiuntur aqua** in 230 is an ironic echo of **percipit auras**
          in 228, as the boy who cannot quite *catch hold of the air* through which
          he "sails" is himself *caught up by the water* in which he drowns.
231. **nec iam pater:** i.e., since Icarus had just perished in the sea.

quae teneram prolem produxit in aera nido,
215 hortaturque sequi, damnosasque erudit artes,
et movet ipse suas et nati respicit alas.
Hos aliquis, tremula dum captat harundine pisces,
aut pastor baculo stivave innixus arator
vidit et obstipuit, quique aethera carpere possent,
220 credidit esse deos.

Icarus' youthful impetuosity precipitates his destruction.

Et iam Iunonia laeva
parte Samos (fuerant Delosque Parosque relictae),
dextra Lebinthos erat fecundaque melle Calymne,
cum puer audaci coepit gaudere volatu
deseruitque ducem caelique cupidine tractus
225 altius egit iter. Rapidi vicinia solis
mollit odoratas, pennarum vincula, ceras.
Tabuerant cerae; nudos quatit ille lacertos,
remigioque carens non ullas percipit auras,
oraque caerulea patrium clamantia nomen
230 excipiuntur aqua, quae nomen traxit ab illo.
At pater infelix, nec iam pater, "Icare," dixit;

"The Fall of Icarus"
Carlo Saraceni, ca. 1608
Museo Nazionale di Capodimonte, Naples, Italy

233. **dicebat:** Ovid's shift to the impf. here *(he kept calling),* after **dixit . . . dixit,** and his triple repetition of Icarus' name add to the pathos of the passage; and the repetition also of **nomen/nomen/nomine** underscores the story's point that Icarus gave his name to both the Icarian Sea (**quae nomen traxit ab illo,** 230) and the island of Icaria (the **tellus,** *land,* of 235).

234. **devovit: devovere,** lit., *to vow away = curse.*
  sepulcro: sepulcrum, *tomb, sepulcher.*

235. **sepulti: sepelire,** *to bury;* set at line's end to echo its cognate **sepulcro** and punctuate the narrative's grim conclusion.

1. **inde:** adv., *thence, from there;* i.e., from Crete, where the marriage god Hymenaeus had attended a wedding (in the story preceding this one at the end of *Metamorphoses* 9).
  croceo: *saffron yellow,* the color of a bride's veil, and so a color naturally enough worn by the god of marriage.
  velatus: velare, *to veil, cover, cloak;* the word is surrounded by **croceo . . . amictu,** producing a WORD-PICTURE.
  amictu: amictus, *robe, cloak.*

2. **Ciconum:** *the Cicones,* a people in Thrace, which was a district north of the Aegean Sea and the homeland of Orpheus.
  oras: ora, *coast, shore.*

3. **Orphea:** adj., *of Orpheus.* A mythical poet, singer, and musician and son of the Muse Calliope, Orpheus was given a lyre by Apollo and instructed by the god; his skill was so great that he could charm with his music not only men and beasts but even trees and stones.
  nequiquam: because of the unhappy end of the marriage.

4. **sollemnia:** *religious, festive, customary.*

6. **fax:** *torch.* An attribute of Hymenaeus, torches were carried in the wedding procession; it was a bad omen for a torch not to burn with a bright flame.
  stridula: *hissing, sputtering.*

7. **motibus:** *with its movement;* i.e., the torch did not flame up even when waved through the air to ignite the sparks.

8. **exitus:** *outcome, result;* sc. **erat.**
  auspicio: auspicium, *omen.*
  nupta . . . nova (9): *the new bride;* i.e., Eurydice, who is curiously not named until line 31.

9. **Naiadum: Nais,** *Naiad* (a water nymph).
  comitata: comitare, *to accompany.*
  vagatur: vagari, *to wander, roam.*

10. **talum: talus,** *ankle, heel;* **in . . . recepto** seems an odd circumlocution and is taken by some readers, along with other curiosities in the narrative, as an intentional deflation of the story's seriousness by way of parodying the grander version in Vergil's *Georgics* (4.452–546).

11. **quam:** Eurydice.
  Rhodopeius . . . vates (12): *the Thracian bard;* from Rhodope, a mountain of Thrace. Note the INTERLOCKED WORD ORDER with **superas . . . auras.**

12. **deflevit: deflere,** *to weep for, bewail;* modified by the rather unheroic **satis.**
  ne non temptaret et: *that he might not* (**ne**) *fail to* (**non**) *try even* (**et**).

"Icare," dixit "ubi es? Qua te regione requiram?"
"Icare," dicebat. Pennas aspexit in undis,
devovitque suas artes, corpusque sepulcro
235   condidit; et tellus a nomine dicta sepulti.

ORPHEUS AND EURYDICE: A DESCENT INTO HADES

Metamorphoses 10.1–77, 11.61–66

Inauspicious omens precede the death of Eurydice.

Inde per immensum, croceo velatus amictu,
aethera digreditur Ciconumque Hymenaeus ad oras
tendit, et Orphea nequiquam voce vocatur.
Adfuit ille quidem, sed nec sollemnia verba
5   nec laetos vultus nec felix attulit omen;
fax quoque quam tenuit lacrimoso stridula fumo
usque fuit nullosque invenit motibus ignes.
Exitus auspicio gravior. Nam nupta per herbas
dum nova, Naiadum turba comitata, vagatur,
10   occidit in talum serpentis dente recepto.

Orpheus' visits the underworld and pleas on behalf of Eurydice.

Quam satis ad superas postquam Rhodopeius auras
deflevit vates, ne non temptaret et umbras,

Orpheus, Eurydice, and Hermes
Marble relief
Roman copy of Greek original
5th century B.C.
Museo Archeologico Nazionale
Naples, Italy

13. **Styga:** Greek acc. of **Styx,** *the Styx,* a river in the Underworld.
     Taenaria . . . porta: *by the gate of Taenarus,* a supposed entrance to Hades in
     the southern tip of Greece; ABL. OF ROUTE.
14. **functa:** fungi, + abl., *to perform, experience;* with **simulacra (simulacrum,**
     phantom, ghost) . . . **sepulcro,** *ghosts which had experienced burial* (with-
     out which they would have to wander in Limbo across the Styx outside
     of Hades).
15. **Persephonen:** Greek acc.; *Persephone,* daughter of the grain-goddess Ceres
     and wife of Pluto, lord of the dead, was queen of the Underworld.
     inamoena: *unpleasant.*
16. **umbrarum dominum:** i.e., Pluto; the circumlocution is made all the more
     effective through ENJAMBEMENT and the booming ASSONANCE, which
     Ovid accentuates by positioning each of the **-um** syllables under the
     ictus.
     ad carmina: i.e., *to accompany his songs;* Orpheus does not merely address
     Pluto and Persephone, but tries to charm them with his singing.
     nervis: nervus, lit., *sinew = string of a lyre.*
17. **numina: numen,** *divine will, divinity, god.*
18. **reccidimus: reccidere,** *to fall back, sink, descend.*
     quidquid: essentially = **qui,** looking back to the subj. of **reccidimus,** hence
     creamur not **creatur.**
19. **positis:** = **depositis.**
     ambagibus: ambages, *circumlocution, ambiguity.*
20. **loqui:** sc. **me** as subj.
     huc: adv., *to this place, here.*
     opaca: *shady, dark.*
21. **Tartara:** n. pl., *Tartarus,* the abode of the dead, Hades.
     uti: = **ut.**
     villosa . . . monstri (22): the INTERLOCKED WORD ORDER of the nouns and
     adjs. (ABACAC) suits the image of Cerberus' three heads *bristling* (**vil-
     losa**) *with snakes* (**colubris,** from **colubra**).
22. **terna:** = **tria;** the distributive numerals (e.g., **ternus,** *three each*) were some-
     times used by poets instead of the cardinals, especially when a pl. noun
     constituted a set, like the three heads of Cerberus, the savage hound who
     guarded the entrance to Hades.
     Medusaei: *Medusa-like;* Cerberus was born of the snake-monster Echidna,
     one of Medusa's sisters, and like Medusa had snakes for hair.
     vincirem: vincire, *to bind, tie;* Hercules had bound and carried off Cerberus
     as one of his labors.
     guttura: guttur, *throat;* Ovid focuses on the **guttura** vs. the **capita** because of
     the vb. **vincire.**
23. **coniunx:** *wife.*
     calcata: *trodden upon, stepped on.*
     venenum: *poison.*
24. **crescentes:** here, *burgeoning, budding.*
25. **pati:** sc. **mortem coniugis.**
     temptasse: = **temptavisse.**

ad Styga Taenaria est ausus descendere porta,
perque leves populos simulacraque functa sepulcro
15 Persephonen adiit inamoenaque regna tenentem
umbrarum dominum, pulsisque ad carmina nervis
sic ait: "O positi sub terra numina mundi,
in quem reccidimus, quidquid mortale creamur,
si licet et, falsi positis ambagibus oris,
20 vera loqui sinitis, non huc, ut opaca viderem
Tartara, descendi, nec uti villosa colubris
terna Medusaei vincirem guttura monstri.
Causa viae est coniunx in quam calcata venenum
vipera diffudit crescentesque abstulit annos.
25 Posse pati volui, nec me temptasse negabo;

"Proserpine" (Persephone)
Dante Gabriel Rossetti
1874
Tate Gallery
London, Great Britain

27. **et:** = **etiam;** with **hic** (adv.).
    auguror: augurari, *to divine, surmise.*
    esse: sc. **eum (Amorem)** as subj.

28. **est mentita: mentiri,** *to lie, speak falsely.*
    rapinae: rapina, *abduction, rape;* Pluto had abducted Persephone and carried her off to Hades to be his queen.

29. **per ego . . . loca:** when **ego** is used in an oath it regularly stands between **per** *(by)* and its object.

30. **Chaos:** n. sg., *Chaos, the Abyss, the Underworld;* modified by **hoc,** which in poetry is often scanned as a long syllable in both the nom. and acc. cases.

31. **Eurydices:** Greek gen. sg.
    properata: *hurried, premature,* from **properare,** *to hurry, rush, hasten.*
    retexite: retexere, *to unweave, reverse;* an allusion to the Fates, who in classical myth weave the tapestry of one's life.

32. **paulum:** adv., *a little, a while.*
    morati: morari, *to linger, delay.*

33. **serius aut citius:** Eng. uses the reverse order, *sooner or later.*
    sedem: sedes, *seat, abode, home, place.*

34. **vosque:** emphatically positioned, to strengthen his appeal (and cp. **vos** in 29).

35. **regna:** pl. for sg., *rule (over)* + OBJ. GEN.

36. **peregerit: peragere,** *to finish, live out.*

37. **iuris erit vestri:** lit., *will be of your law* = *will be under your jurisdiction.*
    pro munere: *as a favor.*
    poscimus: poscere, *to request, demand.*
    usum: *loan;* a technical term for temporary use of another's property. This word, together with **iustos** and **iuris,** gives Orpheus' plea a legalistic tone.

38. **quod si:** *but if.*
    veniam: venia, *kindness, favor, pardon.*
    certum est . . . mihi (39): i.e., *I am resolved (to);* the delay of **mihi** is meant to parallel that of **pro coniuge.**

40. **dicentem . . . moventem:** positioning the first partic. at the caesura emphasizes the internal rhyme, lending a musicality to the verse that suits its meaning.

41. **exsangues:** *bloodless, lifeless, pale.*
    Tantalus: for his sins, *Tantalus* was placed near food and water which always withdrew just beyond his grasp when he reached for it; but for a moment, under the spell of Orpheus' music, he forgot this "tantalizing" torture.

42. **stupuit: stupere,** *to be amazed, stupefied;* with **Ixionis orbis,** *Ixion's wheel,* = *halted in amazement.* Like Tantalus and the others mentioned here, Ixion had committed a crime (the attempted seduction of Juno) for which he was condemned to eternal torment in Hades; Ixion's punishment was to be spread-eagled on a wheel that perpetually turned, but here even the wheel was mesmerized by Orpheus' song and ceased to revolve.

vicit Amor. Supera deus hic bene notus in ora est;
an sit et hic, dubito. Sed et hic tamen auguror esse,
famaque si veteris non est mentita rapinae,
vos quoque iunxit Amor. Per ego haec loca plena timoris,
30   per Chaos hoc ingens vastique silentia regni,
Eurydices, oro, properata retexite fata.
Omnia debentur vobis paulumque morati
serius aut citius sedem properamus ad unam.
Tendimus huc omnes, haec est domus ultima, vosque
35   humani generis longissima regna tenetis.
Haec quoque, cum iustos matura peregerit annos,
iuris erit vestri; pro munere poscimus usum.
Quod si fata negant veniam pro coniuge, certum est
nolle redire mihi; leto gaudete duorum."

*Through the charm of his music Orpheus wins his request for Eurydice's
return, only to lose her again as they near the upper world.*

40   Talia dicentem nervosque ad verba moventem
exsangues flebant animae; nec Tantalus undam
captavit refugam, stupuitque Ixionis orbis,

"Orpheus before Pluto and Proserpina"
François Perrier, 1650
Louvre, Paris, France

43. **iecur:** *liver.*
    volucres: volucris, *winged creature, bird.* The giant Tityus attempted to rape Leto, mother of Diana and Apollo, and was tied to the ground in Hades and exposed to vultures that plucked constantly at his liver.
    vacarunt: vacare, *to be free from.*
44. **Belides:** *Danaids,* the 50 daughters of Danaus, king of Libya and son of Belus; 49 of them murdered their husbands on their wedding night, at their father's bidding, and were punished in the Underworld by forever trying to fill water urns that had holes in the bottom.
    Sisyphe: in an abrupt APOSTROPHE the narrator addresses the Corinthian king *Sisyphus,* who for his deceit and avarice had been condemned in Hades to the unending task of pushing up a hill a huge stone that always rolled back down again when he neared the top.
45. **lacrimis:** with **genas maduisse,** IND. STATE. depending on **fama est.**
    carmine: with **victarum.**
46. **Eumenidum: Eumenides,** *Eumenides, Furies,* three winged demons with snaky hair who relentlessly harassed men for their crimes, both in life and beyond the grave; this was the first time they had ever wept.
47. **sustinet . . . negare:** *endure to deny = have the power to say no (to).*
    oranti: sc. **Orpheo** (dat.).
    ima: sc. **loca.**
48. **Eurydicen:** acc. sg.
    recentes: with **umbras,** obj. of **inter;** ANASTROPHE, reversal of the normal word order, especially in a prep. phrase, was common in poetry.
49. **passu: passus,** *step, pace.*
50. **simul et:** *at the same time as = together with.*
51. **ne flectat:** JUSSIVE NOUN CL. dependent on **legem,** *the stipulation (that).*
    lumina: lumen, *light, eye.*
    donec: conj., *until,* + subjunct. denoting anticipation or purpose.
    Avernas: *of Avernus (Hades).*
52. **exierit:** here transitive with a dir. obj.
    valles: vallis, *valley.*
    irrita: *void, invalid, in vain.*
    futura: sc. **esse,** IND. STATE. depending on the idea of speech in **legem.**
53. **acclivis:** *ascending, sloping upward.*
    trames: *path, trail.*
54. **caligine: caligo,** *fog.*
55. **afuerunt:** vowels normally long, like the **-e-** here, are sometimes shortened in poetry (SYSTOLE), when the syllable was not under the ictus.
    telluris . . . summae: *the highest part of the earth = the upper world.*
56. **hic:** adv.
    deficeret: sc. **Eurydice.**
    avidus videndi: *eager for seeing, eager to see.*
58. **bracchia: bracchium,** *arm.*
    prendi: prendere, *to grasp, seize.*
    certans: certare, *to struggle, strive.*
59. **cedentes:** *yielding, retreating.*

nec carpsere iecur volucres, urnisque vacarunt
Belides, inque tuo sedisti, Sisyphe, saxo.
45 Tunc primum lacrimis victarum carmine fama est
Eumenidum maduisse genas. Nec regia coniunx
sustinet oranti, nec qui regit ima, negare,
Eurydicenque vocant. Umbras erat illa recentes
inter, et incessit passu de vulnere tardo.
50 Hanc simul et legem Rhodopeius accipit Orpheus,
ne flectat retro sua lumina, donec Avernas
exierit valles, aut irrita dona futura.
　　Carpitur acclivis per muta silentia trames,
arduus, obscurus, caligine densus opaca.
55 Nec procul afuerunt telluris margine summae;
hic, ne deficeret metuens avidusque videndi,
flexit amans oculos, et protinus illa relapsa est;
bracchiaque intendens, prendique et prendere certans,
nil nisi cedentes infelix arripit auras.
60 Iamque iterum moriens, non est de coniuge quicquam

"Orpheus and Eurydice"
Peter Paul Rubens, 17th century
Museo del Prado, Madrid, Spain

61. **se . . . amatam:** sc. **esse;** IND. STATE. with the POTENTIAL SUBJUNCT. **quereretur,** *what complaint was she to make except that . . ..*
62. **supremum . . . "Vale":** *a last farewell.*
63. **quod . . . acciperet:** REL. CL. OF CHARACTERISTIC.
     revoluta . . . est: revolvere, *to roll back.*
     rursus: adv., *again.*
     eodem: adv., *to the same place.*
64. **non aliter . . . quam . . . qui . . . quam qui (68):** the tables are turned, and now it is Orpheus who is dumbstruck (**stupuit,** echoing the same vb. in 42); just as his song had momentarily halted the actions of the criminals in the Underworld, and even the turning of Ixion's wheel, so here he is stunned at the sight of Eurydice plummeting backwards into Hades, and his temporary paralysis is compared, in this double simile, with that of two otherwise unknown mythic characters who were transformed into stone. The dactyls in 64–65 help suggest the suddeness of Orpheus' response.
65. **tria:** with **colla** (**collum,** *neck*); though he had not descended into Hades to see Cerberus (21–22), he is stunned as if he had gazed upon the beast.
     medio: sc. **collo;** his neck had been chained by Hercules.
66. **quem . . . oborto (67):** i.e., he was transformed from his human state into stone even before he had stopped trembling in fear at the sight of the dog.
     pavor: *trembling, terror.*
     ante . . . quam (67): conj., *before.*
67. **oborto: oboriri,** *to rise up, spring up.*
68. **quam qui . . . Olenos (69):** = **quam Olenos qui.** Apparently Lethaea had committed some offense (**crimen**), perhaps in boasting about her beauty (**figurae**), and when her spouse or lover Olenos tried to take the blame himself, both were turned to stone.
69. **confisa:** *trusting in,* + dat.
71. **lapides: lapis,** *stone.*
     umida: *wet, moist, rainy.*
     sustinet: i.e., the rocks or boulders were on *Mt. Ida* (**Ide**—there were mountains of this name in Troy and Crete); the myth was perhaps based on some anthropomorphic rock formations.
72. **orantem:** i.e., Orpheus, who had returned towards Hades as far as the Styx.
73. **portitor:** *ferryman,* i.e., Charon, who ferried the dead, and rarely the living, across the Styx.
     arcuerat: arcere, *to keep out, debar, prevent.*
     septem . . . diebus: ABL. OF DURATION OF TIME, instead of the usual acc.
74. **ripa:** *bank* (of a river).
     Cereris sine munere: *without the gift of Ceres* (**Ceres**), i.e., without food.
75. **alimenta: alimentum,** *food.*
76. **Erebi: Erebus** = Hades.
77. **Rhodopen:** acc. of Rhodope (see on 11 above).
     aquilonibus: aquilo, *north wind.*
     Haemum: Haemus, another mountain range in Thrace.

questa suo (quid enim nisi se quereretur amatam?),
supremumque "Vale," quod iam vix auribus ille
acciperet, dixit revolutaque rursus eodem est.
    Non aliter stupuit gemina nece coniugis Orpheus,
65 quam tria qui timidus, medio portante catenas,
colla canis vidit, quem non pavor ante reliquit,
quam natura prior, saxo per corpus oborto;
quam qui in se crimen traxit voluitque videri
Olenos esse nocens, tuque, o confisa figurae
70 infelix Lethaea tuae, iunctissima quondam
pectora, nunc lapides, quos umida sustinet Ide.
    Orantem frustraque iterum transire volentem
portitor arcuerat. Septem tamen ille diebus
squalidus in ripa Cereris sine munere sedit;
75 cura dolorque animi lacrimaeque alimenta fuere.
Esse deos Erebi crudeles questus, in altam
se recipit Rhodopen pulsumque aquilonibus Haemum.

"Orpheus and Eurydice"
Frederico Cervelli
17th century
Galleria Querini Stampalia
Venice, Italy

61.   **umbra:** i.e., Orpheus' ghost. Grieving over the final loss of his wife, he
         scorned all the women of Thrace and thus enraged a band of frenzied
         Maenads (female worshippers of Bacchus), who attacked him and tore
         him to pieces.

62.   **cuncta:** = **omnia.**
         arva: arvum, *field;* with **piorum** *(good, virtuous, blessed)* = the Elysian Fields,
         that region of the Underworld reserved for the virtuous.

63.   **amplectitur:** in Vergil's account Eurydice vanished into the darkness again as
         the two vainly attempted to embrace.
         ulnis: ulna, *arm.*

64.   **spatiantur: spatiari,** *to walk.*

65.   **sequitur: Orpheus** is subj. and **Eurydicen** obj. of the sent.'s three vbs.
         anteit: the **ei** is scanned as a single syllable (SYNIZESIS).

66.   **tuto:** adv., *safely.*

85.   **hoc:** the wine-god Bacchus, outraged by the slaying of his favorite bard, Or-
         pheus, metamorphosed the Thracian women who had killed him into
         oak trees, but this was not punishment enough.

86.   **choro: chorus,** *band* (of followers); i.e., better than the Maenads who had
         slain Orpheus.
         vineta: vinetum, *vineyard.*
         Timoli: T(i)molus, a mountain in Lydia sacred to Bacchus.

87.   **Pactolon:** Greek acc. sg. of **Pactolus,** a river of Lydia in western Asia Minor
         which rose on Mount Timolus and was famous in antiquity for the gold
         found in its sand.

88.   **caris:** here, *dear* in the economic sense, *valuable.*
         invidiosus: lit., *full of envy* = *envied.*
         harenis: harena, *sand;* ABL. OF CAUSE.

89.   **adsueta:** *customary.*
         cohors: *throng, troop.*
         Satyri: *Satyrs,* lascivious woodland creatures who accompanied Bacchus
         in his revels; usually depicted as men with pointed ears, tails, and the
         legs and hooves of goats or horses, they represent the forces of male
         fertility.
         Bacchae: another name for the Maenads, female attendants of Bacchus,
         either semidivine spirits of vegetation and fertility as here or mortal
         women who took part in the orgiastic worship of Bacchus.
         frequentant: frequentare, *to attend in large numbers.*

90.   **Silenus:** an elderly satyr, son of Pan or Hermes, noted for both his wisdom
         and his love of strong drink; he raised Bacchus and was his tutor and
         faithful attendant.
         titubantem: titubare, *to stagger, reel;* sc. **Silenum.**
         meroque: merum (sc. **vinum),** *unmixed wine;* usually the ancients mixed water
         with their wine—but old Silenus took his neat.

91.   **ruricolae . . . Phryges:** *the Phrygian rustics;* Phrygia was a district of Asia
         Minor.
         coronis: corona, *garland,* often worn by the ancients at their festivities.

Orpheus and Eurydice are reunited in Hades.

> Umbra subit terras et, quae loca viderat ante,
> cuncta recognoscit quaerensque per arva piorum
> invenit Eurydicen cupidisque amplectitur ulnis.
> Hic modo coniunctis spatiantur passibus ambo:
> 65   nunc praecedentem sequitur, nunc praevius anteit
> Eurydicenque suam iam tuto respicit Orpheus.

MIDAS AND THE GOLDEN TOUCH

Metamorphoses 11.85–145

Bacchus' tutor Silenus is generously entertained by King Midas of Phrygia, and the wine god grants Midas his wish for the golden touch.

> 85   Nec satis hoc Baccho est: ipsos quoque deserit agros
> cumque choro meliore sui vineta Timoli
> Pactolonque petit, quamvis non aureus illo
> tempore nec caris erat invidiosus harenis.
> Hunc adsueta cohors, Satyri Bacchaeque, frequentant,
> 90   at Silenus abest. Titubantem annisque meroque
> ruricolae cepere Phryges vinctumque coronis

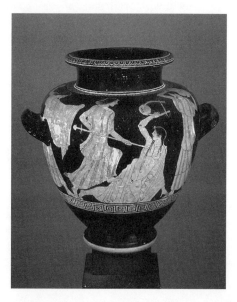

Death of Orpheus
Red-figure stamnos
Hermonax
5th century B.C.
Louvre
Paris, France

92.   **Midan:** acc. sg. of **Midas.** The legendary Phrygian king is best known from this story in Ovid; later in this same book of the *Metamorphoses,* however, Ovid recounts another tale in which Midas was given the ears of an ass by Apollo for judging that god's music inferior to Pan's.

93.   **orgia:** n. pl., *ceremonies, rites,* here, the ecstatic rites of Bacchus.
       Cecropio: *Cecropian* (from Cecrops, the legendary second king of Athens), *Athenian.* The meter of the verse is unusual, with both HIATUS (the lack of elision between **Cecropio** and **Eumolpo**) and a spondee in the fifth foot, which nearly always is dactylic, thus producing a so-called SPONDAIC LINE.
       Eumolpo: *Eumolpus,* a Thracian bard and a pupil of Orpheus, was reputed to have brought the Eleusinian mysteries (the cult of Demeter and Persephone) to Eleusis, near Athens.

94.   **qui:** i.e., **Midas.**
       simul: adv., *at the same time;* here = **simul atque,** *as soon as.*
       comitem: comes, *comrade, companion;* possibly a HENDIADYS WITH **socium,** *his allied comrade.*
       sacrorum: sacra, here, *sacred rites, mysteries.*

95.   **hospitis: hospes,** *guest.*
       festum: *festival.*

97.   **sublime:** *lofty, celestial.*
       coegerat: here, *had driven away.*
       agmen: *band, throng, array.*

98.   **Lucifer:** lit., *Light-bringer,* = the morning star, which ushers in the dawn and thus compels the stars of the night to pale and disappear.
       Lydos: *Lydian.*

99.   **alumno: alumnus,** *foster son.*

100.   **optandi . . . arbitrium (101):** INTERLOCKED WORD ORDER, with **optandi** modifying **muneris,** *of choosing a gift.*
       fecit: with **arbitrium** *(power, opportunity),* = *made available, granted.*

101.   **altore: altor,** *foster father.*

102.   **usurus:** the fut. partic. here has the force of *destined to . . ..*
       effice . . . vertatur (103): sc. **ut.**

103.   **fulvum:** *yellow.*

104.   **solvit: solvere,** *to loosen, free, grant.*

105.   **Liber:** an early Italian god of fertility and vegetation who came to be associated with Bacchus.
       quod . . . petisset: SUBJUNCT. OF QUOTED REASON.

106.   **Berecyntius:** *Berecyntian* = *Phrygian;* Mount Berecyntus in Phrygia was sacred to the fertility goddess Cybele, who in some accounts was mother of Midas.

107.   **polliciti: pollicitum,** *promise.*

108.   **vix . . . credens:** i.e., that he had the power granted to him.
       fronde: frons, *leaf, leafy bough.*
       virentem: virere, *to be green.*

ad regem duxere Midan, cui Thracius Orpheus
orgia tradiderat cum Cecropio Eumolpo.
Qui simul agnovit socium comitemque sacrorum,
95   hospitis adventu festum genialiter egit
per bis quinque dies et iunctas ordine noctes.
Et iam stellarum sublime coegerat agmen
Lucifer undecimus, Lydos cum laetus in agros
rex venit et iuveni Silenum reddit alumno.
100   Huic deus optandi gratum sed inutile fecit
muneris arbitrium, gaudens altore recepto.
Ille male usurus donis ait: "Effice quidquid
corpore contigero fulvum vertatur in aurum."
Adnuit optatis nocituraque munera solvit
105   Liber et indoluit quod non meliora petisset.

Midas' excitement is followed by disillusionment and agony.

Laetus abit gaudetque malo Berecyntius heros,
pollicitique fidem tangendo singula temptat,
vixque sibi credens non alta fronde virentem

"Silenus"
Jusepe de Ribera
17th century
Museo del Prado
Madrid, Spain

109. **ilice: ilex,** *oak tree.*

virgam: virga, *twig, shoot;* the following series of repeated forms of the same word **(virgam/virga, saxum/saxum, glaebam/glaeba, postibus/postes, palmas/palmis, undis/unda),** a favorite device of Ovid's known as POLYPTOTON, focuses attention on the multiple transformations. The effect is amplified through CHIASMUS (**virentem . . . virgam; virga aurea** and **palmas . . . undis, unda . . . palmis**), and etymologizing wordplay (**contigit . . . contactu).**

111. **glaebam: glaeba,** *clod, lump of soil.*

112. **massa:** *mass, lump* (of gold).

arentis: *dried up.*

Cereris: by a common METONYMY = *of wheat.*

decerpsit: decerpere, *to pluck.*

aristas: arista, *ear of grain.*

113. **messis:** *harvest.*

demptum: demere, *to take away, pluck.*

114. **Hesperidas: Hesperides,** *Hesperides, daughters of Hesperus* (the evening star of the west), who tended a garden in which grew golden apples.

donasse: = **donavisse;** sc. **id (pomum).**

postibus: postis, *post, doorpost,* pl. = *a door.*

116. **laverat: lavare,** *to wash, bathe.*

117. **Danaen:** Greek acc. sg. of **Danae;** daughter of Acrisius, king of Argos, *Danae* was impregnated by Zeus in the form of a shower of golden rain and from the union gave birth to the hero Perseus.

118. **animo capit:** lit., *seizes with his mind* = *realizes, comprehends.*

fingens: fingere, *to fashion, mold, imagine.*

119. **gaudenti:** sc. **ei.**

ministri: minister, *servant, attendant.*

120. **exstructas: exstruere,** *to heap up, pile up.*

dapibus: daps, s. and pl. = *feast, banquet.*

tostae: torrere, *to burn, roast.*

frugis: frux, *grain;* **frugis tostae,** = *bread,* with **egere** (which may take the gen. as well as the abl.). Ovid's point is that the feast included all kinds of food, from the simplest to the most elaborate.

121. **sive:** conj., *if;* **sive . . . sive,** *if . . . or if.*

Cerealia: adj., *of Ceres;* with **munera** = *bread.* The repeated phrases, each with slight variation (**Cerealia . . . munera . . . Cerealia dona,** and cp. in 124–25 **dapes . . . dente parabat, . . . dapes . . . dente premebat**), serve much the same purpose as the word repetitions in 109–17.

dextra: sc. **manu.**

122. **rigebant: rigere,** *to be stiff, hard.*

123. **convellere:** *to tear apart, devour.*

124. **lammina:** sometimes spelled **lamina,** *thin metal plate.*

premebat: here, *covered, surrounded.*

125. **auctorem muneris:** = Bacchus and, by METONYMY, wine.

126. **fusile:** *molten, liquefied, fluid.*

ilice detraxit virgam; virga aurea facta est.
110 Tollit humo saxum; saxum quoque palluit auro.
Contigit et glaebam; contactu glaeba potenti
massa fit. Arentis Cereris decerpsit aristas;
aurea messis erat. Demptum tenet arbore pomum;
Hesperidas donasse putes. Si postibus altis
115 admovit digitos, postes radiare videntur.
Ille etiam liquidis palmas ubi laverat undis,
unda fluens palmis Danaen eludere posset.

Vix spes ipse suas animo capit aurea fingens
omnia. Gaudenti mensas posuere ministri
120 exstructas dapibus nec tostae frugis egentes.
Tum vero, sive ille sua Cerealia dextra
munera contigerat, Cerealia dona rigebant;
sive dapes avido convellere dente parabat,
lammina fulva dapes admoto dente premebat.
125 Miscuerat puris auctorem muneris undis;
fusile per rictus aurum fluitare videres.

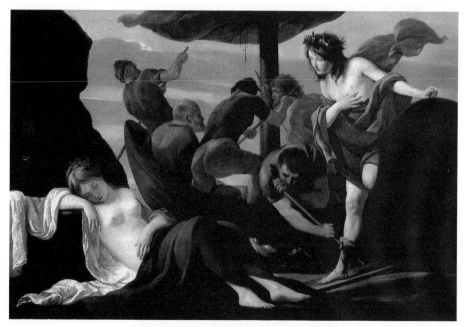

"Bacchus Discovering Ariadne on Naxos"
Louis Le Nain, 1648
Musée des Beaux-Arts, Orleans, France

127. **attonitus:** *thunderstruck, astounded.*
128. **voverat: vovere,** *to vow, pray for.*
129. **famem: fames,** *hunger.*
130. **urit: urere,** *to burn.*
     meritus: lit., *having deserved* = *as he deserved, deservedly.*
     torquetur: torquere, *to twist, torment.*
     inviso . . . ab auro: ABL. OF AGENT, as indicated by the prep., rather than the more prosaic ABL. OF MEANS; with the adj. **inviso** Ovid personifies the gold as a malevolent entity.
131. **splendida:** *shining,* as Midas' arms now are turning to gold.
132. **Lenaee: Lenaeus,** another name for Bacchus.
133. **miserere: misereri,** *to pity.*
     precor: precari, *to pray, beseech.*
     specioso: *beautiful, fine, splendid,* often, as here, with reference to something deceptively attractive.
     eripe: sc. **me.**
     damno: damnum, *injury, loss, curse.*
134. **mite:** *gentle, mild;* sc. **est.**
     deum: = **deorum.**
     peccasse: = **peccavisse;** sc. **se** as subj. of the IND. STATE., dependent on **(eum) fatentem.**
135. **pacti . . . fide:** *as (by) a guarantee of their agreement.*
     solvit: lit., *loosened* = *canceled.*
136. **neve:** *and that . . . not.*
     circumlitus: circumlinere, *to surround;* note the WORD-PICTURE, as Midas/**circumlitus** is "surrounded" by the words **optato . . . auro.**
137. **vade: vadere,** *to go.*
     Sardibus: Sardes, pl., *Sardis,* capital of Lydia.
     amnem: amnis, *river,* i.e., the Pactolus.
138. **iugum Lydum:** *the Lydian ridge,* i.e., Mt. Timolus.
     obvius: *meeting, facing, making your way toward,* + dat.
139. **ortus:** acc. pl., *source.*
140. **spumigero:** *foaming;* the INTERLOCKED WORD ORDER suits the image of the spring waters pouring over and around Midas' head.
     qua: adv., *in what place, where.*
     plurimus: referring to **fonti** but with adv. force, *where it comes out the most,* i.e., where the water comes rushing forth from the spring.
141. **subde: subdere,** *to put under, plunge.*
     subde . . . simul, simul elue: ANAPHORA and CHIASMUS help suggest the simultaneity and finality of the two actions.
     elue: eluere, *to wash away.*
144. **semine: semen,** *seed.*
     venae: vena, *vein* (here, of gold).
145. **madidis:** *wet, soaked.*

Midas confesses his sin and is told how to atone for it.

Attonitus novitate mali, divesque miserque,
effugere optat opes, et quae modo voverat, odit.
Copia nulla famem relevat; sitis arida guttur
130   urit, et inviso meritus torquetur ab auro.
Ad caelumque manus et splendida bracchia tollens,
"Da veniam, Lenaee pater, peccavimus," inquit,
"sed miserere, precor, speciosoque eripe damno!"
Mite deum numen: Bacchus peccasse fatentem
135   restituit pactique fide data munera solvit.
"Neve male optato maneas circumlitus auro,
vade," ait, "ad magnis vicinum Sardibus amnem,
perque iugum Lydum labentibus obvius undis
carpe viam, donec venias ad fluminis ortus;
140   spumigeroque tuum fonti, qua plurimus exit,
subde caput corpusque simul, simul elue crimen."
Rex iussae succedit aquae; vis aurea tinxit
flumen et humano de corpore cessit in amnem.
Nunc quoque, iam veteris percepto semine venae,
145   arva rigent auro, madidis pallentia glaebis.

*Midas turning his
daughter into gold
From a non-Ovidian
version of the tale*

PLINY'S LETTERS

Gaius Plinius Caecilius Secundus (known as "Pliny the Younger," to distinguish him from his famous uncle, the elder Pliny) was born in Comum in northern Italy, ca. A.D. 61. After his father's death, he lived, along with his mother, in the home of his uncle, an assiduous scholar and author of the monumental 37-volume encyclopedia, the *Naturalis Historia;* eventually the young man was adopted by his uncle and inherited his considerable estate. Following his education, which included studying rhetoric with the eminent orator and educator Quintilian, Pliny entered the legal profession, arguing cases throughout his career in the civil courts and prosecuting a number of corrupt provincial governors in the senate. He rose to the praetorship in 93 and the consulship in 100, and had a distinguished career as a civil servant; his series of administrative posts held during the reigns of Domitian, Nerva, and Trajan culminated in the governorship of Bithynia, which he commenced in A.D. 109 or 110 and continued until his death in ca. 112. He had three marriages, the last to Calpurnia Fabata, a younger woman to whom he was deeply and affectionately devoted.

As a literary figure he composed a variety of works, including drama and poetry, which has been almost entirely lost, as well as an extant speech to the senate known as the *Panegyricus,* in which he expresses gratitude for his elevation to the consulship and praises Trajan for the benevolence of his reign in contrast to that of the despotic Domitian. Pliny is best known, however, for his *Epistulae,* nine volumes of personal correspondence carefully edited by him for publication and issued between A.D. 98 and 109 in units of one or more books, as well as a 10th volume, less polished and likely published posthumously, comprising letters both to and from the emperor Trajan. Though the first nine books were written with an eye to publication and consequently lack the spontaneity of Cicero's letters, and though they are occasionally marred by self-consciousness and self-praise, they nevertheless reveal to us much about a Roman of rank who was conscientious, reliable, kind, affectionate, philanthropic, and sensitive—one who, refusing to be dismayed by the evils about him, made the very most of the best of his times. Reading his letters, we feel that we have come to know a decent man, and we are grateful to have this detailed evidence of the good in Roman life as at least a partial corrective to the black and pessimistic pictures painted by such of Pliny's contemporaries as the historian Tacitus (a friend and correspondent), the epigrammatist Martial (an influence on Pliny's own verse), and the scathing satirist Juvenal.

The rich variety of selections from the *Epistulae* chosen for this book include: the dedicatory preface to the first volume; three quite different letters to friends about the pleasures of country life and escape from the urban bustle; another on the suicide of a close friend who had suffered long from disease; one to a young friend on the proper manner of hosting clients and freedmen at a dinner-party (an informative counterpoint to, and an inspiration for, one of Juvenal's satires on the same topic); a long letter to Tacitus, for use in his *Histories,* containing eye-witness accounts of the eruption of Vesuvius in A.D. 79 and the death of Pliny the Elder in that disaster; a brief missive to another friend on the devotion of a wife who had courageously joined her husband in suicide; a tender note to his wife Calpurnia, professing how much he misses her and thinks of her in her absence; and, finally, an exchange of letters between Pliny and Trajan discussing policies for investigating and punishing Christians in the province of Bithynia, invaluable documents for our knowledge of the persecutions and early church ritual.

Page from manuscript of
Pliny's Epistulae
(3.4.8–9 and 3.5.1–3)
Italy, 6th century A.D.
The Pierpont Morgan Library
New York, New York

1. **Septicio Suo S.:** Septicius, an equestrian and praetorian prefect under Hadrian (ca. A.D. 119–121), is little known outside the four letters addressed to him by Pliny; in *Epistulae* 2.9.4 Pliny remarks, **C. Septicium, quo nihil verius, nihil simplicius, nihil candidius, nihil fidelius novi.** The S. = **salutem (dicit),** *says greetings,* a standard salutation in Roman letters.

2. **si quas:** *if any* = *whatever.*
    paulo: adv., *a little, somewhat;* the preserved letters are in general less spontaneous, *more carefully* (**accuratius**) composed and edited than most of Cicero's, as Pliny intended them for publication.

3. **non . . . ordine (4):** although the individual books were published successively, beginning ca. A.D. 99, the arrangement of the letters within a particular book is not strictly chronological.

4. **ut . . . venerat (5):** Pliny's arrangement of the letters was in fact far more calculated than he suggests here.

5. **superest: superesse,** *to be left over, remain;* + dat., *to survive.*
    paeniteat: with the impers. **superest,** *it remains (that);* **paenitet,** also impers., takes an acc. of the repentant person + a gen. of the thing which occasions the repentance, lit., **ut nec . . . te consilii . . . paeniteat** = *that it not repent you of your advice,* i.e., *that you not regret your advice.*

7. **requiram:** NOUN CL. OF RESULT, dependent on **fiet.**
    si . . . addidero: i.e., if he writes any more, as indeed he did.

8. **Cornelio Tacito:** *Publius Cornelius Tacitus,* ca. A.D. 56–118, a close friend of Pliny, addressee of 11 of his letters, and one of the most famous Roman historians; his partially extant *Annals* and *Histories* covered the period from the death of Augustus to the death of Domitian, and his *Germania* is the earliest full-length portrait of the German people.

9. **licet:** impers., + inf. or subjunct.; with **rideas** = *you may laugh* or *you have a right to laugh.*
    nosti: = **novisti.**
    apros: aper, *wild boar.*

10. **ut . . . discederem (11):** RESULT CL.; i.e., he was not so busy with hunting that it distracted him from his rest (**inertia** = **otium**).

11. **retia: rete,** *hunting net;* in the sort of hunt described here, huge nets were spread out and slaves drove animals into them from the woods to be slaughtered by gentleman hunters like Pliny.

12. **in proximo:** i.e., at his side.
    venabulum: *hunting spear* (for thrusting).
    lancea: *lance, spear* (for throwing).
    stilus: the *stilus* was a pointed implement used for writing on *wax tablets* (**pugillares**).

13. **manus vacuas, plenas . . . ceras (14):** CHIASMUS; **cera,** *wax,* and by METONYMY, *tablet.*

14. **non est quod:** *there is no reason why.*

15. **ut:** here, *how,* introducing an IND. QUEST.

17. **venationi: venatio,** *hunt, hunting.*

1.1

Pliny prefaces the first book of his letters with a dedication to his friend Gaius Sep-
ticius Clarus; latest of the letters in this book, published ca. A.D. *99.*

C. Plinius Septicio Suo S.

Frequenter hortatus es ut epistulas, si quas paulo accuratius
scripsissem, colligerem publicaremque. Collegi non servato temporis ordine (neque enim historiam componebam), sed ut quae-
5   que in manus venerat. Superest ut nec te consilii nec me paeniteat obsequii. Ita enim fiet ut eas quae adhuc neglectae iacent
requiram et, si quas addidero, non supprimam. Vale.

1.6

Pliny writes to his friend, the historian Tacitus, about a holiday he has taken for hunt-
ing and study, probably at his Tuscan estate; written ca. A.D. *96–97.*

C. Plinius Cornelio Tacito Suo S.

Ridebis, et licet rideas. Ego, ille quem nosti, apros tres et
10   quidem pulcherrimos cepi. "Ipse?" inquis. Ipse; non tamen ut
omnino ab inertia mea et quiete discederem. Ad retia sedebam;
erat in proximo non venabulum aut lancea, sed stilus et pugillares; meditabar aliquid enotabamque, ut, si manus vacuas, plenas tamen ceras reportarem. Non est quod contemnas hoc stu-
15   dendi genus; mirum est ut animus agitatione motuque corporis
excitetur; iam undique silvae et solitudo ipsumque illud silentium, quod venationi datur, magna cogitationis incitamenta

18. **proinde:** adv., *therefore.*
    venabere: venari, *to hunt.*
    auctore me: ABL. ABS., = *following my example.*
    ut . . . sic (19): *as . . . so* = *not only . . . but (also).*
    panarium: *bread basket, lunch basket.*
19. **lagunculam: laguncula,** *flask.*
    experieris: here, *you will discover,* + IND. STATE.
    Dianam . . . Minervam (20): goddesses of, respectively, hunting and wisdom.
20. **inerrare:** + dat., *to wander in, over.*
21. **Minicio Fundano:** *Minicius Fundanus* was a senator and consul in A.D. 107; we have a few letters Pliny addressed to him, chiefly on political matters, and one he wrote to a mutual friend on the death of Fundanus' daughter.
22. **quam:** *how* (well); cp. **mirum est ut** in 1.6.15 above.
    singulis diebus: i.e., one day at a time.
    ratio . . . constet: *the account balances;* a bookkeeping term meaning that everything is satisfactory.
23. **pluribus iunctisque:** sc. **diebus;** i.e., when several days are considered together.
24. **officio:** here, *ceremony.*
25. **togae virilis:** when the bordered **toga praetexta** of boyhood was laid aside and the plain white *toga of manhood* was assumed, usually between the ages of 14 and 16, a coming-of-age party was held at the boy's home.
    interfui: interesse, + dat., *to be present at, attend.*
    sponsalia: pl., *betrothal,* an often legalistic ceremony.
    nuptias: nuptiae, pl., *wedding.*
    ille . . . ille (26): ANAPHORA and ASYNDETON are used frequently and in combination throughout this letter.
26. **testamentum:** seven witnesses were required at the signing of a will.
    advocationem: advocatio, *assistance at court, legal advice.*
    consilium: various high magistrates and the emperor himself called on senators to serve on their advisory councils.
27. **haec . . . necessaria:** = **haec, eo die quo ea feceris, videntur necessaria.**
    feceris: indef. 2nd pers., *you have done* = *one has done.*
28. **secesseris: secedere,** *to go apart, withdraw* (from the city).
29. **subit: subire,** *to go under, undergo, approach, come to mind.*
    frigidis: here, *dull, unproductive.*
30. **quod:** i.e., this realization.
    Laurentino: sc. **fundo (fundus),** *country estate near Laurentium;* this villa, one of a number that Pliny owned, was near the coast about 15 miles south of Rome.
31. **corpori:** *for the body,* i.e., for exercise, often neglected in busy city life.
    fulturis: fultura, *prop, support.*
34. **reprehendo: reprehendere,** *to seize, blame, censure.*
35. **commode:** adv., *easily.*
    spe: here, an unsettling *expectation, anticipation.*
37. **vitam:** ACC. OF EXCLAMATION.
    honestum: not *honest,* but *fine, respectable.*

20 sunt. Proinde, cum venabere, licebit auctore me ut panarium et lagunculam sic etiam pugillares feras: experieris non Dianam magis montibus quam Minervam inerrare. Vale.

1.9

In this letter to his friend Minicius Fundanus, Pliny contrasts the demands of city life with the leisurely time spent at his villa in Laurentum; written ca. A.D. *97.*

C. Plinius Minicio Fundano Suo S.

Mirum est quam singulis diebus in urbe ratio aut constet aut constare videatur, pluribus iunctisque non constet. Nam, si quem interroges, "Hodie quid egisti?" respondeat, "Officio
25 togae virilis interfui, sponsalia aut nuptias frequentavi, ille me ad signandum testamentum, ille in advocationem, ille in consilium rogavit." Haec quo die feceris, necessaria; eadem si cotidie fecisse te reputes, inania videntur, multo magis cum secesseris. Tunc enim subit recordatio: "Quot dies quam frigidis rebus ab-
30 sumpsi!" Quod evenit mihi, postquam in Laurentino meo aut lego aliquid aut scribo aut etiam corpori vaco, cuius fulturis animus sustinetur. Nihil audio quod audisse, nihil dico quod dixisse paeniteat; nemo apud me quemquam sinistris sermonibus carpit, neminem ipse reprehendo, nisi tamen me, cum parum
35 commode scribo; nulla spe, nullo timore sollicitor, nullis rumoribus inquietor; mecum tantum et cum libellis loquor. O rectam sinceramque vitam, o dulce otium honestumque ac paene

Trapping deer, detail from the "Small Game Hunt" mosaic, 4th century A.D.
Villa del Casale, Piazza Armerina, Sicily, Italy

39. *mouseion:* Greek for Lat. **museum,** a temple or home of the Muses, the god-
desses of that inspiration which Pliny finds in his coastal retreat.

invenitis: *you discover, suggest;* the subjs. of the vb. are **litus** and **mare,** i.e.,
the surroundings.

dictatis: wealthy Romans owned highly trained slaves to whom they could
dictate their compositions; here Pliny fancies himself as the amanuensis.

40. **strepitum: strepitus,** *noise, din.*

multum: adv. modifying **ineptos,** = *very.*

41. **ut primum:** *as soon as.*

42. **Atilius:** *Atilius Crescens,* another of Pliny's close friends.

43. **facetissime:** adv. from **facetus,** *elegant, witty, humorous.*

nihil agere: a play on words, not *to do nothing* but *to be busy at nothing.*

45. **iacturam: iactura,** *throwing away, loss.*

feci: here, *I have experienced, suffered.*

46. **sponte:** sc. **sua,** idiom, *of his own accord, by his own wish;* i.e., by starvation,
in an act of Stoic fortitude.

47. **exulcerat: exulcerare,** *to make extremely sore, aggravate, exacerbate.*

luctuosissimum: *most sorrowful, most lamentable.*

48. **fatalis:** *fated, in accordance with fate.*

utcumque: adv., *somehow, in one way or another.*

50. **arcessita:** *voluntary, self-inflicted;* from **arcessere,** *to call, summon, invite.*

52. **pro necessitate est:** i.e., *takes priority over inevitability.*

53. **quamquam:** conj., *although, and yet.*

55. **pignora: pignus,** *pledge, proof;* used in the pl. of one's *close relatives.*

58. **pretia: pretium,** *price, reward.*

59. **pedum dolore:** probably gout.

60. **patrius:** *inherited from his father,* i.e., not caused by dissolute living.

hic: i.e., **dolor;** sc. **est.**

plerumque: adv., *generally.*

per successiones: i.e., by heredity from one generation to the next.

61. **hunc:** sc. **morbum.**

Boar hunt, detail from the "Small Game Hunt" mosaic, 4th century A.D.
Villa del Casale, Piazza Armerina, Sicily, Italy

omni negotio pulchrius! O mare, o litus, verum secretumque
mouseion, quam multa invenitis, quam multa dictatis! Proinde
40   tu quoque strepitum istum inanemque discursum et multum ineptos labores, ut primum fuerit occasio, relinque teque studiis
vel otio trade. Satius est enim, ut Atilius noster eruditissime
simul et facetissime dixit, otiosum esse quam nihil agere. Vale.

1.12

*In one of several surviving letters to Calestrius Tiro, a senator and his colleague in
both the quaestorship and praetorship, Pliny here discusses the suicide of Corellius
Rufus, consul in* A.D. *78, a noble Roman Stoic, and a man he had often turned to for
advice; written ca.* A.D. *98.*

C. Plinius Calestrio Tironi Suo S.

*It is harder to reconcile oneself to the suicide of a friend than to his
death from natural causes.*

45   Iacturam gravissimam feci, si iactura dicenda est tanti viri
amissio. Decessit Corellius Rufus et quidem sponte, quod dolorem meum exulcerat. Est enim luctuosissimum genus mortis,
quae non ex natura nec fatalis videtur. Nam utcumque in illis
qui morbo finiuntur magnum ex ipsa necessitate solacium est;
50   in iis vero quos arcessita mors aufert, hic insanabilis dolor est,
quod creduntur potuisse diu vivere. Corellium quidem summa
ratio, quae sapientibus pro necessitate est, ad hoc consilium
compulit, quamquam plurimas vivendi causas habentem—optimam conscientiam, optimam famam, maximam auctoritatem,
55   praeterea filiam, uxorem, nepotem, sorores interque tot pignora
veros amicos.

Corellius' suffering lasted long and had broken his body.

Sed tam longa, tam iniqua valetudine conflictabatur, ut haec
tanta pretia vivendi mortis rationibus vincerentur. Tertio et
tricensimo anno, ut ipsum audiebam, pedum dolore correptus
60   est. Patrius hic illi; nam plerumque morbi quoque per successiones quasdam ut alia traduntur. Hunc abstinentia, sanctitate,

62.   **quoad:** conj., *how long, as long as, until.*
       viridis: *green, youthful.*
       fregit: frangere, *to break.*
       ingravescentem: sc. **hunc (morbum)** from the beginning of the sent.
64.   **cruciatus:** acc. pl., *tortures.*
       indignissima: indignus, *unworthy, undeserved,* hence *cruel, harsh.*
65.   **pervagabatur: pervagari,** *to spread throughout, pervade.*
67.   **suburbano:** sc. **praedio,** *estate.*
       iacentem: i.e., sick in bed.
68.   **moris:** PARTITIVE GEN.; i.e., he routinely dismissed his slaves whenever a close
            friend visited.
70.   **capacissima:** *quite worthy of sharing.*
       circumtulit oculos: because of his encouragement of **delatores** *(informers),*
            the tyranny of Domitian (emperor A.D. 81–96) was as dangerous as that
            of Mussolini, Hitler, and Stalin.
71.   **scilicet:** adv., *obviously, of course.*
72.   **latroni: latro,** *bandit, cut-throat;* Domitian, of course.
       vel uno die: *even by one day;* ABL. OF DEGREE OF DIFFERENCE, depending on
            the idea that "to survive" means "to live longer."
       dedisses: indef. 2nd pers.; a conditional cl. without **si,** *had you given.*
73.   **fecisset quod optabat:** i.e., he would have assisted in Domitian's assassination
            (which took place on September 18, A.D. 96).
       voto: votum, *prayer.*
74.   **compos:** *in possession of,* + gen.; with **votum** (here **cuius**), an idiom = *having
            had one's prayer answered.*
       ut: here, *as (one).*
       moriturus: *ready to die;* notwithstanding Pliny's dramatization here, Corellius
            survived Domitian by as much as a year.
75.   **minora:** *too slight, too weak.*
       retinacula: retinaculum, usually pl., *rope, tether, rein.*
       abrumpit: abrumpere, *to break, throw off.*
76.   **perseverantem:** sc. **quam** from the preceding cl., *which continuing = its persis-
            tence.*
       constantia: *by his steadfast resolution* (to commit suicide).
78.   **Hispulla:** perhaps *Calpurnia Hispulla,* an aunt of Pliny's wife.
       C. Geminium: otherwise unknown, as is Julius Atticus below.
79.   **suis:** refers back to Hispulla, not to Geminius.
80.   **a quo . . . posset:** REL. CL. OF PURPOSE.
82.   **nihil . . . ne:** together an emphatic negative.
       impetraturum: sc. **esse;** from **impetrare,** *to obtain, accomplish.*
83.   **induruisse:** sc. **eum** (Corellius).
       sane: adv., *indeed.*
84.   *kekrika:* Greek, *I have decided, my mind is made up.*
89.   **superstitibus suis:** *with his own (family) surviving (him).*
       florente re publica: i.e., during the reign of Nerva (A.D. 96–98) or possibly of
            Trajan (A.D. 98–117).

quoad viridis aetas, vicit et fregit; novissime cum senectute ingravescentem viribus animi sustinebat, cum quidem incredibilis cruciatus et indignissima tormenta pateretur. Iam enim dolor
65   non pedibus solis ut prius insidebat, sed omnia membra pervagabatur.

Corellius' desire to outlive the tyrannous Domitian had buoyed him up for a while.

Veni ad eum Domitiani temporibus in suburbano iacentem. Servi e cubiculo recesserunt (habebat hoc moris, quotiens intrasset fidelior amicus); quin etiam uxor, quamquam omnis se-
70   creti capacissima, digrediebatur. Circumtulit oculos et "Cur," inquit, "me putas hos tantos dolores tam diu sustinere?—ut scilicet isti latroni vel uno die supersim." Dedisses huic animo par corpus, fecisset quod optabat. Adfuit tamen deus voto, cuius ille compos, ut iam securus liberque moriturus, multa illa vitae sed
75   minora retinacula abrumpit. Increverat valetudo, quam temperantia mitigare temptavit; perseverantem constantia fugit.

Corellius' wife, Hispulla, begged Pliny to dissuade him from his resolve to starve himself to death, but Corellius was determined.

Iam dies alter, tertius, quartus: abstinebat cibo. Misit ad me uxor eius Hispulla communem amicum C. Geminium cum tristissimo nuntio destinasse Corellium mori nec aut suis aut filiae
80   precibus flecti, solum superesse me a quo revocari posset ad vitam. Cucurri. Perveneram in proximum, cum mihi ab eadem Hispulla Iulius Atticus nuntiat nihil iam ne me quidem impetraturum; tam obstinate magis ac magis induruisse. Dixerat sane medico admoventi cibum: "*Kekrika,*" quae vox quantum admi-
85   rationis in animo meo tantum desiderii reliquit.

Pliny pays tribute to his friend and asks Tiro to write him some extraordinary words of consolation to suit his extraordinary grief.

Cogito quo amico, quo viro caream. Implevit quidem annum septimum et sexagesimum, quae aetas etiam robustissimis satis longa est; scio. Evasit perpetuam valetudinem; scio. Decessit superstitibus suis, florente re publica, quae illi omnibus

91. **morte:** ABL. OF CAUSE.

morte doleo, doleo . . . nomine (92): CHIASMUS.

licet: here, *although.*

imbecillum: *weak,* suggesting that Pliny lacks the Stoicism of his dear friend.

92. **meo nomine:** *my name = myself.*

testem: testis, *witness;* here, *observer, guardian.*

93. **contubernali: contubernalis,** *comrade.*

94. **Calvisio:** *Calvisius Rufus,* a friend and business advisor of Pliny's from Comum, and the addressee of several of his letters.

neglegentius: i.e., without concern even for his own well-being.

adhibe: adhibere, *to hold to, apply, show, provide.*

96. **audierim:** = **audiverim;** note the difference between **quae audierim,** *the kind which I have (never) heard* (REL. CL. OF CHARACTERISTIC) and **quae audivi,** *those which I have (actually) heard.*

97. **sponte:** here, *spontaneously, naturally.*

100. **longum est:** idiom, *it is long = it would be a long story.*

altius: adv.; i.e., in more detail.

refert: idiom, *it matters.*

acciderit: accidere, *to fall, happen, take place;* impers., *it happens.*

101. **ut . . . cenarem:** NOUN CL. OF RESULT, subj. of **acciderit.**

homo minime familiaris: lit., *(I) a person not at all intimate, only slightly acquainted.*

102. **lautum et diligentem:** *elegant* (lit., *well-washed, clean*) *and* (at the same time) *economical.*

sordidum: *mean, base, stingy;* lit., *dirty, filthy,* and hence contrasting with and balancing *lautum.*

103. **sumptuosum:** *extravagant,* contrasting with **diligentem;** the hissing alliteration of **s** in **sordidum simul . . . sumptuosum** (a brilliant OXYMORON) is perhaps ONOMATOPOETIC, suggesting Pliny's contempt for the man who had been his host.

opima . . . vilia et minuta (104): again note the antithetical balance, **opima** *(rich and abundant)* by itself serving as the opposite of the other two adjs.

104. **parvulis lagunculis:** the two diminutives further suggest Pliny's contempt.

105. **discripserat: discribere,** *to distribute, assign.*

eligendi: eligere, *to choose, select.*

106. **aliud . . . aliud . . . aliud (107):** sc. **genus,** *one kind . . . another . . . another.*

gradatim: adv., *step by step, by grades, graded;* the satirist Juvenal similarly condemns the grading and disparate treatment of dinner-guests in his Satire Five, written just a few years after Pliny's letter.

107. **animadvertit: animadvertere,** *to give attention to, notice.*

108. **recumbebat: recumbere,** *to recline;* the Romans reclined on couches at their meals.

an: conj., *or, whether.*

109. **consuetudinem: consuetudo,** *custom, practice.*

90 suis carior erat; et hoc scio. Ego tamen tamquam et iuvenis et
fortissimi morte doleo, doleo autem (licet me imbecillum putes)
meo nomine. Amisi enim, amisi vitae meae testem, rectorem,
magistrum. In summa dicam quod recenti dolore contubernali
meo Calvisio dixi: "Vereor ne neglegentius vivam." Proinde ad-
95 hibe solacia mihi, non haec, "Senex erat, infirmus erat" (haec
enim novi), sed nova aliqua, sed magna quae audierim numquam, legerim numquam. Nam quae audivi, quae legi sponte
succurrunt, sed tanto dolore superantur. Vale.

2.6.1–5

As Pliny relates to his young friend Junius Avitus, even the freedmen at his dinner-parties enjoy the same food and drink as he does himself, in contrast to some hosts of the day who served lesser fare to their guests of lower rank; written ca. A.D. *98.*

C. Plinius Avito Suo S.

100 Longum est altius repetere, nec refert, quemadmodum acciderit ut homo minime familiaris cenarem apud quendam, ut
sibi videbatur, lautum et diligentem, ut mihi, sordidum simul et
sumptuosum. Nam sibi et paucis opima quaedam, ceteris vilia
et minuta ponebat. Vinum etiam parvulis lagunculis in tria ge-
105 nera discripserat, non ut potestas eligendi, sed ne ius esset recu-
sandi, aliud sibi et nobis, aliud minoribus amicis (nam gradatim
amicos habet), aliud suis nostrisque libertis. Animadvertit, qui
mihi proximus recumbebat, et an probarem interrogavit. Negavi.
"Tu ergo," inquit, "quam consuetudinem sequeris?" "Eadem

*Banquet scene
Etruscan fresco
ca. 500* B.C.
*Tomb of the Leopards
Tarquinia, Italy*

110.   **notam:** *degradation,* referring to the mark **(nota censoria)** which the censor, in revising the citizen lists every five years, placed opposite the names of those guilty of some crime or moral turpitude and thus subject to the loss of voting rights or, in the case of magistrates, expulsion from the senate.

    cunctis: = **omnibus.**

    cunctis . . . rebus (111): ABL. OF SPECIFICATION.

111.   **toro:** torus, *couch, cushion.*

    libertos: libertus, *freedman;* a wealthy **patronus** would periodically invite his freedmen clients to dinner, a courtesy later replaced with the provision of take-out meals (the **sportula**) or cash payments.

112.   **convictores:** convictor, *associate,* lit., *one who lives with another.*

113.   **magno . . . constat:** lit., *it stands at a great price* = *it costs a lot;* ABL. OF PRICE.

    minime: here, *not at all, by no means.*

    qui: adv., *how.*

114.   **idem:** sc. **vinum.**

    quod ego: sc. **bibo.**

115.   **hercule:** originally voc. of **Hercules** *(help me, Hercules)* but regularly used as a mild oath, = *by God!*

    gulae: gula, *gullet, gluttony, appetite.*

    temperes: temperare, + dat., *to control, moderate;* indef. 2nd pers. sg.

116.   **quo:** sc. **id** as antecedent of **quo** and obj. of **communicare.**

117.   **Tacito:** for Tacitus, see note on line 8 above.

118.   **avunculi:** avunculus, *uncle.* Pliny's maternal uncle, known as Pliny the Elder (A.D. 23–79), raised him and in his will adopted him and made him the heir to his entire estate; described by his nephew here and in another letter (3.5), in which his prodigious scholarly activity is recounted, the elder Pliny was a scientist and polymath, best known for his 37-book encyclopedia, the *Naturalis Historia,* which ranges over topics as diverse as art and zoology, medicine and metallurgy.

    exitum: exitus, *end, death.*

    quo: commonly used to introduce a REL. CL. OF PURPOSE containing a comparative degree adj. or adv.

    tradere: here we see Tacitus researching his *Histories,* which covered the period A.D. 68–96; although the section of his work on the eruption of Vesuvius is not extant, we are fortunate to have Pliny's exquisitely detailed account of the event.

120.   **esse propositam:** *has been promised.*

121.   **mansura:** here the fut. partic. has the meaning of *destined to . . ..*

    condiderit: here, *composed.*

123.   **facere scribenda:** *to do things to be recorded, worth recording;* the phrase is subj. of **datum est,** *it has been granted.*

124.   **utrumque:** i.e., **et facere et scribere.**

110 omnibus pono; ad cenam enim non ad notam invito cunctisque
rebus exaequo quos mensa et toro aequavi." "Etiamne libertos?" "Etiam; convictores enim tunc, non libertos puto." Et
ille: "Magno tibi constat." "Minime." "Qui fieri potest?" "Quia
scilicet liberti mei non idem quod ego bibunt, sed idem ego
115 quod liberti." Et hercule, si gulae temperes, non est onerosum,
quo utaris ipse, communicare cum pluribus. Vale.

6.16 (excerpts)

Pliny provides his friend Tacitus, for use in his Histories, *an account of the death
of his uncle, Pliny the Elder, during the catastrophic eruption of Mount Vesuvius, August 24,* A.D. *79; written ca.* A.D. *106–107.*

C. Plinius Tacito Suo S.

*Pliny is pleased to give Tacitus the information he has requested, as it
will perpetuate the memory of his uncle's accomplishments.*

Petis ut tibi avunculi mei exitum scribam, quo verius tradere
posteris possis. Gratias ago; nam video morti eius, si celebretur
120 a te, immortalem gloriam esse propositam. Quamvis ipse plurima opera et mansura condiderit, multum tamen perpetuitati
eius scriptorum tuorum aeternitas addet. Equidem beatos puto,
quibus deorum munere datum est aut facere scribenda aut
scribere legenda; beatissimos vero, quibus utrumque. Horum in
125 numero avunculus meus et suis libris et tuis erit.

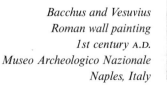

*Bacchus and Vesuvius
Roman wall painting
1st century* A.D.
*Museo Archeologico Nazionale
Naples, Italy*

126. **Miseni: Misenum,** a promontory town and the principal naval base on Italy's west coast, commanding the Bay of Naples.

     classem: classis, *fleet.*

     imperio: i.e., with full authority as prefect of the fleet, a command assigned to members of the equestrian class.

     praesens: *present in person;* i.e., he was not simply at his desk in Rome.

     nonum . . . Septembres (127): the full form of the date would be **ante diem nonum Kalendas Septembres,** *the 9th day before the Kalends* (the first day of any month) *of September = August 24.* The Greek historian Dio identifies the year as the first of the emperor Titus' reign (A.D. 79–81).

127. **hora:** = 1/12 of the day or of the night; the **hora septima,** reckoned from dawn = roughly *1:00 p.m.*

     mater mea: we know little of Pliny's mother, whose name was presumably **Plinia;** Pliny was himself 18 years old at the time of the eruption, and he and his mother were residing with his uncle.

     ei: depends on **indicat.**

128. **inusitata:** *unusual.*

     specie: species, *appearance, kind.*

129. **frigida:** sc. **aqua;** the elder Pliny's routine for relaxing included sunbathing, a cool bath, a snack, and reading.

     poscit: poscere, *to request, demand.*

     soleas: solea, *sandal.*

131. **incertum . . . ex quo monte:** sc. **fuit.** Vesuvius, though an ancient volcano, had no crater, had never erupted within the memory of the Romans, and was ca. 18 miles away, with other mountains in the background—hence the uncertainty.

     procul: adv., *far off, at a distance.*

     intuentibus: intueri, *to look at, contemplate, consider.*

132. **cuius . . . expresserit (133):** a rather involved way of saying "whose shape looked more like that of a pine than anything else"; REL. CL. OF CHARACTERISTIC. Pliny has in mind the Italian umbrella pine, whose branchless lower trunk culminates in a large flattish crown of branches and foliage that flares out around the top; today we might compare the mushroom cloud of a nuclear blast.

134. **velut:** conj., *as, just as, as if.*

135. **maculosa:** *spotted.*

     prout: conj., *as, just as, according as.*

137. **magnum:** sc. **fuit,** *it was an important event.*

     propius: prope, adv., *nearly, closely.*

     ut . . . visum: sc. **est,** *as it seemed (to).*

138. **Liburnicam:** sc. **navem,** a swift galley modeled on those of the Liburnian pirates of the Adriatic.

     aptari: aptare, *to prepare, make ready.*

     una: adv., *along, together.*

     facit copiam: idiom, *he gives the opportunity.*

139. **quod scriberem:** *something to write;* i.e., an exercise in composition.

Pliny the Elder, attracted by the unusual phenomenon, sailed from the naval base at Misenum to study Vesuvius' eruption at close range and to bring assistance to the residents of the area.

Erat Miseni classemque imperio praesens regebat. Nonum Kal. Septembres hora fere septima, mater mea indicat ei apparere nubem inusitata et magnitudine et specie. Usus ille sole, mox frigida, gustaverat iacens studebatque; poscit soleas, as-
130 cendit locum ex quo maxime miraculum illud conspici poterat. Nubes— incertum procul intuentibus ex quo monte (Vesuvium fuisse postea cognitum est)—oriebatur, cuius similitudinem et formam non alia magis arbor quam pinus expresserit. Nam longissimo velut trunco elata in altum quibusdam ramis diffunde-
135 batur, candida interdum, interdum sordida et maculosa, prout terram cineremve sustulerat.

Magnum propiusque noscendum, ut eruditissimo viro visum. Iubet Liburnicam aptari. Mihi, si venire una vellem, facit copiam; respondi studere me malle, et forte ipse quod scriberem

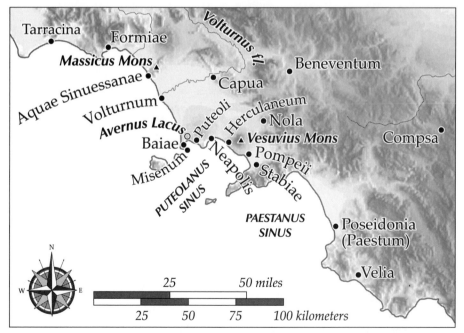

THE BAY OF NAPLES
Map by R. A. LaFleur, Tom Elliott, Nicole Feldl, Alexandra Retzleff, and Joyce Uy. Copyright 2001, Ancient World Mapping Center (http://www.unc.edu/depts/awmc)

140. **egrediebatur ... accipit ... orabat (142):** ASYNDETON emphasizes the tense-
      ness of the situation.

      codicillos: codicillus, *writing tablet;* here, *a message.*

      Rectinae Tasci: *of Rectina (the wife) of Tascius,* the standard formulation for
      a wife's name; the man may be the same as the Pomponianus below, line
      153, but Rectina is not otherwise known.

141. **subiacebat:** *lay at the foot* (of the mountain).

      nec ... fuga (142): the road had doubtless been blocked by debris.

142. **se:** an ind. reflexive in a JUSSIVE NOUN CL., referring to Rectina, the subj.
      of **orabat.**

      discrimini: *danger;* DAT. OF SEPARATION.

143. **incohaverat: incohare,** *to begin.*

      obit: obire, *to go to meet, perform, carry out.*

144. **maximo:** sc. **animo;** i.e., *with courage* vs. scholarly interest.

      quadriremes: *warships* (ships with four banks of oars); switching from a scien-
      tific study expedition to a rescue mission, he needed larger ships, which
      he had at his disposal as admiral of the Roman fleet.

      ascendit: sc. **in navem.**

145. **amoenitas orae:** *the charm of the shore,* a poetic circumlocution for *the charm-
      ing stretch of shore.*

      laturus: *intending to bring;* we do not know either from Pliny's account or
      any other source whether Rectina was saved or not.

146. **properat: properare,** *to hurry.*

147. **gubernacula: gubernaculum,** *helm, rudder.*

      adeo: adv., *to such a degree, so, even.*

148. **motus:** acc. pl.

      figuras: here, *forms, phases.*

      deprenderat: deprendere, *to catch, observe.*

150. **pumices: pumex,** *pumice-stone,* pl., *pieces of pumice.*

151. **ambusti:** *scorched.*

      lapides: lapis, *stone, rock.*

152. **an:** here, *whether.*

      gubernatori: gubernator, *pilot.*

153. **fortes ... iuvat:** a proverb known from several other Roman authors.

      Pomponianum: possibly *Tascius Pomponianus,* the husband of Rectina men-
      tioned earlier (line 140); Pliny fails to inform us of his ultimate fate.

      Stabiis: Stabiae, pl.; the town of *Stabiae* was a few miles south of Vesuvius
      and Pompeii.

154. **erat:** sc. **Pomponianus.**

      diremptus: dirimere, *to take apart, separate;* i.e., he was separated from Pliny.

      sinu: sinus, *bay;* with **medio,** = *lying between them,* i.e., a small arm of the
      Bay of Naples at Stabiae.

      sarcinas: sarcina, *bundle, baggage.*

      certus fugae (155): lit., *determined of flight* = *intending to flee.*

155. **contrarius:** an adverse wind in that it was blowing from the sea so that the
      ships could not sail out from Stabiae; this same wind was favorable **(se-
      cundus)** for Pliny, who was sailing from the bay toward Stabiae.

140   dederat. Egrediebatur domo: accipit codicillos Rectinae Tasci imminenti periculo exterritae (nam villa eius subiacebat, nec ulla nisi navibus fuga); ut se tanto discrimini eriperet, orabat. Vertit ille consilium et, quod studioso animo incohaverat, obit maximo. Deducit quadriremes, ascendit ipse non Rectinae
145   modo, sed multis (erat enim frequens amoenitas orae) laturus auxilium. Properat illuc, unde alii fugiunt, rectumque cursum, recta gubernacula in periculum tenet, adeo solutus metu ut omnes illius mali motus, omnes figuras, ut deprenderat oculis, dictaret enotaretque.

Pliny faced the dangers with extraordinary composure and encouraged the others.

150   Iam navibus cinis incidebat, calidior et densior, iam pumices etiam nigrique et ambusti et fracti igne lapides. Cunctatus paulum an retro flecteret, mox gubernatori ut ita faceret monenti "Fortes" inquit, "fortuna iuvat: Pomponianum pete." Stabiis erat, diremptus sinu medio; sarcinas contulerat in naves, certus
155   fugae, si contrarius ventus resedisset. Quo tunc avunculus meus

Roman warships
Fresco, 1st century A.D.
Casa dei Vettii, Pompeii, Italy

156. **invectus:** i.e., to shore.
   complectitur: complecti, *to embrace.*
   trepidantem: i.e., Pomponianus.
157. **securitate: securitas,** *lack of concern, composure;* CHIASMUS effectively contrasts this word with its antonym **timorem.**
   leniret: lenire, *to calm, soothe.*
   deferri: sc. **se** as subj.
158. **balineum:** *bath.*
   lotus: *having (been) bathed,* from **lavare.**
   accubat: accubare, *to recline at table.*
   hilaris: *cheerful.*
159. **similis hilari:** sc. **viro;** i.e., pretending to be cheerful.
161. **tenebris: tenebrae,** pl., *shadows, darkness, gloom.*
162. **excitabatur:** *were enhanced;* the vb. is sg. to agree with the nearer of the two subjs., and since **fulgor** and **claritas** constitute a single idea.
   agrestium: agrestis, *farmer, peasant;* there were farms throughout the area of Vesuvius, where the volcanically enriched soil was well suited to agriculture.
   relictos: sc. **esse;** in their fear the country people had fled without putting out their fires on the hearth.
163. **per solitudinem:** i.e., in the districts abandoned by the inhabitants.
   in remedium formidinis: indicating purpose, freely = *to allay their terror* (**formido**).
165. **meatus animae:** *the passage of his breath* = *his breathing, snoring.*
166. **obversabantur: obversari,** + dat., *to pass before.*
167. **area:** *open space, courtyard.*
   diaeta: *room, apartment.*
168. **oppleta: opplere,** *to fill, cover.*
169. **mora:** sc. **esset.**
   exitus negaretur: thus explaining the numerous bodies found by archaeologists in the excavations.
170. **in commune:** *for the common good.*
171. **tecta: tectum,** *roof, dwelling, house.*
   subsistant: subsistere, *to stand still, remain, stay;* sc. **utrum.**
   aperto: apertum, *open space.*
   vagentur: vagari, *to wander about.*
172. **nutabant: nutare,** *to nod, totter, sway.*
   sedibus: sedes, *seat, abode, home;* here, *foundation.*
173. **sub dio:** *under the divine element* = *under the open sky.*
   rursus: adv., *back, again.*
174. **quamquam:** to be construed with the adjs.
   exesorum: exedere, *to eat away;* here, *eaten away* (as it were, by fire and gases), *porous.*
   casus: here, *the falling.*

secundissimo invectus complectitur trepidantem, consolatur, hortatur, utque timorem eius sua securitate leniret, deferri in balineum iubet; lotus accubat, cenat aut hilaris aut, quod est aeque magnum, similis hilari.

A description of the eruption and the plight of the people.

160   Interim e Vesuvio monte pluribus locis latissimae flammae altaque incendia relucebant, quorum fulgor et claritas tenebris noctis excitabatur. Ille agrestium trepidatione ignes relictos desertasque villas per solitudinem ardere in remedium formidinis dictitabat. Tum se quieti dedit et quievit verissimo quidem
165   somno, nam meatus animae, qui illi propter amplitudinem corporis gravior et sonantior erat, ab eis qui limini obversabantur audiebatur. Sed area ex qua diaeta adibatur ita iam cinere mixtisque pumicibus oppleta surrexerat, ut, si longior in cubiculo mora, exitus negaretur. Excitatus procedit seque Pomponiano
170   ceterisque, qui pervigilaverant, reddit. In commune consultant, intra tecta subsistant an in aperto vagentur. Nam crebris vastisque tremoribus tecta nutabant et, quasi emota sedibus suis, nunc huc, nunc illuc abire aut referri videbantur. Sub dio rursus quamquam levium exesorumque pumicum casus metuebatur;

"A Dream in the Ruins of Pompeii"
Paul Alfred de Curzon, 1866
Musée Leon Alegre, Bagnois-sur-Ceze, France

175. **quod:** conjunctive use of the rel. referring in general to the preceding point, *but . . . this option;* a comparison **(collatio)** of the risks induced them to take their chances out in the open.

     apud illum: *with him* (Pliny), *in his case.*

176. **ratio rationem . . . timorem timor:** CHIASMUS, ANAPHORA, and ASYNDETON effectively highlight the contrast Pliny is drawing.

     cervicalia: cervical, *pillow.*

177. **linteis: linteum,** *linen cloth, sail;* here, *strips of linen.*

     constringunt: constringere, *to tie, bind.*

179. **dies alibi, illic nox:** this is the second day of the narrative, August 25; CHIASMUS emphasizes the stark difference between normal daylight elsewhere and volcanic night in the stricken area.

180. **faces: fax,** *torch.*

     solabantur: solari, *to console, relieve, mitigate.*

181. **placuit:** lit., *it was pleasing = it seemed best.*

     ecquid: interrog. conj., *whether at all.*

182. **admitteret:** sc. **eos;** the **contrarius ventus** had earlier prevented their sailing.

183. **frigidam:** sc. **aquam.**

184. **hausit: haurire,** *to drink.*

185. **innixus: inniti,** *to lean on, support oneself by.*

186. **colligo:** probably the two **servuli** survived and reported that his uncle had died from the gases.

187. **crassiore:** *thicker, denser.*

     caligine: caligo, *vapor, gas.*

     stomacho: stomachus, *esophagus, stomach;* Pliny uses the term here, rather unscientifically, for *windpipe.* Pliny's uncle had some chronic difficulty with his breathing (doubtless related to his snoring, mentioned in 165–66), perhaps asthma.

188. **interaestuans:** *inflamed.*

189. **dies:** i.e., *daylight.*

     redditus: sc. **est,** as with **inventum** in the next line.

     is . . . tertius: = **is erat tertius dies ab eo . . . .** On August 24 Pliny had sailed to Stabiae and saw daylight for the last time (hence **novissime viderat**); on August 25 he died; and on August 26 the air had cleared somewhat and his body was discovered. Eng. would say "the second day after . . . ," but the Roman counting system regularly included the first and last days in such a series.

190. **corpus . . . indutus (191):** detailed evidence that Pliny had been overcome by volcanic gas only, thus corroborating the statement presumably made by his slaves; **ut fuerat indutus** (from **induere**), *just as he had been clothed,* shows that there had been no harm from fire.

     inlaesum: *uninjured.*

     opertum: operire, *to cover.*

191. **habitus:** *position, appearance.*

175 quod tamen periculorum collatio elegit. Et apud illum quidem ratio rationem, apud alios timorem timor vicit. Cervicalia capitibus imposita linteis constringunt; id munimentum adversus incidentia fuit.

The death of Pliny the Elder.

Iam dies alibi, illic nox omnibus noctibus nigrior densi-
180 orque; quam tamen faces multae variaque lumina solabantur. Placuit egredi in litus et ex proximo aspicere ecquid iam mare admitteret; quod adhuc vastum et adversum permanebat. Ibi super abiectum linteum recubans, semel atque iterum frigidam poposcit hausitque. Deinde flammae flammarumque praenun-
185 tius, odor sulpuris, alios in fugam vertunt, excitant illum. Innixus servulis duobus, adsurrexit et statim concidit, ut ego colligo, crassiore caligine spiritu obstructo clausoque stomacho, qui illi natura invalidus et angustus et frequenter interaestuans erat. Ubi dies redditus (is ab eo, quem novissime viderat, ter-
190 tius), corpus inventum integrum, inlaesum opertumque ut fuerat indutus: habitus corporis quiescenti quam defuncto similior.

A victim of the Vesuvius eruption
Pompeii, Italy

192. **ego et mater:** APOSIOPESIS; in Lat. **ego** was quite lit. the pron. of the first pers. and was so placed in a list, but we say *my mother and I.*

194. **me . . . persecutum (195):** sc. **esse;** *that I have set forth.*
statim: i.e., right after the events.

195. **potissima:** *the most useful things.*

196. **aliud . . . aliud (197):** sc. **scribere** with each of the four instances of **aliud,** *it is one thing to write . . . it is another to . . ..*

198. **Macro:** though the identification is not certain, probably *Publius Calpurnius Macer,* consul in A.D. 103 and the addressee also of *Epistulae* 5.18.

199. **interest:** impers., *it is important.*
a quo . . . fiat: an IND. QUEST. used as subj. of **interest.**

201. **Larium:** *Larius,* modern *Lake Como,* a beautiful Alpine lake in northern Italy, called **nostrum** because Pliny was a native of the city of Comum (modern Como) and Macer was apparently from the same general area.

202. **etiam:** here, *in particular.*

203. **prominet: prominere,** *to jut out, project.*
aliquando: adv., *at some time, once.*
municeps: *citizen (of a free town, a* **municipium**); with **nostra,** *a fellow-citizen of mine, a woman from my town.*

205. **ulceribus:** possibly cancer.
putrescebat: putrescere, *to rot, fester.*

206. **exegit:** here, *demanded (that she).*
indicaturum: sc. **esse;** implied IND. STATE.

207. **vidit . . . hortata est:** the rush of vbs. and the ASYNDETON help suggest the intensity of the wife's concern.

208. **immo:** adv., *on the contrary, indeed.*
necessitas: *the compelling reason.*

209. **mihi:** DAT. OF AGENT, which became fairly common with any pass. form from the first cent. A.D. onward.

210. **municeps:** sc. **sum.**
nisi proxime: here, *until very recently.*
minus: sc. **factum eius fuit,** *her deed was less (noble).*

211. **Arriae:** the allusion is to the famous story of *Arria,* wife of A. Caecina Paetus, known from another of Pliny's letters (3.16); determined to join her husband in suicide, Arria stabbed herself first and then withdrew the dagger from her chest and handed it to her husband, consoling him with the words, **Paete, non dolet.**
minor: *less (famous).*

These details are based largely on eye-witness accounts, and may be used by Tacitus in whatever ways suit his purposes.

Interim Miseni ego et mater—sed nihil ad historiam, nec tu aliud quam de exitu eius scire voluisti. Finem ergo faciam. Unum adiciam, omnia me, quibus interfueram, quaeque statim,
195 cum maxime vera memorantur, audieram, persecutum. Tu potissima excerpes; aliud est enim epistulam, aliud historiam, aliud amico, aliud omnibus scribere. Vale.

6.24 (excerpts)

Pliny tells his countryman, the senator Calpurnius Macer, about the devotion of a woman from Lake Como who courageously joined her diseased husband in death; possibly written A.D. *106.*

C. Plinius Macro Suo S.

Quam multum interest a quo quidque fiat! Eadem enim
200 facta claritate vel obscuritate facientium aut tolluntur altissime aut humillime deprimuntur. Navigabam per Larium nostrum, cum senior amicus ostendit mihi villam atque etiam cubiculum, quod in lacum prominet: "Ex hoc," inquit, "aliquando municeps nostra cum marito se praecipitavit." Causam requisivi. Ma-
205 ritus ex diutino morbo ulceribus putrescebat: uxor, ut inspiceret, exegit; neque enim quemquam fidelius indicaturum possetne sanari. Vidit; desperavit; hortata est ut moreretur, comesque ipsa mortis, dux immo et exemplum et necessitas fuit. Nam se cum marito ligavit abiecitque in lacum. Quod factum ne mihi
210 quidem, qui municeps, nisi proxime auditum est, non quia minus illo clarissimo Arriae facto, sed quia minor ipsa. Vale.

212. **Calpurniae:** *Calpurnia Fabata,* Pliny's third wife, considerably younger than he, whom he married ca. A.D. 100; the two were quite devoted to one another, and Pliny's letters to her, despite a sometimes self-conscious and rhetorical style, reveal their mutual affection and were an important contribution to the theme of conjugal love in classical literature.

213. **in causa:** with **est** (understood), idiom, *is the reason, is responsible.*

214. **inde:** adv., *thence, from this.*
     est quod: *is the reason that,* with **inde,** *this is why;* similarly, though more elliptically, **quod** in 215 and 217.

215. **in imagine tua:** i.e., thinking of you.

216. **interdiu:** adv., *by day, during the day.*
     ipsi . . . ducunt (217): in this delightful image, Pliny insists that his feet have a mind of their own!

217. **aeger:** *sick.*

218. **maestus:** *sad, dejected.*
     excluso: sc. **amatori;** the image deliberately recalls that of the **exclusus amator** common in Latin elegiac poetry.

219. **litibus:** **lis,** *quarrel, controversy, lawsuit.*

223. **olim:** here, *for some time.*

224. **illud:** with **nihil agere** and **nihil esse,** which are also modified by **iners** and **iucundum,** *that . . . doing nothing . . . ..*

226. **secedere:** i.e., to the country, as commonly in Pliny.
     studere: i.e., such subjects as rhetoric, philosophy, and literature.
     nulla studia: much as Pliny longs for his quiet scholarly pursuits, his duty to his friends comes first.

227. **tanti:** sc. **pretii,** GEN. OF INDEF. VALUE, *worth so much, so valuable* (lit., *of such great value*).

228. **studia ipsa:** he probably had in mind such works as Cicero's *De Amicitia.*

Lake Como, with the Alps in the background

7.5

In this charming and tender epistle, one of a series to his wife Calpurnia, Pliny tells her how much he has missed her during her holiday in Campania, apparently their first time apart; written perhaps in the summer of A.D. *107.*

C. Plinius Calpurniae Suae S.

Incredibile est quanto desiderio tui tenear. In causa amor primum, deinde quod non consuevimus abesse. Inde est quod
215   magnam noctium partem in imagine tua vigil exigo, inde, quod interdiu, quibus horis te visere solebam, ad diaetam tuam ipsi me, ut verissime dicitur, pedes ducunt, quod denique aeger et maestus ac similis excluso a vacuo limine recedo. Unum tempus his tormentis caret, quo in foro amicorum litibus conteror. Aes-
220   tima tu quae vita mea sit, cui requies in labore, in miseria curis-que solacium. Vale.

8.9

In this brief note to his friend Cornelius Ursus, the recipient of several other letters on legal matters, Pliny comments on the distractions of city life and the demands of friendship; ca. A.D. *107–108.*

C. Plinius Urso Suo S.

Olim non librum in manus, non stilum sumpsi; olim nescio quid sit otium, quid quies, quid denique illud iners quidem, iu-
225   cundum tamen nihil agere, nihil esse; adeo multa me negotia amicorum nec secedere nec studere patiuntur. Nulla enim studia tanti sunt ut amicitiae officium deseratur, quod religiosissime custodiendum studia ipsa praecipiunt. Vale.

229. **Traiano Imperatori:** *Trajan* (Marcus Ulpius Traianus) was emperor A.D. 98–117; the 10th book of Pliny's letters includes his correspondence with the emperor, the first 14 epistles dating between 98 and his departure to Bithynia, and the remainder to the period of his governorship.

230. **sollemne:** *customary;* the fact that Pliny is inquiring to Trajan is evidence that the emperor had issued no official edict on the matter.

232. **cognitionibus: cognitio,** *trial* (here referring to formal trials at Rome); Pliny knew of these proceedings in Rome but had never participated.

233. **ideo:** adv., *for that reason.*
     quatenus: adv., *to what extent;* the maximum penalty was death.

234. **sitne:** this and all the following subjunct. vbs. are IND. QUESTS.
     discrimen aetatum: i.e., should old and young offenders be treated differently? Entire families were in fact subject to prosecution.

235. **quamlibet teneri:** *those however young* (**tener,** lit., = *tender*).
     robustioribus: lit., *stronger, more robust* = *older.*

236. **ei:** dat. with **prosit** (from **prodesse,** *to benefit, profit*).
     omnino: here, *ever, at all.*
     desisse: i.e., to have recanted and renounced his Christianity.

237. **nomen . . . puniantur (238):** should the mere name of Christian be punished even if the person were not guilty of any crime **(flagitium)**? Certain organizations **(collegia)** had been outlawed by Trajan because they had been sources of disorder in the province, and the Christians might be prosecuted on that account; they were, besides, thought by some to be guilty of such crimes as cannibalism, based on a misunderstanding of the Eucharist.
     cohaerentia: lit., *adhering to* = *associated with.*

239. **in:** here, *in the case of.*
     tamquam: here, simply *as.*
     deferebantur: a technical term for accusations lodged by individuals; Pliny himself was not actively seeking prosecutions but dealt with those that were brought before him.

241. **iterum ac tertio:** adv. modifying **interrogavi;** though it did offer the defendant further opportunity to recant, the repeated questioning was standard procedure and not an extraordinary attempt on Pliny's part to show mercy.

242. **duci:** sc. **ad supplicium,** i.e., execution (generally decapitation by sword).
     qualecumque esset (243): *whatever it was.*

244. **amentiae: amentia,** *madness, folly.*

245. **adnotavi:** a technical term for an entry in the official government records.
     urbem: ordinarily a Roman citizen could not be executed without a trial in Rome (see the case of Gavius in "Cicero's Verrine Orations," above).

246. **tractatu: tractatus,** *handling, treatment,* i.e., of this matter.
     diffundente: diffundere, *to pour forth, spread.*
     crimine: *charge, accusation;* not *crime.*
     species: i.e., of cases.

247. **inciderunt:** here, *occurred.*
     libellus sine auctore: i.e., an anonymous pamphlet.

10.96

As governor of the eastern province of Bithynia (A.D. 109 or 110 until his death in ca. 112), Pliny writes to the emperor Trajan, asking his advice on handling the spread of Christianity among the provincials; our earliest non-Christian account of the religion's practices, this very famous letter (known to Jerome and other early church fathers) was written from either Amisus or Amastris between September 18 and January 3 of the second year of his governorship. The selection following this reading is Trajan's letter of reply.

C. Plinius Traiano Imperatori

Pliny's perplexity about what to do concerning the Christians.

230   Sollemne est mihi, domine, omnia de quibus dubito ad te referre. Quis enim potest melius vel cunctationem meam regere vel ignorantiam instruere? Cognitionibus de Christianis interfui numquam; ideo nescio quid et quatenus aut puniri soleat aut quaeri. Nec mediocriter haesitavi sitne aliquod discrimen aeta-
235   tum, an quamlibet teneri nihil a robustioribus differant; detur paenitentiae venia, an ei, qui omnino Christianus fuit, desisse non prosit; nomen ipsum, si flagitiis careat, an flagitia cohaeren-tia nomini puniantur.

While not actively seeking indictments, Pliny has tried those duly charged with being Christians and has executed the unrepentant.

    Interim in iis qui ad me tamquam Christiani deferebantur,
240 hunc sum secutus modum. Interrogavi ipsos an essent Christi-tiani. Confitentes iterum ac tertio interrogavi, supplicium mina-tus; perseverantes duci iussi. Neque enim dubitabam, quale-cumque esset quod faterentur, pertinaciam certe et inflexibilem obstinationem debere puniri. Fuerunt alii similis amentiae, quos,
245 quia cives Romani erant, adnotavi in urbem remittendos. Mox ipso tractatu, ut fieri solet, diffundente se crimine, plures species inciderunt. Propositus est libellus sine auctore multorum no-mina continens.

249. **praeeunte me (250):** as today an official commonly leads a person or a group in the administration of an oath, dictating the words.
250. **appellarent:** with **deos** (i.e., the official state gods), *invoked.*
     imagini: dat. with **supplicarent,** *worshiped;* though this form of emperor-worship was to most Romans hardly more than an oath of allegiance, it was offensive to Christians because of their intense monotheism.
     propter hoc: i.e., for the purpose of the interrogation.
251. **simulacris: simulacrum,** *image, statue.*
     numinum: numen, *deity, god.*
     ture: tus, *incense.*
252. **maledicerent: maledicere,** + dat., *to curse.*
     quorum nihil: *none of which things.*
253. **re vera:** *in true fact = truly.*
254. **indice: index,** *witness, informer.*
255. **fuisse . . . desisse:** with **quidam (dixerunt se).**
     triennium: ACC. OF DURATION OF TIME with **ante,** *three years earlier.*
256. **non nemo:** (at least) *one person.*
     hi . . . maledixerunt (258): since Pliny does not report here his decision regarding this group of apostates, he had perhaps detained them while awaiting Trajan's reply.
260. **quod:** *that,* introducing a noun cl. in appos. with **summam;** what follows is very important evidence for the ritual of the early Christian church.
     essent soliti: subjunct. in a SUBORDINATE CL. IN IND. STATE.
     stato die: *on a fixed day,* i.e., Sunday.
     ante lucem: the proper time for worship, just as it was for the beginning of the work day.
     carmen: here, *hymn, chant.*
261. **invicem:** adv., *alternately, responsively.*
     sacramento: sacramentum, *oath,* which is explained both by the prep. phrase **non in . . . aliquod** and by the JUSSIVE NOUN CLS. following; the term is taken by some as a reference to baptism or the Eucharist.
262. **non in scelus aliquod:** *not (directed) toward some crime,* an important point since the Christians were commonly misunderstood as some sort of criminal conspirators because of the secretive, exclusive nature of their organization and their seemingly bizarre rituals.
     obstringere: *to tie, bind (by an oath).*
     furta: furtum, *theft;* some see in these prohibitions a reference to the Ten Commandments.
     latrocinia: latrocinium, *robbery, fraud.*
263. **fallerent: fallere,** *to deceive, cheat, betray.*
     depositum: some trustees then, as now, misused funds entrusted to their care.
264. **appellati:** nom., *when called upon* (to return it).
     morem . . . fuisse (265): still IND. STATE. dependent on **adfirmabant.**
265. **cibum: cibus,** *food;* the early Christian "agape," or daily love-feast, involved food, hymns, scripture readings, and prayers.
     promiscuum . . . et innoxium: *ordinary and harmless.*
266. **quod:** = **et hoc.**

Those who denied the charges, cursed Christ, and worshiped the gods and the emperor were released.

Qui negabant esse se Christianos aut fuisse, cum praeeunte
250 me deos appellarent et imagini tuae, quam propter hoc iusseram
cum simulacris numinum adferri, ture ac vino supplicarent,
praeterea maledicerent Christo—quorum nihil posse cogi dicuntur qui sunt re vera Christiani—dimittendos esse putavi.
Alii ab indice nominati esse se Christianos dixerunt et mox ne-
255 gaverunt; fuisse quidem, sed desisse, quidam ante triennium, quidam ante plures annos, non nemo etiam ante viginti. Hi quoque
omnes et imaginem tuam deorumque simulacra venerati sunt et
Christo maledixerunt.

Pliny describes the Christians' rituals as they reported them to him.

Adfirmabant autem hanc fuisse summam vel culpae suae vel
260 erroris, quod essent soliti stato die ante lucem convenire car-
menque Christo quasi deo dicere secum invicem seque sacra-
mento non in scelus aliquod obstringere, sed ne furta, ne latroci-
nia, ne adulteria committerent, ne fidem fallerent, ne depositum
appellati abnegarent; quibus peractis, morem sibi discedendi
265 fuisse rursusque coeundi ad capiendum cibum, promiscuum
tamen et innoxium; quod ipsum facere desisse post edictum

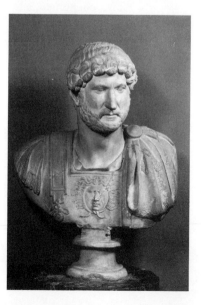

Trajan
Anonymous
17th century
Galleria Borghese
Rome, Italy

267. **secundum:** prep. + acc., *according to.*
   hetaerias: hetaeria, *fraternity, secret society.*
268. **ancillis: ancilla,** *maid-servant, slave;* these are loyal Christians, quite distinct from the recanters above.
   ministrae: the Lat. translation of Greek ***diakonissa, deaconess.***
269. **et per tormenta:** *even by torture;* Pliny apparently thought that these servants of the church were in fact slaves, and the testimony of slaves was acceptable in court only when obtained by torture.
270. **pravam:** *distorted, perverse, wicked.*
272. **periclitantium: periclitari,** *to be in danger.*
274. **in periculum:** i.e., to trial.
275. **civitates:** here, *cities,* which came to be a standard meaning of the word.
   vicos: vicus, *village.*
276. **sisti: sistere,** *to set up, stop, check;* with **posse.**
277. **constat:** impers., *it is agreed.*
   templa: i.e., of the traditional Roman deities.
278. **celebrari: celebrare,** *to visit in large numbers, to throng;* i.e., as a result of the repression of the Christians.
   sollemnia: sollemne, *religious ceremony, rite.*
   passim: adv., *here and there, far and wide, everywhere.*
   venire: veneo, venire, *to go for sale, be sold.*
279. **victimarum:** i.e., animals sacrificed to the gods.
   carnem: carnis, *flesh.*
   adhuc: adv., *up to this time, still, yet.*
   rarissimus emptor: the Christians would not eat meat from the pagan temples.
283. **actum:** here, *procedure.*
   Secunde: in the body of his letters to Pliny, the Emperor Trajan often uses Pliny's cognomen, as here, sometimes with **carissime** added.
   excutiendis: excutere, *to shake out, examine, investigate.*
284. **Christiani:** *as Christians.*
285. **in universum:** *in general;* i.e., there can be no fixed prescription which will cover every single case.
   certam: *fixed, unvarying.*
286. **constitui: constituere,** *to place, establish, determine, decide.*
   conquirendi non sunt: conquirere, *to search out;* Trajan intended no aggressive persecution of the Christians. While generally answering Pliny's initial question regarding the conduct of investigations, the emperor does not give his opinion on the degree of punishment appropriate to the offence (*Epistulae* 10.96, line 233, **quatenus . . . puniri soleat**), thus by silence endorsing the usual penalty of execution.
   arguantur: arguere, *to make clear, prove;* there must be a full trial in court and a formal conviction, not merely an accusation.
287. **ita:** *in such a way (that), with the stipulation (that).*
288. **re ipsa:** *in actual fact* (lit., *by the thing itself*), as defined by **supplicando.**

meum, quo secundum mandata tua hetaerias esse vetueram.
Quo magis necessarium credidi ex duabus ancillis, quae ministrae dicebantur, quid esset veri, et per tormenta quaerere. Nihil
270   aliud inveni quam superstitionem pravam, immodicam.

*Pliny is concerned about humanitarian considerations but feels that the
"superstition" must be curbed.*

Ideo dilata cognitione, ad consulendum te decucurri. Visa
est enim mihi res digna consultatione, maxime propter periclitantium numerum. Multi enim omnis aetatis, omnis ordinis,
utriusque sexus etiam vocantur in periculum et vocabuntur.
275   Neque civitates tantum, sed vicos etiam atque agros supersti-
tionis istius contagio pervagata est; quae videtur sisti et corrigi
posse. Certe satis constat prope iam desolata templa coepisse
celebrari, et sacra sollemnia diu intermissa repeti passimque venire victimarum carnem, cuius adhuc rarissimus emptor inveni-
280   ebatur. Ex quo facile est opinari quae turba hominum emendari
possit, si sit paenitentiae locus.

10.97

*Trajan replies, probably within a few weeks, to the preceding letter, generally approv-
ing Pliny's procedure, advising against witch-hunts and the acceptance of anonymous
accusations, but insisting that Christians who do not renounce their religion, whether
or not guilty of any related crime, must indeed be punished.*

Traianus Plinio

Actum quem debuisti, mi Secunde, in excutiendis causis
eorum qui Christiani ad te delati fuerant, secutus es. Neque
285   enim in universum aliquid, quod quasi certam formam habeat,
constitui potest. Conquirendi non sunt; si deferantur et arguantur, puniendi sunt, ita tamen ut qui negaverit se Christianum
esse idque re ipsa manifestum fecerit, id est supplicando dis

289. **in praeteritum:** *in the past.*
291. **pessimi exempli:** with **est,** *it* (i.e., the practice of crediting anonymous accusations) *is (of) a very bad precedent;* PRED. GEN. OF DESCRIPTION, as also
nostri saeculi.

   nostri saeculi: lit., *of our age* = *appropriate to our age,* i.e., Trajan's relatively
benevolent administration.

290 nostris, quamvis suspectus in praeteritum, veniam ex paenitentia impetret. Sine auctore vero propositi libelli in nullo crimine
locum habere debent. Nam et pessimi exempli nec nostri saeculi est.

Trajan
Louvre, Paris, France

THE VULGATE

The Old Testament, in origin a collection of Jewish writings composed chiefly in Hebrew, was translated into Greek by several different hands beginning in the third century B.C. According to a popular ancient tradition, the translation was produced for the library of the Egyptian king Ptolemy II Philadelphus by a panel of 70 Jewish scholars, hence the title "the Septuagint" often applied to the work.

During the latter half of the first century of our era the New Testament was composed in Greek. As Christianity spread through the Latin-speaking world, including Italy, Gaul, Spain, and North Africa, anonymous Latin versions of various parts of the Bible, the so-called *Vetus Latina,* began to appear from the second century onward. By the fourth century the number of translations and variants had become confusing, and the biblical scholar Eusebius Hieronymus (ca. A.D. 347–420), better known as St. Jerome, was commissioned in the early 380's by Pope Damasus to produce a standard Latin version. Working at first from the Septuagint and later from the original Hebrew for the Old Testament, and directly from the Greek for the New Testament, Jerome ultimately—over a period of about 25 years—produced the "Vulgate," the *Editio Vulgata* of the Bible, so-called from his intention that it serve as a highly readable popular edition for the *vulgus,* the common people. Jerome's edition for centuries was the standard Latin text of the Bible and exercised a profound influence on the church and on European thought generally.

Just as the Greek New Testament had been written in the simple language of the common people, the so-called *koine,* so that it could be easily understood by them, likewise the Vulgate was phrased *ad usum vulgi* and not in the rich elegant style of Cicero (with which Jerome was highly conversant and which he employed in much of his other writing). While his translations from both the Greek and Hebrew were at times highly literal, at others quite free, the structure of his sentences is nearly always eminently simple, with more coordination than subordination. Among other characteristics of Jerome's language are the frequent use of *quod, quia,* or *ut* with either the indicative or the subjunctive to express indirect statement, the use of prepositional phrases instead of simple cases (e.g., *dixit ad eum = dixit ei*), the infinitive to express purpose or result, and the use of new words and of new meanings for old words. Such usages continued and were elaborated throughout medieval

Latin and illustrate the process by which vulgar Latin was gradually transformed into the Romance languages.

The readings excerpted for translation in this text include some of the best known and most influential passages from the Bible, among them the Ten Commandments, Job's views on the inaccessibility of wisdom, Ecclesiastes on the futility of man's earthly existence, selections from Christ's "Sermon on the Mount," and the stories of the "Good Samaritan" and the "Prodigal Son."

Vellum page from Dominican manuscript of
miniature Vulgate bible (Mark 16–Luke 1), ca. 1240
Paris, France

1. **cunctos:** = **omnes.**
    sermones: *words, sayings.*
4. **habebis:** the fut. indic. can be used with the force of a command.
    coram: prep. + abl., *in the presence of.*
5. **sculptile:** *a carved thing, statue.*
    omnem: here (and in 17 below), *any.*
    quae: sc. **eius** as antecedent.
6. **deorsum:** adv., *downward, below.*
8. **zelotes:** a Greek m. nom. sg. form, *one who is jealous.*
    visitans: **visitare,** *to see often, visit,* here *visit upon, send.*
10. **in milia:** balances **in filios** above.
    his: DAT. OF REF., *in the case of the people.*
    diligunt: here, *love* in the sense of *esteem,* a lofty and dignified word, vs.
        amare, *to love* or *like* in a more general or more physical way.
12. **in vanum:** *ostentatiously, in vain.*
15. **memento:** 2nd pers. sg. fut. imper. of the defective vb. **memini.**
    diem sabbati: *the day of the sabbath* (a Hebrew word), *the day of rest.*
    sanctifices: **sanctificare,** eccl. Lat., *to treat as holy, sanctify.*
    diebus: ABL. OF DURATION OF TIME, less common than the acc. construction.
    operaberis: **operari** = **laborare.**
17. **in eo:** a prep. is common with the ABL. OF TIME in eccl. Lat.
18. **ancilla:** *maid-servant.*
    iumentum: *beast of burden, pack animal.*
    advena: m./f., *stranger.*
21. **idcirco:** adv., *on that account, therefore.*
    benedixit: **benedicere** (in class. Lat. usually written **bene dicere**) + dat., *to
        speak well of* = *to bless,* common in eccl. Lat.
23. **longaevus:** *old, aged.*
25. **occides:** from **ob-caedo.**
26. **moechaberis:** **moechari,** *to commit adultery.*
27. **furtum:** *theft.*
28. **proximum:** **proximus,** *neighbor,* a natural later development from the lit.
        meaning of the word ("neighbor" is an Anglo-Saxon word meaning
        "near-dweller"); **vicinus** is the class. term.
29. **concupisces:** **concupiscere,** *to long for, desire eagerly.*
30. **asinum:** **asinus,** *ass.*
33. **quis:** = **quid,** here m. by attraction to **locus.**
    intellegentiae: here, *understanding.*

The Ten Commandments

Locutusque est Dominus cunctos sermones hos:

Ego sum Dominus Deus tuus, qui eduxi te de terra Aegypti, de domo servitutis.

Non habebis deos alienos coram me.

5 Non facies tibi sculptile neque omnem similitudinem quae est in caelo desuper et quae in terra deorsum nec eorum quae sunt in aquis sub terra. Non adorabis ea neque coles; ego sum Dominus Deus tuus fortis, zelotes, visitans iniquitatem patrum in filios, in tertiam et quartam generationem eorum qui oderunt

10 me, et faciens misericordiam in milia his qui diligunt me et custodiunt praecepta mea.

Non adsumes nomen Domini Dei tui in vanum; nec enim habebit insontem Dominus eum qui adsumpserit nomen Domini Dei sui frustra.

15 Memento ut diem sabbati sanctifices. Sex diebus operaberis et facies omnia opera tua. Septimo autem die sabbatum Domini Dei tui est; non facies omne opus in eo, tu, et filius tuus et filia tua, servus tuus et ancilla tua, iumentum tuum, et advena qui est intra portas tuas. Sex enim diebus fecit Dominus caelum et

20 terram, et mare, et omnia quae in eis sunt, et requievit in die septimo; idcirco benedixit Dominus diei sabbati et sanctificavit eum.

Honora patrem tuum et matrem tuam, ut sis longaevus super terram, quam Dominus Deus tuus dabit tibi.

25 Non occides.

Non moechaberis.

Non furtum facies.

Non loqueris contra proximum tuum falsum testimonium.

Non concupisces domum proximi tui; nec desiderabis uxo-

30 rem eius, non servum, non ancillam, non bovem, non asinum, nec omnia quae illius sunt. (*Exodus* 20.1–17)

Job on the Inaccessibility of Wisdom

Sapientia vero ubi invenitur?

Et quis est locus intellegentiae?

Nescit homo pretium eius,

35 nec invenitur in terra suaviter viventium.

36. **Abyssus:** *abyss, bottomless gulf, void;* here personified.

Abyssus ... mecum (37): an example of the parallelism which is one of the major characteristics of Hebrew poetry; the second line of a couplet repeats the thought of the first with different words or expresses a similar idea. This can be observed in the first two lines of this excerpt (32–33) and elsewhere throughout the passage.

38. **aurum obryzum:** *pure gold;* with **non dabitur,** the point is that true wisdom cannot be bought for any price.

39. **appendetur:** *will be weighed out;* similarly **expendo,** from which derives Eng. "spend," both words reflecting the means of exchange **(commutatio)** before the invention of coinage.

40. **tinctis ... coloribus:** probably another reference to gold, for which India was known.

41. **lapidi:** dat. (with the compound vb. **conferetur**) of **lapis,** *stone;* with the adj. **sardonycho,** *of sardonyx.*

42. **ei ... ea (43):** i.e., **sapientia.**

vitrum: *glass;* here, *fine glass,* like our crystal.

44. **excelsa:** *heights.*

eminentia: n. pl. of **eminens,** *things that stand out, project, are lofty;* here = *lofty peaks.*

memorabuntur: memorare, *to mention, recount.*

45. **occultis:** *secret places.*

47. **tincturae:** tinctura, *dyeing, tinting,* here *color* (perhaps again of gold—cp. **tinctis ... coloribus,** 40—or some other precious material).

mundissimae: mundus, *clean, pure.*

48. **unde ... intellegentiae (49):** a recapitulation of the questions in 32–33.

50. **abscondita est:** abscondere, *to conceal.*

51. **volucres:** volucer (avis), *bird.*

latet: latere + acc. = *to escape the notice of, be concealed from.*

52. **perditio:** postclassical, *destruction, ruin.*

56. **intuetur:** intueri, *to look at, contemplate, consider.*

58. **pondus:** *weight.*

59. **mensura:** *measure.*

60. **pluviis:** pluvia, *rain.*

61. **procellis:** procella, *storm.*

65. **ecce:** interj., *look, see, behold.*

Abyssus dicit, "Non est in me";
et Mare loquitur, "Non est mecum."
Non dabitur aurum obryzum pro ea,
nec appendetur argentum in commutatione eius.

40 Non conferetur tinctis Indiae coloribus
nec lapidi sardonycho pretiossimo vel sapphiro.
Non adaequabitur ei aurum vel vitrum,
nec commutabuntur pro ea vasa auri.
Excelsa et eminentia non memorabuntur comparatione eius;

45 trahitur autem sapientia de occultis.
Non adaequabitur ei topazium de Aethiopia,
nec tincturae mundissimae componetur.
Unde ergo sapientia venit?
Et quis est locus intellegentiae?

50 Abscondita est ab oculis omnium viventium,
volucres quoque caeli latet.
Perditio et mors dixerunt,
"Auribus nostris audivimus famam eius."
Deus intellegit viam eius,

55 et ipse novit locum illius.
Ipse enim fines mundi intuetur:
et omnia, quae sub caelo sunt, respicit.
Qui fecit ventis pondus
et aquas appendit mensura,

60 quando ponebat pluviis legem
et viam procellis sonantibus,
tunc vidit illam, et enarravit,
et praeparavit, et investigavit,
Et dixit homini,

65 "Ecce, timor Domini ipsa est sapientia;
et recedere a malo, intellegentia." (*Job* 28.12–28)

"Saint Jerome"
Benvenuto di Giovanni, 15th century
Galleria Sabauda, Turin, Italy

67. **Ecclesiastae: Ecclesiastes, -ae,** m., a Greek word meaning *a member of the assembly, a speaker in the assembly,* hence here perhaps *one who addresses his fellow citizens.* It is intended to translate the Hebrew word "Koheleth," which is said to occur only here in Hebrew literature and may be simply a proper name.

    David: *of David:* the strictly Hebrew names are not inflected, so their case can be determined only from the context. Since scholars agree that the actual date of this book is ca. 200 B.C., Koheleth's claim to be Solomon is a literary convention.

    Hierusalem: *of Jerusalem.*

68. **vanitas:** *vanity* in the sense of *emptiness, futility* (cp. "in vain"), not of *pride, conceit.*

69. **omnia:** sc. **sunt.**

    amplius: modifies **quid,** *what more,* i.e., *what benefit, what profit.*

    universo: here = **omni.**

72. **renascens:** = **renascitur.**

    gyrat: gyrare, *to go around, move in circles;* **spiritus,** here = *wind,* is subj. of all four vbs. in the sent.

    meridiem: here, *the south.*

73. **aquilonem: aquilo,** *north wind, north.*

    lustrans: lustrare, *to move around, circle around (something).*

    pergit: pergere, *to go on, continue, proceed.*

75. **redundat: redundare,** *to overflow.*

77. **saturatur: saturare,** *to satisfy;* i.e., no matter how hard we look or listen, we cannot explain life and the universe.

79. **faciendum est:** a fut. pass. periphrastic with overtones of destiny, *the very thing which shall (must) be done;* i.e., the future repeats the past. There is a fixed round of events; God has predetermined them all; man cannot change them. "To every thing there is a season, and a time to every purpose under the heaven" (*Ecclesiastes* 3.1).

80. **valet:** = **potest,** common in late Lat.

81. **praecessit . . . quae fuerunt:** the antecedent of **quae** is treated as collective sg. subj. of **praecessit,** *whatever things were before us, that has already gone (occurred) before.*

    saeculis: saeculum, *century, generation.*

83. **recordatio:** = **memoria;** the **cor,** *heart,* was regarded as the seat of memory.

    novissimo: the phrase **annus novus** was often used of *the new year* or *the coming year;* similarly **novissimo** here refers to *the distant future.*

84. **Israhel:** *of Israel.*

86. **pessimam:** the point is that God has given humans the power to reason and a desire for knowledge, and yet, despite man's diligence, he is mocked by an inability to understand truly the meaning of life and the universe.

88. **universa:** = **omnia (sunt).**

    perversi: here, *the crooked.*

    difficile: = **difficiliter.**

90. **corde: cor,** *heart.*

91. **sapientia:** ABL. OF SPECIFICATION.

The Futility of Man's Life on Earth

Verba Ecclesiastae, filii David, regis Hierusalem.

"Vanitas vanitatum," dixit Ecclesiastes: "Vanitas vanitatum
et omnia vanitas. Quid habet amplius homo de universo labore
70 suo, quo laborat sub sole? Generatio praeterit, et generatio advenit; terra autem in aeternum stat. Oritur sol, et occidit, et ad
locum suum revertitur ibique renascens. Gyrat per meridiem et
flectitur ad aquilonem; lustrans universa, circuitu pergit spiritus
et in circulos suos regreditur. Omnia flumina intrant in mare, et
75 mare non redundat: ad locum, unde exeunt flumina, revertuntur
ut iterum fluant. Cunctae res difficiles: non potest eas homo
explicare sermone. Non saturatur oculus visu, nec auris auditu
impletur. Quid est quod fuit?—ipsum quod futurum est. Quid
est quod factum est?—ipsum quod faciendum est. Nihil sub
80 sole novum, nec valet quisquam dicere, 'Ecce, hoc recens est.'
Iam enim praecessit in saeculis, quae fuerunt ante nos. Non est
priorum memoria, sed nec eorum quidem quae postea futura
sunt erit recordatio apud eos qui futuri sunt in novissimo.

"Ego Ecclesiastes fui rex Israhel in Hierusalem et proposui
85 in animo meo quaerere et investigare sapienter de omnibus quae
fiunt sub sole. Hanc occupationem pessimam dedit Deus filiis
hominum, ut occuparentur in ea. Vidi cuncta quae fiunt sub
sole, et, ecce, universa vanitas et adflictio spiritus. Perversi difficile corriguntur, et stultorum infinitus est numerus. Locutus
90 sum in corde meo, dicens, 'Ecce, magnus effectus sum, et
praecessi omnes sapientia qui fuerunt ante me in Hierusalem;

"Job"
Leon Bonnat
1880
Musée Bonnat
Bayonne, France

92. **contemplata est: contemplari.**
93. **prudentiam . . . stultitiam (94):** i.e., he sought to understand all life.
94. **agnovi quod:** *I learned that;* in late Lat. **quod** is regularly employed with either a subjunct. or an indic. vb. to introduce IND. STATE.
95. **eo quod:** *for the reason that.*
     indignatio: *occasion for indignation;* i.e., in this world there is no guarantee that men will be rewarded according to their deserts, for the righteous often suffer, the wicked sometimes prosper, and the wise man has the same futile end as the fool—death. Though he lacked belief in an after-life where injustices would be corrected, and acknowledges the ugly real-ities of life, the author did not surrender to despair; rather, he said *carpe diem,* observe the golden mean, be wise, and accept the reality of a God and a universe which you cannot fully understand.
96. **laborem:** here, *sorrow, suffering.*
98. **vobis:** dat. with **maledicere,** *to insult, curse.*
     calumniantibus: calumniari, *to accuse falsely.*
99. **percutit: percutere,** *to strike.*
     maxillam: *jaw;* here, *one side of the jaw* (in view of the following **alteram**).
100. **tibi:** the DAT. OF SEPARATION was often used instead of the abl.
     vestimentum: *clothing,* but here *robe* or some other outergarment, in contrast to **tunicam,** *tunic,* a shirtlike garment worn under the toga or indoors and when working.
101. **petenti te:** = class. **petenti a te.**
     ne repetas: sc. **ab eo;** note **ne** + pres. subjunct. in the 2nd pers. as a variant for expressing a prohibition, where class. Lat. prose would usually have **noli** + inf., as in the preceding line, or **ne** + perf. subjunct.
102. **prout:** *just as* (= **ut** + indic.).
     et: with **facite,** = **etiam.**
103. **vobis:** DAT. OF POSSESSION, with **quae . . . est gratia,** *what thanks do you have,* i.e., *what special regard do you deserve?*
104. **diligentes se:** *who love them.*
105. **siquidem:** conj., *if indeed, since, inasmuch as.*
106. **mutuum:** *a loan.*
108. **faenerantur: faenerari,** *to lend at interest.*
110. **merces:** here, *reward.*
     Altissimi: = **Dei.**
     quia: conj., *since;* in late Lat., *that,* common with IND. STATE.
111. **benignus:** *kind, beneficent.*
     super: prep. + acc., here = *toward.*
     estote: 2nd pers. pl. fut. imper. of **sum,** *you shall be* or simply *be.*
113. **dimittite:** *let go, release,* hence *forgive.*
114. **dabitur:** impers. pass.
     confertam et coagitatam (115): vivid terms *crammed full and shaken down,* referring to the measure **(mensuram).**
115. **supereffluentem:** late Lat., *overflowing.*
     dabunt: sc. **homines.**
     sinum: sinus, *fold, bay gulf; fold (in a garment)* = *pocket, lap, bosom.*

et mens mea contemplata est multa sapienter, et didici.' Dedique cor meum ut scirem prudentiam, atque doctrinam, erroresque et stultitiam; et agnovi quod in his quoque esset labor et afflictio
95 spiritus, eo quod in multa sapientia multa sit indignatio—et qui addit scientiam, addit et laborem." (*Ecclesiastes* 1.1–18)

Thoughts from the Sermon on the Mount

Love your enemies and do good unto others.

Diligite inimicos vestros; bene facite his qui vos oderunt; benedicite maledicentibus vobis; orate pro calumniantibus vos. Et qui te percutit in maxillam, praebe et alteram. Et ab eo qui au-
100 fert tibi vestimentum, etiam tunicam noli prohibere. Omni autem petenti te, tribue; et qui aufert quae tua sunt, ne repetas. Et prout vultis ut faciant vobis homines, et vos facite illis similiter. Et si diligitis eos qui vos diligunt, quae vobis est gratia?—nam et peccatores diligentes se diligunt. Et si bene feceritis his qui
105 vobis bene faciunt, quae vobis est gratia?—siquidem et peccatores hoc faciunt. Et si mutuum dederitis his a quibus speratis recipere, quae gratia est vobis?—nam et peccatores peccatoribus faenerantur, ut recipiant aequalia. Verum tamen diligite inimicos vestros, et bene facite, et mutuum date, nihil inde speran-
110 tes; et erit merces vestra multa, et eritis filii Altissimi, quia ipse benignus est super ingratos et malos. Estote ergo misericordes sicut et Pater vester misericors est. Nolite iudicare, et non iudicabimini; nolite condemnare, et non condemnabimini; dimittite, et dimittemini; date, et dabitur vobis. Mensuram bonam, con-
115 fertam et coagitatam et supereffluentem, dabunt in sinum ves-

"Sermon on the Mount"
Fra Angelico
15th century
Museo di San Marco
Florence, Italy

116. **mensi fueritis:** fut. perf. of **metiri,** *to measure.*
118. **similitudinem:** here, *parable;* lit., *simile, analogy.*
      numquid: a strengthened form of **num.**
119. **ambo:** *both,* nom. pl.
      foveam: *pit, ditch.*
120. **perfectus:** here, *excellent (person).*
121. **quid:** = **cur.**
      festucam: festuca, *straw.*
122. **trabem: trabs,** *beam (of wood), stick.*
123. **sine: sinere,** *to allow,* takes a subjunct. cl., either with or without **ut.**
124. **hypocrita:** Greek for *actor,* but common in eccl. Lat. in the sense of *hypocrite.*
125. **ut educas:** IND. QUEST. with **perspicies,** *how to remove.*
129. **spinis: spina,** *thorn.*
      ficus: acc. pl. of **ficus,** *fig.*
130. **rubo: rubus,** *bramble bush.*
      vindemiant: vindemiare, *to harvest (grapes).*
      uvam: uva, *grape.*
      thesauro: thesaurus, *treasure, treasury.*
133. **legis peritus:** i.e., a lawyer; the gen. is used with many adjs., including those
      denoting *knowledge* and *skill.*
      temptans: temptare, *to test, try, attempt.*
      illum: Jesus.
134. **quid faciendo:** *how;* lit., *by doing what.*
      possidebo: possidere, *to possess, hold.*
135. **ad eum:** eccl. Lat. for dat. **ei** in class. Lat. after verbs of speaking; cp. the
      regular **dixit illi** in 138–39.
      quomodo: here = **quid.**
141. **suscipiens:** *answering;* lit., *taking up (the question).*
142. **in Hiericho:** *into Jericho.*
      incidit: incidere, *to fall.*
      latrones: latro, *robber, bandit.*
      despoliaverunt: despoliare, *to plunder, rob.*
143. **plagis: plaga,** *blow, wound;* with **inpositis,** freely, *after beating him.*
144. **ut ... descenderet:** NOUN CL. OF RESULT with **accidit,** *it happened (that).*

"The Good Samaritan"
Joseph Highmore
1744
Tate Gallery
London, Great Britain

trum; eadem quippe mensura qua mensi fueritis, remetietur vobis.

The beam and the straw.

Dicebat autem illis et similitudinem: Numquid potest caecus caecum ducere? Nonne ambo in foveam cadent? Non est
120   discipulus super magistrum; perfectus autem omnis erit sicut
magister eius. Quid autem vides festucam in oculo fratris tui,
trabem autem quae in oculo tuo est non consideras? Et quomodo potes dicere fratri tuo, "Frater, sine eiciam festucam de
oculo tuo," ipse in oculo tuo trabem non videns? Hypocrita,
125   eice primum trabem de oculo tuo, et tunc perspicies ut educas
festucam de oculo fratris tui.

A tree is known by its fruit.

Non est enim arbor bona quae facit fructus malos; neque
arbor mala, faciens fructum bonum. Una quaeque enim arbor
de fructu suo cognoscitur. Neque enim de spinis colligunt ficus,
130   neque de rubo vindemiant uvam. Bonus homo de bono thesauro cordis sui profert bonum, et malus homo de malo profert
malum: ex abundantia enim cordis os loquitur. (*Luke* 6.27–45)

The Good Samaritan

Et, ecce, quidam legis peritus surrexit, temptans illum et dicens, "Magister, quid faciendo vitam aeternam possidebo?" At
135   ille dixit ad eum, "In lege quid scriptum est? Quomodo legis?"
Ille respondens dixit, "Diliges Dominum Deum tuum ex toto
corde tuo, et ex tota anima tua, et ex omnibus viribus tuis, et ex
omni mente tua, et proximum tuum sicut te ipsum." Dixitque
illi, "Recte respondisti: hoc fac, et vives." Ille autem volens ius-
140   tificare se ipsum, dixit ad Iesum, "Et quis est meus proximus?"
Suscipiens autem Iesus dixit, "Homo quidam descendebat ab
Hierusalem in Hiericho et incidit in latrones, qui etiam despoli-
averunt eum et, plagis inpositis, abierunt, semivivo relicto. Accidit autem ut sacerdos quidam descenderet eadem via; et, viso

145.   **Levita: Levita, -ae,** m., *a Levite,* an assistant to the priests in charge of the tabernacle.

secus: here, prep. + acc., *beside, along, near.*

146.   **pertransiit:** *passed by;* elaborate compounds are common in late and popular Lat.

Samaritanus: a native of Samaria, a district in Palestine; some Jews were hostile toward the Samaritans as being not of Jewish blood.

148.   **appropians: appropiare = appropinquare,** *to approach.*

alligavit: alligare, *to bind up.*

infundens: infundere, *to pour (in, on, over).*

oleum: *(olive) oil.*

149.   **stabulum:** *tavern, inn.*

150.   **altera:** i.e., *the next.*

denarios: the *denarius* was the most common Roman silver coin.

151.   **stabulario: stabularius,** the person who ran the **stabulum.**

quodcumque: quicumque, *whoever, whatever.*

supererogaveris: erogare, *to pay out* + **super,** *in addition,* i.e., beyond the two denarii; fut. perf. in a FUT. MORE VIVID CONDITION (introduced by the rel. **quodcumque** rather than by **si**).

152.   **cum rediero: cum** is often followed by the indic. when the cl. refers to pres. or fut. time.

154.   **vade: vadere,** *to go, rush.*

157.   **substantiae:** *substance = property.*

159.   **peregre:** adv., *abroad* (**per**+**ager,** i.e., through the fields to another country).

161.   **consummasset:** = **consummavisset,** plpf. subjunct. of **consummare,** *to finish off.*

162.   **fames:** *hunger, starvation, famine.*

adhaesit: here, *attached himself to, joined.*

164.   **pasceret:** *to feed, tend.*

porcos: porcus, *pig.*

ventrem: venter, *belly, stomach.*

siliquis: siliqua, *husk.*

165.   **manducabant: manducare,** *to chew, eat.*

166.   **in se . . . reversus:** cp. the Eng. idiom, "having returned to one's senses."

quanti: Cicero would have used **quot.**

171.   **adhuc:** adv., *up to this point, still.*

172.   **osculatus est: osculari,** *to kiss.*

175.   **stolam:** *cloak, robe.*

primam: here, *best.*

induite: induere, *to clothe.*

176.   **date . . . in:** instead of the dat., *put . . . on.*

anulum: anulus, *ring.*

calceamenta: calceamentum, *shoe.*

145   illo, praeterivit. Similiter et Levita, cum esset secus locum et
videret eum, pertransiit. Samaritanus autem quidam, iter faciens, venit secus eum et, videns eum, misericordia motus est.
Et appropians alligavit vulnera eius, infundens oleum et vinum;
et inponens illum in iumentum suum, duxit in stabulum, et

150   curam eius egit. Et altera die protulit duos denarios et dedit
stabulario et ait, 'Curam illius habe; et quodcumque supererogaveris, ego cum rediero reddam tibi.' Quis horum trium videtur
tibi proximus fuisse illi qui incidit in latrones?" At ille dixit,
"Qui fecit misericordiam in illum." Et ait illi Iesus, "Vade, et tu

155   fac similiter." (*Luke* 10.25–37)

The Prodigal Son

His departure and dissipation.

    Homo quidam habuit duos filios, et dixit adulescentior ex
illis patri, "Pater, da mihi portionem substantiae quae me contingit." Et divisit illis substantiam. Et non post multos dies, con-
gregatis omnibus, adulescentior filius peregre profectus est in

160   regionem longinquam et ibi dissipavit substantiam suam vi-
vendo luxuriose. Et postquam omnia consummasset, facta est
fames valida in regione illa, et ipse coepit egere. Et abiit et adhaesit uni civium regionis illius; et misit illum in villam suam ut
pasceret porcos. Et cupiebat implere ventrem suum de siliquis

165   quas porci manducabant, et nemo illi dabat.

The prodigal's return and the father's joy.

    In se autem reversus, dixit, "Quanti mercennarii patris mei
abundant panibus; ego autem hic fame pereo! Surgam, et ibo
ad patrem meum, et dicam illi, 'Pater, peccavi in caelum et coram te, et iam non sum dignus vocari filius tuus; fac me sicut

170   unum de mercennariis tuis.'" Et surgens venit ad patrem suum.
Cum autem adhuc longe esset, vidit illum pater ipsius, et misericordia motus est, et accurrens cecidit supra collum eius, et osculatus est illum. Dixitque ei filius, "Pater peccavi in caelum et
coram te; iam non sum dignus vocari filius tuus." Dixit autem

175   pater ad servos suos, "Cito proferte stolam primam et induite
illum, et date anulum in manum eius et calceamenta in pedes,

177. **vitulum: vitulus,** *calf.*
    saginatum: saginare, *to feed, fatten.*
178. **epulemur: epulari,** *to dine sumptuously, feast.*
181. **symphoniam et chorum:** *music and dancing.*
187. **haedum: haedus,** *young goat, kid.*
189. **meretricibus: meretrix,** *harlot, prostitute.*
194. **purpura:** i.e., expensive *purple cloth.*
    bysso: byssus, *flax, linen.*
195. **mendicus:** *beggar.*
196. **Lazarus:** not the Lazarus who was raised from the dead in *John* 11.1–44.
197. **micis: mica,** *crumb;* class. Lat. would more likely employ an ABL. OF MEANS.
198. **lingebant: lingere,** *to lick.*
    factum est: *it happened, it came to pass;* common in the Vulgate.
199. **Abrahae:** both **Abraham** (indecl.) and **Abraham, -ae,** m.; Abraham was pro-
    genitor of the Hebrews.
200. **sepultus est: sepelire,** *to bury.*
    inferno: infernus, *the lower world* = *hell* in eccl. Lat.
201. **a longe:** *from far off;* the use of **ab** with advs. is rarely found before late Lat.
203. **miserere: misereri** + gen., *to pity.*
    intinguat: intinguere, *to dip.*
204. **crucior: cruciare,** *to torture, torment,* a powerful word involving the **crux,** the
    cross, as an instrument of death.
205. **recordare: recordari,** *to recollect.*
    quia recepisti: IND. STATE.
206. **consolatur:** usually deponent but here passive.
207. **vos:** i.e., *you (sinners).*
208. **chaos:** n. nom., *vast empty space.*

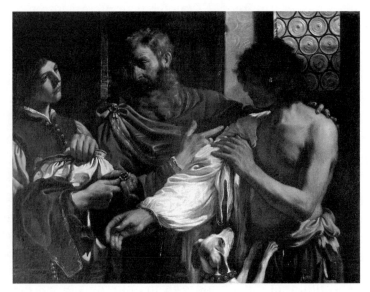

*"Return of the
Prodigal Son"
Guercino
17th century
Galleria Borghese
Rome, Italy*

et adducite vitulum saginatum et occidite, et manducemus et epulemur, quia hic filius meus mortuus erat et revixit, perierat et inventus est." Et coeperunt epulari.

The brother's jealousy and the father's reply.

180   Erat autem filius eius senior in agro; et cum veniret et appropinquaret domui, audivit symphoniam et chorum, et vocavit unum de servis et interrogavit quae haec essent. Isque dixit illi, "Frater tuus venit, et occidit pater tuus vitulum saginatum, quia salvum illum recepit." Indignatus est autem et nolebat introire.
185 Pater ergo illius egressus, coepit rogare illum. At ille, respondens, dixit patri suo, "Ecce tot annis servio tibi et numquam mandatum tuum praeterii, et numquam dedisti mihi haedum ut cum amicis meis epularer; sed postquam filius tuus hic, qui devoravit substantiam suam cum meretricibus, venit, occidisti
190 illi vitulum saginatum." At ipse dixit illi, "Fili, tu semper mecum es, et omnia mea tua sunt; epulari autem et gaudere oportebat, quia frater tuus hic mortuus erat et revixit, perierat et inventus est." (*Luke* 15.11–32)

The Rich Man and the Beggar Lazarus

Homo quidam erat dives, et induebatur purpura et bysso, et
195 epulabatur cotidie splendide. Et erat quidam mendicus, nomine Lazarus, qui iacebat ad ianuam eius, ulceribus plenus, cupiens saturari de micis quae cadebant de mensa divitis; sed et canes veniebant et lingebant ulcera eius. Factum est autem ut moreretur mendicus et portaretur ab angelis in sinum Abrahae. Mor-
200 tuus est autem et dives, et sepultus est in inferno. Elevans autem oculos suos, cum esset in tormentis, videbat Abraham a longe et Lazarum in sinu eius; et ipse, clamans, dixit, "Pater Abraham, miserere mei et mitte Lazarum ut intinguat extremum digiti sui in aquam ut refrigeret linguam meam, quia crucior in hac
205 flamma." Et dixit illi Abraham, "Fili, recordare quia recepisti bona in vita tua, et Lazarus similiter mala; nunc autem hic consolatur, tu vero cruciaris. Et in his omnibus, inter nos et vos chaos magnum firmatum est ut hi qui volunt hinc transire ad

209. **inde:** adv, *thence, from there.*
     huc: adv., *to this place.*
     transmeare: *to cross over.*

212. **Mosen:** acc. of **Moses,** the Hebrew prophet and lawgiver who led the Israel-
     ites from Egypt.

215. **neque:** here, *not even.*

218. **iusti:** here, *righteous,* in their observance of religious ritual.
     aspernabantur: aspernari, *to despise.*
     parabolam: parabola, *comparison, parable.*

219. **Pharisaeus:** *a Pharisee;* the Pharisees, a Jewish sect that insisted on a strict
     interpretation and observation of the law of Moses, were sometimes con-
     demned for their self-righteous attitudes and disdain of those outside
     their sect.

220. **publicanus:** *a tax-collector,* here a native agent of a Roman company collect-
     ing taxes for Rome; because of their association with outsiders and their
     often extortionate practices, the **publicani** were commonly despised.

221. **raptores:** *snatchers* = *robbers.*

222. **velut:** conj., *as, just as, as if.*
     ieiuno: ieiunare, *to fast.*

223. **decimas:** sc. **partes,** *tenth parts, tithes.*

224. **nec:** the double negative, with **nolebat,** is emphatic, *was not even willing.*
     percutiebat: percutere, *to strike.*

225. **propitius:** *gracious, kind.*

226. **iustificatus:** *justified,* i.e., *forgiven.*
     ab illo: *rather than that man.*
     exaltat: exaltare, *to raise on high, exalt;* late and eccl. Lat.

227. **humiliabitur: humiliare,** *to humble, humiliate;* late Lat.

"The Story of Moses"
Raphael, 16th century
Logge, Vatican Palace, Vatican State

210

215

vos non possint, neque inde huc transmeare." Et ait, "Rogo ergo te, pater, ut mittas eum in domum patris mei—habeo enim quinque fratres—ut testetur illis, ne et ipsi veniant in locum hunc tormentorum." Et ait illi Abraham, "Habent Mosen et prophetas; audiant illos." At ille dixit, "Non, pater Abraham: sed si quis ex mortuis ierit ad eos, paenitentiam agent." Ait autem illi, "Si Mosen et prophetas non audiunt, neque, si quis ex mortuis resurrexerit, credent." (*Luke* 16.19–31)

Hypocrisy and Sincerity

220

225

Dixit autem et ad quosdam, qui in se confidebant tamquam iusti et aspernabantur ceteros, parabolam istam: Duo homines ascenderunt in templum ut orarent, unus Pharisaeus et alter publicanus. Pharisaeus, stans, haec apud se orabat, "Deus, gratias ago tibi, quia non sum sicut ceteri hominum—raptores, iniusti, adulteri, velut etiam hic publicanus. Ieiuno bis in sabbato; decimas do omnium quae possideo." Et publicanus, a longe stans, nolebat nec oculos ad caelum levare; sed percutiebat pectus suum, dicens, "Deus, propitius esto mihi peccatori." Dico vobis, descendit hic iustificatus in domum suam ab illo, quia omnis qui se exaltat, humiliabitur, et qui se humiliat, exaltabitur. (*Luke* 18.9–14)

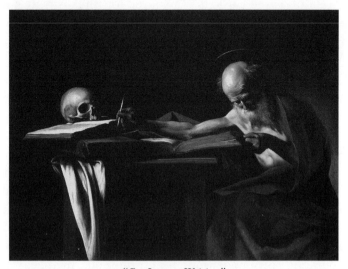

"St. Jerome Writing"
Caravaggio, 17th century
Galleria Borghese, Rome, Italy

MEDIEVAL LATIN

Although the western Roman empire lapsed into political instability in the fifth century of our era, the influence of Rome persisted, even into our own day of course, and Latin remained the primary language of church literature and much of secular literature throughout the Middle Ages and into the Renaissance of the 14th–16th centuries. Medieval Latin, it should be said at the outset, was by no means merely an anemic or imitative extension of its classical parent. Rather, in its vibrant admixture of classical and vulgar Latin (encountered in the previous unit on Jerome's Vulgate), the language became the lingua franca of the ecclesiastical world and the intellectual secular world in the fields of literature, including widely various and often innovative forms in prose and poetry, of religion and philosophy, of politics and diplomacy and law, of education, and of science.

A rich variety of style and expression developed over the centuries and in the many different regions of chiefly western and central Europe where the language continued to be used alongside, and often under the influence of, the local vernacular. This variety is well represented by the selections in this book, which span a period of about 600 years, ranging from the Venerable Bede's accounts in the 8th century of Pope Gregory's mission in England and the poet Caedmon's inspired hymns, to the allegorizing "Tale of Three Caskets" (a source for Shakespeare's *Merchant of Venice*) from the 14th-century *Gesta Romanorum*. Included also are three songs—one a religious meditation on the vanity of human life, one a sprightly celebration of the return of springtime and young love, and the third a raucous drinking song—from the 13th-century *Carmina Burana* (made famous by the cantata of the same name first produced by the German composer Carl Orff in 1937), as well as three of the most famous medieval hymns, from the 12th and 13th centuries, Stephen Langton's reverent *Veni, Sancte Spiritus,* the profoundly sorrowful *Stabat Mater,* and Thomas of Celano's hypnotic prayer on Judgment Day, the *Dies Irae,* which was early on incorporated as a sequence in the requiem mass and later included in arrangements of the requiem composed by Mozart, Verdi, and others.

Although there were many changes and local variations in vocabulary, orthography, pronunciation, and grammar, medieval Latin remained more stable than one might have expected over the 1,000 years of its history from roughly A.D. 500 to 1500, thanks in particular to its preservation by churchmen in Rome and in monasteries throughout Europe. For the selections presented below, classical spelling has been followed, and the meanings of new words, as well as non-classical meanings for classical words, are provided in the notes. Grammatical differences are also pointed out in the notes, generally at the first occurrence or two; following are the commonest variances from classical Latin to be encountered in the readings (some of them already seen in the preceding selections from the Vulgate and many of them approximating the syntax of modern European languages—a fact that often makes for easier reading and comprehension): briefer, less complex sentences (students will be relieved!); indirect statement introduced by *quia, quod,* or *ut,* with either an indicative or subjunctive verb; use of *quod* to introduce purpose and relative clauses; frequent use of the indicative in place of the subjunctive, and occasionally the opposite; use of *debere* and *habere* as auxiliary verbs (indicating, respectively, futurity and obligatory action); use of *sum* as an auxiliary in so-called "analytical" (periphrastic) verb forms such as *eram manens* for *manebam;* increased range of uses for infinitives, e.g., in place of *ut* + subjunctive; use of *non* for *ne;* variance in case uses and gender; frequent use of prepositional phrases in place of simple case uses (e.g., *per* + accusative instead of ablative of means or *de* + ablative instead of the prepositionless ablative of description); and non-reflexive use of *suus/sui.*

Finally, since all these passages, especially the verse selections, should be read aloud, students should note the relatively few major differences between classical and medieval (or ecclesiastical) pronunciation. First, the rules for accent are largely the same; occasionally the accent was shifted to suit a poem's meter, which was accentual (qualitative) not quantitative, as explained in the notes. The consonants *c* and *g* were pronounced soft before the vowels *e* and *i,* as in *agito* ("ajito," like English "agitate") and *cetera* ("chaytera"); *v* was pronounced as in English, not as a "w"; and the diphthongs *ae* and *oe* were pronounced as English long "a," as in *quae* ("kway").

1. **praetereunda:** sc. **est.**

   opinio: here, *story.*

   Gregorio: after living some years in his own monastery in Rome, Gregory (ca. 540–604) was called to be Pope Gregory I in A.D. 590; in 597 he sent to the pagan Anglo-Saxons in England Augustine (the Lesser), who established a monastery at Canterbury and made it the base for missionary work throughout England.

2. **quia … multi … confluxissent et … Gregorium … vidisse (5): dicunt** is followed by two IND. STATES., one a **quia** *(that)* cl. + subjunct. typical of med. Lat. and the other an acc. + inf. construction usual in class. Lat.

3. **mercatoribus: mercator,** *merchant.*

   venalia: *for sale, to be sold.*

4. **fuissent conlata:** = **essent conlata.**

6. **venusti:** *charming.*

7. **egregia:** *unusual, remarkable;* note the combination of ABL. OF DESCRIPTION here with the GEN. OF DESCRIPTION in the preceding phrase.

8. **dictum … est:** impers. pass.

   quia: sc. **adlati essent.**

9. **incolae: incola,** *inhabitant.*

   aspectus: *appearance, aspect;* GEN. OF DESCRIPTION.

   rursus: or **rursum,** adv., *again.*

10. **insulani: insulanus,** *islander;* sc. **essent.**

    paganis: lit., *belonging to a* **pagus** *(village)* = *rustic,* and hence *pagan* (because the old pre-Christian religion survived longest among the country people).

11. **quod:** commonly used in med. Lat., like **quia** (above, line 2), to introduce a subjunct. vb. in IND. STATE.

12. **intimo:** *innermost.*

    corde: cor, *heart.*

    suspiria: suspirium, *sigh.*

    pro: interj., + voc., *oh, ah.*

13. **lucidi:** *bright, shining.*

    tenebrarum: tenebrae, pl., *shadows, darkness;* with **auctor** = the Devil.

14. **possidet: possidere,** *to possess.*

    gratia: here, *grace.*

    frontispicii: frontispicium, *exterior, appearance.*

15. **gestat: gestare,** *to carry about, have.*

16. **vocabulum:** *name.*

18. **angelorum:** depends on **coheredes.**

19. **decet:** impers., *it is proper, fitting.*

    coheredes: coheres, *co-heir.*

20. **Deiri:** *Deirans,* residents of Deira, a kingdom of northern England settled by Angles and encompassing parts of Yorkshire, Northumbria, and East Anglia.

21. **eruti: eruere,** *to pluck out, rescue;* sc. **sunt.**

22. **misericordiam: misericordia,** *mercy.*

THE VENERABLE BEDE

The Venerable Bede (ca. 672–735), a devout English monk and famed scholar and teacher, is best known for his five-volume Historia Ecclesiastica Gentis Anglorum *("Ecclesiastical History of the English People"), which earned him the title of "father of English history." Working at a time when Latin was studied primarily for the sake of reading and understanding the Scriptures and the Church Fathers, he wrote clear and effective, if not entirely classical, Latin.*

Gregory's Interest in British Missions
(Bede *Historia Ecclesiastica* 2.1, excerpts)

Gregory inquires about the provenience of some handsome slaves on sale in the market.

Nec silentio praetereunda opinio quae de beato Gregorio traditione maiorum ad nos usque perlata est. Dicunt quia die quadam cum, advenientibus nuper mercatoribus, multa venalia in forum fuissent conlata, multi ad emendum confluxissent, et
5 ipsum Gregorium inter alios advenisse ac vidisse inter alia pueros venales positos, candidi corporis ac venusti vultus, capillorum quoque forma egregia. Quos cum adspiceret interrogavit, ut aiunt, de qua regione vel terra essent adlati. Dictumque est quia de Britannia insula, cuius incolae talis essent aspectus. Rursus
10 interrogavit utrum idem insulani Christiani an paganis adhuc erroribus essent implicati. Dictum est quod essent pagani. At ille, intimo ex corde longa trahens suspiria, "Heu, pro dolor!" inquit, "quod tam lucidi vultus homines tenebrarum auctor possidet tantaque gratia frontispicii mentem ab interna gratia
15 vacuam gestat."

Learning that they are Angles, Gregory puns on their names.

Rursus ergo interrogavit quod esset vocabulum gentis illius. Responsum est quod Angli vocarentur. At ille, "Bene," inquit, "nam et angelicam habent faciem et tales angelorum in caelis decet esse coheredes. Quod habet nomen ipsa provincia de qua
20 isti sunt adlati?" Responsum est quod Deiri vocarentur idem provinciales. At ille, "Bene," inquit, "Deiri; 'de ira' eruti, et ad misericordiam Christi vocati. Rex provinciae illius quomodo

23. **Aelle:** *Aelle,* the king who founded Deira in 559 and ruled until his death in 588.

adludens: adludere, *to jest at, play with, play on.*

24. **alleluia:** interj., *praise Jehovah, hallelujah.*

26. **pontificem: pontifex,** *pontiff, pope.*

sedis: sedes, *seat;* med., here, *see* (the official seat of a bishop or other church official).

28. **verbi ministros:** here, *ministers of the Word* (of God).

29. **converteretur:** sc. **Britannia;** REL. CL. OF PURPOSE.

se . . . paratum esse: IND. STATE. with an understood speech vb.

in hoc opus . . . perficiendum (30): *to carry out the task.*

31. **papae: papa,** *bishop, pope.*

quod: = **et hoc.**

dum: here with a combined force of circumstance *(when)* and concession *(although),* like Eng. *while* when not used in a strictly temporal sense.

34. **pontificatus:** gen., *of the pontificate.*

functus est: fungi, + abl., *to perform, discharge, complete.*

35. **praedicatores: praedicator,** *preacher.*

36. **fructificaret: fructificare,** *to bear fruit.*

38. **monasterio:** at Streaneshalch (modern Whitby, in Yorkshire), a monastery of both nuns and monks that became one of the major religious centers of northern England during this period.

abbatissae: abbatissa, *abbess,* i.e., St. Hilda (614–680), founder of the abbey at Streaneshalch.

39. **insignis:** *distinguished.*

pietati: pietas, *piety* in the med. Christian sense of the word.

40. **interpretes: interpres,** *expounder, translator.*

41. **pusillum:** *a little* (time).

42. **compunctione: compunctio,** *humility.*

44. **saeculi: saeculum,** med. Lat., *the world.*

accensi: accendere, *to set on fire;* sc. **sunt.**

45. **et:** = **etiam.**

47. **non ab hominibus neque per hominem:** *not by men nor through the agency of a human being* (i.e., one through whom God worked), but by direct divine revelation.

institutus: here, *instructed.*

48. **divinitus:** adv., *divinely* (i.e., directly by God).

gratis: abl. as adv., *gratis, for nothing,* i.e., as a direct gift of God and without training.

49. **nil . . . frivoli et supervacui poematis (49):** *no trifling and unnecessary poem.*

50. **tantummodo:** adv., *only.*

appellatur?" Responsum est quod Aelle diceretur. At ille, adludens ad nomen, ait: "Alleluia, laudem Dei creatoris illis in parti-
25   bus oportet cantari."

Some time later Gregory, when Pope, was able to send missionaries to Britain.

Accedensque ad pontificem Romanae et apostolicae sedis (nondum enim erat ipse pontifex factus), rogavit ut genti Anglorum in Britanniam aliquos verbi ministros, per quos ad Christum converteretur, mitteret; se ipsum paratum esse in hoc
30   opus, Domino cooperante, perficiendum, si tamen apostolico papae hoc ut fieret placeret. Quod dum perficere non posset, quia, etsi pontifex concedere illi quod petierat voluit, non tamen cives Romani ut tam longe ab urbe secederet potuere permittere, mox, ut ipse pontificatus officio functus est, perfecit opus
35   diu desideratum, alios quidem praedicatores mittens, sed ipse praedicationem ut fructificaret suis exhortationibus ac precibus adiuvans.

Caedmon's Anglo-Saxon Compositions on the Scriptures
(Bede *Historia Ecclesiastica* 4.22)

Caedmon, a brother in the monastery of St. Hilda at Streaneshalch (now Whitby), was blessed by God with the ability to turn religious teachings into verse.

In huius monasterio abbatissae fuit frater quidam divina gratia specialiter insignis, quia carmina religioni et pietati apta
40   facere solebat, ita ut, quidquid ex divinis litteris per interpretes disceret, hoc ipse post pusillum verbis poeticis maxima suavitate et compunctione compositis, in sua, id est Anglorum, lingua proferret. Cuius carminibus multorum saepe animi ad contemptum saeculi et appetitum sunt vitae caelestis accensi. Et
45   quidem et alii post illum in gente Anglorum religiosa poemata facere temptabant; sed nullus eum aequiperare potuit. Namque ipse non ab hominibus neque per hominem institutus canendi artem didicit, sed divinitus adiutus gratis canendi donum accepit. Unde nil umquam frivoli et supervacui poematis facere
50   potuit, sed ea tantummodo quae ad religionem pertinent religi-

51. **siquidem:** conj., *since, inasmuch as.*
    habitu: habitus, *appearance, dress, clothes;* with **saeculari,** *secular dress = secular life.*
52. **provectioris:** *rather advanced.*
    constitutus: constituere, *to place, position;* sc. **erat.**
53. **aliquando:** adv., *at any time.*
    nonnumquam: adv., *sometimes.*
    convivio: convivium, *dinner, banquet.*
54. **laetitiae: laetitia,** *entertainment.*
    per ordinem: *in turn.*
    deberent: often used as an auxiliary vb. in med. Lat. (cp. **habes,** below, line 65); for **cantare deberent** class. Lat. might simply have **cantarent.**
55. **citharam: cithara,** at this time a variety of *harp.*
56. **repedabat: repedare,** *to go back, withdraw, retire.*
57. **dum:** here, *when.*
58. **iumentorum: iumentum,** *pack animal, farm animal.*
59. **competenti:** *appropriate.*
61. **Caedmon:** *Caedmon,* a seventh-century churchman and the first Old English Christian poet, adapted Anglo-Saxon verse to religious themes.
62. **et:** = **etiam.**
    ideo: adv., *therefore, for that reason.*
65. **habes:** = **debes;** this common med. Lat. usage is equivalent to Eng. "you have (to) . . . ."
66. **creaturarum: creatura,** *creature, creation.*
67. **in:** *to.*
70. **quomodo:** here exclamatory, not interrog., *in what a manner!*
71. **exstitit: exsistere,** *to step forth, appear, emerge, exist, be.*
72. **culmine: culmen,** *top, summit.*
    tecti: tectum, *roof, home;* here, the home of all mankind, i.e., *the world.*
75. **ad verbum:** *to a word, literally.*
76. **detrimento: detrimentum,** *loss (of), injury (to).*
77. **cuncta:** = **omnia.**
79. **carminis:** with **plura . . . verba.**
80. **mane:** adv., *in the morning.*
    vilicum: vilicus, *steward, reeve.*
83. **universorum:** *of all together.*

osam eius linguam decebant. Siquidem in habitu saeculari usque ad tempora provectioris aetatis constitutus, nil carminum
aliquando didicerat. Unde nonnumquam in convivio, cum esset
laetitiae causa decretum ut omnes per ordinem cantare debe-
55   rent, ille, ubi appropinquare sibi citharam cernebat, surgebat a
media cena et egressus ad suam domum repedabat.

*Caedmon is inspired by a vision in a dream to compose holy verse and
to sing.*

Quod dum tempore quodam faceret, et relicta domu con-
vivii egressus esset ad stabula iumentorum, quorum ei custodia
nocte illa erat delegata, ibique hora competenti membra dedis-
60   set sopori, adstitit ei quidam per somnium, eumque salutans ac
suo appellans nomine, "Caedmon," inquit, "canta mihi aliquid."
At ille respondens, "Nescio," inquit, "cantare; nam et ideo de
convivio egressus huc secessi, quia cantare non poteram." Rursum ille qui cum eo loquebatur, "Attamen," ait, "mihi cantare
65   habes." "Quid," inquit, "debeo cantare?" Et ille, "Canta," inquit, "principium creaturarum." Quo accepto responso, statim
ipse coepit cantare in laudem Dei conditoris versus quos numquam audierat, quorum iste est sensus: "Nunc laudare debemus
auctorem regni caelestis, potentiam creatoris et consilium illius,
70   facta Patris gloriae. Quomodo ille, cum sit aeternus Deus, omnium miraculorum auctor exstitit, qui primo filiis hominum
caelum pro culmine tecti, dehinc terram custos humani generis
omnipotens creavit!" (Hic est sensus, non autem ordo ipse verborum, quae dormiens ille canebat; neque enim possunt carmina,
75   quamvis optime composita, ex alia in aliam linguam ad verbum
sine detrimento sui decoris ac dignitatis transferri.) Exsurgens
autem a somno, cuncta quae dormiens cantaverat memoriter
retinuit, et eis mox plura in eundem modum verba Deo digni
carminis adiunxit.

Caedmon's verses are judged to be the product of divine inspiration.

80   Veniensque mane ad vilicum qui sibi praeerat, quid doni
percepisset indicavit atque, ad abbatissam perductus, iussus est,
multis doctioribus viris praesentibus, indicare somnium et dicere carmen ut universorum iudicio quid vel unde esset quod

84. **probaretur:** the subj. is **quid (esset) vel unde esset (id) quod referebat.**

86. **Honorius:** Roman emperor of the West, A.D. 395–423; but the numerous stories of Rome's emperors in the **Gesta Romanorum** are largely or entirely fabricated.

  valde: adv., *very, very much.*

  unicum: *an only.*

88. **unum:** = **quendam,** or simply the indef. article *a,* as often in med. Lat.

89. **guerram: guerra,** med. = **bellum.**

  cum . . . sustinebat (90): in med. Lat. **cum** circumstantial and causal may be used with the indic. rather than the subjunct.

90. **damna: damnum,** *damage, injury, loss.*

92. **si . . . possem . . . obtinerem (93):** in med. Lat. the impf. subjunct. can be used, as here, in a fut. less vivid condition and, as in class. Lat., in a pres. contrary to fact.

  per aliquam viam: = **aliquo modo;** this is an example of the common use in med. Lat. of prep. phrases to replace cases without a prep. in class. Lat.

93. **copulare:** *to join, unite.*

94. **ut . . . concederet (95):** actually a JUSSIVE NOUN CL. depending on the idea of *asking* implicit in **misit nuntios.**

  saltem: adv., *at least.*

  trewgam: trewga, *truce* (a Germanic word, as the **w** shows).

95. **quod:** can in med. Lat. introduce a PURPOSE CL., as here.

97. **filiam eius filio suo:** the normal possessives are reversed here (**eius** for **suam,** and **suo** for **eius**), a common irregularity in med. Lat.

98. **habeam:** for **habebo.**

99. **decessum: decessus,** *departure, death.*

100. **destinetur: destinare,** here, *to bequeath.*

  conventione: conventio, *agreement, compact.*

101. **charta:** *paper, document.*

  sigillata est: sigillare, *to seal, mark with a seal.*

  vale . . . fecit: med. Lat. for **vale dixit.**

102. **parari fecit:** for class. **fecit ut pararetur.**

103. **quia:** usually + indic. in class. Lat.

The Venerable Bede

85 referebat probaretur. Visumque est omnibus caelestem ei a Domino con cessam esse gratiam.

GESTA ROMANORUM

The Gesta Romanorum *("Deeds of the Romans") is an early 14th-century collection
of medieval exempla, brief narratives designed both to entertain and to edify, each
containing some spiritual message that is explicated in an allegorizing postscript.
Drawn from a variety of Roman, Greek, and near eastern sources, the stories were
enormously popular in the late Middle Ages among churchmen and general readers
alike and were a source for such later writers as Chaucer and Shakespeare. Perhaps
compiled in England, but of unknown authorship, the collection is loosely structured,
the style uneven, and the Latinity far removed from that of the classical period.*

The Story of the Three Caskets

*The emperor Honorius makes a truce with a certain king and agrees to
the marriage of the king's daughter to his own son on two conditions.*

Honorius regnavit, dives valde, qui unicum filium habebat,
quem multum dilexit. Fama eius imperatoris per mundum vola-
bat quod in omnibus probus erat et iustus. Tamen contra unum
regem guerram habebat et eum devastabat. Rex iste, cum mul-
90 tas persecutiones ac damna infinita ab eo sustinebat, tandem
cogitabat, "Tantum unicam filiam habeo et adversarius meus
unicum filium. Si per aliquam viam filiam meam possem filio
suo in matrimonium copulare, pacem perpetuam obtinerem."
Misit sollemnes nuntios ad imperatorem, ut saltem ei trewgam
95 ad tempus concederet quod cum eo personaliter loqui posset.
Imperator, habito consilio, trewgam unius anni concessit. Rex
vero personaliter ad eum accessit et filiam eius filio suo obtulit.
At iste, "Non faciam nisi duo habeam. Primo ut tua filia sit
virgo; secundo ut post decessum tuum totum regnum tuum filio
100 meo destinetur." At ille, "Bene placet mihi." Statim de conventione charta sigillata est. Rex vale imperatori fecit.

The ship carrying the king's daughter is swallowed by a whale.

Cum autem ad regnum suum venerat, navem parari fecit,
quia oporteret ut filia sua per mare ad imperatorem transiret.

104. **facta:** = **parata,** *readied.*
105. **thesaurum: thesaurus,** *treasure,* i.e., her dowry.
106. **dominabus:** *ladies;* cp. **filiabus,** used to distinguish between the f. and the m., which otherwise would have the same form **(dominis).**

   cete: cete, -i, *whale.* The word, which comes from Greek and in the form **cete** looks like a Greek pl., is here nom. m. sg., equivalent to the class. Lat. **cetus;** in line 119 and elsewhere **cete** is treated as n. sg., an inconsistency characteristic of much of med. Lat. (though this particular word had a number of variants in class. Lat. as well).

107. **ei:** the ambiguous antecedent is the **navis.**

   deglutire: *to devour.*

108. **praecipue:** adv., *especially.*
110. **accidit . . . quod . . . dormierunt (111):** for class. **accidit . . . ut . . . dormirent.**
110. **triduum: triduus,** *period of three days.*

   fessi: *weary.*

113. **ventre: venter,** *belly.*
115. **estote:** fut. imper. of **esse.**

   confortati: med. Lat. (especially in the Vulgate), **confortare,** *to strengthen greatly.*

116. **salvabit: salvare,** med. Lat. for **servare.**
117. **erimus salvati:** = **salvabimur.**
119. **cete:** here, n. acc.

   quilibet: *anyone,* here perhaps = **quisque.**

   sicut profundius possit: *just as deeply as he can.*

   ista duo (120): i.e., **ignem et vulnera.**

120. **natabit: natare,** *to swim.*
121. **per omnia:** i.e., *in all its details, in every respect.*
122. **impleverunt: implere,** *to fill up, complete, accomplish.*

   perrexit: pergere, *to go on, proceed.*

123. **iuxta:** prep. + acc., *close to, near.*

   quam: = **hanc.**

   erat . . . manens: = **manebat;** the use of **erat** as an auxiliary is quite comparable to the Eng. formation *was waiting,* just one example of the many ways in which the grammar of med. Lat. comes to approximate that of Eng.; cp. **erimus salvati,** above, line 117.

124. **versus:** = **adversus,** prep. + acc., *toward.*

   hinc inde: *here and there, back and forth.*

126. **cum instrumentis:** ABL. OF MEANS; for the prep., see note on line 92.

   percutere: *to strike.*

127. **sonitum: sonitus,** *sound.*
128. **suaviter:** lit., *sweetly* = *gently.*

   latus: n., *side.*

   aperite: aperire, *to open.*

129. **de . . . sanguine:** here again class. Lat. might use an ABL. OF DESCRIPTION without the prep.

   generoso: *noble.*

Facta nave et omnibus necessariis paratis, puella intravit, ha-
105   bens thesaurum secum in magna copia ac milites quinque cum
dominabus et ancillis. Cum autem per mare navigarent, cete
grandis ei occurrebat in mare et navem deglutire volebat. Nautae hoc percipientes timuerunt valde et praecipue puella. Nautae vero ignem copiosum fecerunt et die ac nocte vigilabant.
110   Sed accidit post triduum quod, fessi propter magnas vigilias,
dormierunt. Cete subito navem cum omnibus contentis de-
glutivit.

The girl and her attendants attack the whale and force it to go ashore.

Puella, cum intellexit quod in ventre ceti esset, fortiter clamabat. Ad cuius clamorem omnes excitati sunt. Nautae vero
115   puellae dixerunt ac militibus, "Carissimi, estote confortati; Deus
nos salvabit. Habeamus bonum consilium quia sumus in ventre
ceti." Ait puella, "Audite consilium meum et erimus salvati."
Qui dixerunt, "Dic." Quae ait, "Accendamus ignem in magna
copia et cete quilibet vulneret sicut profundius possit et per ista
120   duo mortem recipiet et statim ad terram natabit et sic per gratiam Dei evadere poterimus." Illi vero consilium puellae per omnia impleverunt. Cete, cum mortem sensit, ad terram perrexit.

They are rescued out of the whale and sent to the emperor.

Iuxta quam terram erat quidam miles manens, qui, cena
facta, versus litus maris ambulavit. Cum ergo cete hinc inde na-
125   tare vidisset et terrae appropinquare, servos vocat et cete ad terram traxit. Qui inceperunt cum instrumentis percutere. Puella,
cum sonitum audisset, loquebatur pro omnibus et ait, "Carissimi, suaviter percutite et latus ceti aperite; hic sumus in eius
ventre, filii bonorum virorum de generoso sanguine." Miles, cum
130   vocem puellae audisset, ait servis suis, "Carissimi, latus ceti ape-

131.   **lateat: latere,** *to lie hidden, hide.*
       interius: = **intus.**
       apertum fuisset: = **apertum esset.**
132.   **immo quasi:** *nearly.*
133.   **ceteri alii: alii** is pleonastic and would not be used with **ceteri** in class. Lat.
       cuius . . . esset: IND. QUEST.
          et . . . esse deberet (134): *and that she was going to be,* IND. STATE. introduced
             by **quod** (understood); **deberet,** as often in med. Lat., functions simply
             as a temporal auxiliary vb., indicating futurity (see above on line 54).
134.   **aliquot:** indecl. adj., *several.*
135.   **donec:** conj., *as long as, until,* + indic. or, indicating anticipation or pur-
             pose, subjunct.
       statum: i.e., *state of health.*
       recuperabant: recuperare, *to recover, regain;* the impf. here conveys simply a
             general past idea.
140.   **in maritum:** *as a husband.*
141.   **fecit fieri:** = class. **fecit ut fierent;** i.e., he had them brought forth.
       cophinos: cophinus, *chest, casket;* this motif of the three caskets is adapted
             by Shakespeare in the *Merchant of Venice,* act 2, scene 7.
       lapidibus: lapis, *stone.*
143.   **meruit: merere,** *to deserve, earn, merit.*
144.   **ossibus: os,** *bone.*
145.   **ex omni:** we would say, not *from every,* but *in every.*
146.   **elegerit: eligere,** *to choose, select.*
147.   **plumbo: plumbum,** *lead.*
150.   **anuli: anulus,** *ring;* the vb. is sg. because the rings are viewed as a set.
151.   **quemcumque: quicumque,** *whoever, whichever.*
153.   **intime:** adv., *closely, intimately, thoughtfully.*
154.   **illo:** i.e., God.
155.   **deficiam: deficere,** *to fail,* i.e., in one's responsibilities to another, a sense that
             in class. Lat. regularly takes the dat. or **ad** (vs. **de** here).
157.   **exterius:** adv., *on the outside.*
       penitus: adv., *inside, deeply, thoroughly, entirely.*
159.   **quod:** = **ut.**

rite et videamus quid lateat interius." Cum vero apertum fuisset, puella primo exivit immo quasi mortua, deinde milites et
ceteri alii. Coepit narrare cuius filia esset et uxor filii imperatoris
esse deberet. Hoc audiens, miles eam per aliquot dies cum tota
135   familia secum retinuit, donec perfectum statum suum recupera-
bant. Post hoc puellam cum muneribus ad imperatorem misit
cum tota familia.

The emperor tests the king's daughter by requiring her to choose one of three caskets.

Imperator, cum eam vidisset, ait, "Carissima filia, bene tibi
sit nunc et in perpetuum. Sed tibi dico, filia, antequam filium
140   meum habueris in maritum, te probabo per unum actum." Statim
fecit fieri tres cophinos. Primus erat de auro purissimo et lapidibus pretiosis. Et erat talis superscriptio super cophinum: "Qui
me aperiet, in me invenerit quod meruit." Et totus cophinus erat
plenus ossibus mortuorum. Secundus erat de argento purissimo,
145   plenus gemmis ex omni parte, qui talem superscriptionem habebat: "Qui me elegerit, in me invenerit quod natura dedit." Iste
cophinus terra plenus erat. Tertius cophinus erat de plumbo, ha-
bens superscriptionem talem: "Potius eligo hic esse et requiescere, quam in thesauris regis permanere." In cophino isto erat
150   tres anuli pretiosi. Tunc ait imperator puellae, "Carissima, hic
sunt tres cophini; eligas quemcumque volueris; et si bene elege-
ris, filium meum in maritum obtinebis."

Pondering the inscriptions, she makes the right choice and marries the emperor's son.

Illa vero tres cophinos intime respexit et ait in corde suo,
"Deus, qui omnia videt, det mihi gratiam sic eligendi ut de illo
155   pro quo multum laboravi non deficiam." Quae primum cophinum tetigit et scripturam legit: "Qui me," etc. Illa cogitabat,
"Cophinus exterius est pretiosus, sed quid interius lateat penitus
ignoro; ideo eum eligere nolo." Deinde secundum legit, etc.
Quae ait, "Numquam natura dedit quod filia patris mei deberet
160   copulari filio imperatoris. Et ideo," etc. Tertium cophinum legit,
dicens, "Melius est mihi cum filio regis requiescere quam in thesauris patris mei." Et alta voce clamabat, "Istum cophinum ter-

165. **unum . . . tertium:** class. Lat. would have nom. m. adjs., to agree with **anulus.**
    desponsationis: desponsatio, *betrothal, engagement.*

166. **fecit:** here, *he prepared.*
    nuptias: nuptiae, pl., *nuptials, wedding.*

168. **moralitas:** *moral interpretation;* the stories in the *Gesta Romanorum* generally
    conclude with an allegorizing interpretation.

169. **in tantum:** idiom, *to such a degree, to such an extent.*
    quod . . . erat destructa (170): in med. Lat. RESULT CLS. are often introduced
    by **quod** and have an indic. vb.

170. **peccatum:** *sin.*

171. **dominum:** i.e., the **rex** in the story.

174. **ceteris:** i.e., the **dominabus et ancillis** mentioned above.

175. **diabolus:** *the devil.*

178. **eum:** the **diabolus.**

180. **confessores: confessor,** *one who confesses Christianity, a Christian.*

182. **curiam: curia,** originally *senate house,* here = *the court.*
    quod . . . praesentantur (183): i.e., what they are, what they represent.

183. **ei:** = **puellae** = **animae.**

186. **merui:** i.e., *I incurred, have been guilty of.*
    quod est dolendum: *which (circumstance) is to be lamented.*
    vae: sc. **homini,** *woe to the man.*

187. **intellegitur:** strictly this should be pl. to agree with **sapientes,** but even Eng.
    allows the idiom *is understood the wise men.*

188. **eloquia: eloquium,** poetic for **eloquentia.**
    splendunt: splendere, *to shine, glitter.*
    terrenis: *earthly things, base things.*

190. **illi:** i.e., the **sapientes.**
    maritantur: maritare, *to marry.*

192. **aliquo:** here, *anything.*
    mundano: *worldly, of this world.*

193. **scilicet:** adv., *namely, of course.*
    caritas: lit., *dearness* = *love, esteem.*

Saint Gregory
(Pope Gregory I)
Ms. lat. 2287, fol. 1v
French, 12th century
Bibliotheque Nationale
Paris, France

tium eligo." Imperator, cum audisset, ait, "O bona puella, satis
prudenter elegisti. In isto cophino sunt tres anuli mei pretiosi;
165   unum pro me, unum pro filio, tertium pro te in signum despon-
sationis." Statim fecit nuptias celebrare, et tradidit ei filium suum,
et sic in pace vitam finierunt.

The moral interpretation of the story.

Moralitas: Carissimi, imperator est Deus, qui diu guerram
cum homine habuit in tantum quod tota natura humana erat
170   destructa per peccatum. Modo trewgae nobis datae sunt per
dominum, id est, Christum. Filia quae filio imperatoris debet
desponsari est anima. Oportet ergo ut navis paretur pro ea cum
nuntiis, id est, corpus in quo anima residet cum quinque sensi-
bus et ceteris; nautae sunt ratio, voluntas, etc. Sed oportet per
175   mare, id est, per mundum, transire. Cete grande est diabolus,
contra quem debemus vigilare. Sed si nos contingit dormire in
peccatis, deglutiet corpus et animam. Fac ergo sicut fecit puella;
ignem devotionis accende et eum cum instrumentis, id est, bonis
operibus percute, donec recedat et potestatem suam contra te
180   amittat. Tunc servi militis, id est, praedicatores et confessores,
habent eum percutere, donec puella, id est, anima, ab eorum
potestate exeat et ad curiam Dei veniat. Sed est sciendum quod
tres cophini ei praesentantur. Per primum cophinum potentes
ac divites intelleguntur, qui habent talem superscriptionem: "Qui
185   me," etc., id est, quando anima a corpore separetur, nihil in me
Deus inveniet nisi peccata quae merui, quod est dolendum; vae
qui hunc eligit. Per secundum intellegitur mundi sapientes, quorum eloquia splendunt sicut argentum et intus pleni sunt ter-
renis cum tali superscriptione: "Qui me elegerit," etc. Natura
190   semper appetit animae contrarium et illi non maritantur Christo.
Per tertium cophinum designantur boni christiani, qui sunt
plumbei, id est, quod non curant de aliquo mundano; in quibus
sunt tres anuli, scilicet, fides, spes, et caritas; qui istos eligit,
filium Dei habere potest libentius quam in thesauro mundano
195   permanere. Studeamus.

196. **ver:** *spring.*
    redit: some license is taken with the accent, which is here shifted to the second syllable to maintain the trochaic rhythm; in general, though not always, med. Lat. followed the same rules for placement of the stress accent as those applied in class. Lat.
199. **purpureo:** *purple, dark red.*
200. **aves: avis,** *bird.*
    edunt: edere, *to give forth.*
202. **revirescit: revirescere,** *to grow green again.*
    nemus: *grove.*
203. **amoenus:** *charming, delightful.*
208. **reficiant: reficere,** *to repair, restore, refresh.*
209. **virgines:** acc.
    assumant: assumere, *to take to oneself.*
211. **prata: pratum,** *meadow.*

Saint Gregory (Pope Gregory I)
Codex 2907, Italian manuscript
Biblioteca Augusta, Perugia, Italy

CARMINA BURANA

The Carmina Burana *("Songs of Beuern"), so-called from their preservation in a single 13th-century manuscript from the Bavarian monastery of Benedictbeuern, is a collection of 228 poems (many of them songs with musical notation) and six religious plays; the manuscript was rediscovered in 1803 and first published in 1847. The poems were composed by numerous, mostly anonymous wandering scholars and students (the so-called goliards) during the 12th century; the themes are variously satiric, amatory, and celebratory, including some carousing drinking songs; many are quite beautiful, others raucously humorous. Some were composed in German or Occitan (a Romance dialect of southern France), but most are in Latin and characterized by all the spontaneity and naturalness of a living language, as the goliards recorded both the joyous and the melancholy aspects of their student life. While some of the poems employ classical meters, including the dactylic hexameter, and are reminiscent of authors like Ovid, most (including all three selections below) are rhyming lyrics with accentual meters that have much in common with modern verse; the work gained renewed popularity in the 20th century through the selection made by the German composer Carl Orff for his oratorio and ballet, the* Carmina Burana, *produced in 1937 and available in numerous recordings today.*

Ver Redit

Carmina Burana 137. The return of spring and love; the metrical pattern is three trochees in lines 1, 3, 5, 7, and 8 of each stanza and two iambs in the rest; the rhyme scheme is ABABCDEED.

Ver redit optatum	205 Iuvenes, ut flores
Cum gaudio,	Accipiant
Flore decoratum	Et se per odores
Purpureo;	Reficiant,
200 Aves edunt cantus	Virgines assumant
Quam dulciter;	210 Alacriter
Revirescit nemus;	Et eant in prata
Cantus est amoenus	Floribus ornata
Totaliter.	Communiter.

214. **taberna:** *tavern.*
215. **humus:** i.e., **mors.**
216. **ludum:** here, *gaming, gambling;* likewise **ludunt** below.
    properamus: properare, *to hurry.*
217. **insudamus: insudare,** *to sweat at, sweat over.*
219. **nummus:** *coin, money;* with **pincerna** *(cupbearer, host)* a PERSONIFICATION.
220. **hoc est opus:** refers to **quid agatur in taberna,** *this is the business.*
    ut quaeratur . . . audiatur (221): *to be looked into (and) . . . to be . . . .*
224. **morantur: morari,** *to delay, loiter, spend time.*
225. **denudantur:** cp. our idiom "to lose your shirt."
226. **vestiuntur: vestire,** *to clothe;* i.e., they win their clothes, or the money to buy
    them.
227. **saccis: saccus,** *sack.*
    induuntur: induere, *to clothe, cover.*
229. **pro Baccho:** *to Bacchus, in the name of Bacchus.*
    sortem: sors, *lot, fortune;* with **mittunt,** *they cast their lot* (in life) or perhaps
    they gamble.
230. **nummata:** lit., *furnished with money, rich;* the meaning is somewhat obscure
    here (and cp. 261 below), perhaps *expensive,* with some f. noun like **men-
    sura** *(measure)* or **olla** *(jug)* understood.
231. **libertini: libertinus,** originally *freedman;* here = *carouser.*
232. **pro captivis:** in this and the next three stanzas the nouns and adjs. seem to
    be chosen with complete abandon (except for the needs of meter and
    rhyme) to reflect the riotous nature of the scene.
233. **ter . . . tredecies (243):** *three times, four times,* etc.; numeral advs.
234. **Christianis:** the second **i** is treated as a consonant (SYNIZESIS), so the word is
    trisyllabic ("Christyanis," and cp. our pronunciation of "Christian" as
    a disyllable).
235. **defunctis:** = **mortuis.**
236. **vanis:** *empty, vain, false, silly.*
239. **monachis: monachus,** *monk.*
241. **discordantibus: discordare,** *to disagree.*
244. **papa:** *pope.*

In Taberna

Carmina Burana 196. A lively drinking song, included in Orff's cantata; the rhyme scheme of each stanza is AABBCCDD, and the meter is four trochees per line except in 229–39, where the number of syllables is humorously increased to 9, 10, and 11.

In taberna quando sumus,
215   Non curamus quid sit humus,
Sed ad ludum properamus,
Cui semper insudamus.
Quid agatur in taberna,
Ubi nummus est pincerna,
220   Hoc est opus ut quaeratur,
Si quid loquar, audiatur.

Quidam ludunt, quidam bibunt,
Quidam indiscrete vivunt.
Sed in ludo qui morantur,
225   Ex his quidam denudantur,
Quidam ibi vestiuntur,
Quidam saccis induuntur.
Ibi nullus timet mortem,
Sed pro Baccho mittunt sortem:

230   Primo pro nummata vini—
Ex hac bibunt libertini;
Semel bibunt pro captivis,
Post haec bibunt ter pro vivis,
Quater pro Christianis cunctis,
235   Quinquies pro fidelibus defunctis,
Sexies pro sororibus vanis,
Septies pro militibus silvanis,

Octies pro fratribus perversis,
Novies pro monachis dispersis,
240   Decies pro navigantibus,
Undecies pro discordantibus,
Duodecies pro paentitentibus,
Tredecies pro iter agentibus.
Tam pro papa quam pro rege,
245   Bibunt omnes sine lege.

246. **hera . . . herus:** *mistress . . . master* (of a household); lines 246–53 parody a hymn by St. Thomas of Aquinas.
247. **clerus:** *clergy, cleric, scholar, student.*
252. **vagus:** *wandering, roaming.*
253. **rudis:** *rough, unskilled.*
    magus: *a learned man.*
254. **aegrotus:** *sick.*
256. **canus:** *gray-haired, old.*
257. **praesul:** *patron, bishop.*
    decanus: *deacon.*
259. **anus:** *old woman.*
262. **parum:** with **durant.**
    nummatae: here = **nummi,** or perhaps *expensive (cups)* (see note on 230).
263. **ubi:** the **i** elides before the initial **i** of the next word, as in class. Lat.
264. **meta:** lit., *turning post* = *limit.*
266. **rodunt: rodere,** lit., *to gnaw,* here = *to disparage, slander;* often there was animosity between the townspeople and the university students.
    gentes: here, *families,* or, with **omnes,** simply *everybody.*
268. **confundantur: confundere,** *to confound, ruin, destroy.*
269. **iustis . . . scribantur:** i.e., in the book of the righteous.
    non: for **ne,** a very common substitution in med. Lat.
271. **furibundus:** *furious, mad, insane.*
275. **ceu:** adv., *as, just as.*
    campi: campus, *field, plain.*
276. **res mundana:** here, *the mundane world.*
281. **Tartara:** n. pl., *Tartarus* (the region for sinners in Hell).

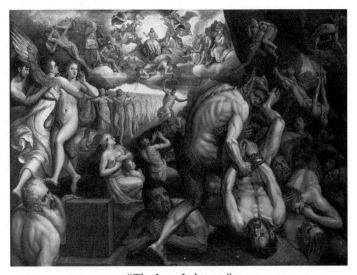

"The Last Judgment"
Frans Floris, 1565
Kunsthistorisches Museum, Vienna, Austria

Bibit hera, bibit herus,
Bibit miles, bibit clerus,
Bibit ille, bibit illa,
Bibit servus cum ancilla,
250 Bibit velox, bibit piger,
Bibit albus, bibit niger,
Bibit constans, bibit vagus,
Bibit rudis, bibit magus,

Bibit pauper et aegrotus,
255 Bibit exul et ignotus,
Bibit puer, bibit canus,
Bibit praesul et decanus,
Bibit soror, bibit frater,
Bibit anus, bibit mater,
260 Bibit ista, bibit ille,
Bibunt centum, bibunt mille.

Parum centum sex nummatae
Durant, ubi immoderate
Bibunt omnes sine meta,
265 Quamvis bibant mente laeta.
Sic nos rodunt omnes gentes,
Et sic erimus egentes.
Qui nos rodunt confundantur,
Et cum iustis non scribantur.

Vita Vana

Carmina Burana 24. On the vanity of our earthly lives; the rhyme scheme is
AABCCB, with lines 3 and 6 of each stanza ending in -a, and the meter is trochaic,
with two trochees in lines 1, 2, 4, and 5 of each stanza and 3 1/2 trochees (7 syllables)
in lines 3 and 6. The last stanza has an additional three lines repeating the metrical
pattern of the first three.

270 Iste mundus
Furibundus
Falsa praestat gaudia,
Quae defluunt
Et decurrunt
275 Ceu campi lilia.

Res mundana,
Vita vana
Vera tollit praemia,
Nam impellit
280 Et summergit
Animas in Tartara.

284. **patria:** here, *world,* i.e., on earth.
287. **quercus:** *oak tree.*
      folia: folium, *leaf.*
291. **frangit: frangere,** *to break,* here used intransitively.
      transit: a play on **transitoria.**
292. **velut:** adv., *as, just as.*
294. **conteramus: conterere,** *to wear away, destroy.*
295. **confringamus: confringere,** *to break to pieces, destroy.*
298. **electis:** *chosen ones.*
300. **gratulari:** here, *enjoy;* with **mereamur,** *let us earn the enjoyment of.*
302. **saecula: saeculum,** *century, generation, age.*
304. **caelitus:** med. Lat. adv., *from heaven.*
305. **radium:** *rod, spoke, ray.*
308. **lumen:** = **lux.**
311. **refrigerium:** lit., *cooling* = *refreshment, consolation.*
313. **aestu: aestus,** lit., *heat, boiling* = *turmoil, commotion* (of life).
      temperies: lit., *tempering* = *calmness, restraint.*
314. **fletu: fletus,** *weeping.*
316. **reple: replere,** *to fill up.*
      intima: here, *innermost parts.*
320. **innoxium:** *harmless, innocent.*
321. **lava: lavare,** *to wash.*
322. **riga: rigare,** *to moisten, water, irrigate.*
323. **saucium:** *wounded.*
325. **fove: fovere,** *to warm, cherish.*
326. **devium:** *off the road, gone astray.*
329. **septenarium:** *seven gifts;* the spiritual gifts mentioned in *Isaiah* 11.2, **sapientia, intellectus, consilium, fortitudo, scientia, pietas, timor Domini.**
330. **meritum:** *desert, benefit.*
331. **exitum: exitus,** *result, outcome.*

"Isaiah"
Raphael
16th century
S. Agostino
Rome, Italy

Quod videmus
Vel tacemus
In praesenti patria,
285 Dimittemus
Vel perdemus,
Quasi quercus folia.

Res carnalis,
Lex mortalis
290 Valde transitoria,
Frangit, transit
Velut umbra,
Quae non est corporea.

Conteramus,
295 Confringamus
Carnis desideria,
Et cum iustis
Et electis
Caelestia gaudia
300 Gratulari
Mereamur
Per aeterna saecula.

VENI, SANCTE SPIRITUS

One of the most famous of all medieval hymns, Veni, Sancte Spiritus *was composed in the late 12th century, possibly by the archbishop of Canterbury Stephen Langton. The meter is trochaic, with seven syllables per line; the rhyme scheme is AABCCB, with the third and sixth lines of each stanza ending in* -ium.

Veni, Sancte Spiritus,
Et emitte caelitus
305 Lucis tuae radium.
Veni, pater pauperum,
Veni, dator munerum,
Veni, lumen cordium.

Consolator optime,
310 Dulcis hospes animae,
Dulce refrigerium,
In labore requies,
In aestu temperies,
In fletu solacium.

315 O lux beatissima,
Reple cordis intima
Tuorum fidelium.
Sine tuo nomine

Nihil est in homine,
320 Nihil est innoxium.

Lava quod est sordidum,
Riga quod est aridum,
Sana quod est saucium;
Flecte quod est rigidum,
325 Fove quod est frigidum,
Rege quod est devium.

Da tuis fidelibus
In te confidentibus
Sacrum septenarium;
330 Da virtutis meritum,
Da salutis exitum,
Da perenne gaudium.

334.   **crucem: crux,** *cross.*
335.   **pendebat: pendere,** *to hang.*
336.   **gementem: gemere,** *to groan.*
337.   **contristantem:** *sorrowing.*
340.   **benedicta:** *blessed.*
341.   **unigeniti:** *the only-begotten.*
342.   **maerebat: maerere,** *to mourn, lament.*
344.   **incliti:** *famous.*
345.   **fleret: flere,** *to weep;* class. Lat. would use the pres. subjunct. here.
347.   **supplicio: supplicium,** *distress, suffering.*
348.   **non posset:** = *could fail (to).*
       contristari: contristare, *to sadden, afflict.*
349.   **contemplari:** *to contemplate;* the inf., which has in med. Lat. a much wider range of usage than in class. Lat., has a kind of explanatory function with **contristari,** *to be saddened to contemplate, in contemplating.*
353.   **flagellis: flagellum,** *scourge.*
       subditum: subdere, *to place under, subject (to).*
357.   **eia:** interj., here, *oh!*
       fons: *fountain.*
358.   **me sentire:** with **fac,** *make me feel;* the inf. phrase is a med. variant for the class. Lat. **fac ut ardeat** in the next line (and cp. the similar alternation of **fac** + inf./**fac** + subjunct. in 377–78 below).
359.   **lugeam: lugere,** *to mourn;* PURPOSE CL.

"What Is the Truth"
(Christ before Pilate)
Nikolai Ge
19th century
Tretyakov Gallery
Moscow, Russia

STABAT MATER

Another of the best known Christian hymns of the Middle Ages, and certainly the most sorrowful one, the Stabat Mater *can be dated to the 13th century, but its authorship is uncertain (though Pope Innocent III and St. Bonaventure have been suggested). The rhyme scheme is AABCCB, the same as that of the* Veni, Sancte Spiritus; *the metrical pattern is four trochees each in lines 1, 2, 4, and 5 of each stanza, and 3 1/2 each in lines 3 and 6.*

Stabat mater dolorosa
Iuxta crucem lacrimosa,
335 Dum pendebat filius,
Cuius animam gementem,
Contristantem et dolentem
 Pertransivit gladius.

O quam tristis et afflicta
340 Fuit illa benedicta
 Mater unigeniti,
Quae maerebat et dolebat
Et tremebat, dum videbat
 Nati poenas incliti.

345 Quis est homo qui non fleret,
Matrem Christi si videret
 In tanto supplicio?
Quis non posset contristari
Piam matrem contemplari
350 Dolentem cum filio?

Pro peccatis suae gentis
Vidit Iesum in tormentis
 Et flagellis subditum;
Vidit suum dulcem natum
355 Morientem, desolatum,
 Dum emisit spiritum.

Eia mater, fons amoris!
Me sentire vim doloris
 Fac, ut tecum lugeam.

360. **ardeat: ardere,** *to burn;* here in a NOUN CL. OF RESULT.

362. **sibi:** = **ei;** the reflexive pron. was often not used reflexively in med. Lat.

363. **agas:** JUSSIVE SUBJUNCT., paralleling the 2nd pers. imper. in the following verse.

364. **crucifixi:** *fixed to the cross, crucified.*
     fige: figere, *to affix, thrust, imprint on.*
     plagas: plaga, *blow, wound.*

366. **nati:** with **poenas.**

367. **dignati: dignari,** *to deign, think it appropriate.*

374. **planctu: planctus,** *lamentation.*

376. **non:** = **ne.**
     amara: *bitter, unkind.*

377. **plangere:** *to lament.*

378. **portem: portare,** *to carry, bear.*

379. **fac:** sc. **me.**
     consortem: *sharing in, a sharer in.*

380. **recolere:** *to cultivate again, feel afresh.*

382. **inebriari: inebriare,** *to intoxicate.*

383. **cruore: cruor,** *blood, gore.*

384. **inflammatus et accensus:** i.e., **passione Christi.**

385. **sim defensus:** in place of the simple, so-called "synthetic" vb. forms of class. Lat. (here, **defendar**), med. Lat. tended to use **esse** + a partic., the so-called "analytical forms" common in Eng. as well as the Romance languages.

386. **in die:** for the prep., see note on **per . . . viam** (92).

388. **praemuniri: praemunire,** *to fortify.*

389. **confoveri: confovere,** *to warm, foster.*

"The Crucifixion of Christ"
Peter Paul Rubens
1620
Koninklijk Museum voor Schone Kunsten
Antwerp, Belgium

360 Fac ut ardeat cor meum
     In amando Christum Deum,
          Ut sibi complaceam.

     Sancta mater, istud agas—
     Crucifixi fige plagas
365   Cordi meo valide;
     Tui nati vulnerati,
     Tam dignati pro me pati,
          Poenas mecum divide.

     Fac me vere tecum flere,
370 Crucifixo condolere,
          Donec ego vixero;
     Iuxta crucem tecum stare,
     Meque tibi sociare
          In planctu desidero.

375 Virgo virginum praeclara,
     Mihi iam non sis amara,
          Fac me tecum plangere;
     Fac ut portem Christi mortem,
     Passionis fac consortem
380   Et plagas recolere.

     Fac me plagis vulnerari,
     Cruce hac inebriari
          Et cruore filii;
     Inflammatus et accensus,
385 Per te, Virgo, sim defensus
          In die iudicii.

     Fac me cruce custodiri,
     Morte Christi praemuniri,
          Confoveri gratia.
390 Quando corpus morietur,
     Fac ut animae donetur
          Paradisi gloria.

394.   **solvet: solvere,** *to loosen, release, dissolve.*
      saeclum: = **saeculum;** here, *the world.*
      favilla: *ashes.*
395.   **teste: testis,** *witness.*
      David: abl. with **teste,** ABL. ABS.; Hebrew names are commonly not declined
          in Lat. texts. David, the second king of Israel, here stands for the Scrip-
          tures which foretold the Day of Judgment.
      Sibylla: *the Sibyl,* a prophetic priestess in classical myth, who here represents
          pagan lore, in which there was also a tradition about the final destruc-
          tion of the world by fire.
396.   **est futurus:** another analytical form (see note on 385), = **erit.**
398.   **stricte:** adv., *severely.*
      discussurus: discutere, *to shatter, scatter, destroy.*
399.   **tuba:** *trumpet.*
402.   **stupebit: stupere,** *to be amazed, gaze at in wonder.*
407.   **iudicetur:** as a rel. adv., **unde** can introduce, as here, a REL. CL. OF PURPOSE.
410.   **inultum:** *unavenged.*

The Cumaean Sibyl, Sistine Chapel
Michelangelo, 1536–41
Vatican Palace, Vatican State

DIES IRAE

This best known and most powerful of the medieval hymns is attributed to the Italian Franciscan Thomas of Celano, who lived in the early 13th century and also wrote a biography of his friend St. Thomas of Assisi and a treatise on the miracles of St. Francis. Cast in the form of a prayer of a person hoping to escape eternal damnation on the "Day of Wrath," the judgment day foretold in the New Testament, the hymn was incorporated as a sequence to the requiem mass and appears in arrangements of the requiem by Mozart, Berlioz, Verdi, and others, as well as in such meditations on death as Rachmaninoff's Isle of the Dead *and Liszt's* Dante Symphony. *The meter is trochaic, with eight syllables per line, except for the two closing verses, which have seven; and the three verses of each stanza have two-syllable end-line rhyme, except the final stanzas, which have an AABB pattern, and the two irregular closing verses. In combination, the hymn's rhyme and rhythms have an almost hypnotic effect.*

      Dies irae, dies illa
      Solvet saeclum in favilla,
395   Teste David cum Sibylla.

      Quantus tremor est futurus,
      Quando iudex est venturus,
      Cuncta stricte discussurus!

      Tuba, mirum spargens sonum
400   Per sepulcra regionum,
      Coget omnes ante thronum.

      Mors stupebit et natura,
      Cum resurget creatura
      Iudicanti responsura.

405   Liber scriptus proferetur,
      In quo totum continetur,
      Unde mundus iudicetur.

      Iudex ergo cum sedebit,
      Quidquid latet apparebit:
410   Nil inultum remanebit.

      Quid sum miser tunc dicturus,
      Quem patronum rogaturus,
      Cum vix iustus sit securus?

414. **tremendae:** lit., *to be trembled at* = *terrifying, dreadful.*
417. **recordare: recordari,** *to remember.*
418. **quod sum:** IND. STATE.
    viae: i.e., his journey to earth.
420. **lassus:** *weary, exhausted.*
421. **redemisti: redimere,** *to buy back, ransom, redeem;* sc. **me.**
422. **cassus:** *useless, futile.*
423. **ultionis: ultio,** *punishment.*
426. **ingemisco: ingemiscere,** *to groan.*
    reus: *defendant, accused.*
427. **rubet: rubere,** *to be red, blush.*
429. **Mariam:** *Mary Magdalene,* a woman in the Bible cleansed by Jesus of her
    seven demons.
430. **latronem: latro,** *robber;* the robber promised salvation by Jesus, when both
    were on the cross.
433. **bonus:** for **bone,** voc.
434. **cremer: cremare,** *to consume by fire.*
436. **haedis: haedus,** *goat.*
437. **statuens: statuere,** *to put, place, set up;* sc. **me.**
438. **confutatis: confutare,** *to check, repress.*
    maledictis: *accursed.*
439. **addictis: addicere,** *to surrender, doom to.*
441. **acclinis:** *bent, bowed down.*
442. **contritum: conterere,** *to wear out, consume, destroy;* sc. **est.**

"The Penitant Magdalene"
Georges de La Tour
17th century
Louvre
Paris, France

Rex tremendae maiestatis,
415　Qui salvandos salvas gratis,
Salva me, fons pietatis.

Recordare, Iesu pie,
Quod sum causa tuae viae,
Ne me perdas illa die.

420　Quaerens me, sedisti lassus;
Redemisti, crucem passus;
Tantus labor non sit cassus.

Iustae iudex ultionis,
Donum fac remissionis
425　Ante diem rationis.

Ingemisco tamquam reus;
Culpa rubet vultus meus;
Supplicanti parce, Deus.

Qui Mariam absolvisti
430　Et latronem exaudisti,
Mihi quoque spem dedisti.

Preces meae non sunt dignae,
Sed tu bonus fac benigne,
Ne perenni cremer igni.

435　Inter oves locum praesta
Et ab haedis me sequestra,
Statuens in parte dextra.

Confutatis maledictis,
Flammis acribus addictis,
440　Voca me cum benedictis.

Oro supplex et acclinis;
Cor contritum quasi cinis;
Gere curam mei finis.

444. **lacrimosa:** sc. **erit.**
446. **reus:** *as a defendant, as a sinner.*
447. **huic:** pronounced and scanned as a disyllable.

"The Last Judgment" triptych
Detail from right panel: fall of the damned
Hans Memling, 15th century
Pomorskie Museum, Gdansk, Poland

Lacrimosa dies illa,
445   Qua resurget ex favilla
Iudicandus homo reus:
Huic ergo parce, Deus.

Pie Iesu Domine,
Dona eis requiem.

"The Last Judgment"
Detail: the archangel Michael weighing the souls
Roger van der Weyden, 1434
Hotel-Dieu, Beaune, France

Vocabulary

An asterisk (*) preceding an entry marks a word that occurs five or more times in the book; such words should be memorized. As an aid to learning the meanings of compound words, verbs in particular, a hyphen has generally been used to separate the prefix from the root word; e.g., the entry *ab-eō* is employed for *abeō = ab + eō*, "to go away from." Words adequately defined in the text, including the occasional Greek word and many proper nouns, are not included in the following list. The abbreviations ML and EL are employed, respectively, for Medieval Latin and Ecclesiastical Latin; compar. and superl. are used for comparative and superlative degrees; and (1) indicates a regular first conjugation verb.

A

* **ā** *or* **ab (abs),** *prep.* + *abl.,* from, away from; by (*agent*); on (the side of); **ā dextrā parte,** on the right
ab-aliēnō (1), transfer to another, sell
abbātissa, -ae, *f.,* abbess (*ML*)
ab-dicō (1), renounce; resign, abdicate
ab-dō, -ere, -didī, -ditum, put away; hide
* **ab-eō, -īre, -iī, -itum,** go away, depart
ab-iciō, -ere, -iēcī, -iectum, throw away *or* down, abandon
ab-lātum: *see* **auferō**

ab-nuō, -ere, -nuī, -nūtum, deny, refuse
* **Abraham,** *indecl., and* **Abraham, -ae,** *m., the Hebrew patriarch*
ab-ripiō, -ere, -ripuī, -reptum, snatch away, hurry away
ab-rogō (1), repeal, abrogate, take away
ab-rumpō, -rumpere, -rūpī, -ruptum, break off, throw off
abs-conditus, -a, -um, concealed, hidden
ab-sēns, *gen.* **-sentis,** absent, remote
ab-solvō, -ere, -solvī, -solūtum, set free, release; absolve, acquit; complete

abs-tinentia, -ae, *f.,* abstinence

abs-tineō, -ere, -tinuī, -tentum, abstain, refrain

abstulī, *perf. of* **auferō**

* **ab-sum, -esse, ā-fuī, ā-futūrus,** be away, be absent

ab-sūmō, -ere, -sūmpsī, -sūmptum, consume, waste away

abundantia, -ae, *f.,* abundance

ab-undō (1), overflow; have an abundance of, abound in (+ *abl.*)

abyssus, -i, *m.,* bottomless pit, abyss (*EL*)

* **ac = atque**

* **ac-cēdō, -ere, -cessī, -cessum,** go to, approach, be added

* **ac-cendō, -ere, -cendī, -cēnsum,** kindle, set on fire, light, stir up, incite

ac-cidō, -ere, -cidī, fall; happen, take place; **accidit,** *impers.,* it happens

ac-cingō, -ere, -cinxī, -cinctum, gird on, arm; **sē accingere** *or passive used reflexively,* gird oneself

ac-ciō (4), summon, send for

* **ac-cipiō, -ere, -cēpī, -ceptum,** receive, accept; hear, learn

ac-clīnis, -e, leaning, inclined, bent

acclīvis, -e, ascending, sloping upward

ac-commodātus, -a, -um, adapted, fit, suitable

ac-commodō (1), adapt, adjust

ac-cubō (1), recline at table

ac-cūrātē, *adv. of* **accūrātus**

ac-cūrātus, -a, -um, careful, exact, accurate

ac-currō, -ere, -currī, -cursum, run to, hurry to

accūsātiō, -ōnis, *f.* accusation, indictment

accūsātor, -ōris, *m.,* accuser

accūsō (1), accuse; blame, reproach

ācer, ācris, ācre, sharp, keen, fierce, severe

* **acerbus, -a, -um,** bitter, harsh, cruel; *adv.* **acerbē**

acētum, -ī, *n.,* sour wine, vinegar

* **aciēs, -ēī,** *f.,* battle-line, battle

acquiēscō, -ere, -quiēvī, -quiētum, become quiet, have peace

ācriter, *adv. of* **ācer**

* **āctiō, -ōnis,** *f.,* a doing, action; action *or* legal process in court

āctor, -ōris, *m., lit.* doer, performer; prosecutor; actor

actus, -ūs, *m.,* action, procedure

acūtus, -a, -um, sharp, keen, intelligent; crafty

* **ad,** *prep.* + *acc.,* to, up to, near to, for the purpose of; *as adv. w. numerals,* about

ad-aequō (1), make equal, compare

ad-dīcō, -ere, -dīxī, -dictum, *lit.* assent; award; surrender; doom to

ad-discō, -ere, -didicī, learn in addition, learn something new

* **ad-dō, -ere, -didī, -ditum,** add

* **ad-dūcō, -ere, -dūxī, -ductum,** lead to, bring in *or* to; induce

* **ad-eō,** *adv., lit.* to this; to such a degree *or* extent, so, even

* **ad-eō, -īre, -iī, -itum,** go *or* come to, approach, visit; undertake, undergo

* **ad-ferō, -ferre, at-tulī, ad-lātum (ad-ferō),** bring (to), convey, cause; report; **manūs adferre,** lay hands on, do violence to

ad-ficiō, -ere, -fēcī, -fectum,
 influence, affect, treat, afflict
ad-fingō, -ere, -finxī, -fictum,
 fashion, invent
ad-firmō (1), strengthen, support;
 assert
ad-flictiō, -ōnis, *f.,* suffering, torment
ad-fligō, -ere, -flīxī, -flīctum, strike
 against, dash down, shatter, afflict
ad-gredior: *see* **aggredior**
ad-haereō, -ēre, -haesī, -haesum,
 cling to, stick to
ad-haerēscō, -ere, -haesī, haesum,
 stick to, cling to
* **ad-hibeō, -ēre, -hibuī, -itum,** hold to,
 apply, employ, show
ad-hortor, -ārī, -hortātus sum, urge,
 exhort, encourage
* **adhūc,** *adv.,* up to this time, still,
 yet
ad-iciō, -ere, -iēcī, -iectum, direct to;
 add
ad-imō, -ere, -ēmī, -ēmptum, take
 away
adipiscor, -ī, adeptus sum, win,
 obtain, acquire
ad-itus, -ūs, *m.,* approach, entrance
ad-iūdicō (1), award, adjudicate,
 assign
adiūmentum, -ī, *n.,* help, assistance
ad-iungō, -ere, -iūnxī, -iūnctum, join
 to, attach, associate
adiūtor, -ōris, *m.,* helper, assistant
adiūtrīx, -īcis, *f.,* (female) helper,
 assistant
* **ad-iuvō, -āre, -iūvī, -iūtum,** help,
 assist, support
ad-liciō, -ere, -lexī, -lectum, allure,
 draw to oneself, entice
ad-ligō (1), bind

ad-loquor, -ī, -locūtus sum, speak to,
 address
ad-lūdō, -ere, -lūsī, -lūsum, jest at,
 play with; play on (a word)
adluviēs, -ēī, *f.,* overflow, pool,
 floodwater
adminiculum, -ī, *n.,* prop (for vines),
 support
ad-mīrābilis, -e, wonderful; strange;
 admirable
admīrātiō, -ōnis, *f.,* wonder,
 amazement, admiration
ad-mīror, -ārī, -ātus sum, wonder at,
 admire
ad-mittō, -ere, -mīsī, -missum, admit;
 commit (a crime)
ad-moveō, -ēre, -mōvī, -mōtum, bring
 up, apply
ad-nectō, -ere, -nexuī, -nexum, bind,
 connect
ad-nītor, -ī, -nīsus (-nīxus) sum, lean
 on, strive toward, exert oneself
ad-notō (1), note down, mark
ad-nuō, -ere, -nuī, -nūtum, nod
 assent, agree
ad-operiō, -īre, -operuī, -opertum,
 cover up
ad-ōrō (1), address, entreat;
 reverence, worship
adp-: *see* **app-**
ad-quiēscō, -ere, -quiēvī, -quiētum,
 become quiet, rest, find comfort
adr-: *see under* **arr-**
ad-sentātor, -ōris, *m.,* flatterer, yes-
 man
ad-sentiō, -īre, -sēnsī, -sēnsum *and as*
 deponent vb. **ad-sentior, -īrī, -**
 sēnsus sum, assent to, agree with
ad-sequor, -sequī, -secūtus sum,
 overtake, reach, attain, gain

ad-servō (1), preserve, keep, watch

adsp-: *see* **asp-**

ad-stō, -āre, -stitī, stand near *or* by

ad-stringō, -ere, -strīnxī, -strictum, bind, oblige

ad-suēscō, -ere, suēvī, -suētum, become accustomed; **adsuētus, -a, -um,** customary, usual; accustomed to

* **ad-sum, -esse, ad-fuī, ad-futūrum,** be near, be present; assist

ad-sumō, -ere, -sūmpsī, -sūmptum, take to oneself, take

ad-surgō, -ere, -surrēxī, -surrēctum, rise up, stand up

adt-: *see* **att-**

* **adulēscēns,** *gen.* **-entis,** young; *as a noun, m./f.,* a young man (*or* woman)

adūlō (1), fawn; *in pass.,* be fawned upon

adūlor, -ārī, -ātus sum, fawn (on), flatter, cringe (before)

adulter, -erī, *m.,* adulterer

adulterium, -ī, *n.,* adultery

ad-ūrō, -ere, -ussī, -ustum, set on fire, scorch

ad-vena, -ae, *m.,* stranger, foreigner

* **ad-veniō, -īre, -vēnī, -ventum,** come to, arrive

* **ad-ventus, -ūs,** *m.,* arrival

adversārius, -a, -um, opposed, hostile; **adversārius, -ī,** *m.,* opponent, adversary

* **adversus,** *prep. + acc. and adv.,* opposite, against; towards

* **ad-versus, -a, -um,** *lit.* turned toward; opposed, hostile, unfavorable

ad-vertō, -vertere, -vertī, -versum, turn toward, direct; draw near

ad-vocātiō, -ōnis, *f.,* assistance at court, legal advice

ad-volō (1), fly (to), hasten

* **aedēs, -is,** *f.,* chamber; sanctuary, temple; *pl.* house, dwelling

aedificium, -ī, *n.,* building, edifice

aedificō (1), build

aedīlis, -is, *m.,* aedile, superintendent of public works and entertainment

aeger, -gra, -grum, sick

aegrē, *adv., lit.* painfully; with difficulty, hardly, scarcely; *superl.* **aegerrimē**

aegritūdō, -dinis, *f.,* sickness; grief, sorrow

aegrōtus, -a, -um, sick

Aegyptus, -ī, *f.,* Egypt

Aemilius, -ī, *m.,* a Roman nomen

aēneus, -a, -um, of bronze

aequābilitās, -tātis, *f.,* uniformity, impartiality, evenness, serenity

aequālis, -e, equal; coeval

aequiperō (1), to equal

aequitās, -tātis, *f.,* fairness, impartiality, justice

* **aequō** (1), make equal, compare, equal; **sē aequāre,** become equal

aequor, -oris, *n.,* level surface, sea

* **aequus, -a, -um,** equal, level, calm; fair, just; **aequē,** *adv.,* equally; **aequē ac, ac sī,** *etc.,* equally with, just as

āēr, āëris (*acc.* **āëra**), *m.,* air

aerārium, -ī, *n.,* public treasury *or* funds

aerumna, -ae, *f.,* hardship

aerumnōsus, -a, -um, full of hardship, distressed, troubled

Aesculāpius, -ī, *m., son of Apollo*

aestās, -tātis, *f.,* summer

aestimō (1), estimate, judge

aestuō (1), boil, burn, blaze

aestus, -ūs, *m.,* a boiling, heat, turmoil

* **aetās, -tātis,** *f.,* time of life, age

aeternitās, -tātis, *f.,* eternity, immortality

aeternus, -a, -um, eternal, everlasting; **in aeternum,** forever

Aethiopia, -ae, *f., a country south of Egypt*

aethēr, -eris (*acc.* **aethera**), *m.,* the upper air, sky

Āff-: *see* **adf-**

Africa, -ae, *f.,* Africa, *espec. the area of Carthage and her possessions*

Agamemnon, -nonis, *m., commander-in-chief of the Greek forces against Troy*

Agathoclēs, -is, *m., tyrant and later king of Syracuse* 317−289 B.C.

* **ager, agrī,** *m.,* field, land; district

ag-gredior, -ī, -gressus sum, approach, attack; begin, undertake, try

agitātiō, -ōnis, *f.,* motion, movement, play, agitation, activity

agitō (1), trouble, vex

* **agmen, -minis,** *n.,* column, line of march

a-gnōscō, -ere, -gnōvī, -gnitum, recognize, observe, perceive

* **agō, -ere, ēgī, actum,** drive, lead, urge, do, act; **rēs agitur,** is at stake; **grātiās agō,** thank; **vītam agō,** lead *or* spend one's life

agrestis, -e, of the fields, rustic; **agrestis, -is,** *m.,* a countryman, a peasant

* **aiō,** *defective vb. chiefly in pres. and*

impf. indic., say; *among the most common forms are* **ais, ait, aiunt**

āla, -ae, *f.,* wing

alacer, -cris, -cre, quick, eager; cheerful, glad

alacritās, -tātis, *f.,* quickness, eagerness

alacriter, *adv. of* **alacer**

* **Albānus, -a, -um,** Alban, *referring to Alba Longa, the old Latin town on the Alban Mountain south of Rome*

albus, -a, -um, white; pale

āles, -itis, *m./f.,* winged creature, bird

aliās, *adv.,* at another time; elsewhere; **aliās . . . aliās,** at one time . . . at another

alibī, *adv.,* elsewhere, at another place

aliēnō (1), take away, transfer, remove

* **aliēnus, -a, -um,** belonging to another, strange, foreign, alien, hostile, unsuitable

alimentum, -ī, *n.,* food, nourishment

aliō, *adv.,* to another place, elsewhere

aliquam-diū, *adv.,* for some time

* **aliquandō,** *adv.,* at some *or* any time, ever, sometimes; at last, finally

aliquantum, *adv.,* somewhat

aliquantus, -a, -um, some, considerable; **aliquantum, -ī,** *n.,* a considerable amount, a good deal

aliquī, aliqua, aliquod, *indef. adj.,* some, any

* **aliquis, -qua, -quid,** *indef. pron.,* someone *or* somebody, something, anyone, anything

* **aliquot,** *indecl. adj.,* several, some

* **alius, alia, aliud,** other, another;
    aliī . . . aliī, some . . . others

all-: *see* **adl-**

allēlūia, *interjection from the Hebrew
    meaning* praise ye Jehovah (*EL*)

alō, -ere, aluī, alitum (altum),
    nourish, bring up, rear

Alpēs, -ium, *f. pl.,* the Alps

Alpīnus, -a, -um, Alpine

altāria, -ium, *n. pl.,* altar

* **alter, -era, -erum,** one of two, the
    other (of two), second

altercātiō, -ōnis, *f.,* dispute, quarrel

altitūdō, -dinis, *f.,* height

altor, -ōris, *m.,* foster father

altus, -a, -um, high, deep; **altum, -ī,**
    n., height, heaven; depth, the
    deep, the sea; *adv.* **altē**

alumnus, -ī, *m.,* foster son, pupil

alveus, -ī, *m.,* trough, tub

amābilis, -e, lovable

amāns, *gen.* **-antis,** loving, friendly;
    amāns, -antis, *m./f.,* a loving
    person, lover

amārus, -a, -um, bitter

ambāgēs, -um, *f. pl.,* ambiguous
    words, riddles

ambitus, -ūs, *m.,* a going around; an
    (illegal) canvassing for votes,
    bribery

* **ambō, -ae, -ō,** both

ambulō (1), walk about

amb-ūrō, -ere, -ussī, -ustum, scorch;
    burn up, consume

ā-mēns, *gen.* **-mentis,** out of one's
    mind, mad

āmentia, -ae, *f.,* madness, folly

* **amīcitia, -ae,** *f.,* friendship

amictus, -ūs, *m.,* robe, veil

* **amīcus, -a, -um,** friendly, kind;
    amīcus, -ī, *m.,* a friend

ā-missiō, -ōnis, *f.,* loss

* **ā-mittō, -ere, -mīsī, -missum,** send
    away = let go, lose

amnis, -is, *m.,* stream, river, current

* **amō** (1), love, like; admire, approve

amoenitās, -tātis, *f.,* pleasantness,
    charm

amoenus, -a, -um, pleasant, lovely,
    charming

* **amor, -ōris,** *m.,* love, affection;
    passion

ā-moveō, -ēre, -mōvī, -mōtum, move
    away, withdraw

amplector, -ī, -plexus sum, embrace

amplitūdō, -dinis, *f.,* size, breadth

amplus, -a, -um, large, spacious,
    ample, splendid

Amūlius, -ī, *m., brother of Numitor
    and usurper of his throne*

* **an,** *conj., in double questions* **utrum
    . . . an,** whether . . . or; *in indirect
    simple questions,* whether; **haud
    sciō an, nesciō an,** I do not know
    whether = I am inclined to think,
    probably, perhaps

anceps, *gen.* **-cipitis,** *lit.* with two
    heads; uncertain, doubtful; on
    both sides

* **ancilla, -ae,** *f.,* maidservant

ānfrāctus, -ūs, *m.,* turn, bend

angelicus, -a, -um, of an angel,
    angelic

angelus, -ī, *m.,* messenger, angel (*EL*)

Anglī, -ōrum, *m. pl.,* the Angles

anguis, -is, *m./f.,* snake

angustiae, -ārum, *f. pl.,* the narrows,
    defile, strait; distress, straits

* **angustus, -a, -um,** narrow; base,
    mean

anhēlitus, -ūs, *m.,* gasping, panting,
    breathing

* **anima, -ae,** *f.,* breath; soul, principle of life, life; soul of the dead, ghost
* **anim-advertō, -ere, -vertī, -versum,** give attention to, notice, observe, consider; punish

  animal, -ālis, *n.,* living creature, animal

  animāns, -antis, *m./f.,* a living being, creature, animal (= **animal**)
* **animus, -ī,** *m.,* soul, spirit, courage, mind; **in animō habēre** *or* **esse,** to be resolved

  ann- *in compounds: see* **adn-**

  annālis, -e, annual; **annālēs, -ium,** *m. pl.,* yearly records, annals

  anniversārius, -a, -um, annual
* **annus, -ī,** *m.,* year

  an-quīrō, -ere, -quīsīvī, -quīsītum, seek, search after
* **ante,** *adv. and prep.* + *acc.: adv.,* forward, previously, before, ago; *prep.,* before (*in time and space*), in front of
* **anteā,** *adv.,* before, formerly

  ante-cellō, -ere, excel, surpass

  ante-cessiō, -ōnis, *f.,* antecedent, cause

  ante-eō, -īre, -iī, -itum, go before, precede; excel

  ante-gredior, -ī, -gressus sum, go before

  ante-pōnō, -ere, -posuī, -positum, place before; prefer

  antequam, *conj.,* before

  antīquitās, -tātis, *f.,* antiquity, men of old, the ancients
* **antīquus, -a, -um,** old-time, ancient, antique

  Antium, -ī, *n.,* Antium (*modern Anzio*)

  Antōnius, -ī, *m.,* Antony

  antrum, -ī, *n.,* cave
* **ānulus, -ī,** *m.,* seal ring

  anus, -ūs, *f.,* old woman
* **aper, aprī,** *m.,* wild boar
* **aperiō, -īre, aperuī, apertum,** open, uncover, reveal

  apertē, *adv.,* openly

  apertus, -a, -um, open, uncovered; clear, evident; **apertum, -ī,** *n.,* an open space

  Apollō, -inis, *m.,* Apollo

  apostolicus, -a, -um, apostolic (*ML*)

  ap-parātus, -a, -um, elaborate, magnificent, sumptuous

  ap-parātus, -ūs, *m.,* preparation, splendor, magnificence
* **ap-pāreō, -ēre, -uī, -itum,** be visible, appear
* **appellō** (1), call, name, address

  ap-pendō, -ere, -pendī, -pēnsum, weigh out

  Appennīnus, -ī, *m.,* the Appennines, *a mountain range extending through the length of Italy*

  appetenter, *adv.,* graspingly, greedily

  ap-petītiō, -ōnis, *f.,* desire
* **ap-petītus, -ūs,** *m.,* longing, desire
* **ap-petō, -ere, -petīvī, -petītum,** strive after, desire, seek

  Appius, -a, -um, Appian; **Via Appia,** the Appian Way, *first of the great Roman roads,* **regīna viārum,** *begun by Appius Claudius, censor in* 312 B.C., *to connect Rome and Capua and ultimately extended to Brundisium*

  ap-plicātiō, -ōnis, *f.,* attachment, inclination

  ap-portō (1), carry, bring to

  ap-positus, -a, -um, suitable, appropriate

ap-probō (1), approve

ap-propinquō (1), approach, draw near, be at hand

ap-propiō (1) = **appropinquō** (*EL*)

aprīcus, -a, -um, sunny, warm

* **aptō** (1), prepare, make ready, adjust

* **aptus, -a, -um,** suitable, appropriate, fit

* **apud,** *prep* + *acc.,* among; at; at the house of, in the presence of, with

* **aqua, -ae,** *f.,* water

aquilō, -ōnis, *m.,* north wind; north

arātor, -ōris, *m.,* plowman, farmer, tenant

arbiter, -trī, *m.,* arbiter, judge

arbitrātus, -ūs, *m.,* decision, discretion, choice, pleasure

arbitrium, -ī, *n.,* judgment; choice, power, opportunity

* **arbitror, -ārī, -ātus sum,** judge, think, believe

* **arbor, -oris,** *f.,* tree

arboreus, -a, -um, of a tree, arboreal

arceō, -ēre, -uī, shut in, keep away, restrain, debar, prevent

arcessō, -ere, -īvī, -ītum, call, summon, derive, obtain

Archimēdēs, -is, *m., famous Greek scientist, killed at the capture of Syracuse in* 212 B.C.

Ardea, -ae, *f.,* a town in Latium

* **ārdeō, -ēre, ārsī, ārsum,** be on fire, burn, blaze; be inflamed *or* aroused.

arduus, -a, -um, steep, high, lofty, difficult

area, -ae, *f.,* open space, courtyard, public square

ārēns, *gen.* **-entis,** dried up, parched

Arethūsa, -ae, *f., name of a spring at Syracuse*

argentāria, -ae, *f.,* banker's shop *or* business

argentum, -ī, *n.,* silver; money

argumentum, -ī, *n.,* proof, argument; subject, story, theme

arguō, -ere, -uī, -ūtum, make clear, show, prove

aridus, -a, -um, dry, parched, arid

arista, -ae, *f.,* ear of grain

Aristaeus, -ī, *m., a son of Apollo*

Aristīdēs, -is, *m., Athenian statesman of the 5th cent.* B.C.

* **arma, -ōrum,** *n. pl.,* weapons, arms, armor

armātūra, -ae, *f.,* armor, equipment; a branch of military service

armātus, -a, -um, armed

* **armō** (1), to arm

ar-ripiō, -ere, -ripuī, -reptum, snatch, catch, lay hold of

arrogantia, -ae, *f.,* arrogance, pride

* **ars, artis,** *f.,* art, skill, occupation; **artēs,** *pl.,* liberal arts

artificium, -ī, *n.,* skill; cunning, scheme

arvum, -ī, *n.,* field

arx, arcis, *f.,* citadel, stronghold

ascendō, -ere, scendī, -scēnsum, go up, mount

ascēnsus, -ūs, *m.,* climbing up, ascent

Asia, -ae, *f.,* Asia, *the Roman province of Asia Minor*

asinus, -ī, *m.,* ass

aspectus, -ūs, *m.,* appearance, aspect

aspergō, -inis, *f.,* spray, sprinkling

aspernor, -ārī, -ātus sum, despise, reject

* **a-spiciō, -ere, -spexī, -spectum,** look at, see

as-portō (1), carry away

asse-: *see under* **adse-**

assu-: *see under* **adsu-**

ast-: *see under* **adst-**

* **at,** *conj.,* but, yet, on the other hand (*an emotional, or surprise, adversative as compared with* **sed,** *which is rather a factual adversative*)

āter, ātra, ātrum, black, dark; gloomy

Athēnae, -ārum, *f. pl.,* Athens

Athēniēnsis, -e, Athenian; **Athēniēnsēs, -ium,** *m. pl.,* the Athenians

* **atque** *or* **ac,** *conj.,* and, and also, and even

at-quī, *conj.,* yet, however; now

atrōciter, *adv.,* savagely, fiercely, cruelly

atrōx, *gen.* **-ōcis,** cruel, fierce, harsh

at-tamen, *conj.,* but yet

at-tendō, -ere, -tendī, -tentum, *lit.* stretch to; **animum attendere,** direct attention to, notice, attend to.

Atticus -ī, *m.,* Titus Pomponius Atticus, *business man and literary figure, long resident of Athens, Cicero's close friend*

at-tineō, -ēre, -tinuī, -tentum, pertain to, concern

* **at-tingō (ad-tangō), -ere, -tigī, -tāctum,** touch, reach, be related to

at-tollō, -ere, raise *or* lift up

at-tonitus, -a, -um, thunderstruck, astonished

at-tulī: *see* **ad-ferō**

* **auctor, -ōris,** *m.,* author, leader, supporter, originator, founder, instigator

* **auctōritās, -tātis,** *f.,* authority, power, influence, decision, bidding; official record

* **audācia, -ae,** *f.,* daring, insolence

audāx, *gen.* **-ācis,** bold, daring

* **audeō, -ēre, ausus sum,** dare

* **audiō** (4), hear, learn; listen to, obey; examine a case in court

audītus, -ūs, *m.,* hearing

* **au-ferō, -ferre, ab-stulī, ab-lātum,** carry away *or* off, remove, steal; destroy

au-fugiō, -ere, -fūgī, flee away, escape

* **augeō, -ēre, auxī, auctum,** increase, enlarge

augurium, -ī, *n.,* augury, interpretation of omens; omen

auguror, -ārī, -ātus sum, *lit.* prophesy by augury; conjecture, surmise

augustus, -a, -um, revered, august

* **aura, -ae,** *f.,* air, breeze, wind

* **aureus, -a, -um,** of gold, golden

* **auris, -is,** *f.,* ear

aurōra, -ae, *f.,* dawn; **Aurōra,** *goddess of the dawn*

* **aurum, -ī,** *n.,* gold

auspicium, -ī, *n.,* divination from omens given by birds, auspices; omen

* **aut,** *conj.,* or; **aut . . . aut,** either . . . or

* **autem,** *postpositive conj.,* however; moreover

auxilium, -ī, *n.,* aid, assistance
avāritia, -ae, *f.,* greed, avarice
avārus, -a, -um, greedy, avaricious;
    adv. **avārē**
avēna, -ae, *f.,* wild oats; shepherd's
    pipe
Aventīnum, -ī, *n.,* Aventine Hill *in*
    Rome
aveō, -ēre, desire
Avernus, -a, -um, of Avernus, *the*
    infernal regions, or Hades
ā-vertō, -ere, -vertī, -versum, turn
    away
avidus, -a, -um, eager, desirous,
    longing; greedy, avaricious
avis, -is, *f.,* bird; omen
avītus, -a, -um, ancestral, hereditary
avunculus, -ī, *m.,* uncle (*on mother's*
    side)

B

Babylōnius, -a, -um, Babylonian
Baccha, -ae, *f.,* a Bacchante, female
    worshipper of Bacchus
Bacchus, -ī, *m., god of fertility, wine,*
    and literary inspiration
baculum, -ī, *n.,* staff
balineum, -ī, *n.,* bath
barbarus, -a, -um, foreign,
    barbarian, uncivilized
basis, -is, *f.,* pedestal, base
* **beātus, -a, -um,** happy, fortunate,
    prosperous; blessed; *adv.* **beātē**
Bēlides, -um, *f. pl.,* the Danaïdes,
    grand-daughters of Belus,
    condemned in Tartarus to draw
    water eternally
bellicus, -a, -um, of war, belonging
    to war
* **bellum, -ī,** *n.,* war

bēlua, -ae, *f.,* beast
* **bene,** *adv.,* well, rightly; quite,
    thoroughly; *compar.* **melius;** *superl.*
    optimē
bene-dīcō, -ere, -dīxī, -dictum, speak
    well of, praise; bless (*EL*)
benedictus, -a, -um, blessed (*EL*)
beneficentia, -ae, *f.,* beneficence,
    charity
beneficium, -ī, *n.,* kindness, favor
* **bene-(beni)volentia, -ae,** *f.,* good will,
    kindness, favor
benignē, *adv.,* kindly, in a friendly
    fashion
benignitās, -tātis, *f.,* kindness,
    friendliness, courtesy
benignus, -a, -um, kind, beneficent
benivolentia: *see* **benevolentia**
Berecyntius, -a, -um, Phrygian
    (**Berecyntus,** *a mountain in*
    Phrygia)
bestia, -ae, *f.,* beast, animal
* **bibō, -ere, bibī,** drink
bīduum, -ī, *n.,* a period of two days
bīnī, -ae, -a, *distrib. numeral,* two
    each, two (*nouns normally pl.*)
bis, *adv.,* twice
blanditia, -ae, *f.,* blandishment
bonitās, -tātis, *f.,* goodness
* **bonus, -a, -um,** good; worthy, loyal;
    bona, -ōrum, *n. pl.,* good things,
    goods, property; *compar.* **melior,**
    -ius, better; *superl.* **optimus,**
    -a, -um, best, very good, excellent
Boōtēs, -ae *or* **-ī** (*acc.* **-ēn**), *m.,*
    constellation of the Plowman
bōs, bovis (*pl. gen.* **boum;** *dat. and*
    abl. **bōbus**), *m./f.,* ox, cow
bracchium, -ī, *n.,* arm, *strictly* the
    forearm
* **brevis, -e,** short, brief; shallow; **brevī,**

as adv. (sc. **tempore**), in a short
time

brevitās, -tātis, *f.,* shortness; brevity,
conciseness

Britannia, -ae, *f.,* Britain

Brundisīnus, -a, -um, of Brundisium,
a port on the heel of Italy

Brutus, -ī, *m., a famous cognomen:*
L. Junius Brutus, *who freed Rome
from Tarquinius Superbus and was
elected to the first Roman
consulship;* M. Junius Brutus,
assassin of Julius Caesar;
D. Junius Brutus, *a conspirator
against Caesar*

bulla, -ae, *f.,* boss, stud; amulet

bustum, -ī, *n., often pl.,* tomb

buxum, -ī, *n.,* wood of the box tree

byssus, -ī, *f.,* cotton, cotton *or* linen
material (*EL*)

C

C., *abbr. of* **Gaius,** *a praenomen*

cacūmen, -minis, *n.,* top, peak

* **cadō, -ere, cecidī, cāsum,** fall,
happen, perish

cadūcus, -a, -um, falling, frail,
perishable

* **caecus, -a, -um,** blind; obscure,
uncertain

* **caedēs, -is,** *f., lit.* a cutting;
slaughter, murder

* **caedō, -ere, cecīdī, caesum,** cut, beat,
slay

caelestis, -e, heavenly, celestial

caelitus, *late Lat. adv.,* from heaven

* **caelum, -ī,** *n.,* sky

caeruleus, -a, -um, blue, dark blue

Caesar, -aris, *m., a cognomen;
especially* Gaius Julius Caesar

calamitās, -tātis, *f.,* misfortune,
disaster, loss

calceāmentum, -ī, *n.,* shoe

calcō (1), tread on

Calendae, -ārum, *f. pl.,* the
calends = the first day of a month

calidus, -a, -um, hot

cālīgō, -inis, *f.,* mist, fog, vapor,
gas

calliditās, -tātis, *f.,* skill; shrewdness

callidus, -a, -um, skilful, shrewd,
crafty, cunning

calor, -ōris, *m.,* heat

calumnia, -ae, *f.,* deceitful pretense,
chicanery, false statement

calumnior, -ārī, -ātus sum, accuse
falsely, misrepresent

Calymnē, -ēs, *f., an island of the
Sporades in the Aegean Sea off
the southwestern coast of Asia
Minor*

campester, -tris, -tre, like a field
(**campus**), level

campus, -ī, *m.,* field, plain

candidus, -a, -um, gleaming white

Canīnius, -ī, *m., a Roman name*

canis, -is, *m./f.,* dog

Cannae, -ārum, *f. pl., a town in
southeastern Italy where Hannibal
disastrously defeated the Romans
in* 216 B.C.

Cannēnsis, -e, of *Cannae*

* **canō, -ere, cecinī, cantum,** *sing,*
compose (poems)

* **cantō** (1), sing, celebrate in song

cantus, -ūs, *m.,* song

cānus, -a, -um, gray; old

Canusium, -ī, *n., a town in Apulia in
southern Italy*

capāx, *gen.* **-ācis,** able to hold;
receptive, fit for

capessō, -ere, -īvī, -ītum, seize
eagerly, enter upon

capillus, -ī, *m.,* hair, hair of the
head; *pl.,* the hair

* **capiō, -ere, cēpī, captum,** take,
receive, get, capture

* **Capitōlium, -ī,** *n.,* the Capitoline
Hill *in Rome*

capra, -ae, *f.,* a she-goat

* **captīvus, -a, -um,** captured in war;
captīvus, -ī, *m.,* a captive,
prisoner

captō (1), *freq. of* **capiō,** try to take,
snatch at, pluck at, desire

Capua, -ae, *f., city in Campania*

* **caput, capitis,** *n.,* head, life

cardō, -inis, *m.,* hinge

* **careō, -ēre, -uī,** be without, lack; be
deprived of, miss; + *abl.*

* **caritās, -tātis,** *f.,* dearness, love,
esteem, affection; high price

* **carmen, -minis,** *n.,* song; lyric poem

carnālis, -e, fleshly, carnal (*EL*)

carō, carnis, *f.,* flesh

* **carpō, -ere, carpsī, carptum,** pluck,
gather, make use of, enjoy; tear to
pieces, censure, slander, revile

Carthāginiēnsis, -e, Carthaginian

Carthāgō, -inis, *f.,* Carthage, *famous
city and rival of Rome in north
Africa*

* **cārus, -a, -um,** dear

Cassius, -ī, *m.,* Cassius, *especially*
C. Cassius Longinus, *the assassin
of Julius Caesar*

cassus, -a, -um, empty, hollow,
useless, vain

castellum, -ī, *n.,* fort

castīgō (1), reprove; punish

* **castra, -ōrum,** *n. pl.,* camp; **castra
pōnere,** pitch *or* make camp

* **cāsus, -ūs,** *m., lit.* a falling *or* fall
(**cadō**); accident, chance;
misfortune; **cāsū,** *abl.,* by chance

catēna, -ae, *f.,* chain

Catō, -ōnis, *m., famous cognomen,
especially* Cato the Censor *and*
Cato of Utica, *his Stoic grandson*

* **causa, -ae,** *f.,* cause, reason; sake;
case, situation; excuse, pretext;
causā *with a preceding genitive,* for
the sake of, on account of

cautus, -a, -um, cautious, careful;
secure

cavea, -ae, *f.,* excavated place;
auditorium, theater

* **caveō, -ēre, cāvī, cautum,** beware of;
take care, see to it (that)

-ce, *demonstrative enclitic added to
some pronouns (and adverbs):*
huius-ce bellī, of this (here) war

cēdō, -ere, cessī, cessum, go,
withdraw; yield to, submit, grant

celebrātiō, -ōnis, *f.,* crowded
assembly; festival, celebration

celebritās, -tātis, *f.,* large crowd,
crowded condition; frequency;
fame

celebrō (1), celebrate; honor, make
famous

cēlō (1), hide, conceal

celsus, -a, -um, high, lofty, noble

cēna, -ae, *f.,* dinner

cēnō (1), dine

* **cēnseō, -ēre, cēnsuī, cēnsum,**
estimate, think, judge; advise,
vote, decree

centuriātus, -a, -um, divided into
centuries (groups of 100)

cēra, -ae, *f.,* wax, writing tablet
covered with wax

Cereālis, -e, of Ceres

Cerēs, Cereris, *f.,* the Roman goddess of agriculture and grain

* **cernō, -ere, crēvī, crētum,** see, discern, distinguish, decide

* **certāmen, -minis,** *n.,* contest, struggle, fight

* **certē,** *adv.,* certainly, surely, at least

certō, *adv.,* with certainty, without doubt, really

* **certō** (1), fight, struggle, contend, compete

* **certus, -a, -um,** definite, certain, sure, fixed, resolved upon, reliable; **aliquem certiōrem facere,** to make someone more certain = to inform him; **certior fīō,** I am informed

cervīcal, -ālis, *n.,* pillow

cessō (1), delay

* **cēterus, -a, -um,** the other, the rest, *mostly in pl.; adv.* **cēterum,** but, however

* **cētus, -ī,** *m.,* whale (*pl.* = **cēte,** *a Greek neuter form, sometimes also used as a singular*)

ceu, *adv.,* as, just as

Chaos, *nom. and acc. n.,* empty space, the lower world

charta, -ae, *f.,* papyrus paper; letter, poem, document, etc.

chorus, -ī, *m.,* choral dance; choral band, chorus

* **Christiānus, -ī,** *m.,* a Christian

* **Christus, -ī,** *m.,* Christ

Chrȳsippus, -ī, *m.,* Stoic philosopher

* **cibus, -ī,** *m.,* food

Cicerō, -ōnis, *m.:* (1) Marcus Tullius Cicero, *orator, statesman, and author,* 106–43 B.C.; (2) *his son,* Marcus Tullius Cicero; (3) *his brother,* Quintus Tullius Cicero

Ciconēs, -um, *m. pl., a Thracian people*

Cilix, -icis, *m.,* a Cilician (from Asia Minor)

cingō, -ere, cīnxī, cīnctum, surround, gird (on)

cinis, -eris, *m.,* ashes

* **circā,** *adv.,* around, round about; *prep.* + *acc.,* around, about

circuitus, -ūs, *m.,* circular path, circuit

circulus, -ī, *m.,* circle, circular space

circum, *adv. and prep.* + *acc.,* around, near

circum-arō (1), plow around

circum-dō, -are, -dedī, -datum, put around; surround with

circum-ferō, -ferre, -tulī, -lātum, carry around, turn around

circum-fluō, -ere, -fluxī, -fluxum, overflow; abound in, be rich

circum-fundō, -ere, -fūdī, -fūsum, pour around; *pass.,* stream around, gather around

circum-linō, -ere, smear around, spread over, cover

circumpadānus, -a, -um, about the Po (river)

circum-pōnō, -ere, -posuī, -positum, place around

circum-spectō (1), look around, look at

circum-stō, -āre, -stetī, stand around, surround

circum-veniō, -īre, -vēnī, -ventum, surround, encircle

cithara, -ae, *f.,* a stringed instrument, lyre

cito, *adv.,* quickly; *compar.* **citius;** *superl.* **citissimē**

citō (1), arouse; call, summon, cite

citrō, *adv.,* to this side

cīvīlis, -e, civil, pertaining to citizens

* **cīvis, -is,** *m./f.,* citizen

* **cīvitās, -tātis,** *f.,* state; citizenship

* **clādēs, -is,** *f.,* injury, damage; calamity, disaster, slaughter, destruction

* **clam,** *adv.,* secretly, privately

clāmitō (1), *frequentative of* **clāmō,** cry out (over and over)

* **clāmō** (1), cry, shout

* **clāmor, -ōris,** *m.,* shout, outcry, clamor, applause, noise

clāritās, -tātis, *f.,* clearness, brightness

* **clārus, -a, -um,** bright, clear; famous, illustrious

* **classis, -is,** *f.,* fleet, navy

* **claudō, -ere, clausī, clausum,** close, shut

clērus, -ī, *m.,* the clergy (*ML*)

cliēns, -entis, *m.,* dependent, client, follower

clīvus, -ī, *m.,* slope; hill

Clūsīnus, -a, -um, of Clusium, *a city in Etruria*

Clytaemnēstra, -ae, *f.,* Clytemnestra, *wife and murderess of Agamemnon*

Cn., *abbr. of the praenomen* **Gnaeus**

co-aedificō (1), build on

co-agitō (1), shake together (*EL*)

cocles, -itis, *m.,* one-eyed man; Horatius Cocles, *who held the Tiber bridge against the Etruscans*

coctilis, -e, *lit.* baked; made of brick

cōdicillus, -ī, *m.,* writing tablet

co-eō, -īre, -iī, -itum, go together, meet, assemble; be joined

* **coepī, -isse, coeptum,** *defective verb in perf. system only,* began

coerceō, -ēre, -uī, -itum, curb, check, repress

coeptum, -ī, *n.,* work begun, undertaking

coetus, -ūs, *m.,* a meeting, assembly

cōgitātē, *adv.,* thoughtfully, deliberately

* **cōgitātiō, -ōnis,** *f.,* thinking; thought, plan, purpose, design

* **cōgitō** (1), think, ponder, intend, plan

cognātiō, -ōnis, *f.,* relationship, family, connection

* **cognitiō, -ōnis,** *f.,* acquaintance with, knowledge of, consideration; legal inquiry, investigation

cognitor, -ōris, *m.,* attorney; witness to one's identity

cognōmen, -nōminis, *n.,* surname, *which follows the* **praenomen** *and the* **nomen**

* **cognōscō, -ere, cognōvī, cognitum,** become acquainted with, learn, recognize; *in perf. tenses,* know

cōgō, -ere, coēgī, coāctum (coagō), drive *or* bring together, assemble; force, compel

co-haereō, -ēre, -haesī, cohere, adhere, hang together

co-hērēs, -ēdis, *m./f.,* coheir

cohors, -ortis, *f.,* division of soldiers; retinue, band, crowd

Collātīnus, -ī, *m.,* L. Tarquinius Collatinus, *colleague with Brutus in the first consulship at Rome*

col-lātiō, -ōnis, *f., lit.* a bringing together, a comparison

col-laudō (1), praise highly

* **collēga, -ae,** *m.,* partner in office, colleague

* **col-ligō, -ere, -lēgī, -lēctum (con-**

legō), gather together, collect; infer, suppose

collis, -is, *m.,* hill

collum, -ī, *n.,* neck

* **colō, -ere, -uī, cultum,** cultivate, cherish, honor, worship

color, -ōris, *m.,* color

coluber, -brī, *m.,* serpent, snake

coma, -ae, *f.,* hair (of the head)

* **comes, -itis,** *m./f.,* companion, comrade

comitātus, -ūs, *m.,* attendance, retinue, escort

* **comitium, -ī,** *n.,* assembly place; **comitia, -ōrum,** *n. pl.,* public assembly, an election

comitō (1), accompany, attend

commeātus, -ūs, *m.,* provisions, supplies

commemorātiō, -ōnis, *f.,* mention, remembrance

* **commemorō** (1), mention, relate

commentārius, -ī, *m.,* memorandum, commentary; record

commentātiō, -ōnis, *f.,* meditation, study, preparation

commentīcius, -a, -um, invented, fictitious

commentor, -ārī, -ātus sum, study, consider, practice (something oratorical or literary)

com-minus, *adv.,* hand to hand, at close quarters

* **com-mittō, -ere, -mīsī, -missum,** commit, entrust; be guilty of; allow it to happen (that)

commoditās, -tātis, *f.,* advantage, comfort

commodō (1), furnish, lend

commodum, -ī, *n.,* convenience, advantage

* **commodus, -a, -um,** suitable, advantageous, favorable, agreeable, easy, pleasant; *adv.* **commodē**

* **com-moveō, -ēre, -mōvī, -mōtum,** move greatly, stir, affect; disturb, alarm

commūnicō (1), make common, share, communicate, confer

com-mūniō (4), fortify on all sides

* **commūnis, -e,** common, general, universal, public; *adv.* **commūniter,** jointly, together

commūnitās, -tātis, *f.,* community, fellowship

com-mūtātiō, -ōnis, *f.,* change; exchange

* **com-mūtō** (1), change completely, alter; exchange

com-parātiō, -ōnis, *f.,* preparation, acquiring; comparison

com-parō (1) [**par,** equal], to match, compare

com-parō (1) [**parare**], prepare, make ready, establish

compellō (1), call; rebuke, chide

com-pellō, -ere, -pulī, -pulsum, bring together, collect; drive, compel

comperiō, -īre, -perī, -pertum, find out, learn, discover

compescō, -ere, -pescuī, check, restrain

competēns, *gen.* **-entis,** appropriate

com-petītor, -ōris, *m.,* competitor

com-placeō, -ēre, -placuī, -placitum, please greatly

com-plector, -ī, -plexus sum, embrace

complexus, -ūs, *m.,* embrace

com-plōrātus, -ūs, *m.,* loud wailing, lamentation

com-plūrēs, -a, *pl.,* several, many

* **com-pōnō, -ere, -posuī, -positum,** put together, compose

compos, -potis, in possession of, endowed with

com-positus, -a, -um, *lit.* put together; well arranged, prepared, calm

com-prehendō, -ere, -hendī, -hēnsum, seize, arrest; perceive, comprehend

com-primo, -ere, -pressī, pressum, press together, embrace; restrain

compunctiō, -ōnis, *f.,* humility, remorse (*EL*)

cōnātus, -ūs, *m.,* attempt

* **con-cēdō, -ere, -cessī, -cessum,** depart; yield, grant, concede

concessus, -ūs, *m.: only in abl.* **concessū,** by permission

con-cidō, -ere, -cidī, fall down in a heap, collapse, perish

conciliātrīx, -īcis, *f.,* uniter

conciliō (1), bring together, win over, reconcile

concilium, -ī, *n.,* council; assembly

con-citō (1), stir up, excite

con-clāmō (1), shout together, cry out, shout loudly

con-clūdō, -ere, -clūsī, -clūsum, shut up, close, conclude

con-cordia, -ae, *f.,* concord, unity, harmony

con-cupīscō, -ere, -pīvī *or* **-piī, -pītum,** long for, eagerly desire

con-currō, -ere, -currī, -cursum run *or* rush together, assemble

concursō (1), run about, travel about

con-cursus, -ūs, *m.,* a running together, attack, encounter

condemnō (1), condemn, blame

condiciō, -ōnis, *f.,* agreement; condition, terms

conditor, -ōris, *m.,* founder

* **con-dō, -ere, -didī, -ditum,** put together, found, establish, build; compose; lay away, bury

con-doleō, -ēre, -uī, -itūrus, feel great pain, suffer greatly; + *dat.,* suffer with another (*EL*)

* **cōn-ferō, -ferre, -tulī, collātum,** bring together, compare, devote, apply; **sē cōnferre,** betake oneself, go

* **cōn-fertus, -a, -um,** closely packed, dense, crowded

confessiō, -ōnis, *f.,* confession, admission

cōnfessor, -ōris, *m.,* one who confesses Christianity, a martyr (*EL*)

cōn-ficiō, -ere, -fēcī, -fectum, accomplish, finish, produce; wear out, weaken, exhaust, destroy

* **cōn-fīdō, -ere, -fīsus sum,** have confidence in, trust, be confident

cōn-fīrmō (1), make firm; assert, affirm

cōn-fiteor, -ērī, -fessus sum, confess, acknowledge

cōn-flīctō (1), *lit.* strike together; ruin; be tormented, be afflicted

cōn-flīgō, -ere, -flīxī, -flīctum, collide, clash, fight

cōn-flō (1), *lit.* blow together; melt metals; forge, produce

cōn-fluō, -ere, -fluxī, flow together, stream in, flock together

cōn-fōrmō (1), form, shape, fashion

cōn-fortō (1), strengthen greatly (*EL*)

cōn-foveō, -ēre, -fōvī, -fōtum, to warm, cherish, foster

cōn-fringō, -ere, -frēgī, -frāctum, break to pieces, destroy

cōn-fugiō, -ere, -fūgī, flee (to), take refuge, have recourse (to)

cōn-fundō, -ere, -fūdī, -fūsum, confuse, disturb, confound

cōnfūtō (1), check, repress, silence

con-glūtinō (1), glue *or* cement together, bind closely

con-gredior, -ī, -gressus sum, come together, meet; fight

con-gregō (1), collect into a flock *or* herd; gather together

con-gruō, -ere, -uī, come together, agree, harmonize

* **con-iciō, -ere, -iēcī, -iectum,** throw together, cast, force; conjecture

con-iectūra, -ae, *f.,* conjecture, inference

con-iūnctiō, -ōnis, *f.,* a joining; union, association, bond; intimacy

* **con-iūnctus, -a, -um** (*partic. of* **coniungō**), joined together, united

* **con-iungō, -ere, -iūnxī, -iūnctum,** join together, unite

* **coniūnx, -iugis,** *f.,* wife; *sometimes* *m.,* husband

con-iūrō (1), swear together; conspire

con-lēga: *see* **collēga**

cōnor, -ārī, -ātus sum, try, attempt

con-queror, -ī, -questus sum, complain (loudly), lament, deplore

con-quiēscō, -ere, -quiēvī, -quiētum, become quiet, find rest

con-quīrō, -ere, -quīsīvī, -quīsītum, search out

cōn-salūtō (1), greet, salute

cōnsānēscō, -ere, -sānuī, become healthy, get well, heal

cōn-sanguineus, -a, -um, of the same blood, related; *as a noun,* brother, *m.,* sister, *f.*

* **Cōnsānus, -a, -um,** of Consa, *a city in south central Italy*

cōn-scendō, -ere, -scendī, -scēnsum, ascend, mount, climb, go on board

cōn-scientia, -ae, *f., lit.* knowledge (in oneself), consciousness, conscience

cōn-scius, -a, -um, *lit.* having knowledge with another; cognizant of, aware, conscious; *m. and f. as a noun,* accomplice

cōnsecrō (1), dedicate, consecrate

cōn-sector, -ārī, -ātus sum, follow, pursue, strive after

cōn-senēscō, -ere, -senuī, become old, grow weak, lose power

cōn-sēnsiō, -ōnis, *f.,* agreement, harmony

cōn-sentāneus, -a, -um, agreeing with, suitable; reasonable, consistent; **cōnsentāneum est,** it is reasonable (+ *inf. or* **ut-***clause as subject*)

cōn-sentiō, -īre, -sēnsī, -sēnsum, agree, be of one accord

* **cōn-sequor, -ī, -secūtus sum,** follow, result; follow up, pursue; gain

cōn-serō, -ere, -seruī, -sertum, connect, join, bind, engage in battle

* **cōn-servō** (1), save, preserve; maintain, observe

cōnsīderātē, *adv.,* thoughtfully, carefully

cōnsīderātus, -a, -um, thoughtful, considerate

cōnsīderō (1), contemplate, consider, weigh

cōn-sīdō, -ere, -sēdī, -sessum, sit down, take up a position

* **cōnsilium, -ī,** *n.,* counsel, advice, plan, purpose; judgment, wisdom; council, panel (of jurors)

* **cōn-sistō, -ere, -stitī,** take one's stand, halt, stop, stay; be based on, consist of (+ **in** + *abl.*)

cōnsōlātor, -ōris, *m.,* consoler

* **cōnsōlō** (1), comfort, console (*According to Lewis and Short this active form is anteclassical and very rare. The regular class. form is the deponent* **cōnsōlor.**)

cōnsōlor, -ārī, -ātus sum, console, comfort

cōnsors, *gen.* **-sortis,** sharing in; *as a noun,* a sharer in, partner

cōn-spectus, -a, -um (*partic. of* **cōnspiciō,** to view), visible

cōn-spectus, -ūs, *m.,* sight, view

* **cōn-spiciō, -ere, -spexī, -spectum,** look at, observe; *pass. often* = be conspicuous

cōn-stāns, *gen.* **-stantis,** standing firm, steady, constant, steadfast

* **cōnstantia, -ae,** *f.,* firmness, steadfastness, strength of character

cōn-sternō, -ere, -strāvī, -strātum, confound, alarm, terrify, dismay

* **cōn-stituō, -ere, -uī, -ūtum,** place, establish, arrange; determine, decide

* **cōn-stō, -āre, -stitī, -stātūrus,** stand firm; consist of, be composed of,

depend on; cost; **cōnstat,** *impers.,* it is agreed; **ratiō cōnstat,** the account balances

cōn-stringō, -ere, -strinxī, -strictum, bind, fasten

cōn-suēscō, -ere, -suēvī, -suētus, be accustomed

cōnsuētūdō, -dinis, *f.,* custom, practice, way of life, close and personal relationship

* **cōnsul, -ulis,** *m.,* consul

cōnsulāris, -e, of a consul, consular; **cōnsulāris, -is,** *m.,* an ex-consul, a person of consular rank

cōnsulātus, -ūs, *m.,* consulship

* **cōnsulō, -ere, -uī, -tum,** deliberate; consult; + *dat.,* have regard for, look out for the interests of

cōnsultātiō, -ōnis, *f.,* deliberation, inquiry, asking for advice

cōnsultō (1), consider carefully, weigh, ponder

cōnsultum, -ī, *n.,* decree, *especially* **senātūs cōnsultum,** a decree of the senate; **cōnsultō,** *as adv.,* intentionally, deliberately

cōn-summō (1), sum up: finish, complete

cōn-sūmō, -ere, -sūmpsī, -sūmptum, use up, consume

con-tāctus, -ūs, *m.,* touch

con-tāgiō, -ōnis, *f., lit.* a touching; contagion, infection

* **contemnō, -ere, -tempsī, -temptum,** scorn, despise, disparage

contemplor, -ārī, -ātus sum, contemplate, consider carefully; look at, view

contemptiō, -ōnis, *f.,* contempt, disregard

contemptus, -ūs, *m.,* disdain,
contempt
con-tendō, -ere, -tendī, -tentum,
strain, strive, contend, hasten
* **contentus, -a, -um,** contented,
satisfied
con-terminus, -a, -um, adjoining
con-terō, -ere, -trīvī, -trītum, wear
out, consume, spend (time),
destroy
con-terreō, -ēre, -terruī, -territum,
terrify, frighten thoroughly
contiguus, -a, -um, touching,
adjoining
con-tinentia, -ae, *f.,* restraint,
temperance
* **con-tineō, -ēre, -uī, -tentum,** hold
together, contain, restrain; *pass.,*
consist of, depend on
con-tingō, -ere, -tigī, -tactum, touch;
happen, befall; concern
continuus, -a, -um, uninterrupted,
successive
* **contiō, -ōnis,** *f.,* meeting, assembly;
a speech made to the assembly
* **contrā,** *adv.,* on the contrary;
prep. + *acc.,* against, contrary to
con-tractus, -a, -um, *partic. of*
contrahō
con-trahō, -ere, -traxī, -tractum,
lit. draw together; transact,
complete a business arrangement,
make a contract; shorten, reduce,
contract
contrārius, -a, -um, opposite,
contrary
con-trīstāns, *gen.* **-antis,** sorrowing
con-trīstō (1), make sad, sadden;
make gloomy
contubernālis, -is, *m.,* comrade

contumācia, -ae, *f.,* obstinacy,
haughtiness
con-turbō (1), throw into disorder,
confound, disturb
con-valēscō, -ere, -valuī, become
strong, recover, convalesce
con-vellō, -ere, -vellī, -vulsum, tear,
rend
con-veniēns, *gen.* **-entis,** agreeing,
harmonious, appropriate
convenientia, -ae, *f., lit.* a coming
together; agreement, harmony,
symmetry
* **con-veniō, -īre, -vēnī, -ventum,** come
together, meet; to be agreed upon;
convenit, it is agreed
conventiō, -ōnis, *f.,* agreement,
compact
conventum, -ī, *n.,* agreement,
compact
* **convertō, -ere, -vertī, -versum,** turn
about, change, reverse; return
convīctor, -ōris, *m., lit.* one who lives
(**vīvere**) with another, associate
con-vincō, -ere, -vīcī, -victum,
overcome, convict, prove guilty
convīvium, -ī, *n.,* feast, banquet;
dinner
co-operor, -ārī, -ātus sum, work
with, cooperate
co-orior, -īrī, -ortus sum, arise,
break out
* **cophinus, -ī,** *m.,* basket, chest
* **cōpia, -ae,** *f.,* abundance, supply,
fullness, opportunity; fluency; *pl.*
wealth, resources, forces, troops
cōpiōsē, *adv. of* **cōpiōsus**
cōpiōsus, -a, -um, well supplied,
abounding, abundant, plentiful,
copious

cōpulō (1), join together, couple, unite

* **cor, cordis,** *n.,* heart; **cordī esse,** be dear to, to please

cōram, *adv.,* face to face, in one's own person, personally; *prep. + abl.,* in the presence of

Corfīnium, -ī, *n., a town in central Italy*

Coriolānus, -ī, *m., an early Roman traitor dissuaded by his mother from attacking the city*

Cornēlius, -ī, *m., name of men of a famous Roman gens (clan) which includes:* P. Cornelius Scipio, *father of the following:* P. Cornelius Scipio Africanus Maior, *conqueror of Hannibal;* P. Cornelius Scipio Aemilianus Africanus Minor, *victor in the Third Punic War in 146* B.C.

cornū, -ūs, *n.,* horn; wing of an army

corōna, -ae, *f.,* wreath, garland

corporeus, -a, -um, corporeal, fleshy

* **corpus, -oris,** *n.,* body

cor-rigō, -ere, -rēxī, -rēctum, set right, correct; reform

cor-ripiō, -ere, -ripuī, -reptum, seize; attack, blame

cor-ruō, -ere, -ruī, fall together, fall to the ground; be ruined

* **cōtīdiē (cōttīdiē),** daily, every day

crassus, -a, -um, thick, dense; fat; rude

Cratippus, -ī, *m., Athenian philosopher of 1st cent.* B.C.

creātor, -ōris, *m.,* creator, maker

creātūra, -ae, *f.,* creature, creation (*EL*)

crēber, -bra, -brum, thick, frequent, crowded

crēbrō, *adv.,* frequently

crēdibilis, -e, credible, worthy of belief

* **crēdō, -ere, crēdidī, crēditum,** believe, give credence to, trust, + *dat. or acc. or both*

cremō (1), consume by fire, burn

* **creō** (1), create, choose, elect

crepitus, -ūs, *m.,* rattling, rustling, noise

crēscō, -ere, crēvī, crētum, increase, grow, thrive, prosper

Crēta, -ae (acc. **-am** *or* **-ēn**), *f.,* Crete

crēterra, -ae, *f.,* mixing bowl

* **crīmen, -minis,** *n.,* charge, accusation; *sometimes* fault, offense, guilt, crime

crīminor, -ārī, -ātus sum, accuse, denounce, charge

croceus, -a, -um, saffron yellow

cruciātus, -ūs, *m.,* torture, torment

cruci-fīgō, -ere, -fīxī, -fīxum, fix to the cross, crucify

* **cruciō** (1), crucify, torture

* **crūdēlis, -e,** cruel

* **crūdēlitās, -tātis,** *f.,* cruelty, severity

crūdēliter, *adv.,* cruelly

cruentātus, -a, -um, stained with blood (*cp.* **cruor**)

cruentus, -a, -um, bloody

* **cruor, -ōris,** *m.,* blood, gore

* **crux, crucis,** *f.,* the cross

cubiculum, -ī, *n.,* bedroom

cucurrī: *see* **currō**

culmen, -minis, *n.,* top, summit

* **culpa, -ae,** *f.,* fault, blame

cultus, -ūs, cultivation; culture, civilization, style of living, refinement

* **cum,** *conj., usually with subjunct.,* when, since, although; *also with*

indic., when; **cum . . . tum,** both
. . . and, not only . . . but also
cum, *prep.* + *abl.,* with
cumulātē, *adv.,* heaped up,
abundantly, completely
cūnctātiō, -ōnis, *f.,* a delaying,
hesitation
cūnctātor, -ōris, *m.,* delayer
cūnctor, -ārī, -ātus sum, delay,
hesitate
* **cūnctus, -a, -um,** all (together as a
whole), whole
* **cupiditās, -tātis,** *f.,* desire, passion;
avarice; partisanship
cupīdō, -inis, *f.,* desire; **Cupīdō, -inis,**
m., Cupid, *son of Venus*
cupidus, -a, -um, desirous, eager,
greedy, avaricious, fond; *adv.*
cupidē
* **cupiō, -ere, -īvī, -ītum,** wish eagerly,
desire, long for
cūr, *adv.,* why?
* **cūra, -ae,** *f.,* care, concern, anxiety
* **cūria, -ae,** *f.,* senate-house; *in EL* the
court (*e.g.,* of God)
Cūriatiī, -ōrum, *m.,* *the three Alban
brothers who fought the three
Horatian brothers*
Cūriō, -ōnis, *m.,* *a Roman cognomen*
Curius, -ī, *m.,* *Roman nomen; espec.
the conqueror of Pyrrhus*
* **cūrō** (1), care (for), cure, attend to,
take care, see to it (that), manage;
with gerundive, have a thing done
* **currō, -ere, cucurrī, cursum,** run,
hurry
currus, -ūs, *m.,* chariot
* **cursus, -ūs,** *m.,* a running, course,
journey; racecourse
curvāmen, -minis, *n.,* a bending, an
arching, curve

* **custōdia, -ae,** *f.,* custody, prison; a
guard, sentinel
custōdiō (4), guard, preserve,
observe
custōs, -ōdis, *m./f.,* guard, watchman

D

Daedalus, -ī, *m.,* *legendary Athenian
craftsman who built the labyrinth
in Crete*
* **damnō** (1), condemn, censure
damnōsus, -a, -um, harmful,
destructive
damnum, -ī, *n.,* damage, injury,
loss
Danaē, Danaēs, *f.,* *daughter of
Acrisius, mother of Perseus by
Jupiter*
daps, -pis, *f.,* feast, banquet (*both sg.
and pl.*)
dator, -ōris, *m.,* giver
David, *indecl.,* *the great king of the
Hebrews*
* **dē,** *prep.* + *abl.,* from, down from;
concerning, about
dea, -ae, *f.,* goddess
* **dēbeō, -ēre, dēbuī, dēbitum,** owe,
ought, must
dēbilitō (1), weaken
decānus, -ī, *m.,* dean (*EL*)
dē-cēdō, -ere, -cessī, -cessum,
withdraw, depart; depart from
life, die
decem, *indecl.,* ten
December, -bris, -bre, of *or*
belonging to December
dē-cernō, -ere, -crēvī, -crētum,
decide, judge, decree
dē-cerpō, -ere, -cerpsī, -cerptum,
pluck off, gather

dē-certō (1), fight out, fight through, fight to a decision

dēcessus, -ūs, *m.,* departure; death

* **decet, -ēre, decuit,** *impers.,* it is proper, fitting, becoming, decent (physically *or* morally), it befits *or* becomes

dē-cĭdō (-cădō), -ere, -cĭdī, fall down, sink; perish

deciēs, *adv.,* ten times

decimus, -a, -um, tenth; **decima, -ae,** *f., sc.* **pars,** a tithe

dē-cipiō, -ere, -cēpī, -ceptum, deceive

dē-clārō (1), make clear, declare; declare as elected to office

dē-clīnō (1) turn away, avoid, shun

decor, -ōris, *m.,* charm, beauty, grace

decorō (1), adorn, beautify

decōrus, -a, -um, fitting, becoming, seemly, proper, decent, graceful; **decōrum, -ī,** *n.,* propriety, grace

dē-currō, -ere, -(cu)currī, -cursum, run down

decus, -oris, *n.,* honor, worth, virtue

dē-decet, -ēre, -decuit, *impers.,* it is unfitting, unbecoming

dē-decus, -oris, *n.,* disgrace, infamy, shame

dē-dicō (1), dedicate, consecrate

dē-dō, -ere, -didī, -ditum, give up, surrender

dē-dūcō, -ere, -dūxī, -ductum, lead away *or* off, draw down; lead, conduct

dē-fatīgō (1), to weary, fatigue, tire

dēfectiō, -ōnis, *f.,* desertion, revolt

* **dē-fendō, -ere, -fendī, -fēnsum,** ward off; defend, protect

dēfēnsiō, -ōnis, *f.,* defense

* **dē-ferō, -ferre, -tulī, -lātum,** bear off; report; accuse

* **dē-ficiō, -ere, -fēcī, -fectum,** fail; revolt, desert

dē-fīgō, -ere, -fīxī, -fīxum, fix, fasten, drive down

dē-fīniō (4), bound, limit, define

dēfīnītiō, -ōnis, *f.,* definition

dē-flagrō (1), burn down, consume by fire; be destroyed by fire

dē-fleō, -ēre, -flēvī, -flētum, weep for, bewail

dē-fluō, -ere, -fluxī, -fluxum, flow down, flow away, vanish

dēfōrmō (1), disfigure, spoil

dē-fungor, -ī, -fūnctus sum, perform, discharge, complete; die

dē-glūtiō (4), swallow down (*EL*)

dēgō, -ere, dēgī (dē-agō), pass (time *or* life), live

dehinc, *adv., lit.* from here; thereupon, henceforth

dē-iciō, -ere, -iēcī, -iectum, throw down, ward off, avert

dein, *adv.* = **deinde**

* **deinde** *or* **dein,** *adv.,* from there, then, next, in the second place

* **dēlectātiō, -ōnis,** *f.,* delight, pleasure

* **dēlectō** (1), delight, please, interest

dē-lēgō (1), assign, delegate

dēleō, -ēre, -ēvī, -ētum, destroy, wipe out, erase

dēlīberātiō, -ōnis, *f.,* deliberation, consideration

dē-līberō (1), weigh carefully, consider

dēlicātē, *adv.,* luxuriously

dēlicātus, -a, -um, charming, luxurious, dainty, fastidious

dēliciae, -ārum, *f., usually only in pl.,*

delight, pleasure; sweetheart, darling

dē-ligō (1), bind

dē-ligō, -ere, -lēgī, -lēctum, pick out, choose, select

dē-līrō (1), be mad, insane, rave

Dēlos, -ī, *f., a small island of the Cyclades in the Aegean Sea, sacred as the birthplace of Apollo and Artemis (Diana)*

dēlūbrum, -ī, *n.,* shrine, temple

dē-migrō (1), emigrate, depart

dē-minuō, -ere, -minuī, -minūtum, diminish

dē-missus, -a, -um (*partic. of* **dēmittō**), *lit.* lowered; low, weak, humble, downcast

dē-mittō, -ere, -mīsī, -missum, *lit.* send down; thrust *or* plunge into, lower, let down

dēmō, -ere, -dēmpsī, -dēmptum, take away, remove

dēmum, *adv.,* at length, at last

dēnārius, -ī, *m., a Roman silver coin*

* **dēnique,** *adv.,* finally, at last

dēns, -ntis, *m.,* tooth

dēnsus, -a, -um, thick, dense

dē-nūdō (1), lay bare, denude

dē-nūntiō (1), announce, declare, proclaim, threaten; *not* denounce

de-orsum, *adv.,* downward, down, below

dē-pecūlātor, -ōris, *m.,* plunderer, embezzler

dē-pecūlor, -ārī, -ātus sum, plunder, rob

dē-pellō, -ere, -pulī, -pulsum, drive away, ward off

dē-plōrō (1), weep, bewail, bewail the loss of, complain of

* **dē-pōnō, -ere, -posuī, -positum,** put

down, deposit; lay aside, give up, abandon, get rid of

dē-portō (1), carry off

dē-positum, -ī, *n.,* deposit, trust

dē-precor, -ārī, -ātus sum, avert by entreaty

* **dēprehendō, -ere, -hendī, -hēnsum,** seize, arrest; detect, observe, understand

dē-primō, -ere, -pressī, -pressum, press down, depress, sink

dē-ripiō, -ere, -ripuī, -reptum, snatch away, pull down

dē-ruptus, -a, -um, steep

* **dē-scendō, -ere, -scendī, -scēnsum,** descend, go down

dē-scrīptiō, -ōnis, *f.,* definition, description

* **dē-serō, -ere, -seruī, -sertum,** desert

dēsertus, -a, -um (*partic. of* **dēserō**), deserted, lonely

* **dēsīderium, -ī,** *n.,* longing (*especially for what one misses or has lost*), desire

* **dēsīderō** (1), long for, miss, desire; require; lose

dē-sīdō, -ere, -sēdī, sink, give way

dē-signō (1), mark out, signify; elect; **dēsignātus, -a, -um,** *as adj.,* chosen, elect

dē-siliō, -īre, -siliī, -sultum, leap down

* **dēsinō, -ere, -siī, -situm,** cease, stop, leave off

dēsolātus, -a, -um, forsaken, desolate

dē-spērātiō, -ōnis, *f.,* hopelessness, despair

dē-spērō (1), give up hope, despair

dē-spicientia, -ae, *f.,* contempt

dē-spiciō, -ere, -spexī, -spectum, look down on, scorn, despise dē-spoliō (1), plunder, rob

dēspōnsātiō, -ōnis, *f.,* betrothal (*EL*)

dēspōnsō (1), betroth

dēstinō (1), determine, resolve,
intend, destine

dē-stituō, -ere, -stituī, -stitūtum, set
down; leave, abandon

dē-stitūtus, -a, -um (*partic. of*
dēstituō), forsaken, helpless

dē-struō, -ere, -struxī, -structum, tear
down, destroy

* dē-sum, -esse, -fuī, -futūrus, be
wanting, fail (+ *dat.*)

dē-super, *adv.,* from above, above

dē-terreō, -ēre, -uī, -itum, frighten
away, prevent, hinder

dētestābilis, -e, detestable,
abominable

dē-trahō, -ere, -traxī, -tractum, take
away, remove

dētrīmentum, -ī, *n.,* loss, damage,
harm

dē-trūdō, -ere, -trūsī, -trūsum, thrust
down *or* away, dislodge

dē-truncō (1), lop off; behead

* deus, -ī, *m.,* god; *voc.* = deus

dē-vāstō (1), lay waste, devastate

dē-vius, -a, -um, out of the way, off
the road; dēvium, -ī, *n.* (*sc.* iter) a
byway

dē-volō (1), *lit.* fly down; rush
down

dē-volvō, -ere, -volvī, -volūtum, roll
down, fall headlong

dēvōtiō, -ōnis, *f.,* a consecrating *or*
vowing (*espec. of one's life*) *in class.
Lat.;* piety, devotion *in EL*

dē-voveō, -ēre, -vōvī, -vōtum, vow,
consecrate; curse

* dexter, -tra, -trum (*or* -tera, -terum),
right, on the right

dextra, -ae, *f.* (*sc.* manus), right hand

diabolus, -ī, *m.,* devil (*EL*)

diaeta, -ae, *f.,* room

Diāna, -ae, *f., virgin goddess of the
moon and of the hunt, sister of
Apollo*

diciō, -ōnis, *f.,* authority, control,
sway

* dīcō, -ere, dīxī, dictum, say, tell,
speak; call, name; proclaim,
appoint

* dictātor, -ōris, *m.,* dictator

dictitō (1), say repeatedly, over and
over

dictō (1), dictate; compose

dictum, -ī, *n., lit.* thing said; a word;
proverb

didicī: *see* discō

* diēs, diēī, *m./f.,* day; (period of)
time; **in diēs,** from day to day; **ad
diem,** at the appointed time,
punctually

dif-ferentia, -ae, *f.,* difference

dif-ferō, -ferre, dis-tulī, dīlātum,
differ, be different; report,
circulate; put off, postpone

* dif-ficilis, -e, not easy, difficult,
hard; surly, obstinate; *compar.*
difficilior; *superl.* **difficillimus;**
adv. **difficiliter** *or post-Augustan*
difficile

dif-fugiō, -ere, -fūgī, -fugitum, flee in
different directions, disperse

dif-fundō, -ere, -fūdī, -fūsum, pour
forth in all directions, spread out,
extend

digitus, -ī, *m.,* finger

* dignitās, -tātis, *f.,* worth, merit,
honor, dignity, prestige

dignor, -ārī, -ātus sum, to deem
worthy; deign, condescend

* **dignus, -a, -um,** worthy (of + *abl. or gen.*)

dī-gredior, -ī, -gressus sum, depart

dī-lēctus, -ūs, *m.,* a levy

dīligēns, *gen.* **-entis,** careful, assiduous, industrioius, diligent; *adv.* **dīligenter**

* **dīligentia, -ae,** *f.,* carefulness, attention, diligence

* **dīligō, -ere, -lēxi, -lēctum,** [*lit.* choose out] value, esteem, love,

dīmicātiō, -ōnis, *f.,* fight, combat, struggle

dīmicō (1), fight, struggle

* **dī-mittō, -ere, -mīsī, -missum,** send away, send forth; let go, release, forgive

dī-moveō, -ēre, -mōvī, -mōtum, move apart, separate

dīreptiō, -ōnis, *f.,* plundering

dī-rigō, -ere, -rēxī, -rēctum, *lit.* guide straight, arrange, direct

dir-imō, -ere, -ēmī, -ēmptum, take apart, separate, break up, end, disturb

dī-ripiō, -ere, -ripuī, -reptum, tear apart, plunder, rob

dī-rumpō, -ere, -rūpi, -ruptum, break apart, burst

dīs = deīs

dis-(di-, dif-, dir-), *prefix* = apart, away, not

dis-cēdō, -ere, -cessī, -cessum, go away, depart

dis-cernō, -ere, -crēvī, -crētum, separate; distinguish, discern, decide

discidium, -ī, *n.,* disaffection, alienation

disciplīna, -ae, *f.,* training, discipline, instruction

discipulus, -ī, *m.,* pupil; disciple

* **discō, -ere, didicī,** learn

* **dis-cordia, -ae,** *f.,* disagreement, dissension, strife

dis-cordō (1), disagree, quarrel

di-scrībō, -ere, -scrīpsī, -scrīptum, distribute, assign

* **discrīmen, -minis,** *n.,* distinction, turning point, crisis, critical moment, peril

dis-crīminō (1), separate, divide

dis-cursus, -ūs, *m., lit.* a running about to and fro, mad rush

dis-cutiō, -ere, -cussī, -cussum, shatter, scatter, destroy

dis-pār, *gen.* **-paris,** unequal

di-spergō, -ere, -spersī, -spersum, scatter, spread abroad

dispersē, *adv.,* here and there

dis-pōnō, -ere, -posuī, -positum, distribute, station at intervals

dis-putātiō, -ōnis, *f.,* discussion

* **dis-putō** (1), discuss, examine

dis-sēnsiō, -ōnis, *f.,* disagreement, dissension

dis-serō, -ere, -seruī, -sertum, discuss, argue

dis-sipō (1), scatter

dis-solvō, -ere, -solvī, -solūtum, dissolve, separate, release

dis-sonus, -a, -um, discordant, confused

dis-tineō, -ēre, -tinuī, -tentum (dis, apart, + **teneō),** hold apart, separate; hinder, distract

di-stō, -āre, stand apart, lie at a distance, be distant

dis-trahō, -ere, -traxī, -tractum, draw apart, distract

* **diū,** *adv.,* long, for a long time; *compar.* **diūtius;** *superl.* **diūtissimē**

dīus, -a, -um: *see* **dīvus**

diūtinus, -a, -um, lasting, of long duration

diūturnus, -a, -um, long-lasting

dī-vellō, -ere, -vellī, -vulsum, tear apart

* **dīversus, -a, -um,** separate, different, various

* **dīves,** *gen.* **dīvitis,** rich, wealthy; *compar.* **dīvitior** *or* **dītior;** *superl.* **dīvitissimus** *or* **dītissimus**

dīvidō, -ere, -vīsī, -vīsum, divide, separate

dīvīnitus, *adv.,* divinely, providentially

dīvīnus, -a, -um, divine; godlike, excellent

dīvitiae, -ārum, *f. pl.,* riches, wealth

dīvus, -a, -um, divine; **dīvus, -ī,** *m.,* a god; **dīva, -ae,** *f.,* goddess; **dīvum, -ī,** *n.,* sky

* **dō, dăre, dedī, dătum,** give, offer, furnish; **litterās dare,** write *or* mail a letter

* **doceō, -ēre, docuī, doctum,** teach, inform, explain

doctor, -ōris, *m.,* teacher

doctrīna, -ae, *f.,* learning, erudition; teaching, instruction

doctus, -a, -um (*partic. of* **doceō**), *lit.* taught; learned, well informed, skilled

documentum, -ī, *n.,* example, instance, pattern; proof

* **doleō, -ēre, -uī, -itūrus,** feel pain, be pained, grieve

* **dolor, -ōris,** *m.,* pain, grief

dolōrōsus, -a, -um, full of sorrow (*late Lat.*)

domesticus, -a, -um, pertaining to the home *or* family, domestic

domicilium, -ī, *n.,* dwelling, abode

domina, -ae, *f.,* mistress of a household, lady

dominātiō, -ōnis, *f.,* rule, dominion; despotism

* **dominus, -ī,** *m.,* master, lord

Domitiānus, -ī, *m., Roman emperor* A.D. *81–96*

* **domus, -ūs,** *f.,* house, home; **domī** (*loc.*) at home; **domum,** (to) home; **domō,** from home

* **dōnec,** *conj.,* as long as, until

dōnō (1), give, bestow

* **dōnum, -ī,** *n.,* gift

* **dormiō** (4), sleep

Druentia, -ae, *f.,* the Durance, *a tributary of the Rhone*

dubitātiō, -ōnis, *f.,* doubt, hesitation

* **dubitō** (1), doubt, hesitate

dubius, -a, -um, doubtful, uncertain, hesitant; **dubium, -ī,** *n.,* doubt, uncertainty

ducentī, -ae, -a, two hundred

* **dūcō, -ere, dūxī, ductum,** lead; consider, think

* **dulcis, -e,** sweet, pleasant, dear

* **dum,** *conj.,* while, as long as; until; provided that

dumtaxat, *adv.,* at least, at any rate, only

* **duo, duae, duo,** two

duodeciēs, *adv.,* twelve times

duplex, *gen.* **-plicis,** *adj.,* twofold, double

dūrō (1), harden; endure; remain, last

dūrus, -a, -um, tough, strong, hard, harsh, cruel; *adv.* **dūrē** *and* **dūriter**

* **dux, ducis,** *m./f.,* leader, guide, commander

E

* **ē:** *see* **ex**

ebur, eboris, *n.,* ivory

* **ecce,** *interj.,* look, see, behold

Ecclēsiastēs, -ae, *m.,* the Preacher, one who addresses the assembly (*EL*)

ecquid, *interrogative conj.,* whether

ē-dīcō, -ere, -dīxī, -dictum, proclaim, declare, decree

ē-dictum, -ī, *n.,* decree, proclamation

ē-dō, -ere, -didī, -ditum, give forth; give birth to; tell, publish

ē-doceō, -ēre, -docuī, -doctum, teach thoroughly, instruct

ē-ducō (1), rear, educate

ē-dūcō, -ere, -dūxī, -ductum, lead out

effēminātē, *adv.,* effeminately, in unmanly fashion

* **ef-ferō, -ferre, extulī, ēlātum,** carry out, lift up, extol, praise; *pass.,* be carried away, be puffed up

* **ef-ficiō, -ere, -fēcī, -fectum,** accomplish, bring about, cause

ef-flōrēscō, -ere, -flōruī, blossom, flourish

* **ef-fugiō, -ere, -fūgī, -fugitum,** flee away, escape, avoid

ef-fugium, -ī, *n.,* escape

ef-fundō, -ere, -fūdī, -fūsum, pour out

ef-fūsē, *adv.,* far and wide, extensively

* **egeō, -ēre, eguī,** be in need, need, lack, want; *often + abl.*

ē-gerō, -ere, -gessī, -gestum, take away

* **ego, meī,** *1st personal pron.,* I; *pl.* **nōs, nostrum/nostrī,** we, *sometimes* = I

* **ē-gredior, -ī, -gressus sum,** go out

ē-gregiē, *adv. of* **ēgregius**

* **ē-gregius, -a, -um,** *lit.* out from the herd; uncommon, extraordinary, excellent, remarkable, distinguished

eia, *interj. indicating surprise, joy, or exhortation,* ah, ha, well then, come on

e-iaculor (1), shoot out, spurt forth

* **ē-iciō, -ere, -iēcī, -iectum,** throw out, reject

ē-lābor, -ī, -lāpsus sum, slip away, escape

ē-labōrātus, -a, -um, *lit.* worked out; carefully finished

ēlātiō, -ōnis, *f.,* exaltation

ēlegāns, *gen.* **-antis,** choice, fine, tasteful, refined; fastidious

elephantus, -ī, *m.,* elephant; ivory

ē-levō (1), lift up, raise

* **ē-ligō, -ere, -lēgī, -lēctum,** pick out, select

ē-loquentia, -ae, *f.,* eloquence

ēloquium, -ī, *n., poetic for* **ēloquentia**

ē-loquor, -loquī, -locūtus sum, utter, say, speak

ē-lūceō, -ēre, -lūxī, shine forth, be conspicuous

ē-lūdō, -lūdere, -lūsī, -lūsum, play to the end; parry, ward off; outplay, outmaneuver

ē-luō, -ere, -luī, -lūtum, wash away

ē-mendō (1), free from faults, correct

ē-mergō, -ere, -mersī, -mersum, come forth, emerge

ē-micō, -āre, -uī, -ātum, spring forth, break forth

ē-mineō, -ēre, -uī, project; stand out, be conspicuous

ē-mittō, -ere, -mīsī, -missum, send forth, let go forth

emō, -ere, ēmī, ēmptum, buy

ē-morior, -ī, -mortuus sum, die off, perish

ē-moveō, -movēre, -mōvī, -mōtum, move out, remove

ēmptiō, -ōnis, *f.,* purchase

ēmptor, -ōris, *m.,* purchaser

ēn, *interjection,* see, lo, behold

ē-narrō (1), narrate, explain

* **enim,** *postpositive conj.,* for, indeed, certainly

enim-vērō, *adv.,* certainly, indeed, to be sure

ē-nītor, -ī, -nīxus (nīsus) sum, struggle, strive

ē-notō (1), make notes on

ēnsis, -is, *m.,* sword

* **eō,** *adv.,* to that place

* **eō, īre, iī, itum,** go

* **eō-dem,** *adv.,* to the same place

epigramma, -atis, *n.,* inscription, epigram

epistula (epistola), -ae, *f.,* letter, epistle

* **epulor (1),** feast, dine

* **eques, equitis,** *m.,* horseman, knight, businessman

equester, -tris, -tre, (of) cavalry, equestrian

* **equidem,** *adv. usually emphasizing the 1st person,* indeed, certainly, (I) for my part

equitātus, -ūs, *m.,* cavalry

* **equus, -ī,** *m.,* horse

era, -ae, *f.,* mistress (of a house)

Erebus, -ī, *m.,* the lower world, Hades

ē-rēctus, -a, -um (*partic. of* **ē-rigō**), erect, intent, excited

ergā, *prep.* + *acc.,* toward, in relation to

ergō, *adv.,* therefore

ē-rigō, -ere, -rēxī, -rēctum, direct *or* guide up; erect; excite

* **ē-ripiō, -ere, -ripuī, -reptum,** snatch away

errō (1), wander astray; err, be mistaken

* **error, -ōris,** *m., lit.* a wandering, straying; error, mistake, fault

ērudiō (4), teach

ērudītus, -a, -um, educated, learned, cultivated

ē-rumpō, -ere, -rūpī, -ruptum, burst forth, break out

ē-ruō, -ere, -ruī, -rutum, pluck out, rescue

erus, -ī, *m.,* master (of a house), owner

ē-scendō, -ere, -scendī, -scēnsum, climb up, ascend

estō, *3rd per. sg. of fut. imper. of* **sum,** granted, *lit.* let it be; *also 2nd per. sg.,* be, you shall be

et, *conj.,* and; **et . . . et,** both . . . and; *adv.,* even, also, too

et-enim, *conj.,* for truly, and in fact

* **etiam,** *adv.,* even, also, still, even now

Etrūria, -ae, *f., a district north of Rome*

Etruscus, -a, -um, Etruscan; an Etruscan

et-sī, *conj.,* even if, although; and yet

Eumenides, -um, *f. pl.,* the (three) Furies, *who harassed men for their crimes*

Eurydicē, -ēs, *f., wife of Orpheus*

* ē-vādō, -ere, -vāsī, -vāsum, *lit.* go forth; escape; travel over

ē-vagor, -ārī, -ātus sum, wander, spread (intrans.); transgress

* ē-veniō, -īre, -vēnī, -ventum, come out, turn out, result, happen

ē-ventus, -ūs, *m., lit.* outcome; result

ē-vertō, -ere, -vertī, -versum, overturn, destroy

ē-vidēns, *gen.* -entis, clear, evident

* ex *or* ē, *prep.* + *abl.,* from within, out of, from; because of; **ex parte,** in part

ex-aequō (1), make equal, place on a level

ex-altō (1), elevate, exalt

ex-animis, -e, breathless, lifeless

ex-ārdēscō, -ere, -ārsī, take fire, become hot, glow

ex-audiō (4), hear, listen

ex-cēdō, -ere, -cessī, -cessum, go away from, go beyond, transgress

excellō, -ere, excelluī, excelsum, be superior, surpass, excel

excelsus, -a, -um, lofty, high

ex-cerpō, -ere, -cerpsī, -cerptum, pick out, choose, select

* ex-cipiō, -ere, -cēpī, -ceptum, take out, except; receive, welcome; capture

* ex-citō (1), arouse, excite

ex-clūdō, -ere, -clūsī, -clūsum, shut out, exclude

excūsātiō, -ōnis, *f.,* excuse

ex-cutiō, -ere, -cussī, -cussum, *lit.* shake out; investigate, examine

ex-edō, -ere, -ēdī, -ēsum, eat up, hollow out

exemplar, -āris, *n.,* image, likeness; model

* exemplum, -ī, *n.,* example, model

* ex-eō, -īre, -iī, -itum, go out

exercitātiō, -ōnis, *f.,* exercise, training, practice

* exercitus, -ūs, *m.,* army

exēsus, -a, -um: *partic. of* exedō

ex-horreō, -ēre, -uī, shudder, shudder at

exhortātiō, -ōnis, *f.,* exhortation

ex-igō, -ere, -ēgī, -āctum, drive out; demand, require; complete

exiguus, -a, -um, scanty, small, little

eximius, -a, -um, extraordinary, excellent

ex-imō, -ere, -ēmī, -ēmptum, take away, remove

exīstimātiō, -ōnis, *f.,* judgment; good name, reputation

* exīstimō (1), estimate, reckon, think, consider

existō: *see* exsistō

exitiōsus, -a, -um, disastrous, destructive

* ex-itus, -ūs, *m.,* a going out, departure, passage; end, death; result, outcome

ex-onerō (1), unburden, release

ex-optō (1), desire (**optō**) greatly (**ex**), long for

ex-orior, -īrī, -ortus sum, arise, spring up, come forth

ex-pallēscō, -ere, -palluī, turn very pale

* ex-pediō (4), let loose, set free; prepare, procure; be profitable, advantageous

expedītus, -a, -um, unimpeded, unencumbered, light-armed

ex-pellō, -ere, -pulī, -pulsum, drive out, expel

expergīscor, -ī, -perrēctus sum, wake up

experior, -īrī, -pertus sum, try, test, learn by experience

ex-pers, *gen.* **-pertis (ex-pars),** having no part in, free from (+ *gen.*)

expertus, -a, -um, experienced

* **ex-petō, -ere, -petīvī, -petītum,** seek after, strive for, desire

expīrō: *see* **exspīrō**

ex-plānō (1), explain

ex-plicō, -āre, -āvī *or* **-uī, -ātum,** unfold, release, explain, set forth

ex-plōrō (1), search out, ascertain; **explōrātus, -a, -um,** certain, sure

* **ex-pōnō, -ere, -posuī, -positum,** set forth, explain, expose

ex-primō, -ere, -pressī, -pressum, express, portray, describe

ex-prōmō, -ere, -prōmpsī, -prōmptum, disclose, tell

ex-pugnō (1), take by storm, capture

ex-quīsītus, -a, -um, diligently sought out, choice, exquisite

ex-sanguis, -e, bloodless, lifeless, pale

ex-siliō, -īre, -uī, leap forth, start up

exsilium, -ī, *n.,* exile

* **ex-sistō, -ere, -stitī,** step forth, emerge, arise, appear; exist, be

exspectātiō, -ōnis, *f.,* a waiting, anticipation, expectation

* **ex-spectō** (1), watch for, wait for, expect; wait to see, fear, dread

ex-spīrō (1), breathe out, expire, die

ex-spoliō (1), plunder, rob

exstinguō, -ere, -stīnxī, -stīnctum, extinguish, destroy

ex-stō, -āre, be extant, exist

ex-struō, -ere, -strūxī, -strūctum, heap up

ex-sul, -sulis, *m./f.,* an exile

ex-sulō (1), go into exile, be banished

ex-sultō (1), leap up, rejoice, exult, revel, boast

ex-surgō, -ere, -surrēxī, get up, stand up

ex-suscitō (1), arouse

extemplō, *adv.,* immediately

* **exter** *or* **exterus, -era, -erum,** outside, outer, foreign; *compar.,* **exterior, -ius,** outer, exterior; *superl.,* **extrēmus, -a, -um** outermost, farthest, last, extreme, the last part of

exterius, *adv., see* **extrā**

externus, -a, -um, external

ex-terreō, -ēre, -uī, -itum, frighten, terrify greatly, alarm

ex-timēscō, -ere, -timuī, greatly fear

extrā, *adv. and prep.* + *acc.,* outside; *compar. adv.* **exterius,** on the outside, externally

ex-trahō, -ere, -trāxī, -tractum, drag out

extrēmus, -a, -um (*superl. of* **exterus**), outermost, furthest, last, extreme, the furthest part of; **extrēmum, -ī,** *n.,* outer edge, end

exul: *see* **exsul**

ex-ulcerō (1), *lit.* make very sore; aggravate, intensify

exultō: *see* **exsultō**

ex-ūrō, -ere, -ussī, -ustum, burn up

F

faber, -brī, *m.,* smith, carpenter, engineer

Fabius, -ī, *m., a Roman nomen; e.g.,* Q. Fabius Maximus Cunctator,

*famous for his tactics of delay
against Hannibal*

Fabricius, -ī, *m., a Roman nomen,
especially a general against
Pyrrhus*

* **fābula, -ae,** *f.,* story; play

facētus, -a, -um, elegant, witty,
humorous

faciēs, -ēī, *f.,* form, face, appearance

facilĕ, *adv. of* **facilis,** easily; *compar.*
facilius; *superl.* **facillimē**

* **facilis, -e,** easy

facilitās, -tātis, *f.,* facility, fluency;
courteousness, affability, good
nature

facinorōsus, -a, -um, criminal

* **facinus, -oris,** *n.,* a deed; a bad deed,
misdeed, crime

* **faciō, -ere, fēcī, factum,** make, do,
accomplish, bring about; see to it
(that), take care

* **factum, -ī,** *n., lit.* a thing done; deed,
act

facultās, -tātis, *f.,* ability, skill;
opportunity, means

faeneror, -ārī, -ātus sum, lend at
interest

* **fallō, -ere, fefellī, falsum,** deceive,
cheat, disappoint; be false to;
violate; escape the notice of

* **falsus, -a, -um** (*cp.* **fallō**), false,
deceptive

* **fāma, -ae,** *f.,* rumor, report, tradition

* **famēs, -is,** *f.,* hunger, starvation,
famine

* **familia, -ae,** *f.,* household, family
property, slaves; family; group

familiāris, -e, belonging to a **familia,**
friendly; intimate; **familiāris, -is,**
m., intimate friend

familiāritās, -tātis, *f.,* intimacy, close
friendship

famulus, -ī, *m.,* servant, slave

fānum, -ī, *n.,* temple, shrine

fascis, -is, *m.,* bundle; **fascēs, -ium,**
pl., fasces (*bundle of rods with an
imbedded ax, a sign of high office
with the* **imperium**)

fāstīdium, -ī, *n.,* scorn, disdain,
aversion, haughtiness,
fastidiousness

fātālis, -e, fated, in accordance with
fate; fatal, deadly

* **fateor, -ērī, fassus sum,** confess,
admit

fatīgō (1), tire, weary, exhaust;
harass

fātum, -ī, *n.,* fate

faveō, -ēre, fāvī, fautum, support,
favor

favilla, -ae, *f.,* glowing ashes

favor, -ōris, *m.,* favor

fax, facis, *f.,* torch

fēcundus, -a, -um, fertile, rich

fēlīcitās, -tātis, *f.,* happiness, good
fortune

fēlīx, -līcis, lucky, fortunate, happy

fera, -ae, *f.,* wild animal

* **ferē,** *adv.,* generally, as a rule, about,
almost; **nōn ferē,** scarcely, hardly

fermē = ferē

* **ferō, ferre, tulī, lātum,** bear, carry;
endure; report, say

ferōx, *gen.* **-ōcis,** fierce, bold,
warlike, defiant

* **ferrum, -ī,** *n.,* iron; sword

ferus, -a, -um, wild, savage

fervēns, *gen.* **-entis** (*partic. of* **ferveō**),
boiling, foaming

ferveō, -ēre, ferbuī, boil, foam; rage

* **fessus, -a, -um,** tired, exhausted
festīnātiō, -ōnis, *f.,* haste
festīnō (1), hurry, hasten
festūca, -ae, *f.,* straw, stem
fēstus, -a, -um, festal, festive;
  fēstum, -ī, *n.,* festival, holiday
fētus, -ūs, *m.,* offspring, progeny,
  fruit
fictus, -a, -um (*partic. of* **fingō**),
  fashioned, fictitious, false
fīcus, -ūs, *or* **-ī,** *f.,* fig tree; fig
* **fidēlis, -e,** faithful
* **fidēs, -eī,** *f.,* faith, trust, reliance,
  belief; loyalty, fidelity; pledge,
  word of honor; protection
fidūcia, -ae, *f.,* confidence, reliance,
  trust
fīdus, -a, -um = **fidēlis**
* **fīgō, -ere, fīxī, fīxum,** attach, fasten,
  affix, fix, set up
figūra, -ae, *f.,* form, shape
* **fīlia, -ae,** *f.,* daughter
* **fīlius, -ī,** *m.,* son
fīlum, -ī, *n.,* thread; form, style
findo, -ere, fidī, fissum, cleave,
  split
fingō, -ere, fīnxī, fictum, fashion,
  mold, imagine, pretend, invent
fīniō (4), limit, bound, restrain,
  restrict; end, finish
* **fīnis, -is,** *m.,* end, limit, boundary;
  purpose, aim, goal
* **fīō, fierī, factus sum,** be made, be
  done, become, happen, come
  about
firmō (1), make firm, strengthen,
  fortify
* **firmus, -a, -um,** strong, firm,
  steadfast
fistula, -ae, *f.,* tube, pipe,
  waterpipe

flagellum, -ī, *n.,* scourge
* **flāgitium, -ī,** *n.,* shameful act,
  outrage, disgrace
flāgitō (1), demand
flagrō (1), blaze, be inflamed
Flāminīnus, -ī, *m., Roman general
  who defeated Philip V of Macedon
  in 197* B.C.
Flāminius, -ī, *m.,* C. Flaminius,
  *consul defeated and killed by
  Hannibal at Lake Trasimene in
  217* B.C.
* **flamma, -ae,** *f.,* flame, blaze
flāvus, -a, -um, yellow, reddish
  yellow
* **flectō, -ere, flexī, flexum,** bend, turn;
  change
fleō, -ēre, flēvī, flētum, weep; bewail,
  lament
flētus, -ūs, *m.,* weeping, lamentation
flōrēns, *gen.* **-entis,** blooming,
  flourishing
* **flōs, flōris,** *m.,* flower
fluitō (1), flow; float
* **flūmen, -minis,** *n.,* stream, river
fluō, -ere, fluxī, fluxum, flow
fōculus, -ī, *m., lit.* a little fire; a
  brazier
fodiō, -ere, fōdī, fossum, dig up
foederātus, -a, -um, allied
* **foedus, -a, -um,** foul, hideous, base,
  shameful
foedus, -eris, *n.,* treaty
folium, -ī, *n.,* leaf
* **fōns, -ntis,** *m.,* spring, source,
  fountain
forāmen, -inis, *n.,* hole, perforation
fore (= **futūrus esse**), *an old fut. inf.
  of* **sum; fore ut** + *subjunct. (result)
  can be used as a circumlocution for
  the fut. inf. of a verb*

forēnsis, -e, of the forum, public, forensic

foris, -is, *f.,* door; *pl.,* entrance

* **fōrma, -ae,** *f.,* form, appearance, beauty

Formiānus, -a, -um, of *or* near Formiae, *a coastal town of Latium;* **Formiānum (praedium),** an estate near Formiae

formīdō, -inis, *f.,* dread, terror

fōrmula, -ae, *f.,* rule, regulation, formula

* **fors, fortis,** *f.,* chance, luck; **forte,** *abl. as adv.,* by chance, accidentally

forsitan, *adv. w. subjunct.,* perhaps

fortasse, *adv.,* perhaps

* **forte,** *abl. of* **fors** *as adv.,* by chance

* **fortis, -e,** strong, brave; *adv.* **fortiter**

* **fortitūdō, -dinis,** *f.,* strength, bravery, fortitude

fortuītō, *adv.,* by chance, fortuitously

* **fortūna, -ae,** *f.,* luck, fortune (*good or bad*)

fortūnātus, -a, -um, lucky, fortunate, prosperous

* **forum, -ī,** *n.,* forum, market-place: place of business, law, and government

fovea, -ae, *f.,* pit, pitfall

foveō, -ēre, fōvī, fōtum, warm, cherish

fragilis, -e, easily broken, frail, weak

fragor, -ōris, *m.,* a breaking, crash, noise

* **frangō, -ere, frēgī, frāctum,** break, shatter; subdue

* **frāter, -tris,** *m.,* brother

fraus, fraudis, *f.,* deceit, fraud

frequēns, *gen.* **-entis,** full, crowded

frequenter, *adv.,* in large numbers; frequently

frequentō (1), attend (in large numbers), visit often

fretum, -ī, *n.,* strait, channel

fretus, -ūs, *m.,* = **fretum**

frīgidus, -a, -um, cold; insipid, trivial

frīgus, -oris, *n.,* cold

frīvolus, -a, -um, trifling, worthless

frōns, -ndis, *f.,* leaf, leaves, foliage, leafy bough

frōns, -ntis, *f.,* forehead, brow, appearance

frontispicium, -ī, *n.,* façade, exterior (*ML*)

frūctificō (1), bear fruit (*EL*)

* **frūctus, -ūs,** *m.,* fruit, enjoyment, profit

frūgifer, -era, -erum, fruitful, profitable

frūmentum, -ī, *n.,* grain

* **fruor, fruī, frūctus sum,** enjoy

frūstrā, *adv.,* in vain, without reason

frūx, frūgis, *f.,* grain

* **fuga, -ae,** *f.,* flight

* **fugiō, -ere, fūgī, fugitum,** flee, escape

fugitīvus, -ī, *m.,* runaway slave

fulciō, -īre, fulsī, fultum, prop up, support

fulgeō, -ēre, fulsī, flash, gleam, shine

fulgor, -ōris, *m.,* flash, brightness

fulmen, -minis, *n.,* lightning, thunderbolt

fultūra, -ae, *f.,* prop, support

fulvus, -a, -um, yellow, tawny

fūmō (1), to smoke, steam

fūmus, -ī, *m.,* smoke

funda, -ae, *f.,* sling, sling-stone

fundamentum, -ī, *n.,* base, foundation

funditus, *adv.,* utterly, completely

fundō, -ere, fūdī, fūsum, pour, pour forth; spread, scatter, rout

fūnestus, -a, -um, fatal, calamitous

fungor, -ī, fūnctus sum, perform, discharge, complete

furibundus, -a, -um, furious, mad

furor, -ōris, *m.,* rage, madness

fūrtum, -ī, *n.,* theft; stolen property

fūsilis, -e, molten, liquified, fluid

fūsus, -a, -um: *see* **fundō**

G

Gāius, -ī, *m., a common Roman praenomen; see also under* **C.**

Gallia, -ae, *f.,* Gaul, *the territory extending roughly from the Pyrenees to the Rhine*

Gallus, -a, -um, Gallic; **Gallus, -ī,** *m.,* a Gaul; **Gallus, -ī,** *m., a Roman name*

* **gaudeō, -ēre, gāvīsus sum,** rejoice, be glad

* **gaudium, -ī,** *n.,* joy, gladness

Gāvius, -ī, *m., a Roman citizen crucified by Verres*

gelidus, -a, -um, icy, cold

gelū, -ūs, *n.,* frost, cold

geminō (1), double, repeat

* **geminus, -a, -um,** double, twin

gemitus, -ūs, *m.,* groan

gemma, -ae, *f.,* bud; jewel, gem

gemō, -ere, -uī, -itum, groan, lament

gena, -ae *f.,* cheek

gener, -erī, *m.,* son-in-law

generātiō, -ōnis, *f.,* generation (*EL*)

generōsus, -a, -um, noble, excellent, magnanimous

geniāliter, *adv.,* gaily, joyfully

* **gēns, gentis,** *f.,* clan, tribe, nation

* **genus, -eris,** *n.,* kind, sort, class, category, nature, race

* **gerō, -ere, gessī, gestum,** bear, wear; manage, conduct, carry on, perform; **bellum gerere,** wage war; **sē gerere,** conduct oneself, behave; **rēs gestae, rērum gestārum,** *f. pl.,* exploits, history

gestiō (4), exult, be excited *or* transported, desire eagerly

gestō (1), carry about, bear, wear

gignō, -ere, genuī, genitum, beget, bring forth

gladiātor, -ōris, *m.,* gladiator, robber

gladius, -ī, *m.,* sword

glaeba, -ae, *f.,* clod, lump of soil

* **glōria, -ae,** *f.,* glory, fame

Gnaeus, -ī, *m., a Roman praenomen; e.g.,* Gnaeus Pompeius Magnus

Gorgō, -gonis, *f., one of 3 sisters of whom the most famous was Medusa*

gradātim, *adv.,* step by step, by degrees

gradus, -ūs, *m.,* step, position, degree, rank; stand, stance

Graeculus, -ī, *m.,* a Greekling

* **Graecus, -a, -um,** Greek; **Graecus, -ī,** *m.,* a Greek

grāmineus, -a, -um, grassy; of bamboo

grandis, -e, grownup, large; important, lofty

grassor, -ārī, -ātus sum, proceed, act; attack

* **grātia, -ae,** *f.,* charm, grace; favor, regard; thankfulness, gratitude; **grātiās agere,** to thank; **grātiam habēre,** be thankful, feel grateful

grātīs *or* **grātiīs,** *abl. of* **grātia,** out of favor *or* kindness, without recompense, for nothing

grātulor, -ārī, -ātus sum, rejoice; congratulate

* **grātus, -a, -um,** pleasing, grateful

* **gravis, -e,** heavy, weighty, important, grave, serious, severe

gravitās, -tātis, *f.,* weight, gravity, seriousness, importance

graviter, *adv.,* heavily, severely, deeply, grievously

gravō (1), make heavy, weigh down

gravor, -ārī, -ātus sum, be weighed down; be reluctant

gubernāculum, -ī, *n.,* helm, rudder

gubernātor, -ōris, *m.,* pilot

guerra, -ae, *f.* = **bellum** (*ML*)

gula, -ae, *f.,* throat; appetite

gustō (1), taste, take a snack

guttur, -uris, *n.,* throat

Gȳgēs, -is, *m.,* *a king of Lydia*

gymnasium, -ī, *n.,* gymnasium, *which, in addition to the exercise area, usu. had rooms for intellectual and artistic activities*

gyrō (1), go around, move in circles

H

* **habeō, -ēre, habuī, habitum,** have, hold, possess; consider, regard, think

habilis, -e, skillful

habitō (1), inhabit; dwell

habitus, -ūs, *m.,* appearance; dress; condition, nature

hāc-tenus, *adv.,* thus far, up to this time *or* point

haedus, -ī, *m.,* a kid, young goat

Haemus, -ī, *m.,* *a mountain range in Thrace*

haereō, -ēre, haesī, haesum, cling, stick; hesitate, be perplexed

haesitō, (1), *lit.* to stick fast, remain fixed; hesitate

Hamilcar, -caris, *m.,* *a Carthaginian name, espec.* Hamilcar Barca, *father of Hannibal and general in the First Punic War*

Hannibal, -balis, *m.,* *Carthaginian general in 2nd Punic War; see Livy*

harēna, -ae, *f.,* sand

harundō, -inis, *f.,* reed, rod

Hasdrubal, -balis, *m.,* *a Carthaginian name, espec. the brother of Hannibal*

hasta, -ae, *f.,* spear

haud, not, not at all; **haud sciō an,** I am inclined to think

hauriō, -īre, hausī, haustum, draw out, drain, drink up *or* in; exhaust

haustus, -ūs, *m.,* drink, draft

Helicē, -ēs, (*acc.* **-ēn**), *f.,* the Great Bear *or* Dipper, *constellation of Ursa Major*

hera = **era**

herba, -ae, *f.,* grass; plant

hercule, *or* **hercle,** *interjection,* by Hercules, good Heavens, certainly

hērōs, -ōis (*acc.* **-ōa**), hero

herus = **erus**

Hesperides, -um (*acc.* **-as**), *f., pl.,* daughters of Hesperus (*the Evening Star in the west*) *and guardians of the golden apples*

hetaeria, -ae, *f.,* fraternity, secret society

heu, *interjection,* oh! ah! alas!; *actually the spelling of a sigh*

heus, *interjection,* come now, see
   here, say

hiātus, -ūs, *m.,* opening, cleft

Hibērus, -ī, *m.,* the river Ebro *in
   eastern Spain*

* **hīc,** *adv.,* in this place, here

* **hic, haec, hoc,** *demonstrative adj. and
   pron.,* this, the latter; *at times
   hardly more than* he, she, it

hiems, hiemis, *f.,* winter, storm

Hierusalem, *indecl. n.,* Jerusalem
   (*EL*)

hilaris, -e, cheerful, glad

hilaritās, -tātis, *f.,* enjoyment,
   amusement, gayety

hinc, *adv.,* from this place, hence;
   here; henceforth; for this reason

Hippolytus, -ī, *m., son of Theseus*

Hispānia, -ae, *f.,* Spain (*including
   Portugal*)

historia, -ae, *f.,* history, historical
   work

ho-diē, *adv.,* today

hodiernus, -a, -um, of this day,
   today's

* **homō, hominis,** *m./f.,* human being,
   man, person

* **honestās, -tātis,** *f.,* honor, virtue,
   worth

* **honestus, -a, -um,** honorable, worthy,
   noble; **honestum, -ī,** *n.,* morality,
   moral excellence, virtue

* **honor (honōs), -ōris,** *m.,* honor,
   esteem, respect, public office

honōrō (1), to honor

* **hōra, -ae,** *f.,* hour; time

Horātius, -a, -um, *belonging to the
   Horatian gens; espec. the three
   Roman Horatii who fought the
   three Alban Curiatii;* Horatius
   Cocles, *who defended the Tiber*

bridge against Porsenna; Q.
   Horatius Flaccus, *the lyric poet*

horror, -ōris, *m.,* a shuddering,
   dread, terror, horror

* **hortor, -ārī, -ātus sum,** urge,
   encourage

hortus, -ī, *m.,* garden

hospes, -pitis, *m.,* guest; host;
   stranger

hostīlis, -e, of an enemy, hostile

Hostīlius, -a, -um, Hostilian,
   *referring espec. to Tullus Hostilius,
   third king of Rome*

* **hostis, -is,** *m.,* an enemy (*of the
   state*); *pl.,* **hostēs,** the enemy

* **hūc,** *adv.,* to this place, to this;
   hūcine, *the interrog. form*

* **hūmānitās, -tātis,** *f.,* kindness,
   courtesy, refinement, culture

hūmāniter, *adv. of* **hūmānus,** in a
   cultured, refined manner; kindly

hūmānus, -a, -um, human; humane,
   kind; cultured, refined

humiliō (1), to humble (*EL*)

humilis, -e, *lit.* on the ground;
   humble, insignificant, lowly

humus, -ī, *f.,* earth, ground; **humī,**
   loc., on the ground

Hymenaeus, -ī, *m.,* Hymen, *the god
   of marriage*

hȳpocrita, -ae, *m.,* actor; hypocrite
   (*EL*)

I

* **iaceō, -ēre, -uī,** lie; lie dead

* **iaciō, -ere, iēcī, iactum,** throw

iactūra, -ae, *f., lit.* a throwing away;
   loss; **iactūram facere,** suffer a loss

* **iam,** *adv.,* now, already, soon; **iam
   diū** *or* **prīdem,** long ago

Iāniculum, -ī, *n., a hill across the Tiber from Rome*

iānua, -ae, *f.,* door, *espec.* outside door

Iānuārius, -a, -um, of January

* **ibī,** *adv.,* there; thereupon

Īcarus, -ī, *m., son of Daedalus*

īcō, -ere, īcī, ictum, strike, hit, stab; **foedus īcere,** strike *or* make a treaty

* **ictus, -ūs,** *m.,* blow, stroke

id-circō, *adv.,* on that account, therefore

* **īdem, eadem, idem,** *demonstr. adj. and pron.,* the same

* **ideō,** *adv.,* on that account, therefore

idōneus, -a, -um, fit, suitable, proper

iecur, -oris, *n.,* the liver

iēiūnō (1), fast (*EL*)

Iēsus, -u, *m.,* Jesus

* **igitur,** *postpositive conj.,* therefore, then

ignārus, -a, -um, not knowing, ignorant; not known, unknown

ignāvia, -ae, *f.,* idleness, inactivity; cowardice

* **ignis, -is,** *m.,* fire

ignōminia, -ae, *f.,* disgrace, dishonor

ignōrantia, -ae, *f.,* ignorance

* **ignōrō** (1), not to know, be ignorant, be unacquainted with

* **ignōscō, -ere, -nōvī, -nōtum,** pardon, forgive

ignōtus, -a, -um, unknown, strange

īlex, -icis, *f.,* oak tree

īlia, -ium, *n. pl.,* abdomen, groin, genitals, entrails

illāc (*sc.* **viā**), *adv.,* that way

* **ille, illa, illud,** *demonstrative adj. and pron.,* that, the former; *at times weakened to* he, she, it

illinc, *adv.,* from that place, thence; there

illūc, *adv.,* to that place

illūstris: *see* **inlūstris**

imāgō, -ginis, *f.,* image, portrait

imbēcillitās, -tātis, *f.,* weakness

imbēcillus, -a, -um, weak, feeble

im-bellis, -e, unwarlike

imber, -bris, *m.,* violent rain, storm; shower

imitor, -ārī, -ātus sum, copy, imitate

immānis, -e, enormous, horrible

im-memor, *gen.* **-oris,** unmindful, forgetful

immēnsus, -a, -um, immeasurable, immense

im-migrō (1), move into, migrate

im-mineō, -ēre, hang over, threaten, be imminent

im-misceō, -ēre, -miscuī, -mixtum, mix, mingle

immō, *adv.,* nay rather, on the contrary; indeed

im-moderātē, *adv.,* without measure, immoderately

im-modicus, -a, -um, immoderate, excessive, unrestrained

im-molō (1), to sacrifice

im-mortālis, -e, immortal

im-mūtābilis, -e, unchangeable

im-mūtō (1), change, transform

impedīmentum, -ī, *n.,* hindrance; *pl.* = baggage

impediō (4), entangle, impede, hinder, prevent

im-pellō, -ere, -pulī, -pulsum, push forward, impel, urge

im-pendeō, -ēre, hang over, threaten, impend

* **imperātor, -ōris,** *m.,* commander, general; emperor

imperitō (1), govern, command

* **imperium, -ī,** *n.,* command, military authority, power, rule; dominion, empire; the supreme power of command *held by the consuls*

imperō (1), give commands to, command, order

impertiō, -īre, -īvī, -ītum, share *or* divide with

* **im-petrō** (1), get, obtain, gain by request, accomplish, succeed in a request

* **im-petus, -ūs,** *m.,* violent movement, violence, attack

im-piger, -gra, -grum, not lazy, energetic

* **im-pleō, -ēre, -plēvī, -plētum,** fill up, complete, satisfy, accomplish, fulfil

im-plicō, -āre, -uī *or* **-āvī, -ātum,** enfold, involve, entangle

implōrātiō, -ōnis, *f.,* an imploring

im-plōrō (1), implore, beseech

im-pōnō, -ere, -posuī, -positum, put on *or* in

importūnitās, -tātis, *f.,* insolence, ruthlessness

im-probus, -a, -um, not good, base, wicked, shameless

im-prōvidus, -a, -um, *lit.* not foreseeing; heedless, imprudent

imprūdentia, -ae, *f.,* lack of foresight; ignorance

impudēns, *gen.* **-entis,** shameless, impudent

impūnē, *adv.,* with impunity, safely

im-pūnitās, -tātis, *f.,* impunity

im-pūrus, -a, -um, unclean, foul, shameful

īmus, -a, -um, *a superl. of* **īnferus**

* **in,** *prep.* (1) + *abl.,* in, on, among, in the case of; (2) + *acc.,* into, toward, against

in-amoenus, -a, -um, unpleasant, unlovely, dismal

in-animus, -a, -um, without life, inanimate

inānis, -e, empty, vain, useless, idle

inaugurō (1), take the auguries; consecrate

* **in-cēdō, -ere, -cessī, -cessum,** advance, attack

incendium, -ī, *n.,* fire, heat, conflagration

in-cendō, -ere, -cendī, -cēnsum, set on fire, inflame, excite, enrage

inceptus, -ūs, *m.,* beginning, undertaking

* **in-certus, -a, -um,** uncertain

in-cǐdo, -ere, -cǐdi, -cāsum (cadō), fall into *or* upon, come upon, fall in with; happen, occur

in-cīdo, -ere, -cīdī, -cīsum (caedō), cut into, inscribe

in-cipiō, -ere, -cēpī, -ceptum, begin

incitāmentum, -ī, *n.,* inducement, incentive

incitō (1), arouse, stir up, incite

in-clāmō (1), cry out to, call upon

in-clinō (1), lean, bend, incline

inclitus, -a, -um, famous

in-cognitus, -a, -um, unknown, unexamined

incohō (1), begin

incola, -ae, *m.,* inhabitant, resident

in-colō, -ere, -uī, -cultum, dwell, inhabit, live in

in-columis, -e, uninjured, safe

in-commodum, -ī, *n.,* inconvenience, trouble, disadvantage, harm

incōnsīderātē, *adv.,* without consideration

in-continenter, *adv.,* intemperately

in-corruptus, -a, -um, uncorrupted, unspoiled, trustworthy

* **incrēdibilis, -e,** incredible, extraordinary

in-crepitō (1), call out to; reproach, rebuke

in-crepō, -āre, -uī, -itum, rattle, make a din; speak angrily; reproach, rebuke

in-crēscō, -ere, -crēvī, grow, increase

in-cultus, -a, -um, uncultivated; unrefined, rude

in-cumbō, -ere, -cubuī, -cubitum, lie on, lean on, throw oneself on, fall on

* **in-de,** *adv.,* thence; after that, thereupon

in-decōrus, -a, -um, unbecoming, unseemly, disgraceful; *adv.* **indecōrē**

index, -dicis, *m.,* witness, informer

India, -ae, *f.,* India

indicium, -ī, evidence, proof

* **in-dicō** (1), declare, make known

* **in-dīcō, -ere, -dīxī, -dictum,** proclaim, declare; impose

in-dictus, -a, -um, unsaid; **indictā causā,** *lit.* the case not having been said = without a hearing

indigentia, -ae, *f.,* need, want

indignātiō, -ōnis, *f.,* indignation; a cause for indignation

indignitās, -tātis, *f.,* shamefulness, indignity

in-dignor, -ārī, -ātus sum, consider as unworthy; be offended, indignant

* **in-dignus, -a, -um,** unworthy; undeserved, cruel, harsh; *adv.,* **indignē**

in-discrētus, -a, -um, without distinction; not distinguishing, indiscreet; *adv.,* **indiscrētē,** indiscriminately, indiscreetly

in-dō, -ere, -didī, -ditum, put into, apply

indolēs, -is, *f.,* nature, disposition, talents

indolēscō, -ere, -doluī, grieve

in-dūcō, -ere, -dūxī, -ductum, bring in, introduce

in-dulgeō, -ēre, -dulsī, -dultum, be indulgent to, gratify, give oneself up to

* **induō, -ere, -uī, -ūtum,** put on, dress; wrap, entangle

in-dūrēscō, -ere, -dūruī, become hard, be hardened

industria, -ae, *f.,* diligence, industry; **dē** *or* **ex industriā,** intentionally, on purpose

indūtiae, -ārum, *f. pl.,* truce

inēbriō (1), intoxicate

in-eō, -īre, -iī, -itum, go into, enter upon, undertake, commence

in-eptē, *adv.,* unsuitably, foolishly

in-eptus, -a, -um (in-aptus), unsuitable, silly, absurd

in-errō (1), wander over

in-ers, *gen.* **-ertis,** *lit.* without skill; lazy, idle; dull

inertia, -ae, *f.,* inactivity, laziness

* **īn-fāmia, -ae,** *f.,* ill report, ill repute, disgrace, reproach

īn-fāmis, -e, disreputable, infamous, disgraceful

īn-fāns, -fantis, *m./f.,* infant

īn-fēlīx, *gen.* **-īcis,** unhappy, unfortunate, miserable

īnfēnsus, -a, -um, hostile

īnfernus, -a, -um, underground, infernal; **īnfernum, -ī,** *n.,* the depths of the earth

* **īn-ferō, -ferre, intulī, inlātum,** bring in, introduce; occasion, produce; **bellum īnferre** + *dat.,* make war on

īnferus, -a, -um, below; **īnferī, -ōrum,** *m. pl.,* those below, the dead; *compar.* **īnferior, -ius,** lower, inferior; *superl.* **īnfimus, -a, -um** (also **īmus, -a, -um**), lowest, lowest part of; meanest, basest

* **īnfestus, -a, -um,** unsafe, dangerous; hostile

īn-fīdus, -a, -um, unfaithful, untrue

īn-fīnītus, -a, -um, infinite

īnfirmitās, -tātis, *f.,* weakness

īn-firmus, -a, -um, week, feeble

īn-flammō (1), inflame, stir up, rouse

īn-flātus, -a, -um, blown up, puffed up, haughty

īn-flexibilis, -e, inflexible

īn-fōrmis, -e, shapeless, hideous

īn-fōrmō (1), to form, shape; describe; educate

īn-fundō, -ere, -fūdī, -fūsum, pour in, on, over

ingemēscō, -ere, -gemuī, groan

in-generō (1), implant

* **ingenium, -ī,** *n.,* inborn ability, nature, talent, genius

* **ingēns,** *gen.* **-entis,** vast, huge, immense

ingenuus, -a, -um, native, free born

in-grātus, -a, -um, ungrateful; displeasing

in-gravēscō, -ere, become heavy, become a burden, grow worse

in-gredior, -gredī, -gressus sum, go into, go forward, advance; undertake

in-hibeō, -ere, -uī, -itum, hold back, restrain

in-hūmānus, -a, -um, inhuman, savage, cruel

* **in-imīcus, -a, -um (-amīcus),** unfriendly, hostile; **inimīcus, -ī,** *m.,* personal enemy

inīquitās, -tātis, *f.,* unevenness, unfavorableness; injustice, unfairness; iniquity, sin (*EL*)

in-īquus, -a, -um (-aequus), unequal, uneven; unfair, unjust, adverse

initium, -ī, *m.,* beginning

* **iniūria, -ae,** *f.,* injury, injustice, wrong, harm

in-iussū, *idiomatic abl.,* without orders *or* command

in-iūstitia, -ae, *f.,* injustice

* **in-iūstus, -a, -um,** unjust; *adv.* **iniūstē**

in-laesus, -a, -um, uninjured

inlūstris, -e, bright, clear, illustrious, famous

in-nītor, -ī, -nīxus *or* **-nīsus sum,** lean on, support oneself by

in-nocēns, *gen.* **-entis,** guiltless, innocent, harmless

innocentia, -ae, *f.,* innocence

in-noxius, -a, -um, *lit.* not harming; harmless; innocent

in-numerābilis, -e, countless

inopia, -ae, *f.,* want, lack, need

in-ops, *gen.* **-opis,** *adj.,* poor, needy, lacking, destitute

in-pōnō: *see* **im-pōnō**

* **inquam,** I say; **inquis,** you say; **inquit,**

he says: *defective verb used parenthetically in direct quotations and repetitions*

in-quiētō (1), disturb, disquiet

inquīsītiō, -ōnis, *f.,* inquiry

in-rīdeō, -ēre, -rīsī, -rīsum, laugh at, mock, ridicule

in-ritus, -a, -um, not valid, invalid, void, useless

īn-sānābilis, -e, incurable

īn-sāniō (4), be mad, be insane

īn-serō, -ere, -sēvī, -situm, sow in, implant, instill

īn-serō, -ere, -seruī, -sertum, put in, insert, introduce, join

īn-sideō, -ēre, -sēdī, -sessum, *lit.* sit in; possess, occupy

īnsidiae, -ārum, *f. pl.,* ambush; plot, treachery

īnsidiātor, -ōris, *m.,* a man in ambush, waylayer, plotter

īn-sīdō, -ere, -sēdī, -sessum, sit down on, settle in

īnsignis, -e, distinguished, notable

īn-sipiēns, *gen.* **-entis,** unwise, foolish; *as a noun, m.,* fool

īn-situs, -a, -um, implanted, innate

īn-sōns, *gen.* **-ntis,** innocent, guiltless

īn-spērātus, -a, -um, unhoped for, unexpected

īn-spiciō, -ere, -spexī, -spectum, examine, inspect; investigate

īnstar, *indecl. n. noun,* image, likeness; + *gen.,* like, as large as

īn-stituō, -ere, -tuī, -tūtum, establish, appoint; determine; instruct

īnstitūtiō, -ōnis, *f.,* = **īnstitūtum**

* **īnstitūtum, -ī,** *n.,* custom, institution; instruction, principles

īnstrūmentum, -ī, *n.,* tool, instrument

īn-struō, -ere, -struxī, -structum, draw up, arrange, make ready; teach, instruct

īn-sūdō (1), sweat at

īnsula, -ae, *f.,* island

īnsulānus, -ī, *m.,* islander

īn-sum, -esse, -fuī, -futūrus, be in, be contained in

in-tāctus, -a, -um, untouched, uninjured

* **integer, -gra, -grum,** untouched, uninjured, blameless, honest; pure, fresh; **dē integrō,** afresh

intellegentia, -ae, *f.,* intelligence, understanding, perception

* **intellegō, -ere, -lēxī, -lēctum,** understand, perceive

in-tempestīvus, -a, -um, untimely, unseasonable

* **in-tendō, -ere, -tendī, -tentum,** stretch, aim, direct, intend

in-tentus, -a, -um (*cp.* **tendō**), *lit.* stretched; intent, attentive, alert

* **inter,** *prep.* + *acc.,* between, among, amid

inter-aestuō (1), be inflamed (in places)

inter-diū, *adv.,* by day

interdum, *adv.,* sometimes, from time to time, occasionally

intereā, *adv.,* meanwhile, in the meantime

inter-ficiō, -ere, -fēcī, -fectum, kill, slay, murder

interim, *adv.,* meanwhile

inter-imō, -ere, -ēmī, -ēmptum, take away; destroy, kill

interior, -ius, inner, interior

inter-itus, -ūs, *m.,* destruction, ruin

interius, *adv.,* on the inside, within

inter-mittō, -ere, -mīsī, -missum, interrupt, neglect, omit

internus, -a, -um, internal

interpres, -pretis, *m./f.,* messenger, expounder, translator

interpretātiō, -ōnis, *f.,* interpretation

interpretor, -ārī, -ātus sum, explain, interpret

* **inter-rogō** (1), ask, question; examine

inter-rumpō, -ere, -rūpī, -ruptum, break down

* **inter-sum, -esse, -fuī,** *lit.* be between *or* in the midst of; be present at, take part in, attend (+ *dat.*); **interest,** *impers.,* it is of importance *or* interest, it concerns, it makes a difference, *with the subject commonly an inf. clause, an* **ut-**clause, *or an ind. quest.*

inter-vallum, -ī, *n.,* space between, interval

inter-veniō, -īre, -vēnī, -ventum, come between, interrupt

inter-vīsō, -ere, -vīsī, -vīsum, visit (from time to time)

intimus, -a, -um (*superl. of* **interior**), innermost, intimate, most profound; *adv.* **intimē**

in-tinguō, -ere, -tīnxī, -tīnctum, dip

in-tolerābilis, -e, unendurable, intolerable

in-tōnsus, -a, -um, unshorn

intrā, *adv.,* within; *prep.* + *acc.,* into, within

intrō, *adv.,* inside, within

intrō (1), go into, enter

intro-eō, -īre, -iī, -itum, enter

intro-itus, -ūs, *m.,* a going within, entrance

* **in-tueor, -ērī, -tuitus sum,** look at, contemplate, consider

intus, *adv.,* within

in-ultus, -a, -um, unavenged

in-ūsitātus, -a, -um, unusual

in-ūtilis, -e, useless, injurious

in-vādō, -ere, -vāsī, -vāsum, go in, attack, invade, befall, seize

in-validus, -a, -um, weak

in-vehō, -ere, -vexī, -vectum, carry into, bring in; *w. reflex. pron. or in passive,* carry oneself against, attack (*physically or with words*), inveigh against

* **in-veniō, -īre, -vēnī, -ventum,** come upon, find, discover

inventor, -ōris, *m.,* discoverer, inventor

in-vertō, -ere, -vertī, -versum, turn about

investīgātiō, -ōnis, *f.,* investigation

investīgō (1), search out, track out

inveterāscō, -ere, -veterāvī, grow old, become fixed *or* established

in-vicem, *adv.,* in turn, by turns, alternately; mutually

in-victus, -a, -um, unconquered; unconquerable, invincible

* **in-videō, -ēre, -vīdī, -vīsum,** look askance at, envy, be jealous of, begrudge

invidia, -ae, *f., lit.* a looking askance at; envy, jealousy; odium, unpopularity

invidiōsus, -a, -um, envious; envied; hated

invidus, -a, -um, envious, jealous

inviolātus, -a, -um, unhurt, inviolable

in-vīsitātus, -a, -um, unseen; strange

in-vīsus, -a, -um, hated, hateful

invītō (1), invite

invītus, -a, -um, unwilling, against one's will

invius, -a, -um, pathless, impassable; **invia, -ōrum,** *n. pl.,* trackless places

Īphigenīa, -ae, *f., daughter of Agamemnon, who sacrificed her to win a safe voyage against Troy*

* **ipse, ipsa, ipsum,** *intensive pron.,* himself, herself, itself, etc.

* **īra, -ae,** *f.,* anger, wrath

īrācundia, -ae, *f.,* irascibility, wrath

īrātus, -a, -um, angry

irr-: *see* **inr-**

* **is, ea, id,** *demonstrative pron. and adj.,* this, that; he, she, it

* **iste, ista, istud,** *demonstrative adj. and pron.,* that of yours, that, such; *sometimes with contemptuous force*

istūc, *adv.,* to where you are, to what you mention

* **ita,** *adv.,* so, thus

Ītalia, -ae, *f.,* Italy

* **itaque,** and so, therefore

* **item,** *adv.,* also, likewise

* **iter, itineris,** *n.,* journey, way, road

* **iterum,** *adv.,* again, a second time

* **iubeō, -ēre, iussī, iussum,** bid, order

iūcunditās, -tātis, *f.,* pleasantness, delight

iūcundus, -a, -um, pleasant, agreeable

* **iūdex, -dicis,** *m.,* judge, juror; **iūdicēs** (*voc.*), gentlemen of the jury

* **iūdicium, -ī,** *n.,* trial, judgment; court, jury

iūdicō (1), decide, judge

iugulō (1), cut the throat of, slay, destroy

iugulum, -ī, *n.,* throat

* **iugum, -ī,** *n.,* yoke; ridge

* **iūmentum, -ī,** *n.,* beast of burden, pack animal

* **iungō, -ere, iūnxī, iūnctum,** join, unite

iūnior, -ōris, *m./f.,* rather young *or* youthful (person); **iūniōrēs, -um,** *m. pl., often =* men of military age (under 46 years)

Iūnōnius, -a, -um, belonging to *or* sacred to Juno

Iuppiter, *gen.* **Iovis,** *m.,* Jupiter *or* Jove, *king of the gods*

iūris-dictiō, -ōnis, *f.,* administration of justice

* **iūrō** (1), take an oath, swear; **iūrātus, -a, -um,** having sworn, under oath, on oath

* **iūs, iūris,** *n.,* right, law; privilege; **iūs iūrandum, iūris iūrandī,** *n.,* oath

iussū, *idiomatic abl.,* by order *or* command

iūstificō (1), do justice to; justify, forgive

* **iūstitia, -ae,** *f.,* justice

iūstus, -a, -um, just, right; proper, regular; *adv.* **iūstē**

* **iuvenis,** *gen.* **-is,** *m./f.,* young, youthful; *as a noun,* a young man *or* woman (*of 20–45 years*)

iuventūs, -tūtis, *f.,* youth; young man in the army

* **iuvō, -āre, iūvī, iūtum,** help

iuxtā: *adv.,* near, nearby, equally, in like manner; *prep.* + *acc.,* close *or* near to

Ixīōn, -onis, *m., legendary king of*

Thessaly condemned to the torture
of the wheel in Tartarus for an
insult to Juno

K

Kal., *abbr. of* **Kalendae:** *see* **Calendae**

L

L., *abbr. of* **Lūcius,** *a praenomen*
Labeō, -ōnis, *m., a cognomen*
labēs, -is, *f.,* ruin; disgrace
labō (1), totter, waver
* **labor, -ī, lapsus sum,** slip, fall; err
* **labor, -ōris,** *m.,* labor, toil; hardship,
   difficulty, distress, suffering
labōriōsus, -a, -um, full of toil *or*
   hardship, laborious
labōrō (1), labor, toil; suffer, be in
   distress
Lacedaemonius, -a, -um, Spartan; *m.*
   pl. as a noun, Spartans
lacertus, -ī, *m.,* (upper) arm
lacessō, -ere, -īvī, -ītum, provoke,
   irritate, harass
* **lacrima, -ae,** *f.,* tear
lacrimōsus, -a, -um, tearful;
   mournful
lacus, -ūs, *m.,* lake
Laelius, -ī, *m., a Roman nomen,*
   especially Gaius Laelius,
   commemorated in Cicero's **Dē**
   Amīcitiā
laetitia, -ae, *f.,* joy, delight;
   entertainment
laetor, -ārī, -ātus sum, rejoice, be
   glad
* **laetus, -a, -um,** glad, joyful
laevus, -a, -um, left, on the left
   side

laguncula, -ae, *f.,* flask
lambō, -ere, lick, lap
lāmmina, -ae, *f.,* thin plate *or* layer;
   plate of iron (*heated for torture*)
lancea, -ae, *f.,* lance, light spear
languidus, -a, -um, weak, languid,
   dull, inactive
laniō (1), tear to pieces, mangle
lapis, -idis, *m.,* stone
lāpsus, -ūs, *m.,* sliding, slipping
Larius, -ī, *m.,* Lake Como, *Alpine*
   lake in northern Italy
Lars, Lartis, *m., an Etruscan name*
   or title
lassus, -a, -um, weary, tired
lātē, *adv. of* **lātus**
* **lateō, -ere, -uī,** lie hidden, hide;
   escape the notice of, be concealed
   from (+ *acc.*)
latibulum, -ī, *n.,* hiding place, shelter
Latīnus, -a, -um, Latin; **Via Latīna,**
   a very old Roman road running
   southeast from Rome; adv. **Latīnē,**
   in Latin, *espec. w.* **dīcere, loquī,**
   etc.
latrō, -ōnis, *m.,* robber, bandit,
   cutthroat
latrōcinium, -ī, *n.,* robbery; fraud
lātum: *see* **ferō**
* **lātus, -a, -um,** broad, wide,
   extensive; copious; *adv.* **lātē,**
   broadly, widely; **longē lātēque,** far
   and wide
latus, -eris, *n.,* side
laudābilis, -e, praiseworthy, laudable
* **laudō** (1), praise, approve
Laurentīnus, -a, -um, Laurentine, of
   Laurentum (*a town on the coast*
   south of Ostia); **Laurentīnum** (*sc.*
   praedium), Laurentine estate
laus, laudis, *f.,* praise, renown

lautumiae, -ārum, *f. pl.,* stonequarry, *used as a prison at Syracuse*

lautus, -a, -um (*see* **lavō**), washed; elegant, refined

Lāvīnium, -ī, *n., a town said to have been founded in Latium by Aeneas*

lavō, -āre, lāvī, lautum *or* **lōtum,** wash, bathe

laxō (1), relax, slacken

Lazarus, -ī, *m., the beggar in the parable of Dives and Lazarus* (*EL*)

lea, -ae, *f.,* lioness

leaena, -ae, *f.,* lioness

Lebinthos, -ī, *f., a small island of the Sporades in the Aegean Sea off the southwestern coast of Asia Minor*

lectīcula, -ae, *f.,* small litter

lēgātus, -ī, *m.,* ambassador; lieutenant

legiō, -ōnis, *f.,* legion

lēgitimus, -a, -um, legal, legitimate, proper; *adv.* **lēgitimē**

* **lēgō** (1), appoint, send as an ambassador; bequeath

* **legō, -ere, lēgī, lēctum,** gather, pick, choose; read

Lēnaeus, -a, -um, Lenaean, *epithet of Bacchus*

lēniō (4), alleviate, soothe

lēnis, -e, soft, mild, gentle, kind

leō, -ōnis, *m.,* lion

lepos, -ōris, *m.,* charm, grace, wit

lētum, -ī, *n.,* death, ruin

* **levis, -e,** light, trivial

Lēvītā, -ae, *m., a Levite* (*EL*)

levitās, -tātis, *f.,* lightness, levity, fickleness, weakness

levō (1), lighten; raise, lift up; relieve, console

* **lēx, lēgis,** *f.,* law

libellus, -ī, *m.,* little book; notebook; pamphlet

libenter, *adv.,* gladly, with pleasure, willingly

* **liber, -brī,** *m.,* book

* **līber, -era, -erum,** free, unrestricted

Līber, -erī, *m., Roman equivalent of the Greek Bacchus*

Lībera, -ae, *f., Italian equivalent of Proserpina, daughter of Ceres*

līberālis, -e, *lit.* worthy of a free man; noble, honorable, generous

līberālitās, -tātis, *f.,* kindness, generosity

līberātor, -ōris, *m.,* liberator

līberē, *adv.,* freely

līberī, -ōrum, *m. pl.,* children

* **līberō** (1), free, liberate

* **lībertās, -tātis,** *f.,* liberty

lībertīnus, -ī, *m.,* a freedman; a libertine

* **lībertus, -ī,** *m.,* a freedman, ex-slave

libet, -ēre, libuit, *impers.,* it is pleasing, it gives one pleasure

libīdinōsē, licentiously, lustfully; wilfully, arbitrarily

libīdinōsus, -a, -um, licentious, lustful; wilful, arbitrary

* **libīdō, -dinis,** *f.,* desire; lust

librārius, -ī, *m.,* scribe, copyist

lībrō (1), balance, poise

Liburnica, -ae, *f., a swift ship* (*like those of Liburnian pirates of the Adriatic*)

licentia, -ae, *f.,* license

* **licet, -ēre, licuit,** *impers.,* it is permitted, one may

lignum, -ī, *n.,* wood

ligō (1), bind

līlium, -ī, *n.,* lily

līmen, -minis, *n.,* threshold

līmes, līmitis, *m.,* path, road, way

līneāmentum, -ī, *n.,* line; features

lingō, -ere, līnxī, līnctum, lick

* **lingua, -ae,** *f.,* tongue; speech, language

linteum, -ī, *n.,* linen cloth; sail

līnum, -ī, *n.,* linen; thread, cord

lippitūdō, -inis, *f.,* inflammation of the eyes

liquidō, *adv.,* clearly, certainly

līs, lītis, *f.,* quarrel, controversy, lawsuit

* **littera, -ae,** *f.,* letter of the alphabet; **litterae, -ārum,** *f. pl.,* a letter (epistle); literature

lītus, -oris, *n.,* seashore, coast

* **locō** (1), place, put

locuplēs, *gen.* **-plētis,** wealthy

* **locus, -ī,** *m. in sg.* (*pl. usually* **loca, -ōrum,** *n.*), place, region, space; opportunity, situation; a passage in literature (*pl. here =* **locī, -ōrum**), topic

longaevus, -a, -um, old, aged

* **longē,** *adv.,* far, a long way off

longinquus, -a, -um, distant, foreign

* **longus, -a, -um,** long

* **loquor, -ī, locūtus sum,** say, speak, converse

lūbricus, -a, -um, slippery

lūceō, -ēre, lūxī, be light, shine; be clear

lūcidus, -a, -um, bright, shining

Lūcifer, -ferī, *m.,* the morning star

Lucrētius, -ī, *m., a Roman nomen, espec.* (*1*) Sp. Lucretius, *father of Lucretia and hero in the founding of the Roman republic;* (*2*) T. Lucretius Carus, *author of* **Dē Rērum Nātūrā**

lūctuōsus, -a, -um, sorrowful, lamentable

* **lūctus, -ūs,** *m.,* grief, sorrow, distress

lūdibrium, -ī, *n.,* mockery, derision

* **lūdō, -ere, lūsī, lūsum,** play (*at a game or on an instrument*); mock, ridicule

* **lūdus, -ī,** *m.,* play, game; *especially pl.,* public games; school

lūgeō, -ēre, lūxī, mourn, lament

* **lūmen, -minis,** *n.,* light; eye

lūna, -ae, *f.,* moon

lupa, -ae, *f.,* a she-wolf

lūstrō (1), purify; move round, circle round

lustrum, -ī, *n.,* den, brothel, debauchery

lūsus, -ūs, *m.,* a playing, play, sport

* **lūx, lūcis,** *f.,* light; **prīmā lūce,** at daybreak

luxuria, -ae, *f.,* excess, dissipation, extravagance

luxuriōsus, -a, -um, luxurious, dissolute, excessive

luxus, -ūs, *m.,* luxury, extravagance, debauchery

Lȳdia, -ae, *f., a kingdom in west-central Asia Minor*

Lȳdus, -a, -um, Lydian, of Lydia (*in Asia Minor*)

M

M., *abbr. of* **Mārcus,** *a praenomen*

M.', *abbr. of* **Mānius**

Macedonēs, -um, *m. pl.,* the Macedonians

Macedonia, -ae, *f., country north of Mt. Olympus*

Macedonicus, -a, -um, Macedonian

macte virtūte, *a phrase of salute* = good luck, bravo, congratulations

maculōsus, -a, -um, spotted

made-faciō, -ere, -fēcī, -factum, wet, drench

madeō, -ēre, -uī, be wet

madidus, -a, -um, wet, soaked

maereō, -ēre, grieve, lament

maestus, -a, -um, sad, dejected

* **magis,** *adv. (compar. of* **magnopere)** more, rather; **eō** *or* **quō magis,** *lit.* more by that = all the more

* **magister, -trī,** *m.,* master; teacher; **magister equitum,** master of the horse (*second in command to a dictator*)

* **magistrātus, -ūs,** *m.,* public office, magistracy; public official, magistrate

magn-animus, -a, -um, high-minded, high-spirited, magnanimous

magnificentior, -ius, *compar. of* **magnificus**

magnificus, -a, -um, great, fine, splendid; sumptuous

* **magnitūdō, -dinis,** *f.,* large size, greatness, magnitude, extent

magn-opere, *adv.,* greatly, earnestly; *compar.* **magis;** *superl.* **maximē**

* **magnus, -a, -um,** large, great, important; *compar.* **maior, maius;** *superl.* **maximus, -a, -um; maiōrēs, -um,** *m. pl.,* ancestors

Māgō, -ōnis, *m., youngest brother of Hannibal*

magus, -ī, *m.,* a learned man (*among the Persians*); a magician

Maharbal, -alis, *m., a Carthaginian officer under Hannibal*

maiestās, -tātis, *f.,* greatness, dignity, majesty

maior: *see* **magnus**

Maius, -a, -um, of (the month of) May

* **male,** *adv. of* **malus,** badly, wickedly; *with words of good connotation,* not, scarcely, with difficulty (**male fīdus,** not faithful; **male sustinēns arma,** scarcely supporting his armor); *with words of bad connotation,* excessively, greatly (**male ōdisse,** to hate excessively; **male metuere,** to fear greatly); *compar.* **peius;** *superl.* **pessimē**

male-dīcō, -ere, -dīxī, -dictum, speak ill of, revile, curse (+ *dat.*)

male-dictus, -a, -um (*partic. of* **maledīcō**), accursed

malitia, -ae, *f.,* malice

malitiōsus, -a, -um, wicked, malicious

* **mālō, mālle, māluī (magisvolō),** wish more, prefer, rather

malum, -ī, *n. of* **malus,** evil, misfortune, crime

* **malus, -a, -um,** bad, evil, wicked; *compar.* **peior, peius;** *superl.* **pessimus, -a, -um**

Māmertīnus, -a, -um, Mamertine, of the Mamertini (*Campanian mercenaries who in the early third cent.* B.C. *had made themselves masters of Messana*)

mamma, -ae, *f.,* breast, teat, dug

mandātum, -ī, *n.,* an order, command, injunction

mandō (1), commit, entrust; order, command

mandūcō (1), chew, eat

māne, *adv.,* early in the morning

* **maneō, -ēre, mānsī, mānsum,** remain, stay; await

mānēs, -ium, *m. pl. (used of one person or more than one),* ghost, shade, spirit of the dead

manifestus, -a, -um, clear, plain, evident

* **manus, -ūs,** *f.,* hand; band, force; handwriting

Marcellus, -ī, *m., a cognomen; espec.* M. Claudius Marcellus, who *recaptured Syracuse in 212* B.C.

Mārcus, -ī, *m.,* Marcus, *a common praenomen*

* **mare, -is,** *n.,* sea; **terrā marīque,** by *or* on land and sea

margō, -inis, *m.,* border, edge

Maria, -ae, *f.,* Mary (*EL*)

marītō (1), marry; give in marriage

* **marītus, -ī,** *m.,* husband

Mārs, Mārtis, *m., Roman god of agriculture, and war;* war, battle

Mārtius, -a, -um, of Mars, from Mars

massa, -ae, *f.,* mass, lump

Massicus, -a, -um, Massic, *referring to an area in Campania noted for its wine*

* **māter, -tris,** *f.,* mother

mātrimōnium, -ī, *n.,* marriage, matrimony

mātrōna, -ae, *f.,* married woman, matron

mātūrus, -a, -um, ripe, mature, seasonable

Māvors, -vortis, *m., an archaic name for Mars*

maxilla, -ae, *f.,* jaw

* **maximē,** *adv. (superl. of* **magnopere**), very greatly, especially, most

* **maximus, -a, -um,** *superl. of* **magnus;** *also cognomen of* Q. Fabius Maximus, *hero against Hannibal*

meātus, -ūs, *m.,* course, passage

medeor, -ērī, + *dat.,* heal, cure; correct

medicīna, -ae, *f.,* medicine, remedy

medicus, -ī, *m.,* doctor, physician

mediocris, -e, moderate, medium; ordinary, mediocre; *adv.* **mediocriter**

meditor, -ārī, -ātus sum, think over, plan; practice

* **medius, -a, -um,** middle; *with partitive force,* the middle of, the midst of; **medium, -ī,** *n.,* the middle, center

Medūsaeus, -a, -um, Medusa-like

mehercule *or* **-cle** (= **mē Herculēs iuvet**), *interjection,* by Hercules, certainly; *cp.* **hercule**

mel, mellis, *n.,* honey

membrum, -ī, *n.,* limb, member

meminī, -isse, *defective in perf. system with "present" meaning,* remember, think of (+ *gen. or acc.*)

memor, *gen.* **memoris,** *(adj. of 1 ending in nom.),* mindful

memorābilis, -e, memorable

* **memoria, -ae,** *f.,* memory

memoriter, *adv.,* from memory, by heart

memorō (1), mention, recount

mendīcus, -a, -um, poor, beggarly; **mendīcus, -ī,** *m.,* beggar

* **mēns, mentis,** *f.,* mind, reason, understanding; soul, spirit; intention

mēnsa, -ae, *f.,* table; food, course

mēnsis, -is, *m.,* month

mēnsūra, -ae, *f.,* measure, amount

mentiō, -ōnis, *f.,* mention
mentior, -īrī, -ītus sum, lie, say
    falsely, break one's word
mercātor, -ōris, *m.,* merchant,
    trader
mercēnnārius, -ī, *m.,* hireling,
    mercenary
mercēs, -ēdis, *f.,* reward, pay, wages,
    income
* **mereō, -ēre, -uī, -itum,** *and deponent*
    mereor, -ērī, meritus sum, deserve,
    earn, merit; serve as a soldier
mereor, *deponent: see* **mereō**
meretrīcius, -a, -um, of a prostitute,
    meretricious
meretrīx, -trīcis, *f.,* prostitute
mergō, -ere, mersī, mersum, sink,
    drown, overwhelm
merīdiēs, -diēī *m.,* midday; south
meritō, *adv.,* deservedly
meritum, -ī, *n.,* merit, desert, worth;
    benefit, service
merum, -ī, *n.,* unmixed wine
Messāna, -ae, *f., a town in*
    northeastern Sicily on the Straits of
    Messina
messis, -is, *f.,* harvest
-met, *intensive suffix added to certain*
    pronominal forms, self, own
mēta, -ae, *f.,* a turning post (*on a*
    racecourse); goal, end, boundary
Metellus, -ī, *m., a Roman nomen*
mētior, -īrī, mēnsus sum, measure
    out, measure
* **metuō, -ere, metuī,** dread, fear, be
    afraid
* **metus, -ūs,** *m.,* fear, dread, anxiety
* **meus, -a, -um,** my, mine
    mī, *voc. of* **meus;** *also short form of*
    mihi
mīca, -ae, *f.,* crumb, morsel

micō, -āre, -uī, shake, shine, flash,
    sparkle
Midās, -ae, *m., a king of Phrygia*
migrō (1), depart; transgress
* **mīles, mīlitis,** *m.,* soldier
mīlia: *see* **mīlle**
mīlitāris, -e, military, warlike
mīlitia, -ae, *f.,* military service,
    warfare
* **mīlle,** *indecl. adj. in sg.,* thousand;
    mīlia, -ium, *n. pl. noun,* thousands
mināciter, *adv.,* threateningly
minae, -ārum, *f. pl.,* threats
mināx, *gen.* **minācis** (*adj. of 1 ending*
    in nom.), threatening
Minerva, -ae, *f., goddess of wisdom*
    and arts
* **minimē,** *adv.,* (*superl. of* **parum**),
    least, very little; not at all, by no
    means
minister, -trī, *m.,* servant, attendant,
    helper, accomplice
ministra, -ae, *f.,* servant
minitābundus, -a, -um, threatening
minitor, -ārī, -ātus sum (+ *dat. of*
    pers.), threaten
minor, -ārī, -ātus sum, threaten
minor, minus, *compar. of* **parvus**
Mīnos, -ōis, *m., legendary king of*
    Crete
Minucius, -ī, *m., a Roman nomen;*
    e.g., M. Minucius Rufus, **magister**
    equitum *of the dictator Q. Fabius*
    Maximus in the Second Punic
    War
* **minus,** *compar. adv.* (*see* **parum**), less,
    too little; not
minūtus, -a, -um, small, trifling
mīrābilis, -e, wonderful, marvelous,
    extraordinary
mīrāculum, -ī, *n.,* wonder, miracle

mīrandus, -a, -um, wonderful, remarkable

* **mīror, -ārī, -ātus sum,** wonder at, admire

* **mīrus, -a, -um,** wonderful, extraordinary

misceō, -ēre, miscuī, mixtum, mix, mingle

Mīsēnum, -ī, *n., promontory near Naples*

* **miser, -era, -erum,** wretched, unhappy, sad, miserable

miserābilis, -e, pitiable

miserandus, -a, -um, = **miserābilis**

misereor, -ērī, -itus sum, + *gen.,* pity

miseria, -ae, *f.,* misery, unhappiness, misfortune

* **misericordia, -ae,** *f.,* pity, mercy, sympathy

misericors, *gen.* **-cordis,** pitiful, compassionate

miseror, -ārī, -ātus sum, pity

mītigō (1), soften, lighten, ease, alleviate

mītis, -e, mild, soft, gentle

* **mittō, -ere, mīsī, missum,** send; throw, cast; let go, omit, pass over

moderātiō, -ōnis, *f.,* moderation, self-control, temperance

moderātus, -a, -um, moderate, temperate, restrained; *adv.* **moderātē**

modestia, -ae, *f.,* moderation (*cp.* **modus**), sobriety, modesty

modicus, -a, -um, moderate

* **modo,** *adv.,* only, merely, just; just now; **modo . . . modo,** now . . . now, at one time . . . at another

* **modus, -ī,** *m.,* measure, quantity, limit, due measure, moderation; mode, way, manner, method; kind, sort; **quem ad modum,** in what way, how, as; **eius modī,** of that sort, of such sort

moechor, -ārī, -ātus sum, commit adultery

* **moenia, -ium,** *n. pl.,* city walls, fortifications

mōlēs, -is, *f.,* mass, large structure, difficulty

molestia, -ae, *f.,* trouble, annoyance

molestus, -a, -um, troublesome, annoying, disagreeable

molliō (4), soften; moderate

mollis, -e, soft

mōmentum, -ī, *n., lit.* movement, motion, moment; influence, importance

monachus, -ī, *m.,* monk (*ML*)

monastērium, -ī, *n.,* monastery (*EL*)

* **moneō, -ēre, -uī, -itum,** advise, warn, instruct

monitus, -ūs, *m.,* admonition, advice

* **mōns, -ntis,** *m.,* mountain

mōnstrum, -i, *n.,* monster

montānus, -a, -um, of the mountains, mountainous; **montānus, -ī,** *m.,* a mountaineer

* **monumentum, -ī,** *n.,* reminder; monument, record

* **mora, -ae,** *f.,* delay

mōrālitās, -tātis, *f.,* moral interpretation (*EL*)

morbus, -ī, *m.,* disease, sickness

* **morior, -ī, mortuus sum,** die

moror, -ārī, -ātus sum, delay

* **mors, -rtis,** *f.,* death

morsus, -ūs, *m.,* a biting, bite; teeth

mortālis, -e, mortal

* **mortuus, -a, -um,** dead
 mōrum, -ī, *n.,* mulberry
 mōrus, -ī, *f.,* mulberry tree
* **mōs, mōris,** *m.,* habit, custom,
 manner; **mōrēs, -um,** *m. pl.,* habits,
 character
 Mōses, -is *or* **-ī** (*acc.* **Mōsēn),** *m., the*
 great Hebrew leader
* **mōtus, -ūs,** *m.,* movement; impulse;
 commotion
 mouseion = **musēum, -ī,** *n.,* abode of
 the muses, museum, library
* **moveō, -ēre, mōvī, mōtum,** move;
 arouse, affect, disturb; **castra**
 movēre, break camp
* **mox,** *adv.,* soon; thereupon
 Mūcius, -ī, *m., a Roman nomen; e.g.,*
 C. Mucius Scaevola, *for whose plot*
 against the Etruscan king Porsenna
 see Livy, Bk. II
 mūcro, -ōnis, *m.,* sharp point (of
 sword)
 multiplicō (1), multiply, increase
 multitūdo, -dinis, *f.,* large number,
 crowd, multitude
* **multum,** *adv.,* much; *compar.* **plūs,**
 more; *superl.* **plūrimum,** very much
* **multus, -a, -um,** much, many;
 compar. **plūs, plūris,** *n. noun in sg.,*
 more, *and* **plūrēs, plūra,** *adj. in pl.,*
 more, several, many; *superl.*
 plūrimus, -a, -um, most, very
 much *or* many (*see* **plūrimus)**
 mūlus, -ī, *m.,* mule
 mundānus, -a, -um, of the world,
 worldly
 mundus, -a, -um, clean, pure, elegant
* **mundus, -ī,** *m.,* world
* **mūni-ceps, -cipis,** *m./f.,* citizen of a
 free town

 municipālis, -e, belonging to a free
 town or towns
 mūnificē, *adv.,* generously
 mūnīmentum, -ī, *n.,* defense,
 fortification
 mūniō (4), to wall in, fortify, defend;
 viam mūnīre, build a road
* **mūnus, -eris,** *n.,* duty, function,
 service, gift
 murmur, -uris, *n.,* murmur
 mūrus, -ī, *m.,* wall
 mūtō (1) change; take in exchange
 mūtus, -a, -um, mute, dumb; silent,
 still
 mūtuum, -ī, *n.,* a loan
 mūtuus, -a, -um, mutual, reciprocal;
 borrowed, lent

N

 Naïas, -adis, *f.,* Naiad, water nymph
* **nam,** *conj.,* for
 nancīscor, -ī, nactus sum, find, get,
 obtain
 nārrō (1), tell, relate
* **nāscor, -ī, nātus sum,** be born; arise
 nātālis, -e, of birth, natal
 nātiō, -ōnis, *f.,* a people, nation
 natō (1), swim
* **nātūra, -ae,** *f.,* birth; nature, laws of
 nature
 nātūralis, -e, natural
* **nātus, -ī,** *m.,* son (= **fīlius,** *espec. in*
 poetry)
 nauarchus, -ī, *m.,* captain of a ship
 naufragium, -ī, *n.,* shipwreck
 nausea, -ae, *f.,* seasickness, nausea
* **nauta, -ae,** *m.,* sailor
* **nāvigō** (1), sail, sail over
* **nāvis, -is,** *f.,* ship

* **nē** (*sometimes* **ut nē**), *neg. w.
  subjunctive,* not, in order that . . .
  not, not to; *after verbs of fearing,*
  that, lest; *as adv.,* **nē . . . quidem,**
  not even
ne, *a Greek interjection,* surely
-ne, *interrog. suffix introducing either
  a direct or an indirect question*
nē . . . quidem, *adv.,* not . . . even
Neāpolis, -is, *f., Greek for* 'New
  City': (1) *part of Syracuse;*
  (2) Naples *in Campania*
Neāpolitānus, -a, -um, belonging to
  Naples
* **nec:** *see* **neque**
necessāriō, *adv.,* necessarily
* **necessārius, -a, -um,** necessary;
  necessārius, -ī, *m.,* a necessary
  person, a relative; **necessāria,
  -ōrum,** *n. pl.,* necessities
necesse, *indecl. adj.,* necessary
necessitās, -tātis, *f.,* necessity
* **necō** (1), kill, slay
* **nefārius, -a, -um,** impious, wicked;
  adv. **nefāriē**
neglegēns, *gen.* **-entis,** careless,
  indifferent, negligent
neglegenter, *adv.,* carelessly
neglegentia, -ae, *f.,* carelessness,
  negligence
* **neglegō, -ere, -lēxī, -lēctum,** neglect,
  disregard
* **negō** (1), deny, say that . . . not;
  refuse
negōtior, -ārī, -ātus sum, be in
  business, trade
* **negōtium, -ī,** *n.,* business,
  assignment, task
* **nēmō (nūllīus), nēminī, nēminem,
  (nūllō, -ā),** nobody, no one

nemus, -oris, *n.,* grove
nepōs, -ōtis, *m.,* grandson
Neptūnus, -ī, *m.,* Neptune, *god of the
  sea*
nē-quam, *indecl. adj.,* worthless, bad,
  wicked; *compar.* **nēquior, -ius;**
  superl. **nēquissimus, -a, -um**
nēquāquam, *adv.,* by no means
* **ne-que** *or* **nec,** *conj.,* and not, nor;
  neque . . . neque, neither . . . nor
ne-queō, -īre, -quiī (-īvī), -itum, be
  unable
nēquior: *see* **nēquam**
nēquīquam, *adv.,* in vain, to no
  purpose
nervus, -ī, *m.,* sinew; string of a
  lyre
* **nesciō** (4), not to know, be ignorant;
  nesciō + *complementary inf.,*
  know how to; **nesciō quis (quid**
  etc.) as an indef. pron., somebody
  (-thing, *etc.*) or other; **nesciō quī
  (quae, quod)** *as indef. adj.,*
  somebody (-thing, *etc.*) or other
  (**nesciō quā ratiōne,** in some way
  or other); **nesciō an,** I do not
  know whether = probably,
  perhaps
neuter, -tra, -trum, neither (of two)
nē-ve *or* **neu,** and not, or not; **nēve
  (neu) . . . nēve (neu),** neither . . .
  nor
nex, necis, *f.,* murder, violent death
nī = **nisi**
nīdus, -ī, *m.,* nest
niger, -gra, -grum, black, dark
* **nihil,** *or* **nīl,** *n. nom. and acc.,*
  nothing; **nōn nihil,** something; **nihil**
  as adv., not at all
nihilum, -ī, *n.,* nothing; **nihilō minus,**

adv., lit. less by nothing =
nevertheless

nīl = nihil

nīmīrum, *adv.,* doubtless, of course,
to be sure

* **nimis** *or* **nimium,** *adv.,* too much,
excessively

nimius, -a, -um, too much, too great,
excessive

Ninus, -ī, *m., king of Assyria*

* **nisi,** if . . . not, unless; except

niveus, -a, -um, snowy, snow-white

* **nix, nivis,** *f.,* snow

* **nōbilis, -e,** well known, celebrated,
famous; of high birth; excellent

nōbilitās, -tātis, *f.,* fame; noble birth;
the nobility, the nobles

nōbilitō (1), make known *or* famous

nocēns, *gen.* **-entis,** harmful; wicked,
guilty

* **noceō, -ēre, nocuī, nocitum** (+ *dat.*),
harm, injure

noctū, *adv.,* at night, by night

nocturnus, -a, -um, nocturnal

Nōlānus, -a, -um, belonging to Nola,
a town in Campania

* **nōlō, nōlle, nōluī,** be unwilling, not
wish

* **nōmen, -inis,** *n.,* name; *technically
the 'gentile' name (indicating the
gēns, clan), the second of the three
regular parts of the formal Roman
name:* **praenōmen, nōmen,
cognōmen** *(family branch of the
gēns);* renown, power, status;
pretext

* **nōminō (1),** name, call

* **nōn,** *adv.,* not

nōnae, -ārum, *f. pl.* the nones, *i.e.,
the 5th day of the month, except in*

*March, May, July, and October,
when the nones are the 7th day*

nōn-dum, *adv.,* not yet

nōn-ne, *adv.,* not? *in questions which
expect the answer "yes":* **nōnne
vidēs?** You see, do you not *or* don't
you?

nōn-nūllus, -a, -um, some, several

nōn-numquam, *adv.,* sometimes

nōnus, -a, -um, ninth

nōs: *see* **ego;** *sometimes the plural is
used of one person, where we should
ordinarily use 'I'.*

* **nōscō, -ere, nōvī, nōtum,** become
acquainted with, learn; *perf.
system* = have become acquainted
with, *etc., and so* know, *etc.*

* **noster, -tra, -trum,** our, ours

nota, -ae, *f.,* mark; disgrace *(as in a
censor's mark),* brand

nōtitia, -ae, *f.,* acquaintance,
knowledge; fame

notō (1), notice, observe

* **nōtus, -a, -um,** known, famous

novem, *indecl.,* nine

noverca, -ae, *f.,* stepmother

noviēs, *adv.,* nine times

novissimē, *adv.,* lately, recently

novitās, -tātis, *f.,* novelty,
strangeness

novō (1), make new; change, alter

* **novus, -a, um,** new; strange

* **nox, noctis,** *f.,* night

nūbēs, -is, *f.,* cloud

nūdō (1), strip; rob

nūdus, -a, -um, naked, bare

* **nūllus, -a, -um,** not any, no, none

num, *interrogative adv.:* (1)
*introduces direct questions which
expect a negative answer;* (2)

introduces ind. quests. and means whether

nūmen, -minis, *n., lit.* nod; divine will *or* power, divinity, god

* **numerus, -ī,** *m.,* number; rank, company

Numidae, -ārum, *m.,* the Numidians, *in northern Africa*

Numitor, -ōris, *m., a king of Alba Longa, grandfather of Romulus and Remus*

nummulus, ī, *m.,* little sum of money

nummus, -ī, *m.,* coin; *pl.* money; *any small coin like* a penny or a nickel

* **numquam,** *adv.,* never; **nōn numquam,** sometimes (*also written as one word*)

numquid, *interrogative adv., introducing quests. expecting a negative answer,* is it really possible that, surely . . . not?

* **nunc,** *adv.,* now, at present; in these circumstances

nuncupō (1), name

* **nūntiō** (1), announce, report

* **nūntius, -ī,** *m.,* messenger, message, news

nūper, *adv.,* recently

nūpta, -ae, *f.,* bride

nūptiae, -ārum, *f. pl.,* nuptials, wedding

nūtō (1), nod; totter

nūtus, -ūs, *m.,* nod, command

O

Ō, *interjection,* O! Oh!

* **ob,** *prep. + acc.,* towards, to; in front of, over against; on account of, because of

ob-eō, -īre, -iī, -itum, go to meet, meet; visit; undertake, perform, carry out; die

* **ob-iciō, -ere, -iēcī, -iectum,** *lit.* throw against *or* before; offer, present; oppose; cite (*as grounds for disapproval*)

oblātus: *see* **offerō**

oblectāmentum, -ī, *n.,* delight, pleasure

ob-linō, -ere, -lēvi, *or* **-līvī, -litum,** smear

oblītus, -a, -um (*see* **oblīvīscor**); *and* **oblitus, -a, -um** (*see* **oblinō**)

ob-līvīscor, -ī, oblītus sum, forget (+ *gen. or acc.*)

oboedientia, -ae, *f.,* obedience

ob-oediō, -īre, -īvī, -ītum, harken to, obey (+ *dat.*)

ob-orior, -orīrī, -ortus sum, rise up, spring up

ob-ruō, -ere, -ruī, -rutum, overwhelm, oppress; cover, bury

obryzum, -ī (*sc.* **aurum**) *n.,* pure gold (*EL*)

obscūritās, -tātis, *f.,* obscurity, darkness

obscūrō (1), hide, conceal

obscūrus, -a, -um, dark, obscure, unknown

obsecrō (1), beg, beseech

obsequium, -ī, *n.,* compliance, obedience

ob-servō (1), guard, keep, observe, honor

ob-sideō, -ēre, -sēdī, -sessum, *lit.* sit down against, besiege

ob-sidiō, -ōnis, *f.,* siege, blockade

ob-sistō, -ere, -stitī, -stitum, *lit.* stand in the way; withstand, resist (+ *dat.*)

obstinātiō, -ōnis, *f.,* persistence, obstinacy

obstinātus, -a, -um, resolute, firm, obstinate

ob-stipēscō, -ere, -stipuī, be amazed, astounded

ob-stō, -āre, -stitī, -statūrus, stand in the way, stand against, resist, hinder

ob-stringō, -ere, -strīnxī, -strictum, tie, bind (*by an oath*)

ob-struō, -ere, -strūxī, -strūctum, block up, hinder

ob-stupefaciō, -ere, -fēcī, -factum, astonish, amaze

ob-temperō (1), obey, submit

ob-testor, -ārī, -ātus sum, call to witness; implore, entreat

ob-tineō, -ēre, -tinuī, -tentum, hold, possess, maintain

ob-truncō (1), cut down, kill

ob-vertō, -ere, -vertī, -versum, turn towards *or* against

ob-viam, *adv.,* in the way, towards, to meet, to oppose

obvius, -a, -um, in the way, meeting, to meet

* **occāsiō, -ōnis,** *f.,* opportunity, occasion

occāsus, -ūs, *m.,* setting; fall

occidēns, *gen.* **-entis** (*pres. partic. of* **occidō**), *as adj.* setting; *as m. noun* (*sc.* **sōl**), the setting sun, the west

* **oc-cĭdō, -ere, -cĭdī, -cāsum** (**ob-cadō,** fall), fall down, go down, set; die, perish

* **oc-cīdō, -ere, -cīdī, -cīsum** (**ob-caedō,** cut), cut down, kill

occultō (1), hide, conceal

occultus, -a, -um, hidden, concealed, secret

occupātiō, -ōnis, *f.,* business, employment, occupation

occupō (1), seize, occupy; employ

oc-currō, -ere, -currī, -cursum, run to meet, hurry to, arrive

octāvus, -a, -um, eighth

octiēs, *adv.,* eight times

octō, *indecl.,* eight

* **oculus, -ī,** *m.,* eye

* **ōdī, ōdisse, ōsūrus,** hate

* **odium, -ī,** *n.,* hate, hatred, aversion

odor, -ōris, *m.,* odor, scent

odōrātus, -a, -um, fragrant

offendō, -ere, -fendī, -fēnsum, dash against; come upon; offend, displease; receive an injury, suffer grief

of-ferō, -ferre, obtulī, oblātum, offer, present, show

officiōsus, -a, -um, dutiful, obliging, courteous

* **officium, -ī,** *n.,* service, kindness; duty, obligation; ceremony

oleum, -ī, *n.,* (olive) oil

ōlim, *adv.,* at that time; formerly, once upon a time; hereafter, in times to come

Olympius, -a, -um, of Olympus (*the home of the gods*)

ōmen, ōminis, *n.,* omen, sign, token

* **omittō, -ere, -mīsī, -missum,** let go, pass over, omit

* **omnīnō,** *adv.,* wholly, entirely, altogether, completely

omni-potēns, *gen.* **-potentis,** all-powerful, omnipotent

* **omnis, -e,** all, every

onerōsus, -a, -um, burdensome

onus, -eris, *n.,* load, burden

opācus, -a, -um, dark, obscure

* **opera, -ae,** *f.,* effort, pains, attention,

care, work, help; **operā meā,** thanks to me; **operam dare,** see to, take pains

operārius, -ī, *m.,* day-laborer

operiō, -īre, operuī, opertum, cover

operor, -ārī, -ātus sum, work, labor, toil

opi-fex, -ficis, *m./f.,* worker, artisan

opīmus, -a, -um, fat; rich, splendid

* **opīniō, -ōnis,** *f.,* opinion, thought, expectation, belief, repute

opīnor, -ārī, -ātus sum, be of an opinion, think, suppose

* **oportet, -ēre, oportuit,** *impers.,* it behooves, it is proper, necessary, becoming; one ought

op-petō, -ere, -petīvī, -petītum, go to meet; suffer, encounter

oppidum, -ī, *n.,* town

op-pleō, -ēre, -plēvī, -plētum, fill, cover

op-pōnō, -ere, -posuī, -positum, oppose, put forward, allege

opportūnitās, -tātis, *f.,* advantage, opportunity

opportūnus, -a, -um, appropriate, serviceable, advantageous

op-primō, -ere, -pressī, -pressum, overwhelm, overpower, crush

* **op-pugnō** (1), attack

* **ops, opis,** *f.,* help, aid, power; **opēs, opum,** *pl.,* power, resources, wealth

optātiō, -ōnis, *f.,* wish

optātum, -ī, *n.,* wish

optimē, *superl. of* **bene**

optimus, -a, -um, *superl. of* **bonus**

* **optō** (1), wish, wish for, desire

* **opus, operis,** *n.,* work, achievement; **opus est,** there is need of (+ *gen.*

or *abl.*), it is necessary (*often + inf.*)

* **ōra, -ae,** *f.,* seashore, coast

* **ōrātiō, -ōnis,** *f.,* speech, oration; discourse; eloquence; language

orbis, -is, *m.,* orb, circle; **orbis terrārum,** the world

orbō (1), deprive (*of parents or children*)

ōrdior, -īrī, ōrsus sum, begin, commence

* **ōrdō, -dinis,** *m.,* order, rank, class; arrangement, regularity

Orestēs, -is, *m., son of Agamemnon and Clytemnestra, and close friend of Pylades*

orgia, -ōrum, *n. pl.,* orgies, secret festival (of Bacchus)

oriēns, -entis, *m., lit.* the rising sun (*sc.* **sōl**); the east, orient

orīgō, -inis, *f.,* origin, source, lineage

Ōrīōn, -ōnis, *m., a famous hunter slain by Artemis and changed into a constellation*

* **orior, -īrī, ortus sum,** rise, arise; spring from, descend, originate

* **ōrnāmentum, -ī,** *n.,* distinction, honor, decoration, ornament

* **ōrnātus, -a, -um,** adorned, decorated; distinguished, illustrious

* **ōrnātus, -ūs,** *m.,* ornament, decoration, embellishment, dress

* **ōrnō** (1), equip; adorn, decorate, embellish

* **ōrō** (1), speak, plead, beg, pray

Orpheus (-a, -um, of) Orpheus

ortus, -ūs, *m.,* a rising; origin; source

* **ōs, ōris,** *n.,* mouth, face; tongue, speech

os, ossis, *n.,* bone
ōscular (1), kiss
ōsculum, -ī, *n.,* kiss
* **os-tendō, -ere, -dī, ostentum,** *lit.*
stretch out; show, exhibit; declare
ostentātiō, -ōnis, *f.,* ostentation,
boasting, false show
ostentō (1), *frequentative of* **ostendō,**
display, exhibit, show
ōtiōsus, -a, um, at leisure,
unoccupied
* **ōtium, -ī,** *n.,* leisure; peace, quiet
ovis, -is, *f.,* sheep
ovō (1), rejoice, exult

P

P., *abbr. of* **Publius,** *a praenomen*
pābulum, -ī, *n.,* fodder
pacīscō, -ere, pactum, arrange,
negotiate, agree upon
Pactōlus, -ī, *m., Lydian river famous*
for the gold found in its sand
pactum, -ī, *n.,* agreement, pact; **quō**
pactō, in what way
pactus, -a, -um, agreed upon,
stipulated
Pācuvius, -ī, *m., a Roman writer of*
tragedy in the 2nd cent. B.C.
Paean, -ānis, *m., epithet of Apollo*
the healer
* **paene,** *adv.,* almost, nearly
paenitēns, *gen.* **-entis,** penitent,
repentant
paenitentia, -ae, *f.,* repentance
* **paenitet, -ēre, paenituit,** *impers. with*
acc. of person and gen. of thing or
the inf. of a **quod** *clause:* **mē huius**
reī paenitet, *lit.* it causes me regret
or repentance of this thing = I

repent, regret, am sorry for this
thing
pāgānus, -a, -um, belonging to a
country district *or* village, rural;
pagan; **pāgānus, -ī,** *m.,* a
countryman, villager; a pagan
pāla, -ae, *f.,* bezel of a ring
palam, *adv.,* openly
Palātium, -ī, *n.,* Palatine Hill *in*
Rome
palleō, -ēre, be pale
pallēscō, -ere, -palluī, grow pale *or*
yellow
pallidus, -a, -um, pale, pallid
palma, -ae, *f.,* palm (of hand)
palus, -ūdis, *f.,* swamp
Pamphȳlia, -ae, *f., a district in*
southern Asia Minor
pānārium, -ī, *n.,* bread basket
pandō, -ere, pandī, passum, extend,
spread, lay open
pangō, -ere, pepigī, pāctum, fasten;
compose; agree on, contract
pānis, -is, *m.,* bread
Panormus, -ī, *f.,* Palermo
pāpa, -ae, *m.,* father, papa; *in eccl.*
Lat., bishop, pope
pār, *gen.* **paris,** *adj.,* equal,
adequate
parabola, -ae, *f.,* comparison;
parable
paradīsus, -ī, *m.,* a park; Paradise
parātus, -a, -um (*partic. of* **parō**),
prepared, ready
parcō, -ere, pepercī, parsum, + *dat.,*
spare, preserve
* **parēns, -entis,** *m./f.,* parent
* **pāreō, -ēre, pāruī, pāritum,** + *dat.,*
be obedient to, obey
pariēs, -etis, *m.,* wall (of a house)

* **pariō, -ere, peperī, partum,** beget, produce

pariter, *adv.,* equally, as well

parō (1), prepare, furnish, provide; acquire, get

Paros, -ī, *f., a large island of the Cyclades in the Aegean Sea, famous for its beautiful marble*

parricīdium, -ī, *n.,* murder of a parent *or* relative; murder; treason

* **pars, partis,** *f.,* part, share; side, direction; role; party, faction; **ā dextrā (laevā) parte,** on the right (left) hand *or* side; **maximam partem,** *as adv.,* for the most part.

parsimōnia, -ae, *f.,* thrift, frugality

parti-ceps, *gen.* **-cipis,** *adj.,* sharing, participating; *as noun, m.,* sharer, participant, partner

partim, *adv.,* partly

partiō (4), divide, share, distribute

partītiō, -ōnis, *f.,* partition, division

partus, -ūs, *m.,* offspring, bearing offspring

parum, *adv. of* **parvus,** too little, not enough; *compar.* **minus,** less; *superl.* **minimē,** very little, least of all, not at all

parumper, *adv.,* for a little while

parvulus, -a, -um, small, tiny

parvus, -a, -um, little, small; *compar.* **minor, minus;** *superl.* **minimus, -a, -um**

pāscō, -ere, pāvī, pāstum, feed, lead to pasture

passim, *adv.,* here and there, far and wide

passiō, -ōnis, *f.,* suffering, passion (*EL*)

passus, -ūs, *m.,* step, pace

pāstor, -ōris, *m.,* shepherd

pāstus, -ūs, *m.,* food, fodder

patefaciō, -ere, -fēcī, -factum, throw open, expose

* **pateō, -ēre, -uī,** lie open, extend, be exposed, be revealed *or* clear

* **pater, -tris** *m.,* father

patientia, -ae, *f.,* endurance, patience

* **patior, -ī, passus sum,** suffer, endure; permit, allow

* **patria, -ae,** *f.,* fatherland, native land

patrius, -a, -um, of a father, father's, paternal; ancestral

patrōnus, -ī, *m.,* protector, patron; advocate (in a trial)

* **paucī, -ae, -a,** *adj. usu. in pl.,* few, a few

paucitās, -tātis, *f.,* small number

paulātim, *adv.,* gradually, little by little

* **paulus, -a, -um,** little, small; *very commonly in the abl. (degree of difference) as an adv.,* **paulō,** a little, somewhat

Paulus (*or* **Paullus**), **-ī,** *m., a cognomen in the gens Aemilia, e.g.,* L. Aemilius Paulus, *consul and general who lost his life at Cannae in 216* B.C.; L. Aemilius Paulus Macedonius, *son of the above and victor at Pydna in 167* B.C.

pauper, *gen.* **-eris,** poor (not rich)

paupertās, -tātis, *f.,* poverty

pavor, -ōris, *m.,* trembling, terror

* **pāx, pācis,** *f.,* peace

* **peccātor, -ōris,** *m.,* sinner (*EL*)

peccātum, -ī, *n.,* sin, error, fault

* **peccō** (1), make a mistake, commit a fault, sin

pectus, -oris, *n.,* breast; heart, feelings

* **pecūnia, -ae,** *f.,* money, property, wealth

pecūniōsus, -a, -um, moneyed, wealthy

pecus, -oris, *n.,* cattle, herd

* **pedes, peditis,** *m.,* foot soldier; *pl.* = infantry

peditātus, -ūs, *m.,* infantry

peior: *see* malus

pelagus, -ī, *n.,* sea

* **pellō, -ere, pepulī, pulsum,** strike, push; move; drive out, exile, defeat

penātēs, -ium, *m. pl.,* household gods, penates

pendeō, -ere, pependī, hang, hang down, be suspended

penes, *prep.* + *acc.,* in the possession *or* power of

penetrō (1), enter, penetrate

penitus, *adv.,* deeply, thoroughly, wholly

* **penna, -ae,** *f.,* feather

pēnsō (1), weigh

pēnūria, -ae, *f.,* want, scarcity

pependī: *see* pendeō

peper_cī: *see* parcō

peperī: *see* pariō

pepulī: *see* pellō

* **per,** *prep.* + *acc.,* through, across; by; *as adverbial prefix,* very (**permagnus,** very large), thoroughly

per-agō, -ere, -ēgī, -āctum, *lit.* do thoroughly; complete, finish; live through

per-angustus, -a, -um, very narrow

* **per-cipiō, -ere, -cēpī, -ceptum,** obtain, get, acquire, perceive

per-contor (*or* **-cunctor**), **-ārī, -ātus sum,** question, ask, investigate

per-crēbrēscō, -ere, -bruī, become very frequent; spread abroad

per-cunctor: *see* **per-contor**

* **per-cutiō, -ere, -cussī, -cussum,** strike

perditiō, -ōnis, *f.,* ruin, perdition (*EL*)

perditus, -a, -um, lost, corrupt, depraved

* **per-dō, -ere, -didī, -ditum,** destroy, ruin; lose

peregrē, *adv.,* away from home, abroad

peregrīnātiō, -ōnis, *f.,* foreign travel

peregrīnor, -ārī, -ātus sum, travel abroad; ramble

perennis, -e, lasting, perennial

* **per-eō, -īre, -iī, -itum,** pass away, be destroyed, perish

perfectus, -a, -um, complete, finished; excellent, carefully wrought, perfect

per-ferō, -ferre, -tulī, -lātum, bear through, endure; report, relate, announce

* **per-ficiō, -ere, -fēcī, -fectum,** *lit.* do thoroughly; complete, accomplish, bring about, achieve

perfidia, -ae, *f.,* faithlessness, treachery

per-fuga, -ae, *m.,* fugitive, deserter

per-fugiō, -ere, -fūgī, -fugitum, flee, escape

per-fungor, -ī, -fūnctus sum, + *abl.,* perform, complete, execute

pergō, -ere, perrēxī, perrēctum, go on, keep on, continue, proceed

per-grātus, -a, -um, very pleasing

perīclitor, -ārī, -ātus sum, test; run a risk, be in danger

perīclum = **perīculum**

perīculōsē, *adv.,* dangerously

perīculōsus, -a, -um, dangerous

* **perīculum, -ī,** *n.,* danger, risk

per-imō, -ere, -ēmī, -ēmptum, kill, destroy

perītus, -a, -um, experienced, expert, skilled (+ *gen. or abl.*)

per-iūrium, -ī, *n.,* perjury

periūrus, -a, -um, perjured, lying

per-magnus, -a, -um, very large *or* great

* **per-maneō, -ēre, -mānsī, -mānsum,** remain, abide, continue

per-māturēscō, -ere, -mātūruī, become ripe

per-mittō, -ere, -mīsī, -missum, permit, allow

per-molestē, *adv.,* with much vexation, with great distress, annoyance, irritation

per-multum, *adv.,* very much

per-multus, -a, -um, very much, very many

perniciēs, -ēī, *f.,* destruction, ruin, death

perniciōsus, -a, -um, destructive, dangerous, pernicious

per-nōbilis, -e, very famous

per-ōsus, -a, -um, hating, loathing (+ *acc.*)

per-pellō, -ere, -pulī, -pulsum, drive on, urge

perpetuitās, -tātis, *f.,* continuity, duration

* **perpetuus, -a, -um,** continuous, uninterrupted, constant, lasting, perpetual

Persae, -ārum, *m. pl.* the Persians

per-saepe, *adv.,* very often

per-secūtiō, -ōnis, *f.,* a chase, pursuit; prosecution; persecution

per-sequor, -ī, -secūtus sum, follow closely, pursue; record, relate, describe; perform, accomplish

Persephonē, -ēs, *f., Greek for* Proserpina, *the queen of Hades*

per-sevērō (1), persevere, persist, insist, continue

persōna, -ae, *f.,* mask (in drama); character, person

persōnāliter, *adv.,* personally (*late Lat.*)

perspicientia, -ae, *f.,* full knowledge

* **per-spiciō, -ere, -spexī, -spectum,** see clearly, perceive

per-stringō, -ere, -strinxī, -strictum, affect deeply, strike, move

per-suadeō, -ēre, -suāsī, -suāsum, persuade

per-timēscō, -ere, -timuī, become *or* be thoroughly frightened, fear greatly

pertinācia, -ae, *f.,* obstinacy, stubbornness, defiance

per-tināx, *gen.* **-ācis,** tenacious; obstinate, stubborn

* **per-tineō, -ēre, -tinuī, -tentum,** pertain to, relate to, concern

per-trāns-eō, -īre, -iī, -itum, go *or* pass through, pass by

* **per-turbātiō, -ōnis,** *f.,* disturbance, disorder; emotion, passion

per-turbō (1), agitate, disturb

per-ūtilis, -e, very useful

per-vagor, -ārī, -ātus sum, wander about; spread over

* **per-veniō, -īre, -vēnī, -ventum,** come through, arrive, reach

per-versē, *adv.,* perversely

perversus, -a, -um, crooked, distorted, perverse

per-vigilō (1), stay awake throughout the night

pēs, pedis, *m.,* lower leg, foot

pessimus: *see* **malus**

pestifer, -fera, -ferum, destructive, injurious

pestilentia, -ae, *f.,* plague, pestilence

pestis, -is, *f.,* pestilence, destruction, death

petītiō, -ōnis, *f.,* attack; pursuit; petition, request

* **petō, -ere, -īvī, -ītum,** seek, aim at, ask, beg

Phaëthōn, -ontis, *m., son of the sun god, killed while trying to drive his father's chariot through the sky*

Pharisaeus, -ī, *m.,* a Pharisee

Philippus, -ī, *m., name of several Macedonian kings, especially* Philip II, *the father of Alexander and in his conquest of Greece opposed by Demosthenes*

* **philosophia, -ae,** *f.,* philosophy

philosophus, -ī, *m.,* philosopher

Phryges, -um, *m. pl.,* the Phrygians *of Asia Minor*

pictūra, -ae, *f.,* a painting, picture

pietās, -tātis, *f.,* devotion, loyalty; piety

piger, -gra, -grum, lazy

pignus, -oris, *n.,* pledge, proof; *pl.,* pledges of love (= children)

pigritia, -ae, *f.,* laziness, indolence, sluggishness, disinclination (*to act*)

pincerna, -ae, *m.,* cupbearer (*late Lat.*)

pingō, -ere, pinxī, pictum, paint, portray

pīnus, -ī, *f.,* pine tree

pīrāta, -ae, *m.,* pirate

piscis, -is, *m.,* fish

Pīsō, -ōnis, *m.,* Piso, *a cognomen; espec.* L. Calpurnius Piso, *Caesar's father-in-law*

pius, -a, -um, pious, religious, loyal, devoted

* **placeō, -ēre, -uī, placitum,** + *dat.,* be pleasing to, please; *especially impersonal* **placet,** it is pleasing, is thought best, is decided, + *inf.* or ut-*clause*

* **plāga, -ae,** *f.,* blow, wound

planctus, -ūs, *m., lit.* a beating of the breast; lamentation

plangō, -ere, planxī, planctum, strike, beat; lament, bewail

plangor, -ōris, *m.,* a striking, blow; lamentation, wailing

* **plānus, -a, -um,** level, plain, clear; **plānum, -ī,** *n.,* a plain; *adv.* **plānē**

Platō, -ōnis, *m., the famous Greek philosopher*

plaudō, -ere, plausī, plausum, strike together, clap the hands, applaud

* **plēbs, plēbis, plēbēs, -ēī,** *f.,* the common people

* **plēnus, -a, -um,** full (+ *gen. or abl.*)

* **plērīque, -aeque, -aque,** *pl.,* the majority, very many

plērumque, *adv.,* generally

plūma, -ae, *f.,* soft feather, down

plumbeus, -a, -um, made of lead, leaden; dull; heavy

plumbum, -ī, *n.,* lead

plūrimum, *adv.: see under* **plūrimus** *and* **multum**

* **plūrimus, -a, -um,** *superl. of* **multus; plūrimum, -ī,** *n.,* very much, a

great deal; **plūrimum,** *adv.,* very
much, for the most part; **plūrimum
posse,** to be very powerful

* **plūs,** *compar.: see both adj.* **multus**
and adv. **multum**

pluvia, -ae, *f.,* rain

poēma, -atis, *n.,* poem

poena, -ae, *f.,* punishment, penalty

Poenus, -ī, *m.,* a Carthaginian; the
Carthaginian = Hannibal; **Poenī,
-ōrum** *m. pl.,* the Carthaginians

poēta, -ae, *m.,* poet

poēticus, -a, -um, poetic

polītus, -a, -um, polished, refined,
polite

pollex, -icis, *m.,* thumb

* **polliceor, -ērī, -licitus sum,** promise

pollicitum, -ī, *n.,* promise

Polybius, -ī, *m., Greek historian of
the 2nd cent.* B.C.

Pompēius, -ī, Gnaeus Pompeius
Magnus, Pompey the Great,
triumvir and rival of Caesar

pōmum, -ī, *n.,* fruit

pondus, -eris, *n.,* weight

* **pōnō, -ere, posuī, positum,** put,
place, set; set before, serve (food)

* **pōns, -ntis,** *m.,* bridge

pontifex, -ficis, *m.,* a Roman high
priest; a Christian bishop *or* the
Pope

pontificātus, -ūs, *m.,* the pontificate

Pontus, -ī, *m.,* the Black Sea

poposcī: *see* **poscō**

populāris, -e, of the people,
belonging to the people; **populāris,
-is,** *m.,* a fellow-countryman,
accomplice

populātiō, -ōnis, *f.,* plundering,
devastation

populor, -ārī, -ātus sum, plunder,
devastate

* **populus, -ī,** *m.,* people, nation; the
multitude

porcus, -ī, *m.,* pig

porrō, *adv.,* forward, furthermore,
moreover, in turn

Porsenna, -ae, *m., Etruscan king of
Clusium*

* **porta, -ae,** *f.,* gate

porticus, -ūs, *f.,* colonnade, portico

portiō, -ōnis, *f.,* part, portion

portitor, -ōris, *m.,* ferryman

* **portō** (1), carry, take

portus, -ūs, *m.,* port, harbor

poscō, -ere, poposcī, request,
demand

* **possideō, -ēre, -sēdī, -sessum,**
possess, hold

* **possum, posse, potuī,** be able, can,
have power; **plūrimum possum,** be
very powerful, have very great
power

* **post,** *prep.* + *acc. and adv.: prep.,*
behind, after, since; *adv.,* behind,
afterwards, later

* **post-eā,** *adv.,* afterwards; **posteā
quam** *or* **posteāquam** = **postquam,**
conj., after

posteritās, -tātis, *f.,* future ages, time
to come, posterity

* **posterus, -a, -um,** following, future;
posterī, -ōrum, *m. pl.,* posterity; **in
posterum,** for the future; *compar.*
posterior, -ius, later, inferior;
superl. **postrēmus, -a, -um,** last,
worst

post-hāc, *adv.,* hereafter, henceforth

postis, -is, *m.,* post; *pl.,* door

* **postquam,** *conj.,* after

postrēmus, -a, -um, *superl. of*
  posterus, last; worst
* **postulō** (1), demand, request;
  prosecute, accuse
potēns, *gen.* **-entis,** powerful
* **potentia, -ae,** *f.,* power, rule
* **potestās, -tātis,** *f.,* power, authority;
  opportunity
pōtiō, -ōnis, *f.,* drink
potior, -īrī, potītus sum, + *abl. or*
  gen., be powerful over, get
  possession of, possess
* **potis, pote,** powerful, able, possible;
  compar. **potior, -ius,** better, more
  important; **potissimus, -a, -um,**
  most important
potissimum, *superl. adv. of* **potius,**
  especially, above all
potius, *compar. adv., of* **potis;** rather,
  preferably; *superl.* **potissimum,**
  especially, above all
prae, *prep.* + *abl.,* before, in front of;
  in comparison with; **prae-** *as*
  prefix, before, very (*intensive*)
praebeō, -ēre, -uī, -itum, hold out,
  offer, present, furnish; show
prae-cēdō, -ere, -cessī, -cessum, go
  before, precede
praeceps, *gen.* **-cipitis,** headlong,
  unchecked
praeceptum, -ī, *n.,* precept,
  injunction, rule
* **prae-cipiō, -ere, -cēpī, -ceptum,**
  advise, instruct, prescribe,
  command
praecipitō (1), cast down headlong,
  destroy; hasten
prae-cipuus, -a, -um, especial,
  peculiar, distinguished; *adv.*
  praecipuē

praeclārē, *adv. of* **praeclārus**
* **prae-clārus, -a, -um,** brilliant,
  illustrious, magnificent, excellent
prae-clūdō, -ere, -clūsī, -clūsum, shut
  off, close
prae-currō, -ere, -cucurrī, -cursum,
  run ahead, exceed, surpass
prae-dicātiō, -ōnis, *f.,* proclamation;
  commendation; *in eccl. Lat.,*
  preaching
prae-dicātor, -ōris, *m.,* a eulogist; *in*
  eccl. Lat., a preacher
prae-dīcō, -ere, -dīxī, -dictum, warn;
  instruct
prae-ditus, -a, -um (-datus), gifted *or*
  endowed with
* **praedō, -ōnis,** *m.,* robber, pirate,
  plunderer
praedor, -ārī, -ātus sum, plunder
prae-eō, -īre, -iī, -itum, *lit.* go ahead;
  lead the way, dictate a formula
prae-fectus, -ī, *m.,* overseer,
  commander, prefect
prae-ferō, -ferre, -tulī, -lātum, carry
  before, display; prefer, choose
* **prae-ficiō, -ere, -fēcī, -fectum,** *lit.* to
  make *or* put ahead; put in
  command
prae-gredior, -ī, -gressus sum, go
  ahead of, precede
prae-gressus, -ūs, *m.,* previous
  development
prae-lūceō, -ēre, -lūxī, shine before,
  throw a light before; outshine,
  surpass
praemium, -ī, *n.,* reward, prize
prae-mūniō (4), fortify, make safe
prae-nūntius, -ī, *m.,* foreteller, sign,
  token
prae-parō (1), prepare

prae-pōnō, -ere, -posuī, -positum, put before; put over, appoint; prefer

prae-potēns, *gen.* **-entis,** *adj.,* very powerful

* **praesēns,** *gen.* **-entis,** *adj.,* present, at hand, in person

praesentō (1), show, present

praesertim, *adv.,* especially

* **praesidium, -ī,** *n.,* protection, assistance; garrison, post, station

prae-stābilis, -e, = prae-stāns

prae-stāns, *gen.* **-stantis,** excellent, eminent, distinguished, important

* **prae-stō, -āre, -stitī, -stitum,** stand out; offer, show, exhibit; excel

praestō, *adv.,* on hand, ready, waiting for

praesul, -ulis, *m.,* patron, bishop (*ML*)

prae-sum, -esse, -fuī, -futūrus, be set over, be in command, command, rule (+ *dat.*)

praeter, *adv. and prep.* + *acc.,* past, beyond, by; except, contrary to

* **praptereā,** *adv.,* beyond, besides, moreover

praeter-eō, -īre, -iī, -itum, go *or* pass by, pass; omit, neglect; transgress

praeter-itus, -a, -um, past, gone by

praeter-mittō, -ere, -mīsī, -missum, let pass, pass over, neglect, omit

praeter-vectiō, -ōnis, *f.,* passing place for ships

praeter-vehor, -ī, -vectus sum, *lit.* be carried by; pass by, ride by

prae-textātus, -ī, *m.,* a boy who wore the **toga praetexta** (*w. a purple border*), *i.e., till the age of 15 or 16*

* **praetor, -ōris,** *m.,* praetor, *a Roman magistrate with judicial duties*

praetōrium, -ī, *n.,* general's tent; residence of the governor

prae-vius, -a, -um, going before

prātum, -ī, *n.,* meadow

prāvus, -a, -um, distorted, perverse; wicked

precātiō, -ōnis, *f.,* prayer

precēs, -um, *f., pl.* (**prex, precis,** *sg. rare*), prayers, entreaty

precor, -ārī, -ātus sum, pray, beseech, invoke

premō, -ere, pressī, pressum, press, pursue, oppress; load, cover, bury

prēndō, -ere, prēndī, prēnsum, grasp, seize

* **pretiōsus, -a, -um,** valuable, costly, precious

* **pretium, -ī,** *n.,* price, value; reward

prīdem, *adv.,* long ago

prīdiē, *adv.,* on the day before

prīmordium, -ī, *n.,* beginning

prīmum, *adv.,* first, in the first place; **quam prīmum,** as soon as possible; **cum (ut) prīmum,** as soon as

* **prīmus, -a, -um,** (*superl. of* **prior**), first, foremost; earliest, principal; **in prīmīs,** (*or* **imprīmīs**), especially; **prīmō,** *as adv.,* at first, at the beginning; **prīmum,** *adv., see* **prīmum**

* **prīnceps,** *gen.* **-cipis,** *adj.,* foremost; *also as a noun m./f.,* leader, chief

prīncipātus, -ūs, *m.,* pre-eminence, rule, leadership

* **prīncipium, -ī,** *n.,* beginning, origin; element, principle; **prīncipiō,** in the beginning, at first

prior, prius, *compar.,* former, previous, prior; **prius,** *adv.,* previously

prīscus, -a, -um, of former times,

ancient, olden, venerable, old-
fashioned

prius, *adv. of* **prior**

prius-quam, *conj.,* before; until *after
a negative*

prīvātim, *adv.,* privately

prīvātus, -a, -um, private, individual;
prīvātus, -ī, *m.,* private citizen

* **prō,** *prep.* + *abl.,* in front of, on
behalf of, for, in return for, in
place of, in view of

* **prō,** *interjection,* oh! ah! alas!

probābilis, -e, acceptable,
commendable, probable, likely

* **probitās, -tātis,** goodness,
uprightness, honesty

* **probō** (1), test, examine, prove,
demonstrate; approve, commend

probus, -a, -um, upright, honest,
good; *adv.* **probē,** well, rightly,
properly

Proca, -ae, *m., a king of Alba Longa*

prō-cēdō, -ere, -cessī, -cessum, go
forth, advance

procella, -ae, *f.,* storm; onset

procer, -eris, *m.,* a chief, noble

prōclīvis, -e, sloping down; steep

prō-cōnsul, -sulis, *m.,* proconsul, *a
consul whose power was extended
beyond his term of office, often to
serve as governor of a province*

prō-creō (1), beget, produce,
procreate

* **procul,** *adv.,* far off, at a distance

prō-cūrātiō, -ōnis, *f.,* a taking care
of, management, administration,
conduct

prō-cursātiō, -ōnis, *f.,* sally, charge

prod-eō, -īre, -iī, -itum, go forth,
advance

prōditor, -ōris, *m.,* traitor

prō-dūcō, -ere, -dūxī, -ductum, lead
forth, produce; prolong

* **proelium, -ī,** *n.,* battle

pro-fānus, -a, -um, *lit.* in front of the
temple; not sacred, profane,
common

profectō, *adv.,* surely, actually, really

* **prō-ferō, -ferre, -tulī, -lātum,** carry
forward, bring forth, make
known, invent, mention

* **prō-ficiō, -ere, -fēcī, -fectum,** gain,
accomplish

* **proficīscor, -ī, -fectus sum,** set out,
depart; arise from

pro-fiteor, -ērī, -fessus sum, declare
openly, avow, profess

prō-fluō, -ere, -flūxī, -fluxum, flow

pro-fugiō, -ere, -fūgī, -fugitum,
escape

profundus, -a, -um, extending a long
way down, deep

* **prō-gredior, -ī, -gressus sum,** go
forward, advance, proceed

prohibeō, -ēre, -uī, -itum, hold off,
check, prevent, prohibit

proinde, *adv.,* therefore

prō-lābor, -ī, -lāpus sum, slip
forward, fall down

prōlēs, -is, *f.,* offspring, progeny

prō-mineō, -ēre, jut out, project

prō-miscuus, -a, -um, *lit.* mixed;
indiscriminate, in common

prō-missum, -ī, *n.* (*from partic. of*
prō-mittō), a thing promised, a
promise

* **prō-mittō, -ere, mīsī, -missum,**
promise

prō-mulgō (1), make known,
publish, promulgate

prōmunturium, -ī, *n.,* headland

prō-palam, *adv.,* publicly, openly

* **prope,** *prep.* + *acc.,* near, close to; *as adv.,* nearly, almost, closely; *comp.* **propius,** more nearly, nearer; *superl.* **proximē,** nearest, very recently

pro-pellō, -ere, -pulī, -pulsum, drive forth

properātus, -a, -um, (*partic. of* **properō**), hurried, untimely

properē, *adv.,* quickly

* **properō** (1), hasten, act in haste, be quick

prophēta, -ae, *m.,* prophet (*EL*)

propinquus, -a, -um, near, neighboring, related; **propinquus, -ī,** *m.,* kinsman

propitius, -a, -um, favorable, gracious

propius, *adv.; see* **prope**

* **prō-pōnō, -ere, -posuī, -positum,** set forth, display; propose

proprius, -a, -um, one's own, peculiar, proper, characteristic of

* **propter,** *prep.* + *acc.,* on account of, because of

prō-pulsō (1), repel, ward off, avert

prō-cēdō, -ere, -cessī, cessum, go forward, advance

prō-ripiō, -ere, -ripuī, -reptum, drag forth

prōrsus (prō-versus), *adv.,* by all means, certainly, absolutely; in short

prō-sequor, -ī, -secūtus sum, accompany, attend

prō-siliō, -īre, -siluī, leap forth

prō-spectus, -ūs, *m.,* view

* **prosperus, -a, -um,** fortunate, prosperous; *adv.* **prosperē**

prō-spiciō, -ere, -spexī, -spectum, look out toward: foresee, provide for

prō-sum, prōdesse, prōfuī, prōfutūrus (+ *dat.*), be useful, benefit, profit

prō-tegō, -ere, -tēxī, -tēctum, *lit.* cover in front; defend, protect

prōtinus, *adv., lit.* forward; at once, immediately

pro-ut, *conj.,* just as, according as

prō-vectus, -a, -um, *lit.* carried forward; advanced (in years)

prōverbium, -ī, proverb

* **prōvincia, -ae,** *f.,* province; sphere of duty

prōvinciālis, -e, of a province, provincial; **prōvinciālēs, -ium,** *m. pl.,* inhabitants of a province, provincials

prō-vocō (1), call forth, provoke, challenge

* **proximus, -a, -um,** (*superl. of* **propior**), nearest, next, very near; **proximum, -ī,** *n.,* neighborhood; **proximus, -ī,** *m.,* neighbor (= **vīcīnus**)

prūdēns, *gen.* **-entis,** foreseeing, skilled, wise, prudent

prūdenter, *adv. of* **prūdēns**

prūdentia, -ae, *f.,* foresight, discretion; knowledge, skill

pruīnōsus, -a, -um, covered with frost, frost-laden

prytanēum, -ī, *n.,* town hall

pūblicānus, -ī, *m.,* tax-collector, publican

pūblicō (1), make public, publish

* **pūblicus, -a, -um,** belonging to the people, public, common, general; **rēs pūblica,** commonwealth, state, republic, government; **pūblicum,**

-ī, *n.,* a public place; **pūblicē,** *adv.,* publicly

pudor, -ōris, *m.,* modesty, decency; shame, disgrace

* **puella, -ae,** *f.,* girl, maiden, young woman

* **puer, puerī,** *m.,* boy; child

puerīlis, -e, boyish, childish

pugillārēs, -ium, *m. pl.,* writing tablets

* **pugna, -ae,** *f.,* fight, battle

* **pugnō** (1), fight

* **pulcher, -chra, -chrum,** beautiful

* **pulchritūdō, -inis,** *f.,* beauty

pullus, -a, -um, dark

pulsō (1), beat, strike

pulvis, -eris, *m.,* dust

pūmex, -icis, *m.,* pumice

Pūnicus, -a, -um, Punic, Carthaginian; Phoenician

* **pūniō** (4), punish

pūrgō (1), cleanse, clean, clear up

purpura, -ae, *f.,* purple garment, robe

purpureus, -a, -um, purple, dark red; bright, shining

pūrus, -a, -um, pure, undefiled

pusillus, -a, -um, very little, very small; **pusillum, -ī,** *n.,* a very little, a trifle

* **putō** (1), think, suppose, consider

putre-faciō, -ere, -fēcī, -factum, make rotten *or* friable

putrēscō, -ere, become rotten, decay

Pyladēs, -is, *m., alter ego of Orestes*

Pȳramus, -ī, *m., lover of Thisbe (see Ovid)*

Pyrrhus, -ī, *m., king of Epirus, finally defeated by the Romans in 275* B.C.

Pȳrēnaeus, -a, -um, of *or* belonging to Pyrene *(a local heroine buried amid the Pyrenees mountains, which lie between Spain and France),* Pyrenean

Q

* **quā,** *adv.,* in which place, where

quadrāgintā, *indecl.,* forty

quadrīduum, -ī *n.,* period of four days

quadringentiēns, *adv.,* four hundred times

quadrirēmis, -is, *f.,* quadrireme *(a ship with four banks of oars)*

* **quaerō, -ere, quaesīvī, quaesītum,** seek, search for, inquire, investigate

quaestiō, -ōnis, *f.,* seeking, inquiry, examination, investigation

quaestus, -ūs, *m.,* gain, profit

quālis-cumque, quāle-cumque, of whatever sort

quālis, -e, of what kind, what sort; such as, as

* **quam,** *adv., after a compar.,* than; *with a superl.,* as . . . as possible; how, how greatly; **tam . . . quam,** as . . . as

quam-diū, *adv.,* how long?, as long as

quam-libet, *adv.,* ever so (much), however (much)

quam-ob-rem, why?, wherefore, therefore

* **quamquam,** *conj.,* although; *transitional at the beginning of a sent. or of a main cl. in a sent.,* and yet, in fact, to be sure

* **quam-vīs,** *lit.* as you wish; *adv.* ever

so (much), however; *conj.*
although, however much

* **quandō,** *interrog adv. and conj.,*
when?; *indef. after* **sī** *and* **nē,** at
any time, ever; *causal,* since,
because

* **quantus, -a, -um,** *interrogative and
rel.,* how great, how much; **tantus
. . . quantus,** as great/much . . . as

quā-propter, *adv.,* wherefore,
therefore

quārē (quā-rē), *adv., lit.* because of
which thing, wherefore, why

quārtāna, -ae, *f.,* quartan fever
(febris), *recurring every 4th day*

quārtus, -a, -um, fourth

* **qua-si,** *conj.,* as if; *adv.,* as it were, so
to speak, nearly

quā-tenus, *adv.,* how far? up to what
point? to what extent? inasmuch
as, since

quater, *adv.,* four times

quatiō, -ere, quassī, quassum, shake

* **quattuor,** *indecl.,* four

* **-que,** *enclitic conj.,* and

quem-ad-modum, *adv.,* how

queō, quīre, quīvī, quitum, *defective
vb. chiefly in pres. tense,* can, be
able

quercus, -ūs, *f.,* the oak (tree)

querēlla, -ae, *f.,* complaint

querimōnia, -ae, *f.,* lament,
complaint

* **queror, -ī, questus sum,** complain,
lament

* **quī? quae? quod?** *interrogative adj.,*
what? which? what kind of?

* **quī, quae, quod,** *rel. pron.,* who,
which, what, that; *often with
conjunctive force at the beginning*

of a sentence = **et hic (haec, hoc,**
etc.); **quam ob rem,** on account of
this thing, wherefore; **quod sī,** but
if; **quī-cum,** *an old form* = **quō-
cum; quī,** *adv.,* how

* **quī, quae/qua, quod,** *indef. adj. after*
sī, nisi, nē *and* **num,** any, some

* **quia,** *conj.,* because, since

* **quīcumque, quaecumque,
quodcumque,** *rel. and indef. pron.
and adj.,* whoever, whatever

quid, *as adv.: see* **quis?**

* **quī-dam, quae-dam, quid-dam** (*pron.*)
or **quod-dam** (*adj.*), *indef.,* a
certain; a certain one *or* person

* **quidem,** *postpositive adv.,* indeed, to
be sure, at least, even; **nē . . .
quidem,** not even

* **quiēs, -ētis,** *f.,* rest, quiet

quiēscō, -ere, quiēvī, quiētum, be
quiet, be neutral, do nothing

quiētus, -a, -um, quiet

quī-libet, quae-libet, quod-libet (*adj.*)
or **quid-libet** (*pron.*), any, any you
please

quīn, how not? why not? that *after
verbs of doubting; from after
negative vbs. of hindering,
preventing, etc.;* **quīn** = **quī nōn**
after a general negative; **quīn
etiam,** why even, more than that

* **quī-nam, quae-nam, quod-nam**
interrogative adj., who, which,
what (in the world)?

quīndecim, *indecl.,* fifteen

quīngentī, -ae, -a, five hundred

* **quīnque,** *indecl.,* five

quīnquiēs, *adv.,* five times

* **quīntus, -a, -um,** fifth

Quīntus, -ī, Quintus, *a praenomen*

* **quippe,** *adv.,* of course, to be sure, naturally, for, indeed

Quirīnus, -ī, *m., an ancient name given to Romulus*

* **quis quid,** *interrogative pron.,* who? what? **quid** *often* = why?; what! why! *indef. pron. after* **sī, nisi, nē** *and* **num,** anyone, anything, someone, something

quis-nam, quae-nam, quid-nam, *interrog. pron.,* who/what pray? who/what in the world?

* **quis-piam, quae-piam, quid-piam,** someone, something

* **quisquam, quidquam** *or* **quicquam,** *indef.,* anyone, anything, *usually in negative clauses*

* **quisque, quaeque, quidque** (*pron.*) *or* **quodque** (*adj.*), *indef.,* each one, every one, each, every; **unus quisque,** each one

* **quisquis, quaequae, quidquid,** whoever, whatever

quīvīs, quaevīs, quidvīs *or* **quodvīs,** *indef. pron. and adj.,* anyone, anything

* **quō,** *adv. interrogative or rel.,* where (*i.e.,* whither = to what *or* which place); *also conj. introducing a purpose cl. containing a comparative,* in order that

quo-ad, *conj.,* how long? as long as, until

quōcircā, *adv.,* therefore

quō-cumque, *adv.,* to whatever place, wherever

* **quod,** *conj.,* because; the fact that, as to the fact that; **quod sī,** but if. *In EL and ML* **quod** = that, *a "universal conj." introducing ind.* state. *and* command, purpose, result, etc.

quōmodo, *adv.,* in what way, how

quō-minus, *lit.* by which the less; in order that the less, from (**quōminus faciat,** from doing) *after verbs of hindering and preventing*

quondam, *adv.,* once, formerly; sometimes

* **quoniam,** *conj.,* since, because

* **quoque,** *adv.,* also, too

quō-quō, *adv.,* to whatever place, wherever

* **quot,** *indecl.,* how many; as many

quotiēns, *adv.,* how often?, as often as

quotiēnscumque, *adv.,* however often, as often as

quo-usque, *adv.,* how far, how long

R

radiō (1), send out rays, gleam

radius, -ī, *m.,* rod, spoke (of a wheel), ray

rādix, -īcis, *f.,* root

Raecius, -ī, *m., a Roman name*

rāmus, -ī, *m.,* branch

rapidus, -a, -um, *lit.* snatching; consuming, rapacious, fierce; rapid, swift

rapīna, -ae, *f.,* seizure; plundering, robbery

rapiō, -ere, rapuī, raptum, seize, snatch, carry off, hurry off

raptim, *adv.,* hurriedly

raptor, -ōris, *m.,* snatcher, robber

rārus, -a, -um, scattered, rare, uncommon, remarkable

* **ratiō, -ōnis,** *f.,* reckoning, business account; reason, method, plan, theory, consideration, regard

Rēa (Rhēa) Silvia, -ae, *f., mother of Romulus and Remus by Mars*

rec-cidō: *see* **re-cidō**

re-cēdō, -ere, -cessī, -cessum, go back, retire, withdraw, go away

recēns, *gen.* **-entis,** recent; new, just come

receptrīx, -īcis, *f.,* receiver, concealer

re-cidō, -ere, reccidī, recāsum (cadō), fall back, return, be reduced

re-ciperō (1): *see* **recuperō**

* **re-cipiō, -ere, -cēpī, -ceptum,** take back, regain, recover, receive; **sē recipere,** betake oneself, withdraw, retire

re-cognōscō, -ere, -cognōvī, -cognitum, recognize

re-colō, -ere, -coluī, -cultum, cultivate again, feel afresh

re-conciliō (1), regain, win back, reconcile

re-condō, -ere, -didī, -ditum, put back, store away; *with* **oculōs,** close again

re-cordātiō, -ōnis, *f.,* recollection

re-cordor, -ārī, -ātus sum, call to mind, recollect, remember

re-creō (1), *lit.* create again; refresh, revive, restore; recover

re-crūdēscō, -ere, -crūduī, become raw again

* **rēctē,** *adv.,* rightly, properly

rēctor, -ōris, *m.,* director, governor

rēctus, -a, -um, straight, right, proper, just; **rēctā** (*sc.* **viā**) *as adv.,* straight, directly

recubō, -āre, lie back, recline

re-cumbō, -ere, -cubuī, recline

* **recuperō** (1), recover, regain

re-cūsō (1), decline, refuse, protest

* **red-dō, -ere, -didī, -ditum,** give back, return, restore

* **red-eō, -īre, -iī, -itum,** go back, return

red-imō, -ere, -ēmī, -ēmptum, buy back, ransom, buy

red-itus, -ūs, *m.,* a going back, return

red-undō (1), overflow, flow freely, abound in

re-fellō, -ere, -fellī, disprove, refute

* **re-ferō, -ere, rettulī, relātum,** bring back, report; record

rē-fert, -ferre, -tulit, *impers.,* it matters, it is important

refertus, -a, -um (refarciō), crammed, crowded with (+ *gen. or abl.*)

re-ficiō, -ere, -fēcī, -fectum, repair, restore, refresh

refrīgerium, -ī, *n., lit.* a cooling; refreshment, consolation (*EL*)

refrīgerō (1), to cool (off)

re-fugus, -a, -um, fugitive, receding

rēgia, -ae, *f.,* royal palace

rēgīna, -ae, *f.,* queen

Rēgīnī, -ōrum, *m.,* people of Regium, *a town in southern Italy opposite Messina*

* **regiō, -ōnis,** *f.,* region, district

Rēgium, -ī, *n., town in southern Italy*

* **rēgius, -a, -um,** royal

* **rēgnō** (1), be king, reign

* **rēgnum, -ī,** *n.,* kingdom, realm

* **regō, -ere, -rēxī, rēctum,** guide, direct; rule

re-gredior, -ī, -gressus sum, go back, retreat, withdraw

Rēgulus, -ī, *m., Roman cognomen;*

espec. M. Atilius Regulus, *famous for loyalty to his oath in 1st Punic War*

rē-iectiō, -ōnis, *f.,* rejection

re-labor, -ī, -lapsus sum, slip, glide, *or* sink back

relaxō (1), relax, loosen

re-levō (1), lift up; relieve, lighten

* religiō, -ōnis, *f.,* religious ceremony *or* scruples, worship, sacred obligation

religiōsē, *adv.,* conscientiously, devoutly

* religiōsus, -a, -um, holy; pious, devout

* relinquō, -ere, -līquī, -lictum, leave; abandon, desert, give up

* reliquus, -a, -um, remaining, rest (of), other

re-lūceō, -ēre, -lūxī, shine out

re-maneō, -ēre, -mānsī, -mānsum, remain, continue, abide

remedium, -ī, *n.,* remedy

re-mētior, -īrī, -mēnsus sum, measure again, measure back

rēmigium, -ī, *n., lit.* a rowing; rowing motion (of wings), wing power

remissiō, -ōnis, *f.,* a relaxing, relaxation, slackening, remission, forgiveness

re-mitto, -ere, -mīsī, -missum, send back, send off, give up, forgive, remit

re-moror, -ārī, -ātus sum, linger, tarry

re-mōtus, -a, -um, removed, distant, remote, free from

* re-moveō, -ēre, -mōvī, -mōtum, remove, lay aside

re-mūneror, -ārī, -ātus sum, repay, reward

Remus, -ī, *m., brother of Romulus*

re-nāscor, -ī, -nātus sum, be born again, return

renīdeō, -ēre, shine, beam, smile

re-novō (1), renew

reor, rērī, ratus sum, think, suppose

re-pedō (1), step back, turn back; retire

re-pellō, -ere, reppulī, repulsum, drive back *or* away

repente, *adv.,* suddenly, unexpectedly

repentīnus, -a, -um, sudden, unexpected

re-percussus, -a, -um, (*partic. of* repercutiō), re-echoing

re-periō, -īre, repperī, repertum, find, discover

* re-petō, -ere, -petīvī, -petītum, seek again, return to; repeat

re-pleō, -ēre, -plēvī, -plētum, fill up

re-portō (1), carry back, bring back

re-prehendō, -ere, -hendī, -hēnsum, seize; blame, censure

re-prehēnsō (1), hold back repeatedly *or* eagerly

re-pudiō (1), reject, refuse, repudiate

re-pugnō (1), resist, oppose; be inconsistent with

re-putō (1), think over, consider

requiēs, -ētis, *f.,* rest

re-quiēscō, -ere, -quiēvī, rest, repose

* re-quīrō, -ere, -sīvī, -sītum, search for, ask for, require

* rēs, reī, *f., a noun of innumerable meanings according to the context,* thing, matter, business, affair, *etc.;* rēs pūblica, reī pūblicae, state, commonwealth, republic, government; rē vērā, *as adv.,* really, actually

re-scindō, -ere, -scidī, -scissum tear away, tear down

re-servō (1), keep back, reserve; preserve

re-sīdo, -ere, -sēdī, -sessum, sit down; abate, subside

* **re-sistō, -ere, -stitī,** halt, remain; resist (+ *dat.*)

* **re-spiciō, -ere, -spexī, -spectum,** look back; reflect upon, consider

* **respondeō, -ēre, -spondī, -spōnsum,** answer

re-stituō, -ere, -stituī, -stitūtum, set up again, restore, renew

re-supinus, -a, -um, lying on the back

re-surgō, -ere, -surrēxī, -surrēctum, rise up again

rēte, -is, *n.,* net

re-texō, -ere, -uī, -tum, unweave, reverse

retināculum, -i, *n., usually pl.,* rope, tether, rein

* **re-tineō, -ēre, -tinuī, -tentum,** hold back, retain, restrain

re-trahō, -ere, -trāxī, -trāctum, drag back, bring back

retrō, *adv.,* back, backwards

* **reus, -ī,** *m.,* defendant, accused person; a sinner (*in ML*)

re-vellō, -ere, -vellī, -vulsum, tear away, pull off

* **re-vertor, revertī** (*pres. inf.*), **revertī** (*perf. indic. act. and perf. system act.*), **reversus, -a, -um** (having returned), turn back, come back, return

re-virēscō, -ere, -viruī, become green again

re-vīvīsco, -ere, re-vīxī, come back to life again, revive

re-vocō (1), call back, recall

re-volvō, -ere, -volvī, -volūtum, roll back; think over; *pass.,* return

* **rēx, rēgis,** *m.,* king; despot; a rich *or* mighty person

Rhodopē, -ēs (*acc.* **-ēn**), *f., mountain range in Thrace*

Rhodopēius, -a, -um, Thracian (*from the mountain Rhodope*)

rictus, -ūs, *m., sg. or pl.,* the open mouth, jaws

rīdeō, -ēre, rīsī, rīsum, laugh, laugh at

rigeō, -ēre, be stiff, stiffen

rigēns, *gen.* **-entis,** stiff, hard

rigidus, -a, -um, stiff, rigid, inflexible

rigō (1), moisten, to water

rīma, -ae, *f.,* crack

rīpa, -ae, *f.,* bank (of a river)

rīvus, -ī, *m.,* brook, stream

rōbur, -boris, *n., lit.* oak; strength

robustus, -a, -um, *lit.* of oak; firm, strong, robust

rōdō, -ere, rōsī, rōsum, gnaw, nibble at; disparage, slander

rogātus, -ūs, *m.,* asking, request

rogātiō, -ōnis, *f.,* proposed law, bill; request

* **rogō** (1), ask, request; propose for election, elect

rogus, -ī, *m.,* funeral pyre

Rōma, -ae, *f.,* Rome

Rōmānus, -a, -um, Roman

Rōmulus, -ī, *m., reputed founder of Rome*

rōstrum, -ī, *n.,* beak; ramming beak of a warship; **rōstra, -ōrum,** *pl.,* speakers' platform in Forum, *which was adorned with ships' beaks*

rubeō, -ēre, be red, blush

rubus, -ī, *m.,* bramble-bush
rudis, -e, rough, unskilled, uncultivated
ruīna, -ae, *f.,* a falling down, ruin, disaster
rūmor, -ōris, *m.,* report, rumor
rumpō, -ere, rūpī, ruptum, burst, break open, destroy
* **rūpēs, -is,** *f.,* rock, cliff
rūri-cola, -ae, *m./f.,* inhabitant of the country, a farmer
* **rūrsus,** *adv.,* back, again
rūsticānus, -a, -um, of the country, rustic
rūsticātiō, -ōnis, *f.,* rural life, visit to the country
rūsticus, -a, -um, of the country, rural, rustic

S

S. = salūtem (dicit)
sabbatum, -ī, *n.,* the Sabbath
saccus, -ī, *m.,* sack, bag
* **sacer, -cra, -crum,** sacred, holy; **sacrum, -ī,** *n.,* religious rite; sacrifice
sacerdōs, -ōtis, *m./f.,* priest, priestess
sacrāmentum, -ī, *n.,* oath
sacrificium, -ī, *n.,* sacrifice
saeculāris, -e, of a generation *or* a century; worldly, profane, secular
* **saeculum, -ī,** *n.,* century; generation; the world (*in ML*)
* **saepe,** *adv.,* often; *compar.* **saepius**
saepiō, -īre, -psī, -ptum, hedge in, enclose; protect
saevus, -a, -um, savage, fierce
sagīnō (1), feed, fatten
sagulum, -ī, *n.,* military cloak

Saguntīnī, -ōrum, *m.,* the people of Saguntum *in eastern Spain*
saltem, *adv.,* at least
saltus, -ūs, *m.,* mountain pass
salūbris, -e, healthful, salutary, beneficial
* **salūs, -ūtis,** *f.,* health, safety, welfare, preservation; greeting **(salūtem dīcere),** *usually abbreviated to* **S.** *or* **Sal.**
salūtāris, -e, healthful, salutary, beneficial
salūtō (1), greet, salute
* **salvō** (1), save, preserve (*ML*)
* **salvus, -a, -um,** safe
Samarītānus, -a, -um, Samaritan
Samos, -ī, *f., an island in the Aegean Sea off the central western coast of Asia Minor, birthplace of Pythagoras*
sanciō, -īre, sanxī, sānctum, make sacred
sāncti-ficō (1), treat as holy, sanctify (*EL*)
sānctitās, -tātis, *f.,* sanctity, purity
* **sānctus, -a, -um,** sacred, holy, venerable, virtuous
sānē, *adv.* indeed, truly, by all means, certainly, to be sure
* **sanguis, -inis,** *m.,* blood; bloodshed
sānō (1), heal, cure
* **sānus, -a, -um,** sound, healthy
sapiēns, *gen.* **-entis,** wise, sensible; *as a noun, m.,* a wise man, philosopher
sapienter, *adv.,* wisely
* **sapientia, -ae,** *f.,* wisdom; intelligence
* **sapiō, -ere, -īvī,** be sensible *or* wise, understand

sapphīrus, -ī, *m.,* sapphire

Sapphō, -ūs, *f., the famous Greek lyric poetess*

sarcina, -ae, *f.,* soldier's pack, baggage

Sardēs, -ium, *f. pl.,* Sardis, *capital of Lydia*

sardonychus, -a, -um, of sardonyx

satelles, -itis, *m./f.,* attendant

satietās, -tātis, *f.,* satiety, sufficiency

* **satis,** *indecl. adj., n., and adv.,* enough; *compar.* **satius,** better

satis-faciō, -ere, -fēcī, -factum, *lit.* do enough for; satisfy

saturō (1), satisfy, fill

satyrus, -ī, *m.,* a satyr, *a sylvan divinity with animal traits (horns, horse's tail, goat's feet), an attendant of Bacchus*

saucius, -a, -um, wounded, injured

* **saxum, -ī,** *n.,* rock

scaena, -ae, *f.,* stage, theater

scaenicus, -a, -um, of the stage *or* theater, dramatic, theatrical

Scaevola, -ae, *m.,* the left-handed, *the cognomen given to C. Mucius*

scelerātus, -a, -um, criminal, wicked, accursed

* **scelus, -eris,** *n.,* crime, wickedness

* **scientia, -ae,** *f.,* knowledge

scī-licet, *adv.,* obviously, to be sure, of course; namely

scindō, -ere, scidī, scissum, cut, split

* **sciō, -īre, scīvī, scītum,** know, understand; know how

Scīpiō, -ōnis, *m., a Roman cognomen; see* **Cornelius**

scīscitor, -ārī, -ātus sum, seek to know, inquire

scopulus, -ī, *m.,* crag, cliff

* **scrība, -ae,** *m.,* secretary

* **scrībō, -ere, scrīpsī, scrīptum,** write, compose; enroll (soldiers)

scrīptum, -ī, *n.,* a writing, treatise

scrīptūra, -ae, *f.,* a writing, composition

sculptilis, -e, carved, sculptured

scūtum, -ī, *n.,* shield

sē, *reflex. pron.: see* **suī**

sē-, *inseparable prefix,* apart, aside, without

sē-cēdō, -ere, -cessī, -cessum, go away, withdraw

sē-crētus, -a, -um, remote, hidden, secret; **sēcrētum, -ī,** *n.,* a secret

secundum, *prep. + acc.,* following, after; according to

* **secundus, -a, -um,** *lit.* following; second, favorable; **secundō,** *as adv.,* secondly

secūris, -is, *f.,* ax

sē-cūritās, -tātis, *f.,* freedom from care, confidence; safety, security

sē-cūrus, -a, -um, free from care, safe, secure

secus, *adv.,* otherwise; *prep. + acc. (ante-class. and late Lat.)* along, near, beside

* **sed,** *conj.,* but

sēdātiō, -ōnis, *f.,* an allaying, soothing; see (*EL, official seat of a bishop or other church official*)

* **sedeō, -ēre, sēdī, sessum,** sit

* **sēdēs, -is,** *f.,* seat, abode, home, place

sēd-itiō, -ōnis, *f., lit.* a going apart; dissension, quarrel

sēd-itiōsus, -a, -um, turbulent, rebellious, quarrelsome

sēdō (1), settle, soothe, check, stop

sēdulō, *adv.,* earnestly; purposely, designedly

sēgnis, -e, slow, sluggish

sēgniter, *adv.,* sluggishly, slowly

sē-gregō (1), separate, set apart

sē-iungō, -ere, -iūnxī, -iūnctum, separate

semel, *adv.,* once

sēmen, -inis, *n.,* seed

Semīramis, -idis, *f., wife of Ninus, king of Assyria*

sēmi-vīvus, -a, -um, half alive = half dead

* **semper,** *adv.,* always

sempiternus, -a, -um, everlasting, eternal

senātor, -ōris, *m.,* senator

* **senātus, -ūs,** *m.,* senate

senectūs, -tūtis, *f.,* old age

senex, senis, *m./f. adj. or noun,* old *or* an old man (woman); *compar.* **senior, -ōris,** *m.,* older, elderly *or* an elderly man (*between 45 and 60 years of age*)

senīlis, -e, of an old man, old man's

senior: *compar. of* **senex**

sēnsus, -ūs, *m.,* feeling, sensation, understanding, opinion, meaning

* **sententia, -ae,** *f.,* thought, opinion; vote

* **sentiō, -īre, sēnsī, sēnsum,** feel, think, perceive

sēparātim, *adv.,* separately, apart

sē-parō (1), separate

sepeliō, -īre, -īvī, sepultum, bury

septem, *indecl.,* seven

September, *gen.* **-bris,** *adj.,* belonging to September, of September; **September** (*sc.* **mēnsis**), **-bris,** *m.,* September

septem-decim = **septendecim**

septēnārium, -ī, *n.,* that which consists of seven = the seven gifts

of the Spirit (*see* **Veni Sancte Spiritus**)

septen-decim, *indecl.,* seventeen

septiēs, *adv.,* seven times

septimus, -a, -um, seventh

septingentī, -ae, -a, seven hundred

sepulcrum, -ī, *n.,* grave, tomb

sepultūra, -ae, *f.,* burial

sequestrō (1), separate (*late Lat.*)

* **sequor, -ī, secūtus sum,** follow

* **sermō, -ōnis,** *m.,* conversation, talk

sērō, *adv. of* **sērus,** late, too late; *compar.* **sērius;** *superl.* **sērissimē**

serpēns, -entis, *m./f.,* snake

serpō, -ere, -psī, crawl, creep, spread

sērus, -a, -um, late, belated

servīlis, -e, of a slave, servile

* **serviō** (4), be a slave, serve

servitium, -ī, *n.,* slavery, servitude; slaves

servitūs, -tūtis, *f.,* slavery, servitude, subjection

* **servō** (1), save, preserve

servulus, -ī, *m.,* young slave

* **servus, -ī,** *m.,* slave, servant

sescentī, -ae, -a, six hundred; *often simply an indefinitely large number, as we use 1000*

sēstertium, -ī, *n.,* a thousand sesterces

* **seu** = **sīve**

sevēritās, -tātis, *f.,* severity, sternness

sex, *indecl.,* six

sexāgēsimus, -a, -um, sixtieth

sexiēs, *adv.,* six times

sexus, -ūs, *m.,* sex

* **sī,** *conj.,* if, in case; whether; **quod sī,** but if

Sibylla, -ae, *f.,* a Sibyl, *prophetic priestess of Apollo*

* **sīc,** *adv.,* so, thus

siccō (1), to dry

siccus, -a, -um, dry

Sicilia, -ae, *f.,* Sicily

Siculus, -a, -um, Sicilian; **Siculus, -ī,**
m., a Sicilian

* **sīc-ut** (*or* **-utī**), just as

sīdus, -eris, *n.,* constellation, star

sigillō (1), to seal (*ML*)

significātiō, -ōnis, *f.,* sign, token

significō (1), indicate, make known;
mean, signify

* **signō** (1), to seal

* **signum, -ī,** *n.,* sign, signal, standard
(banner); seal; statue

silēns, *gen.* **-entis,** silent, still

* **silentium, -ī,** *n.,* silence

Sīlēnus, -ī, *m., oldest of the satyrs
and tutor and attendant of
Bacchus*

siliqua, -ae, *f.,* husk, pod

silva, -ae, *f.,* forest

silvānus, -a, -um, of the woods,
sylvan (*ML*)

* **similis, -e,** like, similar (+ *gen. or
dat.*); *compar.,* **similior;** *superl.*
simillimus

similiter, *adv.,* similarly, likewise

* **similitūdō, -inis,** *f.,* likeness,
resemblance; comparison, simile;
parable (*EL*)

simplex, *gen.* **-icis,** plain, simple,
sincere

* **simul,** *adv.,* at the same time, along
with; **simulatque,** as soon as

* **simulācrum, -ī,** *m.,* image, portrait,
statue; phantom, shade

simulātiō, -ōnis, *f.,* false show,
pretence, hypocrisy

simulātus, -a, -um (**simulō**), feigned,
pretended

simulō (1), feign, pretend

* **sīn,** *conj.,* but if

sincērus, -a, -um, unadulterated,
whole; candid, sincere, genuine

* **sine,** *prep + abl.,* without

* **singulī, -ae, -a,** *distributive pl.,* one
each, one at a time; single,
individual

sinister, -tra, -trum, left, on the left
hand; awkward, wrong, perverse

* **sinō, -ere, sīvī, situm,** allow, permit

Sinuessānus, -a, -um, of Sinuessa, *a
town in Latium*

sinus, -ūs, *m.,* fold; bay, gulf; fold
(*in a garment*) = pocket, lap,
bosom

sīquidem, *conj.,* if indeed; since,
inasmuch as

* **sistō, -ere, stitī, statum,** set up, stop,
check

Sīsyphus, -ī, *m., wicked king of
Corinth condemned in Tartarus to
roll a boulder eternally uphill*

sitiēns, *gen.* **-entis,** thirsty

sitis, -is, *f.,* thirst

situs, -a, -um, *perf. partic. of* **sino,**
placed, situated; **situs esse in** +
abl., to rest *or* depend on

* **sī-ve** (*or* **seu**), *conj.,* or if; **sīve . . .
sīve,** if . . . or if, whether . . . or

socer, -erī, *m.,* father-in-law

* **societās, -tātis,** *f.,* fellowship,
association; alliance, society,
union

sociō (1), unite, join, associate

* **socius, -ī,** *m.,* ally, partner, associate

Sōcratēs, -is, *m., famous Athenian
philosopher of the 5th cent.* B.C.

* **sōl, sōlis,** *m.,* sun

* **sōlācium, -ī,** *n.,* consolation, solace

solea, -ae, *f.,* sandal

* **soleō, -ēre, solitus sum,** be
accustomed

solidus, -a, -um, firm, solid, complete

sōlitārius, -a, -um, solitary, lonely, unsocial

sōlitūdō, -dinis, *f.,* solitude, wilderness

solitus, -a, -um (*partic. of* **soleō**), usual, customary

sollemne, -is, *n.,* festival, ceremony, rite

sollemnis, -e, annual; solemn; usual, customary, festive

sollertia, -ae, *f.,* skill, expertness, cleverness, quickness of mind, keen understanding; shrewdness, trickery

sollicitō (1), agitate, disturb, harass

sollicitus, -a, -um, stirred up, agitated, disturbed

sōlor, -ārī, -ātus sum, comfort, console; soothe, lessen

solum, -ī, *n.,* soil, earth

* **sōlum,** *adv.,* (*cp.* **sōlus**) only, merely; **nōn sōlum . . . sed etiam,** not only . . . but also

* **sōlus, -a, -um,** alone, only, sole

solūtus, -a, -um (*from* **solvō**), loosened, free (from); unrestrained, careless

solvō, -ere, solvī, solūtum, loosen, release, dissolve; fulfill, pay

somnium, -ī, *n.,* dream

somnus, -ī, *m.,* sleep

sonāns, *gen.* **-antis,** sounding, noisy

sonitus, -ūs, *m.,* sound, noise

sonus, -ī, *m.,* sound, noise

sopor, -ōris, *m.,* deep sleep

* **sordidus, -a, -um,** dirty, base, disgraceful

soror, -ōris, *f.,* sister

sors, sortis, *f.,* lot, fate

spargō, -ere, sparsī, sparsum, scatter

spatior, -ārī, -ātus sum, walk, walk about

spatium, -ī, *n.,* space, place, room; interval, time, opportunity

speciāliter, *adv.,* particularly, especially

* **speciēs, -ēī,** *f.,* sight, view; appearance, mien, semblance; vision; kind, species

speciōsus, -a, -um, beautiful, fine, splendid

spectāculum, -ī, *n.,* sight, spectacle

spectātiō, -ōnis, *f.,* the sight

* **spectō** (1), look at, see, watch; consider; look toward, face

speculātor, -ōris, *m.,* a spy

speculor, -ārī, -ātus sum, spy

spernō, -ere, sprēvī, sprētum, despise, spurn, reject

* **spērō** (1), hope, hope for; expect

* **spēs, -eī,** *f.,* hope, expectation

spīna, -ae, *f.,* thorn

* **spīritus, -ūs,** *m.,* breath, breathing; spirit, soul, mind, courage; air, wind

splendeō, -ēre, -uī, shine, glitter, be bright, be glorious

splendidus, -a, -um, shining, splendid, fine, illustrious; *adv.* **splendidē,** splendidly, with splendor

splendor, -ōris, *m.,* brightness, splendor

spoliātiō, -ōnis, *f.,* plundering, robbing

spoliō (1), strip, despoil, rob, plunder

spolium, -ī, *n.,* booty, spoil, arms taken from the enemy

spōnsālia, -ium, *n. pl.,* a betrothal

sponte, *f. abl. sg. as an adv. (often with* **suā, meā**), of one's own accord, voluntarily, freely

spūmi-ger, -era, -erum, foaming

spūmō (1), to foam

squālidus, -a, -um, dirty, squalid

Stabiae, -ārum, *f. pl., town near Vesuvius*

* **stabilis, -e,** stable, steadfast, constant, firm

stabilitās, -tātis, *f.,* stability, firmness, steadfastness

stabulārius, -ī, *m.,* innkeeper

stabulum, -ī, *n.,* stable; tavern, lodging

stadium, -ī, *n.,* racecourse, stadium

stāgnum, -ī, *n.,* standing water, pool

* **statim,** *adv.,* at once, immediately

statiō, -ōnis, *f.,* station, post

statīvus, -a, -um, stationary, fixed; **statīva, -ōrum,** *n. pl. (sc.* **castra**) permanent camp

statua, -ae, *f.,* statue

* **statuō, -ere, -uī, -ūtum,** put, place, set up; decide, determine, resolve

status, -ūs, *m.,* standing, condition, state

status, -a, -um (*partic. of* **sisto**), fixed, appointed

stēlla, -ae, *f.,* star

stilus, -ī, *m.,* stylus, pointed instrument *for writing on wax tablets*

stīpendiārius, -a, -um, required to pay tax *or* tribute, tributary

stīpendium, -ī, *n.,* pay; tribute

* **stirps, stirpis,** *f.,* trunk, stock; family, lineage

stīva, -ae, *f.,* plowhandle

* **stō, -āre, stetī, statum,** stand, stand still

Stōicus, -a, -um, Stoic; **Stōicus, -ī,** *m.,* a Stoic philosopher

stola, -ae, *f.,* long robe

stomachus, -ī, *m.,* gullet; stomach; liking, taste

strāgēs, -is, *f.,* ruin; slaughter

strātum, -ī, *n.,* bed; blanket

strēnuē, *adv.,* actively, promptly

strepitus, -ūs, *m.,* noise, din

strictus, -a, -um (*partic. of* **stringō**), drawn together, tight; severe, strict; *adv.* **strictē**

strīdō, -ere, strīdī, hiss

strīdulus, -a, -um, hissing, creaking

stringō, -ere, strīnxī, strictum, touch lightly, graze; draw tight, bind; draw, unsheath

struēs, -is, *f.,* heap

* **studeō, -ēre, -uī,** be eager, be devoted to, study

studiōsē, *adv. of* **studiōsus**

studiōsus, -a, -um, eager, zealous, devoted

* **studium, -ī,** *n.,* eagerness, zeal, pursuit, study; loyalty, devotion

stultitia, -ae, *f.,* foolishness, stupidity

* **stultus, -a, -um,** foolish

stupeō, -ēre, -uī, be amazed, gaze at with wonder

stuprum, -ī, *n.,* debauchery, sexual intercourse, dishonor

Styx, Stygis, *f., the hated river which surrounded Hades*

suādeō, -ēre, suāsī, suāsum, advise, urge, recommend

suāsor, -ōris, *m.,* recommender, promoter, advocate

suāvitās, -tātis, *f.,* sweetness, pleasantness

suāviter, *adv.,* sweetly, pleasantly; gently

* **sub,** *prep.* + *acc. and abl.: with acc. of motion,* under, close up to; *with abl. of place where,* under, at the foot of

sub-dō, -ere, -didī, -ditum, put *or* place under, plunge; subject, subdue

sub-dūcō, -ere, -dūxī, -ductum, draw up, draw ashore

sub-eō, -īre, -iī, -itum, *lit.* go under; undergo, undertake, endure, come to mind; approach

sub-iaceō, -ēre, -uī, lie below

sub-iciō, -ere, -iēci, -iectum, *lit.* throw under; subject, subordinate; place near; **subiectus, -a, -um,** lying under *or* at the foot of, adjacent; subjected

sub-invītō (1), gently (**sub-**) invite, suggest, hint

subitō, *adv.,* suddenly

subitus, -a, -um, sudden

sublicius, -a, -um, built on piles

sublīmis, -e, lofty, on high

sub-m: *see* **sum-m**

sub-sistō, -ere, -stitī, stand still, halt; remain, stay

substantia, -ae, *f.,* substance; property

subter-fugiō, -ere, -fūgī, escape, evade

subtīliter, *adv.,* nicely, accurately

sub-urbānum, -ī, *n.,* estate near the city

sub-vehō, -ere, -vexī, -vectum, carry up, transport

suc-cēdō, -ere, -cessī, -cessum, go under, approach; succeed

suc-cendō, -ere, -cendī, -cēnsum, set on fire

suc-cessiō, -ōnis, *f.,* succession

suc-cessus, -ūs, *m.,* success

suc-cumbō, -ere, -cubuī, -cubitum, yield, succumb, be overcome

suc-currō, -ere, -currī, -cursum, *lit.* run up under; rush to the aid of, help; come to mind

suf-ficiō, -ere, -fēcī, -fectum, supply, substitute, appoint (*in place of another*)

suffrāgium, -ī, *n.,* vote

suī (sibi, sē, sē), *reflexive pron. of 3rd pers.,* himself, herself, itself, themselves

Sulla, -ae, *m.,* L. Cornelius Sulla, *dictator in 81* B.C., *infamous for his proscriptions*

Sulpicius, -ī, *m., a Roman nomen*

sulpur, -uris, *n.,* sulphur

* **sum, esse, fuī, futūrus,** be, exist; **est, sunt** *may mean* there is, there are; **fore,** *an old fut. inf.*

* **summa, -ae,** *f.,* sum, amount, whole, chief point

sum-mergō, -ere, -mersī, -mersum, plunge under water, overwhelm, drown

sum-missus, -a, -um, gentle, calm, humble, submissive

sum-mittō, -ere, -mīsī, -missus, let down, lower

* **summus, -a, -um,** *superl. of* **superus,** highest, greatest, most important; highest part of, top of; **summum bonum,** the highest good *or* goal in life

sūmō, -ere, sūmpsī, sūmptum, take, consume; assume, choose

sūmptuōsus, -a, -um, expensive; extravagant

supellex, supellectilis, *f.,* furniture, equipment

* **super,** *adv.,* above, besides, moreover; *prep.* + *acc.* over, above, upon; + *abl.* over, above, concerning

superbia, -ae, *f.,* pride; haughtiness, insolence

* **superbus, -a, -um,** haughty, proud

super-effluō, -ere, -fluxī, -fluctum, flow over (*EL*)

super-ērogō (1), spend over and above

superior: *see* **superus**

super-in-cidō, -ere, -cidī, -cāsum, fall on from above

supernē, *adv.,* from above

* **superō** (1), surpass, overcome, defeat; surmount, pass over; survive

* **superscrīptiō, -ōnis,** *f.,* inscription, superscription (*EL*)

super-stes, *gen.* **-stitis,** surviving, outliving

superstitiō, -ōnis, *f.,* superstition

super-sum, -esse, -fuī, be more than enough (for), be left over, survive

superus, -a, -um, high up, upper, above; *compar.* **superior, -ius,** higher, superior, earlier, former; *superl.* **summus, -a, -um,** highest, highest part of, *and* **suprēmus, -a, -um,** highest, last, final, extreme

super-vacāneus, -a, -um, superfluous, needless

supervacuus, -a, -um, superfluous, unnecessary

super-veniō, -īre, -vēnī, -ventum, follow up, overtake; appear unexpectedly

suppeditō (1), supply, furnish, suffice

sup-plantō (1), trip up

sup-pleō, -ēre, -plēvī, -plētum, fill up

supplex, -plicis, *m.,* a suppliant

* **supplicium, -ī,** *n., lit.* a kneeling; supplication; punishment, penalty; pain, distress, suffering

sup-plicō (1), kneel down to, pray to, worship, entreat

sup-primō, -ere, -pressī, -pressum, hold back, suppress

* **suprā,** *adv. and prep.* + *acc.,* above, over, beyond; upon

suprēmus, -a, -um, *a superl. of* **superus**

* **surgō, -ere, surrēxī, surrēctum,** arise, get up

sur-ripiō, -ere, -ripuī, -reptum, snatch (secretly), steal

* **sus-cipiō, -ere, -cēpī, -ceptum,** undertake; incur, suffer

suspectus, -a, -um, suspected

sus-pēnsus, -a, -um, (*partic. of* **suspendō,** hang up), doubtful, in suspense, fearful, anxious

suspiciō, -ere, -spexī, -spectum, suspect

suspīciō, -ōnis, *f.,* suspicion, distrust

suspicor, -ārī, -ātus sum, suspect, conjecture

suspīrium, -ī, *n.,* sigh, deep breath

sustentō (1), sustain, bear, endure

* **sus-tineō, -ēre, -tinuī, -tentum,** hold up, support, sustain, endure, withstand

sustulī, *perf. of* **tollō**

* **suus, -a, -um,** *reflexive possessive adj.,* his own, her own, its own, their own

symphōnia, -ae, *f.,* musical concert

Syrācūsae, -arum, *f. pl.,* Syracuse

Syrācūsānus, -a, -um, of Syracuse;
  Syrācūsānī, -ōrum, *m.,* the
  Syracusans

T

T., *abbr. of* **Titus,** *a praenomen*
tabellārius, -ī, *m.,* letter-carrier
taberna, -ae, *f.* shop, tavern, inn
tābēscō, -ere, tābuī, waste away,
  melt, be dissolved
* **tabula, -ae,** *f.,* board; writing-tablet;
  document, record; picture,
  painting
taceō, -ēre, tacuī, tacitum, be silent;
  be silent about, pass over in
  silence
tacitus, -a, -um, silent
taeda, -ae, *f.,* torch; wedding torch
  (*carried in the procession*), wedding
taedium, -ī, *n.,* weariness, disgust
Taenarius, -a, -um, Taenarian =
  Spartan (*from Taenarus, a city in
  Laconia*)
taeter, -tra, -trum, foul, offensive,
  repulsive
* **tālis, -e,** such, of such a sort
tālus, -ī, *m.,* ankle; heel
* **tam,** *adv. used with adjs. and advs.,*
  so, to such a degree
* **tamen,** *adv.,* nevertheless, still
tam-etsī, *conj.,* although
* **tamquam,** *adv.,* as, just as, as it
  were
* **tandem,** *adv.,* finally, at last; *in
  questions,* pray, now then
* **tangō, -ere, tetigī, tāctum,** touch
Tantalus, -ī, *m., legendary king
  condemned to be tantalized in
  Tartarus for an insult to the gods*

tantisper, *adv.,* just so long
* **tantum,** *as adv. of* **tantus,** so much,
  only
tantummodo, *adv.,* only
* **tantus, -a, -um,** so great, so much;
  tantus . . . quantus, as great . . . as;
  tantum *as adv.,* so much; only
tantus-dem, tanta-dem, tantun-dem,
  just so great *or* large
tardus, -a, -um, slow, tardy, late; *adv.*
  tardē
Tarquinius, -ī, *m., name of two
  Etruscan kings at Rome, Priscus
  and Superbus; the latter was the
  last of the kings at Rome and was
  expelled in 510* B.C.
Tartara, -ōrum, *n.,* Tartarus, *in
  Hades, the region for evil-doers*
Tauromenitānus, -a, -um, of
  Taormina, *a town on the east coast
  of Sicily*
tēctum, -ī, *n.,* roof; dwelling, house
* **tegō, -ere, tēxī, tēctum,** cover, hide;
  protect
tellūs, -ūris, *f.,* earth, land, region
* **tēlum, -ī,** *n.,* missile, javelin, spear,
  weapon
Temenītēs, -is, *m., a title of Apollo as
  god of the sacred precinct at
  Syracuse*
temerārius, -a, -um, rash, foolhardy
temerē, *adv.,* rashly, heedlessly
temeritās, -tātis, *f.,* rashness,
  foolhardiness; chance, accident
temperantia, -ae, *f.,* moderation,
  temperance, self-control, restraint,
  avoidance of excess
temperiēs, -ēī, *f.,* moderate
  temperature; calmness, restraint
temperō (1), control, observe proper

limits, use with moderation,
refrain from

tempestās, -tātis, *f.,* weather; storm;
misfortune

* **templum, -ī,** *n.,* sacred area; temple

temptābundus, -a, -um, attempting,
feeling one's way

* **temptō** (1), test, try, attempt

* **tempus, -oris,** *n.,* time, period,
season, opportunity; crisis,
misfortune, extremity; **ad tempus,**
for the time

tendō, -ere, tetendī, tentum *or*
tēnsum, stretch; strive, struggle,
contend; travel, direct one's course
(*sc.* **iter**)

tenebrae, -ārum, *f. pl.,* shadows,
darkness, gloom

* **teneō, -ēre, -uī, tentum,** hold,
contain, possess, check, hold
back, restrain

tener, -era, -erum, tender, delicate

tenor, -ōris, *m.,* course, continuance

* **tenuis, -e,** slender, thin, weak,
humble, simple; fine, exact

tepeō, -ēre, -uī, be warm

ter, *adv.,* three times

Terentia, -ae, *f.,* Terentia, *wife of
Cicero*

Terentius, -ī, *m.,* a Roman nomen;
e.g., C. Terentius Varro, *defeated at
Cannae in 216* B.C.; M. Terentius
Afer, *writer of comedy*

tergum, -ī, *n.,* back (*part of the
body*); **ā tergō,** in the rear

terminō (1), limit, restrict, bound,
define

ternī, -ae, -a, *pl.,* three each,
triple

terō, -ere, trīvī, trītum, rub, wear
out, consume

* **terra, -ae,** *f.,* earth, land; territory,
country; **terrā marīque,** by *or* on
land and sea

terrēnus, -a, -um, belonging to the
earth, terrestrial

terreō, -ēre, -uī, -itum, terrify

terrestris, -e, terrestrial, on the earth

* **terror, -ōris,** *m.,* terror, fear, dread

tertiō, *adv.,* for the third time;
thirdly

tertium, *adv.,* thirdly, in the third
place, for the third time

* **tertius, -a, -um,** third

testāmentum, -ī, *n.,* last will,
testament

testimōnium, -ī, *n.,* evidence,
testimony

* **testis, -is,** *m./f.,* witness

testor, -ārī, -ātus sum, bear witness
to, declare, assert; call to witness

tetendī, *perf. of* **tendō**

tetigī, *perf. of* **tangō**

theātrum, -ī, *n.,* theater

Themistoclēs, -is, *m., Athenian
general victorious at Salamis in
480* B.C.

* **thēsaurus, -ī,** *m.,* treasure; treasury

Thēseus, -eī, *m., a famous king of
Athens*

Thisbē, -ēs, *f., sweetheart of Pyramus
of Babylon (see Ovid)*

Thrācius, -a, -um, Thracian

thronus, -ī, *m.,* throne

Ti., *abbr. of* **Tiberius,** *a praenomen*

Tiberīnus, -a, -um, of *or* belonging to
the Tiber river

Tiberis, -is, *acc.* **-berim,** *abl.* **-berī,**
m., Tiber River

* **timeō, -ēre, -uī,** fear, be afraid of; be
afraid

* **timidus, -a, -um,** cowardly, timid

Timōlus (Tmōlus), -ī, *m., mountain in Lydia, Asia Minor*

* **timor, -ōris,** *m.,* fear, dread

Tīcīnus, -ī, *m.,* the Ticino river, *in northern Italy*

tīnctūra, -ae, *f.,* dyeing, tinting

tingō, -ere, tinxī, tinctum, wet, dip, dye, stain

Tīrō, -ōnis, *m.,* Tiro, *Cicero's very dear freedman and secretary*

titubō (1), stagger, reel

toga, -ae, *f.,* toga (*the Roman citizen's voluminous outer garment worn in formal, civic situations and regarded as the garb of peace*)

tolerābilis, -e, bearable, tolerable

toleranter, *adv.,* patiently

* **tollō, -ere, sustulī, sublātum,** lift up, take away, destroy

topazium, -ī, *n.,* precious stone, topaz, green jasper

* **tormentum, -ī,** *n.,* torture, torment, rack

torpeō, -ēre, be stiff, numb, stupefied, sluggish

torpidus, -a, -um, stiff, numb

torqueō, -ēre, torsī, tortum, twist, torture, distress

torreō, -ēre, -uī, tostum, burn, roast

torridus, -a, -um, parched, burnt

torus, -ī, *m.,* couch, cushion

* **tot,** *indecl.,* so many

totaliter, *adv.,* totally, completely (*ML*)

totiēns, *adv.,* so many times, so often

* **tōtus, -a, -um** (*gen.* **tōtīus**), whole, entire

trabs, trabis, *f.,* a beam of wood

tractātus, -ūs, *m.,* handling, treatment

tractō (1), handle, manage, treat

trāditiō, -ōnis, *f.,* a handing over, surrender; a handing down, instruction, tradition

* **trā-dō, -ere, -didī, -ditum,** hand over, surrender; hand down, transmit

trā-dūcō, -ere, -dūxī, -ductum, lead across, conduct; spend, pass

* **trahō, -ere, traxī, tractum,** drag; draw, assume, acquire; influence, cause

trā-iciō, -ere, -iēcī, -iectum, throw across, bring across, transfer

trames, -itis, *m.,* path

trā-nō (1), swim across

tranquillitās, -tātis, *f.,* quietness, calmness, peace, tranquility

tranquillus, -a, -um, quiet, calm

trāns, *prep.* + *acc.,* across

trānscendō, -ere, -scendī, -scēnsum, climb over, pass over

* **trāns-eō, -īre, -iī, -itum,** go across, pass beyond, transgress, violate; (*of time*) go by, pass

trāns-ferō, -ferre, -tulī, -lātum, bring across, transfer, transport; translate

trāns-fuga, -ae, *m.,* deserter

trānsiliō, -īre, -siluī, leap over *or* across

trānsitōrius, -a, -um, having a passage through; passing, transitory (*EL*)

trāns-itus, -ūs, *m.,* a crossing, passage

trāns-meō (1), go over *or* across

trāns-mittō, -ere, -mīsī, -missum, send over *or* across; go over, cross over; intrust

trāns-verberō, *lit.* strike through; pierce

trāns-versus, -a, -um, transverse, crosswise

Trasumennus, -ī, *m.,* Lake Trasimeno (Lago di Perugia), *where Hannibal defeated Flaminius in 217* B.C.

Trebia, -ae, *m., a tributary of the Po River in northern Italy*

tre-centī, -ae, -a, three hundred

tredeciēs, *adv.,* thirteen times

tremebundus, -a, -um, trembling, quivering

tremō, -ere, -uī, tremble, shudder

tremor, -ōris, *m.,* a trembling; earthquake

tremulus, -a, -um, trembling, quivering

trepidātiō, -ōnis, *f.,* agitation, alarm, nervousness

trepidō (1), be agitated, alarmed, anxious

trepidus, -a, -um, alarmed, disturbed

* **trēs, tria,** three

trewga, -ae, *f.,* truce (*ML*)

tribūnal, -ālis, *n.,* raised platform

tribūnicius, -a, -um, of a tribune, tribunician

* **tribūnus, -ī,** *m.,* tribune, *a Roman official originally appointed to protect the interest of the plebeians;* a military officer

* **tribuō, -ere, -uī, -ūtum,** assign, ascribe, attribute, give

trīcēnsimus *or* **trīcēsimus, -a, -um,** thirtieth

trīduum, -ī, *n.,* period of three days

* **triennium, -ī,** *n.,* period of three years

trigeminus, -a, -um, threefold; triplet

trīginta, *indecl.,* thirty

trīstis, -e, sad, saddening, sorrowful

trītus, -a, -um, well-worn, familiar

triumphus, -ī, *m.,* triumphal procession, triumph; victory

Troezēn, -zēnis, *f., a town in Argolis across the Saronic Gulf from Athens*

Troiānus, -a, -um, Trojan

truncus, -ī, *m.,* trunk

trux, *gen.* **trucis,** savage, fierce

* **tū, tuī,** *personal pron.,* you *sg.* (thou)

tuba, -ae, *f.,* trumpet

* **tueor, -ērī, tuitus sum,** look at, watch, protect, defend, preserve

tulī: *see* **ferō**

Tullia, -ae, *f.,* Tullia, *Cicero's beloved daughter*

Tullius, -ī, *m., a Roman gentile name; see especially under* **Cicero**

* **tum,** *adv.,* then, at that time, thereupon

tumultuōsus, -a, -um, confused, noisy, tumultuous

* **tumultus, -ūs,** *m.,* uproar, confusion, tumult

* **tumulus, -ī,** *m.,* mound, hill; grave

* **tunc,** *adv.,* then

tunica, -ae, *f.,* tunic, *the shirt-like garment worn under the robe* (*toga*) or without the robe

* **turba, -ae,** *f.,* disorder, disturbance, confusion; mob, crowd

* **turpis, -e,** ugly, shameful, base, foul

turpiter, *adv. of* **turpis**

turpitūdō, -dinis, *f.,* baseness, disgrace, ugliness

turris, -is, *f.,* tower

tūs, tūris, *n.,* incense

Tusculānum, -ī, *n., sc.* **praedium,** villa at Tusculum, *a town just southeast of Rome*

tūtēla, -ae, *f.,* protection, defense

tūtō, *adv.,* safely

* **tūtus, -a, -um,** safe, guarded, protected; **tūtum, -ī,** *n.,* a safe place, safety

* **tuus, -a, -um,** your (*sg.*)

tycha, -ae, *f., Greek* = **fortuna**

tyrannus, -ī, *m.,* tyrant, despot

U

ūber, *gen.* **ūberis,** fertile, fruitful, abounding in

* **ubĭ,** *rel. adv. and conj.,* where, when; *interrogative adv. and conj.,* where?

ubī-cumque, *adv.,* wherever, anywhere, everywhere

ulcīscor, -ī, -ultus sum, avenge; take vengeance on, punish

ulcus, -eris, *n.,* ulcer, sore

* **ūllus, -a, -um,** any

ulna, -ae, *f.,* elbow, arm

ultimus, -a, -um (*superl. of* **ulterior;** *cp.* **ultrō**), farthest, most distant, last, utmost

ultiō, -ōnis, *f.,* vengeance, punishment

ultor, -ōris, *m.,* avenger

ultrō, *adv.,* to the farther side, beyond; voluntarily; without provocation; **ultrō citrōque,** up and down, back and forth

* **umbra, -ae,** *f.,* shade; ghost

umerus, -ī, *m.,* shoulder

ūmidus, -a, -um, wet, moist

* **umquam,** *adv.,* ever

* **ūnā** *as adv.: see* **ūnus**

* **unda, -ae,** *f.,* wave

* **unde,** *adv.* from which place, whence; from whom

ūndeciēs, *adv.,* eleven times

ūn-decimus, -a, -um, eleventh

* **undique,** *adv.,* from *or* on all sides, everywhere

ūnicus, -a, -um, one, only, sole; unique

ūni-genitus, -a, -um, only-begotten, only (*EL*)

* **ūniversus, -a, -um,** all together, entire, universal

* **ūnus, -a, -um,** one, single, only; **ūnā** (*sc.* **viā**) *as adv.,* together, along; **ūnus quisque,** each one. *In ML* **ūnus** *is often used as the indefinite article* a, an.

urbānus, -a, -um, belonging to a city, urban

* **urbs, -is,** *f.,* city; *the* city, *i.e.,* Rome

urna, -ae, *f.,* jug, urn

ūrō, -ere, ussī, ustum, burn, destroy by fire

usquam, *adv.,* anywhere, in any way

* **usque,** *adv.,* all the way, as far as, up (to), even (to); continuously

ūsūrpātiō, -ōnis, *f.,* employment, a making use of

ūsūrpō (1), claim, employ, repeatedly mention

* **ūsus, -ūs,** *m.,* use, practice, experience; enjoyment, profit

* **ut,** *conj.: A. with subjunctive introducing* (1) *purpose,* in order that, that, to; (2) *indirect command,* that, to; (3) *result,* so that, that; *B. with indicative,* as, when; as for example, as being

utcumque, *conj.,* in whatever way, however; *adv.,* somehow

* **uter, utra, utrum,** which of two

uterque, -traque, -trumque, each of two, both; *in pl. usually* each side, both parties

* **utī** = **ut**

* **ūtilis, -e,** useful, advantageous, profitable
* **ūtilitās, -tātis,** *f.,* use, profit, advantage, expediency

  utinam, *adv., introducing wishes,* oh that, would that

  ūtor, -ī, ūsus sum, + *abl.,* use, enjoy

  utrimque, *adv.,* from both sides, on both sides

  utrō-que, *adv.,* in both directions

  utrum, *adv.,* whether; **utrum . . . an,** whether . . . or

  ūva, -ae, *f.,* bunch of grapes
* **uxor, -ōris,** *f.,* wife

V

* **vacō** (1), be empty; be free from, be without; have (leisure) time for
* **vacuus, -a, -um,** empty, unoccupied, free

  vādō, -ere, go, rush

  vae, *interjection of pain or anger,* ah! alas! woe (to)

  vāgītus, -ūs, *m.,* a crying

  vagor, -ārī, -ātus sum, wander about

  vagus, -a, -um, wandering

  valdē, *adv.,* greatly, thoroughly, very much

  valēns, -entis, *partic. of* **valeō** *as adj.,* powerful, strong

  Valentīnī, -ōrum, *m.,* the people of Valentia *in southern Italy*
* **valeō, -ēre, valuī, valitūrus,** be strong, have power; be able, prevail; be well, fare well; **valē (valēte),** good-bye, farewell

  Valerius, -ī, *m., a Roman nomen*
* **valētūdō, -dinis,** *f.,* health

  validus, -a, -um, strong, powerful; *adv.* **validē**

vallis, -is, *f.,* valley
* **valvae, -ārum,** *f. pl.,* folding door (the leaves)
* **vānitās, -tātis,** *f.,* emptiness, vanity
* **vānus, -a, -um,** empty, vain, false; ostentatious

  varius, -a, -um, different, various, manifold, diverse; fickle

  Varrō, -ōnis, *m., a Roman cognomen; e.g.,* C. Terentius Varro *in 2nd Punic War*

  vās, vāsis, *n.,* vessel; *pl.* **vāsa, -ōrum**

  vāstus, -a, -um, empty, waste; vast, immense

  vātēs, -is, *m./f.,* soothsayer; bard, poet

  -ve, *enclitic conj.,* or

  vectīgal, -ālis, *n.,* tax

  vectīgālis, -e, subject to taxation
* **vehementer,** *adv.,* violently; earnestly, greatly, very much
* **vel,** *conj.,* or (if you please); **vel . . . vel,** either . . . or; *adv.,* even, very

  vēlāmen, -minis, *n.,* veil

  vēlō (1), to veil, cover, cloak

  vēlōx, *gen.* **-ōcis,** quick, swift
* **vel-ut,** *adv.,* as, just as, as if

  vēna, -ae, *f.,* vein, blood-vessel

  vēnābulum, -ī, *n.,* hunting spear

  vēnālis, -e, on sale, to be sold

  vēnātiō, -ōnis, *f.,* hunting; a hunt, *especially as a spectacle at the games*

  vendō, -ere, -didī, -ditum, sell

  venēnum, -ī, *n.,* poison

  vēneō, -īre, -iī, be on sale, be sold

  veneror, -ārī, -ātus sum, revere, worship
* **venia, -ae,** *f.,* pardon, favor, indulgence
* **veniō, -īre, vēnī, ventum,** come

  vēnor (1), to hunt

venter, -tris, *m.,* belly, stomach

ventus, -ī, *m.,* wind

Venus, -eris, *f., goddess of love*

Venusia, -ae, *f., a town not far from Cannae*

venustās, -tātis, *f.,* loveliness, charm

venustus, -a, -um, charming, lovely, attractive

* **vēr, vēris,** *n.,* spring, springtime

verber, -eris, *n.,* blow, lash

verberō (1), beat, scourge

* **verbum, -ī,** *n.,* word; **ad verbum,** to a word = word for word, literally

vērē, *an adv. of* **vērus,** truly, rightly, actually, really

verēcundia, -ae, *f.,* respect, reverence; modesty, propriety, shame

vereor, -ērī, -veritus sum, fear, be anxious; reverence, have respect for

vēritās, -tātis, *f.,* truth; sincerity, honesty

* **vērō,** *an adv. of* **vērus,** indeed, in fact; but in fact

Verrēs, -is, *m., the* Verres *prosecuted by Cicero*

* **versō** (1), turn, turn about; agitate, disturb; consider; *see also deponent* **versor**

versor, -ārī, -ātus sum, *deponent of* **verso,** *lit.* turn oneself about (in); be busy, engaged, occupied; be concerned with; dwell

versus, *as adv.,* towards; *as a prep.* = **adversus** *in ML*

* **vertō, -ere, vertī, versum,** turn; *see also deponent* **vertor**

vertor, vertī, versus sum, *as pass. and deponent of* **vertō,** turn oneself, turn about; be engaged in

* **vērum,** *conj.,* but, nevertheless, still; **nōn modo . . . vērum etiam,** not only . . . but also

* **vērus, -a, -um,** true, actual, real, reliable; **vērum, -ī,** *n.,* truth, reality; **vērē,** *adv., and* **rē vērā** *as adv.,* truly, really, actually; **vērum** *as conj. (see under* **vērum**)

Vestālis, -is, *f.,* a Vestal virgin, *one who tended the sacred fire of Vesta in the Forum*

* **vester, -tra, -trum,** your *(pl.),* yours

vestibulum, -ī, *n.,* entrance, vestibule

vestīgium, -ī, *n.,* footprint, track; trace, sign, evidence

vestīmentum, -ī, *n.,* clothing, garment, robe

vestiō (4), clothe; cover, adorn

vestis, -is, *f.,* clothing, clothes, garment

vestītus, -ūs, *m.,* clothing, clothes

Vesuvius, -ī, *m., the famous volcano near Naples*

veterānus, -ī, *m.,* a veteran

veterātor, -ōris, *m.,* an experienced person, an old hand (*often pejorative*)

vetō, -āre, -uī, -itum, forbid, veto

* **vetus,** *gen.* **veteris,** old; aged

vetustus, -a, -um, old, ancient

vexātiō, -ōnis, *f.,* hardship, harassment

vexātor, -ōris, *m.,* harasser

vexō (1), harass, molest, damage, maltreat

* **via, -ae,** *f.,* way, road, street

vīcīnia, -ae, *f.,* proximity, nearness, neighborhood

vīcīnus, -a, -um, neighboring, near; *noun m. or f.,* neighbor

vicis (= *gen.; nom. not found*), **vicem**

(*acc.*), **vice** (*abl.*); *pl.* **vicēs, vicibus,** change, interchange, vicissitude, plight, lot, fate; **in vicem** and **in vices,** in turn

vicissim, *adv.,* in turn

victima, -ae, *f.,* sacrificial animal

* **victor, -ōris,** *m.,* victor, conqueror; *sometimes as adj.,* **victōrī hostī,** victorious enemy

* **victōria, -ae,** *f.,* victory

victus, -ūs, *m.,* a living, food, provisions; way of life

vīculus, -ī, *m.,* hamlet

vīcus, -ī, *m.,* village; estate, property; street

vidē-licet, *adv.,* clearly; of course, to be sure

* **videō, -ēre, vīdī, vīsum,** see, observe, understand; **videor, -ērī, vīsus sum,** *passive voice,* be seen, seem; seem best

vigil, vigilis, awake, wakeful

vigilāns, *gen.* **-antis,** watchful, vigilant

vigilia, -ae, *f.,* a being awake, wakefulness, vigil; watch (*a quarter of the night*); sentinel

vigilō (1), keep awake

vīgintī, *indecl.,* twenty

vigor, -ōris, *m.,* vigor, energy

vīlicus, -ī, *m.,* steward, overseer of an estate

vīlis, -e, cheap, worthless

* **vīlla, -ae,** *f.,* villa, country house, farm

villōsus, -a, -um, shaggy, rough

vīllula, -ae, *f.,* small country house, small farm

* **vinciō, -īre, vinxī, vinctum,** bind

* **vincō, -ere, vīcī, victum,** conquer

vinculum, -ī, *n.,* bond, fetter

vindemiō (1), gather (grapes), harvest

vindicō (1), deliver, defend, protect; avenge, punish

vīnētum, -ī, *n.,* vineyard

* **vīnum, -ī,** *n.,* wine

violō (1), injure, outrage, violate

vīpera, -ae, *f.,* snake, viper

* **vir, virī,** *m.,* man; hero

vireō, -ēre, -uī, be green, be vigorous

vīrēs: *see* **vis**

virga, -ae, *f.,* twig, shoot; wand, rod

virginitās, -tātis, *f.,* virginity, chastity

* **virgō, -ginis,** *f.,* virgin, maiden

virgultum, -ī, *n.,* shrub, bush

viridis, -e, green; youthful

virīlis, -e, male, manly

virīliter, *adv.,* manfully, courageously

* **virtūs, -tūtis,** *f.,* courage, virtue, excellence

* **vīs, vīs,** *f.,* force, power, violence; *pl.* **vīrēs, vīrium,** strength

vīscera, -um (*pl. of* **vīscus, -eris,** flesh), *n.,* vitals, entrails

vīsitō (1), see often, visit

* **vīsō, -ere, vīsī, vīsum,** go to see, visit

vīsus, -ūs, *m.,* seeing, sight

* **vīta, -ae,** *f.,* life; way of life

vītālis, -e, vital

vitiātus, -a, -um, faulty, defective

* **vitium, -ī,** *n.,* fault, crime, vice

vītō (1), avoid, shun, escape

vitrum, -ī, *n.,* glass

vitulus, -ī, *m.,* calf

vituperō (1), blame, censure

* **vīvō, -ere, vīxī, vīctum,** live

vīvus, -a, -um, living, alive

* **vix,** *adv.,* hardly, scarcely, barely, with difficulty

vocābulum, -ī, *n.,* name, appellation

vocō (1), call, name; invite

vōc-ula (*dimin. of* **vōx**), **-ae,** *f., lit.*
little voice; weak voice, poor voice

volātus, -ūs, *m.,* a flying, flight

volgus: *see* **vulgus**

* **volō, velle, voluī,** will, be willing,
wish; intend, mean

volō (1), to fly

volucer, -cris, -cre, *lit.* flying; winged,
swift; *as a noun* (*sc.* **avis**), bird

voluntārius, -a, -um, willing,
voluntary, of one's own accord

* **voluntās, -tātis,** *f.,* will, wish, desire;
good will

* **voluptās, -tātis,** *f.,* pleasure, delight;
sensual pleasure, passion

vomō, -ere, -uī, -itum, vomit

* **vōs, vestrum** *or* **vestrī,** *pl. of* **tu,** you

vōtum, -ī, *n.,* vow; prayer

voveō, -ere, vōvī, vōtum, vow; pray
for, desire

* **vōx, vōcis,** *f.,* voice, word, cry; a
saying

vulgātus, -a, -um, commonly known,
public

vulgō (1), spread among the
common people, communicate,
publish

vulgō (*abl. of* **vulgus** *as adv.*),
commonly, openly

vulgus, -ī, *n.,* the common people,
crowd, throng, masses

* **vulnus, -eris,** *n.,* wound

vulnerō (1), wound

vultur, -uris, *m.,* vulture

Vulturnus, -ī, *m.,* the Volturno, *a
river in Campania*

* **vultus, -ūs,** *m.,* face, looks, mien,
appearance

X

Xerxēs, -is, *m., king of the Persians,
defeated at Salamis in 480* B.C.

Z

zēlotēs, -ae, *m.,* one who is jealous

ABOUT THE AUTHORS

Frederic M. Wheelock (1902–1987) received the A. B., A.M., and Ph.D. degrees from Harvard University. His long and distinguished teaching career included appointments at Haverford College, Harvard University, the College of the City of New York, Brooklyn College, Cazenovia Junior College (where he served as Dean), the Darrow School for Boys (New Lebanon, New York), the University of Toledo (from which he retired as full Professor in 1968), and a visiting professorship at Florida Presbyterian (now Eckerd) College. He published a number of articles and reviews in the fields of textual criticism, palaeography, and the study of Latin; in addition to *Wheelock's Latin Reader* (previously titled *Latin Literature: A Book of Readings*), his books include the classic introductory Latin textbook, *Wheelock's Latin,* as well as *Quintilian as Educator* (translation by H. E. Butler, introduction and notes by Professor Wheelock). Professor Wheelock was a member of the American Classical League, the American Philological Association, and the Classical Association of the Atlantic States.

Richard A. LaFleur, received the B. A. and M. A. in Latin from the University of Virginia and the Ph.D. in Classical Studies from Duke. He has taught since 1972 at the University of Georgia, where he served for 21 years as head of one of the largest Classics programs in North America and has held since 1998 the chair of Franklin Professor of Classics. He has numerous publications in Latin language, literature, and pedagogy, including the books *The Teaching of Latin in American Schools: A Profession in Crisis, Latin Poetry for the Beginning Student, Love and Transformation: An Ovid Reader, Latin for the 21st Century: From Concept to Classroom, Wheelock's Latin* (revised 5th and 6th eds.), and (with Paul Comeau) *Workbook for Wheelock's Latin* (revised 3rd ed.). Professor LaFleur is also editor of *The Classical Outlook* (since 1979) and a past President of the American Classical League (1984–1986). He has been recipient of state, regional, and national awards for teaching and professional service, including, in 1984, the American Philological Association's award for Excellence in the Teaching of Classics.